WORLD HISTORY VOLUME II
1500 to 20th Century

Second Edition

Editor

David McComb
Colorado State University

David McComb received his Ph.D. from the University of Texas and is currently a professor of history at Colorado State University. He has written five books, numerous articles and book reviews, and teaches courses in the history of technology, cities, sport, and the world. He has traveled twice around the world as a Semester at Sea faculty member of the University of Pittsburgh, and spent additional time in India.

Annual Editions
A Library of Information from the Public Press

Cover illustration by Mike Eagle

The Dushkin Publishing Group, Inc.
Sluice Dock, Guilford, Connecticut 06437

The Annual Editions Series

Annual Editions is a series of over fifty volumes designed to provide the reader with convenient, low-cost access to a wide range of current, carefully selected articles from some of the most important magazines, newspapers, and journals published today. Annual Editions are updated on an annual basis through a continuous monitoring of over 200 periodical sources. All Annual Editions have a number of features designed to make them particularly useful, including topic guides, annotated tables of contents, unit overviews, and indexes. For the teacher using Annual Editions in the classroom, an Instructor's Resource Guide with test questions is available for each volume.

VOLUMES AVAILABLE

Africa
Aging
American Government
American History, Pre-Civil War
American History, Post-Civil War
Anthropology
Biology
Business and Management
Business Ethics
Canadian Politics
China
Comparative Politics
Computers in Education
Computers in Business
Computers in Society
Criminal Justice
Drugs, Society, and Behavior
Early Childhood Education
Economics
Educating Exceptional Children
Education
Educational Psychology
Environment
Geography
Global Issues
Health
Human Development

Human Resources
Human Sexuality
Latin America
Macroeconomics
Marketing
Marriage and Family
Middle East and the Islamic World
Money and Banking
Nutrition
Personal Growth and Behavior
Psychology
Public Administration
Social Problems
Sociology
Soviet Union and Eastern Europe
State and Local Government
Third World
Urban Society
Violence and Terrorism
Western Civilization, Pre-Reformation
Western Civilization, Post-Reformation
Western Europe
World History, Pre-Modern
World History, Modern
World Politics

Library of Congress Cataloging in Publication Data
Main entry under title: Annual editions: World history, vol. II: 1500 to 20th Century.
     1. World history—Periodicals. 2. Civilization, Modern—Periodicals. 3. Social problems—Periodicals. I. McComb, David, comp. II. Title: World history, vol. II: 1500 to 20th Century.
905   ISBN 0-87967-819-4

Second Edition

Manufactured by The Banta Company, Harrisonburg, Virginia 22801

Editors/
Advisory
Board

EDITOR

David McComb
Colorado State University

ADVISORY BOARD

STAFF

To The Reader

In publishing ANNUAL EDITIONS we recognize the enormous role played by the magazines, newspapers, and journals of the *public press* in providing current, first-rate educational information in a broad spectrum of interest areas. Within the articles, the best scientists, practitioners, researchers, and commentators draw issues into new perspective as accepted theories and viewpoints are called into account by new events, recent discoveries change old facts, and fresh debate breaks out over important controversies.

Many of the articles resulting from this enormous editorial effort are appropriate for students, researchers, and professionals seeking accurate, current material to help bridge the gap between principles and theories and the real world. These articles, however, become more useful for study when those of lasting value are carefully *collected, organized, indexed,* and *reproduced* in a *low-cost format*, which provides easy and permanent access when the material is needed. That is the role played by *Annual Editions*. Under the direction of each volume's *Editor*, who is an expert in the subject area, and with the guidance of an *Advisory Board*, we seek each year to provide in each *ANNUAL EDITION* a current, well-balanced, carefully selected collection of the best of the public press for your study and enjoyment. We think you'll find this volume useful, and we hope you'll take a moment to let us know what you think.

After 1500 the world was increasingly taken up with the power and problems of the West. Europe and its offspring in North America experienced a unique transformation during the industrial and scientific revolutions. Western technology allowed a global extension of Western culture. Ideas, not only about science and technology, but also about liberalism, socialism, capitalism, Christianity, democracy, human rights, and nationalism followed in the wake of caravels and steamboats. It was a European who dispelled the myth of the "sea of pithy darkness" on the west coast of Africa where sea dragons ate sailors. It was also a European who discovered the "New World," and carried trade to the distant Orient. It was not a Chinese mariner who sailed up the Hudson River, nor an African who forced open the Japanese ports at gunpoint. It was not an Indian who transferred potatoes to Ireland and corn to France. For all of their faults, it was the Europeans, and later the Americans, who ventured forth around the globe and on to the surface of the moon.

The history of the world in the modern period, therefore, intimately concerns the circumstances of the West and the ambitions of its people. As shown by William H. McNeill and L. S. Stavrianos in their texts, the West expanded into the rest of the world and the peoples there reacted in one way or another. First, there was colonialism and the carving out of overseas empires. Early conquerors in the Americas and the Pacific used swords, horses, disease, and gunpowder. Later invaders in Africa and India utilized railroads, telegraphs, quinine, steamboats, and Maxim guns. Then, after the disasters of two world wars and a depression in the twentieth century, the West retreated. It left behind a residue of ideas, an interest in technology, and the English language.

The purpose of this anthology is to give the reader a sense of this modern world history. It is organized topically, with a chronological arrangement within the topics. For those with different needs I recommend the use of the topic guide, which arranges the articles according to subject, including region of reference. The articles were selected to reflect current thinking, to engender interest, and to be readable.

It is not a perfect world, and this is not a perfect anthology. World history by its nature must be selective, and not everything can be covered. You may have some suggestions for improving this edition and some alternative articles to recommend. Please use the article rating form at the back of this volume to submit your thoughts and ideas.

David McComb
Editor

Contents

Unit 1

The Industrial and Scientific Revolutions

Eleven selections discuss the revolution in the industrial and scientific world. Topics include the change from cottage industry to factory, the impact of the Copernican revolution, the importance of Galileo, and the effect of agriculture on world development.

The concepts in bold italics are developed in the article. For further expansion please refer to the Topic Guide and the Index.

Unit 2

The Cultural Ferment of the West

Seven articles examine the cultural development of the West including such topics as early religious thinking, early economic interpretations of capitalism, music, women in eighteenth-century society, and the importance of the American Constitution in world events.

The concepts in bold italics are developed in the article. For further expansion please refer to the Topic Guide and the Index.

Unit 3

The Expansion and Domination of the West

Six articles show how the West extended and dominated much of the world. Topics include the emergence of Western colonial powers, the importance of the Anglo-Zulu War, and feudal Japan.

Unit 4

Twentieth-Century Warfare

Nine articles examine the effect of war and depression on modern world history. Topics include the causes of war, the impact of the First World War, the rise of Hitler, the Vietnam War, and the seeming inevitability of war.

The concepts in bold italics are developed in the article. For further expansion please refer to the Topic Guide and the Index.

Unit 5

The Retreat of the West

Seven articles discuss how Western colonialism has
impacted on the world. Topics include African
independence, India, the Middle East, the legacy of
English colonization, and Japan's success.

Unit 6

World Problems and Interdependence

Six selections examine the effects of interdependence
on some world problems including population growth,
Japanese women, global climatic changes, and the
internationalization of history.

The concepts in bold italics are developed in the article. For further expansion please refer to the Topic Guide and the Index.

Topic Guide

This topic guide suggests how the selections in this book relate to topics of traditional concern to world history students and professionals. It can be very useful in locating articles which relate to each other for reading and research. The guide is arranged alphabetically according to topic. Articles may, of course, treat topics that do not appear in the topic guide. In turn, entries in the topic guide do not necessarily constitute a comprehensive listing of all the contents of each selection.

TOPIC AREA	TREATED AS AN ISSUE IN:	TOPIC AREA	TREATED AS AN ISSUE IN:
Africa	19. Portugal's Impact on Africa 21. The Struggle for Land 22. West Africa's Mary Kingsley 34. Whose Dream Was It Anyway? 41. Population and Economic Growth	**Europe**	1. An Early Energy Crisis and Its Consequences 2. Cottage Industry and the Factory System 3. From Astronomy to Astrophysics 4. Galileo's Science and the Trial of 1633 5. The Alchemical Roots of Chemistry 9. Driving Toward a World Car? 12. Luther: Giant of His Time and Ours 13. The Body of Bach 15. What Was Revolutionary? 16. Scotland's Greatest Son 17. The First Feminist 18. Freudian Myths and Freudian Realities 19. Portugal's Impact on Africa 20. The Emergence of the Great Powers 24. Southern Barbarians and Red-Hairs 26. Sarajevo: The End of Innocence 27. The Dangerous Summer of 1940
Agriculture	8. The Green Revolution		
America	7. New Light on Edison's Light 14. The Great Compromise 29. To Cleave an Atom 41. Population and Economic Growth		
Asia	9. Driving Toward a World Car? 24. Southern Barbarians and Red-Hairs 30. Reborn From Holocaust 31. Lessons From a Lost War 37. The 10 Years of Chaos 40. The Price of Success 41. Population and Economic Growth 43. Japanese Women: A World Apart	**Geography**	3. From Astronomy to Astrophysics 8. The Green Revolution 11. Scientists Go North 19. Portugal's Impact on Africa
China	37. The 10 Years of Chaos 41. Population and Economic Growth	**Great Britain**	1. An Early Energy Crisis and Its Consequences 2. Cottage Industry and the Factory System 16. Scotland's Greatest Son 17. The First Feminist 20. The Emergence of the Great Powers 21. The Struggle for Land 22. West Africa's Mary Kingsley 23. A Whole Subcontinent Was Picked Up 42. A "Satanic" Fury
Colonization	20. The Emergence of the Great Powers 21. The Struggle for Land 22. West Africa's Mary Kingsley 23. A Whole Subcontinent Was Picked Up 34. Whose Dream Was It Anyway? 39. The New English Empire		
Culture	13. The Body of Bach 17. The First Feminist 30. Reborn From Holocaust 35. India's Estranged Communities 37. The 10 Years of Chaos 39. The New English Empire 42. A "Satanic" Fury 43. Japanese Women: A World Apart 44. A Matter of Honor	**Historiography**	46. The Internationalization of History
		India	23. A Whole Subcontinent Was Picked Up 35. India's Estranged Communities 41. Population and Economic Growth
Economics	2. Cottage Industry and the Factory System 9. Driving Toward a World Car? 16. Scotland's Greatest Son 19. Portugal's Impact on Africa 22. West Africa's Mary Kingsley 23. A Whole Subcontinent Was Picked Up 24. Southern Barbarians and Red-Hairs 40. The Price of Success 41. Population and Economic Growth	**Industrial Revolution**	1. An Early Energy Crisis and Its Consequences 2. Cottage Industry and the Factory System 9. Driving Toward a World Car? 45. Global Climatic Change
		Islam	36. Islam 42. A "Satanic" Fury
Environment	1. An Early Energy Crisis and Its Consequences 3. From Astronomy to Astrophysics 45. Global Climatic Change	**Japan**	9. Driving Toward a World Car? 24. Southern Barbarians and Red-Hairs 30. Reborn From Holocaust 40. The Price of Success 43. Japanese Women: A World Apart

TOPIC AREA	TREATED AS AN ISSUE IN:	TOPIC AREA	TREATED AS AN ISSUE IN:
Middle East	32. The Dismal Chronology of Foolish War 33. Weapons, Deadly Weapons 36. Islam 42. A "Satanic" Fury 44. A Matter of Honor	**Technology**	1. An Early Energy Crisis and Its Consequences 2. Cottage Industry and the Factory System 7. New Light on Edison's Light 8. The Green Revolution 9. Driving Toward a World Car? 10. The Conquering Machine
Politics	14. The Great Compromise 15. What Was Revolutionary? 20. The Emergence of the Great Powers 23. A Whole Subcontinent Was Picked Up 25. The Causes of Wars 34. Whose Dream Was It Anyway? 35. India's Estranged Communities 38. Marx Had It Wrong. Does Gorbachev? 40. The Price of Success	**Terrorism**	28. Social Outcasts in Nazi Germany 37. The 10 Years of Chaos 42. A "Satanic" Fury
		United States	7. New Light on Edison's Light 9. Driving Toward a World Car? 14. The Great Compromise 29. To Cleave an Atom 31. Lessons From a Lost War 33. Weapons, Deadly Weapons
Pollution	1. An Early Energy Crisis and Its Consequences 45. Global Climatic Change		
Population	11. Scientists Go North 28. Social Outcasts in Nazi Germany 35. India's Estranged Communities 39. The New English Empire 41. Population and Economic Growth	**Urbanization**	1. An Early Energy Crisis and Its Consequences 2. Cottage Industry and the Factory System
Religion	4. Galileo's Science and the Trial of 1633 12. Luther: Giant of His Time and Ours 36. Islam 42. A "Satanic" Fury	**Warfare**	21. The Struggle for Land 23. A Whole Subcontinent Was Picked Up 25. The Causes of Wars 26. Sarajevo: The End of Innocence 27. The Dangerous Summer of 1940 28. Social Outcast in Nazi Germany 29. To Cleave an Atom 30. Reborn From Holocaust 31. Lessons From a Lost War 32. The Dismal Chronology of Foolish War 33. Weapons, Deadly Weapons
Science	3. From Astronomy to Astrophysics 4. Galileo's Science and the Trial of 1633 5. The Alchemical Roots of Chemistry 6. Life's Recipe 7. New Light on Edison's Light 8. The Green Revolution 11. Scientists Go North 18. Freudian Myths and Freudian Realities 22. West Africa's Mary Kingsley 29. To Cleave an Atom 45. Global Climatic Change		
		Women	17. The First Feminist 22. West Africa's Mary Kingsley 24. Southern Barbarians and Red-Hairs 43. Japanese Women: A World Apart 44. A Matter of Honor
Soviet Union	20. The Emergence of the Great Powers 33. Weapons, Deadly Weapons 38. Marx Had It Wrong. Does Gorbachev?		
Sports	37. The 10 Years of Chaos		

The Industrial and Scientific Revolutions

In 1500, it can be argued, the Chinese were at the same technological level as the Europeans. What brought supremacy to the West were the revolutions in industry and science; other civilizations did not experience these changes. Industrialization started in England, where favorable conditions in the areas of economics, government, and religion prevailed. England also had both the resources and the need for industrialization. The nation had used up its forests and turned to coal as a fuel. As the

shafts went deeper the need for drainage became severe, and the result was the Newcomen steam engine, a device designed to pump water from the mines. This gave the world a portable energy source; people no longer had to depend upon the vagaries of wind and streams.

Mechanization spread into the English textile industry through a series of inventions that increased the output of weavers and spinners. Factories replaced the small-scale cottage weavers, but the shift was gradual. Nevertheless, it was stressful for the workers, and between 1811 and 1816 the band of laborers known as the Luddites were severely repressed for destroying factory equipment. From England the innovations spread to the mainland, as Europe began its industrialization, and later to the United States. The change was not a revolution in the sense of a quick, dramatic shift. It was slower than that; its roots can be found in the later Middle Ages. Interestingly, the Industrial Revolution continues today, and has spread worldwide, as the article about the "world car" demonstrates: since automobile parts are made in various countries, it has become increasingly difficult to name the nation where a car is manufactured.

At the same time as the Industrial Revolution, science as an objective means of discovering the truth about natural phenomena emerged from the shift of interest to mundane affairs during the Renaissance and the loosening of the hold of the Roman Catholic Church during the Reformation. Copernicus started the revolution in astronomy by placing the sun at the center of the solar system and the earth as a planet in orbit. Galileo, who combined his technical skills at telescope construction with his scientific curiosity, discovered four new planets, the stars of the Milky Way, eighty stars in the constellation Orion, the mountains of the moon, and the moons of Jupiter, which lent credence to the Copernican system. Galileo was a transitional man, however, with one foot in the medieval world and the other in the modern. His arguments for Copernicus, as William A. Wallace points out, were based more on intuition than fact.

Until the latter part of the nineteenth century, science and technology operated separately, for the most part. Thomas A. Edison, however, bridged the gap by using scientific principles for his inventive endeavors. The story of the incandescent lamp, as told in "New Light on Edison's Light," illustrates his approach—the use of library resources, a laboratory, division of labor, rational analysis of the problem to be solved, and adequate financing. Since this marriage, science and technology have worked together. This can be seen in the Green Revolution, which has utilized new plant types in combination with balanced supplies of water and fertilizer to increase crop yields. How far the Green Revolution can be taken remains to be seen; the potential has not been realized for a variety of reasons.

A combination of science and technology also produced the computer, which now is creating what some writers call the second industrial revolution. The first revolution substituted inanimate power and mechanization for muscle power and human dexterity; the second revolution replaced the control function of humans with automatic devices that could analyze and make decisions. One of the simplest examples of this is a thermostat, which monitors room temperature and switches on the furnace when it gets too cold. The development of the computer has raised questions about artificial intelligence, and whether or not computers with electric circuits can think like human beings with "wet" circuits. Can it be that human beings with their science and technology have created a machine that is smarter than they are?

Scientists and innovators tend to gather together to stimulate each other's thoughts. This may actually be necessary for the advancement of science and technology. As Isaac Newton once commented, "If I have seen further it is by standing on the shoulders of giants." The article by Anthony de Souza demonstrates this phenomenon. Not only are there heavy concentrations of scientists in the United States, but also in the northern half of the globe in general. This underscores in a special way the growing split between the rich and poor nations, a split that also seems to divide the north and south.

Following 1500, the West began to reach out around the world. At that time there was nothing extraordinary about the civilization except the scientific and technological phenomenon that was still unfolding; it was this phenomenon, however, that brought the West to global dominance.

Looking Ahead: Challenge Questions

What were the characteristics of the cottage industry, and why was it defeated by the factory system?

Why was astronomy the leading discipline of scientific inquiry?

How "scientific" was Galileo?

Dispute the image that Thomas A. Edison liked to project of himself—that of a simple garage tinkerer.

Why is the genetic code an important discovery?

What is the Green Revolution, and what has happened to it?

Can a computer think?

An Early Energy Crisis and Its Consequences

In the 16th century Britain ran out of wood and resorted to coal.
The adoption of the new fuel set in motion a chain of events that
culminated some two centuries later in the Industrial Revolution

John U. Nef

JOHN U. NEF ("An Early Energy Crisis and Its Consequences") is professor emeritus of economic history at the University of Chicago. Born in 1899, Nef attended Harvard College and the Robert Brookings Graduate School in Washington, where he received his Ph.D. in economics in 1927. After teaching for two years at Swarthmore College he joined the Chicago faculty. In 1942 he founded the Committee on Social Thought, a small interdisciplinary faculty devoted to the study of historical and cultural development. The committee attracted many eminent thinkers and artists to Chicago, among them Friedrich von Hayek and Saul Bellow (who became the committee's chairman after Nef's retirement). Nef is the author of 15 books, including a two-volume history of the British coal industry and, a memoir titled *Search for Meaning: The Autobiography of a Nonconformist.*

In medieval Europe wood was utilized not only in many types of construction but also in most domestic and industrial heating. Then in Britain in the second half of the 16th century coal came into widespread use as a substitute for wood as fuel. The earliest coal-burning economy the world has known was established first in England and then in Scotland between about 1550 and 1700.

This transition from woodcutting to coal mining as the main source of heat was part of an early British economic revolution. The first energy crisis, which has much to do with the crisis we now face, was a crisis of deforestation. The adoption of coal changed the economic history of Britain, then of the rest of Europe and finally of the world. It led to the Industrial Revolution, which got under way in Britain in the last two decades of the 18th century. The substitution of coal for wood between 1550 and 1700 led to new methods of manufacturing, to the expansion of existing industries and to the exploitation of untapped natural resources.

To make these assertions is not to belittle the role of other changes during the Middle Ages and the Renaissance in the coming of our industrialized world. The century before Britain's wood crisis—the 100 years from about 1450 to 1550—was characterized by a new spirit of expansion. Voyages of discovery were launched, carrying explorers to the ends of the earth. The art of printing with movable type spread across Europe, and the production of paper expanded; millions of books were printed and put in circulation. In central Europe, where the major centers of mining and metallurgy were to be found, the output of ores, particularly silver-bearing copper ores, multiplied severalfold. The years between 1494 and 1529 have been described as bringing about a "revolution in the art of war." With the help of the new firearms Spain conquered Mexico and Peru.

These and other innovations increased, directly or indirectly, the need for all existing kinds of energy: the heat provided by wood and the power provided by wind, animals and running water. The need for larger amounts of wood for construction and for heating, particularly for the smelting and refining of ores, called for a substantial increase in the felling of trees.

All Europe felt these pressures, and yet the first large area to experience an acute shortage of wood was Britain. Why did the fuel revolution that led to new uses of heat energy begin in that particular place? Was wood particularly scarce there? It seems to be true that the most populous parts of Scotland (the areas surrounding the Firth of Forth) were barren of trees; a wit from England is said to have observed in the reign of James I that if Judas had repented in the king's native land (Scotland), he would have been hard put to find a tree on which to hang himself! Such an explanation does not fit England. The wood crisis there has to be attributed to the requirements of expanding agriculture, industry and commerce, all stimulated by a growing, shifting population.

It appears that Sweden and the Netherlands were the only other European countries to experience anything comparable to the growth and resettlement of the British population in the period from 1550 to 1700. The population of England and Wales, about three million in the early 1530's, had nearly doubled by the 1690's. The resulting demand for wood for various purposes was further increased by changes in the distribution of the population. In this period the inhabitants of London multiplied at least eightfold, from some 60,000 in 1534 to some 530,000 in 1696.

According to Gregory King's estimate for the latter year, the British capital had by then become the largest city in Europe and perhaps the world. King estimates that England's other "cities and...market towns" had a total population of about 870,000. This means that although only one person in 10 was a "townsman" in the 1530's, one person in four was a townsman in the 1690's. Larger towns meant heavier demands on nearby wood supplies. Moreover, outside the towns there was much migration of the unemployed across the country in search of work. Wherever they found employment, shelter had to be provided, putting still another strain on the forests.

During the reigns of Elizabeth I (1558–1603) and James I (1603–25) this pressure on the supply of trees was reflected in the soaring cost of firewood and lumber for construction. The period from 1550 to 1640 was a time of inflation throughout Europe, but the price of wood in England rose very much faster than that of any other commodity in general use anywhere. Complaints of deforestation came from all parts of the kingdom.

Wherever coal seams outcropped in Europe, coal had been burned in small quantities since the 12th century. (It had been more extensively burned in China earlier than that and also to some degree in Roman Britain.) In Europe during the later Middle Ages peasants had occasionally warmed their homes or stoked their lime kilns and smithies with these "black stones." Why then was coal not widely adopted as a fuel on the Continent and in Britain before the forests were seriously depleted?

In societies earlier than the one that arose in western Europe in medieval times mining was looked on with disfavor. It was often regarded as robbery, even as a kind of rape. Unlike the plow, which made the earth fertile, the pick and shovel removed what seemed to be irreplaceable soil and subsoil.

By the early 16th century a different attitude toward the exploitation of the more valuable underground resources found expression in two books. In *De re metallica* (1556) Georgius Agricola (1494–1555) ranked the miner's calling higher than "that of the merchant trading for lucre." And in *Pirotechnia* (1540) Vannoccio Biringuccio (1480–1539) advocated an all-out assault on these underground riches. He advised "whoever mines ores...to bore into the center of the mountains...as if by the work of necromancy or giants. They should not only crack the mountains asunder but also turn their very marrow upside down in order that what is inside may be seen and the sweetness of the fruit despoiled as soon as possible."

COAL WAS BRITAIN'S PRINCIPAL FUEL by the end of the 17th century. Coal heavers, such as the ones shown in this print from 1805, handled coal destined for homes and industries across Britain and for many foreign countries as well. In background are coal barges.

The new dignity attached to mining was reserved for metallic ores. It did not extend to coal. The medieval craftsmen who needed fuel wanted their work to be beautiful, whether it was for their church or for rich laymen. The unpleasant smoke and fumes of coal therefore limited the market for it. There was little incentive before the mid-16th century to dig deep into the soil in search of this dirty fuel as long as wood was available, and there seemed to be an abundance of that. Biringuccio himself believed the forests of Europe could fill all conceivable future demands for fuel. In *Pirotechnia* he wrote: "Miners are more likely to exhaust the supply of ores than foresters the supply of the wood needed to smelt them. Very great forests are found everywhere, which makes one think that the ages of man would never consume them...especially since Nature, so very liberal, produces new ones every day." Coal is mentioned only once in his long treatise and then just to dismiss it: "Besides trees, black stones, that occur in many places, have the nature of true charcoal, [but] the abundance of trees makes [it] unnecessary...to think of that faraway fuel."

Less than a generation later the English turned to coal under pressure from the high price of wood. By the early 17th century efforts by the government to stop deforestation were felt to be imperative because the shortage of lumber for shipbuilding seemed to threaten Britain's existence. A royal proclamation of 1615 laments the former wealth of "Wood and Timber," the kind of wood that is "not only great and large in height and bulk, but hath also that toughness and heart, as it is not subject to rive or cleave, and thereby of excellent use for shipping, as if God Almightie, which had ordained this Nation to be mighty by Sea and navigation, had in his providence indued the same with the principall materiall conducing thereunto." By the middle of the 17th century coal had proved so useful and was already so widely burned that the British had come to make necessity a virtue. They reconciled themselves to the disappointing failure of their explorers to locate sources of precious metal and of their miners to find much of it in Britain itself. In spite of the smoke and fumes of coal and in spite of a widespread distaste for it, by the time of the civil war in the 1640's Londoners were dependent on the coastwise shipment of coal to keep warm. In 1651 the anonymous author of *News from Newcastle* wrote verses in praise of the new fuel. "England's a perfect World! Has Indies too! / Correct your Maps; New-castle is Peru!... / Let th' naughty Spaniard triumph, 'til

BEFORE THE ADVENT OF COAL wood was the main source of heat energy in Europe. Industrial power was provided by wind, animals and running water. It was often necessary to convert the wood to charcoal by partially burning it in furnaces such as the ones shown here. The wood was piled in stacks, covered with earth and powdered charcoal dust and then burned. The covering kept combustion at a minimum so that the end product was charcoal rather than ashes. For some manufacturing processes charcoal was preferred to wood because it is mostly pure carbon and so yields a greater amount of heat per unit volume of fuel. Illustration is from Diderot's *Encyclopédie, ou Dictionnaire Raisonné des Sciences, des Art et des Métiers.*

'tis told / Our sooty mineral purifies his gold."

Even earlier, as is made clear by William Harrison's *Description of Britain* (1577) and by a petition London brewers addressed to Sir Francis Walsingham, Queen Elizabeth's secretary of state (1578), coal was acquiring a new and important place in domestic and industrial heating. The surviving records of customs officials at Newcastle-on-Tyne (and later records of other towns) reveal a continuous and rapid growth in the shipments of coal between 1550 and 1700, first from Newcastle-on-Tyne and then from other ports. These records suggest that the coastwise shipments increased at least twentyfold between 1550 and 1700. Coastwise imports to London grew even faster, probably more than thirtyfold, which is not surprising in view of the multiplication of the city's population in that period. Lord Buckhurst, who became Queen Elizabeth's lord treasurer at the end of the 16th century, required the customs officials during the 1590's to determine the

"rate of growth" in coal shipments from Newcastle, thereby introducing a new concept into human affairs. The calculations on which Buckhurst insisted indicated that taxes on coal shipments could be counted on to provide a continually increasing source of revenue, and so taxes on coal shipments were imposed in 1599 and 1600.

The most impressive rises in the growth rate of coal production occurred in the second half of the 16th century and at the beginning of the 17th. In fact, the growth rate in the volume of coal mined between 1556 and 1606 may even exceed the growth rate (computed from less incomplete statistics) in the volume mined during the first part of the 19th century, that is, at the height of Britain's Industrial Revolution. The actual quantities involved in the rapid growth of coal production in the earlier period may seem insignificant today, but it is the viewpoint of the Elizabethans and their immediate successors that needs to be recaptured. To them the expansion in the output of coal must have seemed extraordinarily rapid.

Coal was not only a source of energy but also a spur to technological development. Most products that could be manufactured with open wood fires were damaged by contact with coal fumes. John R. Harris has commented that as a result "coal was hardly ever adopted without significant alteration of industrial processes." Indeed, the technological advances of the Industrial Revolution were largely the culmination of the innovative period associated with the conversion to coal.

New methods of firing had to be developed in which the materials to be heated were protected from direct contact with the burning coals and the gases evolved in their combustion. Otherwise the coal would have had to be reduced to coke and so purged of its noxious properties. After about 1610 glass began to be manufactured with mineral fuel in a variant of the reverberatory furnace, a system that later played an important role in the growth of other major industries. In this type of furnace an arched roof reflects the heat of the burning coal onto the material to be heated, thereby preventing the contamination of the material by substances originating with the fuel. The potash and sand to be melted down to form glass were enclosed in a clay crucible to further protect them from the fumes. Like the reverberatory furnace, the crucible was later employed in many other manufacturing processes.

Over the decades following 1610 new technology brought coal into many kinds of manufacturing. The cementation process for converting wrought iron into steel with coal was introduced between 1612 and 1620. By 1618 a method of baking bricks in coal fires near London was described by the Venetian ambassador in words showing that Italians were no longer disposed to ignore this "faraway fuel" as Biringuccio had recommended. Before the British civil war of the 1640's coke was introduced for the drying of malt in connection with the brewing industry, which had expanded rapidly during most of the 16th century with the spread of hop gardening from the Netherlands.

One of the most important applications of coal following the restoration of the British monarchy in 1660 was in the adaptation of the reverberatory furnace for smelting nonferrous metals. This innovation of the 1680's made it possible to smelt the lead, copper and tin ores of Britain with coal. By the end of the 17th century only the production of

pig and bar iron remained dependent on wood. Although the problem was not completely solved until the 1780's, an important step toward its solution was taken in 1709, when coke was introduced by Abraham Darby the elder at

THE WOOD CRISIS of the 16th century coincided with the expression of a changed attitude toward mining. Until the Middle Ages mining had been widely considered an affront to nature. In *De re metallica*, published in 1556, however, Georgius Agricola expressed a new respect for mining. This careful account of metallurgy and mining gives a good picture of those industries at about the time when it was first necessary to increase coal production. In this illustration from *De re metallica* a tunnel, *D*, has been cut into a hill and three shafts have been dug from above. Although the mining was facilitated when a shaft connected with the tunnel, not all the shafts were meant to do so. In this case the shaft at *A* will be mined only from the surface; the shaft at *B* connects with the tunnel, and the tunnel will soon connect with the shaft at *C*. Material was hauled vertically out of a shaft with a windlass, which was usually covered with a shed to keep rain out of the shaft. Agricola pointed out that it was desirable to construct a separate building as a dwelling because "sometimes boys and other living things fall into the shafts."

his blast furnace in Shropshire. In this kind of furnace the fuel and the ore are in contact. The trouble with Darby's process was that it yielded a kind of pig iron that, unlike the pig iron produced with wood, could not be converted to wrought iron, the form of iron then most in demand. In 1784 Henry Cort invented the puddling process, in which pig iron (even pig iron from a blast furnace) is remelted and manipulated in a coal-fired reverberatory furnace to produce wrought iron. Until Cort's invention the making of iron remained largely dependent on charcoal. Thus although iron production in England had increased several times between 1540 and about 1620, this growth had been arrested by the shortage of wood for making charcoal in the 1620's. Beginning in that decade, however, an increase in iron imports, notably from Sweden, made possible a continuous slow growth in the output of finished iron wares, which were already produced by processes utilizing mineral fuel.

Samuel Eliot Morison has observed about innovations in shipbuilding and navigation that there is always "a gap between the invention of a device and persuading owners to supply it or sailors to use it." The same can be said about the spread of inventions connected with the introduction of coal in Britain after 1550. It took a substantial period of experimentation to make the new coal-based methods efficient. For example, in brickmaking (as also in the baking of clay tobacco pipes) there was much waste through breakage when coal-burning furnaces were introduced. Before the end of the 17th century, however, few bricks were lost in the course of coal firing.

As it became clear that coal could mean cheaper and more efficient production more industries turned to it as a fuel. Before the end of the 17th century in Britain's growing textile industry, where processes such as steaming and dyeing called for large quantities of fuel, that fuel was usually coal. Before 1700 the expanding manufactures of salt, alum, copperas (vitriol, or ferrous sulfate), saltpeter, gunpowder, starch and candles depended on coal. Coal was then also being employed extensively in the preparation of preserved foods, vinegar and Scotch whisky, and in brewing, soap boiling and sugar refining. A French visitor studying English technology in the Midlands in 1738–39 reported that the new coal-burning kilns (made of coal-baked bricks) had produced such a superior lime fertilizer that the yield of arable land had tripled. He considered coal "the soul of English manufactures."

The spread of coal into British homes that began early in Elizabethan times was continuous throughout the 17th century. This was not the only residential change brought about by the conversion of Britain to mineral fuel. The kingdom was extensively rebuilt under Queen Elizabeth and her Stuart successors. Brick and stone structures (with mortar made from coal-burned limestone) were replacing wood ones. Windows made of glass (produced in coal furnaces) were installed in buildings to retain the heat from the new coal-burning fireplaces (which had iron grates and brick chimneys manufactured with coal). In spite of its grime and stench coal had brought a new comfort to Britain's damp, chilly climate. Already in 1651 the author of *News from Newcastle* observed that the sacks of coal had heightened the joys of intimacy!

Coal had been so successfully incorporated into the British technology and economy that during the last four decades of the 17th century wood prices stopped rising. Some years ago I ventured a rough estimate of three million tons for Britain's annual coal production in the 1690's. In Harris' opinion that figure "may eventually prove conservative rather than excessive." It appears that at least as much as four times more heating was done at that time with coal than was done with wood. Never before had a major country come to depend on underground resources for the bulk of its fuel.

Although the exploitation of coal had largely solved the fuel shortage before 1700, there was still a wood shortage because other demands for wood had increased. In 1618 a traveler from London described his time as a "rattling, rowling, rumbling age" and remarked that "the World runnes on [wood] Wheeles." Great quantities of lumber were required for the construction of the growing number of ships and horse-drawn vehicles needed to transport people and goods across water and land. Moreover, although there was some reforestation during the 17th century, more and more forest was being cleared for farms and pastures. In addition smaller areas were being cleared for the growing metallurgical industries and for the expansion of mining, particularly of coal mining. Britain's forests simply could not keep up with the island's demand for wood.

The British were forced to supplement their domestic supply with imports, mostly from the American colo-

REVERBERATORY FURNACE made possible the utilization of coal in spite of the fuel's reactive smoke and flames. The arched roof of a reverberatory furnace reflects the heat of combustion onto the material to be heated. When the fuel being burned is coal, the arrangement prevents contamination of the product by the substances in the coal fumes. This view of a reverberatory annealing furnace is from the section on coinmaking in Diderot's *Encyclopédie*. Blanks, such as one shown in furnace, had to be annealed before coins could be struck.

nies and from the Baltic region. (In his *Wealth of Nations,* published in 1776, Adam Smith remarked that in his native Edinburgh "there [was] not perhaps a single stick of Scotch timber.") The imports of wood were paid for in part by the mounting exports of coal and probably in greater part by the mounting exports of textiles manufactured in varying degrees with coal fuel. This foreign trade, and even more the rapidly expanding coastwise trade, had already resulted in the 17th century in the development of a large British merchant marine. New colliers, or coal ships, were designed to carry more coal with a smaller crew, and the coastwise coal trade was considered the chief training ground for seamen, a major factor in Britain's emergence as a sea power.

Yet in some instances coal made Britain less dependent on imported commodities, for example salt. As Robert Multhauf explains in his forthcoming book *Neptune's Gift: A History of Common Salt,* this commodity was an essential one in Europe during the 16th and 17th centuries. In Britain, where food from the sea was coming to occupy a more important place in an increasingly abundant diet, salt was indispensable for preserving fish. In southern and western France salt was obtained by allowing the sun to evaporate seawater in shallow pans, or ponds, but this method was impractical in Britain's climate. In the early 16th century two thirds of the salt consumed in England had to be imported, mostly from France. Britain's almost total conversion to coal changed the situation. At the end of the 17th century some 300,000 tons, or nearly 10 percent of the coal mined annually in Britain, was burned to evaporate water for the production of salt in England and Scotland. As a result the country had become virtually self-sufficient in terms of salt.

The conversion to a new kind of fuel might have had less effect on the British economy if Britain had been poorly, or even only moderately, endowed with coal. Before the end of the 17th century, however, it had become clear that Britain possessed enormous coal reserves. A piece of coal-inspired technology provided new and reassuring information. The device, called a boring rod, was introduced at the beginning of the 17th century. Early boring-rod surveys were inaccurate, but before the 17th century had ended mining experts were able to determine the thickness and quality of coal seams without sinking shafts. Boring rods had become reliable tools and had revealed a newfound land of plenty under the soil and even under the sur-

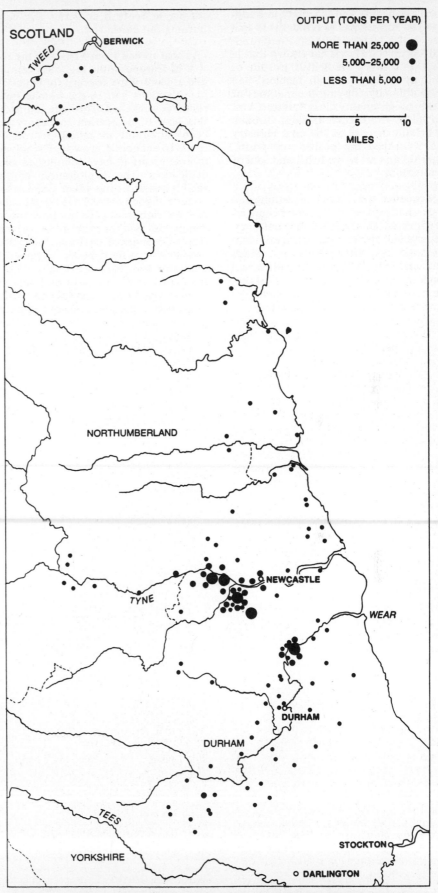

MAP OF DURHAM AND NORTHUMBERLAND COUNTIES in England shows the approximate locations of collieries in 1635. There were probably more collieries than are shown on the map. Illustration is adapted from map in author's *The Rise of the British Coal Industry.*

quest for beauty and harmony in buildings and furnishings as remarkable as it was in the Netherlands of Rembrandt and Vermeer.) Harris has shown that in the 18th century the British, in spite of their aspirations to high fashion, had great difficulty copying the methods of making high-quality glass that were employed by the French at Saint-Gobain. In Britain the rise of the coal industry had weakened the position of craftsmanship and art as the heart and soul of production.

Moreover, the rise of coal mining had cast a shadow over the laborers connected with coal. Coal miners and coal carriers, stained by the black mineral, were often outcasts. They were seen as black men, and in the 17th century, when real black men were being shipped as slaves from Africa to America, coal laborers were being subjected to a new form of slavery in Scottish collieries and coal-burning salt pans.

As coal spread from Britain to the rest of Europe in the late 18th century and afterward the concern for beauty in manufactures and in the human environment weakened. Throughout history this kind of dedication to beauty has been important in setting reasonable limits to economic growth. The advent of coal seems to have diminished such dedication. The exploitation of the earth's resources has often violated the bounds of good taste. To make the most of these resources calls not only for ingenuity but also for restraint. At present man's dependence on fossil fuels is as problematic as his dependence on wood was some 400 years ago. The best hope for the fruitful exploitation of fuel resources may lie in a renewal and an amplification of the standards of beauty. If humanity is to advance, the making of history must become an art, that is, a search for beauty.

Bibliography

THE RISE OF THE BRITISH COAL INDUSTRY: VOLS. I AND II. John U. Nef. George Routledge & Sons, Ltd, 1932.

NOTE ON THE PROGRESS OF IRON PRODUCTION IN ENGLAND, 1540–1640. John U. Nef in *The Journal of Political Economy*, Vol. 44, No. 3, pages 398–403; June, 1936.

SILVER PRODUCTION IN CENTRAL EUROPE, 1450–1618. John U. Nef in *The Journal of Political Economy*, Vol. 49, No. 4, pages 575–591; August, 1941.

THE AGRICULTURAL REVOLUTION. Eric Kerridge. Allen & Unwin Ltd, 1967.

WAR AND HUMAN PROGRESS: AN ESSAY ON THE RISE OF INDUSTRIAL CIVILIZATION. John U. Nef. W. W. Norton & Co., 1968.

COTTAGE INDUSTRY AND THE FACTORY SYSTEM

Duncan Bythell

AT THE CENTRE OF MOST PEOPLE'S picture of Britain's industrial revolution in the nineteenth century stands the dark, satanic mill, where an exploited and dispirited army of men, women and children is engaged for starvation wages in a seemingly endless round of drudgery: the pace of their labour is determined by the persistent pulse of the steam engine and accompanied by the ceaseless clanking of machines; and the sole beneficiary of their efforts is the grasping, tyrannical, licentious factory master, pilloried by Charles Dickens in that loud-mouthed hypocrite and philistine, Mr. Bounderby. Crude and exaggerated though this image is, it depicts very clearly the main features of the pattern of production which became widespread in the manufacturing industries, not only of Britain, but also of the other advanced countries, by the end of the nineteenth century. For it highlights the emergence of the factory, where hundreds labour together under one roof and one direction, as the normal type of work-unit; it stresses the new importance of complex machine-technology in the process of production; and it emphasises that, because ownership of these machines, of the building which houses them and the engine which drives them, rests with the private capitalist, there exists an unbridgeable gulf between him and his property-less wage-earning employees.

This system of production, which is usually assumed to have been pioneered and rapidly adopted in Britain's textile industries around the end of the eighteenth century, did not, of course, emerge in a wholly non-industrial world. The popular picture suggests that it replaced – or rather, brutally displaced – an earlier type of organisation, variously referred to as 'the domestic system', the 'outwork system', or simply as 'cottage industry', which differed totally from the factory system. Whereas the latter concentrates workers under one roof in an increasingly urban enviroment, the former disperses employment into the homes of the workers, most of whom live in the countryside. Although the modern mill is filled with the factory master's costly machinery, the domestic workshop houses simple and traditional hand-tools – the spinner's wheel, the weaver's loom, the cordwainer's bench, the nail-maker's forge, and the seamstress' humble pins and needles – which actually belong to the worker. And whilst the factory system implies clear class division, with the wage-earner firmly subordinated to, and perpetually at odds with, his employer, the domestic system gives the head of the household an independent, quasi-managerial status, which enables him to control his own time and to direct, in a 'natural' fatherly way, the efforts of his family team.

The unspoken assumption is that, in the undisciplined, fulfilling, and relatively classless world of cottage industry, the common man was certainly happier, even if he was materially worse off, than his grandson. Only in the last desperate phase, when the dwindling band of domestic handworkers found themselves competing hopelessly against the new generation of factory machine-minders, is the idyllic image tarnished; and the haunting picture of the doomed handloom weaver, striving in his cellar to match the output of his wife and children who have been forced into the factory, reinforces the notion that, between old and new systems, there is nothing but contrast, conflict, and competition.

Any concept of historical change based on snapshots taken on separate occasions tends to emphasise differences and discontinuities. In the caricature of the domestic and factory systems just presented, they appear to be completely antithetical. Yet on closer examination, the story of most industries which 'modernised' in the course of the nineteenth century is full of important elements of *continuity* and *complementarity* between the factory and the pre-factory stages of their development; and it is on these two dimensions, rather than on the stark contrasts suggested by the traditional stereotype, that I want to focus attention.

Let us consider continuity first. A number of historians have recently suggested that the existence of the domestic system of production in such industries as textiles was one of the main features

Factory spinning

distinguishing the pre-industrial economies of Europe from the Third World countries of today; and although they prefer the abstract concept of 'proto industrialisation' to the well-established and perfectly adequate term 'domestic system', they are essentially claiming that the industrial revolutions of the nineteenth century could not have taken place without the prior development of a form of production which, in their view, was to provide both the capital and the labour needed for modern industrial development.

In making this claim, proponents of the theory of 'proto industry' are drawing attention to one of the most important, but often misunderstood, features of the classic domestic system – the fact that it already showed a clear distinction between the capitalists who controlled it and the wage-earners who depended upon it for their livelihood. For the domestic system, no less than the factory system which replaced it, was a method of mass-production which enabled wealthy merchant-manufacturers to supply not only textile fabrics, but also items as diverse as ready-made clothes, hosiery, boots and shoes, and hardware, to distant markets at home and abroad. In order to do so, they, like the factory masters who followed them, bought the appropriate raw materials and hired wage-labour to convert them into finished products. The pay roll of some of these merchant-manufacturers could run into many hundreds: in the late 1830s, for example, Dixons of Carlisle, cotton manufacturers, employed 3,500 handloom weavers scattered over the border counties of England and Scotland and in Ulster; a decade or so later, Wards of Belper, hosiers, provided work for some 4,000 knitting frames in the counties of Derbyshire, Nottinghamshire, and Leicestershire; and as late as the 1870s, Eliza Tinsley and Co. put out work to 2,000 domestic nail- and chain-makers in the west Midlands.

To service and co-ordinate such large and scattered forces required an elaborate system of communication and control in which the key figures were the agents – variously known as 'putters-out', 'bagmen', and 'foggers' – who were the equivalents of the modern supervisor or shop-floor manager. Certainly, the workers whom these great men employed generally owned their own tools, although in the case of an elaborate piece of machinery like the knitting frame they often had to hire it; and most of

them worked on their own premises – although, again, it was by no means rare for the individual weaver, knitter, or nail-maker to rent space and tools in another man's shop. But except in a few minor rural trades like straw-plaiting and lace-making in the south and east Midlands, they neither provided their own raw materials, nor had they any interest in marketing the goods they helped to make. They were, in short, wage-earners who happened to own some of the tools of their trade. But the trade in which they worked was organised by capitalists; and far from making goods to sell to local customers, they were often, all unknowing, supplying the wants of West Indian slaves and North American frontiersmen.

The crux of the argument about continuity between domestic and factory systems of mass-production turns on whether it was actually the case that the firms which set up the first modern factories in a particular industry were already active in it on a putting-out basis, and whether the last generation of domestic workers transformed themselves into the new race of factory hands. Of course, no one is maintaining that continuity was direct and complete in every single industry or region where such a transition occurred: indeed, there were areas such as East Anglia or the Cotswolds where the change-over simply did not take place, and where a once important industry gradually vanished as the old domestic system dwindled and died. But where 'modernisation' did happen in traditional outwork industries in the course of the nineteenth century, as it did in the textile industries of Lancashire and Yorkshire and in the hosiery trade of the east Midlands, historians seem to be agreed that it was existing firms which played a leading role, albeit cautiously and belatedly in some instances, in setting-up the factory system and in embodying some of their capital in buildings and machines; in other words the fortunes made, and the expertise in marketing and managing acquired, in the old system of production were important in enabling the new system to develop.

There is less agreement, however, as to how far the existing hand-workers in any particular industry really did shift over to the factory. The theory of 'proto industry' suggests that the domestic system had created a country-dwelling but landless proletariat in many ways at odds with the traditional rural society around

them: they had only a minimal involvement in the agrarian economy, and were therefore rootless and prone to migration; they possessed manual skills irrelevant to farming activities; and as wage-earners, they were obliged to respond to the pressures and the opportunities of a market economy in which the price of survival was adaptability. In terms of both work-skills and mental outlook, that is to say, they were already well-equipped to form the first generation of the modern industrial labour force.

But did this actually happen? The traditional picture suggests not, because it depicts a stubborn refusal to come to terms with changed circumstances and, indeed, a downright hostility to 'machinery' which, in the Luddite movement of 1811-16 in the Midlands and the various outbreaks of loom-smashing in Lancashire and elsewhere, sometimes erupted in violence. Clearly, the worker's readiness to change with the times depended partly on age, and partly on opportunity. Case studies based on census returns for Lancashire weaving villages during the crucial phase of transition in the middle of the nineteenth century suggest that, once a powerloom shed had been started locally, the younger married men were ready enough to take work in it, but that the elderly were either reluctant to do so, or were debarred by the employer, and therefore stuck to the handloom. But until there was a mill virtually on the spot, most of these villagers believed they had little option but to stick to the handloom, and for want of other opportunity they continued to bring their children up to it. Probably the most important strand of continuity in the labour force was in fact provided by the children of the last generation of hand-workers: by and large, a trade dies out because it stopped recruiting sometime before; and the demise of occupations like handloom weaving was finally assured when families were willing and able to put their offspring into something different, instead of forcing them to follow automatically in father's footsteps.

By highlighting the division between capital and labour which characterised the domestic no less than the factory system of production, and by considering the continuity which this engendered, the new theory of 'proto industry' has pinpointed certain popular misconceptions about the nature of cottage industry. First of all, it must be clear that when economic historians refer to 'outwork' or 'cottage industry' they are *not* talking about a world where each family simply makes manufactured goods for its own use – although in even the most advanced societies elements of the home-made and the do-it-yourself survive. Nor are they discussing the self-employed craftsman or genuine artisan – the village shoe-maker and tailor, or the more sophisticated urban wig-maker and cabinet-maker – who produced and sold 'one-off' goods directly to the order of their local customers, and whose successors are still to be found in some parts of the modern economy. Indeed – and this is a second error which needs to be corrected – in the strict sense they are not dealing with 'skill' or 'craft' at all. As a method of mass-production, the greater part of cottage industry involved the

The weaver at his domestic hand loom (above) contrasts sharply with work on a factory power loom (below).

making of plain, simple, inexpensive goods by hands which, although they became more nimble and adept with experience, had neither needed nor received much initial training. Weaving heavy woollens and hammering nails and chains required a certain strength; but weaving plain calico, knitting coarse stockings, sewing buttons on shirts, plaiting straw, and sticking matchboxes together with glue called for neither brain nor brawn. A seven-year apprenticeship to learn the 'mysteries' of most domestic industries was unnecessary, when the work merely involved the monotonous repetition of a few simple

movements of the fingers; and because the work was unskilled and undemanding it was considered particularly suitable for women and children. Domestic industry, like factory industry, involved the worker in much mindless drudgery; the chief difference was that, in working at home with hand-tools, the wage-earner could go at his or her own pace, instead of having to keep up with the steam engine.

Thirdly, just as we need to abandon the notion that the domestic system was all about skilled craftsmen, so we must reject the idea that it was predominantly about 'men' at all. One of the advantages

which the old terms 'domestic system' and 'cottage industry' have over 'proto industry' is that they suggest an important feature which old-style mass-production shared with the early textile mills: a domestic or cottage workshop called on the efforts of housewife, grandparents, and children of both sexes, as well as those of the household's head. Thus the average weaving or knitting family would run two or three looms or frames, and in addition would operate any ancillary machinery needed to prepare or finish the work. Because it worked as a team, the domestic work unit could also practice division of labour, so that each member could specialise on just one stage in the sequence of production. Like any other family business, a workshop involved in the domestic system was a collective enterprise to which all contributed who could: and only when the household included no children old enough to do even the simplest tasks did it depend for its income on what a man could earn by his own unaided efforts. Because the capitalist-controlled outwork industries made particular use of women's and children's labour in this way, female workers were generally in a clear majority in the work force; and in the mass-production section of the needlework trades, where outwork remained particularly important until late in the nineteenth century, and which included men's tailoring and shirt-making as well as dress-making and lace stitching, the preponderance of women was especially striking.

Fourthly, we must not imagine that, in a capitalist controlled industrial system such as outwork was, relations between masters and operatives were marked by much sweetness and light. Since the main tie between them was the cash nexus, disputes about wages could be frequent and bitter. Most employers in the industries which used the domestic system operated in a tough competitive environment, and their likely reaction to a spell of bad trading conditions would be to cut the piece-rates they paid their workers. Most of the scattered rural outworkers were disorganised and docile, and could offer little, if any, resistance; and in any case, for women and children a pittance was deemed better than no work at all. But the adult men – especially those who lived in the towns, and did the better-class work which needed more strength or skill – were another matter. They had a clear

1. INDUSTRIAL AND SCIENTIFIC REVOLUTIONS

conception of the work and wages proper for a man, and they were better able to take collective action against underpaying masters and weak-willed blacklegs who broke the conventional rules.

As a result, at different times in the late eighteenth and early nineteenth centuries, fierce strikes broke out in such towns as Manchester, Coventry, Barnsley and Norwich, major centres of handloom weaving; among the urban framework knitters of Nottingham and Leicester; and among the nail-makers of the Black Country. At a time when

formal trade unionism was a shadowy affair, and in difficult political and economic circumstances, some at least of Britain's industrial outworkers played their part in sustaining patterns of collective bargaining which, *faute de mieux*, sometimes involved great violence; whilst the support these disgruntled men gave to the various campaigns for parliamentary reform between the 1790s and the 1850s has been frequently noted by historians.

Once we have abandoned such misconceptions about the nature of the domestic system as it had come to exist

by the end of the eighteenth century, it is easier to see the similarities and the points of continuity between it and the factory system which was eventually and gradually to supersede it. And when we realise that the domestic system, far from being some prehistoric monster which expired when the first cotton factory was built, actually expanded and persisted in many industries and regions until well into the second half of the nineteenth century, we become aware, not only that the two types of mass-production overlapped in time, but also that they complemented each other,

(Above left) The Domestic Rope Maker; from *The Book of Trades*, 1804. (Above right) Making ropes by Huddart's Machinery.
(Below left) An outworker making pins at home: (below right) a needle pointer at work in a factory in Redditch, Worcester.

rather than competed. The textile industries usually occupy the forefront of any discussion of the domestic and factory systems; and in view of their wide geographic dispersal, their rapid expansion, and the hundreds of thousands they had come to employ by the late eighteenth century, this is entirely appropriate. But because, starting with the spinning branch of the British cotton industry in the 1770s, it was in these industries that the complete triumph of the factory system was achieved earliest, attention has been deflected from the many other trades – particularly shoe-making, clothing, and some branches of hardware – where the domestic system actually became more, rather than less, important. For although the first half of the nineteenth century saw the disappearance into the factory first of spinning and then of weaving in Lancashire and Yorkshire, it also witnessed the expansion of mass-production by outwork methods in the ready-made clothing trades and in the boot and shoe industries. And apart from the fact that these growing industries increased output by traditional rather than modern methods, there were other, less expansionary trades – such as Midlands hosiery and Black Country nail-making – which remained fossilised at the 'domestic' stage of development until well after 1850. In addition, the latter part of the nineteenth century actually saw a number of new, small scale manufactures, such as paperbag and cardboard-box making, establish themselves as cottage industries. Thus, if outwork had more or less disappeared from the staple textile industries by the 1850s, it was more firmly entrenched than ever in and around many of the industrial towns of the Midlands and the south of England, and, above all, in what were to become known as the 'sweated trades' of London. Why was this?

The pioneering experience of the textile industries suggests some of the answers. Contrary to popular belief, even in the cotton industry, the transition from the domestic to the factory system was a slow, piecemeal affair, which took three generations; and in wool, linen and silk, the process was even more protracted. The reason was simple: the first power-driven machines of the 1770s revolutionised *spinning* only; and by making it possible to produce thread on a scale and at a price which would have been inconceivable in the days of the spinning wheel, they simply created a good deal more work for a great many more work-

ers – in this case, the weavers – at the next stage in the production process. And so long as enough extra weavers could be found at wages the employers were prepared to pay, there was no need to think of replacing the handloom with some labour-saving device, as yet uninvented. Thus between 1780 and 1820, the growth of spinning factories marched *pari passu* with a vast increase in the number of handloom weavers' shops; and technical progress in one section of the industry merely led to the multiplication of traditional handwork in associated sections.

The same thing was to happen in other industries later: when lace-making was mechanised in Nottingham from the 1820s, there was a consequent increase in the amount of stitching, finishing and mending for hand-sewers in their homes; when machines were first used to cut out the components of a stock-sized shoe or coat, they made more unskilled assembly work for domestic workers; and even when the sewing machine had transformed the traditional needlework trades, it did not necessarily drive them out of the home into the factory, because, as a compact, hand-powered, and relatively inexpensive tool, it could be used in a domestic workshop as effectively as in a large factory. In all these ways, factory and domestic systems often co-existed and complemented each other in a given industry. Since it was rarely either possible or necessary for new techniques to be

introduced simultaneously at every stage in the process of manufacture, flexible combinations of centralised factory work at one stage, and cottage industry at the next, were perfectly practicable.

There was often a regional dimension to the co-existence of these two types of mass-production, and it was here that elements of competition emerged between them. In the classic case of cotton weaving, for example, the handloom survived as the dominant machine in some parts of Lancashire for almost a generation after it had largely given way to the powerloom in others: in large

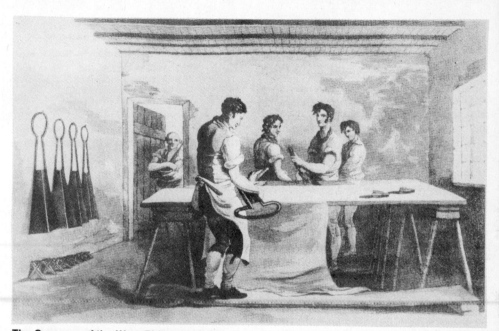

The Croppers of the West Riding of Yorkshire were much involved in the machine-wrecking Luddite movement of 1812.

towns such as Stockport, Oldham and Blackburn, factory production was taken up in the 1820s by manufacturers who already operated spinning mills; but it made little progress in the small towns and villages of north-east Lancashire, such as Padiham, Colne and Haggate before the 1840s. In part, this reflected local differences in the availability of labour and capital, for the more remote rural areas were richer in the former than in the latter. But independent of such regional differences, there was also a qualitative side to this 'staggered' adoption of the powerloom, because the early, clumsy factory looms could cope better with the plain types of cloth than with fancy or patterned goods. Other industries were later to show similar disparities in the rate at which different districts and sections adopted new techniques: for example, the boot and shoe industry of Leicester

Merchants in the Cloth Hall, Leeds in 1814. Merchants used cottage industries as a method of mass-production to supply their buyers.

seems to have relied more on factory production and less on outwork than did that of Northampton in the second half of the nineteenth century; whilst in the 1890s, cottage industry was more apparent in the ready-made clothing trade of London than in that of Leeds.

In short, the domestic system of mass-production in British industry took a long time a-dying during the nineteenth century. It might expand in one trade at the very time that it was contracting in another; in some industries, it could enjoy a harmonious co-existence with factory production for many years, whilst elsewhere it might struggle on in arduous competition for a generation or more. Why was this? How could this technically primitive form of large-scale production remain viable for so long in important parts of the world's first industrial economy?

To find the answer, we must try to fathom the minds of the entrepreneurs in the different industries, as they calculated how best, in a complex and competitive world, to get their goods to market with least cost and least trouble to themselves. A manufacturer who had grown up with the domestic system as the dominant mode of production in his trade would need strong inducements to abandon it, because under normal circumstances it offered him many advantages. If his employees provided their

own tools and workrooms, he himself was spared the need to tie up his own capital in bricks and mortar and in machinery; and in times of periodic trade depression or slack seasonal demand – and most of these industries were subject to one or other of these risks, if not, indeed, to both of them – it was the worker, not his employer, who suffered when plant and equipment were standing idle. It was not that these great merchant-manufacturers lacked capital – indeed it required remarkably little fixed capital in most of these industries to build or rent a small factory and fill it with new or second-hand machinery; nor was it generally the case that appropriate new techniques were not available – the time-lag between invention and adoption of a new machine is a recurrent feature in many of these trades; it was rather the case that their capital under the domestic system was embodied in unused raw materials, goods 'in the make', and stocks in the warehouse.

Nevertheless, because it involved more sophisticated machinery, the application of power, and the construction of large, purpose-built work premises, the factory system of production was capital-intensive, rather than labour-intensive. By contrast, what an employer had to rely on to keep cottage industry viable was an abundance of

cheap, unskilled, and unorganised labour. So long as he could find enough workers who had no choice but to take his work at the wages he was prepared to offer – no matter how low these might be – he could meet his production targets and reap his expected profits. From the late eighteenth to the late nineteenth centuries, there were many regions of Britain which could provide just such supplies of labour: a high and sustained rate of population increase, together with the greater commercialisation of agriculture, tended to create pools of unemployed or under-employed workers in many rural areas; and in so far as these impoverished country people moved off to the towns in search of more work and better wages, they often merely added to the chaos and confusion in the unskilled urban labour markets.

But what kept the domestic system alive after the mid-nineteenth century more than anything else was the continued availability – long after most adult men had deserted these low paid, dead-end jobs – of female and child labour: incapable of collective self-defence, and often deliberately ignored by their better organised menfolk, accustomed to regarding any earnings, however minute, as a worthwhile contribution to family income; and often only able to work on a part-time or casual basis – they were ideal for many employers' purposes. And in a perverse way, because it thrived on family labour, the domestic system actually helped to perpetuate its own labour force: because cottage industry, by enabling the whole household to earn, acted as a great inducement to early marriages and large families, and thus contributed to the 'population explosion' which was so important a feature of Britain's industrial revolution.

Because labour could be much cheaper in one part of the country than in another, an old-fashioned employer who stuck to outwork could still hope to compete with his more ambitious and enterprising fellows elsewhere who had switched over to factory production. Only in the last quarter of the nineteenth century did a combination of new circumstances – including rural depopulation, compulsory schooling (which both kept young children out of the labour market and widened their horizons) rising real incomes (which made small supplementary earnings less essential to a family), and more 'chivalrous' male

Gathering Teasels in the West Riding of Yorkshire, an aquatint after George Walker. Teasels are still used to raise the nap on woollen cloth.

(Below) *The Preemer Boy,* 1814; aquatint after George Walker. 'Preeming' is detaching, with an iron comb, the bits of wool on the teasel.

only stay in business if they themselves adopted American methods of production. Both the cotton manufacturers of the 1820s and the boot and shoe manufacturers of the 1890s had to overcome strong opposition from workers still suspicious of machinery and still attached (in spite of the precarious economic position in which it left them) to the domestic system: but once the entrepreneurs in any industry had concluded, for whatever reasons, that the disadvantages of cottage industry outweighed the benefits, its days were numbered.

From the worker's point of view, even if we forget the caricature, the dark satanic mill offered an uninviting prospect; but it is hard to escape the conclusion that the domestic system was in many ways even less agreeable. Even where cottage workers were not directly competing with factory workers – and I have suggested that it would be wrong to put too much emphasis on this side of the story – most of them were poorly paid, and likely to be alternately overworked and under-employed. Worst of all, they were subject to all kinds of abuses, not only from employers and their agents, but often from heads of households and fathers of families who connived, however reluctantly, in the exploitation of their own wives and children. Men may have been unwilling to accept the separation of home and workplace which the gradual replacement of the domestic system by the factory system involved: but in its long-term implications for family life, it was probably one of the most beneficial, as well as one of the most fundamental, of all the changes brought about by the industrial revolution.

attitudes towards women as workers – help gradually to eliminate some of the sources of cheap labour and thus undermine one of the domestic system's chief props.

Changes in market conditions, as well as the increasing difficulty of finding suitable labour, could also be instrumental in persuading entrepreneurs to abandon old-style mass-production in favour of the factory. When, for example, attractive new export markets opened up

for the English cotton industry in Latin America in the early 1820s, Lancashire manufacturers knew that they would be better able to increase output by introducing powerlooms than by seeking out more handloom weavers at higher wages; and when, more than two generations later, British boot and shoe manufacturers were faced with an 'invasion' of their own home market by cheap mass-produced, factory-made American imports, they recognised that they could

FOR FURTHER READING:
D. Bythell, *The Sweated Trades* (Batsford, 1978); J. L. and B. Hammond, *The Skilled Labourer* (London, 1919); G. Stedman Jones, *Outcast London* (Oxford University Press, 1971); P. Kriedte, H. Medick and J. Schlumbohm, *Industrialization before Industrialization* (Cambridge University Press, 1981); D. Levine, *Family Formation in an Age of Nascent Capitalism* (Academic Press, 1977); J. M. Prest, *The Industrial Revolution in Coventry* (Oxford University Press, 1960); E. P. Thompson, *The Making of the English Working Class* (Gollancz, 1963; Penguin Books).

FROM ASTRONOMY TO ASTROPHYSICS

James Trefil

. James S. Trefil, is professor of physics at the University of Virginia. Born in Chicago, Illinois, he received a B.S. (1960) from the University of Illinois, a B.A. and an M.A. (1962) from Oxford University, and an M.S. (1964) and a Ph.D. (1966) from Stanford University. He is the author of Meditations at Ten Thousand Feet *(1986).*

Nicolaus Copernicus (1473–1543) was a Pole, a churchman, an intellectual recluse, and a somewhat enigmatic figure. Much is unknown about him, yet he sparked a scientific revolution that powerfully influenced the subsequent five centuries. Today, looking back at his life and work, it is difficult to comprehend the magnitude of the Copernican Revolution, how momentous a change it really was for 16th-century Europe. But altering civilized man's view of the cosmos is exactly what he did.

Guided by his uncle, a Roman Catholic bishop, Copernicus was elected to a position as canon (business manager) at the Cathedral of Frauenburg in his native Poland. He traveled widely, studied in Italy, and was a model scholar and churchman. From roughly 1512 on, he developed a scheme of a planetary system in which the planets moved and the Sun stood still. He confided his manuscript to a printer only in 1540, at age 67. As the story goes, he received a copy of his published book on the day he died, three years later.

The book, *On the Revolutions of the Celestial Spheres*, is an odd mixture of revolutionary and traditional ideas. Since Claudius Ptolemy (circa A.D. 100–178), the ancient Greek astronomer who advocated a geocentric model of the universe, Europeans had envisioned the Sun, stars, and planets embedded in concentric spheres around the Earth, with God, in effect, cranking the mechanism from the outside.

Copernicus realized that the daily motion of the stars across the sky resulted from the Earth's rotation, and that the complex motions of planets were the natural effect of their movement around the Sun. His system, of course, was not identical to the modern one. To account for the true planetary orbits, Copernicus had to put his planets on epicycles (small circles centered on the rims of larger ones). The centers of the larger circles lay not in the Sun, but at a point in space between the Sun and the Earth. Even if it could not be proved, his view had an immense allure for adventuresome minds.

Copernicus's scheme was only somewhat simpler than Ptolemy's, but it prompted astronomy students (at least from 1543 on) to realize that they could question traditional wisdom. Human reason was freeing itself from burdens of the past—another major step for Europeans who had just experienced the throes of the Reformation, Martin Luther's break with the monolithic authoritarianism of Rome.

Another consequence of the Copernican system—one often overlooked—is that it expanded mankind's concept of the universe. Formerly, with a seemingly stationary Earth, the realm of the stars lay just beyond Saturn's orbit; the entire universe seemed only as big as the solar system. But with Earth orbiting the Sun, the stars had to

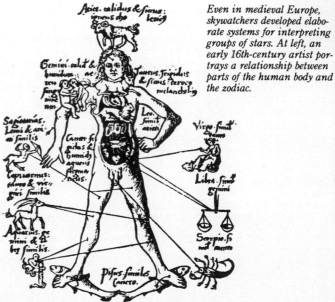

Even in medieval Europe, skywatchers developed elaborate systems for interpreting groups of stars. At left, an early 16th-century artist portrays a relationship between parts of the human body and the zodiac.

be far away to appear stationary. In one fell swoop, Copernicus moved the Earth from the center and set it moving in a new heaven of wider horizons. He and Christopher Columbus were contemporaries. Each man revealed a new world to Europe—but Copernicus was charting a realm whose outer boundaries have yet to be discovered.

As it happened, *On the Revolutions of the Celestial Spheres* spread quickly throughout Europe, encountering far less ecclesiastical opposition than Galileo would later face. For one thing, Copernicus was well connected in the church. For another, the unsigned preface of his book presents the Copernican system as a mathematical exercise, not necessarily a statement about the real world. This pretension left plenty of maneuver room for theologians and scholars.

Among Copernicus's readers was the Danish nobleman Tycho Brahe (1546–1601), who had a lifelong obsession with measuring the heavens accurately. During the 16th century, observation was not much more accurate than it had been during the time of Ptolemy. Tycho, born before the invention of the telescope, pushed the accuracy of naked-eye astronomy to its limit. He built astronomical instruments, such as a huge brass quadrant and a four-cubit sextant, to reduce errors associated with reading small scales. He compensated for the expansion and shrinkage of his brass instruments due to temperature changes, devising tables to correct for these effects. He even built an underground observatory to reduce wind vibrations.

Reprinted from *The Wilson Quarterly*, Summer 1987, pp. 50-63. From **Space, Time, Infinity** by James S. Trefil. © 1985 Smithsonian Institute. Published by Pantheon Books, Random House. Reprinted by permission.

In part, the quest for precision grew out of the desire to distinguish between the Copernican and Ptolemaic systems, and because people of the mid-16th century had witnessed some unusual events in the heavens. On November 11, 1572, for instance, a new star appeared in the constellation of Cassiopeia—one so bright that during the next month it could be seen in daylight. Repairing to his beautifully crafted instruments, Tycho took a series of readings. He established beyond a doubt that the object (now called Tycho's supernova) moved less than the most distant planet in the sky and was therefore beyond the sphere of the stars. This feat established the 25-year-old Dane as one of Europe's premier astronomers.

So impressed was King Frederick II of Denmark that he installed Tycho on the Baltic island of Hven and provided the money to construct the world's largest astronomical observatory. There Tycho built instruments and gathered data unprecedented in both volume and accuracy.

All was well, until Tycho ran afoul of Frederick's successor, Christian IV, over a number of issues—such as whether or not Tycho had the right to throw peasants into his private dungeon. So the astronomer packed up his data, instruments, and court jester, and quit Hven for the court of Emperor Rudolf II in Prague.

Tycho's Undoing

All told, Tycho lived an unusual life. At an early age, he was kidnapped by his wealthy and childless uncle Jorgen, who raised him in a castle in Tostrup. Sent to the University of Copenhagen to study jurisprudence, Tycho—profoundly impressed by an eclipse of the Sun in 1560—instead spent his time studying the stars. Prone to emotional outbursts, at the age of 20 he dueled a fellow student over the question of who was a better mathematician. During the battle, Tycho lost a piece of his nose and had to wear a gold alloy prosthesis. Even his death was bizarre. At a banquet attended by much of Prague's nobility, he partook copiously of Bohemian beer. Not wishing to appear impolite—so the story goes—he ate and drank without excusing himself. Bladder stones may have been his undoing; he fell into a fever that night and died 11 days later.

Tycho's data tables went to an impecunious Austrian mathematician he had hired after his arrival in Prague—Johannes Kepler.

Kepler (1571–1630) was a mystic by nature. But, when confronted with all the data that Tycho had collected over a lifetime, he felt compelled to question some of his basic assumptions. Instead of trying to force Tycho's data into preconceived patterns, Kepler returned to the basics and considered which shapes best described the motions of the known planets.

Galileo as Martyr

Kepler's results are stated in what are now known as Kepler's first and second laws of planetary motion. The first law says that a planet's orbit assumes the shape of an ellipse—rather than a circle—with the Sun at one focus; the second law indicates that planets move faster when near the Sun than they do when farther away. In other words, as a planet passes near to the Sun it "swings around," speeding up as it does so.

Kepler published these two laws in 1609. A third and final law was published in 1619, relating the length of a planet's "year" to its distance from the Sun. Thus it became possible to shed excess conceptual baggage that scientists had developed to justify a false notion, namely, that celestial objects move along circular orbits.

Following the observational work of Copernicus, Tycho, and Kepler, Galileo Galilei (1564–1642) was the first to study the sky through a telescope.

Ironically, Galileo is one of those men in history who is famous for the wrong reasons. Because of his notorious trial in 1633 by the Roman Inquisition he has, perhaps undeservedly, become enshrined as a "martyr of science." Legend has it that he stood alone as a champion of the heliocentric universe against the forces of dogma-

---

GOING BACK TO STONEHENGE

Today most people take the sky for granted. Not so the ancients. They used the sky as clock, calendar, navigational aid, and oracle.

Among the oldest observatories, according to British astronomer Gerald S. Hawkins, is Stonehenge—a series of concentric circles, marked by large stones, standing on a plain near Salisbury, England. In 1963, Hawkins argued that Stonehenge enabled skywatchers, perhaps as early as 3100 B.C., to mark the solstices (when viewed correctly, the Sun rises over a 35-ton Heel Stone), the lunar cycles, and eclipses. Similar ruins stand around the world, in places as disparate as Scotland, Kenya, and the central United States.

Cro-Magnon people were probably the first humans to note the stars. Animal bones with markings that correspond to lunar phases, dated 9,000 to 30,000 years old, have been found in Europe. Between 3000 B.C. and 2000 B.C., Babylonians in Mesopotamia devised the first systematic calendar, based on 235 lunar months (29.5 days apiece) in 19 solar years. Between 1646 and 1626 B.C., they made the first detailed astronomical records, and later (circa 400 B.C.) used mathematics to predict celestial events. They were astrologers too. Atop immense, stepped, mud-brick towers, such as the ziggurat of Ur in southeastern Iraq (construction began in 2100 B.C.), Babylonian priests prayed to the Moon god Nanna-Sin while surveying stars.

•

Ancient Egyptians also were stargazers. Many of their great monuments—such as the Great Pyramid of Cheops and the temple at Karnak—are aligned with key positions of the Sun, Moon, and stars. Yet, despite Egypt's creation of a "modern" calendar (12 30-day months, plus five extra days), the Babylonians surpassed the Egyptians in astronomical sophistication.

The Greeks were the first scientists, not only recording celestial motion but wondering why stars and planets moved along particular paths. They sought physical rather than religious explanations. Thales of Miletus (circa 585 B.C.) predicted eclipses; Pythagoras (circa 580–500 B.C.) and his school deduced that the Earth is round, and Eratosthenes of Cyrene (circa 276–194 B.C.) devised a method for measuring its circumference at the equator—250,000 stadia (the width of a stadium, 607 feet), a figure quite close to the actual 24,902 miles. By the second century A.D., Claudius Ptolemy summarized four

The Mayan Caracol of Chichén Itzá, as it may have appeared circa 1000 A.D.

centuries of Greek astronomy in his treatise *Almagest*. As early as 720 B.C., Chinese astronomers kept watch for "portentous" events: eclipses, comets, meteors, planetary alignments. But their observations were not "scientific"; they tended simply to record, not analyze, unusual phenomena.

In Central America, circa 1000 A.D., Mayan astronomers on the Yucatán Peninsula constructed an observatory, the Caracol of Chichén Itzá. It demonstrates in its architecture alone—through alignments with certain stars and planets—a knowledge of solstices, lunar cycles, and the motions of the Morning and Evening Star (Venus). Their astronomical records, detailed on the bark leaves of an almanac called the Dresden Codex (it is now in a Dresden museum), reveal great sophistication: They calculated the length of a 365-day solar year, a 29.5 day lunar cycle, and the cycles of Venus within minutes of their true periods.

Throughout North America, Indian tribes, too, practiced astronomy. Atop Medicine Mountain, in Wyoming's Bighorn Range, lies a circular arrangement of "loaf-sized" rocks. This "medicine wheel," in which 28 35-foot-long lines of rocks, seemingly spokes, reach out from a central hub to a surrounding circle of rocks, is believed to have been used for astronomical purposes. Similarly, the Hohokam Indian structure at Casa Grande near Phoenix, Arizona, contains 14 windowlike openings, eight of which are aligned with the rising and setting Sun during solstices and equinoxes. Other Sun-marking sites exist at Chaco Canyon, New Mexico, and Hovenweep, Utah. And, at Cahokia, Illinois, the American "woodhenge"—concentric circles comprised of 49 poles, with the largest circle measuring 410 feet across—is thought to have been a tool for measuring solstices and equinoxes, and possibly to predict eclipses.

tism and authority. This is unfortunate, because Galileo did many other things during his lifetime that were worthy of lasting fame. He was, for example, the founder of modern experimental physics. He also made the first break with naked-eye astronomy by starting a systematic study of the heavens with a telescope. He was largely responsible for bringing the ideas of Copernicus to the attention of the intellectual community of 17th-century Europe. It was this seemingly heretical activity, of course, that eventually caused him to draw the attention of the Inquisition.

The son of a musician in Pisa, Galileo studied at the local university and embarked on a career teaching mathematics. As the story goes, his early interest in physics is associated with observations conducted at the Pisa cathedral. He noted that a cathedral lamp required the same amount of time to complete a swing no matter how wide the range of the swing. Later, Galileo suggested that this principle could be used to develop a pendulum clock. His studies of physics and mathematics helped him to win a position in the Medici court in Florence in 1610.

While in Venice in 1609, Galileo learned of the recent invention of the telescope in the United Netherlands. He devised a superior lensmaking technique and produced a telescope capable of magnifying an image 32 times. It was an immense step forward. Astronomers could thereupon examine the heavens with more than the power of the unaided human eye. He opened a window on the cosmos and was not slow to exploit it.

During the years after the building of his telescope, Galileo and others saw many new things. Mountains loomed on the Moon where no mountains were supposed to be. The apparently unblemished Sun had spots. Venus was seen to go through phases as does the Moon. Galileo observed the four largest moons of Jupiter and caught a hint of Saturn's rings. As has happened ever since, whenever a new window on the sky is opened, the first glimpse shows an undreamed-of richness and complexity.

Why were these discoveries so important? The first two—lunar mountains and sunspots—showed that the Greek ideal of heavenly perfection was incorrect. Also, the fact that Venus could be observed to pass through Moonlike phases proved that at least one other planet orbited the Sun. And Jupiter's four moons belied the assumption that everything orbited Earth. These facts had enormous psychological impact during the 17th century.

Enter Newton

Galileo announced the first of these findings in his book *The Starry Messenger*. He called Jupiter's satellites the Sidera Medici (Medicean Stars), attempting to flatter his hoped-for patrons, the Medici family. The ploy worked. He received support from Florence, and today those satellites are called the Galilean Moons.

Furthermore, the maestro had a way with words, writing—unlike Copernicus and Kepler—in the vernacular, Italian in this case. Through his writings, Copernican ideas spread throughout Europe. Galileo's trial did not curb the spread of these ideas—indeed, its only effect was to guarantee that the center of astronomical studies would move across the Alps to the Protestant countries of Europe and eventually to England.

In the same year that Galileo died, 1642, Isaac Newton was born. It is a coincidence, of course, but one that symbolizes the continuity of the development of scientific ideas about the universe during the 17th century.

The scientific revolution of the 17th century culminated in the work of Isaac Newton, who developed a view of the universe still held today. His most important contribution to astronomy is the law of universal gravitation, which states that any two objects in the universe will experience a force of attraction proportional to their masses and to the distance between them. The laws that Kepler deduced from Tycho's data can also be derived from Newton's work.

In later years, a legend grew about how Newton realized that one gravitational law governed the entire universe. The part that sticks in the public fancy is the fall of an apple in an orchard.

To understand Newton's insight in that orchard, one must remember that, until his time, the science of astronomy and the science of mechanics (which dealt with the motions of things on Earth) were totally separated. No one had yet connected the stately turning of the planets with the fall of an apple on Earth. Newton's gift to humanity

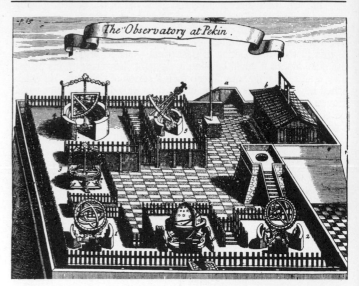

17th-century Chinese skywatchers at the Imperial Observatory observed the stars with astronomical instruments, some imported from Europe.

was to show that such artificial distinctions do not hold in nature—that the universe is a single, seamless web, and that the forces guiding the Moon also cause apples to fall.

To demonstrate the unity of the gravitational force, Newton imagined what would happen if a cannon were placed on a mountaintop, firing successive projectiles, with an increase in the charge of each shot. Eventually, with just enough gunpowder, the cannonball would fly around the world, overcoming gravity's downward pull and maintaining a constant altitude.

This hypothetical missile, he concluded, was behaving like the Moon, or any other satellite. In his own words, "[I] compared the force requisite to keep the Moon in her Orb with the force of gravity at the surface of the Earth, and found them to answer pretty nearly." In effect, Newton had seen that the Moon and the Earth continually fall toward each other, offset by their orbital motion. With this realization, any simple distinction between terrestrial and celestial science—a notion accepted since ancient Greece—crumbled. Using calculus, a method that he originated, Newton worked out the planets' orbits and demonstrated that they followed Kepler's laws.

His vision of the solar system in perpetual motion led naturally to a model of the universe resembling a geared clock. Once the solar system had been created, its future history lay ordained. But a debate ensued along these lines: mathematician G. W. Leibniz argued that God had made an automated universe; theologian Samuel Clarke contended that God was continually adjusting the works. Either way, the Creator had more leisure than with Ptolemy's system, which ascribed to God (or appointed angels) the turning of cranks. Newton believed that God created a mechanistic universe and then fine-tuned the machinery while it operated.

It is difficult to overemphasize the importance of this new scientific movement, and of Newton's place as its prime mover. He completed the work begun by Copernicus and his successors.

In fact, the Newtonian Synthesis gave rise to another powerful idea: Events anywhere in the universe can be studied in laboratories on Earth. And, if nature's laws are constant, then all events of the past—right back to the creation of the universe—are accessible to investigation.

It is comforting, in the face of such advances in scientific knowledge, to reflect on how it all started. An obscure Polish scholar was able to set in motion a scientific revolution capped by, of all things, a view of space and time based on an inspired interpretation of a fallen apple in an English orchard.

On to Mount Palomar

During the 200 years that followed Newton's discovery of the workings of the solar system, astronomers developed two improved tools. First, bigger, and sometimes better, telescopes allowed astronomers to collect more light from objects farther away. And second, improved theoretical tools, based on calculus and Newton's laws, enabled scientists to analyze (and therefore predict) the behavior of more complex celestial phenomena. The delicate interplay of instrumental and theoretical advances was like a waltz through history—first one partner would lead, then the other.

Galileo turned a primitive telescope toward the heavens. But to go beyond Galileo, it was necessary to build better telescopes. This was no easy task.

Newton saw no future in the type of telescope used by Galileo. Called the refractor, it uses a series of lenses to collect and focus incoming light. Unfortunately, it also suffers from a defect known as "chromatic aberration," in which colored fringes appear around an image's edges. Consequently, Newton built a telescope without lenses. Such a *reflector* telescope uses curved mirrors, made of polished metal, to focus light at the back of the instrument. However, his first models had little more power than did Galileo's refractor.

By the mid-18th century, techniques for fashioning mirrors from metal had been perfected. By the 20th century, mirrors were ground from glass and then coated with reflective metal. Today, such highly efficient light collectors are the workhorses of astronomy. The most famous (and most productive) of these giants is the 200-inch telescope located at the Hale Observatory on Mount Palomar near San Diego, California.

Completed in 1948, Hale's main mirror is 17 feet (five meters) across and weighs 14.5 tons. Technicians ground away more than five tons of glass from the original 20-ton disk to form a concave surface, which became reflective when polished and coated with a thin layer of aluminum. To construct the immense disk, molten Pyrex glass was poured into a form, then allowed to cool for eight months to keep the glass from cracking.

The telescope itself is so big that at one time an astronomer sat inside it to observe the stars. Today, however, a computer monitors observations. It is so well balanced that an electric motor no more powerful than one found in a food processor can rotate it. Although the Soviets now have a larger optical telescope operating in the Caucasus Mountains, technical troubles have limited its usefulness.

Improved telescope designs enabled astronomers to expand their inventory of the solar system. William Herschel (1738–1822), born in Germany, was a musician-turned-astronomer who lived in England during the 18th century. He built his own reflecting telescopes because he could not afford to buy one made by craftsmen. Believing that studying the heavens was one way to peer into the mind of God, Herschel set out to catalogue everything in the sky.

Finding Neptune

On March 13, 1781, Herschel observed a fuzzy object, hitherto unknown. His telescope allowed him to see that this new object was not just a point (as most stars appear), but something with an extended structure. Since the object moved against a background of fixed stars, it had to be a planet or a comet. And, given that 2,000 years of skywatching had turned up only six planets, European astronomers looked carefully before concluding that Herschel really had found another planet—one located too far from the Sun to be seen by the naked eye. It was christened Uranus, and became the first planet discovered in modern times.

Astronomers throughout Europe worked to chart its orbit. It quickly became apparent that applying Newton's law of gravitation to the new planet did not give a correct description of its path in the sky. Working independently, an English and a French astronomer came to the same conclusion. In 1845, John Couch Adams and Urbain-Jean-Joseph Le Verrier showed that this orbital discrepancy could be explained if there were yet another planet beyond Uranus. On September 23, 1846, astronomers in Berlin saw it—the planet we now call Neptune.

While the discovery of Uranus depended on the development of better telescopes, the discovery of Neptune depended on the ability

---

NEW EFFORTS IN ASTRONOMY

Since the discovery in 1932 that radio waves emanate from the Milky Way's center, astronomers have been scanning the "invisible" universe. That task requires special instruments. Because only visible light, radio waves, and some infrared radiation can penetrate the atmosphere, special devices are sent into space aboard satellites. Below, some details about the latest efforts to analyze specific kinds of electromagnetic radiation:

• RADIO WAVES (wavelength: one millimeter to 10 meters): The first radio telescope—a bowl-shaped antenna measuring 9.4 meters across—was built in Illinois in 1937. Today, "interferometry"—a computerized system that merges signals from an array of radio telescopes—allows astronomers to simulate one enormous dish. The Very Large Array in New Mexico synchronizes 27 radio telescopes to form images equivalent to those of one 24-kilometer dish. Currently, the National Science Foundation is building the Very Long Baseline Array; with 10 antennas spanning Hawaii to St. Croix, its "baseline" will measure 7,500 kilometers.

• INFRARED RADIATION (wavelength: one micron to one millimeter): Infrared radiation carries crucial data about star and planet formation. NASA's Kuiper Airborne Observatory, a 0.9 meter telescope aloft at 41,000 feet, has charted infrared sources since 1975. More impressive, the joint U.S.–Dutch–British Infrared Astronomical Satellite mapped more than 250,000 sources during 1983. On the drawing board for the 1990s are two space-based observatories: NASA's $600 million Shuttle Infrared Telescope Facility and the European Space Agency's Infrared Space Observatory.

• VISIBLE LIGHT (wavelength: 300 nanometers to one micron): Delayed because of space shuttle troubles, NASA's $1.5 billion Hubble Space Telescope awaits launch in 1988. Its 2.4-meter telescope will capture visible, infrared, and ultraviolet radiation, detecting objects 50 times fainter and seven times farther away than those detectable by Earth's best telescopes. Still, ground-based observatories with larger apertures remain important in spectral analysis. By the mid-1990s, Hawaii may house two giant optical telescopes; the $87 million Keck Telescope, using a honeycomb design, will join 36 mirrors into a single 10-meter mirror, while the proposed $125 million National New Technology Telescope will achieve a 15-meter aperture—the world's largest.

• ULTRAVIOLET RADIATION (wavelength: 10–300 nanometers). The

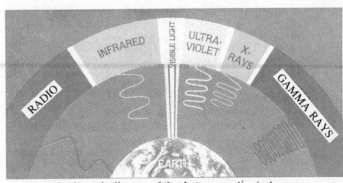

A schematic diagram of the electromagnetic spectrum.

first ultraviolet telescopes were hoisted aloft on high-altitude balloons. Today, the International Ultraviolet Explorer, a U.S.–European satellite launched in 1978, examines radiation from intergalactic matter and the outer layers of stars. Soon, NASA's Extreme Ultraviolet Explorer, now being developed, will study high-energy ultraviolet rays, so far uncharted.

• X-RAYS (wavelength: .01–10 nanometers). So energetic are x-rays that studying them requires a unique telescope design: cylindrical mirrors to deflect x-rays into focus. Between 1978 and 1981, the orbiting Einstein Observatory satellite used this method (as did its European counterpart, Exosat) to collect data on pulsars, neutron stars, and galactic nuclei. The latest x-ray space observatory is Japan's Astro-C, launched in February 1987 (approximate cost: $40 million). By 1995, NASA hopes to place in orbit the Advanced X-Ray Astrophysics Facility, a $1 billion telescope 100 times more sensitive than the Einstein Observatory.

• GAMMA RAYS (wavelength: less than .01 nanometers): Gamma rays are more energetic than x-rays, and difficult to measure. Thus the European gamma ray observatory, Cos-B, took seven years (1975–82) to make a gamma ray chart of the sky. In 1990, NASA plans to launch a $500 million space-based Gamma Ray Observatory, 10 times more sensitive than Cos-B, which will carry instruments supplied by the United States and Germany.

of theoreticians to predict the orbit of the new planet. In fact, once told of its general location, observers at Berlin took less than one night to pinpoint Neptune. The ninth planet, Pluto, was also found through computation and observation.

About the same time that Herschel was expanding our perception of the solar system, the return of a comet in 1758 as predicted served to provide dramatic confirmation of the clockwork universe developed by Newton. In 1682, Edmund Halley (1656–1742) had observed a large comet approach the Sun and swing away. Looking at historical records, he found that a bright comet with roughly the same orbit had appeared in 1531 and 1607. Using Newton's laws and the positions of the planets, Halley calculated the orbit of the comet and predicted that it would again be near the Sun in 1758. Its appearance, on Christmas Day of that year, provided a major verification of Newton's description of the universe.

With telescopes and satellites routinely probing the farthest reaches of the universe, one would expect few surprises in the relatively mundane study of our own neighborhood in space. Not so. In 1978, scientists at the U.S. Naval Observatory in Flagstaff, Arizona, obtained high-grade photographs of Pluto, showing that the planet has a moon. It was christened Charon, after the boatman charged with conducting souls of the dead to the underworld, Pluto's realm. This discovery allowed astronomers to estimate the mass of Pluto, a value insufficient to explain all of the vagaries of the orbits of Neptune and Uranus. Thus, there still may be pages to be written in the story of the solar system—a possible 10th planet.

Seeing the Spectrum

Beyond our own star system lie other stars, perhaps with their own planets. From a science concerned with determining *where* stars and planets are, the new discoveries changed the focus of astronomy to the question of *what* they are. A new science, astrophysics, emerged as a complement to astronomy. It seeks to reveal the nature of the stars through an understanding of the laws of physics.

The basis for this new departure in man's view of the heavens was a famous experiment by Isaac Newton. He noted that a glass prism held up to a beam of sunlight broke the light into its constituent colors—a "spectrum" of sunlight.

For a long time, this peculiar property of light was merely a nuisance to lensmakers. Then, in 1802, physician William Hyde Wollaston found narrow bands of missing color in the spectrum of sunlight. By 1814, a physicist, Joseph von Fraunhofer, made the first map of these lines, which now bear his name. Their origin remained a mystery until 1859, when Gustav Kirchhoff, working with Robert Bunsen at Heidelberg, showed that the lines were caused by familiar chemical elements in the Sun's outer atmosphere that absorb certain wavelengths of light.

Such "spectral analysis" works something like this: Each kind of element (e.g., hydrogen, nitrogen), when pushed to an "excited" state, emits a unique spectrum of light—a kind of atomic fingerprint.

In fact, burning an element gives off a specific "emission spectrum," while passing light *through* an element causes certain colors to be absorbed, creating an "absorption spectrum." The correspondence between atoms and their unique spectra is daily evident: A neon light glows red; sodium-vapor street lamps emit yellow light; mercury-vapor lamps are bluish-white. Each element has its own colors.

Discovering this connection between atoms and light was enormously important. As early as 1868, bright lines were observed in the Sun's spectrum—lines that had no counterpart in any known element on Earth. Scientists concluded that a new element was present on the Sun, one that they named helium (from the Greek word for Sun, *helios*).

There was, as far as anyone could tell, no helium on the Earth. In 1895, however, helium was discovered in certain uranium-bearing minerals. Once again, it turned out that the Earth was not as different from the rest of the universe as some people had thought.

From these early days, the technique of identifying chemicals by their light spectra has penetrated every corner of modern technology. Spectroscopy is today used in industrial quality control (to monitor the presence of impurities), in medicine (to identify substances taken from the body), and in many other areas where one must determine the chemical constituents of materials. It even figures in courtroom dramas, where substances identified by this sort of analysis are accepted as legal evidence.

Once scientists had proven that known elements make up the Sun and other stars, another question arose: How could the stars shine so brightly for so long? Astrophysicists had calculated that, even if the Sun were made of pure anthracite coal, it could have shone for only 20,000 years—instead of the 4.5 billion years so far.

Throughout the last decades of the 19th century, scientists tried to determine the Sun's fuel source. The answer came from a completely unexpected quarter—the study of radioactive materials. By the 1930s, a number of things had become clear: First, certain nuclear processes alter the weight of atoms; second, the weight change is related to energy by means of Einstein's famous formula, $E = mc^2$. Arthur (later Sir Arthur) Eddington, working in England during the 1920s, had suggested that the conversion of mass to energy might be the process that provided the Sun's energy. But no one knew enough about nuclear physics at that time to consider Eddington's suggestion as anything more than an educated guess.

In fact, the Sun shines through a fusion process in which lighter elements are transmuted into heavier ones, liberating energy. Detailed knowledge of this phenomenon grew out of a small conference held in Washington, D.C., in April 1938. The gathering had aimed to unite astrophysicists and nuclear physicists. The former knew about stellar structure; the latter understood something of the reactions taking place in stars. The interchange must have been extraordinarily effective: Shortly thereafter Hans Bethe of Cornell University worked out the earliest model of fusion in stars.

The theory was so successful that Bethe was awarded a Nobel Prize for physics in 1967. His idea of nuclear reactions in our Sun allowed scientists to begin to understand the very fires of creation.

Galileo's Science And the Trial of 1633

"Nature . . . is inexorable and immutable; she never transgresses the laws imposed upon her." Thus did Galileo argue in 1615 for the authority of science over that of Scripture in the physical world. The Catholic Church's 1633 condemnation of Galileo is popularly seen as the response of theological dogmatism. But the issue debated by scholars today is whether Galileo actually *proved* that the Earth revolves around the sun. Here, as he analyzes Galileo's ordeal, historian William A. Wallace explores the complexities of demonstrating truth in science.

William A. Wallace

William A. Wallace, O.P., is professor of philosophy and history at the Catholic University of America (CUA). Born in New York City, he received a B.E.E. from Manhattan College (1940), an M.S. from CUA (1952), and a Ph.D. from University of Fribourg, Switzerland (1959). He was ordained in 1953, and his most recent book is Prelude to Galileo: Medieval and 16th-Century Sources of Galileo's Thought *(1981).*

The casual tourist in Rome, should he climb the Spanish Steps and approach the imposing palace to which they lead, might notice a green marble pillar bearing an inscription in Italian that translates as follows:

The next palace is the Trinità dei Monti, once belonging to the Medici; it was here that Galileo was kept prisoner of the Inquisition when he was on trial for seeing that the Earth moves and the sun stands still.

The first part of that inscription is undoubtedly true, but less certain is the claim that Galileo was brought to trial "for seeing that the Earth moves and the sun stands still." One cannot actually observe the Earth's movement; proof of this now commonplace notion is considerably more complex.

Notwithstanding the conservatism, overzealousness, and incompetence of the Catholic Church officials who prosecuted him, Galileo's defense, scientifically speaking, was not nearly so strong as is commonly thought. All of the evidence marshaled *after* his time distorts modern judgments of the trial. We must return to Galileo's assessment of his own work to appreciate his real achievements.

Polish astronomer Nicolaus Copernicus (1473–1543) brought the theory of a rotating Earth that revolved around the sun into public discourse with the publication in 1543 of *On the Revolutions of the Heavenly Spheres*. But it was Galileo's work that sparked debate, almost 70 years later, over this heliocentric theory.

Galileo Galilei was born at Pisa on February 15, 1564, and in his early years he apparently thought of becoming a monk. His father persuaded him to study medicine instead, and he pursued courses at the University of Pisa with that intention from 1581 to 1585, when he dropped out, without a degree, and devoted himself increasingly to the study of mathematics.

Such was his competence in mathematics, both pure and applied, that the University of Pisa called him back in 1589 to teach courses in geometry and astronomy. In 1592, he was offered a more prestigious position at the University of Padua, and there, for the next 18 years—which Galileo recalled as "the happiest of my life"—he flourished as professor of mathematics. He taught courses in astronomy; experimented with pendulums, inclined planes, and falling bodies; and perfected the telescope as a reliable instrument for astronomical observations.

On the basis of such observations, he published his *Sidereus nuncius (The Starry Messenger)* in Venice in 1610, and soon won acclaim throughout Europe as the foremost astronomer of his time.

Galileo's teaching notes from his stays at Pisa and Padua have survived, and from these we know that he was aware of the Copernican theory. But he preferred to teach the geocentric theory of Ptolemy (second century A.D.), which at the time was the dominant theory in the universities. Half a century after the appearance of Copernicus's book, only a few scholars had seriously entertained his views.

One such scholar was the German astronomer Johann Kepler (1571–1630), who corresponded with Galileo, and to whom Galileo wrote in 1597 that he himself had become a committed Copernican. Recent research suggests, however, that Galileo wavered in his commitment; his treatises on astronomy published during the early 1600s show him still arguing for the Ptolemaic system. What transformed Galileo after 1610 into an enthusiastic supporter of the Polish astronomer were his own discoveries with the telescope.

Between 1609 and 1611, he discovered the moons of Jupiter, which showed that not all motions in the heavens had to be around the Earth as a center. He saw mountains on Earth's moon, which suggested that Earth and moon were made of the same material and possibly underwent similar motions. He discerned the phases of Venus, which showed that its orbit had to be around the sun, not around the Earth as had previously been supposed.

Citing the Cardinal

On the strength of the publication of *Sidereus nuncius*, Galileo obtained the patronage of the Grand Duke of Tuscany, Cosimo II de Medici. He gave up his teaching duties at Padua and moved to Florence where he served as mathematician and philosopher to the Grand Duke.

His advocacy of the Copernican theory as the true explanation of the universe soon came under attack from two camps. On the one hand, Italian philosophers were concerned over the Copernican system's apparent violation of the principles of Aristotelian physics. Theologians, on the other hand, claimed that Copernicanism violated Scripture, notably the Old Testament's assertions that the sun moves across the heavens (e.g., Joshua commanded the sun to stand still, Josh. 10:12), and that the Earth is the immovable center around which God made the heavenly luminaries rotate (e.g., Ps. 93:1).*

Encouraged, it seems, by his patron, Galileo responded to both parties: to the conservative Aristotelian philosophers with a *Discourse on Floating Bodies* (1612), and to the theologians with a *Letter to Castelli*, later enlarged as the *Letter to Christina* (1615), wherein he suggested that the Scriptures could be reconciled with the Copernican system by interpreting the Bible allegorically rather than literally. He cited Caesar Cardinal Baronius, a contemporary who said: "The intention of the Holy Spirit is to teach us how one goes to heaven, not how heaven goes."

Meanwhile, a Carmelite friar, Paolo Foscarini, had published in 1615 a theological treatise in which he interpreted the Scriptures in a fashion similar to Galileo's. The works of both men were brought to the atten-

DIALOGO
DI
GALILEO GALILEI LINCEO
MATEMATICO SOPRAORDINARIO
DELLO STVDIO DI PISA.
E Filosofo, e Matematico primario del
SERENISSIMO
GR. DVCA DI TOSCANA.
Doue ne i congreffi di quattro giornate fi difcorre
fopra i due
MASSIMI SISTEMI DEL MONDO
TOLEMAICO, E COPERNICANO;
*Proponendo indeterminatamente le ragioni Filosofiche, e Naturali
tanto per l'vna, quanto per l'altra parte.*

CON PRI   VILEGI.

IN FIORENZA, Per Gio: Batifta Landini MDCXXXII.
CON LICENZA DE' SVPERIORI.

Aristotle, Ptolemy, and Copernicus (left to right) are depicted in the frontispiece to the first edition of Galileo's Dialogue *(1632).*

---

tion of Robert Cardinal Bellarmine, a learned Jesuit in Rome who at that time was investigating the criticisms of the Reformers and what the Roman church regarded as their heretical interpretations of Scripture.

In April 1615, Bellarmine wrote to both Foscarini and Galileo, advising them that the Copernican system was as yet only a hypothesis, since the motion of the Earth had not been conclusively demonstrated. He cautioned that until such time as solid proof was offered, the commonly accepted interpretation of Scripture was to be preserved.

Shortly thereafter, in 1616, the Congregation of the Index (a church agency that judged works as heretical or correct) published a decree against the Copernican teaching, condemning Foscarini's book outright and suspending publication of Copernicus's work of 1543 pending correction of its text.

Necessary Demonstrations

Oddly enough, in his *Letter to Christina*, Galileo had agreed with Bellarmine that the traditional interpretation of Scripture was to stand unless the new system could be "well founded on manifest experiences and necessary demonstrations." He apparently felt that he would soon provide such evidence. But, as we shall see, he subsequently ran into difficulties.

In February 1616, when he was in Rome, Galileo had an important meeting with Cardinal Bellarmine. In the files of the Holy Office, a much-discussed document is pre-

served, dated February 26, which states that Galileo, while in Bellarmine's household, was enjoined not to hold, teach, or defend the Copernican system "in any way whatever."

The document seems to be a record of an injunction that was to be served on Galileo should he not agree to Bellarmine's instructions. It appears that the injunction was never actually served on Galileo, and thus there is some doubt whether he was told that he could teach the Copernican system as a mathematical *hypothesis* that simplified astronomical predictions, or whether he was told that he was not to hold, teach, or defend it in any way whatsoever.

I will return to this matter later, for the question of whether the injunction was actually served on Galileo assumed some importance at the trial of 1633.

Difficult Dialogue

Galileo's early relations with the papacy and the Jesuits were, on the whole, good. Cardinal Bellarmine had questioned the Jesuit astronomers at the Collegio Romano about the accuracy of the new observations with the telescope; they had promptly confirmed Galileo's findings. The Collegio's greatest mathematician, Christopher Clavius, knew of Galileo's work and had helped him get his teaching positions.

Clavius died in 1612, however, and soon after, Galileo got into a nasty dispute with a German Jesuit, Christopher Scheiner, over the nature and motion of sunspots. The situation worsened a few years later, in 1618,

---

*According to Aristotelian physics (which St. Thomas Aquinas and other Scholastics had followed), the Earth's position in the center of the universe explained local motions such as the downward fall of bodies. Further, the heavenly bodies appeared to be immutable; such perfect spheres, it was thought, could only move in circles. The Earth appeared to be so unlike the celestial luminaries that it seemed impossible to attribute to it the same heavenly motion. Even before Galileo's time, astronomical observations had cast some doubt on some features of this cosmology, and philosophers were divided into those committed to preserving it (the Peripatetics) and those willing to revise it (the more progressive Scholastics).

when Galileo launched another attack on one of Clavius's successors at the Collegio, Orazio Grassi, over the paths and appearances of comets.

While this argument was raging, in 1621 three important figures died: Pope Paul V, Cardinal Bellarmine, and Galileo's patron, Cosimo de Medici. Fortunately, Paul V was succeeded by a Florentine cardinal, Matteo Barberini, who had been sympathetic to Galileo during the troubles of 1616 and who generally took Galileo's side in his battles with the more orthodox Jesuits.

When Barberini assumed the papacy in 1623 as Urban VIII, Galileo took the opportunity to dedicate his definitive answer to Grassi on comets, *The Assayer*, to the new pope. No doubt Urban VIII was pleased and flattered by this action; Galileo was granted the favor of six papal audiences. Most scholars agree that Galileo secured some kind of permission from Urban to resume work on the Copernican system.

By 1630, he had finished his great work, the *Dialogue on the Two Chief Systems of the World*. In it he evaluated all of the evidence and arguments for and against the Ptolemaic and Copernican systems, coming down rather hard on the side of the Copernicans and making the Ptolemaists and the Aristotelians look somewhat foolish in the process. Galileo caricatures their positions through a fictional character, the inept Simplicio, a Peripatetic who finds his philosophy in the text of Aristotle rather than in the book of nature.

The importance of the *Dialogue* is twofold. It was the first frontal attack on the whole of Aristotelian physics. It focused on the weakest point of Aristotelian physics—its account of the motions of bodies.

Galileo had difficulty obtaining permission to have the *Dialogue* published. The Dominican Niccolò Riccardi, charged with censoring the work, was mindful of the decree against Copernicanism handed down in 1616. But, by doctoring the manuscript, Galileo was able to get Riccardi's approval, and his book was printed by Landini at Florence in 1632. He had added a preface and a note at the end, wherein he disclaimed giving any actual proof of the Copernican system and labeled it a pure mathematical hypothesis.

The "dialogue" takes place over four days among the fictional characters Salviati, Sagredo, and Simplicio, with a different series of

Portrait by Flemish painter Justus Susterman of Galileo, who was elected in 1611 to the Academy of the Lynx-eyed, Europe's first scientific society.

arguments being developed in the course of each day. On the first day, Salviati, Galileo's mouthpiece, argues that there is no clear dichotomy between the celestial and terrestrial regions, a central tenet of Aristotelian cosmology. He says the world is one, probably constructed of the same kind of material (e.g., the mountains on the moon, just like those on Earth) and probably undergoing the same kinds of motion.

On the second day, the main topic is the rotation of the Earth on its axis. Here Galileo rebuts most of the proofs that the Earth is at rest (such as the fact that a stone dropped from a tower always falls at its foot) and shows that, if one knows the proper principles of mechanics, the proofs offered yield the same results whether the Earth is still or turning.

Rejecting Kepler

The arguments, he admits, do not *prove* that the Earth is rotating. They simply destroy the proofs of his adversaries that it must be at rest. The Earth's diurnal rotation is thus left an open question.

The third day is devoted to a more difficult problem: whether the Earth is immobile in the center of the universe or actually travels in a large, annual orbit around the sun. Arguing by analogy, Galileo asks: Since the other planets revolve around the sun, why should not the Earth do likewise? Further, earthly revolution can explain the movement of sunspots.

Finally, on the fourth day, Galileo

puts together the conclusions of the second and third days' discussions, showing how they provide a simple explanation of a universally observed phenomenon, the motion of the tides.

His argument, in summary, is that the combination of the Earth's daily rotation on its axis with its annual revolution around the sun results in unequal forces being exerted daily on the waters on the Earth's surface. These unequal forces give rise to the tides.

To make his point, Galileo had to reject Kepler's theory of tides—that they are caused by lunar attraction—the theory that is accepted by scientists today. In the preface, Galileo himself refers to his argument on tides as an "ingenious fantasy"; he labored over it for years without removing all its flaws.

Coming to Trial

With the publication of the *Dialogue* in 1632, Galileo found himself in deeper trouble than he had ever imagined. Pope Urban VIII was furious, probably because he felt Galileo had betrayed his earlier pledge that he would write impartially, and almost certainly because he felt that Galileo had misused, and ridiculed, Urban's own preferred answer to the Ptolemaic-Copernican controversy, namely that it could not be definitively resolved by human intellect.

In August 1632, all further publication and sales of the book were prohibited by the Holy Office. Galileo was summoned to Rome from Florence to be tried by a tribunal of 10 cardinals on the charge that he had willfully taught the Copernican doctrine despite its condemnation as contrary to Scripture. In preparing for the trial, the clerical prosecutors discovered the written injunction that had putatively been given to Galileo on February 26, 1616, enjoining him not to hold, teach, or defend the Copernican system in any way.

Accordingly, a number of theologians examined the *Dialogue* to ascertain whether Galileo had or had not actually held, taught, or defended Copernicanism in that work. The results were, predictably, that Galileo had undoubtedly *taught* the motion of the Earth and the immobility of the sun in the *Dialogue*, and that he had also *defended*, without a doubt, the same teaching.

House Arrest

But had Galileo actually *held* a belief in this teaching? Basing their judgment on the preface Galileo had written (presumably to please Riccardi and so get his work approved for publication), the theologians gave him the benefit of the doubt and decided that he might not have proffered the work as a statement of his own personal conviction.

During the course of the trial, Galileo, for whatever motive, took the obvious way out and said that the theologians' finding on the third point was correct. As a devout son of the church, he would not personally believe anything that was contrary to sacred Scripture. He was made to swear that he did not believe in the Earth's motion, and on this basis he was given a salutary penance ("for the spiritual benefit of former heretics who had returned to the faith") and confined to house arrest. The *Dialogue* was banned, and Galileo was forbidden to write any more on Copernicanism.

Galileo then retired to his villa at Arcetri, outside Florence, and there spent the remaining years of his life studying and writing. In 1638 (four years before his death), he published *Two New Sciences*, a work regarded by scientists as laying out the principles of the modern science of mechanics. It has earned him the title "Father of Modern Science."

The work is replete with claims that the author has founded a "new science," that he has provided demonstrations or strict proofs pertaining to the motions of earthly bodies. Such claims are conspicu-

ously absent from the earlier *Dialogue on the Two Chief Systems of the World*, and their absence, I argue, necessitates reevaluation of what Galileo did and thought he did in *that* book, and of why he recanted.

Return to the inscription on the pillar in Rome and its implication that Galileo actually *saw* the Earth's motion, i.e., that he was able to prove, on the basis of incontrovertible evidence, that the Earth was rotating on its axis and revolving in a closed orbit around the sun. Did Galileo believe he had done this? To answer this, one must know precisely what he took to be scientific proof.

Galileo's Sources

Unfortunately, this has proved difficult for historians of science to discover. My study, over the past 15 years, of three notebooks that Galileo composed while he was a young math professor at Pisa, has turned up an unsuspected possibility. These notebooks, now in the Biblioteca Nazionale Centrale in Florence, cast an entirely new light on the way Galileo structured his *Dialogue*.

What is surprising about the notebooks is that they summarize and explore the logical and physical treatises of Aristotle, not in the conservative and textual style of the Peripatetics in the Italian universities, but rather in a progressive application of Aristotle's principles to current problems. For example, in the third notebook, Galileo applies Aristotelian principles to the motions of heavy bodies.

Even more surprising are the sources on which the notebooks draw, since Galileo has been so often cast in opposition to both the church and the Aristotelians. The first two volumes were drawn from Latin notes used by Jesuit lecturers at the Collegio Romano on logic and natural philosophy, respectively. The third is an adaptation of the same materials to Galileo's own study of the motion of projectiles and falling bodies. Galileo apparently obtained the lecture notes through his correspondence with the Jesuit Clavius.

Using Suppositions

The key to my solution is an expression that occurs repeatedly throughout Galileo's writings from his earliest to his last years, namely, the Latin term *suppositio*, especially as applied to a type of demonstration. Reasoning *ex suppositione* is rarely discussed in the present day, but it assumed considerable impor-

tance at the end of the 16th century among progressive Aristotelians. It is in these notebooks that the clearest statement of Galileo's methodology, that of *ex suppositione*, is found, and its debt to Aristotle is unmistakable.

Identifying the Jesuit Aristotelian precursors of his thought gives us a new appreciation of Galileo's later contacts with Jesuits such as Bellarmine, Scheiner, and Grassi, particularly in evaluating Galileo's claims for demonstration and proof. All of these men used precisely the same terminology employed in Galileo's early notebooks. When we reread the *Dialogue*, we can assume that his later Jesuit protagonists understood and to some extent shared both the concept of *ex suppositione* and the methods for evaluating such reasoning as applied therein.

What is reasoning *ex suppositione*? Unlike the hypothetico-deductive method scientists use today (which denies that there can be positive, incontestable proof of any conclusions based on hypotheses), it allows the possibility of *demonstrating* the truth and certainty of some results through the use of appropriate suppositions. Both Galileo and the Jesuits recognized that there were two types of *suppositiones:* some would be merely imagined situations that could not be verified, whereas others would be capable of verification, either by induction from sense experience or by measurement to within a specified degree of accuracy.*

In all of Galileo's serious scientific writings up to, but not including, the *Dialogue*, he is at pains to identify and verify the suppositions on which his reasoning is based, to justify his claims for strict proof. He follows the same procedure in *Two New Sciences*, where the new science of local motion is finally worked out. But in the *Dialogue*, such claims are strangely absent. Thus one must wonder whether Galileo really did think in 1632 that he had proved the Earth's motion. Was the question, in his own eyes, still debatable?

My suspicion is that Galileo himself was aware, in 1632, that he lacked rigorous proof of the Earth's motion. He supported the Coperni-

---

*For example, the supposition of epicycles in the geocentric theory was postulated *merely* for predicting planets' positions—not because it was believed to be physically true. On the other hand, Galileo's supposition in the *Two New Sciences* that a body falls with uniformly increasing velocity is mathematically formulated in terms of time and distance; this formula he then verifies experimentally.

THE COPERNICAN CHALLENGE... VS. THE TYCHONIAN COMPROMISE...

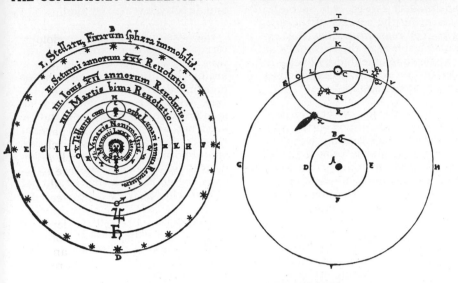

VS. THE MEDIEVAL WORLDVIEW

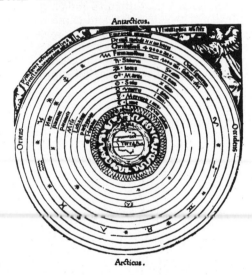

The Copernican system's (above left) main attraction was its mathematical simplicity. Galileo sought the same simplicity in motions on Earth. The Tychonian system (above right) appealed to those who believed the Earth could not possibly move as fast as Copernicus's theory required. It, too, simplified the Aristotelian model (right), whose defects Ptolemy had sought to remedy with complex devices such as epicycles and equants

can system anyway on the grounds that the arguments he had been able to muster, though not conclusive, were better than his opponents'.

We now know that during his 1592–1610 stay at Padua, Galileo continued to work on problems of motion and mechanics and that he made drafts of proofs and demonstrations on which his "science of motion" would one day be erected. By 1609, when he started to work with the telescope, he had completed all the investigations that would be required to write the *Two New Sciences*—a book that would not be published for another 30 years.

Galileo's familiarity with the subject was such that in 1609 he had implicitly grasped the demonstrative force of the arguments he would later formalize in the *Two New Sci-*

ences. He had already experimentally validated the *suppositiones* (e.g., the definition of accelerated motion; the negligible effects of friction) on which his work would be based, and he spoke with confidence of the book's imminent appearance.

It was a confident Galileo, then, who gazed through the telescope, and his intuition was this: If he could systematize his new observations, and couple these with the principles of motion he was soon to formulate, he could quickly extend his demonstrations to cover the Earth's motion—not only in its diurnal rotation but in its revolution around the sun as well. Such a comprehensive system would be an imposing rival to Aristotelian physics.

It was the prospect of these demonstrations that led him to make the

extravagant claims in the *Letter to Christina.* And it was the same prospect that was to haunt him when he came to write his definitive treatise defending the Copernican system. He had to cast it as a dialogue precisely because the proof of the suppositions on which the reasoning was based (i.e., the Earth's rotation and revolution, and the sun's immobility) still eluded him in 1632.

Both before and after the publication of the *Dialogue*, then, Galileo gives abundant evidence of his awareness of and adherence to the canons of demonstrative proof as required by the method of reasoning *ex suppositione*. In the *Dialogue* itself, persuasive argumentation is used, not demonstration, and no mention is even made of the Tychonian system, favored by Galileo's real opponents, which could just as readily explain all of the observational evidence provided with the telescope.*

Finally, as if to add insult to injury, the rebuttal to Galileo's proof of the tides—perhaps dictated by Urban VIII—is voiced at the end of the work by Simplicio, the "simpleton," whose judgment and credibility have already been questioned at every turn. Urban's argument was that God in his infinite power could effect the tidal motion in many ways beyond the reach of man's intellect, and thus that no human explanation, however ingenious, should be regarded as true and conclusive.

But the rebuttal also leads one to wonder whether Galileo was really forced to make the statements in the preface and endnote. Did he use them freely, aware that his arguments for the Earth's motion had barely progressed beyond the level of hypothetical reasoning, appealing enough, but still short of incontestable proof? More important, did he perjure himself when he swore after his trial that he personally did not believe in the Earth's motion?

If his concept of proof was indeed the one outlined of necessity *ex suppositione*, then one must conclude that he did not verify the mathematical principles on which the *Dialogue* was based. And only if one concludes that Galileo himself was aware of this shortcoming, do we give proper credit to his intelligence and to his

---

*Danish astronomer Tycho Brahe (1546–1601) maintained that the other planets circled the sun, and that this system as a whole revolved around the Earth, thus preserving the geocentric theory of the universe.

character, to both his brilliance and his will. He was perceptive enough to recognize the limitations of his argument, skillful though it was, and he was honest enough, as a believer, to acquiesce in the church's interpretation of the Scriptures when he lacked the "necessary demonstrations" to show it was otherwise.

Such a resolution of the problem posed by Galileo's abjuration of Copernicanism is not easy to grasp in the late 20th century, when there is no clear and accepted demarcation between the provinces of faith and reason. But in Galileo's day, in the Italy of the late 16th and early 17th centuries, an important teaching of Aquinas prevailed: Faith and reason have radically different spheres.

This means that a person cannot assent to one and the same truth by faith and by reason at the same time. If one *knows* something by reason, for example, one cannot assent to it by faith. If one *believes* something, on the other hand, one does so only because one's *reason* is unable to decide whether it is true or not.

In light of this teaching, the human intellect can go only so far in penetrating the secrets of the universe. Yet reasoning does not exhaust the sphere of the knowable, as it can be supplemented by faith—in those instances where God chooses to reveal something important.

Galileo, on such an accounting, would have two options on the matter of the Earth's motion: either he could *prove* it, and so *know* the truth of the proposition "the Earth moves" on the basis of his own reasoning; or he could *not prove* it, leaving it an open question which could still be decided by faith.

Early on in his investigations, if my analysis is correct, Galileo thought that convincing proof of the Earth's motion was within his grasp. Later, he saw the difficulty and complexity of the situation and came to admit, begrudgingly, that the opposite conclusion would have to be accepted on faith—because the church was proposing it to him as some-

thing beyond man's knowing powers and directly revealed by God.

Galileo's only "crime," to use historian Giorgio de Santillana's term, was that he was too precipitate in urging his intuitions on others, too presumptuous in expecting others to "see" what he could "see." Very human are faults such as these. But we need not add to these the further charges of arrogance and insincerity, of stubborn adherence to a position he was finally unable to defend, of swearing under oath that he did not believe what he truly believed.

It is much better, in my view, to see him as a true son of his church, willing to accept its teachings when his reason—despite its strong intuitions—was unable to establish their opposite. And, as a true scientist, he not only admitted that he failed to meet the standards of his profession but also persevered during his last years in the quest for a new science that would, one day, be able to furnish the proofs that eluded his grasp.

THE ALCHEMICAL ROOTS OF CHEMISTRY

Chemists have often denied any debts to the old alchemists, but centuries of attempts to make gold yielded much basic chemical knowledge.

B.J.T. DOBBS

B.J.T. Dobbs is professor of history at Northwestern University, and is the author of two books and a number of articles on early modern history of science. Currently on leave from Northwestern, she holds an NEH visiting fellowship at the Huntington Library in San Marino, California.

"Gold! Gold!"

The cry that sent Americans rushing to California in 1849 has thrilled human beings since prehistoric times. Singularly beautiful among the substances on earth, gold adorned the royalty of antiquity. Uniquely stable in its chemical properties, it became a symbol of the stability of royal power. Philosophers saw in it a state of physical perfection and a symbol of immortality; alchemists, in turn, sought to make it by a thousand different methods.

Gold was probably the first naturally occurring chemical element to be discovered in pure form. It was once widely distributed on earth in surface rocks, and the erosion of less stable materials has also progressively exposed the incorruptible golden grains and nuggets to view or washed them downstream among the sands and pebbles.

By the second or third century A.D., however, the gleaming natural substance became increasingly rare in the ancient world, and about that time efforts to make gold artificially began in the cosmopolitan city of Alexandria—efforts that led to the theory and practice of alchemy. Alchemy flourished in Egyptian Alexandria, later in the great Islamic centers of learning in the tenth through twelfth centuries, and finally in Christian Europe from the twelfth through the seventeenth centuries. Alchemy was essentially a quest for perfection, and since gold was the "perfect" metal, one alchemical goal was to transform base metals into gold. But other forms of perfection were sought as well, such as "the philosopher's stone"—an agent of perfection that would provide for salvation, health, and immortality as well as the transmutation of metals. The alchemical pursuit of perfection ultimately failed, but not before it had yielded a rich harvest of chemical concepts, laboratory equipment, and techniques that nurtured the growth of modern chemistry in the eighteenth century.

ALCHEMY'S HIERARCHY OF METALS

METAL	CELESTIAL BODY	DEITY	SYMBOL
Gold	Sun	Apollo	☉
Silver	Moon	Diana	☽
Mercury	Mercury	Mercury	☿
Copper	Venus	Venus	♀
Iron	Mars	Mars	♂
Tin	Jupiter	Jupiter	♃
Lead	Saturn	Saturn	♄

THE CHEMICAL ELEMENTS IN ANTIQUITY

With the discovery of gold began the saga of the discovery and characterization of the several building blocks, called chemical elements, that make up the many different materials of the world. Fewer than one hundred chemical elements occur naturally, yet some three thousand years of laborious experimentation and theorizing were required before that simple fact was fully understood. That laborious work was to a great extent done under the rubric of alchemy.

Metals other than gold soon came to be known: silver, copper, lead, iron, tin, and mercury. Silver, copper, and mercury sometimes occur in a free state, but more often in ores that are easily reduced. Lead and tin also are fairly easily obtained from their ores, but the smelting of iron ore to obtain the metal is more difficult and requires higher temperatures, so the discovery of metallic iron came somewhat later.

Gold was the most valuable, and a hierarchy of the seven ancient metals became one of the basic assumptions of alchemical doctrine. Assimilated to organic ideas of growth and maturation, the hierarchy ranked gold as the most mature fruit of the

Medieval alchemists sought many methods to transform base metals into gold, the "perfect metal," as shown in this scene from Goethe's *Faust*.

metallic tree. It was assumed that all the metals grew from one root in the womb of the earth, but the alchemist might aid nature by suitable processes and bring to maturity those "green fruits" such as lead or mercury that had been plucked from the matrix too soon. Although many other rationales for metallic transmutation were put forward over the centuries, a hierarchical ranking of the metals was assumed in most of them, and the doctrine of the "vegetation," or growth, of metals was common through the seventeenth century, accepted even by the great Isaac Newton.

In addition to the seven metals, at least two nonmetallic elements were also known in relatively pure form in antiquity: carbon and sulfur. By the end of the alchemical period, quite a few nonelementary working reagents were also well known: the mineral acids now called nitric, sulfuric, and hydrochloric; large numbers of binary salts, "vitriols" (sulfates), and alums; mild alkalis (carbonates) and strong ones (oxides); and *aqua vitæ* (the water of life, ethyl alcohol). Alchemists played a large part in the discovery and characterization of these substances, along with chemical artisans such as tanners, metallurgists, glassmakers, and pharmacists.

Pre-Modern 'Chemical Theory'

In no case did any chemical or alchemical worker in the Middle Ages describe any of those known substances as either elementary or nonelementary (compound) in a modern sense. Even the seven metallic and two nonmetallic substances now recognized as chemical elements were described as composed of other things, according to theoretical schemes derived from certain philosophical considerations. Pre-Socratic philosophers adhered to a very basic philosophical urge: an ontological unity behind the overwhelming multiplicity of things. Modern science still searches for a "theory of everything" that will satisfactorily unite gravitation with the other forces operating in the universe. Thales said

everything was made of water; Anaximander insisted that the primal substance was an indefinite and unbounded one. Anaximenes argued for air, Heraclitus for fire, and Empedocles for earth.

The ideas of Thales, Anaximenes, Heraclitus, and Empedocles composed the first list of "chemical elements"—fire, air, water, earth—which became in turn the canonical list in the works of Aristotle in the fourth century B.C. and subsequently passed with his immense authority into the philosophies of both Islam and Christendom. It is still embedded in common language, where "the raging of the elements" may mean the quaking of the element earth, the explosive ejection of elemental fire from a volcano, or turbulence in air and water. In actuality the list constitutes a primitive description of the three states of matter—liquid (water), solid (earth), gas (air)—plus what is now called energy (fire).

Everyone agreed that everything was composed of the four "elements" in varying proportions, but the Arabic alchemists had also adopted another of Aristotle's ideas to explain both the growth of metals and their associated properties. They created a concept of "chemical" principles, which evolved eventually into the modern chemical form. Aristotle had spoken of two exhalations in the bowels of the earth, watery and smoky. Assuming the two exhalations to be equivalent, respectively, to principles of liquidity and combustibility, the Arabic alchemists identified an abstract, nonempirical "mercury" and "sulfur" with the two principles, and declared that those two principles were the principles of all metals.

That was a very clever idea (even though it was wrong), for it seemed to explain many things about the metals. A very pure mercury and a very pure sulfur meeting under suitable conditions in the bowels of the earth produced gold. Unsuitable subterranean conditions, or an impurity in either principle, produced the less desirable metals. But the alchemist could perhaps correct the problem by separating and purifying each principle separately and then recom-

In 1789, Antoine-Laurent Lavoisier, shown here with his wife, produced the first modern list of chemical elements (painting by Jacques Louis David).

bining them. The doctrine of the mercury/sulfur composition of metals then passed to Western Europe in the twelfth and thirteenth centuries, with interesting results for chemical/alchemical theory.

EARLY MODERN ELEMENTS AND PRINCIPLES

While everyone still agreed that the ultimate constituents of all forms of matter were elemental fire, air, water, and earth, many alchemists and chemists came to regard mercury and sulfur as constituents of matter more or less obtainable in the laboratory. By melting a metal or reducing its ore, one could obtain a liquid "running mercury" from all metals. Most of the metals were also combustible under certain conditions, so by inference they also contained a "sulfur," the principle of combustibility. Any metal that was not combustible, such as gold, was said to have its "sulfur" very strongly "fixed." Thus the doctrine that intermediate chemical states existed between the ordinary substance and its ultimate elemental constituents seemed to have sound empirical justification.

In the sixteenth century a radical medical alchemist named Paracelsus added a third principle to the "mercury" and "sulfur" of Arabic alchemy: the principle of "salt," which he conceived as the principle of solidity. Then followed more than two centuries of creative confusion, in which practically every individual alchemist or chemist produced his own idiosyncratic list of elements and/or principles.

Yet truly innovative steps came in response to the general confusion. Ancient concepts were falling right and left in Renaissance Europe in any case, as conflicting systems generated new critical attitudes. Copernicus and Paracelsus were contemporaries, and the Copernican attack on Ptolemaic, earth-centered astronomy was in some ways comparable to the Paracelsian attack on the Aristotelian elements. There had always been a nonempirical aspect to the Aristotelian elements in that they did not purport to describe the actual products of chemical analysis, except in the most general way. The Paracelsian principles were only a little less abstract, since they were general principles of fluidity, combustibility, and solidity. With the concept of chemical principles, however, came the notion that the analyst really could obtain them from the substance being analyzed. In the state of confusion engendered by the conflict between systems of Aristotelian elements and Paracelsian principles, that notion became increasingly prominent.

The systems proposed in chemical and alchemical literature were often complex combinations of Aristotelian and Paracelsian ideas, lists of constituents of bodies that might contain five, six, or even seven or eight elements or principles. That was not very satisfying philosophically, as it conflicted with the basic desire to discern unity behind multiplicity. No list was any more accurate than another from the modern perspective, but every writer claimed empirical justification for his list and increasingly de-

scribed his substances as the actual products of chemical analysis.

The abstract, supra-physical nature of the elements or principles did not exactly disappear during the alchemical period, or even in early chemistry, but within each classification more and more differentiation appeared. Within the principle of solidity, that process of differentiation was most apparent, so that what had formerly been described as "earth" or "salt" became "a sweet earth," "a friable yellow earth," "nitre" (potassium nitrate), "vitriol," and so forth. By the third quarter of the eighteenth century, 17 distinct "earths" had been isolated and identified as obtainable by chemical analysis, as had a large number of salts. The recognition of these substances as "chemical individuals" that could *not* be transmuted formed the base of chemical knowledge necessary for modern chemistry.

ROBERT BOYLE

In the seventeenth century the chemist, alchemist, and "corpuscularian" Robert Boyle had tried to put a stop to this process in a famous book called *The Skeptical Chymist*. Boyle was convinced that all matter was made up of small corpuscles or particles that were essentially composed of the same type of matter—"one catholick and universal matter," as he called it. Various combinations of the corpuscles were possible, he thought, and those combinations produced the variety and multiplicity in the world. To Boyle the transmutation of metals seemed perfectly feasible. All that was required was the reduction of complex materials to their basic corpuscles, which could then be put together again in some other form.

In his works Boyle attacked all contemporary ideas about elements and principles by pointing out that chemical analysis and chemical theory were often inconsistent. Boyle's scathing critique of both Aristotelian and Paracelsian chemistry had little practical historical effect, however—his theoretical analysis reduced multiplicity to unity in a satisfactory way, but his particles of common matter were unobtainable in a seventeenth-century laboratory.

Practicing chemists and alchemists continued to produce lists of elements and principles that were more or less obtainable by laboratory analysis. By the end of the eighteenth century their approach had been justified by the first modern list of chemical elements, a list that clearly grew out of their analytical work. Boyle's ideas about fundamental corpuscles of matter were later to prove fruitful, but only in the nineteenth century with the work of John Dalton on chemical atomism. Fundamental to Dalton's work was the empirically derived list of nontransmutable chemical elements that stemmed from the many centuries of laboratory analysis and, ironically, from the theoretical structure erected by the alchemists in their efforts to effect transmutation.

1. INDUSTRIAL AND SCIENTIFIC REVOLUTIONS

ALCHEMICAL CHEMISTRY

For a number of reasons, mercury was always for alchemists a special substance. Named in antiquity for the god Mercury, the winged messenger of the gods, apparently for its property of lively motion, mercury was also called quicksilver in English and *argentum vivum* (living silver) in Latin. A liquid possessing a splendid silvery sheen at room temperatures, mercury races from place to place, often shattering into droplets that then coalesce with lifelike spontaneity.

Mercury's peculiar properties convinced alchemists that it was an immature metal, a substance that had the luster of metals and their relative heaviness, but not their other usual properties. Consequently, it was the starting point of a great many alchemical operations. Coupled with the Arabic doctrine that all metals contain a "mercury" as a fundamental principle, the special properties of mercury insured that its chemistry would be explored exhaustively over the centuries.

Gold's top ranking in the hierarchy of metals ensured it the same attention. In addition, gold was thought to have special medicinal properties. Because the heart was conceived as "the sun of the body," correlative to the celestial sun as a source of heat and vital spirits, and because gold was anciently associated with the sun, gold was conceived as a medicine especially apt to strengthen the heart. Chaucer's physician in the fourteenth-century *Canterbury Tales* knew gold to be a wonderful medicine for that purpose, though he also liked to line his pockets with it.

The alchemists wanted to make a universal medicine, a "panacea," almost as much as they wanted to make gold itself, and they constantly sought a "potabile gold," a means of conveying gold in solution into the human body. In the course of their search they discovered *aqua regia*, a "water" that would dissolve gold, the king of metals. Actually a combination of nitric and hydrochloric acids, *aqua regia* was hardly potable. Yet again, the chemistry of gold was systematically explored because of its special significance in alchemy.

In many ways the seventeenth century was the apex of alchemy in general. The alchemical lore that had been circulating in manuscript form during the Middle Ages went into print after the invention of movable type, thereby reaching a much wider public. In the seventeenth century much new work was done in elucidating the chemistry of metals. Since one alchemical goal was to transform base metals into gold, the alchemists wanted to understand all the metals as thoroughly as possible. The seventeenth century also brought the discovery of phosphorus, one of the last great experimental achievements of the alchemical era.

THE CHEMICAL REVOLUTION

Alchemy and chemistry have distinctly different aims and goals. Alchemy, though it might employ ordinary chemical techniques, had as its overarching goal the preparation of an agent of perfection (the philosopher's stone) or the achievement of some form of perfection itself—in metals, gold; in medicine, a universal medicine or panacea. Still other aspects of alchemy involved the search for personal or cosmic salvation, similar to a search for the Holy Grail. Chemistry, on the other hand, even in antiquity and certainly by the seventeenth and eighteenth centuries, had much more limited goals of a practical nature.

Yet the alchemists also produced much empirical information that contributed to the chemical revolution at the end of the eighteenth century. They laid the foundation for the fundamental notion that a chemical element or principle must be the product of chemical analysis. When Lavoisier's first modern list of chemical elements appeared in 1789, few alchemists of the old sort remained. Yet the ancient search for perfection had finally yielded the fruitful product of modern chemistry.

The early seventeenth-century philosopher and herald of modern science, Francis Bacon, had this to say of alchemy:

> Surely to alchemy this right be due, that it may be compared to the husbandman whereof Aesop makes the fable; that, when he died, told his sons that he had left unto them gold buried underground in his vineyard; and they digged over all the ground, and gold they found none; but by reason of their stirring and digging the mould about the roots of their vines, they had a great vintage the following year; so assuredly the search and stir to make gold hath brought to light a great number of good and fruitful inventions and experiments.

ADDITIONAL READING

Dobbs, B.J.T. *The Foundations of Newton's Alchemy, or "The Hunting of the Greene Lyon".* The Cambridge Paperback Library. Cambridge: Cambridge University Press, 1983.

Ferchl, Fritz, and Süssenguth, A. *A Pictorial History of Chemistry.* Translated from the German. London: William Heinemann, 1939.

Multhauf, Robert P. *The Origins of Chemistry.* London: Oldbourne, 1966.

Partington, J.R. *A Short History of Chemistry.* Second edition. London: Macmillan and Co., 1951.

Read, John. *Through Alchemy to Chemistry: A Procession of Ideas & Personalities.* London: G. Bell and Sons, 1961.

Rickard, T.A. *Man and Metals. A History of Mining in Relation to the Development of Civilization.* 2 vols. New York/London: Whittlesey House, McGraw-Hill Book Co., 1932.

Weeks, Mary Elvira. *Discovery of the Elements.* Completely revised and new material added by Henry M. Leicester. Illustrations collected by F.B. Dains. Seventh edition. Easton, Pa.: *Journal of Chemical Education,* 1968.

Life's recipe

This brief is about genes and science's greatest achievement this century: deciphering the code in which are written the instructions for building, running and reproducing bodies. The text is still being read.

In the 1940s and 1950s, several clever physicists turned themselves into biologists. Flushed with their success within the atom, they decided the next problem to be solved was life itself. It was a shrewd move. Between 1944 and 1972, discoveries came thick and fast: first, the nature of hereditary material, called genes; then the ingenious molecular structure of genes; then the code in which their hereditary message was written; and then a way to tinker with that code.

Since then, genetics has become a significant part of the biotechnology industry. It has also invaded the rest of biology as a tool. Medicine, agriculture and the study of evolution have all adopted the techniques and insights of molecular biology, along with its jargon of clones, sequences and mutants.

Since 1972, genetics has made few big breakthroughs. This is not because it has nothing left to discover. Progress is being held up because scientists now know practically all there is to know about bacteria (the simple one-cell creatures on which early genetic studies were done), but little about man and other animals.

In the past few years, however, biotechnology has given scientists the tools to explore the genes of mice and even men. Molecular biologists now hope they can tackle two pressing questions: how does a fertilised egg manage to turn into a human being, and how does a healthy cell turn into a cancer tumour?

Before 1860, ideas about heredity were few and vague. Charles Darwin, for example, thought that a child somehow inherited a blended mixture of vital fluid from its father and mother. Then Gregor Mendel, a Bohemian monk, crossed some pea plants and showed that the offspring were not blended versions of their parents, but that they inherited discrete "factors" from each parent and passed those factors on unchanged to their offspring in predictable ratios.

Mendel's experiments, rescued from obscurity by British and American biologists in the early part of the twentieth century, seemed to prove that heredity relied on particles carried within eggs and sperm. The particles became known as genes.

In 1871, a substance called deoxyribonucleic acid (DNA) was found to be common in the sperm of trout from the river Rhine. It, too, had to be rescued from obscurity by a series of elegant experiments in the 1940s by a Canadian physician, Oswald Avery, and his colleagues. They proved, to the surprise of most biologists, that genes are made of DNA and not, as expected, of protein—out of whose molecules most of the body's machinery and structure are made.

Yet DNA was known to be just a long, thin molecular string, made of a repeating sequence of sugars, phosphates and chemical bases. How could it possibly carry the instructions for building and running bodies? Clearly, its secret must lie in its structure. In 1953, the race to work out the structure of DNA was won by two young Cambridge scientists, Mr James Watson and Dr Francis Crick, working largely in their spare time. The ingenuity of the structure was immediately obvious: it was Mendel's factors made flesh.

Two intertwined helices of DNA are linked by weak bonds between the bases. The bases come in four kinds (A, C, G and T) and links can be made only between given pairs of them: G to C and A to T (see chart on this page). Thus a sequence of bases can spell out a code and that code can be faithfully passed on to offspring by untwining the two helices and copying them.

Code crackers

Next, to crack the code. Were it not for some great leaps of imagination, mainly on the part of Dr Crick, this problem might have remained intractable for decades. It was already fairly widely agreed that the code must be principally a set of instructions for making proteins. Proteins depend largely on their shapes to do their jobs, so somehow the code must spell out that shape. Proteins, like DNA, are made of long unbranching strings. Dr Crick realised that the protein shape was determined by the sequence of amino acids in the strings, and he guessed that the sequence was somehow determined directly by the sequence of bases (letters) on the DNA.

He was right. By 1970, the last letter of the code had been cracked: the code is written in three-letter words (called codons), each of which specifies one of the 20 amino acids in the protein alphabet, except for a few which act as signals to the copying machinery to start and stop. Each gene is faithfully transcribed to make a temporary single-stranded copy from a material called RNA (which is very like DNA, except that it is unable to form double helices).

This transcript, known as the messenger, is then used as the blueprint for building a protein by a neat little machine tool in the form of a cell called a ribosome (see diagram on next page). The ribosome reads the messenger by moving from codon to codon along it.

The replicating helix
How DNA copies itself

At each stop, a small tug-like RNA molecule called transfer-RNA brings along the appropriate amino acid to attach to a growing protein chain: each transfer molecule has on its head the three-letter word corresponding to the code for the amino acid it carries. The code is the same in man, mouse and all living creatures—with one exception found so far, a tiny slipper-shaped protozoan (called Paramecian) that uses different words for certain amino acids.

One big problem remained—and it has not been fully solved to this day. Every cell in the human body contains the complete recipe for the whole body. Yet cells differ in their sizes, shapes, biochemistry and abundance. Skin cells, blood cells, nerve cells, muscle cells—all must somehow receive instructions to differentiate in the growing embryo. How?

The first part of that question is, how do the cells switch on different sets of genes and so produce different sets of proteins? The hunt for gene switches began in bacteria. A common bacterium like *E. coli*, from the human gut, is able to switch on the gene for an enzyme called beta-galactosidase when lactose sugar (essentially its food) is present, and switch it off when there is no lactose. The enzyme breaks down the lactose into simpler sugars on which the bacteria can feed.

In the 1960s, two French scientists, Jacques Monod and François Jacob, worked out how the gene is switched on and off. Lactose itself boosts the amount of beta-galactosidase by somehow increasing the activity of another enzyme that transcribes the beta-galactosidase gene. Lactose thus speeds up the production of messenger RNAs and hence of beta-galactosidase protein which, in turn, digests the lactose. Its abundance controls the means of its own destruction.

However, certain mutant bacteria can produce lots of enzyme whether their lactose food supply is there or not. Jacques Monod came up with an explanation: a specific repressor molecule attaches itself to the DNA, blocking the transcription of the beta-galactosidase gene. Lactose unblocks it by attaching itself to the repressor and putting it out of action. In mutant bacteria, the genes to which the repressor molecule attaches itself do not work, so the main gene is always switched on.

This may sound complicated, but it was in fact the system's simplicity that excited scientists. Similar switches have been found to control most bacterial genes. Do the same mechanisms control human genes? Dr Monod, in a fit of optimism, declared that "what is true for *E. coli* is also true for an elephant."

Unfortunately, it is not. Elephant and human genes turn out to be much more complicated—which is not surprising, since bacteria are single cells. Elephants are made up of billions of different sorts of cells.

The first thing scientists found about switches in human cells was that a short distance "upstream" of a gene (ie, at the end that is transcribed first), there usually lies a short sequence of four bases, TATA. This turned out to be a red herring. The TATA grouping is merely a signal to tell the transcribing mechanism where the gene starts; it is not the switch itself.

To find the switches, scientists had to isolate pure genes in test tubes, add basic ingredients such as the transcribing enzyme and any other proteins necessary to switch on the gene, and then try to work out where the proteins attached to the DNA. In theory, these points could be where the switches are.

What scientists found was a series of short sequences (or "boxes") upstream of the gene and a series of new proteins that attach to these boxes. For example, one gene, to be switched on, requires two proteins called SP1 to attach to boxes that read GGGCGG, and one other protein to attach to a third box between those boxes reading GCCAAT.

Moreover, these boxes (known as promoters) have to be in exactly the right place relative to the gene. Other sequences, known as enhancers, can be anywhere, not even close by, and still control the gene. This gap between the gene and an enhancer took some explaining, until experiments revealed that the protein that attaches to the enhancer can cause the DNA to bend into a loop, bringing the enhancer into contact with the gene.

So some switches have been found. Nobody knows how the proteins that control the switches are themselves controlled, and nobody knows exactly how switches control development. There are tantalising clues, though. One comes from fruit flies, in which certain genes cause young flies to develop abnormally: to grow a leg instead of an antenna, for example.

In 1984, several scientists discovered that such genes all had a single sequence of 180 DNA letters in them. Even more remarkable, these sequences (called homeo-boxes) were found in the genes that affect development in mice and even human beings. It was as if this sequence were somehow a universal switch for genes that control growth and differentiation.

Sceptics point out, however, that the universality of the homeo-box is likely to mean that it is the least interesting part of the machinery. All computers use the same plugs to plug into the electricity supply. Perhaps the homeo-box is the developmental gene's plug.

To understand embryonic development is one of the reasons for studying gene switches. The other is to understand cancer. The discovery that healthy cells harbour special genes called oncogenes that can cause cancer has transformed the way scientists think about this disease.

It now looks as if the proteins made by oncogenes control a series of master switches that are responsible for controlling the cell's growth. Cancer, which is nothing more than a cell gone berserk, growing and dividing continuously, is therefore caused by somebody leaving the growth genes switched on.

Scientists realised this in 1983, when they read the sequence of bases in one human oncogene. It turned out to resemble closely the sequence of a human gene that encoded a protein called a growth factor. In healthy cells, growth factors set off a chain of events via so-called receptors on the cell's surface, so that the cell reproduces itself—for instance, when blood clots, healing cells multiply. Normally, the cells that make a growth factor do not respond to it, and vice versa. If a cell that responds to a growth factor switches on the gene for that factor, it tells itself continuously to grow and multiply. It becomes a cancer.

Two other kinds of oncogenes work in similar ways. One makes a faulty version of the receptor for the growth factor—faulty in the sense that it acts as if it were continuously receiving the factor. Again, it continuously tells the cell to grow. A third class of oncogenes encodes proteins that are themselves switches for other genes.

Gene dreams

These discoveries were quite unexpected. Before 1982, when the first human oncogene was found, nobody expected cancer to be so readily explicable through genetics. Thanks to molecular biology, cancer is now understood, though not conquered. The aim of most molecular biologists is to uncover enough information so that cures can be found to treat hitherto intractable diseases. One possibility is that agents could be developed which block the binding of the growth factors to the receptor. They could turn out to be promising anti-cancer drugs.

These are distant dreams, but they are not fantasies. Already molecular biology has begun to transform medicine in many different ways. It has enabled scientists to track down the genes responsible

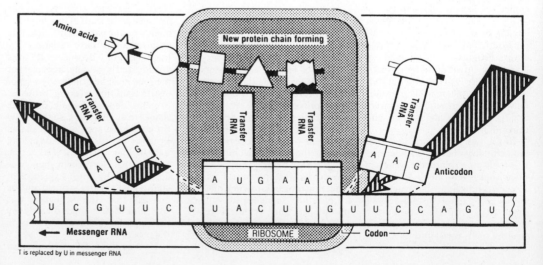

Amino acids
New protein chain forming
Transfer RNA
Anticodon
A U G A A C
U C G U U C C U A C U U G U U C C A G U
← Messenger RNA
RIBOSOME
Codon
T is replaced by U in messenger RNA

for inherited diseases like cystic fibrosis. It has enabled them to find the cause of diseases like AIDS and to design drugs and vaccines that fight disease.

Molecular biology has given scientists two especially useful tools: sequencing and genetic engineering. Sequencing is a clumsy term for reading the sequence of letters in a gene and translating it to work out what protein it spells out. As the cancer story illustrates, it is useful mainly because of the coincidences it reveals: a computer first spotted that oncogenes are like the genes which code for growth-factor proteins by comparing their sequences.

In 1986, encouraged by the recent invention of a machine to read the sequences of genes automatically, a bold plan was aired by a group of American scientists: to read the sequences of the entire set of 50,000 human genes (called the genome).

The result would be a list of bases 3.5 billion characters long—or enough characters to fill about 5,000 average-sized books. Even with the new machines, it would take about ten years and $1 billion a year to do the job. Moreover, genomes are as idiosyncratic as people: whose would you choose to read?

Genetic engineering means taking a gene from one creature and putting it in another. It was first invented in 1972 and perfected during the late 1970s, for transferring genes from human cells to bacteria. The advantage of doing this is that the bacteria can then be encouraged to churn out large amounts of some human protein that can then be used as a drug.

Insulin for diabetics and growth hormone for young dwarfs are both made this way. Drugs to fight cancer and heart disease have also been mass-produced in bacteria—without any great success, as yet, simply because scientists do not know enough about the body's biochemistry to predict which proteins they want to mass-produce.

Genes can now also be put into plants and even animals. For example, a gene was taken from a bacterium that kills insects and put into a tobacco plant. That plant was then left alone by insects. Putting genes into animals is less easy, but it has been done. Human globin genes, which encode the protein responsible for carrying oxygen in the blood, have been transferred to mice. Scientists hope this will reveal how the switches controlling globin genes work. But they could, conceivably, have more practical ambitions—to make cattle grow wool, for instance.

The most ambitious scheme is to put human genes into other human beings. The point would be to cure certain inherited diseases, such as Huntington's chorea, that are caused by the absence of a working copy of the gene. "Gene therapy" would add a working copy of the gene using a special virus called a retrovirus that inserts its genes into human DNA when it infects a cell.

The virus would first be disarmed by removing the genes that enable it to make more viruses, and the experiment would be done only on the bone marrow, not on the germ cells that carry genes to the next generation. Nonetheless, the idea of playing with human genes and retroviruses—AIDS is a retrovirus—alarms people. The alternative, though, for diseases like Huntington's chorea, is to do nothing.

New Light on Edison's Light

Digging anew through the voluminous papers of Thomas Edison, scholars are constructing a fresh, more accurate and revealing understanding of his greatest invention

Robert Friedel

Robert Friedel, an associate professor of history at the University of Maryland, is the author (with Paul B. Israel) of Edison's Electric Light: Biography of an Invention, *published by Rutgers University Press.*

No tale in all the chronicles of American invention would seem to be better known than the story of Thomas Edison's incandescent electric light. The electric light, after all, quickly became the epitome of the bright idea, and its creator was for more than fifty years the living symbol of America's inventive genius. But in truth it is only in recent years that we have begun to piece together the complete story of history's most famous invention.

That the full picture of Edison's work on the electric light in the late 1870s should be obscure is a bit strange, for few inventions before the twentieth century are better documented. The records of the famous laboratory at Menlo Park, New Jersey, were voluminous and have been well preserved over the years. Dozens of laboratory notebooks, hundreds of drawings and sketches, a wealth of letters, patents, and other documents all give testimony to the work and lives of the light's inventors. The importance of the effort to invent a practical electric light was widely evident to contemporary observers, so we have, in addition, an unusual number of journalists' accounts of their trips to Menlo Park. Finally, the fame that Edison achieved with not only this invention but also dozens of others made him an object of attention and adulation for more than half a century after. Journalists, biographers, popularizers, and other writers besieged Edison with regularity, and accounts of the invention of the electric light were among their most popular works. So how can there be more to be known about such an event?

It is perhaps because there has been *too much* information. The vast numbers of documents, now residing in a large vault at Edison's last laboratory, in West Orange, New Jersey, have so intimidated scholars and other researchers that few have attempted a careful combing of them for evidence. The reports in newspapers were always better sources of color and human interest than of reliable technical information. And the half-century of interviews has resulted in a tale jumbled by romantic recollection and the faulty memories of old men.

From all of this have come two pictures of the electric light's creator. The one that has the larger place in the public mind is of the rough-and-ready inventor whose pursuit of the electric light was a dogged hunt through nature's storehouse, a tireless search through thousands of possible substances for the right filament to make a light bulb work. The second, and very different, image is that of the scientific-laboratory chief, a prototype of the modern research manager, who was guided by a vision of a complete electric light and power system and who left the technical details to a skilled, educated staff. As contradictory as these two pictures are, both of them—or some fuzzy composite of the two—have a firm place in not only the popular mythology but in the history books as well.

The new, clearer picture that we are now piecing together comes from a systematic search through the archives at West Orange. For the first time, scholars are recognizing the great potential of the Edison records for revealing the character of the great technological transformations that made over American society in the last decades of the nineteenth century and the first years of the twentieth. Invention, it turns out, is neither a haphazard tinkering nor is it a mechanical application

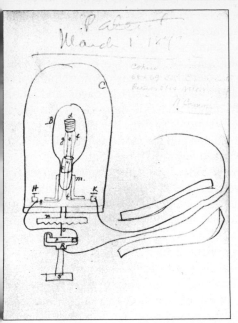 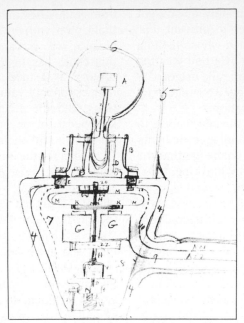 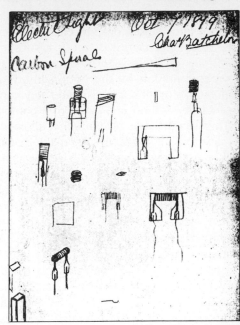

The sketch at left, drawn by Edison in March 1879, shows a would-be lamp with a pneumatic regulator; at center, also from Edison's notebooks, is a slightly later version with an especially complex regulator; the doodles of the carbon spirals, at right, are by Charles Batchelor.

of scientific knowledge. It is a very human activity, filled with the accomplishments and the failings of most endeavors.

The story of the invention of the electric light is a chronicle of people in the midst of the most exciting creative challenge of their lives, working at a frontier of technology. Edison and his colleagues were participants in an enterprise that was part puzzle-solving, part system-building, and part hoopla. When Thomas Edison began to think seriously about the problem of the electric light, he was only thirty-one years old, but already he was the most famous inventor in America. Beginning with an improved stock ticker in 1869, his contributions to telegraphy had made him indispensable to the financiers who controlled the most visible "high technology" of the day. In 1876 he had taken his profits and built in the New Jersey countryside an "invention factory," promising a "minor invention every ten days and a big thing every six months or so." The only thing more astonishing than the young Midwesterner's bravado was his success. Challenged to find a way around Alexander Graham Bell's telephone patents, Edison devised the carbon telephone transmitter and other components for telegraphy's latest wrinkle. Experimenting with means for recording telegraph signals, he came up with his most surprising invention, the phonograph. With this last wonder, Edison became a celebrity.

The burdens of being a celebrity were little different in the 1870s from today. By the middle of 1878 Edison was described as "very tired and ill," worn out by traveling around the country showing off the "machine that talked." That summer he sought a break and took off to the West with a group of scientists who invited him to accompany them to Wyoming to view a solar eclipse. The vacation was, apparently, a great tonic, but conversations with the scientists turned Edison's attention to a new challenge: creating a practical electric light to replace the gas and oil lamps used everywhere.

When he returned east, Edison headed to the workshop of William Wallace in Connecticut. There Wallace, the country's premier brass founder, had on display an electric arc lighting system of his own devising. The newspaper reporter who tagged along described the scene: "Mr. Edison was enraptured . . . eight electric lights were kept ablaze at one time, each being equal to 4,000 candles, the sub-division of electric lights being a thing unknown to science. This filled up Mr. Edison's cup of joy. He sprawled over the table with the simplicity of a child, and made all kinds of calculations." The source of Edison's pleasure was not simply what he saw in Connecticut, it was also what he didn't see. A few weeks later he explained to a newspaper reporter: "I saw the thing had not gone so far but that I had a chance. . . . The intense light had not been subdivided so that it could be brought into private homes." Edison was certain that he could "subdivide the light."

There were known to inventors two ways to derive light from electricity. The first was the electric arc, a blindingly bright spark sustained between two pieces of carbon. This was the form of light made by William Wallace and a host of other inventors. By the 1870s the availability of practical (though very inefficient) generators made the use of arc lights possible in large public areas, in lighthouses, and on streets. By its nature the electric arc was many times brighter than an ordinary interior lamp—perhaps four thousand candlepower as compared with the ten or twenty of gaslight. The other form of electric light used a current to heat up a material so hot that it became "incandescent." It was well known that an incandescent light, if sustained, could be made moderate enough for common indoor usage. But all substances that could be heated to incandescence were in the process either melted or burned up in the heat. This had been demonstrated by the futile efforts of inventors for several decades. Two distinct approaches emerged: one was to use a material with a moderately high melting point that did not oxidize, such as platinum. This substance, unfortunately, always got too hot and melted despite clever devices to prevent this. The other approach was to use a substance whose melting point was so high as to pose no problem. Carbon was the obvious candidate for this option, but despite the use of vacuum pumps or inert gases, no one had managed to sufficiently protect the carbon in a lamp from combustion.

This was the state of affairs that allowed the newspapers to remark that subdivision—the making of small electric lights —was "unknown to science." Here was a challenge that the superconfident Edison felt was both worthy and ripe. Upon his return to Menlo Park he plunged into several days of intensive experimenting. With the help of his closest assistant, Charles Batchelor, a clever and nimble-fingered Englishman, Edison constructed several lamps using spirals of platinum wire as "burners." These devices were distinguished by regulating mechanisms designed to cut off the current if the platinum approached its melting point. These regulators were combinations of electromagnets, switches, resistances, and levers, familiar features of Edison's telegraph inventions. Certain that finding the right sort of regulator posed little problem, Edison brashly announced that in a matter of weeks he would have all problems in hand.

Nothing emerges more vividly out of the laboratory records, letters, and newspaper interviews from Menlo Park in the early fall of 1878 than Edison's supreme confidence. The confidence was infectious, and Edison's announcement was greeted on the stock exchanges by a precipitious fall in gas stocks and by a clamor from some to secure a piece of the new technology.

Little time was wasted in organizing the Edison Electric Light Company, among whose backers were J.P. Morgan and the Vanderbilt interests. The company assured Edison the funds he needed to perfect his invention, including resources to expand Menlo Park and hire experts. All of this was comforting to Edison, and for several weeks the workers at Menlo Park went about constructing models of the new lamp, testing generators to power the system, and preparing patent applications. Only one problem clouded the picture—the light didn't work. Dozens of regulators were made, using several approaches, all designed to cut off current to the platinum wires or strips as they exceeded safe temperatures. The platinum was formed into a variety of shapes, with the intent of conserving the heat energy put into the lamp while allowing the maximum amount of light to be emitted. In every case the lamp flickered intolerably, the burner melted or broke, or the light was too faint. At this point Edison had made little effort to systematically investigate prior work on incandescent lights or to work out the various elements of the generation and distribution system that he would need. By late fall it was apparent that what he didn't know about electric lighting was at least as important as what he did.

Unfortunately for the inventor's giant ego, this was as clear to some of his financial backers as it was to Edison. In November, therefore, Edison was prevailed upon to hire a young Princeton-trained physicist, Francis Upton, recently returned from graduate training in Germany. In later years some claimed that Upton, with his advanced knowledge of mathematics and physics, was the key member of the Menlo Park team, and this claim has become part of the image of Edison's laboratory as a modern scientific establishment. Upton was unquestionably valuable, for he was sharp, eager, and ambitious. But the electric light did not depend on the latest knowledge of physics. Upton's hiring was more important for what it said about Edison and his new line of attack in late 1878 than for the advanced learning it brought to the project. Edison now resolved to find out all he could about every aspect of lighting systems. He and his workers studied old patents, analyzed the work of current rivals, subscribed to the gas-light journals, and set about to begin all over again, still confident but now driven by both the challenges before them and the promises behind them.

At just this point, as the year was ending and the work in the laboratory began to take on the rhythm of a long, hard slog, a technical discovery was made that would set Edison's system apart from all others and provide a key to long-term success. In looking at some rival efforts, Edison and his associates noticed that the amount of electrical current required to operate the systems was quite large. Since Edison was determined to make a lamp that could be used with all the convenience of gaslight and, in particular, could be turned on and off without affecting other lamps, he realized that the lamps would have to be on a "parallel" circuit. In such a circuit, as opposed to a "series" circuit, electric current would be delivered independently to each lamp from the main wires of the circuit. This much was generally known, but the team at Menlo Park observed something else. If a circuit had many lamps on it (and Edison always felt that would be the only economical approach), the delivery of sufficient energy to light each lamp would require either a high voltage or a large current (energy equals voltage times current). Large currents, which everyone else's system relied on, could be carried only by large conductors— resulting in an enormously expensive use of copper. A combination of smaller currents and large voltages would require that each lamp have a high resistance (voltage equals current times resistance). Edison thus decided that his lamp would have to have a high-resistance burner.

This compounded the technical challenge, however. Short pieces of platinum had low resistances, so long spirals of thin thin platinum wire were required. The spirals, on the other hand, always broke easily once they were heated to incandescence. For many months in 1879 Edison and his co-workers struggled to make spirals that would last, all to little avail. Only one thing seemed to improve matters. When the platinum burner was enclosed in a glass globe and the best vacuum pump available had exhausted the air, the life of the glowing burner was measurably longer—reaching a few hours. Edison's response to this discovery was typical: he insisted on having the finest vacuum pump possible and hired a glass-blower to make it and keep it operating.

As 1879 dragged on, progress on the lamp was frustratingly slow. Still, Edison's confidence never flagged. He set his workers to designing and building the other pieces of equipment that would be necessary to make the light work. Much time and energy went into constructing a generator for a high-voltage system, and the result in the summer of 1879 was a radical new design that was the most efficient in the world. Smaller details were not forgotten as Menlo Park yielded meters, switches, fuses, insulators, and other paraphernalia.

All this took place in the public eye. Even though Edison's early claims of the imminent demise of gas lighting were now discounted and a few voices of disenchantment could be heard, the general fascination with the happenings in the rural New Jersey laboratory was still lively. This was in part due to the continuing backing of Wall Street for Edison's efforts, although mutterings of dismay were being heard even there. The main source of wonderment, however, was Edison himself and the still fresh image of the Wizard of Menlo Park. The press loved it, of course, and Edison was ever mindful of the advantages of a reputation for working miracles. Eager readers devoured reporters' descriptions of laboratory life, as in this story from the New York *Herald* of January 17, 1879:

"The ordinary rules of industry seem to be reversed at Menlo Park. . . . At six o'clock in the evening the machinists and electricians assemble in the laboratory. Edison is already present, attired in a suit of blue flannel, with hair uncombed and straggling over his eyes . . . his hands and face somewhat begrimed and his whole air that of a man with a purpose and indifferent to everything save that purpose. By a quarter past six the quiet laboratory has become transformed into a hive of industry. The hum of machinery drowns all other sounds and each man is at his particular post. . . . Edison himself flits about, first to one bench, then to another, examining here, instructing there; at one place drawing out new fancied designs, at another earnestly watching the progress of some experiment. Sometimes he hastily leaves the busy throng of workmen and for an hour or more is seen by no one. . . . In these moments he is rarely disturbed. If any important question of construction arises on which his advice is necessary the workmen wait. Sometimes they wait for hours in idleness, but at the laboratory such idleness is considered far more profitable than any interference with the inventor while he is in the throes of invention . . ."

The main laboratory at Menlo Park was a two-story white clapboard building one hundred feet long and thirty feet wide. Most of the activity was on the second floor, a single room lined with bottle-laden shelves and filled with tables cluttered with electrical and chemical apparatus. The most conspicuous feature of the room was a large pipe organ on the back wall, a gift from an admirer who felt Edison and "the gang" needed some diversion in their long nights of work. The sound of organ music in the middle of the night coming from the hilltop building marked by the occasional strange glow from the windows heightened the mysterious atmosphere that seemed to surround Menlo Park. When, in May 1879, Edison publicly announced a worldwide search for new sources of platinum, a New York tabloid featured him on its cover, complete with wizard's robe and hat. Never before or since was one man or one place so closely identified with the strange miracles of the modern age.

In mid-1879, however, it looked as though only a true miracle would salvage the reputation of Menlo Park. The platinum lamp simply could not be made to work. When investors insisted on inspecting the work that had already cost them tens of thousands of dollars, Edison's staff made a number of low-resistance lamps that, at best, lasted a few hours. High-resistance devices were impossible to keep glowing for any time at all. The only thing that improved the behavior of the lamps was increasing the vacuum in their bulbs, so better vacuum pumps continued to be made. By fall Edison had reached the limits for improving the platinum lamp.

Nothing emerges more vividly than Edison's supreme confidence during the fall of 1878.

Such limits are constantly encountered in the chronicles of human creativity. An individual, driven by vision, imagination, and ambition into new and uncharted territory, will often reach the boundaries of the possibilities held out by a once promising direction. What then determines the changes in direction that yield up the special prize—the creation that makes a difference in the world and that marks the creator forever as different from his fellows? In the case of Edison's electric light, as in so many others, this is not an easily solved puzzle. In October 1879, faced with the unhappy results of more than a year of arduous and expensive labor, Edison changed direction. In a matter of weeks, the missing element of his invention was put in place; no one from that time forth was allowed to doubt the success of the electric light.

The missing element was carbon. But this time it was not the carbon lamp tried by dozens of inventors before, only to burn up or disintegrate—it was carbon in the incredibly high vacuum of Edison's bulbs. Carbon was a familiar material, indispensable to the telephone inventions that still occupied Edison's attention from time to time. In the middle of October, Batchelor and Upton jotted down in their notebooks measurements of carbon's resistance and some ideas on how it might be shaped into spirals. The efforts to make spirals, however, turned out to be fruitless—they always broke in the attempt to put them in bulbs. Finally, on the twenty-second of the month, Batchelor recorded "some very interesting experiments" using just a few inches of carbonized cotton thread. Put into a lamp, the short length of thread measured a resistance of a hundred ohms—many times that of platinum. What was more, the carbon lamp glowed almost as brightly as a gas lamp without flickering out.

1. INDUSTRIAL AND SCIENTIFIC REVOLUTIONS

One of the legends to grow up around the electric light was the story of a lamp, lit on October 21 and lasting forty hours, that provided a moment of clear triumph for the group at Menlo Park. For many years, electric companies celebrated the date as Electric Light Day, and October 21, 1929, was chosen as the day to honor Edison at Light's Golden Jubilee. But records from the laboratory give no evidence of this "breakthrough" lamp. The dramatic moment was perhaps a necessary creation of the memories of people who, understandably, recalled in later years their work as a romantic quest, capped by a single shining moment. We learn, however, that invention is rarely romantic but instead shares the messiness and uncertainty of most creative human endeavors.

After a few more days of testing it became clear that the carbon lamp was the answer. During the next few weeks Edison and his assistants made variations on the new lamp to learn all they could about it. They clearly marveled at the result, for the lamp that emerged was as wonderful for its simplicity as for its light. A simple evacuated glass globe, in it mounted nothing but a short, black piece of carbonized sewing thread, the new lamp was very different from the bulky, expensive, and complex platinum devices around which the experimenters had built their hopes. Francis Upton, in a letter home in mid-November, exclaimed: "Just at the present I am very much elated at the prospects of the Electric Light. During the past week Mr. Edison has succeeded in obtaining the first lamp that answers the purpose we have wished. It is cheap—much more so than we ever hoped to have."

Little time was wasted in letting the anxious investors know that an important discovery had been made. Several of them took the Pennsylvania Railroad to the little Menlo Park stop to see for themselves that Edison was not bluffing. The inventor showed an unusual reluctance, however, to let the press in on the story—at least until he was ready. Finally he invited a reporter to get a full account of the invention, swearing him to secrecy. When the New York *Herald* for December 21 appeared carrying Marshall Fox's full-page story on the lamp, Edison was reported to be livid at the breach of confidence. The displeasure was short-lived, however, for, in truth, preparations for a public demonstration were well advanced. The workers in the laboratory had been kept busy for weeks making lamps, having discovered that bristol board made more reliable filaments than thread, while others had begun to install lamps in nearby homes, including Edison's and Upton's. A grand public display was scheduled for New Year's Eve, and hundreds of the curious, aroused by a steady stream of newspaper stories, flocked to the laboratory, heedless of a winter storm.

The crowds that thronged into Menlo Park were made up of curiosity seekers and newshounds after the latest sensation. But they represented something more; they stood for a new relationship between advanced technology and the common man. Edison's electric light was as mystifying and awe-inspiring as any invention of the age. Few things could have been more marvelous than the piece of charred paper glowing bright enough in its glass container to light up a room and yet not burning up. The magic represented by scientific technology was a source of unalloyed hope, not distrust. This attitude toward the powers of science and technology is one of the nineteenth century's most important legacies, and no single instance better represents it than the enthusiasm with which the crowds ushered in the new decade at Menlo Park.

> **W**e learn that invention shares the messiness and uncertainty of most human endeavors.

The Green Revolution

Robert E. Huke

Robert E. Huke was educated at Dartmouth College and Syracuse University, and he is currently Professor of Geography, Dartmouth College, Hanover, NH 03755. His teaching and research interests focus on agriculture, especially in South and Southeast Asia where he has completed a number of village and regional level research projects. A second major interest lies with the development of computer-assisted instruction modules for use in teaching and in training agricultural extension workers.

The Green Revolution refers to a complex package that includes improved seeds and a wide range of management practices. The new plant types show a strong positive response to fertilizer because of a high leaf area index, short stature, and stiff straw that resists lodging. These plant varieties have resistance to many insect pests and plant diseases. The management package is concerned with timing; rate and method of application of various inputs; appropriate spacing of plants; thorough weeding; careful monitoring and control of pests; and improved harvesting, drying, and threshing methods. Of all the management practices, the control of water is

perhaps the most important, because its timely application is essential to efficient utilization of fertilizer and the attainment of high yields (Anderson et al. 1982).

The Green Revolution is not a miracle of modern agricultural technology, but rather an evolution that differs only in time and place from earlier developments in industrialized countries. In both cases, the route to significant yield improvements involved plant materials having high genetic potential farmed with improved management practices that included considerably increased levels of input.

This paper provides a brief historic and geographic

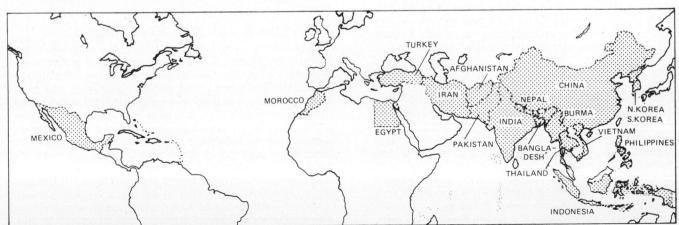

Figure 1. Chief benefiting countries. Source: Author.

From *Journal of Georgraphy*, Vol. 84, No. 6, November/December 1985, pp. 248-254. Reproduced with permission of the National Council for Geographic Education.

view of the genetic and technological developments that led to the Green Revolution. It describes some of the characteristics of the area where these developments were most readily applied and raises questions concerning the unequal impact of the revolution.

Targeted Areas

Yield increases and improved food availability have been particularly important in a group of eighteen heavily populated countries where wheat and/or rice are major food crops. These countries, which are the chief beneficiaries of the Green Revolution, extend across the subtropical part of the world from Korea in the east to Mexico in the west (Figure 1). Fifteen of these countries are contiguous, describing an arc in southern Asia, and are characterized by high rural and farming populations. The benefiting countries include eighteen percent of the earth's land surface, thirty-two percent of its cultivated area, and are home to fifty-six percent of the world's population. Except for China, their population numbers are increasing at a markedly higher rate than that for the world as a whole, and population density is already at extraordinary levels. In mid-1985, there were 290 persons per square mile (750 per square kilometer) compared to forty-nine (127) for the remainder of the world. Population density is almost six times higher than that of the rest of the world; and the nutritional density, or population per square mile of cultivated land, is over 1,500.

The high population-to-land ratio helps to explain other characteristics of the area as well. Grain is raised chiefly on small farms without mechanization and often in monocultivation. The annual crop provides a major portion of the total farm income, and frequently a significant portion of the crop stays on the farm to provide food for the coming year. The farm population dependent on either wheat or rice as a major crop totals at least 1.7 billion people, or 320 million families. Many of these families have no land at all and depend on farm employment for their income. Even those who own or rent land have an average of less than 2.5 acres (about one hectare) per family. The vast majority of these Third World farmers live close to the margin of existence. Surpluses of food and money are minimal.

Unfortunately for these and other underdeveloped countries, the Green Revolution promises more than it can deliver. The term "Green Revolution" implies that a solution has been found for the problem of providing adequate food for a population that grows exponentially. A solution has not been found. The Green Revolution has provided for a quantum leap in food production per unit area, but further increases will be slower, smaller, and probably more expensive. What the Green Revolution has done is to provide time—a breathing space—for people to find a more permanent solution to the population-food problem.

Genetic History: The Green Evolution

The term, "Green Revolution," was originally inspired by work with wheat and rice during the late 1960s, but today is applied to developments in a broad range of food crops throughout the tropics and subtropics. Much of the fundamental research is done at a series of international centers that conduct basic research and train scientists from and in underdeveloped countries. National research centers adapt this research to local needs.

The genes that sparked the Green Revolution were brought to the attention of the post-World War II scientific community by S.C. Salmon who carried seeds of an obscure, short, stiff-strawed, heavy-seeded Japanese wheat (Norin No. 10) to the US in 1946. In 1953 a small packet of second-generation seeds (Norin crossed with a tall North American wheat) was received in Mexico and became the foundation for a breeding program that eventually resulted in a Nobel Peace Prize for Norman Borlaug. In 1962 the first few of Borlaug's Mexican semi-dwarf, rust-resistant seeds were matured in New Dehli. M.S. Swaminathan, then head of the Indian Agricultural Research Institute's Division of Genetics, was so impressed that Borlaug was invited to India where the two scientists launched a program of agricultural innovation in the subcontinent (CIMMYT Economics Program 1983).

Also in 1962, Peter Jennings at the International Rice Research Institute in the Philippines crossed Peta (a tall Indonesian rice variety) with Dee-geo-woo-gen (a short statured variety from Taiwan) (Chandler 1982), and 130 seeds were formed. From these seeds, IR8 (the first of the IRRI modern high-yielding varieties) was identified and named. IR8 was short and sturdy, tillered well, had great seedling vigor, responded well to fertilizer, had moderate seed dormancy, was reasonably resistant to tungro virus, and was essentially insensitive to photoperiod. (Varieties that are insensitive to photoperiod can be planted and harvested in any season without regard to the number of hours of daylight.) IR8 produced record yields almost everywhere it was tested. Unfortunately, it also had several disadvantages. The grain was bold and chalky in appearance, which detracted from its value; it was subject to considerable breakage in the milling process; and the amalose content of its starch was so high as to cause a hardening after cooking and cooling (a distinct handicap for sales to Asian consumers). It was also susceptible to bacterial blight and several races of rice blast. IR8 was soon replaced by a sequence of newer varieties that overcame IR8's disadvantages but maintained most of its yield advantage.

Contact with rice scientists in China was difficult and limited until the 1970s. Nonetheless, a small but steady exchange of genetic material and published research was maintained through Hong Kong and East Pakistan (now called Bangladesh). In China the breeding efforts in rice were divided between the development of improved varieties and hybrids, for which new seeds had to be developed for each planting. The emphasis on hybrids was so strong that by the early 1980s almost twenty percent of China's total rice area was planted to hybrids (Huke 1982). In other rice growing countries, the cost and effort of raising hybrid seed was not considered worth the gains to be realized from hybrid vigor until recently.

Innovations Through Breeding

The breeding of rice and wheat in the mid-twentieth century developed along three distinctive and equally important lines. The first innovation was the introduction of the dwarfing gene that allowed plants to use high levels of fertilizer and achieve yield levels far above those previously possible. Along with this change came the elimination of photoperiod sensitivity. This innovation was of greatest benefit to farmers on the highest quality land that could be irrigated year round. But even for farmers on rainfed land, it allowed increased flexibility and the opportunity to adjust planting dates to the soil moisture levels of individual seasons. It also allowed some spreading out of labor demands in areas where monocultivation was the normal mode of operation and, therefore, moderated the "boom" and "bust" character of the labor market.

The second innovation was the genetic capability to resist attacks by various insect pests and diseases. One reason for the rapid and widespread acceptance of wheat varieties from Mexico in the early 1960s was a strong resistance to various rusts. With rice, early releases were not as resistant to attack. In many parts of Asia, losses to insects and diseases were often severe, especially during the monsoon season. Several early varieties produced yields up to their genetic potential only with heavy and frequent application of chemical insect controls. Farmer resistance to the use of expensive systemics, inappropriate use of sprays, increasing environmental concerns, and the development of resistant genotypes among insect populations hastened the development of grain types with genetic resistance. Newer varieties of both rice and wheat require smaller amounts of pesticides than varieties used in the 1970s.

The third innovation was the development of plants with much shorter growing seasons. Before this innovation, the normal practice in Asia was for farmers to plant rice with the first monsoon rains in June and to harvest in mid-December. A 180-day growing season was common. The growing season, however, was reduced to 150 days with IR8 and 110 days with IR36. The adoption of IR36 allows farmers in areas subject to erratic, early rains to evade moisture problems by planting late, and it allows farmers more favorable conditions to supplement the rice crop with an early planting or post-rice planting of a vegetable or a pulse.

The importance of these innovations may be appreciated with reference to wheat in Bangladesh, where output increased from 100,000 metric tons to over 1,000,000 metric tons in twelve years. When the country was established as an independent nation in 1971, many writers believed the problem of producing sufficient food for over 90,000,000 people on a land area the size of New York State, and whose farm base is subject to annual deep flooding as well as to periodic devastation by typhoons, was close to hopeless. Rice is the major food

crop, and wheat a secondary crop used chiefly for making chapatis. The environment for rice production is probably the most difficult of any rice-growing country. Of 24.7 million acres (ten million hectares) planted annually, only ten percent is irrigated; twelve percent is flooded to a depth of greater than three feet (one meter); almost ten percent is dryland, lacking even bunds to pond rainfall; and the remainder is rainfed, frequently subject to massive but temporary flooding. Despite such handicaps, Bangladesh has converted about fifteen percent of its rice area to modern varieties and has improved its national rice yield by almost thirty percent. At the same time, wheat acreages, yields, and production increased sharply (Figure 2). This shift came about only after changes had been made in rice and wheat seeds. The shortened rice growing season provided a window of opportunity for Bangladeshi farmers; and the rust-resistant, short growing season wheat allowed farmers to take advantage of the opportunity. Wheat is now grown as a winter season crop on large areas that previously produced only a rainy season, long-duration rice crop.

It is improbable, however, that wheat expansion would have taken place rapidly were it not for the fact that farmers had prior experience with modern rice varieties and had received help from extension agents. In less than fifteen years, wheat yields more than doubled. The area planted to wheat expanded five times, and wheat production increased ten times (CIMMYT 1982). In the world's most crowded country where food shortages and natural disasters occur frequently, the food situation by mid-1985 in Bangladesh was marginally better than it was a decade earlier. In Bangladesh, modern agricultural technology has already proven that it can provide the time for the country to tackle the population-food problem.

Inputs and Yield

Modern plant varieties give higher yields than do traditional ones. They are planted on the best land, tend to occupy irrigated or at least reliable water control areas, receive

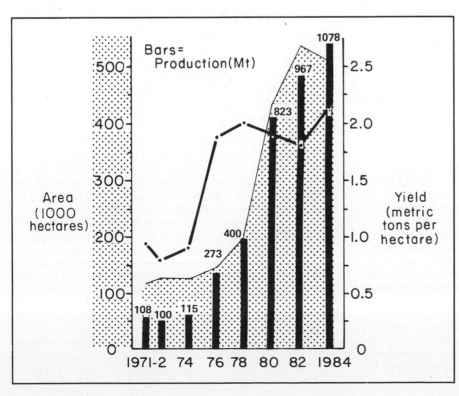

Figure 2. Bangladesh wheat: area, yield, production. Source: US Department of Agriculture (1984).

1. INDUSTRIAL AND SCIENTIFIC REVOLUTIONS

Table 1.

Percentage Change in Area, Production, and Yield of Rice: 1965-67 to 1982-84

Country	Change in rice area		Change in rice production		Change in rice yield	
	million hectares	percentage	million metric tons	percentage	metric tons per hectare	percentage
China	3.1	10	67.9	73	1.76	57
India	4.0	11	31.5	69	0.66	51
Indonesia	1.6	21	18.8	122	1.72	83
Bangladesh	1.4	15	7.0	46	0.44	27
Thailand	2.8	43	5.2	42	− 0.02	− 1
Burma	0.1	2	7.0	97	1.45	94
Vietnam	0.9	19	5.3	60	0.66	75
Philippines	0.3	10	3.8	93	0.99	75
S. Korea	<.1	0	2.3	45	1.96	47
Pakistan	0.6	43	3.2	160	1.20	83
N. Korea	0.2	33	2.7	117	2.47	66
Total	+ 15.0	+ 14	+ 154.7	+ 74	+ 1.05	+ 52
World less 11 above	+ 3	+ 15	+ 5.3	+ 11	− 0.10	− 4

Source: Palacpac (1982) and US Department of Agriculture (1984).

Table 2.

Percentage Change in Area, Population, and Yield of Wheat: 1965-1984

Country	Change in wheat area		Change in wheat production		Change in wheat yield	
	thousands of hectares	percentage	thousands of metric tons	percentage	metric tons per hectare	percentage
Egypt	47	+ 9	728	+ 57	1.08	+ 45
Morocco	318	+ 19	874	+ 80	.34	+ 52
Afghanistan	294	+ 13	800	+ 36	.20	+ 21
Bangladesh	405	+ 405	960	+ 813	.96	+ 81
China	4106	+ 17	51671	+ 173	1.63	+ 135
India	9685	+ 72	25900	+ 156	.61	+ 50
Iran	2000	+ 50	2582·	+ 66	.10	+ 10
Pakistan	2052	+ 39	6284	+ 103	.54	+ 47
Turkey	1574	+ 22	3264	+ 33	.12	+ 9
Total	20481	+ 39	93063	+ 131	.82	+ 66
World less 9 above		− 4		+ 24		+ 29

Source: US Department of Agriculture (1984) and FAO (1967).

higher levels of fertilizer, and are often more carefully weeded than traditional varieties. Plant protection is more commonly extended to modern varieties; the net labor input is higher, and the modern varieties are first adopted by the most innovative farmers. For almost every input controlled by farmers, modern varieties have an advantage over traditional ones.

Changes in area planted, production, and yield for rice and wheat for Green Revolution countries are shown in Tables 1 & 2. In the case of rice, area increased by a modest fifteen percent over eighteen years, reflecting the fact that land was already at a premium and that the best land had already been developed. The new area was land previously avoided for rice because of poor soils, excessive flooding, excessive drainage, remoteness, or some other physical or locational handicap. Despite this modest increase in area, the production of rice rose by seventy-four percent over the same period because of a remarkable increase in yield per unit area.

Output of modern grain varieties increases sharply with the application of the first unit of a new input, but an additional unit of that same input results in a lower additional increase. For example, a first weeding may result in a yield increase of fifteen percent over that of no weeding, but a second weeding may result in only a ten percent additional increase. Eventually, one further weeding will cost more than the value of the resulting yield increase. With chemical fertilizers, the response will be more dramatic. At some level, a point will be reached where one additional unit of input will result in a decrease in yield. Nonetheless, at all levels of fertilizer input, the expected yield of modern varieties exceeds that of traditional varieties. The general formula describing this relationship is:

Final Yield = Base Yield + A(Fertilizer) − B(Fertilizer)^2.

The case of Indonesia provides an example of the differential impact of high nitrogen fertilizer on irrigated rice (Figure 3). The coefficients for (Fertilizer) and

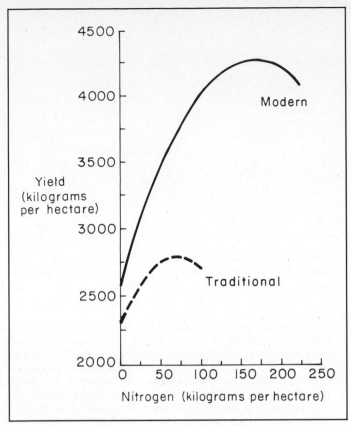

Figure 3. Yield response of nitrogen on irrigated rice in Indonesia. Source: Herdt and Capule (1983).

(Fertilizer)[2] vary with rice variety, water control, soil character, and season but always show a more rapid response on the part of improved grain types. The observation that modern varieties require more fertilizer is only partly correct. Although they do require more fertilizer to reach their maximum potential, modern varieties outyield traditional types even without the application of fertilizer (Barker and Herdt 1985).

Impact of the Green Revolution

From 1965 through 1983, underdeveloped countries outperformed developed countries in terms of the rate of increase in food production (Figure 4). Unfortunately, population growth was so high in underdeveloped countries that their per capita gain was no more than in developed countries, about one percent per year.

On a regional scale, the impact of the improved technology is illustrated in Tables 1 & 2. In the case of rice, the benefiting countries increased their average yield by an impressive fifty-two percent between 1965 and 1983, representing almost 2.5 percent per year. In the same period, their total production went up by seventy-

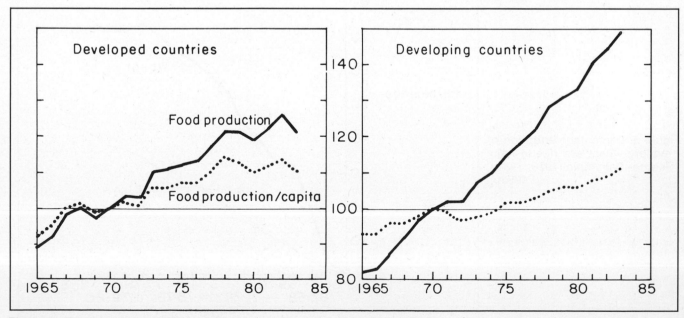

Figure 4. Food indexes (1970 = 100 percent). Source: After FAO (1984).

Table 3.

Rice Area and Nitrogen Used 1979-1980

Country	Rice area planted thousand hectares	Nitrogen kilograms per hectare	Yield rough rice metric tons per hectare
Burma	5,013	11	2.19
Bangladesh	10,308	21	2.02
India	40,200	19	2.01
Pakistan	2,026	52	2.37
Indonesia	8,495	73	3.29
Philippines	3,543	33	2.15
Thailand	8,288	10	1.82
S. Korea	1,314	131	5.90

Source: Martinez and Diamond (1982) and FAS (1983).

four percent. For the rest of the world, yield decreased by four percent, and production advanced by only eleven percent. Higher yields among the beneficiaries were related to improved irrigation, increased use of fertilizers, better weeding, and plant protection, all applied to a stronger genetic stock.

High yielding modern varieties of wheat and rice have not been universally adopted, nor have their full potentials been realized by the farmers using them. On experimental farms, the new seeds commonly produce four times the yield of traditional varieties, but on farmers' fields the advantage is far smaller. The difference is often called the "yield gap" and probably occurs because the environment on the farmers' fields is less ideal than on experimental farms where neither flood nor drought is a problem, where soil conditions are most favorable, where each field is carefully monitored by specialists, and where the level of inputs, especially fertilizer, is well above that used by farmers. On experimental farms, the new varieties maximize their yield on most soil types at levels of nitrogen ranging from 130 to 200 pounds per acre (150 to 225 kilograms per hectare). Depending on the relative price of fertilizer and the market value of rough

rice, the optimum level of application to maximize returns without measurable damage to the ecosystem is between ninety and 130 pounds per acre (100 to 150 kilograms per hectare). These levels are seldom achieved in Third World countries.

In South and Southeast Asia, modern wheat seeds have been planted to roughly eighty percent of the wheat area compared to under fifty percent for rice. The lower figure for rice is related to the character of the new seed and the physical geography of Asia's rice lands. The seed produces a plant about three feet (about one meter) tall that matures in roughly 110 days. The plant does poorly when subject to submergence, and it does not have time to recover from drought stress that may occur early in the growing season. Modern rice cannot be grown at all on areas normally subject to more than three feet (about one meter) of standing water during the wet season. Rice varieties also provide only modest yield advantage under saline conditions or in high sulfate soils (IRRI 1985). Large areas of the great delta regions of South and Southeast Asia, therefore, are unsuitable for today's modern rice varieties. With this in mind, the fifty-two percent mean yield increase already achieved is even more remarkable.

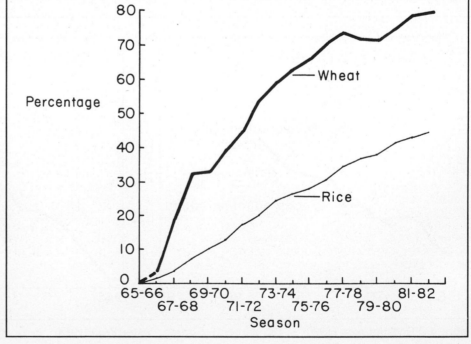

Figure 5. Percentage adoption of modern wheat and rice in Asia. Source: Dalrymple (1978, 1985a, 1985b).

It is difficult to identify and document those factors beyond the physical environment that have contributed directly to unequal benefits, and many questions have been raised. Has the Green Revolution resulted in unfair advantages accruing to the already well-to-do, or have the poor benefited as well? Do farmers with large holdings reap disproportionately more profit than those with small holdings? Do owners of land prosper while tenants and the landless become poorer?

In 1982, The American Association for the Advancement of Science published the results of a symposium devoted to discussing these questions (Anderson et al. 1982). The publication consists of eighteen well-documented papers that provide different answers to these fundamental questions. In a much briefer report, more than 100 sources reporting on modern rice varieties in Asia are analyzed for answers to the same questions (Herdt and Capule 1983). The evidence is strongly conflicting across time, place, and cultural setting and, therefore, the authors conclude that there are no consistent findings relating successful adoption of the Green Revolution package to either farm size or tenure.

In a report on two Indonesian and two Philippine villages, strong evidence was found supporting the environment as the principal determinant of success in adoption.

The four village cases invariably show that farm size was not a factor in the adoption of MV [modern varieties]. In the three villages with environmental conditions suitable for MV, both large and small farmers planted MV in nearly 100% of their paddy areas. On the other hand, both large and small farmers rejected MV when they found the MV to be unsuited to their environment. In neither case was a significant difference observed in the levels of either yield or application of modern inputs such as fertilizers (Hayami and Kikuchi 1982, pp. 212-13).

Conclusion

In the years ahead, there are two groups of challenges facing agricultural scientists and social scientists in regard to the Green Revolution. The first is to continue research on breeding and farm systems. The objective of breeding should be to develop plants that will adapt more readily to the less than ideal environments where most of the poorest farmers of the world live. The objective of farming systems research should be to maximize year-round food production on a given plot of land and to substitute home-grown or home-produced inputs for purchased industrial inputs where possible.

The second objective is to continue to extend the improved technology to those farmers who have not yet participated and to encourage those who have adopted one-half the package to intensify their operations. For example, a majority of farmers in Asia apply very low levels of nitrogen to their crop. In environments as different as Indonesia and South Korea where nitrogen levels are high, yields are significantly above those of neighboring countries. For the other countries, much unexploited potential remains to be developed through fertilizers and other management inputs.

Success in these broad research objectives holds promise for possibly a fifty percent increase in yields. Such a result would provide the world with two or three decades to find a more permanent solution to the population-food question.

References

Anderson, R.S., ed. et al. 1982. *Science, Politics and the Agricultural Revolution in Asia.* Boulder, CO: Westview Press.

Barker, R., and Herdt, R.V. 1985. *The Rice Economy of Asia.* Resources for the Future Series. Baltimore: Johns Hopkins University Press, forthcoming.

Chandler, R.F., Jr. 1982. *An Adventure in Applied Science: A History of the International Rice Research Institute.* Manila, Philippines: International Rice Research Institute.

CIMMYT. 1982. "Wheat in Bangladesh." *CIMMYT Today No. 15.* Mexico, D.F. Mexico: Centro Internacional de Mejoramiento de Maiz y Trigo.

CIMMYT Economics Program. 1983. *World Wheat Facts and Trends.* Report 2: An Analysis of Rapidly Rising Third World Consumption and Imports of Wheat. Mexico, D.F. Mexico: Centro Internacional de Mejoramiento de Maiz y Trigo.

Dalrymple, D.G. 1978. *Development and Spread of High-Yielding Varieties of Wheat and Rice in the Less Developed Nations.* Report No. 95. Washington, DC: US Department of Agriculture.

_____. 1985a. *Development and Spread of High Yielding Rice Varieties in the Developing Countries.* AID Technical Bulletin Series. Washington, DC: United States Agency for International Development.

_____. 1985b. *Development and Spread of High Yielding Wheat Varieties in the Developing Countries.* AID Technical Bulletin Series. Washington, DC: United States Agency for International Development.

FAO. 1967. *FAO Production Yearbook 1967.* Rome.

_____. 1984. *FAO Production Yearbook 1984.* Rome.

FAS. 1983. *Foreign Agriculture Circular FG 26 83 World Rice Reference Tables.* Washington, DC: US Department of Agriculture.

Hayami, Y., and Kikuchi, M. 1982. *Asian Village Economy at the Crossroads: An Economic Approach to Institutional Change.* Baltimore: Johns Hopkins Press.

Herdt, R.V., and Capule, C. 1983. *Adoption, Spread, and Production Impact of Modern Rice Varieties in Asia.* Manila, Philippines: International Rice Research Institute.

Huke, R.E. 1982. *Rice Area by Type of Culture: South, Southeast and East Asia.* Manila, Philippines: International Rice Research Institute.

IRRI. 1985. *International Rice Research: 25 Years of Partnership.* Manila, Philippines: International Rice Research Institute.

Martinez, A., and Diamond, R.B. 1982. *Fertilizer Use Statistics in Crop Production.* Muscle Shoals, AL: International Fertilizer Development Center.

Palacpac, A.C. 1982. *World Rice Statistics.* Los Banos, Philippines: IRRI, Department of Agricultural Economics.

US Department of Agriculture. 1984. *Agriculture Statistics 1984.* Washington, DC: US Government Printing Office.

Driving Toward a World Car?

U.S. automakers go abroad to find partners

For years, top American auto executives railed against their Japanese competitors at every turn of the wheel. Chrysler chairman Lee Iacocca launched some of his best barbs to protest what he considered unfair Japanese tactics. Lately, the big guns have been remarkably silent. But then again, who would criticize his business partner? The old antagonists have suddenly started working together on the same assembly lines.

Customers may not realize it, but the world auto industry is fast becoming one great partnership. Consider this: Mazda designed and built Ford's sporty new Probe. The classic Japanese Toyota Corolla now rolls out of an American plant half owned by General Motors. The peppy "American" Pontiac LeMans was engineered by Opel (GM's West German subsidiary) and is built by Daewoo in South Korea. The Corvette, often described as the epitome of the American-made sports car, comes with a high-performance transmission built by ZF, a West German company.

Over all, experts say approximately 25 major car and truck manufacturers worldwide have combined in nearly 300 joint relationships, a pace worthy of "Dangerous Liaisons." Some automakers have bought stock in their competitors; others jointly assemble parts like engines. While U.S. car makers don't yet produce cars in tandem—their agreements are basically with foreign manufacturers—they are moving closer. Last year GM, Ford and Chrysler agreed to conduct joint research on structural materials for cars and trucks in a so-called "precompetitive" venture sanctioned by the government. The pace of joint deals is "faster than an evolution and slower than a revolution," says Chrysler Corp. vice chairman Gerald Greenwald: "No car company will be successful in the '90s that doesn't learn to develop strategic international alliances."

Fierce competition among car makers has spurred this maze of transocean connections. By one estimate, American customers have about 600 different car and truck models to choose from. Many of these vehicles are targeted for "niche" markets with expected annual sales of a relatively small 100,000 to 300,000 units. No company, not even GM, the largest of them all, can afford on its own to design, build and market the vehicles they need to satisfy all their customers. (GM has gotten involved in 50 joint deals since 1980.)

Far from stifling competition, the companies typically develop a car together and then sell it in the same niche of the marketplace. Mazda, for instance, builds the Ford Probe and Mazda MX-6 in the same plant in Flat Rock, Mich. The cars, essentially the same underneath but with different exteriors, compete for the same buyers. The deal benefits both: Ford couldn't afford to build a sports car from scratch and Mazda couldn't sell enough MX-6s to justify a new plant. "The main rationale is to spread and reduce costs," says Christopher Cedergren of J.D. Power and Associates, an auto consulting firm. Without the deals, says Oppenheimer & Co. analyst Charles Brady, many automakers would face serious financial trouble because huge costs, including overcapacity, already burden the industry.

The joint auto deals come in all shapes. GM bought interests in three Asian manufacturers (Isuzu and Suzuki in Japan, Daewoo in South Korea) to assure itself a flow of subcompact cars—which it could not make profitably itself. Chrysler and Mitsubishi set up a new American company, Diamond-Star Motors, to build no fewer than three look-alike sports cars in Normal, Ill. Mitsubishi provided the technology, Chrysler the marketing muscle. Diamond-Star makes the Eclipse for Mitsubishi and the Plymouth Laser for Chrysler; this fall it will start producing the Eagle Talon for Chrysler. Chrysler will import Alfa Romeo luxury cars from Italy's Fiat to fill another hole in its line.

Old hands: Ford and Mazda helped pioneer the globalization movement. Twenty years ago Mazda began making cars for Ford to sell in Asia; 10 years later Ford bought 25 percent of Mazda's stock. Mazda dealers in Japan now import Tauruses and Probes. Following up their sports-car venture, Ford will expand a plant in Louisville, Ky., to make light trucks for Mazda. Ford now works with other Japanese companies too. It buys the engine for its souped-up Taurus SHO from Yamaha. (Some experts say Ford

---

Who Made This Vehicle, Anyway?

Car makers have agreed to nearly 300 joint deals, including a venture to make the Ford Probe (below left) and the Mazda MX-6 in the same Michigan plant.

GM/Toyota
Joint venture in America now produces Geo Prizms for General Motors and Corollas for Toyota.

Ford/Yamaha
Japanese company supplies souped-up engine that it designed and engineered for Taurus SHO.

Chrysler/Mitsubishi
Jointly owned Diamond-Star Motors makes look-alike sports cars in the United States for both companies.

Ford/Nissan
A joint-owned U.S. plant to make a Nissan-designed minivan to be sold under both Ford and Nissan nameplates.

could not have afforded to produce the SHO if it had to develop its own engine.) A joint Ford-Nissan plant in Avon Lake, Ohio, will make Nissan-designed front-wheel-drive minivans with similar innards but different skins, one for Ford, one for Nissan.

Chrysler also plans to make minivans with Renault—giving the American company its first manufacturing operation in Europe in years. "We certainly didn't want to go back into Europe the way Chrysler did in the '70s, which was to buy up all the dogs and almost get eaten by them," says Greenwald. "Our best choice is a project that involves a European partner."

One of the most successful joint ventures resulted from the shotgun marriage of Volkswagen and Ford in Brazil and Argentina. Large losses by both automakers in the Latin market led them to merge into Autolatina in 1987. The new company, the largest private enterprise in South America, produces Volkswagens and Fords under one roof but sells them through competing marketing organizations. Autolatina showed a profit in 1988.

Political pressures force some partnerships. Toyota, for example, formed New United Motor Manufacturing Inc. (NUMMI) with GM in 1984 to make cars in California. The United States wanted Toyota to manufacture here—and to create American jobs instead of erasing them. The venture, which now builds Geo Prizms and Toyota Corollas, also paid off for Toyota in a more strictly business sense. It found out how to deal with an American work force, a skill that was needed when Toyota opened its 100 percent-owned Camry plant in Georgetown, Ky. NUMMI benefits GM too. Jack Smith, executive vice president for GM's international operations, says his company is learning how the Japanese build cars.

While joint ventures have a quick-fix attraction, they could produce long-term pain. David Andrea of the University of Michigan's Office for the Study of Automotive Transportation says the decision by GM and Ford to sell imported subcompacts under their own names might backfire. Many first-time car buyers know they are getting a vehicle made in Japan or South Korea. When the time comes to trade up, Andrea says, these consumers may bypass American dealers and buy a medium-priced car with a Japanese nameplate.

Opting out? The rush to cooperative deals may benefit some of Japan's top automakers in another way. Right now, Toyota and Honda have agreed to very few joint ventures. Toyota plans to build pickup trucks with Volkswagen in West Germany and Honda produces the Sterling luxury car with Great Britain's Rover. The lack of deals partly reflects European automakers' fears of coming out second best to Japan. But if the Japanese can continue to build most of their own cars, they might end up with a substantial advantage over competitors: they won't have to split their profits with anyone.

Experts say the joint-venture trend will help American consumers get just the kind of cars they want at decent prices. But globalization of the industry presents a problem for any lingering patriot who wants a car made in the U.S.A. At the rate things are going, even the most savvy tire kicker won't be able to tell if it really is.

FRANK WASHINGTON *in Detroit*
and DAVID PAULY

THE CONQUERING MACHINE

It was first developed in England to break
Nazi codes. Computers now prescribe
cancer chemotherapy and prospect for oil.

Pamela McCorduck

Today's digital computer was born in Great Britain and the United States during World War II, in the frenzy of technological innovation that war invariably spawns. In Great Britain, mathematician Alan Turing helped design an electronic computer named Colossus in absolute secrecy to help crack the ciphers of Enigma, the Nazi code machine. Turned on in December of 1943, it was the first computer to employ vacuum tubes as digital on-off switches—some 2,000 of them—instead of the slow, noisy electromagnetic relays its predecessors had used. Some military analysts say that Colossus was the pivotal factor in Hitler's defeat, for the Germans never knew the computer was breaking codes almost as fast as Enigma was cranking them out.

So tight was the secrecy around Colossus that the U.S. designers of Eniac, the first general-purpose electronic computer, began their work confident that their machine would be first. Physicist John William Mauchly and a 22-year-old engineer named J. Presper Eckert at the University of Pennsylvania started building Eniac (for Electronic Numerical Integrator and Computor) in 1943. It passed its tests in the fall of 1945 and went to work the following February, calculating bomb and missile trajectories for the Army—a job that had been done by as many as 200 people using desktop tabulating machines. The heat thrown off by Eniac's 17,468 vacuum tubes sent the temperature in the room to 120 degrees and the tubes to premature deaths; whenever the computer malfunctioned, teams of technicians would search the racks of equipment looking for burned-out glass corpses. But the monstrous machine did work, cost less than $500,000, and spent nearly a decade calculating trajectories and performing such civilian work as weather forecasting.

In the four decades since Eniac, computers have moved through a continuing series of improvements: vacuum tubes, transistors, integrated circuits with dramatically increasing density, the microprocessor chip, and advances in memory devices.

The computer's performance improved with its hardware, allowing it to move beyond simple numerical symbols to the manipulation of complex visual and aural symbols. Computing thus transformed virtually any task that can be expressed symbolically: design, manufacturing, and information gathering, for example.

Medicine is a convenient microcosm. Computerized billing, and hospital records that can be called up and displayed immediately instead of stored in space-consuming and slow-to-retrieve folders, are already common. Communications networks are slowly being set up for fast transfer of information about suitable organ transplant donors and recipients; statistics about the incidence of disease, whether geographical, occupational, by age, or any other characteristic, are being gathered and sorted for the epidemiological tale they tell. Such gathering and sorting of data by computer is already mundane and familiar, but it is just such tasks that have profound effects on our health and well-being. They also illustrate one of the most important changes wrought by the computer, the so-called order of magnitude effect, where a large change in quantity brings about a marked change in quality. When people began to ride in cars, the social effect was profound far beyond the obvious fact that riding at 40 mph is 10

From *Science 84*, November 1984, pp. 131-132, 138. Reprinted by permission of the American Association for the Advancement of Science and the author.

times faster than walking at four mph. Moving from car to airplane at 400 mph works a similar qualitative transformation. And so does adding a large number of computers where few or none existed before.

Some changes in the medical microcosm have occurred behind the scenes. Computers routinely analyze specimens that human lab assistants once painstakingly examined, and the tirelessness of the machines, coupled with their sophistication, makes them not only cheaper than the humans they replaced but more accurate and dependable. Physicians can receive these analyses and test results on a desk-top terminal, eliminating delays of human couriers.

If we quickly become blasé about routine applications of the computer, we are justifiably awed by the new. Noninvasive diagnostic techniques produce high-resolution images of the body's interior, whether organ or cell, in some cases at relatively small risk to the patient. The early 1970s, for example, marked the introduction of the computerized axial tomographic scanner, which makes images of "slices" of the body, particularly soft tissues.

In its decade of use, the CAT scanner has proven a valuable tool. Even more sophisticated probes have been invented. The most advanced nuclear magnetic resonance scanners can exhibit the sodium level in a single cell, an important sign of cellular health.

Soon every professional, whether doctor, engineer, or manager, will have a computer work station and every client will demand it be used. Even as computers have become more powerful, cheaper, and smaller, roughly doubling in power and halving in cost every two years, they have also become progressively easier to use. High-level programming languages, such as For-

tran and Lisp in the early 1960s, allowed users to enter more powerful commands in a format that more closely approximated ordinary English, the machine automatically translating those instructions into the more cryptic but faster language it used internally. The siblings and offspring of those first high-level languages are even faster and come closer to English, so that effective programming can be done with only modest expertise. The ultimate goal, of course, is natural language dialogue with computers. This, along with conveniences such as symbols and menus that appear on the screen, will make computers even easier to use. Miniaturization at ever lower cost will allow microprocessors to be embedded anywhere human wit perceives a need.

As a symbol-processing machine, the computer moves everywhere symbols matter—perhaps most portentously into intelligence. To attempt artificial intelligence it is necessary to discover what intelligence really is; the field of cognitive psychology has been changed utterly by this machine that is simultaneously laboratory instrument and model for experiment and discovery.

One important intellectual concept that has emerged is the notion of expert systems, based on the work of Edward Feigenbaum, Joshua Lederberg, Bruce Buchanan, and their colleagues. An expert system is a program that mimics the behavior of experts in a narrowly defined field, reasoning and inferring from data to arrive at plausible conclusions. Because of its ability to move so quickly through large masses of data, it sometimes does better than the human experts who taught it.

At the Stanford Medical Center, for example, an expert system called Oncocin helps physicians choose the right type and regimen of chemotherapy for

patients with certain forms of cancer. It offers therapeutic advice after reasoning through a large number of variables with a consistency from patient to patient that human physicians cannot match. Expert systems are also at work prospecting for minerals and designing computer systems. And the notion of the ultimate expert system—a program that can learn, as people do, from experience—is at the center of Japan's Fifth Generation Project, which has been underway for three years with the aim of turning out useful computers in the 1990s.

Theoretical computer science has also contributed to human knowledge. Information can be treated in ways that allow it to be quantified and manipulated mathematically; this can lead to unexpected insights into intelligent behavior. For example, Michael Rabin has proved that when the quality of randomness, or chance, is introduced into the decision-making processes of large groups, whether computers or people, there is increased order instead of chaos, a surprising and counter-intuitive result. Since the computer system of the future will likely take the form of many personal computers that normally function alone but can talk together when necessary to share stored data or exchange messages, a dose of deliberate randomness may help insure order, control, and integrity.

Computing is so lively and pregnant, predicting its future is nearly impossible. The level of certainty and precision in our lives will rise, as the medical example shows, but so will our expectations. The machine's power will introduce further complexity at the same time it helps us deal with complexity. For symbol systems, from language to mathematics, have always accelerated and amplified our intellectual grasp, and the computer is the symbol processor *par excellence*.

SCIENTISTS GO NORTH

Anthony de Souza

Anthony R. de Souza is professor of geography at the University of Wisconsin-Eau Claire and editor of the Journal of Geography (USA).

THE contrast between the rich, developed 'North' and the poorer developing 'South' is nowhere wider than in scientific research. The scientific divide is so enormous that it is tempting to argue that countries must have vigorous and productive scientific communities if they are to develop.

The development potential of a country may be measured by the size of its pool of publishing scientists. This measure is crude because it does not take into account country-by-country variations in the quality of work published, yet it is an easier base from which to make comparisons than one which is dependent on budget data, such as the proportion of GNP a country spends on science.

Data on the number of publishing scientists in 164 countries, produced by the Institute for Scientific Information in Philadelphia show a remarkable imbalance: 47 countries account for 99 per cent of scientific authorship. Within this, the USA alone accounts for 36 per cent and 10 countries produce 80 per cent.

Industrial market economies and East European non-market economies have nearly 95 per cent of all publishing scientists. India, which has a venerable history of technical and scientific education and which is one of the biggest contributors of scientists in the world, is home to nearly 50 per cent of all the publishing scientists of the South. China and a handful of newly industrializing and oil-exporting countries such as Singapore, Nigeria and Mexico, account for much of the remainder.

The information that is so vital to the conduct of scientific research is most abundant in major metropolitan areas and specialized science centres. And, although it can be communicated to scientists elsewhere by various methods, there are inherent advantages in personal exchanges. However, the geographical concentration of scientists may often operate against such exchanges since it varies considerably both within the 'North' and between the 'North' and 'South'.

In the USA, patterns of communication and cooperation among scientists are informal and no single city or region has a monopoly of talented scientists. New York is the leading US scientific city and has universities, medical centres, industrial laboratories, zoological and botanical parks, and museums. Yet it has only three per cent of the publishing scientists.

Outside the USA, scientific effort tends to be more concentrated geographically. Moscow, the world's largest scientific city, supports 38 per cent of the USSR's publishing scientists. Moscow, Leningrad, and Kiev together have 55 per cent of the country's scientific capacity.

The concentration of scientists in most West European countries and Japan falls somewhere between that of the USA and East Europe.

Largest scientific cities of the 'South' in 1984		
city	number of publishing scientists	percentage share of national scientific effort
Beijing	2334	38.0
Buenos Aires	2109	59.1
Bombay	1539	8.0
Santiago	1496	71.1
New Delhi	1292	6.7
Cairo	1266	60.0
Calcutta	1221	6.3
Mexico City	1211	70.2
Shanghai	1143	18.6
Sao Paulo	1079	23.2

Largest scientific cities in 1984		
Moscow	25,511	37.8
London	25,511	37.8
London	14,784	23.7
Tokyo	10,875	18.9
Paris	10,707	23.3
New York	8994	3.1
Boston	7300	2.5
Washington	6982	2.4
Philadelphia	6275	2.1
Los Angeles	6183	2.1
Leningrad	6120	9.1
Chicago	5777	2.0
Bethesda, Maryland	5443	1.9
Kiev	5431	8.1
Houston	5106	1.7
Toronto	4143	13.4

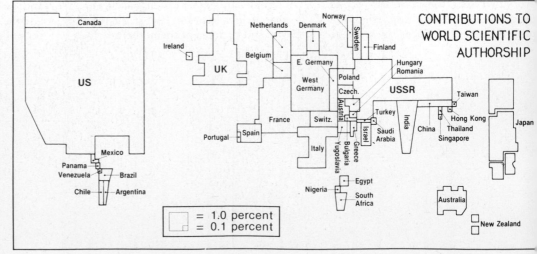

CONTRIBUTIONS TO WORLD SCIENTIFIC AUTHORSHIP

□ = 1.0 percent
□ = 0.1 percent

From *The Geographical Magazine*, London, England, April 1986, p. 170. Reprinted by permission.

London has 24 per cent of Britain's publishing scientists; Paris 23 per cent of France's; and Tokyo, 19 per cent of Japan's. London has more than five times the number of scientists of Britain's second- and third-ranked scientific cities — Cambridge and Oxford.

In the 'South', scientific research is concentrated in a few institutions in capital cities. For example, Mexico City boasts 70 per cent of Mexico's scientific community. India is among the few countries of the poor 'South' where scientific effort is dispersed among a number of regional centres. Only 21 per cent of India's publishing scientists live in Bombay, New Delhi and Calcutta.

Countries with a large pool of publishing scientists have a high technological potential. If countries are classified by technological levels, high technology countries with industries such as aeronautics and aerospace, telecommunications and telematics, nuclear energy, computers and bio-industry, account for 80 per cent of all scientific authorship. The USA, Canada, Japan, Sweden, Denmark, Italy, Switzerland, West Germany, Netherlands, Belgium, UK, Australia, USSR, and East Germany fall into this category. In only two of these, USSR and East Germany, is science highly regulated by government. The countries with a classic technology, that is all the remaining countries in the study except for Panama, Nigeria, and Saudi Arabia, account for 19 per cent of scientific authorship. The vast majority of the third group of technologically dependent countries do not appear in the statistics because they have too few publishing scientists.

Development is not primarily a scientific but a political and social process. Nonetheless, a commitment to basic scientific effort appears to be necessary for development to succeed. Unfortunately the opportunities for talented scientists from developing countries are mainly in the universities, research institutes, and industrial laboratories of the 'North'. This drain of intellectual resources from the 'South' helps to widen the North-South intellectual gap so that the 'South' looks likely to remain scientifically undermanned and technologically dependent in the foreseeable future.

The Cultural Ferment of the West

The circumstances which produced the new attitudes toward science and technology also inspired other intellectual accomplishments which became a part of the cultural baggage of the West. In religion, Martin Luther started the Protestant Reformation with his protests against the excesses of the Roman Catholic Church. He started a landslide of debate which not only contributed to theology, but also fed the skepticism of the time. If people could doubt the church fathers, they could challenge the status quo elsewhere as well.

The West produced more than its quota of prominent composers and artists. Michelangelo, Leonardo da Vinci, Titian, Rembrandt, Van Dyke, Hogarth, and later Delacroix, Goya, Monet, and Picasso are but a few of its artists. In music, the classical tradition began in the eighteenth century and continued into the twentieth. It included composers such as Mozart, Beethoven, Paganini, Schubert, Chopin, Tchaikovsky, Rimsky-Korsakov, Puccini, and Rachmaninoff. In his article about Bach, Edward Rothstein reveals that great musicians, like others, carry their share of the cares of the world.

Late in the eighteenth century, the young United States reconstructed its government to improve efficiency and to state with clarity the ideas of the patriots regarding the relationship of the government to the people. Federalism, control of the economy, property rights, representation, and division of powers were all discussed. The Constitution might well be considered America's most important intellectual export. Shortly afterwards, the French Revolution brought many of the same issues to the forefront on the European mainland. In France, however, the revolutionary ideals ended in a reign of terror and a dictatorship by Napoleon. Nonetheless, the seeds of liberty, equality, and fraternity were deeply planted and gave forth fruit in later times.

A compatible economic system—capitalism—was described by Adam Smith to explain the workings of the Industrial Revolution. Smith, the first of the economists, argued that laissez-faire and the invisible hand in the marketplace would work to supply the goods people demanded. His concept has been much modified by changing conditions—the regulations of government, social welfare, large multinational corporations—but it was not destroyed by downtrodden workers. John Kenneth Galbraith, an outstanding economist himself, describes this son of Scotland in the section's next article.

In yet another area, psychology, the West led the way. Sigmund Freud was one of the great intellects of the twentieth century. He discovered a whole new dimension of human existence when he opened the door to the recesses of the mind. According to Peter F. Drucker, however, Freud fooled himself about the realities of his own life; for instance, he believed that he was ignored and poor, which was not true.

In his practice Freud often treated women, and he once lamented, "What do women want?" Mary Wollstonecraft, the subject of the article by Shirley Tomkievicz, had an answer. She believed that women wanted recognition of the fact that the female mind was just as good as the male mind. Through much of history women had groaned under the weight of the patriarchal attitudes that confined them in space and action. During the American Revolution and the Constitutional period, women began to hope for greater freedoms. In the nineteenth century, they agitated for suffrage and property rights. In the twentieth century, the women of the West won equality before the law and the right to vote, but still the patriarchy prevailed in employment, politics, and public attitudes.

Women's rights fall under the heading of liberalism, a movement characterized by a concern for the freedom of the individual. Liberalism, socialism, capitalism, democracy, communism, Christianity, industrialism, and science were products of the Western mind. They were carried to the rest of the world as intellectual baggage when Western merchants, soldiers, and diplomats set forth from their homelands.

Looking Ahead: Challenge Questions

Why are the people featured in this section considered "great"?

Do great people make history, or does history produce great people?

Why did Luther's protest have an effect?

What is the significance of music in a culture? Does it merely reflect the nature of society, or does it have the power to shape it?

Why did the liberal revolutions occur in the West?

What is a feminist? Does Mary Wollstonecraft fit the definition?

LUTHER SCHLÄGT DIE 90 SÄTZE AN.

Luther: Giant of His Time and Ours

Half a millennium after his birth, the first Protestant is still a towering force

It was a back-room deal, little different from many others struck at the time, but it triggered an upheaval that altered irrevocably the history of the Western world. Albrecht of Brandenburg, a German nobleman who had previously acquired a dispensation from the Vatican to become a priest while underage and to head two dioceses at the same time, wanted yet another favor from the Pope: the powerful archbishop's chair in Mainz. Pope Leo X, a profligate spender who needed money to build St. Peter's Basilica, granted the appointment—for 24,000 gold pieces, roughly equal to the annual imperial revenues in Germany. It was worth it. Besides being a rich source of income, the Mainz post brought Albrecht a vote for the next Holy Roman Emperor, which could be sold to the highest bidder.

In return, Albrecht agreed to initiate the sale of indulgences in Mainz. Granted for good works, indulgences were papally controlled dispensations drawn from an eternal "treasury of merits" built up by Christ and the saints; the church taught that they would help pay the debt of "temporal punishment" due in purgatory for sins committed by either the penitent or any deceased person. The Pope received half the proceeds of the Mainz indulgence sale, while the other half

went to repay the bankers who had lent the new archbishop gold.

Enter Martin Luther, a 33-year-old priest and professor at Wittenberg University. Disgusted not only with

the traffic in indulgences but with its doctrinal underpinnings, he forcefully protested to Albrecht—never expecting that his action would provoke a sweeping uprising against a corrupt church.

RUDI FREY

A statue of the reformer stares defiantly across Eisenach, East Germany
To some Catholic scholars, he has even become a "father in the faith."

Luther's challenge culminated in the Protestant Reformation and the rending of Western Christendom, and made him a towering figure in European history. In this 500th anniversary year of his birth (Nov. 10, 1483), the rebel of Wittenberg remains the subject of persistent study. It is said that more books have been written about him than anyone else in history, save his own master, Jesus Christ. The renaissance in Luther scholarship surrounding this year's anniversary serves as a reminder that his impact on modern life is profound, even for those who know little about the doctrinal feuds that brought him unsought fame. From the distance of half a millennium, the man who, as Historian Hans Hillerbrand of Southern Methodist University in Dallas says, brought Christianity from lofty theological dogma to a clearer and more personal belief is still able to stimulate more heated debate than all but a handful of historical figures.

Indeed, as the reformer who fractured Christianity, Luther has latterly become a key to reuniting it. With the approval of the Vatican, and with Americans taking the lead, Roman Catholic theologians are working with Lutherans and other Protestants to sift through the 16th century disputes and see whether the Protestant-Catholic split can some day be overcome. In a remarkable turnabout, Catholic scholars today express growing appreciation of Luther as a "father in the faith" and are willing to play down his excesses. According to a growing consensus, the great division need never have happened at all.

Beyond his importance as a religious leader, Luther had a profound effect on Western culture. He is, paradoxically, the last medieval man and the first modern one, a political conservative and a spiritual revolutionary. His impact is most marked, of course, in Germany, where he laid the cultural foundations for what later became a united German nation.

When Luther attacked the indulgence business in 1517, he was not only the most popular teacher at Wittenberg but also vicar provincial in charge of eleven houses of the Hermits

BILDARCHIV JURGENS

The room where Luther translated the New Testament; title page of his Bible

CROSSROAD PUBLISHING

of St. Augustine. He was brilliant, tireless and a judicious administrator, though given to bouts of spiritual depression. To make his point on indulgences, Luther dashed off 95 theses condemning the system ("They preach human folly who pretend that as soon as money in the coffer rings, a soul from purgatory springs") and sent them to Archbishop Albrecht and a number of theologians.*

*Despite colorful legend, it is not certain he ever nailed them to the door of the Castle Church.

The response was harsh: the Pope eventually rejected Luther's protest and demanded capitulation. It was then that Luther began asking questions about other aspects of the church, including the papacy itself. In 1520 he charged in an open letter to the Pope, "The Roman Church, once the holiest of all, has become the most licentious den of thieves, the most shameless of brothels, the kingdom of sin, death and hell." Leo called Luther "the wild boar which has invaded the Lord's vineyard."

The following year Luther was summoned to recant his writings before the Diet of Worms, a council of princes convened by the young Holy Roman Emperor Charles V. In his closing defense, Luther proclaimed defiantly: "Unless I am convinced by testimony from Holy Scriptures and clear proofs based on reason—because, since it is notorious that they have erred and contradicted themselves, I cannot believe either the Pope or the council alone—I am bound by conscience and the Word of God. Therefore I can and will recant nothing, because to act against one's conscience is neither safe nor salutary. So help me God." (Experts today think that he did not actually speak the famous words, "Here I stand. I can do no other.")

This was hardly the cry of a skeptic, but it was ample grounds for the Emperor to put Luther under sentence of death as a heretic. Instead of being executed, Luther lived for another 25 years, became a major author and composer of hymns, father of a bustling household and a secular figure who opposed rebellion—in all, a commanding force in European affairs. In the years beyond, the abiding split in Western Christendom developed, including a large component of specifically "Lutheran" churches that today have 69 million adherents in 85 nations.

The enormous presence of the Wittenberg rebel, the sheer force of his personality, still broods over all Christendom, not just Lutheranism. Although Luther declared that the Roman Pontiffs were the "Antichrist," today's Pope, in an anniversary tip of the zucchetto, mildly speaks of Luther as "the reformer." Ecumenical-minded Catholic theologians have come to rank Luther in importance with Augustine and Aquinas. "No one who came after Luther could match him," says

Father Peter Manns, a Catholic theologian in Mainz. "On the question of truth, Luther is a lifesaver for Christians." While Western Protestants still express embarrassment over Luther's anti-Jewish rantings or his skepticism about political clergy, Communist East Germany has turned him into a secular saint because of his influence on German culture. Party Boss Erich Honecker, head of the regime's *Lutherjahr* committee, is willing to downplay Luther's antirevolutionary ideas, using the giant figure to bolster national pride.

Said West German President Karl Carstens, as he opened one of the hundreds of events commemorating Luther this year: "Luther has become a symbol of the unity of all Germany. We are all Luther's heirs."

After five centuries, scholars still have difficulty coming to terms with the contradictions of a tempestuous man. He was often inexcusably vicious in his writings (he wrote, for instance, that one princely foe was a "faint-hearted wretch and fearful sissy" who should "do nothing but stand like a eunuch, that is, a harem guard, in a fool's cap with a fly swatter"). Yet he was kindly in person and so generous to the needy that his wife despaired of balancing the household budget. When the plague struck Wittenberg and others fled, he stayed behind to minister to the dying. He was a powerful spiritual author, yet his words on other occasions were so scatological that no Lutheran periodical would print them today. His writing was hardly systematic, and his output runs to more than 100 volumes. On the average, Luther wrote a major tract or treatise every two weeks throughout his life.

The scope of Luther's work has made him the subject of endless reinterpretation. The Enlightenment treated him as the father of free thought, conveniently omitting his belief in a sovereign God who inspired an authoritative Bible. During the era of Otto von Bismarck a century ago, Luther was fashioned into a nationalistic symbol; 70 years later, Nazi propagandists claimed him as one of their own by citing his anti-Jewish polemics.

All scholars agree on Luther's importance for German culture, surpassing even that of Shakespeare on the English-speaking world. Luther's masterpiece was his translation of the New Testament from Greek into German, largely completed in ten weeks while he was in hiding after the Worms confrontation, and of the Old Testament, published in 1534 with the assistance of Hebrew experts. The Luther Bible sold massively in his lifetime and remains today the authorized German Protestant version. Before Luther's Bible was published, there was no standard German, just a profusion of dialects. "It was Luther," said Johann Gottfried von Herder, one of Goethe's mentors, "who has awakened and let loose the giant: the German language."

Only a generation ago, Catholics were trained to consider Luther the arch-heretic. Now no less than the Vatican's specialist on Lutheranism, Monsignor Aloys Klein, says that "Martin Luther's action was beneficial to the Catholic Church." Like many other Catholics, Klein thinks that if Luther were living today there would be no split. Klein's colleague in the Vatican's Secretariat for Promoting Christian Unity, Father Pierre Duprey, suggests that with the Second Vatican Council (1962–65) Luther "got the council he asked for, but 450 years too late." Vatican II accepted his contention that, in a sense, all believers are priests; while the council left the Roman church's hierarchy intact, it enhanced the role of the laity. More important, the council moved the Bible to the center of Catholic life, urged continual reform and instituted worship in local languages rather than Latin.

One of the key elements in the Reformation was the question of "justification," the role of faith in relation to good works in justifying a sinner in the eyes of God. Actually, Catholicism had never officially taught that salvation could be attained only through pious works, but the popular perception held otherwise. Luther recognized, as University of Chicago Historian Martin Marty explains, that everything "in the system of Catholic teaching seemed aimed toward appeasing God. Luther was led to the idea of God not as an angry judge but as a forgiving father. It is a position that gives the individual a great sense of freedom and security." In effect, says U.S. Historian Roland Bainton, Luther destroyed the implication that men could "bargain with God."

Father George Tavard, a French Catholic expert on Protestantism who teaches in Ohio and has this month published *Justification: an Ecumenical Study* (Paulist; $7.95), notes that "today many Catholic scholars think Luther was right and the 16th century Catholic polemicists did not understand what he meant. Both Lutherans and Catholics agree that good works by Christian believers are the result of their faith and the working of divine grace in them, not their personal contributions to their own salvation. Christ is the only Savior. One does not save oneself." An international Lutheran-Catholic commission, exploring the basis for possible reunion, made a joint statement along these lines in 1980. Last month a parallel panel in the U.S. issued a significant 21,000-word paper on justification that affirms much of Luther's thinking, though with some careful hedging from the Catholic theologians.

There is doubt, of course, about the degree to which Protestants and Catholics can, in the end, overcome their differences. Catholics may now be permitted to sing Luther's *A Mighty Fortress Is Our God* or worship in their native languages, but a wide gulf clearly remains on issues like the status of Protestant ministers and, most crucially, papal authority.

During the futile Protestant-Catholic reunion negotiations in 1530 at the Diet of Augsburg, the issue of priestly celibacy was as big an obstacle as the faith *vs.* good works controversy. Luther had married a nun, to the disgust of his Catholic contemporaries. From the start, the marriage of clergy was a sharply defined difference between Protestantism and Catholicism, and it remains a key barrier today. By discarding the concept of the moral superiority of celibacy, Luther established sexuality as a gift from God. In general, he was a lover of the simple

pleasures, and would have had little patience with the later Puritans. He spoke offhandedly about sex, enjoyed good-natured joshing, beer drinking and food ("If our Lord is permitted to create nice large pike and good Rhine wine, presumably I may be allowed to eat and drink"). For his time, he also had an elevated opinion of women. He cherished his wife and enjoyed fatherhood, siring six children and rearing eleven orphaned nieces and nephews as well.

But if Luther's views on the Catholic Church have come to be accepted even by many Catholics, his anti-Semitic views remain a problem for even his most devoted supporters. Says New York City Rabbi Marc Tanenbaum: "The anniversary will be marred by the haunting specter of Luther's devil theory of the Jews."

Luther assailed the Jews on doctrinal grounds, just as he excoriated "papists" and Turkish "infidels." But his work titled *On the Jews and Their Lies* (1543) went so far as to advocate that their synagogues, schools and homes should be destroyed and their prayer books and Talmudic volumes taken away. Jews were to be relieved of their savings and put to work as agricultural laborers or expelled outright.

Fortunately, the Protestant princes ignored such savage recommendations, and the Lutheran Church quickly forgot about them. But the words were there to be gleefully picked up by the Nazis, who removed them from the fold of religious polemics and used them to buttress their 20th century racism. For a good Lutheran, of course, the Bible is the sole authority, not Luther's writings, and the thoroughly Lutheran Scandinavia vigorously opposed Hitler's racist madness. In the anniversary year, all sectors of Lutheranism have apologized for their founder's views.

Whatever the impact of Luther's anti-Jewish tracts, there is no doubt that his political philosophy, which tended to make church people submit to state authority, was crucial in weakening opposition by German Lutherans to the Nazis. Probably no aspect of Luther's teaching is the

subject of more agonizing Protestant scrutiny in West Germany today.

Luther sought to declericalize society and to free people from economic burdens imposed by the church. But he was soon forced, if reluctantly, to deliver considerable control of the new Protestant church into the hands of secular rulers who alone could ensure the survival of the Reformation. Luther spoke of "two kingdoms," the spiritual and the secular, and his writings provided strong theological support for authoritarian government and Christian docility.

The Lutheran wing of the Reformation was democratic, but only in terms of the church itself, teaching that a plowman did God's work as much as a priest, encouraging lay leadership and seeking to educate one and all. But it was Calvin, not Luther, who created a theology for the democratic state. A related aspect of Luther's politics, controversial then and now, was his opposition to the bloody Peasants' War of 1525. The insurgents thought they were applying Luther's ideas, but he urged rulers to crush the revolt: "Let whoever can, stab, strike, kill." Support of the rulers was vital for the Reformation, but Luther loathed violent rebellion and anarchy in any case.

Today Luther's law-and-order approach is at odds with the revolutionary romanticism and liberation theology that are popular in some theology schools. In contrast with modern European Protestantism's social gospel, Munich Historian Thomas Nipperdey says, Luther "would not accept modern attempts to build a utopia and would argue, on the contrary, that we as mortal sinners are incapable of developing a paradise on earth."

Meanwhile, the internal state of the Lutheran Church raises other questions about the lasting power of Luther's vision. Lutheranism in the U.S., with 8.5 million adherents, is stable and healthy. The church is also growing in Third World strongholds like racially torn Namibia, where black Lutherans predominate. But in Lutheranism's historic heartland, the two Germanys and Scandinavia, there are deep problems. In East Germany, Lutherans are under pressure from the Communist regime. In West Germany, the Evangelical Church in Germany (E.K.D.), a church federation that includes some non-Lutherans, is wealthy (annual income: $3 billion), but membership is shrinking and attendance at Sunday services is feeble indeed. Only 6% of West Germans— or, for that matter, Scandinavians— worship regularly.

What seems to be lacking in the old European churches is the passion for God and his truth that so characterizes Luther. He retains the potential to shake people out of religious complacency. Given Christianity's need, on all sides, for a good jolt, eminent

Historian Heiko Oberman muses, "I wonder if the time of Luther isn't ahead of us."

The boldest assertion about Luther for modern believers is made by Protestants who claim that the reformer did nothing less than enable Christianity to survive. In the Middle Ages, too many Popes and bishops were little more than corrupt, luxury-loving politicians, neglecting the teaching of the love of God and using the fear of God to enhance their power and wealth. George Lindbeck, the Lutheran co-chairman of the international Lutheran-Catholic commission, believes that without Luther "religion would

have been much less important during the next 400 to 500 years. And since medieval religion was falling apart, secularization would have marched on, unimpeded."

A provocative thesis, and a debatable one. But with secularization still marching on, almost unimpeded, Protestants and Catholics have much to reflect upon as they scan the five centuries after Luther and the shared future of their still divided churches.

—By Richard N. Ostling.
Reported by Roland Flamini and
Wanda Menke-Glückert/Bonn,
with other bureaus.

The pipe-smoking man and his heavenly music.

THE BODY OF BACH

EDWARD ROTHSTEIN

THERE would seem to be very little mysterious about Bach. He has reached his 300th birthday with a reputation unmatched in the musical pantheon. He is neither neglected nor overrated; no revisions of the repertory are taking place; no discoveries are changing our understanding of his achievement. There is, simply, the music itself, extravagant in its range and invention: the *Goldberg Variations*, the *St. Matthew Passion*, the *B minor Mass*, the cantatas, the *Well-tempered Clavier*, the cello suites, the violin sonatas, assorted toccatas and suites and fugues and partitas.

The man behind the music also would seem to offer few secrets—no hints of syphilis as with his Romantic successors, no passionate letters like Beethoven's to his "Immortal Beloved," no arcane musical programs with autobiographical clues buried in scores as with Berlioz or Elgar or Berg. Bach simply looked at himself as a craftsman. "I was obliged to work hard," he said; "whoever is equally industrious will succeed just as well." We know him through that industry—a cantata written every week for two years, a set of collected works that took more than 50 years to edit. He was part of a dynasty of musicians who were so influential that in Eisenach the family name became generic; town musicians were called "die Baache." And Johann Sebastian embodied in his career the variety of that dynasty's social roles. He was a virtuoso organist, a court composer, a church composer, a teacher, a producer of secular concerts. The facts about his life are known through those roles,

in public documents, city records, petitions, announcements, resignations. The private man is seemingly irrelevant: he worked hard, married twice, and in domestic harmony fathered 20 children.

But there is something missing in this apparently clear portrait. We are used to enshrining composers as gods in a temple of art, divorcing earthly facts from our understanding of the music. But in no other composer is the disparity between the man and his work so immense. Bach's life is considered stupefyingly ordinary, but his music is divine, dealing in essence rather than in accident, in being rather than in appearance. Indeed, who can listen to the *D sharp minor Fugue* in Book I of the *Well-tempered Clavier* and not feel, in the ways in which a single theme is contemplated, combined with itself, inverted, expanded, contracted, and dissected, that this work has transcendent concerns? Even the turns of the melodic theme, which hint at something vulnerable, even melancholy, ultimately become aspects of architecture rather than of sentiment. Albert Schweitzer, who wrote one of the more profound studies of the composer, put it this way: "The artistic personality exists independently of the human, the latter remaining in the background as if it were something almost accidental. Bach's works would have been the same even if his existence had run quite another course." As a man, he remains mundane; his music, meanwhile, dwells in the eternal.

It is remarkable how consistent this view of Bach has been. Even during

the years of Bach's supposed eclipse just after his death, when his works were not performed and were compared unfavorably with Handel's, he still had a profound impact on music's greatest practitioners—on Mozart, Haydn, Beethoven, and even Chopin. Bach's son, Carl Philipp Emanuel, made money by renting unpublished scores of his father's works; his wife continued the tradition, and so did Bach's granddaughter.

And, soon enough, devotion to Bach as transcendent artist entered the heart of German musical and intellectual life. On hearing the *Well-tempered Clavier* for the first time on June 21, 1827, Goethe felt, he wrote, "as if the eternal harmony were communing with itself, as might have happened in God's bosom shortly before the creation of the world. It was thus that my inner depths were stirred, and I seemed neither to possess nor to need ears, still less eyes, or any other sense." Wagner presented Bach as a musical savior of the German people itself:

> If we would comprehend the wonderful originality, strength, and significance of the German mind in one incomparably eloquent image, we must look keenly and discerningly at the appearance, otherwise almost inexplicably mysterious, of the musical marvel Sebastian Bach. . . . Look at this head, hidden in its absurd French full-bottomed wig, look at this master, a miserable cantor and organist in little Thuringian towns whose names we hardly know now, wearing himself out in poor situations, always so little considered that it needed a whole century after his death to rescue his works from oblivion; even in his music taking up with an art-form

which externally was the complete likeness of his epoch, dry, stiff, pedantic, like perruques and pigtails in notes; and see now the world the incomprehensibly great Sebastian built up out of these elements!

The amazement and worship endure even in the most scholarly musicological circles of this century. Bach has always been at the center of the "authenticity" movement, which attempts to reconstruct the instruments, ensembles, and performance practice of Bach's time. Arguments over "authentic performance" can resemble disputations over holy texts; they have split the musical community along more than scholarly lines. "You play Bach your way," the harpsichordist Wanda Landowska commented to a colleague, "I will play him his way."

Behind these invocations of the sacred there was, however, a man whose life and character must have been bound up in his music. Even the physical traces of Bach are suggestive. His skeleton was found in 1894 in an oak coffin, with its skull bearing—in Schweitzer's words—a "prominent lower jaw, high forehead, deep-set eyesockets, and marked nasal angle." He continues: "Among the interesting peculiarities of Bach's skull may be mentioned the extraordinary toughness of the bone of the temple that encloses the inner organ of hearing, and the quite remarkable largeness of the fenestra rotunda." The skull bears some resemblance to the only two portraits of Bach that have been authenticated. Both were probably painted by Elias Gottlieb Haussmann, the later (1748) a copy of the earlier (1746). A few years before his death the composer is shown holding, angled against his stomach, the score of a puzzle canon: the canon challenges the player to figure out how and when and where a version of the theme is to be played against itself. Bach's right hand is fleshy, feminine, delicately proffering the sheet of paper, while the rest of his body takes no cognizance of his presented art. He stares directly out at the viewer, bewigged in perruques and pigtails, his face as well fed as his belly, the mouth in a pose of slight tension, neither a smile nor a sneer, possessing some degree of self-satisfaction. His left eyebrow is raised, as if in inquiry, his right brow slightly lowered. It is not quite what we expect of the composer either of the canon or the great *Passions*. The body is so solidly there,

the eyes so surely presenting a claim, their glance so skeptical—and so ambiguous—that the gentility of the musical offering seems posed, unconvincing, artificial.

WAS THAT the pose in which he made his true "Musical Offering" to King Frederick II, based on a theme that the king composed? With a slight irony, and more than a slight ego? When Bach visited Potsdam, the king had presented him with a theme on which to improvise. Most immodestly, Bach improvised extravagantly, and just two months later had engraved two fugues, ten canons, and a trio sonata based upon the king's theme. This is surely the gesture of a man at once making an effusive offering while raising his eyebrow in pride over his invention and his powers. As in the portrait, this is not a man out of touch with his surroundings. Bach is very much in control, choosing to write his puzzle canons, knowing full well how they will be received, and how anomalous such taut structures are in a world beginning to love sentimental novels.

THERE IS also something in the composer's thick neck and corpulent chest covered in white silk and a gold-buttoned coat that suggests a physical body that can be sensed even in Bach's most abstract music—in its dance rhythms, surprising accents, and swirl of figuration. Bach was, in fact, hot-tempered and stubborn. He was censured for getting into a sword fight after calling one of his players a "nanny-goat bassoonist." His taste for wine is evident in the substantial sums that appear on many of his accounts. But in Haussmann's portrait there is also that feminine hand, so split apart in manner from the physically commanding pose of the man. Indeed, in dealing with those in authority, those who controlled the means of patronage, Bach presented that most fleshy delicate hand, the pinky lightly floating in deference. Bach *served* all his life. Servile epistolary salutations were, for example, conventions of the time, but Bach never missed an opportunity to exploit the style when approaching patrons. There is this remarkable opening to an argumentative missive:

> Their Magnificences, the Most Noble, Most Reverend, Most Distinguished, Respected and Most Learned Members of the Most Worshipful Royal and Electoral

Saxon Consistory at Leipzig, My Most Honored Masters and High and Mighty Patron. YOUR MAGNIFICENCES, MOST NOBLE, MOST REVEREND, MOST DISTINGUISHED, RESPECTED AND MOST LEARNED, MOST HIGHLY ESTEEMED MASTERS AND HIGH PATRONI!

But after that very salutation comes the stern and skeptical glance, a demand, an appeal, a complaint—a man discontent with his place and his role.

The letter following that fawning address was, in fact, to Bach's masters at Leipzig, the city where Bach spent most of his mature musical life, from 1723 to 1750. There he produced his great sacred works, including five complete cycles of cantatas, the *Mass* and *Passions*, and the great fugues and canons of his late years. It was the place, in other words, where the transcendental Bach took shape, after he had written most of his organ and keyboard masterpieces. As Kantor of the Thomaskirche and Director Musices, he was the most important musician in Leipzig, responsible for the music in the four principal churches, and for the town's musical life. These were the years of musical grandeur, in which Bach, one would assume, had the religious and public support of Leipzig behind him.

STILL, as any number of his letters to the Leipzig Council indicate, the situation was in fact far different. Before going to Leipzig, Bach was remarkably content at Köthen, where he was a court composer to a prince who loved music. Then the prince married a rather unmusical woman. Sensing the change in his status, Bach made inquiries in other towns. Kuhnau, who held the position at Leipzig, had died. Telemann, then the most renowned musician in Germany, was first offered the position; next in line was Christoph Graupner, who was something of an alumnus. Only when they both declined was Bach considered. To the councillors Bach was a mediocrity and, conversely, the position was a compromise for Bach. From his place at the center of court life with a sensitive prince, he moved to Leipzig, where he had to answer to several dozen civic and church superiors, who included the 15 members of the city council who hired him, the ecclesiastical authority of the consistory, which supervised the church services, and the rector of the school itself, within which Bach had to teach Latin along with music. Bach was paid less than a quarter of what he had received at Köthen, living expenses were higher, and he was dependent upon "freelance" playing at funerals and weddings. (Bach later complained that a "healthy wind was blowing" one year in Leipzig so he made almost nothing from funerals.)

Bach's new position also demanded rising at four or five in the morning to maintain discipline in the school until the students retired at eight in the evening. He was expected to write and prepare music for all the church services; he composed a cantata every week for the first two years. Moreover, as soon as he arrived in Leipzig, Bach was embroiled in a dispute over whether he would have charge of the music at St. Paul's, the university church. Bach needed the income and pressed his case. In 1725 he went over his superiors' heads and wrote three petitions to the Elector of Saxony, pleading a tightly argued case. This did not make for good relations with the council; Bach lost his appeal, and the composer found commissions passing him by, leading to other conflicts. In 1729, just after his first performance of the *St. Matthew Passion*, the council ignored both Bach's selections of new pupils and his musical priorities. At a council meeting, according to the minutes, Bach was called "incorrigible." The council decided "he must be reproached and admonished."

Eschewing his usual salutation, Bach sent a memo to the council, biting in its graciousness and title: "Short but most necessary draft for a well-appointed church music; with certain modest reflections on the decline of the same." The climactic conflict, lasting more than two years, came in 1734, when Johann August Ernesti was appointed rector of the school. One historical account, dating from 1776, describes how the men became bitter enemies: "Bach began to hate those students who devoted themselves completely to the *humaniora* and treated music as a secondary matter, and Ernesti became a foe of music. When he came upon a student practicing on an instrument he would exclaim, 'What? You want to be a beer-fiddler too?'" Finding deaf ears at the council with more than four lengthy complaints and responses, Bach again appealed over their heads, "To His Most

Serene Highness, the Mighty Prince and Lord, Frederick Augustus, King in Poland," etc., etc.

These confrontations, which occurred earlier in Bach's career as well, show a keen sense of political hierarchy in Bach's language, along with a peremptory dismissal of political manners in his actions. When it came to musical matters, there was no compromise. Yet Bach came to Leipzig at a moment when music was becoming less and less important in schools and the community, ironically, because of the dawn of the Enlightenment, which Ernesti represented. Bach's role was peculiar; he was even dependent at the end of his life on contributions from the community, because he essentially had no social position. When he died, one member of the council cautioned against replacing him with anyone resembling a "Kapellmeister." His successor gave his first performance in a concert hall, not a church.

Christoph Wolff, the distinguished Bach scholar, points out that Bach understood these matters quite well. In the cantata of homage to the municipal council (BWV 216a), Mercury, the god of commerce, declares his gift to the council: "My trade, which here / I firmly plant, / shall provide you with / the greatest part of your lustre." That trade, and the world of the bourgeoisie that developed in its wake, did indeed leave the Kantor and Director Musices looking somewhat quaint. Haussmann's portrait captures the paradox, in Bach's face and body and hand, the gracious offer of music, and the ironic awareness that the music was posing more than a trivial puzzle to its listeners.

The biggest puzzle is that this most contentious man working at this peculiar historical moment produced such works as the *St. Matthew Passion* and the *B minor Mass*—music that seems to speak without ambiguities about faith and belief, in a tone of voice and with a technical assurance that make the music seem not just pre-modern, but otherworldly. There would seem to be scarcely a hint of Bach treating the religious realm as he did the political, of offering praise out of duty rather than belief, or of demonstrating the raised eyebrow and ambiguous lips of the Haussmann portrait. There is a certainty in Bach's harmonies. However much they meander into painful realms, the foundation is never left behind.

Moreover, the texts themselves are never subordinate to technical aspects of the music. In fact, they determine the music's central figurations. In the common practice of the period, the music *paints* the texts being set, illustrating them, commenting upon them, knowing its own laws are subordinate to the word. This means that words like "descent" are illustrated with descending melodic lines. Relations between meaning and musical sign can become still more intricate. Sometimes the music intentionally bears mystical or numerological meanings—a bass line, for example, repeated 13 times, underscoring the tragedy of the "Crucifixus" in the *Mass*. And always in the vocal music, there are the chorales—the heart of Lutheran music—which Bach harmonizes and re-harmonizes, treating them with as much care as if they too were sacred texts. Scores also bear dedicatory abbreviations, wholly sincere, like "S.D.G." ("Soli Deo Gloria," To god alone be praise) or "J.J." ("Jesu juva," Help me, Jesus). Bach writes that even so rudimentary an element of music as the figured bass—the fundamental bass line to be filled in by the player—merits attention. In instructing his pupils, he wrote: "Like all music, the figured bass should have no other end and aim than the glory of God and the recreation of the soul; where this is not kept in mind there is no true music, but only an infernal clamor and ranting."

WHAT THEN of the clamor and ranting that comes of Bach's own life? And what are its echoes in the music itself? Theodor Adorno noted that if we treat Bach simply as an archaic man of faith, we have missed the most important aspect of his music: it is a product of its time, anticipating the Enlightenment even as it seems to nestle itself in formal rigors.

Even the work that would seem furthest from the Enlightenment—the *B minor Mass*—acknowledges the new age by attempting to swerve away from it. The *Mass* was written over a period of 20 years; its Credo is now believed to be one of Bach's final works. It is deliberately archaic, orthodox, exaggerating aspects of formality and faith. Bach divided the Credo text into nine sections, grouped into a trinity of three parts each. There is also a formal symmetry around the center group of three, with the Crucifixus lying at its heart. That tripartite center is framed by two arias: "Et in unum Deum" (I believe in one Lord Jesus Christ) and "Et in Spiritum sanctum" (And I believe in the Holy Ghost). Each chorus is suffused with numerical symbolism and pictorial references, so that in "Et incarnatus," for example, the pulsing three tones of the bass line shift upon the words "and was made man"; the breathing sighs of the violins descend, and become incarnated, musically, in that low-pitched earthly realm, like the described movement of the Holy Ghost. Such a musical symbol is not subliminal. It can, in performance, elicit a gasp, as if the music itself had incarnated a spiritual idea and was presenting it, not for appreciation, but as the simple truth.

This gives the Credo an orthodoxy and a seriousness far more extreme than the most impassioned cantatas. But even in this case, the effect of the music is far different from a simple assertion of faith. As the arias and the instrumental solos make clear, there is an *interior* world being presented as well. The communal fugues and proclamations of the choruses are contrasted with the meditative arias of personal belief that frame the central section of the Credo. "Et in unum Deum" is a duet in which the proclamation of belief in one god becomes a sensuous intertwining of imitative voices; similarly, the oboe duet in "Et in Spiritum" is lyrically intimate. The choruses of the central section—the Incarnation, Crucifixion, and Resurrection—also convey a sense of human drama, sounding hushed and eerie at first and finally blazing forth with communal force.

All is so tightly controlled here that the tensions between individual and community, will and authority, sentiment and law, feeling and faith—all the tensions so evident elsewhere in Bach's music—are muted. The cantatas, though, celebrate those tensions, placing them at the core of Bach's religious music. The erotic arias between the soprano soul and bass Christ in *Cantata No. 140*, the variations on the single chorale theme in *Cantata No. 4*, the sharp contrasts between choral fugues and mellifluous arias in nearly all of the cantatas, show Bach moving constantly between the public demands of faith

and its interior trials. In these works, as in the *Passions*, the style becomes almost operatic, dramatic, very different from earlier sacred works. The subject in much of Bach's sacred music is man—man in the particular—represented religiously in the figure of Christ. This shares certain elements with Pietism—the movement that attacked Lutheran orthodoxy, stressing personal and mystical devotion. There are anticipations of similar attitudes in other Baroque composers such as Heinrich Schütz, now celebrating his quadricentennial. But this religious emphasis on the individual links Bach more to the world that came after him than to the world that came before.

THIS IS TRUE even in the most serious secular works. The *Goldberg Variations*, as Glenn Gould pointed out, does not guide the listener through a structure or a narrative that develops in a certain direction. Instead, said Gould, it seems, despite its intricate architecture, to be "a community of sentiment" possessing "a fundamental coordinating intelligence which we [label] ego." It is the path of an individual will at play in the realm of musical structure. Bach is so sure of musical law that it grants him freedom. The canons at each interval are as ecstatic in spirit as the regularly appearing dance movements. And the *Variations'* piety is limited: the return of the magisterial theme at the end is preceded by a "quodlibet"—a playful interweaving of popular songs of the period, *"Ich bin so lang nicht bei dir g'west"* (Long have I been away from you) and *"Kraut und Rüben haben mich vertrieben"* (Cabbage and turnips have put me to flight). It has even been suggested that these songs refer to the theme itself. First heard at the beginning of the work, it returns an hour later; its foundations—its bass line and harmonies—have been transmuted and transformed, put in flight with sophisticated techniques that Bach may have modestly considered as commonplace as cabbages and turnips.

BACH'S musical style, in fact, may almost be defined as the play of an ego in a highly structured world. Such, for example, is the texture of the fugue, which seems to govern every note Bach penned. His fugues construct musical orders in which each individual voice is playfully free—maintaining its identity but capable of the most fantastical diversions—while having its position verified and reinforced by other voices. The

fugue establishes a community of like minds and distinct parts, very different from the polyphony of the Renaissance, where the focus is less on individual voices than on the overall texture. It also contrasts with earlier Baroque fugues, where propriety and sobriety govern the behavior of the voices. Bach's achievement is to make each voice seem completely independent, while showing again and again their links, and even identities, with other free voices. Bach turned the Baroque fugue into a sign of the Enlightenment.

The fugue as used by Bach presents an order known not through faith, but through persistent examination and exploration. His themes are not mere organizations of musical material; instead they venture forth into the fugue fully formed, with shape and character and tensions all their own. Bach, it was said, could glance at a theme and, as if judging its character, tell immediately how it should be treated in a fugue— whether there should be stretti (multiple entrances overlapped in a short time), inversion (the theme played upside down), retrogression (the theme played backward), and so on.

The theme's character is defined as a character by no other composer before Bach. The fugue thus becomes reflective as well as rational. A single voice explores and creates its own musical universe. The fugue as a style can be seen as a prelude, historically, to its own extinction in a style of "feeling," where one voice finds itself thoroughly alone, without such mirrorings and reflections and architectural structures; it wanders through sentiment and fantasy. The fugue and the canon began to seem archaic in the rococo world of Bach's sons. The canon could even seem, as C. P. E. Bach told Charles Burney, a "certain proof to him of a total want of genius." But C. P. E. Bach's successors in the Romantic era understood quite clearly the powers of canon and fugue. The most autobiographical music of the 19th century invokes the fugue in attempts to turn personal feeling into something more metaphysical, as in Beethoven's last piano sonatas or the finale to Liszt's piano sonata.

There is indeed something metaphysical about Bach's concern with the fugue: the belief that the world and the self are images of each other, that the word and music and the world are linked in their structure and their substance. Hence the nearly mystical concern with musical signs and symbols, from the most mundane illustration of joy with dotted rhythms to the use of themes with notes corresponding to the letters of Bach's name.

There is no way in this metaphysical vision to separate the world of daily life from a transcendent spiritual realm. So Bach did not think it at all peculiar to include in a book of music composed and collected for his wife, Anna Magdalena, a poem (attributed to him) about a most mundane pleasure. It is entitled "Edifying Thoughts of a Tobacco Smoker":

Whene'er I take my pipe and stuff it
And smoke to pass the time away,
My thoughts, as I sit there and puff it,
Dwell on a picture sad and gray;
It teaches me that very like
Am I myself unto my pipe.

Like the pipe, he is made of but earth and clay; like the pipe, which glows leaving ash, so will his fame pass and his body turn to dust.

Thus o'er my pipe, in contemplation
Of such things, I can constantly
Indulge in fruitful meditation,
And so, puffing contentedly,
On land, on sea, at home, abroad,
I smoke my pipe and worship God.

Similar speculation suffuses Bach's musical universe. In his compositions, with their word-painting and affects and symbolism, metaphoric and metaphysical links are made between the most mundane and the most spiritual. The world is full of echoes and allusions. Nothing is arbitrary. Into this world comes the ego, the musical subject, Bach himself, whose work is craft rather than art because he does not create a world, he attempts to mirror it. In doing so, of course, he also catches part of himself. His presence slightly disrupts that metaphysical mirror because he begins to sense in his own peculiar position something awry—earthly hierarchies and authorities not quite matching the heavenly. So there is a double perspective: Bach serves, but he also serves himself. "J.J." (Help me, Jesus), he writes, but he also inscribes his own name musically in his final work. He is the voice in the fugues, the solitary individual ironically sensing his own freedom while remaining linked to a larger order. We can see him in the Haussmann portrait questioning, daring, stern and patient, and we can imagine him relishing his glass of port as well as his own skills, smoking his pipe and worshiping God.

BACH ON RECORD

Most Bach playing may still be execrable: consider the "spinning wheel" textures of the most publicly acclaimed modern virtuosos (Jean-Pierre Rampal, Alexis Weissenberg, Pinchas Zukerman, virtually any conductor with any symphony orchestra). But Bach has become the most well-performed composer on record. Herewith, a prejudiced selection on the occasion of Bach's tricentenary:

In the last six months, Archiv has released a generous selection of its Bach recordings dating as far back as the 1950s, on budget-priced disks that lack only English liner notes. The selections range from the large-scale, subtly detailed cantata performances of Karl Richter and the classic organ playing of the great blind virtuoso Helmut Walcha to Nathan Milstein's noble version of the violin sonatas and partitas, and lyrical, idiosyncratic chamber performances by the Musica Antiqua Köln. Most are lush, modern performances; nearly all are elegantly musical, some profoundly so.

Teldec has similarly repackaged for budget collecting its important recordings of the authentic performances of Nikolaus Harnoncourt. These include an introspective B minor Mass, plangent Easter cantatas, the Brandenburg concertos, the St. John Passion. Harnoncourt is at once orthodox and impassioned.

Pro Arte records is releasing here the "Leipzig Bach Edition" of recordings from East Germany. Some are distressingly unfocused (Max Pommer leading Cantatas 56 and 82—M CP27062). Others are unusually rewarding, including "Music in the Bach Household" (M CP27065), and a recording of Hannes Kästner playing a recently built organ in Bach's own Thomaskirche (M CP27069). East Germany's musicians are traditional in style—living near the source and rarely traveling beyond it.

The Cantatas: Nikolaus Harnoncourt and Gustav Leonhardt have been involved in a nearly 20-year project, recording the complete 200-some cantatas in authentic performances, packaged with complete scores. Now well past the halfway

mark, the recordings have helped redefine Bach performance style, bringing introspection and sentiment into the authenticity movement.

The Goldberg Variations: Glenn Gould (CBS M3X-38610). Here, in a boxed set, are two important performances, Gould's 1955 debut recording along with his 1982 rethinking of the work. These should stand alongside Wanda Landowska's grandly scaled performance (RCA AGM1-5251), and all of Gould's other Bach recordings.

The Well-tempered Clavier: Edwin Fischer (Vol I: EMI GR-70028-29—imported from Japan). This important piano performance from the 1930s is full of character and inauthentic nuance—a complement to Gould's pianistic Bach.

Ralph Kirkpatrick (five disks, available only through Quarry Communications, P.O. Box 3168, Stony Creek, Connecticut 06405). This re-release of the Deutsche Grammophon harpsichord version is transparent, restrained, and illuminating. The performance by Kirkpatrick's teacher, Wanda Landowska, is no longer available (originally RCA).

The Brandenburg concertos: Christopher Hogwood and the Academy of Ancient Music (L'Oiseau-Lyre 414 187-1) and Ton Koopman and the Amsterdam Baroque Orchestra (Erato 751342) present two newly recorded authentic performances; parts of each would form a single collection giving brio and tension to these worn divertimenti.

The Violin sonatas and partitas: Sigiswald Kuijken (Harmonia Mundi 1C 3LP 157). This first successful authentic Baroque interpretation should be heard alongside Milstein's modern renderings.

Other recordings of note include: Karl Münchinger's lush, pre-authentic string version of the "Musical Offering" (London STS-15063); the Anna Magdalena Notebooks with Igor Kipnis and Judith Blegen (Nonesuch DB-79020), showing Bach as pedagogue; and recordings by harpsichordist, organist, and conductor Trevor Pinnock, whose freewheeling energy and rigorous authentic style exemplify the qualities that mark a renaissance in Bach performance.

E.R.

'The Great Compromise'
DRAFTING THE AMERICAN CONSTITUTION, 1787

Jack N. Rakove

'The miracle at Philadelphia' 200 years ago was an amalgam of high principles and backroom wheeler-dealing to provide safeguards for the smaller states.

IN 1878, WHEN THE UNITED States Constitution was less than a century old, an inspired William Gladstone described it as 'the most wonderful work ever struck off at a given time by the hand and purpose of man'. Grateful Americans who still relish the approval of their former mother-countrymen have been quoting him ever since. But the appeal of Gladstone's aphorism rests on a deeper foundation – on the conviction that 'the miracle at Philadelphia' was just that. This image of the Federal Convention of 1787 is as venerable as the Constitution itself. 'The real wonder', James Madison observed:

> Is that so many difficulties should have been surmounted, and surmounted with a unanimity almost as unprecedented as it must have been unexpected. It is impossible for any man of candor to reflect on this circumstance without partaking of the astonishment. It is impossible for the man of pious reflection not to perceive in it a finger of that Almighty hand which has been so frequently and signally extended to our relief in the critical stages of the revolution.

Whether one locates this miracle in the character of the delegates who gathered at Philadelphia in late May 1787, or in the compromises they struck before the Convention adjourned on September 17th, or in the simple durability of the Constitution, ultimately matters little.

Historians, of course, have little use for miracles. Against the popular tendency to romanticise both the Founders and the Founding, several generations of scholars have struggled to explain the adoption of the Constitution in more hard-headed terms. Charles Beard (1874-1948) and his disciples portrayed the framers as the spokesmen for an élite intent on protecting the rights of property against the levelling jealousy of 'the lower orders'. Other writers have stressed the pragmatic character of the deliberations, casting the delegates as skilled politicians who knew how to cut deals and seal bargains with a network of compromises that gave every state and region of the new republic a stake in adopting the Constitution.

Certainly no account of the Convention can ignore the intensity of its politics, for concessions were made to almost every interest that had a voice at Philadelphia. Small states received their equal vote in the Senate; the three-fifths clause allowed the South to count its slaves for purposes of representation, and South Carolina and Georgia received a grace period of twenty years to continue importing slaves; northern commercial interests were pleased that laws regulating trade could be enacted by simple majorities; and future migrants to the west were promised fair and equal representation in Congress.

Yet when all is said and done, the great challenge is to balance this image of the Convention with equally persuasive evidence that a concern with principle and theory played a powerful role in the debates of 1787. For what gives the Convention its deeper appeal is the delegates' self-consciousness about their greater task and indeed, their place in history. As Madison once noted when the Convention was poised near deadlock, the decisions the delegates reached would 'decide for ever the fate of republican government'. The belief that this in fact is what the Convention did decide remains a vital part of American political culture today – naive, romantic, and celebratory as that conviction and culture so often seem. But the origins of this image are virtually contemporaneous with the event it exalts.

One reason why the Convention so quickly acquired this character is that many contemporaries – and indeed many of the delegates themselves – were rightly pessimistic about its prospects for success. As late as April, Madison still wondered whether his chief political asset – George Washington – should 'postpone his actual attendance, until some judgment can be formed of the result of the meeting'. The great hero's immense prestige would be squandered, Madi-

First published in *History Today*, September 1987, pp. 19-25. Reproduced by kind permission of History Today, Ltd., 83-84 Berwick Street, London W1V 3PJ, England.

Actors in the drama; James Madison, moving spirit behind the Philadelphia Convention and later Fourth President of the United States, 1809-17.

James Wilson, the Scots-born member of the Pennsylvania delegation who backed proportional representation on the basis of population for both houses of Congress.

Alexander Hamilton, 'the arch-Federalist' enfant terrible from New York, who was to become the first Secretary of the US Treasury and a leading advocate of strengthening central government.

son feared, if he were to 'participate in any abortive undertaking' like the Annapolis Convention which had drawn only twelve commissioners from five states the previous September.

The Annapolis meeting had been called only after a series of efforts to amend the existing Articles of Confederation had failed to secure the required approval of all thirteen states. Rather than adjourn empty-handed, desperation had led the Annapolis commissioners (who included Madison and Alexander Hamilton) to issue a call for a general convention to assemble in Philadelphia the following May. By itself, desperation offered few grounds for optimism, but it had its uses nonetheless. The failure of all earlier attempts to amend the Articles liberated the Convention of 1787 to think about the problems of the American Republic afresh, with a sophistication that ran far beyond the familiar spectrum of public discourse.

Much of the credit for this goes to James Madison, the shy and bookish but politically astute Virginian who is now regarded as 'the father of the Constitution'. The eldest son of a wealthy planter family in Orange County, Virginia, Madison (born 1751) had been educated at the College of New Jersey (now Princeton University). When war broke out in 1775, Madison had yet to discover his own ambitions. The Revolution quickly changed all

that. In politics Madison found the vocation that neither the management of a plantation nor the practice of law could have offered, first as a member of the Virginia assembly and council of state, then in Congress (1780–83), and finally as a reform-minded legislator back in the state legislature (1784–86).

Madison went to Philadelphia in 1787 in the grips of a great intellectual passion, convinced that he had fashioned a plan of reform that would not only save the union from the states, but the states from themselves. The central lesson he drew from his experiences was that state legislators and the popular majorities they represented could never be trusted to respect the general national interest, the permanent good of their own communities, or the rights of individuals and minorities within the states. A Convention that set out to remedy only the manifest failings of the Confederation would leave the deeper 'vices of the political system of the United States' untreated.

From this analysis, Madison drew a number of specific conclusions that were largely incorporated in the fifteen-point Virginia Plan that his colleague, Governor Edmund Randolph, read on May 29th, the first day the Convention was prepared to turn

to serious business.

First, to free the union from its 'imbecilic' dependence on the states, Madison concluded that the new government had to be empowered to make, execute, and adjudicate its own laws, and to exercise its power directly upon the American people, not the states (upon whose good will Congress relied to have its various resolutions and requisitions executed).

This perception led to a second conclusion. Under the Articles, only the unicameral Congress had formal constitutional status. A union vested with full legal authority had to become a government in the full sense of the term, with three independent branches and a legislature divided into two houses.

In some general sense, of course, Madison and his colleagues drew their ideas about government from the great theorists of the seventeenth and eighteenth centuries – 'the celebrated Montesquieu' (as he was called, although often with tongue-in-cheek), John Locke, James Harrington, David Hume, and William Blackstone. But the lessons they applied to their task were rooted less in what they had read than in what they had done – less in the *Second*

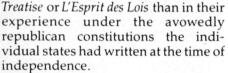

Benjamin Franklin — a bust by Houdon; at 81 he was the 'great sage' of the Convention.

Elbridge Gerry, the maverick from Massachusetts who played a key part in drafting the 'compromise'.

The 'national hero' who presided at Philadelphia — Joseph Wright's portrait of George Washington, soon to be America's first President under the 1787 Constitution.

Treatise or *L'Esprit des Lois* than in their experience under the avowedly republican constitutions the individual states had written at the time of independence.

The distinctive feature of these constitutions was their concentration of power in the legislative branches of government, and especially in the lower houses of assembly. How to prevent these sovereign legislatures from running roughshod over both the state constitutions and the two weaker branches of government – the executive and judiciary – had emerged as the central problem of American constitutionalism. 'Experience had proved a tendency in our governments to throw all power into the Legislative vortex', Madison reminded the delegates in mid-July. 'If no effectual check be devised for restraining the instability and encroachments' of popularly elected legislatures, he concluded, 'a revolution of some kind or another would be inevitable'.

This analysis of legislative misrule cut in two directions. At the national level, it required not only strengthening the authority of the executive and judiciary against that of Congress, but also devising modes of election that would enable the right sort of men to enter Congress. But Madison remained concerned with the residual danger of 'vicious' legislation within the states, which would continue to

hold responsibility for day-to-day governance. So obsessed was Madison with this evil that he wanted the union to enjoy the same authority to veto state laws that the crown had exercised before the Revolution.

These were the central theoretical concerns that Madison carried to Philadelphia in early May. But his agenda rested on one other calculation. He was convinced that the large states would block any major increase in federal power unless principles of proportional representation were applied to *both* houses of the new Congress. A change in the principle of representation, he wrote to Washington shortly before the Convention, was the the 'ground-work' upon which all else depended.

The debate over representation had a dual aspect. The great conflict lay between the large states of Virginia, Pennsylvania, and Massachusetts, and the small states of Delaware, New Jersey, Maryland, and Connecticut, which hoped to retain some vestige of the equal vote they currently enjoyed in Congress. But any scheme of proportional representation inescapably raised the question of slavery: would apportionment be based on total population or simply on the number of free inhabitants?

Madison's strategy on representation was seconded by other large state delegates, notably James Wilson of

Pennsylvania, the Scottish immigrant who was the Convention's leading legal mind, Rufus King of Massachusetts, and Alexander Hamilton of New York. A few delegates – like the temporising John Dickinson – sought to avert confrontation. But Madison's ultimatum set the course the Convention followed during its first seven weeks, until the so-called 'Great Compromise' of July 16th allowed the states to retain an equal vote in the Senate.

Seizing the agenda of debate was one thing, controlling its outcome proved another matter entirely. The small states had able advocates of their own: Roger Sherman of Connecticut, a self-educated shoemaker and storekeeper whose crabbed speech masked dogged parliamentary skill; his colleague, Oliver Ellsworth; the Irish-born William Paterson of New Jersey, a small-town lawyer who had gained political prominence with the Revolution; and Dickinson. These men understood that any scheme of proportional representation would sharply reduce the weight their states enjoyed in national politics, and they were quick to mount a holding action designed to give the states an equal vote in at least one house of Congress.

The debate over representation gave the Convention its great dramatic moments. Principled appeals and heartfelt pleas for accommodation mingled with heavy-handed threats and poker-faced bluffs. On balance, the stronger arguments belonged to Madison, Wilson, and their allies. Time and again, they battered their opponents in debate. Individuals and the interests they possessed were the true constituent elements of society, they insisted, not chunks of territory or the fictitious legal personality of statehood. Moreover, the small states really had no reason to fear domination by the large states. What interests, they asked, did such diverse societies as Virginia, Pennsylvania, and Massachusetts share in common?

These were powerful arguments, and in practice the small state spokesmen rarely confronted them on their merits. Instead they simply replied that their constituents could hardly be expected to place their interests entirely in the hands of their more populous neighbours, especially when the Virginia Plan proposed granting Congress not only broad legislative authority but a right to veto state laws. As opposed to the 'justice' that Madison and Wilson found in majority rule, Sherman, Ellsworth, and Paterson argued that 'security' required an equal state vote in one house at least.

Early tests of strength went mostly to the large state coalition. But a critical vote of July 2nd found the Convention evenly deadlocked on a motion for an equal state vote in the Senate. With little progress having yet been made on any other issue, this vote gave calls for compromise their own logic. The Convention immediately appointed an eleven-man com-

mittee (one from each state) to break the impasse. The small states were represented by their leading spokesmen, but for the large states the Convention revealingly named not 'hard-liners' but rather three men who had already taken conciliatory stances: the great sage, Benjamin Franklin (at eighty-one the senior delegate); the independent-minded George Mason of Virginia, a crusty whig of the old school; and Elbridge Gerry of Massachusetts, a true maverick.

The committee met on July 3rd, joined the celebrations of the eleventh anniversary of Independence on the 4th, and delivered its report the next day. The purported 'compromise' hinged on giving the states an equal vote in the Senate while allowing the lower house to initiate all bills relating to taxes. Further debate led to the adoption of a rule counting five slaves as equivalent to three free whites for purposes of apportioning representation in the lower house (the 'three-fifths clause').

Madison and Wilson scoffed that the proffered compromise was worthless. If the Senate could not 'alter or amend money bills', it could simply reject them until the lower House came into line. Few minds in fact were changed during these debates. But, after final impassioned pleas from Madison, Wilson, and King, the key vote of July 16th found Gerry and Caleb Strong splitting the vote of Massachusetts, allowing the compromise to pass by the narrow margin of five states to four, with one divided.

In its inception, then, the Great Compromise was that in name only.

One side had gained its point, the other had lost. But when a dispirited group of large state delegates met the next morning, they realised that their bluff had been called. No one would break up the Convention over this one issue, unjust as its resolution might be. 'The time was wasted in vague conversation', Madison noted; then they filed back into the main chamber on the first floor of the Pennsylvania State House.

The vote of July 16th had three major consequences for the course that the remaining two months of debate would take.

First, the decision in favour of the small states reinforced the notion that ratification of the Constitution would finally depend on persuading the individual states that their particular interests and concerns had been duly treated. Appeals to the need for mutual accommodation became both more candid and acceptable after July 16th, and led even Madison to concede, grudgingly, that the 'interfering pretensions' of local interests 'compelled [the Convention] to sacrifice theoretical propriety to the force of extraneous considerations'.

A second major consequence of the Great Compromise lay in the more realistic – or limited – conception of the range of powers and responsibilities the national government would be asked to exercise. The Virginia Plan had proposed vesting Congress with a broad and indeed open-ended grant of legislative power. But in emphasising the need to 'secure' particular states and regions against potential abuses of power, the debate over representation led to a

Approval of the new Constitution by the state assemblies was a painstaking and difficult process — this July 1788 cartoon shows New York's pillar of unity coming into line, but North Carolina and Rhode Island still reluctant to ratify the Philadelphia agreement.

On the erection of the Eleventh PILLAR of the great National DOME, we beg leave most sincerely to felicitate " OUR DEAR COUNTRY."

Rise it will.

The foundation good—it may yet be SAVED.

The FEDERAL EDIFICE.

different conclusion. The legislative authority of the union would reach only to well-defined, 'enumerated' objects. Indeed, many of the framers left Philadelphia imagining that once the early sessions of Congress had framed laws for revenue, commerce, and the organisation of the western territories, the national legislature might not even have to meet annually. Within its sphere, the national government could govern as it wished; but that sphere was more constricted than many delegates had originally imagined.

One casualty (in fact the first) of this diminished notion of legislative power was the scheme for a national veto on state laws that Madison had seen as the cure for the evils of law-making within the states. In agreeing that the Senate would represent the states as states, the Convention had also given the power of electing senators to the state legislatures. But this in turn made it extremely unlikely that Congress would ever muster the will to overturn state laws. In place of the veto, the Convention adopted a clause declaring national acts and treaties to be 'the supreme law of the land' and binding the *state* judiciaries to enforce them, 'anything in the respective laws of the individual states to the contrary notwithstanding'.

Over time, the supremacy clause became the principal basis for both the superiority of federal over state law and for the greatly expanded role that both federal and state judiciaries would play in the American constitutional order. The delegates to the 1787 Convention clearly had some grasp of the still quite novel doctrine of judicial review – the distinctively American idea which gives the judiciary the great duty of defending the Constitution (and the individual rights it came to protect) against violations by the political branches of government.

Even so, the framers spent little time exploring the judicial function. It was instead in designing the presidency that they were at their most creative. The dramatic growth of executive power that occurred during the Convention's final weeks marked the third major consequence of the Great Compromise.

Serious debate about the executive had been largely deferred while the Convention wrestled with the prob-

lem of representation. In early June the Convention had agreed that efficiency and responsibility in administering the laws required vesting the executive power in one person. At the same time, they resisted the idea, as Wilson put it on June 1st, that 'the prerogatives of the British monarch' offered 'a proper guide in defining the executive powers'. As late as August, the delegates assumed that the Senate would conduct foreign relations and have the power to appoint major executive and judicial officials. Largely absent from their initial thinking, too, was any idea of the president as prime minister or chief architect of national policy.

Two factors, however, worked to enhance the stature of the presidency the more the delegates pursued the issue. First, the framers agreed, with Madison, that a faithful administra-

tion of the laws required the executive to be insulated from the meddlesome interference of the legislature. Second, the fear that a Senate elected by the state legislatures might too faithfully reflect the parochial wishes of its constituents led many of the framers to begin to think of the president, in the words of Gouverneur Morris, as 'the general guardian of the national interests' and potentially as an active force in politics

The first of these convictions made

'A New Display of the United States' — Amos Doolittle's 1799 engraving showing the population of the thirteen states and their representation in both Houses of Congress on the basis of the Convention's agreement.

modes of election and re-eligibility the crucial issues under debate, as the framers struggled to find a way to render the president politically independent of the legislature whose decisions he was supposed to enforce. The strange device of the Electoral College was the answer the framers finally adopted – less than a fortnight before adjournment – to solve the problem of election. Today this body is often dismissed as a relic of the framers' fear of democracy. But what they actually feared was that a scattered population could never 'be sufficiently informed of characters', as Roger Sherman put it, to choose wisely among a large field of candidates. Believing that popular election was impractical, many delegates at first saw no alternative to election by Congress.

But the proposed Electoral College, awkward as it seemed at first, gradually made converts. An élite body that would convene in the separate states, meet once and then disband, would permit an informed choice by qualified electors who would be difficult to corrupt and incapable of exerting any improper influence over the president once elected. Moreover, the electoral formula itself was artfully designed to repeat the Great Compromise. Votes would be apportioned among the states according to their total representation in Congress, thus giving the large states the initial advantage in promoting candidates. Should no candidate gain a majority, the election would fall to the lower house of Congress, which would vote *by states*, thus giving the small states greater weight in the final selection.

To modern critics of the American system, this desire to make a bicameral Congress and the president independent of each other is the great curse the framers bequeathed to post-

erity, since it greatly complicates the task of framing policies and legislation and renders presidential leadership ever vulnerable to congressional resistance. What such criticism ignores is the fact that the Convention also sought to give the executive more authority than it had initially been inclined to delegate to an office that some feared would prove 'the foetus of monarchy'. The existence of the Electoral College allowed the president to be eligible for re-election, and thus provided a spur to executive ambitions. Equally important, in its final decisions on executive *power*, the Convention transferred the authority to make treaties (and thus conduct foreign relations) and to appoint major officials (including judges) to the president – subject, in both cases, to the 'advice and consent' of the Senate. In so doing, it laid a broad foundation for the growth of the modern presidency.

The development of the executive nicely illustrates the striking mixture of principled and interested concerns that operated throughout the Convention. Some of the delegates left Philadelphia fearful that the compromises they had been forced to strike would still leave the national government too enfeebled to discharge its duties, much less cure the mischiefs of republican government within the states. This was certainly the private opinion of both Madison and Hamilton.

But it took only a little reflection for both men to accept the wisdom in the concluding speech that Benjamin Franklin had asked James Wilson to read just before the delegates signed the finished Constitution. 'I doubt', Franklin had written:

> ...whether any other Convention we can obtain may be able to make a better Constitution. For when you assemble a

number of men to have the advantage of their joint wisdom, you inevitably assemble with those men, all their prejudices, their passions, their errors of opinion, their local interests, and their selfish views. From such an assembly can a perfect production be expected?

Franklin confessed that he was thus 'astonish[ed] ... to find this system approaching as near to perfection as it does', and he went on to note that he consented to the Constitution 'because I expect no better, and because I am not sure that it is not the best'. What he understood was that no second convention could enjoy the same intellectual liberty and political flexibility that the delegates had just exploited. The framers had come to Philadelphia largely unfettered by the instructions of their constituents, but should their proposed Constitution be rejected and a second convention found necessary, its members would likely have far less room for manoeuvre and thus for compromise.

Franklin's appeal failed to sway the three known dissenters at whom it was aimed (Gerry, Mason and Randolph), but his image of the Convention and the Constitution it produced quickly became the dominant one. The irony is that the success of the Federal Convention has left most Americans convinced that it was not so much an experiment that could be repeated as the changing situation of the republic warranted, but a miracle – and even those who believe in miracles do not expect to see them repeated.

FOR FURTHER READING:
Max Farrand, *The Records of the Federal Convention of 1787* (rev. ed., Yale University Press, 1987) contains the journals, notes of debates, and other source material. For the background to the Convention, Forrest McDonald, *Novus Ordo Seclorum* (Kansas, 1985); Gordon S. Wood, *The Creation of the American Republic* (North Carolina, 1969); and Jack N. Rakove, *The Beginnings of National Politics* (Knopf, 1979).

What Was Revolutionary about the French Revolution?

Robert Darnton

1.

What was so revolutionary about the French Revolution? The question might seem impertinent at a time like this, when all the world is congratulating France on the two hundredth anniversary of the storming of the Bastille, the destruction of feudalism, and the Declaration of the Rights of Man and of the Citizen. But the bicentennial fuss has little to do with what actually happened two centuries ago.

Historians have long pointed out that the Bastille was almost empty on July 14, 1789. Many of them argue that feudalism had already ceased to exist by the time it was abolished, and few would deny that the rights of man were swallowed up in the Terror only five years after they were first proclaimed. Does a sober view of the Revolution reveal nothing but misplaced violence and hollow proclamations—nothing more than a "myth," to use a term favored by the late Alfred Cobban, a skeptical English historian who had no use for guillotines and slogans?

One might reply that myths can move mountains. They can acquire a rock-like reality as solid as the Eiffel Tower, which the French built to celebrate the one hundredth anniversary of the Revolution in 1889. France will spend millions in 1989, erecting buildings, creating centers, pro-ducing concrete contemporary expressions of the force that burst loose on the world two hundred years ago. But what was it?

Although the spirit of '89 is no easier to fix in words than in mortar and brick, it could be characterized as energy—a will to build a new world from the ruins of the regime that fell apart in the summer of 1789. That energy permeated everything during the French Revolution. It transformed life, not only for the activists trying to channel it in directions of their own choosing but for ordinary persons going about their daily business.

The idea of a fundamental change in the tenor of everyday life may seem easy enough to accept in the abstract, but few of us can really assimilate it. We take the world as it comes and cannot imagine it organized differently, unless we have experienced moments when things fall apart—a death perhaps, or a divorce, or the sudden obliteration of something that seemed immutable, like the roof over our heads or the ground under our feet.

Such shocks often dislodge individual lives, but they rarely traumatize societies. In 1789 the French had to confront the collapse of a whole social order—the world that they defined retrospectively as the Ancien Régime—and to find some new order in the chaos surrounding them. They experienced reality as something that could be destroyed and recon-structed, and they faced seemingly limit-less possibilities, both for good and for evil, for raising a utopia and for falling back into tyranny.

To be sure, a few seismic upheavals had convulsed French society in earlier ages—the bubonic plague in the four-teenth century, for example, and the religious wars in the sixteenth century. But no one was ready for a revolution in 1789. The idea itself did not exist. If you look up "revolution" in standard diction-aries from the eighteenth century, you find definitions that derive from the verb to revolve, such as "the return of a planet or a star to the same point from which it parted."

The French did not have much of a political vocabulary before 1789, because politics took place at Versailles, in the remote world of the king's court. Once ordinary people began to participate in politics—in the elections to the Estates General, which were based on something approximating universal male suffrage, and in the insurrections of the streets—they needed to find words for what they had seen and done. They developed fun-damental new categories, such as "left" and "right," which derive from the seat-ing plan of the National Assembly, and "revolution" itself. The experience came first, the concept afterward. But what was that experience?

Only a small minority of activists joined the Jacobin clubs, but everyone was touched by the Revolution because the Revolution reached into everything. For example, it re-created time and space. According to the revolutionary calendar adopted in 1793 and used until 1805, time began when the old monarchy ended, on September 22, 1792—the first of Vendémiaire, Year I.

By formal vote of the Convention, the revolutionaries divided time into units that they took to be rational and natural. There were ten days to a week, three weeks to a month, and twelve months to a year. The five days left over at the end became patriotic holidays, *jours sans-culottides*, given over to civic qualities: Virtue, Genius, Labor, Opinion, and Rewards.

Ordinary days received new names, which suggested mathematical regularity: *primidi*, *duodi*, *tridi*, and so on up to *décadi*. Each was dedicated to some aspect of rural life so that agronomy would displace the saints' days of the Christian calendar. Thus November 22, formerly devoted to Saint Cecilia, became the day of the turnip; November 25, formerly Saint Catherine's day, became the day of the pig; and November 30, once the day of Saint Andrew, became the day of the pick. The names of the new months also made time seem to conform to the natural rhythm of the seasons. January 1, 1989, for example, would be the twelfth of Nivôse, Year 197, Nivôse being the month of snow, located after the months of fog (Brumaire) and cold (Frimaire) and before the months of rain (Pluviôse) and wind (Ventôse).

The adoption of the metric system represented a similar attempt to impose a rational and natural organization on space. According to a decree of 1795, the meter was to be "the unit of length equal to one ten-millionth part of the arc of the terrestrial meridian between the North Pole and the Equator." Of course, ordinary citizens could not make much of such a definition. They were slow to adopt the meter and the gram, the corresponding new unit of weight, and few of them favored the new week, which gave them one day of rest in ten instead of one in seven. But even where old habits remained, the revolutionaries stamped their ideas on contemporary consciousness by changing everything's name.

Fourteen hundred streets in Paris received new names, because the old ones contained some reference to a king, a queen, or a saint. The Place Louis XV, where the most spectacular guillotining took place, became the Place de la Révolution; and later, in an attempt to bury the hatchet, it acquired its present name, Place de la Concorde. The Church of Saint-Laurent became the Temple of Marriage and Fidelity; Notre Dame became the Temple of Reason; Montmartre became Mont Marat. Thirty towns took Marat's name—thirty of six thousand that tried to expunge their past by name changes. Montmorency became Emile, Saint-Malo became Victoire Montagnarde, and Coulanges became Cou Sans-Culottes (*anges* or angels being a sign of superstition).

The revolutionaries even renamed themselves. It wouldn't do, of course, to be called Louis in 1793 and 1794. The Louis called themselves Brutus or Spartacus. Last names like Le Roy or Lévêque, very common in France, became La Loi or Liberté. Children got all kinds of names foisted on them—some from nature (Pissenlit or Dandelion did nicely for girls, Rhubarb for boys) and some from current events (Fructidor, Constitution, The Tenth of August, Marat-Couthon-Pique). The foreign minister Pierre-Henri Lebrun named his daughter Civilisation-Jémappes-République.

Meanwhile, the queen bee became a "laying bee" ("*abeille pondeuse*"); chess pieces were renamed, because a good revolutionary would not play with kings, queens, knights, and bishops; and the kings, queens, and jacks of playing cards became liberties, equalities, and fraternities. The revolutionaries set out to change everything: crockery, furniture, law codes, religion, the map of France itself, which was divided into departments—that is, symmetrical units of equal size with names taken from rivers and mountains—in place of the irregular old provinces.

Before 1789, France was a crazy-quilt of overlapping and incompatible units, some fiscal, some judicial, some administrative, some economic, and some religious. After 1789, those segments were melted down into a single substance: the French nation. With its patriotic festivals, its tricolor flag, its hymns, its martyrs, its army, and its wars, the Revolution accomplished what had been impos-

sible for Louis XIV and his successors: it united the disparate elements of the kingdom into a nation and conquered the rest of Europe. In doing so, the Revolution unleashed a new force, nationalism, which would mobilize millions and topple governments for the next two hundred years.

Of course, the nation-state did not sweep everything before it. It failed to impose the French language on the majority of the French people, who continued to speak all sorts of mutually incomprehensible dialects, despite a vigorous propaganda drive by the revolutionary Committee on Public Instruction. But in wiping out the intermediary bodies that separated the citizen from the state, the Revolution transformed the basic character of public life.

It went further: it extended the public into the private sphere, inserting itself into the most intimate relationships. Intimacy in French is conveyed by the pronoun *tu* as distinct from the *vous* employed in formal address. Although the French sometimes use *tu* quite casually today, under the Old Regime they reserved it for asymmetrical or intensely personal relations. Parents said *tu* to children, who replied with *vous*. The *tu* was used by superiors addressing inferiors, by humans commanding animals, and by lovers—after the first kiss, or exclusively between the sheets. When French mountain climbers reach a certain altitude, they still switch from the *vous* to the *tu*, as if all men become equal in the face of the enormousness of nature.

The French Revolution wanted to make everybody *tu*. Here is a resolution passed on 24 Brumaire, Year II (November 14, 1793), by the department of the Tarn, a poor, mountainous area in southern France:

> Considering that the eternal principles of equality forbid that a citizen say "vous" to another citizen, who replies by calling him "toi"... decrees that the word "vous," when it is a question of the singular [rather than the plural, which takes *vous*], is from this moment banished from the language of the free French and will on all occasions be replaced by the word "tu" or "toi."

A delegation of sans-culottes petitioned the National Convention in 1794 to abolish the *vous*, "...as a result of which there will be less pride, less discrimination, less social reserve, more open familiarity, a stronger leaning toward fraternity, and therefore more equality." That may sound laughable today, but it was deadly serious to the revolutionaries: they wanted to build a new society based on new principles of social relations.

So they resdesigned everything that smacked of the inequality built into the conventions of the Old Regime. They ended letters with a vigorous "farewell and fraternity" ("*salut et fraternité*") in place of the deferential "your most obedient and humble servant." They substituted Citizen and Citizeness for Monsieur and Madame. And they changed their dress.

Dress often serves as a thermometer for measuring the political temperature. To designate a militant from the radical sections of Paris, the revolutionaries adopted a term from clothing: *sansculotte*, one who wears trousers rather than breeches. In fact, workers did not generally take up trousers, which were mostly favored by seamen, until the nineteenth century. Robespierre himself always dressed in the uniform of the Old Regime: culottes, waistcoat, and a powdered wig. But the model revolutionary, who appears on broadsides, posters, and crockery from 1793 to the present, wore trousers, an open shirt, a short jacket (the carmagnole), boots, and a liberty cap (Phrygian bonnet) over a "natural" (that is, uncombed) crop of hair, which dropped down to his shoulders.

Women's dress on the eve of the Revolution had featured low necklines, basketskirts, and exotic hair styles, at least among the aristocracy. Hair dressed in the "hedgehog" style ("*en hérisson*") rose two or more feet above the head and was decorated with elaborate props—as a fruit bowl or a flotilla or a zoo. One court coiffure was arranged as a pastoral scene with a pond, a duck hunter, a windmill (which turned), and a miller riding off to market on a mule while a monk seduced his wife.

After 1789, fashion came from below. Hair was flattened, skirts were deflated, necklines raised, and heels lowered. Still later, after the end of the Terror when the Thermidorian Reaction extinguished the Republic of Virtue, fast-moving society women like Mme. Tallien exposed their breasts, danced about in diaphanous gowns, and revived the wig. A true *merveilleuse* or fashionable lady would have a wig for every day of the *décade*; Mme. Tallien had thirty.

At the height of the Revolution, however, from mid-1792 to mid-1794, virtue was not merely a fashion but the central ingredient of a new political culture. It had a puritanical side, but it should not be confused with the Sunday-school variety preached in nineteenth-century America. To the revolutionaries, virtue was virile. It meant a willingness to fight for the fatherland and for the revolutionary trinity of liberty, equality, and fraternity.

At the same time, the cult of virtue produced a revalorization of family life. Taking their text from Rousseau, the revolutionaries sermonized on the sanctity of motherhood and the importance of breast-feeding. They treated reproduction as a civic duty and excoriated bachelors as unpatriotic. "Citizenesses! Give the Fatherland Children!" proclaimed a banner in a patriotic parade. "Now is the time to make a baby," admonished a slogan painted on revolutionary pottery.

Saint-Just, the most extreme ideologist on the Committee of Public Safety, wrote in his notebook: "The child, the citizen, belong to the fatherland. Common instruction is necessary. Children belong to their mother until the age of five, if she has [breast-]fed them, and to the Republic afterwards...until death."

It would be anachronistic to read Hitlerism into such statements. With the collapse of the authority of the Church, the revolutionaries sought a new moral basis for family life. They turned to the state and passed laws that would have been unthinkable under the Old Regime. They made divorce possible; they accorded full legal status to illegitimate children; they abolished primogeniture. If, as the Declaration of the Rights of Man and of the Citizen proclaimed, all men are created free and equal in rights, shouldn't all men begin with an equal start in life? The Revolution tried to limit "paternal despotism" by giving all children an equal share in inheritances. It abolished slavery and gave full civic rights to Protestants and Jews.

To be sure, one can spot loopholes and contradictions in the revolutionary legislation. Despite some heady phrasing in the so-called Ventôse Decrees about the appropriation of counterrevolutionaries' property, the legislators never envisaged anything like socialism. And Napoleon reversed the most democratic provisions of the laws on family life. Nevertheless, the main direction of revolutionary legislation is clear: it substituted the state for the Church as the ultimate authority in the conduct of private life, and it grounded the legitimacy of the state in the sovereignty of the people.

2.

Popular sovereignty, civil liberty, equality before the law—the words fall so easily off the tongue today that we cannot begin to imagine their explosiveness in 1789. We cannot think ourselves back into a mental world like that of the Old Regime, where most people assumed that men were unequal, that inequality was a good thing, and that it conformed to the hierarchical order built into nature by God himself. To the French of the Old Regime, liberty meant privilege—that is, literally, "private law" or a special prerogative to do something denied to other persons. The king, as the source of all law, dispensed privileges, and rightly so, for he had been anointed as the agent of God on earth. His power was spiritual as well as secular, so by his royal touch he could cure scrofula, the king's disease.

Throughout the eighteenth century, the philosophers of the Enlightenment challenged those assumptions, and pamphleteers in Grub Street succeeded in tarnishing the sacred aura of the crown. But it took violence to smash the mental frame of the Old Regime, and violence itself, the iconoclastic, world-destroying, revolutionary sort of violence, is also hard for us to conceive.

True, we treat traffic accidents and muggings as everyday occurrences. But compared with our ancestors, we live in a world where violence has been drained out of our daily experience. In the eighteenth century, Parisians commonly passed by corpses that had been fished out of the Seine and hung by their feet along the riverbank. They knew a "*mine patibulaire*" was a face that looked like one of the dismembered heads exposed on a fork by the public executioner. They had witnessed dismemberments of criminals at public executions. And they could not walk through the center of the city without covering their shoes in blood.

Here is a description of the Paris butcheries, written by Louis-Sébastien Mercier a few years before the outbreak of the Revolution:

> They are in the middle of the city. Blood courses through the streets; it coagulates under your feet, and your shoes are red with it. In passing, you are suddenly struck with an agonized cry. A young steer is thrown to the

ground, its horns tied down; a heavy mallet breaks its skull; a huge knife strikes deep into its throat; its steaming blood flows away with its life in a thick current.... Then bloodstained arms plunge into its smoking entrails; its members are hacked apart and hung up for sale. Sometimes the steer, dazed but not downed by the first blow, breaks its ropes and flees furiously from the scene, mowing down everyone in its paths.... And the butchers who run after their escaped victim are as dangerous as it is.... These butchers have a fierce and bloody appearance: naked arms, swollen necks, their eyes red, their legs filthy, their aprons covered with blood, they carry their massive clubs around with them always spoiling for a fight. The blood they spread seems to inflame their faces and their temperaments.... In streets near the butcheries, a cadaverous odor hangs heavy in the air; and vile prostitutes—huge, fat, monstrous objects sitting in the streets—display their debauchery in public. These are the beauties that those men of blood find alluring.

A serious riot broke out in 1750 because a rumor spread through the working-class sections of Paris that the police were kidnapping children to provide a bloodbath for a prince of the royal blood. Such riots were known as "popular emotions"—eruptions of visceral passion touched off by some spark that burned within the collective imagination.

It would be nice if we could associate the Revolution exclusively with the Declaration of the Rights of Man and of the Citizen, but it was born in violence and it stamped its principles on a violent world. The conquerors of the Bastille did not merely destroy a symbol of royal despotism. One hundred and fifty of them were killed or injured in the assault on the prison; and when the survivors got hold of its governor, they cut off his head, and paraded it through Paris on the end of a pike.

A week later, in a paroxysm of fury over high bread prices and rumors about plots to starve the poor, a crowd lynched an official in the war ministry named Foulon, severed his head, and paraded it on a pike with hay stuffed in its mouth as a sign of complicity in the plotting. A band of rioters then seized Foulon's son-in-law, the intendant of Paris, Bertier de Sauvigny, and marched him through the streets with the head in front of him, chanting "Kiss papa, kiss papa." They murdered Bertier in front of the Hôtel de Ville, tore the heart out of his body, and threw it in the direction of the municipal government. Then they resumed their parade with his head beside Foulon's. "That is how traitors are punished," said an engraving of the scene.

Gracchus Babeuf, the future leftist conspirator, described the general delirium in a letter to his wife. Crowds applauded at the sight of the heads on the pikes, he wrote:

Oh! That joy made me sick. I felt satisfied and displeased at the same time. I said, so much the better and so much the worse. I understood that the common people were taking justice into their own hands. I approve that justice...but could it not be cruel? Punishments of all kinds, drawing and quartering, torture, the wheel, the rack, the whip, the stake, hangmen proliferating everywhere have done such damage to our morals! Our masters...will sow what they have reaped.

It also would be nice if we could stop the story of the Revolution at the end of 1789, where the current French government wants to draw the line in its celebrating. But the whole story extends through the rest of the century—and of the following century, according to some historians. Whatever its stopping point, it certainly continued through 1794; so we must come to terms with the Terror.

3.

We can find plenty of explanations for the official Terror, the Terror directed by the Committee of Public Safety and the Revolutionary Tribunal. By twentieth-century standards, it was not very devastating, if you make a body count of its victims and if you believe in measuring such things statistically. It took about 17,000 lives. There were fewer than twenty-five executions in half the departments of France, none at all in six of them. Seventy-one percent of the executions took place in regions where civil war was raging; three quarters of the guillotined were rebels captured with arms in their hands; and 85 percent were commoners—a statistic that is hard to digest for those who interpret the Revolution as a class war directed by bourgeois against aristocrats. Under the Terror the word "aristocrat" could be applied to almost anyone deemed to be an enemy of the people.

But all such statistics stick in the throat. Any attempt to condemn a person by suppressing his individuality and by slotting him into abstract, ideological categories such as "aristocrat" or "bourgeois" is inherently inhuman. The Terror *was* terrible. It pointed the way toward totalitarianism. It was the trauma that scarred modern history at its birth.

Historians have succeeded in explaining much of it (not all, not the hideous last month of the "Great Terror" when the killing increased while the threat of invasion receded) as a response to the extraordinary circumstances of 1793 and 1794: the invading armies about to overwhelm Paris; the counterrevolutionaries, some imaginary, many real, plotting to overthrow the government from within; the price of bread soaring out of control and driving the Parisian populace wild with hunger and despair; the civil war in the Vendée; the municipal rebellions in Lyons, Marseilles, and Bordeaux; and the factionalism within the National Convention, which threatened to paralyze every attempt to master the situation.

It would be the height of presumption for an American historian sitting in the comfort of his study to condemn the French for violence and to congratulate his countrymen for the relative bloodlessness of their own revolution, which took place in totally different conditions. Yet what is he to make of the September Massacres of 1792, an orgy of killing that took the lives of more than one thousand persons, many of them prostitutes and common criminals trapped in prisons like the Abbaye?

We don't know exactly what happened, because the documents were destroyed in the bombardment of the Paris Commune in 1871. But the sober assessment of the surviving evidence by Pierre Caron suggests that the massacres took on the character of a ritualistic, apocalyptic mass murder.* Crowds of sans-culottes, including men from the butcheries described by Mercier, stormed the prisons in order to extinguish what they believed to be a counterrevolutionary plot. They improvised a popular court in the prison of the Abbaye. One by one the prisoners were led out, accused, and summarily judged according to their demeanor. Fortitude was taken to be a sign of in-

---

*Pierre Caron, *Les Massacres de Septembre* (Paris: La Maison du Livre Français, 1935).

nocence, faltering as guilt. Stanislas Maillard, a conqueror of the Bastille, assumed the role of prosecutor; and the crowd, transported from the street to rows of benches, ratified his judgment with nods and acclamations. If declared innocent, the prisoner would be hugged, wept over, and carried triumphantly through the city. If guilty, he would be hacked to death in a gauntlet of pikes, clubs, and sabers. Then his body would be stripped and thrown on a heap of corpses or dismembered and paraded about on the end of a pike.

Throughout their bloody business, the people who committed the massacres talked about purging the earth of counterrevolution. They seemed to play parts in a secular version of the Last Judgement, as if the Revolution had released an undercurrent of popular millenarianism. But it is difficult to know what script was being performed in September 1792. We may never be able to fathom such violence or to get to the bottom of the other "popular emotions" that determined the course of the Revolution: the Great Fear of the peasants in the early summer of 1789; the uprisings of July 14 and October 5–6, 1789; and the revolutionary "days" of August 10, 1792, May 31, 1793, 9 Thermidor, Year II (July 27, 1794), 12 Germinal, Year III (April 1, 1795), and 1–4 Prairial, Year III (May 20–23, 1795). In all of them the crowds cried for bread and blood, and the bloodshed passes the historian's understanding.

It is there, nonetheless. It will not go away, and it must be incorporated in any attempt to make sense of the Revolution. One could argue that violence was a necessary evil, because the Old Regime would not die peacefully and the new order could not survive without destroying the counterrevolution. Nearly all the violent "days" were defensive—desperate attempts to stave off counterrevolutionary coups, which threatened to annihilate the Revolution from June 1789 until November 1799, when Bonaparte seized power. After the religious schism of 1791 and the war of 1792, any opposition could be made to look like treason, and no consensus could be reached on the principles of politics.

In short, circumstances account for most of the violent swings from extreme to extreme during the revolutionary decade. Most, but not all—certainly not the Slaughter of the Innocents in September 1792. The violence itself remains a mystery, the kind of phenome-

non that may force one back into metahistorical explanations: original sin, unleashed libido, or the cunning of a dialectic. For my part, I confess myself incapable of explaining the ultimate cause of revolutionary violence, but I think I can make out some of its consequences. It cleared the way for the redesigning and rebuilding that I mentioned above. It struck down institutions from the Old Regime so suddenly and with such force that it made anything seem possible. It released utopian energy.

The sense of boundless possibility— "possibilism" one could call it—was the bright side of popular emotion, and it was not restricted to millenarian outbursts in the streets. It could seize lawyers and men of letters sitting in the Legislative Assembly. On July 7, 1792, A.-A. Lamourette, a deputy from Rhône-et-Loire, told the Assembly's members that their troubles all arose from a single source: factionalism. They needed more fraternity. Whereupon the deputies, who had been at each other's throats a moment earlier, rose to their feet and started hugging and kissing each other as if their political divisions could be swept away in a wave of brotherly love.

The "kiss of Lamourette" has been passed over with a few indulgent smiles by historians who know that three days later the Assembly would fall apart before the bloody uprising of August 10. What children they were, those men of 1792, with their overblown oratory, their naive cult of virtue, their simple-minded sloganeering about liberty, equality, and fraternity!

But we may miss something if we condescend to people in the past. The popular emotion of fraternity, the strangest in the trinity of revolutionary values, swept through Paris with the force of a hurricane in 1792. We can barely imagine its power, because we inhabit a world organized according to other principles, such as tenure, take-home pay, bottom lines, and who reports to whom. We define ourselves as employers or employees, as teachers or students, as someone located somewhere in a web of intersecting roles. The Revolution at its most revolutionary tried to wipe out such distinctions. It really meant to legislate the brotherhood of man. It may not have succeeded any better than Christianity christianized, but it remodeled enough of the social landscape to alter the course of history.

How can we grasp those moments of madness, of suspended disbelief, when anything looked possible and the world appeared as a tabula rasa, wiped clean by

a surge of popular emotion and ready to be redesigned? Such moments pass quickly. People cannot live for long in a state of epistemological exhilaration. Anxiety sets in—the need to fix things, to enforce borders, to sort out "aristocrats" and patriots. Boundaries soon harden, and the landscape assumes once more the aspect of immutability.

Today most of us inhabit a world that we take to be not the best but the only world possible. The French Revolution has faded into an almost imperceptible past, its bright light obscured by a distance of two hundred years, so far away that we may barely believe in it. For the Revolution defies belief. It seems incredible that an entire people could rise up and transform the conditions of everyday existence. To do so is to contradict the common working assumption that life must be fixed in the patterns of the common workaday world.

Have we never experienced anything that could shake that conviction? Consider the assassinations of John F. Kennedy, Robert Kennedy, and Martin Luther King, Jr. All of us who lived through those moments remember precisely where we were and what we were doing. We suddenly stopped in our tracks, and in the face of the enormity of the event we felt bound to everyone around us. For a few instants we ceased to see one another through our roles and perceived ourselves as equals, stripped down to the core of our common humanity. Like mountaineers high above the daily business of the world, we moved from *vous* to *tu*.

I think the French Revolution was a succession of such events, events so terrible that they shook mankind to its core. Out of the destruction, they created a new sense of possibility—not just of writing constitutions nor of legislating liberty and equality, but of living by the most difficult of revolutionary values, the brotherhood of man.

Of course, the notion of fraternity comes from the Revolution itself rather than from any higher wisdom among historians, and few historians, however wise, would assert that great events expose some bedrock reality underlying history. I would argue the opposite: great events make possible the social reconstruction of reality, the reordering of things-as-they-are so they are no longer experienced as given but rather as willed, in accordance with convictions about how things ought to be.

Possibilism against the givenness of things—those were the forces pitted against one another in France from 1789 to 1799. Not that other forces were absent, including something that might be called a "bourgeoisie" battling something known as "feudalism," while a good deal of property changed hands and the poor extracted some bread from the rich. But all those conflicts were predicated on something greater than the sum of their parts—a conviction that the human condition is malleable, not fixed, and that ordinary people can make history instead of suffering it.

Two hundred years of experimentation with brave new worlds have made us skeptical about social engineering. In retrospect, the Wordsworthian moment can be made to look like a prelude to totalitarianism. The poet bayed at a blood moon. He barked, and the caravan passed, a line of generations linked together like a chain gang destined for the gulag.

Maybe. But too much hindsight can distort the view of 1789 and of 1793-1794. The French revolutionaries were not Stalinists. They were an assortment of unexceptional persons in exceptional circumstances. When things fell apart, they responded to an overwhelming need to make sense of things by ordering society according to new principles. Those principles still stand as an indictment of tyranny and injustice. What was the French Revolution all about? Liberty, equality, fraternity.

Scotland's Greatest Son

In *The Wealth of Nations* Adam Smith gave the world a new
and witty and literate perception of
the dismal science. But what would he have said about ITT?

JOHN KENNETH GALBRAITH

In June of 1973 economists gathered from all over the world in the Royal Burgh of Kirkcaldy, immediately across the Firth of Forth from Edinburgh, to celebrate the two hundred and fiftieth anniversary of the birth of the town's — most would say Scotland's—greatest son. That was Adam Smith, who was born there in 1723, the son of the local collector of customs, and who, after study at the evidently excellent local school, went on to the University of Glasgow and then to Balliol for six years. Returning to Scotland, he became, first, professor of logic and then, in 1752, professor of moral philosophy at Glasgow. This chair he resigned in 1764 to travel on the Continent as the well-paid tutor of the young Duke of Buccleuch, a family possessed to this day of a vast acreage of dubious land on the border. In Europe Smith made the acquaintance of the physiocratic philosophers and economists Quesnay and Turgot, as well as Voltaire and other notable contemporaries, and used his time and mind well. He then returned to Kirkcaldy where, for the next twelve years, subject to lengthy sojourns in London and to the despair of some of his friends who feared he would never finish, he engaged himself in the writing of *The Wealth of Nations*.

This great book was published in 1776, a few weeks before the Declaration of Independence, and if there is coincidence in the dates, there was also association in the events. Unlike his friend

David Hume (who died that August), Smith deplored the separation. He had wanted instead full union, full and equal representation of the erstwhile colonies in Parliament, free trade within the Union, equal taxation along with equal representation, and the prospect that, as the American part developed in wealth and population, the capital would be removed from London to some new Constantinople in the West. Practical men must have shuddered.

However, *The Wealth of Nations*, at least among the knowledgeable, was an immediate success. Gibbon wrote, "What an excellent work is that with which our common friend Mr. Adam Smith has enriched the public . . . most profound ideas expressed in the most perspicacious language." Hume, in a much quoted letter, was exuberant:

Euge! Belle! Dear Mr. Smith. I am much pleased with your performance, and the perusal of it has taken from me a state of great anxiety. It was a work of so much expectation, by yourself, by your friends, and by the public, that I trembled for its appearance, but am now much relieved . . . it has depth and solidity and acuteness, and is so much illustrated by curious facts that it must at last attract the public attention.

The public response—to two volumes costing £1 16s., the equivalent of perhaps thirty dollars today—was also good. The first edition was soon sold out, although this intelligence would be more valuable were the size of the edition known. Smith spent the next couple

of years in London being, one gathers, much fêted by his contemporaries for his accomplishment, and then, having been appointed Commissioner of Customs in Edinburgh, an admirable sinecure, he returned to Scotland. He died in Edinburgh in 1790.

By this time, *The Wealth of Nations*, though at first ignored by politicians, was having an influence on men of affairs. A year and a half after Smith's death, Pitt, introducing his budget, said of Smith that his "extensive knowledge of detail and depth of philosophical research will, I believe, furnish the best solution of every question connected with the history of commerce and with the system of political economy." Not since, in the nonsocialist world at least, has a politician committed himself so courageously to an economist.

Smith has not been a popular subject for biographers. He was a bachelor. His best-remembered personal trait was his absent-mindedness. Once, according to legend, he fell into deep thought and walked fifteen miles in his dressing gown before regaining consciousness. His manuscripts, by his instruction, were destroyed at his death. He disliked writing letters, and few of these have survived. The papers of those with whom he did correspond, or which reflected his influence, were destroyed, mostly because of lack of interest, and some, it appears, as late as 1941 or 1942. Adam Smith's only other major published work, *The Theory of Moral Sentiments*, reflects in terests antecedent to those in political economy. It is often cited by scholars but little read. No biography of Adam Smith has superseded that by John Rae, published nearly eighty years ago.

If Smith's life has attracted little attention, perhaps it is because so much attention has centered on *Inquiry into the Nature and Causes of the Wealth of Nations*, to give the title of his masterpiece its full resonance. With *Das Kapital* and the Bible, *Wealth of Nations* enjoys the distinction of being one of the three books that people may refer to at will without feeling they should have read it. Scholarly dispute over what is Smith's principal contribution has gone on endlessly. This is partly because there is so much in the book that every reader has full opportunity to exercise his own preference.

Exercising that preference, I have always thought that two of Smith's achievements have been neglected. One, mentioned by Gibbon, is his gift for language. Few writers ever, and certainly no economist since, have been as amusing, lucid, or resourceful—or on occasion as devastating. Most rightly remember his conclusion that "People of the same trade seldom meet together, even for merriment and diversion, but the conversation ends in a conspiracy against the public, or in some contrivance to raise prices." There are many more such gems. He noted that "The late resolution of the Quakers in Pennsylvania to set at liberty all their negro slaves may satisfy us that their number cannot be very great." And, anticipating Thorstein Veblen, that "With the greater part of rich people, the chief enjoyment of riches consists in the parade of riches." On the function or nonfunction of stockholders, no one in the next two centuries was more penetrating in however many words: "[Stockholders]

seldom pretend to understand anything of the business of the company, and when the spirit of faction happens not to prevail among them, give themselves no trouble about it, but receive contentedly such half-yearly or yearly dividend, as the directors think proper to make to them." One of Smith's most famous observations, it may be noted, is not in *Wealth of Nations*. On hearing from Sir John Sinclair in October, 1777, that

MARY EVANS PICTURE LIBRARY, LONDON

Gussied up and properly shod (he usually wore his bedroom slippers), Smith appears in an engraving of 1790, the year of his death.

Burgoyne had surrendered at Saratoga and of his friend's fear that the nation was ruined, Smith said, "There is a great deal of ruin in a nation."

Also neglected now are the "curious facts" that enchanted Hume and of which *Wealth of Nations* is a treasure house. Their intrusion has, in fact, been deplored. As a writer Smith was a superb carpenter but a poor architect. The facts appear in lengthy digressions

that have been criticized as such. But for any discriminating reader it is worth the interruption to learn that the expenses of the civil government of the Massachusetts Bay Colony "before the commencement of the present disturbances," meaning the Revolution, were only £18,000 a year and that this was a rather sizable sum compared with New York and Pennsylvania at £4,500 each and New Jersey at £1,200. (These and numerous other details on the Colonies reflect an interest John Rae believes was stimulated by Benjamin Franklin, with whom Smith was closely acquainted.)

Also, were it not for Smith we might not know that after a bad storm, or "inundation," the citizens of the Swiss canton of Underwald (Unterwalden) came together in an assembly where each publicly confessed his wealth to the multitude and was then assessed *pro rata* for the repair of the damage. Or that, at least by Smith's exceptionally precise calculation, Isocrates earned £3,333 6s. 8d. (upward of 50,000 dollars) for what "we would call one course of lectures, a number which will not appear extraordinary from so great a city to so famous a teacher, who taught, too, what was at that time the most fashionable of all sciences, rhetoric." Or that Plutarch was paid the same. Or, continuing with professors, that those who are subject to reward unrelated to their capacity to attract students will perform their duty in "as careless and slovenly a manner" as authority will permit and that in "the university of Oxford, the greater part of the public professors [those with endowed chairs] have, for these many years, given up altogether even the pretence of teaching."

So no one should neglect Smith's contribution to expository prose and "curious facts." Now as to economic thought and policy. Here a sharp and

2. CULTURAL FERMENT OF THE WEST

ADAM SMITH ON SELF-INTEREST:

"It is not from the benevolence of the butcher, the brewer, or the baker that we expect our dinner but from their regard to their self-interest. We address ourselves not to their humanity, but to their self-love, and never talk to them of our necessities, but of their advantages."

obvious distinction must be made between what was important in 1776 and what is important now. The first is very great; the second, save in the imagination of those who misuse Smith as a prophet of reaction, is much less so. The business corporation, which Smith deplored, and the wealth that accumulated in consequence of his advice combined against him. But first we must consider his meaning in 1776.

Smith's economic contribution to his own time can be thought of as falling into three categories—method, system, and advice. The second, overflowing onto the third, is by far the most important.

As to method, Smith gave to political economy, later to become economics, the basic structure which was to survive almost intact at least for the next hundred and fifty years. This structure begins with the problem of value—how prices are set. Then comes the question of how the proceeds are shared—how the participants in production are rewarded. This latter involves the great trinity of labor, capital, and land. Along the way is the role of money. Thereafter come banking, international trade, taxation, public works, defense, and the other functions of the state. Other writers, notably the physiocrats, had previously given political economy a fairly systematic frame, although, as Alexander Gray observed, they had "embellished it with strange frills." But it was Smith who, for the English-speaking world, provided the enduring structure.

The structure, in turn, was more important than what it enclosed. Although Smith's treatment of value, wages, profits, and rents was suggestive and often incisive, it was, in all respects, a begin-

ning and not an end. So it was regarded by Ricardo, Malthus, and the two Mills. Thus, as one example, Smith held that the supply of workers would increase *pari passu* with an increase in the sustenance available for their support. Ricardo translated this thought into the iron law of wages—the rule that wages would tend always to fall to the bare minimum necessary to sustain life. And Malthus, going a step further, adduced his immortal conclusion that people everywhere would proliferate to the point of starvation. Subsequent scholars—the marginal-utility theorists, Alfred Marshall, others—added further modifications to the theory of prices, wages, interest, profits, and rent, and yet further transmutations were of course to follow. Smith was left far behind.

For Smith, the structure he gave to economics and the explanation of economic behavior that it contained were only steps in the creation of his larger system—his complete view of how economic life should be arranged and governed. This was his central achievement. It provides a set of guiding rules for economic policy that are comprehensive and consistent without being arbitrary or dogmatic.

The Smithian system requires that the individual, suitably educated, be left free to pursue his own interest. In doing so, he serves not perfectly, but better than by any alternative arrangement, the common public purpose. Self-interest or selfishness guides men, as though by the influence of an unseen hand, to the exercise of the diligence and intelligence that maximize productive

effort and thus the public good. Private vice becomes a public virtue.

In pursuit of private interest, producers exploit the opportunities inherent in the division of labor—in, broadly speaking, the specialized development of skill for the performance of each small part of a total task of production. Combined with the division of labor is the natural propensity of man "to truck, barter or exchange." The freedom of the individual to do his best both in production and in exchange is inhibited by regulation and taxation. Thus the hand of the state should weigh on him as lightly as possible. The limiting factor on the division of labor—roughly, the scale of specialized productive activity—is the size of the market. Obviously, this should be as wide as possible.

There follows Smith's special case against internal, monopolistic, or international restrictions on trade. The case against international barriers gains force from the fact that both well-being and national strength derive not from the accumulation of precious metal, as Smith's mercantilist precursors had held, but—as one would now say and as Smith in effect did say—from the productivity of the labor force. Given an industrious and productive labor force, in the most majestic of Smith's arguments, the supply of gold will take care of itself.

Such, in greatest compression, is the Smithian system—the one that Pitt proclaimed as "the best solution of every question connected . . . with the system of political economy."

Smith's third contribution was in the field of practical policy. His advice—on banking, education, colonies, taxation (including the famous canons and extending even to recommendations for the reform of taxation in France), public works, joint-stock companies, agriculture—was infinitely abundant. It could be that no economist since has offered so much. With many exceptions and frequent modifications to fit the circumstance, it is in keeping with Smith's system. The bias in favor of freeing or unburdening the individual to pursue his

"Poverty, though it no doubt discourages, does not always prevent marriage. It seems even to be favourable to generation. A half-starved Highland woman frequently bears more than twenty children, while a pampered fine lady is often incapable of bearing any, and is generally exhausted by two or three. . . . But poverty . . . is extremely unfavourable to the rearing of children. The tender plant is produced, but in so cold a soil and so severe a climate, soon withers and dies."

interest is omnipresent, and so is his belief that men will toil effectively only in the pursuit of pecuniary self-interest. There will be occasion for a further word on this advice; now we must see what of Smith survives.

Needless to say, the mordant language and the curious facts survive; it is too bad they are not more read and enjoyed. Also, Smith's concept of the economic problem—and the division of the subject between value and distribution—are still to be found in that part of the textbooks that economists call microeconomics (and those given to tasteless insider abbreviation call "micro"). His particular conclusions as to how prices, wages, rents, and return to capital are determined, and his views on gold, paper currency, banks, and the like, are now only of antiquarian interest.

Nor does much of the abundant advice just mentioned have modern meaning. It better illuminates life in the eighteenth century than any current problems. Until recently the textbooks on taxation included reverent mention of Smith's four great canons. But no one now coming to them without knowledge of their author would think them very remarkable. That taxes should be certain or predictable and arbitrary in their bite; that they should be so levied and collected as to fit the reasonable convenience of the taxpayer; and that the cost of collection should be a modest part of the total take was important in 1776. But these three things are pretty well accepted now.

Smith's fourth canon, that the "subjects of every state ought to contribute towards the support of the government, as nearly as possible, in proportion to their respective abilities; that is, in proportion to the revenue which they respectively enjoy under the protection of the state," could be taken as an enduring prescription for a proportional (i.e., fixed percentage) as distinct from a progressive income tax. Some beleaguered rich have so argued. In fact, Smith was speaking only of what seemed possible and sensible in his own time. He would have moved with the times. It might be added that his modest prescription gives no comfort to tax shelters, special treatment of state and municipal bonds, the oil-depletion allowance, or those who believe that they were intended by nature to be untroubled by the IRS. Numerous of the big rich in the United States would find even Adam Smith's proportional prescription rather costly as compared with what they now pay.

The next and more interesting question concerns Smith's system—his rules for guiding economic life. What of that survives? Is economic life still guided in appreciable measure by the unseen hand of self-interest—in modern language, by the market? What has happened to the notion of the minimal state, and is it forever dead? And what of Smith's plea for the widest possible market both within and between nations?

In truth, time has dealt harshly with Smith's system. On one important mat-

ter he was simply wrong. Further damage was done by an institution, the business corporation, for which he saw little future and which, on the whole, he deplored. And his system was gravely impaired by the very success of the prescription that he offered.

Smith's error was his underestimate of man's capacity, perhaps with some social conditioning, for co-operation. He thought it negligible. Men would work assiduously for their own pecuniary advantage; on shared tasks, even for shared reward, they would continue to do as little as authority allowed. Only in defeating or circumventing that authority—in minimizing physical and intellectual toil, maximizing indolence and sloth—would they bring real effort and ingenuity to bear. But not otherwise. People work only if working for themselves. There is no more persistent theme in *Wealth of Nations*. It is why government tasks are poorly performed. It is why civil servants are an uncivil and feckless crew. It is his case against the British bureaucracy in India. It is why the Oxford professors lapse into idleness. And it is why, in Smith's view, joint-stock companies, except for routine tasks, have little to commend them. Their best chance for survival, one to which the minds of the directors almost invariably turn, is to obtain a monopoly of their industry or trade, a tendency to which Smith devotes some of his finest scorn. Otherwise, their employees or servants devote themselves not to enriching the company but to enriching themselves or not enriching anyone.

In fact, experience since Smith has shown that man's capacity for co-operative effort is very great. Perhaps this was the product of education and social conditioning, something that no one writing in the eighteenth century could have foreseen. Perhaps Smith, handicapped by his environment, judged all races by the Scotch (as we are correctly called). Most likely he failed to see the pride people could have in their organization, their desire for the good opinion or esteem of their co-workers, maybe what Veblen called their instinct to workmanship.

In any case, governments in the performance of public tasks, some of great technical and military complexity, corporations in pursuit of growth, profit, and power, and socialist states in pursuit of national development and power have been able to enlist a great intensity of co-operative effort. And both corporate and socialist economic activities have been able to unite an instinct to co-operation with a promise of individual economic reward and gain from both. At least in the industrialized world, highly organized forms of economic activity enlist a great intensity of co-operative effort.

The most spectacular example of co-operative effort—or perhaps, to speak more precisely, of a successful marriage of co-operative and self-serving endeavor—has, of course, been the corporation. This, for the reasons just noted, Smith did not think possible. And the development of the corporation, in turn, was destructive of the minimal state that Smith prescribed.

For this there were several reasons. The corporation had needs—franchises, rights-of-way, capital, qualified manpower, technical support, highways for its motor cars, airways for its airplanes—which only the state could supply. A state that served its corporations satisfactorily quickly ceased, except in the hopes of truly romantic conservatives, to be minimal.

Also, a less evident point, the economy of the great corporation, when combined with that of the unions (which were in some measure the response to it), was no longer stable. The corporation retained earnings for investment; there was no certainty that all of such savings would be invested. The resulting shortage of demand could be cumulative, for wages and prices would no longer adjust to arrest the downward spiral. And in other circumstances wages and prices might force each other

up to produce an enduring and cumulative inflation. The state was called upon to offset the tendency to recession by stabilizing the demand for goods. This was the message of Keynes. And the state had to intervene to stabilize prices and wages if inflation were to be kept within tolerable limits. Both actions were heavy blows at the Smithian state.

The corporation, as it became very large, also ceased to be subordinate to the market. It fixed prices, sought out supplies, influenced consumers, and otherwise exercised power not different in kind from the power of the the state itself. As Smith would have foreseen, this power was exercised in the interest of its possessors, and on numerous matters— the use of air, water, and land—the corporate interest diverged from the public interest. It also diverged where, as in the case of the weapons firms, the corporation was able to persuade the state to be its customer. Corporate interest did not coincide with the public interest as the Smithian system assumed. And there were yet further appeals to the government for redress and further enhancement of the state. This development, on which I will have a later word, has proceeded with explosive speed, especially since World War II.

Finally, Smith's system was destroyed by its own success. In the nineteenth century and with a rather deliberate recognition of their source, Britain was governed by Smith's ideas. So, though more by instinct than by deliberate philosophical commitment, was the United States. And directly, or through such great disciples as the French economist J. B. Say, Smith's influence extended to Western Europe. In the context of time and place, the Smithian system worked; there was a vast release of productive energy, a great increase in wealth, a large though highly uneven increase in living standards. Then came the corporation with its superior access to capital (including that reserved from its own earnings), its great ability to adapt science and technology to its purposes, and its strong commitment to its

own growth through expanding sales and output. This, and by a new order of magnitude, added to the increase in output, income, and consumption.

This was the next nail. It is not possible to combine a highly productive economy with a minimal state. Public regulation had to develop in step with private consumption; public services must bear some reasonable relationship to the supply of private services and goods. Both points are accepted in practice if not in principle. A country cannot have a high consumption of automobiles, alcohol, medication, transportation, communications, or even cosmetics, without rules governing their use. The greater the wealth, the more men needed to protect it, and the more required to pick up the discarded containers in which so much of it comes. And in rough accord with increased private consumption goes an increased demand for public services—for education, health care, parks and public recreation, postal services, and the infinity of other things that must be provided, or are best provided, by the state.

Among numerous conservatives there is still a conviction that the society of the minimal state was deliberately destroyed by socialists, planners, *étatists* and other wicked men who did not know what they were about, or knew all too well. Far more of the responsibility lies with Smith himself. Along with the corporation, his system created the wealth that made his state impossible.

In one last area, it will be insisted Adam Smith does survive. Men still respect his inspired and inspiring call for the widest possible market, one that will facilitate in the greatest degree the division of labor. And after two centuries the dominant body of opinion in industrial nations resists tariffs and quotas. And in Europe the nation-states have created the ultimate monument to Adam Smith, the European Economic Community. In even more specific tribute to Smith, it is usually called the Common Market.

Even here, however, there is less of Smith than meets the eye. Since the eighteenth century, or, for that matter, in the last fifty years, domestic markets have grown enormously. That of insular Britain today is far greater than that of imperial Britain at the height of empire. The technical opportunities in large-scale production have developed enormously since 1776. But national markets have developed much, much more. Proof lies in the fact that General Motors, IBM, Shell, Nestlé, do not produce in ever larger plants as would be the case if they needed to realize the full opportunities inherent in the division of labor. Rather, they produce the same items in numerous small plants. Except perhaps in the very small industrial countries — Holland, Belgium, Luxembourg — domestic markets have long been large enough so that even were they confined to the home market, producers would realize the full economies of scale, the full technical advantages of the division of labor.

The Common Market, and the modern enlightenment on international trade, owe much more to the nontechnical needs of the modern multinational corporation than they do to Adam Smith. The multinational corporation stands astride national boundaries. Instead of seeking tariff support of the state against countries that have a comparative advantage, it can go to the advantaged countries to produce what it needs. At the same time, modern marketing techniques require that it be able to follow its products into other countries to persuade consumers and governments and, in concert with other producers, to avoid the price competition that would be disastrous for all. So, for the multinational corporation, tariffs, to speak loosely and generally, are both unnecessary and a nuisance. It would not have escaped the attention of Adam Smith, although it has escaped the attention of many in these last few years, that where there are no corporations, the Common Market is less than common and very

much less than popular. The tariff enlightenment following World War II has resulted not from a belated reading of *Wealth of Nations* but from the much more powerful tendency for what serves the needs of large enterprises to become sound public policy.

But if time and the revolution that he helped set in motion have overtaken Smith's system and Smith's advice, there is one further respect in which he remains wonderfully relevant. That is in the example he sets for professional economists — for what, at the moment, is a troubled, rather saddened discipline. Smith is not a prophet for our time, but, as we have seen, he was magnificently in touch with his own time. He broke with the mercantilist orthodoxy to bring economic ideas abreast of the industrial and agricultural changes that were only then just visible on the horizon. His writing in relation to the Industrial Revolution involved both prophecy and self-fulfilling prophecy. He sensed, even if he did not fully see, what was about to come, and he greatly helped to make it come.

The instinct of the economist, now as never before, is to remain with the past. On that, there is a doctrine, a theory — one that is now wonderfully refined. And there are practical advantages. An economist's capital lies in what he knows — sometimes what he learned in graduate school. Or he has investment in a textbook. To adhere to and articulate the accepted view protects this investment. It also keeps a scholar clear of controversy, something that is usually regarded as a trifle uncouth or indecent. To stay with what is accepted is also consistent with the good life — with the fur-lined comfort of the daily routine between suburb, classroom, and office. To this blandishment, economists are no more immune than other people. The tragedy lies in their resulting obsolescence. As the economic world changes, that proceeds relentlessly, and it is a painful thing.

Remarkably, the same institution, the corporation, which helped to take the

economic world away from Adam Smith, has, in its explosive development in modern times, taken it away from the mature generation of present-day economists. As even economists in their nonprofessional life concede, the modern corporation controls prices and costs, organizes suppliers, persuades consumers, guides the Pentagon, shapes public opinion, buys presidents, and is otherwise a dominant influence in the state. It also, alas, in its modern and comprehensively powerful form, figures not at all in the accepted economic theory. That theory still holds the business firm to be solely subordinate to the market, solely subject to the authority of the state, and ultimately the passive servant of the sovereign citizen. There is no ITT in the system. So there is no control of prices, no weapons culture, no dangerously laggard industries, no deeply endemic inequality — there is only incidental damage to the environment arising from minor and hitherto uncelebrated defects (what are called external diseconomies) in the price system. To have to lose touch with reality is the tragedy. And matters are made worse by a younger generation of scholars that accepts and explores the problem of economic power and struggles, sometimes rather crudely, to come to terms with it. Older scholars are left with the barren hope that they can somehow consolidate their forces and thus exclude the threat. It is a fate that calls less for criticism than for compassion.

It is not a fate that Adam Smith would have suffered. Given his avid empiricism, his deep commitment to reality, his profound concern for practical reform, he would have made the modern corporation and its power, and the related power of the unions and the state, an integral part of his theoretical system. His problem would have been different. With his contempt for theoretical pretense, his intense interest in practical questions, he might have had trouble getting tenure in a first-rate modern university.

The First Feminist

In 1792 Mary Wollstonecraft wrote
a book to prove that her sex was as intelligent
as the other: thus did feminism
come into the world. Right on, Ms. Mary!

SHIRLEY TOMKIEVICZ

The first person—male or female—to speak at any length and to any effect about woman's rights was Mary Wollstonecraft. In 1792, when her *Vindication of the Rights of Woman* appeared, Mary was a beautiful spinster of thirty-three who had made a successful career for herself in the publishing world of London. This accomplishment was rare enough for a woman in that day. Her manifesto, at once impassioned and learned, was an achievement of real originality. The book electrified the reading public and made Mary famous. The core of its argument is simple: "I wish to see women neither heroines nor brutes; but reasonable creatures," Mary wrote. This ancestress of the Women's Liberation Movement did not demand day-care centers or an end to woman's traditional role as wife and mother, nor did she call anyone a chauvinist pig. The happiest period of Mary's own life was when she was married and awaiting the birth of her second child. And the greatest delight she ever knew was in her first child, an illegitimate daughter. Mary's feminism may not appear today to be the hard-core revolutionary variety, but she did live, for a time, a scandalous and unconventional life—"emancipated," it is called by those who have never tried it. The essence of her thought, however, is simply that a woman's mind is as good as a man's.

Not many intelligent men could be found to dispute this proposition today, at least not in mixed company. In Mary's time, to speak of *anybody's* rights, let alone woman's rights, was a radical act. In England, as in other nations, "rights" were an entity belonging to the government. The common run of mankind had little access to what we now call "human rights." As an example of British justice in the late eighteenth century, the law cited two hundred different capital crimes, among them shoplifting. An accused man was not entitled to counsel. A child could be tried and hanged as soon as an adult. The right to vote existed, certainly, but because of unjust apportionment, it had come to mean little. In the United States some of these abuses had been corrected—but the rights of man did not extend past the color bar and the masculine gender was intentional. In the land of Washington and Jefferson, as in the land of George III, human rights were a new idea and woman's rights were not even an issue.

In France, in 1792, a Revolution in the name of equality was in full course, and woman's rights had at least been alluded to. The Revolutionary government drew up plans for female education—to the age of eight. "The education of the women should always be relative to the men," Rousseau had written in *Emile*. "To please, to be useful to us, to make us love and esteem them, to educate us when young, and take care of us when grown up, to advise, to console us, to render our lives easy and agreeable: these are the duties of women at all times, and what they should be taught in their infancy." And, less prettily, "Women have, or ought to have, but little liberty."

Rousseau would have found little cause for complaint in eighteenth-century England. An Englishwoman had almost the same civil status as an American slave. Thomas Hardy, a hundred years hence, was to base a novel on the idea of a man casually selling his wife and daughter at public auction. Obviously this was not a common occurrence, but neither is it wholly implausible. In 1792, and later, a woman could not own property, nor keep any earned wages. All that she possessed belonged to her husband. She could not divorce him, but he could divorce her and take her children. There was no law to say she could not grow up illiterate or be beaten every day.

Such was the legal and moral climate in which Mary Wollstonecraft lived. She was born in London in the spring of 1759, the second child and first daughter of Edward Wollstonecraft, a prosperous weaver. Two more daughters and two more sons were eventually born into the family, making six children in all. Before they had all arrived, Mr. Wollstonecraft came into an inheritance and decided to move his family to the country and become a gentleman farmer. But this plan failed. His money dwindled, and he began drinking heavily. His wife turned into a terrified wraith whose only interest was her eldest son, Edward. Only he escaped the beatings and abuse that his father dealt out regularly to every other household member, from Mrs. Wollstonecraft to the family dog. As often happens in large and disordered families, the eldest sister had to assume the role of mother and scullery maid. Mary was a bright, strong child, determined not to be broken, and she undertook her task energetically, defying her father when he was violent and keeping her younger brothers and sisters in hand. Clearly, Mary held the household together, and in so doing forfeited her own childhood. This experience left her with an everlasting gloomy streak, and was a strong factor in making her a reformer.

At some point in Mary's childhood, another injustice was visited upon her, though so commonplace for the time that she can hardly have felt the sting. Her elder brother was sent away to be educated, and the younger children were left to learn their letters as best they could. The family now frequently changed lodgings, but from her ninth to her fifteenth year Mary went to a day school, where she had the only formal training of her life. Fortunately, this included French and composition, and somewhere Mary learned to read critically and widely. These skills, together with her curiosity and determination, were really all she needed. The *Vindication* is in some parts long-winded, ill-punctuated, and simply full of hot air, but it is the work of a well-informed mind.

Feminists—and Mary would gladly have claimed the title—inevitably, even deservedly, get bad notices. The term calls up an image of relentless battle-axes: "thin college ladies with eye-glasses, no-nonsense features, mouths thin as bologna slicers, a babe in one arm, a hatchet in the other, grey eyes

bright with balefire," as Norman Mailer feelingly envisions his antagonists in the Women's Liberation Movement. He has conjured up all the horrid elements: the lips with a cutting edge, the baby immaculately conceived (one is forced to conclude), the lethal weapon tightly clutched, the desiccating college degree, the joylessness. Hanging miasmally over the tableau is the suspicion of a deformed sexuality. Are these girls man-haters, or worse? Mary Wollstonecraft, as the first of her line, has had each of these scarlet letters (except the B.A.) stitched upon her bosom. Yet she conformed very little to the hateful stereotype. In at least one respect, however, she would have chilled Mailer's bones. Having spent her childhood as an adult, Mary reached the age of nineteen in a state of complete joylessness. She was later to quit the role, but for now she wore the garb of a martyr.

Her early twenties were spent in this elderly frame of mind. First she went out as companion to an old lady living at Bath, and was released from this servitude only by a call to nurse the dying Mrs. Wollstonecraft. Then the family broke up entirely, though the younger sisters continued off and on to be dependent on Mary. The family of Mary's dearest friend, Fanny Blood, invited her to come and stay with them; the two girls made a small living doing sewing and handicrafts, and Mary dreamed of starting a primary school. Eventually, in a pleasant village called Newington Green, this plan materialized and prospered. But Fanny Blood in the meantime had married and moved to Lisbon. She wanted Mary to come and nurse her through the birth of her first child. Mary reached Lisbon just in time to see her friend die of child-bed fever, and returned home just in time to find that her sisters, in whose care the flourishing little school had been left, had lost all but two pupils.

Mary made up her mind to die. "My constitution is impaired, I hope I shan't live long," she wrote to a friend in

February, 1786. Under this almost habitual grief, however, Mary was gaining some new sense of herself. Newington Green, apart from offering her a brief success as a schoolmistress, had brought her some acquaintance in the world of letters, most important among them, Joseph Johnson, an intelligent and successful London publisher in search of new writers. Debt-ridden and penniless, Mary set aside her impaired constitution and wrote her first book, probably in the space of a week. Johnson bought it for ten guineas and published it. Called *Thoughts on the Education of Daughters*, it went unnoticed, and the ten guineas was soon spent. Mary had to find work. She accepted a position as governess in the house of Lord and Lady Kingsborough in the north of Ireland.

Mary's letters from Ireland to her sisters and to Joseph Johnson are so filled with Gothic gloom, so stained with tears, that one cannot keep from laughing at them. "I entered the great gates with the same kind of feeling I should have if I was going to the Bastille," she wrote upon entering Kingsborough Castle in the fall of 1786. Mary was now twenty-seven. Her most recent biographer, Margaret George, believes that Mary was not really suffering so much as she was having literary fantasies. In private she was furiously at work on a novel entitled, not very artfully, *Mary, A Fiction*. This is the story of a young lady of immense sensibilities who closely resembles Mary except that she has wealthy parents, a neglectful bridegroom, and an attractive lover. The title and fantasizing contents are precisely what a scribbler of thirteen might secretly concoct. Somehow Mary was embarking on her adolescence—with all its daydreams—fifteen years after the usual date. Mary's experience in Kingsborough Castle was a fruitful one, for all her complaints. In the summer of 1787 she lost her post as governess and set off for

London with her novel. Not only did Johnson accept it for publication, he offered her a regular job as editor and translator and helped her find a place to live.

Thus, aged twenty-eight, Mary put aside her doleful persona as the martyred, set-upon elder sister. How different she is now, jauntily writing from London to her sisters: "Mr. Johnson . . . assures me that if I exert my talents in writing I may support myself in a comfortable way. I am then going to be the first of a new genus . . ." Now Mary discovered the sweetness of financial independence earned by interesting work. She had her own apartment. She was often invited to Mr. Johnson's dinner parties, usually as the only female guest among all the most interesting men in London: Joseph Priestley, Thomas Paine, Henry Fuseli, William Blake, Thomas Christie, William Godwin—all of them up-and-coming scientists or poets or painters or philosophers, bound together by left-wing political views. Moreover, Mary was successful in her own writing as well as in editorial work. Her *Original Stories for Children* went into three editions and was illustrated by Blake. Johnson and his friend Thomas Christie had started a magazine called the *Analytical Review*, to which Mary became a regular contributor.

But—lest anyone imagine an elegantly dressed Mary presiding flirtatiously at Johnson's dinner table—her social accomplishments were rather behind her professional ones. Johnson's circle looked upon her as one of the boys. "Wollstonecraft" is what William Godwin calls her in his diary. One of her later detractors reported that she was at this time a "philosophic sloven," in a dreadful old dress and beaver hat, "with her hair hanging lank about her shoulders." Mary had yet to arrive at her final incarnation, but the new identity was imminent, if achieved by an odd route. Edmund Burke had recently published his *Reflections on the Revolution in France,* and the book had enraged Mary. The statesman who so readily supported the quest for liberty in the American colonies had his doubts about events in France.

Mary's reply to Burke, *A Vindication of the Rights of Men,* astounded London, partly because she was hitherto unknown, partly because it was good. Mary proved to be an excellent polemicist, and she had written in anger. She accused Burke, the erstwhile champion of liberty, of being "the champion of property." "Man preys on man," said she, "and you mourn for the idle tapestry that decorated a gothic pile and the dronish bell that summoned the fat priest to prayer." The book sold well. Mary moved into a better apartment and bought some pretty dresses—no farthingales, of course, but some of the revolutionary new "classical" gowns. She put her auburn hair up in a loose knot. Her days as a philosophic sloven were over.

Vindication of the Rights of Woman was her next work. In its current edition it runs to 250-odd pages; Mary wrote it in six weeks. *Vindication* is no prose masterpiece, but it has never failed to arouse its audience, in one way or another. Horace Walpole unintentionally set the style for the book's foes. Writing to his friend Hannah More in August, 1792, he referred to Thomas Paine and to Mary as "philosophizing serpents" and was "glad to hear you have not read the tract of the last mentioned writer. I would not look at it." Neither would many another of Mary's assailants, the most virulent of whom, Ferdinand Lundberg, surfaced at the late date of 1947 with a tract of his own, *Modern Woman, the Lost Sex.* Savagely misogynistic as it is, this book was hailed in its time as "the best book yet to be written about women." Lundberg calls Mary the Karl Marx of the feminist movement, and the *Vindication* a "fateful book," to which "the tenets of feminism, which have undergone no change to our day, may be traced." Very well, but then, recounting Mary's life with the maximum possible number of errors per line, he warns us that she was "an extreme neurotic of a compulsive type" who "wanted to turn on men and injure them." In one respect, at least, Mr. Lundberg hits the mark: he blames Mary for starting women in the pernicious habit of wanting an education. In the nineteenth century, he relates, English and American feminists were hard at work. "Following Mary Wollstonecraft's prescription, they made a considerable point about acquiring a higher education." This is precisely Mary's prescription, and the most dangerous idea in her fateful book.

"Men complain and with reason, of the follies and caprices of our Sex," she writes in Chapter 1. "Behold, I should answer, the natural effect of ignorance." Women, she thinks, are usually so mindless as to be scarcely fit for their roles as wives and mothers. Nevertheless, she believes this state not to be part of the feminine nature, but the result of an equally mindless oppression, as demoralizing for men as for women. If a woman's basic mission is as a wife and mother, need she be an illiterate slave for this?

The heart of the work is Mary's attack on Rousseau. In *Emile* Rousseau had set forth some refreshing new ideas for the education of little boys. But women, he decreed, are tools for pleasure, creatures too base for moral or political or educational privilege. Mary recognized that this view was destined to shut half the human race out of all hope for political freedom. *Vindication* is a plea that the "rights of men" ought to mean the "rights of humanity." The human right that she held highest was the right to have a mind and think with it. Virginia Woolf, who lived through a time of feminist activity, thought that the *Vindication* was a work so true "as to seem to contain nothing new." Its originality, she wrote, rather too optimistically, had become a commonplace.

Vindication went quickly into a second edition. Mary's name was soon known all over Europe. But as she savored her fame—and she did savor it—she found that the edge was wearing off and that she was rather lonely. So far as anyone knows, Mary had reached this point in her life without ever having had a love affair. Johnson was the only man she was close to, and he was, as she wrote him, "A father, or a brother—you have been both to me." Mary was often now in the company of the Swiss painter Henry Fuseli, and suddenly she developed what she thought was a Platonic passion in his direction. He rebuffed her, and in the winter of 1792 she went to Paris, partly to escape her embarrassment but also because she wanted to observe the workings of the Revolution firsthand.

Soon after her arrival, as she collected notes for the history of the Revolution she hoped to write, Mary saw Louis XVI, "sitting in a hackney coach . . . going to meet death." Back in her room that evening, she wrote to Mr. Johnson of seeing "eyes glare through a glass door opposite my chair and bloody hands shook at me . . . I am going to bed and for the first time in my life, I cannot put out the candle." As the weeks went on, Edmund Burke's implacable critic began to lose her faith in the brave new world. "The aristocracy of birth is levelled to the ground, only to make room for that of riches," she wrote. By February France and England were at war, and British subjects classified as enemy aliens.

Though many Englishmen were arrested, Mary and a large English colony stayed on. One day in spring, some friends presented her to an attractive American, newly arrived in Paris, Gilbert Imlay. Probably about four years Mary's senior, Imlay, a former officer

in the Continental Army, was an explorer and adventurer. He came to France seeking to finance a scheme for seizing Spanish lands in the Mississippi valley. This "natural and unaffected creature," as Mary was later to describe him, was probably the social lion of the moment, for he was also the author of a best-selling novel called *The Emigrants*, a farfetched account of life and love in the American wilderness. He and Mary soon became lovers. They were a seemingly perfect pair. Imlay must have been pleased with his famous catch, and—dear, liberated girl that she was—Mary did not insist upon marriage. Rather the contrary. But fearing that she was in danger as an Englishwoman, he registered her at the American embassy as his wife.

Blood was literally running in the Paris streets now, so Mary settled down by herself in a cottage at Neuilly. Imlay spent his days in town, working out various plans. The Mississippi expedition came to nothing, and he decided to stay in France and go into the import-export business, part of his imports being gunpowder and other war goods run from Scandinavia through the English blockade. In the evenings he would ride out to the cottage. By now it was summer, and Mary, who spent the days writing, would often stroll up the road to meet him, carrying a basket of freshly-gathered grapes.

A note she wrote Imlay that summer shows exactly what her feelings for him were: "You can scarcely imagine with what pleasure I anticipate the day when we are to begin almost to live together; and you would smile to hear how many plans of employment I have in my head, now that I am confident that my heart has found peace . . ." Soon she was pregnant. She and Imlay moved into Paris. He promised to take her to America, where they would settle down on a farm and raise six children. But business called Imlay to Le Havre, and his stay lengthened ominously into weeks.

Imlay's letters to Mary have not survived, and without them it is hard to gauge what sort of man he was and what he really thought of his adoring mistress. Her biographers like to make him out a cad, a philistine, not half good enough for Mary. Perhaps; yet the two must have had something in common. His novel, unreadable though it is now, shows that he shared her political views, including her feminist ones. He may never have been serious about the farm in America, but he was a miserably long time deciding to leave Mary alone. Though they were seprated during the early months of her pregnancy, he finally did bring her to Le Havre, and continued to live with her there until the child was born and for some six months afterward. The baby arrived in May, 1794, a healthy little girl, whom Mary named Fanny after her old friend. Mary was proud that her delivery had been easy, and as for Fanny, Mary loved her instantly. "My little Girl," she wrote to a friend, "begins to suck so manfully that her father reckons saucily on her writing the second part of the Rights of Woman." Mary's joy in this child illuminates almost every letter she wrote henceforth.

Fanny's father was the chief recipient of these letters with all the details of the baby's life. To Mary's despair, she and Imlay hardly ever lived together again. A year went by; Imlay was now in London and Mary in France. She offered to break it off, but mysteriously, he could not let go. In the last bitter phase of their involvement, after she had joined him in London at his behest, he even sent her—as "Mrs. Imlay"—on a complicated business errand to the Scandinavian countries. Returning to London, Mary discovered that he was living with another woman. By now half crazy with humiliation, Mary chose a dark night and threw herself in the Thames. She was nearly dead when two rivermen pulled her from the water.

Though this desperate incident was almost the end of Mary, at least it was the end of the Imlay episode. He sent a doctor to care for her, but they rarely met again. Since Mary had no money, she set about providing for herself and Fanny in the way she knew. The faithful Johnson had already brought out Volume I of her history of the French Revolution. Now she set to work editing and revising her *Letters Written during a Short Residence in Sweden, Norway, and Denmark,* a kind of thoughtful travelogue. The book was well received and widely translated.

And it also revived the memory of Mary Wollstonecraft in the mind of an old acquaintance, William Godwin. As the author of the treatise *Political Justice,* he was now as famous a philosophizing serpent as Mary and was widely admired and hated as a "freethinker." He came to call on Mary. They became friends and then lovers. Early in 1797 Mary was again pregnant. William Godwin was an avowed atheist who had publicly denounced the very institution of marriage. On March 29, 1797, he nevertheless went peaceably to church with Mary and made her his wife.

The Godwins were happy together, however William's theories may have been outraged. He adored his small stepdaughter and took pride in his brilliant wife. Awaiting the birth of her child throughout the summer, Mary worked on a new novel and made plans for a book on "the management of infants"—it would have been the first "Dr. Spock." She expected to have another easy delivery and promised to come downstairs to dinner the day following. But when labor began, on August 30, it proved to be long and agonizing. A daughter, named Mary Wollstonecraft, was born; ten days later, the mother died.

Occasionally, when a gifted writer dies young, one can feel, as in the example of Shelley, that perhaps he had at any rate accomplished his best work. But so recently had Mary come into her full intellectual and emotional growth that her death at the age of thirty-eight is bleak indeed. There is no knowing what Mary might have accomplished now that she enjoyed domestic stability. Perhaps she might have achieved little or nothing further as a writer. But she might have been able to protect her daughters from some part of the sadness that overtook them; for as things turned out, both Fanny and Mary were to sacrifice themselves.

Fanny grew up to be a shy young girl, required to feel grateful for the roof over her head, overshadowed by her prettier half sister, Mary. Godwin in due course married a formidable widow named Mrs. Clairmont, who brought her own daughter into the house—the Claire Clairmont who grew up to become Byron's mistress and the mother of his daughter Allegra. Over the years Godwin turned into a hypocrite and a miser who nevertheless continued to pose as the great liberal of the day. Percy Bysshe Shelley, born the same year that the *Vindication of the Rights of Woman* was published, came to be a devoted admirer of Mary Wollstonecraft's writing. As a young man he therefore came with his wife to call upon Godwin. What he really sought, however, were Mary's daughters—because they were her daughters. First he approached Fanny, but later changed his mind. Mary Godwin was then sixteen, the perfect potential soul mate for a man whose needs for soul mates knew no bounds. They conducted their courtship in the most up-to-the-minute romantic style: beneath a tree near her mother's grave they read aloud to each other from the *Vindication.* Soon they eloped, having pledged their "troth" in the cemetery. Godwin, the celebrated freethinker, was enraged. To make matters worse, Claire Clairmont had run off to Switzerland with them.

Not long afterward Fanny, too, ran away. She went to an inn in a distant town and drank a fatal dose of laudanum. It has traditionally been said that unrequited love for Shelley drove her to this pass, but there is no evidence one way or the other. One suicide that can more justly be laid at Shelley's door is that of his first wife, which occurred a month after Fanny's and which at any rate left him free to wed his mistress, Mary Godwin. Wife or mistress, she had to endure poverty, ostracism, and Percy's constant infidelities. But now at last her father could, and did, boast to his relations that he was father-in-law to a baronet's son. "Oh, philosophy!" as Mary Godwin Shelley remarked.

If in practice Shelley was merely a womanizer, on paper he was a convinced feminist. He had learned this creed from Mary Wollstonecraft. Through his verse Mary's ideas began to be disseminated. They were one part of that vast tidal wave of political, social, and artistic revolution that arose in the late eighteenth century, the romantic movement. But because of Mary's unconventional way of life, her name fell into disrepute during the nineteenth century, and her book failed to exert its rightful influence on the development of feminism. Emma Willard and other pioneers of the early Victorian period indignantly refused to claim Mary as their forebear. Elizabeth Cady Stanton and Lucretia Mott were mercifully less strait-laced on the subject. In 1889, when Mrs. Stanton and Susan B. Anthony published their *History of Woman Suffrage,* they dedicated the book to Mary. Though Mary Wollstonecraft can in no sense be said to have founded the woman's rights movement, she was, by the late nineteenth century, recognized as its inspiration, and the *Vindication* was vindicated for the highly original work it was, a landmark in the history of society.

Freudian Myths
and
Freudian Realities

Peter F. Drucker

If Sigmund Freud had not been so visible and prominent in the Vienna of my childhood, I would never have paid attention to the glaring discrepancy between the Freudian myths and the Freudian realities.

My parents had both known Freud for many years. But Freud was more than twenty years older than my father. And so my father would bow with great respect when he encountered Freud on the paths around the Alpine lake on which the Freuds had their summer villa, next to Genia Schwarzwald's resort. And Freud would bow back. My mother had had an interest in psychiatry as a medical student, and had worked for a year in the Psychiatric Clinic in Zurich headed by Bleuler, a psychiatrist whom Freud greatly respected. She had bought Freud's books as a young woman, well before her marriage. I own her copy of the first edition, dated 1900, of *Die Traumdeutung (The Interpretation of Dreams)*—one of the pitiful 351 copies which was all the first edition sold—and her copy of the definitive 1907 edition of *Zur Psychopathologie des Alltagslebens (Psychopathology of Everyday Life)* with its famous analysis of the "Freudian slips"—both with bookmarks still in my mother's maiden name. Before her marriage, she also attended one of his lecture series, whether at the University or at the Psychoanalytic Society I do not know, where she apparently was the only woman; she used to recount with some amusement how her presence embarrassed Freud in discussing sex and sexual problems.

I myself had been introduced to Dr. Freud when I was eight or nine years old. One of Genia Schwarzwald's co-op restaurants during World War I was in the Berggasse, next to the Freud apartment. In those hunger years in Vienna Dr. Freud and his family sometimes ate lunch there—and so did we. On one of those days the Freuds' and we sat at the same table. Dr. Freud recognized my parents and I was presented and asked to shake hands.

But this was my only contact with Dr. Freud. And the only reason why I even remember it when I have, of course, forgotten all the other adults with whom I had to shake hands as a boy, is that my parents afterwards said to me: "Remember today; you have just met the most important man in Austria, and perhaps in Europe." This was apparently before the end of the war, for I asked, "More important than the Emperor?" "Yes," said my father, "more important than the Emperor." And this so impressed me that I remembered it, even though I was still quite a small child.

This is the point. My parents were not disciples of Freud—indeed, my mother was quite critical of both the man and his theories. But they still knew that he was "the most important man in Austria and perhaps in Europe."

Three "facts" about Sigmund Freud's life are accepted without question by most people, especially in the English-speaking world: That all his life Freud lived with serious financial worries and in near-poverty; that he suffered greatly from anti-Semitism and was denied full recognition and the university appointments that were his due, because he was a Jew; and that the Vienna of his day, especially medical Vienna, ignored and neglected Freud.

All three of these "facts" are pure myths. Even as a youngster Freud was well-to-do; and from the beginning of his professional life as a young doctor he made good money. He never suffered from discrimination as a Jew until Hitler drove him into exile at the very end of his life. He received official recognition and academic honors not only earlier than almost any person in Austrian medical history; he received at an early age honors and recognition to which, according to the fairly strict Austrian canon, he was not entitled at all. Above all, medical Vienna did not ignore or neglect Freud. It took him most seriously. No one was discussed as much, studied as much, or argued about more. Medical

2. CULTURAL FERMENT OF THE WEST

Vienna did not ignore or neglect Freud, it *rejected* him. It rejected him as a person because it held him to be in gross violation of the ethics of the healer. And it rejected his theory as a glittering half-truth, and as poetry rather than medical science or therapy.

The myths about Freud and his life in Vienna of his days would be trivial and quite irrelevant to the man and to psychoanalytic theory but for one fact: Freud himself believed them. Indeed he invented them and publicized them. In his letters, above all, these myths are stressed again and again. And it was in his letters that the proud, disciplined, and very private man unburdened himself of his own concerns. These myths, in other words, were extremely important to Freud himself. But why?

Freud was a stoic who never complained, abhorred self-pity, and detested whiners. He bore great physical pain without a sound of complaint. And he was equally stoical about sufferings in his private and family life. But he complains incessantly about imaginary sufferings—lack of money, anti-Semitic discrimination, and being ignored by the Viennese physicians.

Freud was in everything else ruthlessly candid, above all with himself. He was merciless in his own self-examination and tore out root and branch what to an ordinary mortal would have been harmless self-indulgence. It is inconceivable that Freud could have knowingly created and propagated fairy tales and myths about himself. But it seems equally inconceivable that Freud could not have been known that these assertions and complaints were not "facts," but pure myths. Everyone else in the Vienna of Freud's time knew it and commented on Freud's strange "obsessions."

The only answer is a Freudian one: these myths are "Freudian slips." They are symptoms of deep existential realities and traumas that Freud could not face despite his self-analysis, his uncompromising truthfulness, his stoic self-discipline. And it is Freud who has taught us that "Freudian slips" are never trivial. The Freud of official legend is a stern monolithic god—a Zeus on Olympus or an Old Testament Jehovah. The Freud of his own "Freudian slips" is a tormented Prometheus. And it was Prometheus who of all the gods of classical mythology is mentioned most often in Freud's works.

The Freuds were not "Rothschild-rich," to use the Viennese term for the super-rich. They were comfortable middle class. Freud's father was a fairly successful merchant. In the Vienna of Freud's youth—he was born in 1856, just when the rapid growth of Vienna into a metropolis began—this meant a high-ceilinged apartment in one of the new four- or five-story apartment buildings just outside the old "Inner City": fairly spacious though dark, overcrowded with furniture, and with one bathroom only. It meant two or three servants, a weekly cleaning woman, and a seamstress every month, a summer vacation in a spa near Vienna or in the mountains, Sunday walks in the Vienna Woods for the whole family, high school (Gymnasium) for the children, books, music, and weekly visits to opera and theaters. And this is precisely how the Freuds lived. Freud's brother, Alexander—he published a reference book on railroad freight tariffs for the Ministry of Commerce when my father was the ministry's head—always resented Sigmund's insistence on the dire poverty in which he

grew up as maligning their dead father's memory, "who was such a good provider." All the sons got university educations, he would point out. Young Sigmund was being supported in considerable comfort in Paris for three or four more years of study, even after he had finished both his medical and his speciality training; and the young Freuds always had enough pocket money to buy books and tickets to opera and theater. Of course, they kept no horse and carriage—that was being "Rothschild-rich." But they rented one when they went for their summer vacation to Baden or Voeslau, the two popular spas near Vienna. And from the day on which Freud went into practice after his return from Paris, he had patients. For his skill in treating neuroses was immediately recognized.

But he also received official recognition very early. The title "Professor" given to an Austrian physician was a license to coin money; the holder automatically tripled or quadrupled his fees. For that reason alone, it was almost never given to a physician before he was in his late fifties. Freud had it in his late forties. A firm rule reserved this title to the medical directors of major hospitals as a way to compensate them for the substantial income they gave up in treating hospital and charity patients for free. Freud received the title, even though he held no hospital appointment and treated only private and paying patients.

But what of his oft-repeated complaint about "anti-Semitic discrimination," in that he was not going to have the title of "full professor" but only that of "extraordinary" or "associate professor" when offered the chair of neurology at the University's medical school? The fact is that the university chairs at the medical school were established by law and required an act of Parliament for any change. The only clinical chairs in the medical school that carried a "full professorship" were the ones in the "old," i.e., eighteenth-century disciplines—in internal medicine, obstetrics, and surgery. Every other chair was an "extraordinary professorship." Any such professor who headed a university hospital, such as the neurological unit that was offered to Freud—again at an earlier age than a university hospital had been offered to a Viennese physician before—received, however, within a year or two, the "personal" rank and title of "full professor." Freud was going to receive it too, had he accepted the offer instead of turning it down and then complaining that "anti-Semitism" had denied him a full professorship.

However strong anti-Semitism was becoming among the small shopkeepers and craftsmen of Vienna in the late 1800s, it was frowned upon at the Imperial court, in the government service, among "educated" people, and above all in the Viennese medical community. In the very years of Freud's professional growth, from 1880 through 1900 or so, the majority of the leadership positions in Viennese medicine were taken over by men who were Jews, if not by religion, then by birth. In 1881, at the time when Freud started on his professional career, more than 60 percent of Veinna's physicians were already Jewish, according to C. A. McCartney, the leading historian of Austria-Hungary. By 1900, Jews held the great majority of clinical chairs at the University's medical school, of the medical directorships in the major hospitals, and such positions as surgeon-general of the Army, personal physician to the Emperor, and obstetrician to the ladies of the Imperial family. "Anti-Semitism" was not the reason why Freud did not have the professorship in neurology; it played altogether no role in his practice, in his standing in official medicine, or in his acceptance by a Viennese medical community that was as Jewish as he was.

Indeed a main reason why this Viennese medical community found Freud unacceptable was that it was Jewish. For the first criticism of Freud, voiced even by believers in psychoanalysis, was always that Freud violated the basic Jewish ethics of the healer. Freud did not accept charity patients, but taught instead that the psychoanalyst must not treat a patient for free, and that the patient will benefit from treatment only if made to pay handsomely. This was absolutely "unethical" to the Jewish tradition out of which so many of Vienna's physicians came. There were of course plenty of physicians, Jewish ones included, who were out for the buck. They were called "rippers"—*Reisser.* A physician might have to refer patients to a "ripper" if they needed the special skill of one of them—if, for instance, they suffered from some sort of skin problem or some kind of stomach ailment. But the "rippers" were held in contempt. And even the most outrageous "ripper" would serve as medical director of a hospital or as department head in one of the university clinics, and thus take care of the indigent sick. And all of them, for all their greed, would at least preach the traditional ethic of the healer, the ethic of selfless giving. Not Freud, however: he spurned it. And thus he challenged head-on the deepest, most cherished values of the Jewish tradition of the healer. He made medicine a *trade.* Worse still, the Veinnese doctors came to suspect that Freud might be right. At least for emotional and psychic ailments, insistence by the physician on a good fee was therapeutic and selflessness did damage.

Even more disturbing was Freud's insistence on emotional detachment of physician from patient. The physicians knew of course that the doctor has to learn to be hard-skinned and to get used to suffering, death, and pain. They knew that there were good reasons for the rule that physicians do not treat members of their own families. But central to their creed was the belief that tender, loving care is the one prescription that fits all symptoms. Admittedly, a broken bone would knit without it—though still better with it. But the wounded *person* needed a caring physician above all. And here was Dr. Freud demanding that the physician divest himself of sympathy for—indeed of human interest in— the patient, and that for the physician to become involved with the human being meant damaging the patient, made him or her dependent, and inhibited recovery and cure. Instead of being a brother, the suffering patient became an object.

That however was tantamount to degrading the physician from healer to mechanic. To all those Jewish physicians of Vienna—and not only to the Jewish ones—this was express denial of the very reasons why they had become physicians, and an affront to what they respected in themselves and in their calling. What made this doubly offensive was again that many sus-

pected Freud might be right, at least with respect to psychoanalysis. "But," once said the elder of Vienna's Jewish surgeons at our dinner table—Marcus Hajek, the head of the University's ear, nose, and throat hospital and one of those "extraordinary" professors with the "personal" title of full professor—"if Freud is right, then psychoanalysis is a narcotic; and for a physician knowingly to create addiction—or even the risk thereof—is both a crime and a breach of his sacred duty."

There was even more discussion of psychoanalysis as therapy and scientific method than of its ethics. Freud belonged to the second generation of "modern" medicine in Vienna. "Modern" medicine, after a century or more of slow gestation, had finally emerged fully developed—at Vienna—only a few years before Freud was born. Freud's medical generation was therefore conscious of what had made possible the giant step from "prescientific" medicine—the medicine of the contemptible quacks of Molière's plays—to medicine that could diagnose, could heal, could be learned, and could be taught. And during this generation's own lifetime "modern" medicine had yielded its greatest gains, in the development of bacteriology, for instance, and with it in the capacity to prevent and to treat infectious diseases; in anesthesia that made surgery bearable; or in the antisepsis and asepsis that made surgery possible without killing the patient through subsequent infection.

The fundamental step from quackery to medicine— the step first taken by such revered ancestors as Boerhave in Holland or Sydenham in England around 1700—had been abstention from big theory and from global speculation. Diseases are specific, with specific causes, specific symptoms, and specific cures. The great triumph of the bacteriologist—that is, of Freud's own generation—was precisely that he showed that every infection is specific, each with its specific bacterial cause carried and spread by its own unique carriers, whether flea or mosquito, and each acting in its own specific way on specific tissue. And whenever anyone in the history of modern medicine had forgotten the lesson of Boerhave and Sydenham as, for instance, the homeopathic school of Hahnemann had done (Hahnemann was only recently dead when Freud was born), his teachings immediately degenerated into the quackery of the "humors" and "vapors." Yet here was psychoanalysis, which postulated one universal psychological dynamism for *every* emotional disorder; and many of its practitioners (though not Freud himself) even claimed that many psychoses too were "emotional" rather than "physical," caused by the same forces of ego, id, and superego acting out sexual repression in the subconscious. Around 1900, I was once told, the Vienna Medical Society put on a skit at one of its parties. It was a parody of Molière's *Le Malade Imaginaire* in which the scurrilous quack was made to say: "If the patient loved his mother, it is the reason for this neurosis of his; and if he hated her, it is the reason for the same neurosis. Whatever the disease, the cause is always the same. And whatever the cause, the disease is always the same. So is the cure: twenty one-hour sessions at 50 Kronen each." Of course, that was gross caricature of psychoanalytic theory and practice. But it was close enough to bring the house down; even the psychoanalysts in the audience, I was told by one of them who had been there as a medical student, laughed until the tears came.

But if the basic method was so controversial to anyone familiar with the history of medicine, what about results? The leaders of the medical fraternity had seen enough to know that medicine is not entirely rational and that things do work which no one can explain. Hence their emphasis on demonstrable results and on the controlled test. But when the Viennese physicians asked for the results of psychoanalysis, they found themselves baffled. That Freud himself was a master healer was beyond doubt. But the results of psychoanalysis were something else again. In the first place Freud and the Freudians refused to define "results." Was it restoration of ability to function? Or relief from anxiety? Was psychoanalysis "curing" anybody? If so, what explained the obvious fact that so many of its patients became permanent patients, or at the least came back to the psychoanalyst again and again? Was it alleviation of a chronic condition—and was it then good enough that the patient became addicted to the treatment and "felt better" for it? And however one defined the "results" of this strange therapy, what was the appropriate control to test its results? Every Viennese doctor saw obviously "neurotic" people in his practice; a large number of them got better without any treatment—especially, of course, adolescents. At least the symptoms disappeared or changed quite drastically. What was the natural rate of remissions in neuroses, and how significantly better did the patient of the psychoanalyst do? It was not only that all the data were lacking. The psychoanalysts, beginning with Freud, refused to discuss the question.

And then it seemed that all methods of psychotherapy had the same results, or non-results. There were some rivals in the field by 1910, offsprings of the Freudian school, Alfred Adler, for instance, or Carl Jung. There was also, in Germany, Oskar Kohnstamm—the forerunner of today's "humanist" psychologists, a respected and successful psychotherapist, and totally non-Freudian in his approach in that he stressed the therapist's personal involvement in the life and problems of the patient. But there were also all kinds of assorted faith healers and "consciousness-raisers" around: spiritualists, hypnotists, people with mysterious magnetic boxes, not to mention pilgrimages to Lourdes and Hassidic "miracle rabbis." The studies of the results of psychotherapies which began to be done around 1920 always showed the same results and still do: psychotherapies might have significant results. The data are inconclusive; but no one method has results that are significantly better than or different from any other. This can mean two things: Freud's psychoanalysis is a specific treatment for some, but not for all, emotional disorders; or emotional problems improve or are even cured by having a fuss made over them. Either conclusion was, of course, unacceptable to Freud and the psychoanalysts; it was a rejection of Freud's entire claim.

I recall a discussion of a big study of the results of psychotherapy—again at our dinner table—between Karl Buehler, a moderately pro-Freudian, who taught

psychology at the University (and whose wife, Charlotte, was a Freudian psychoanalyst), and, as I recall it, Oskar Morgenstern, then probably still a student and later, at Princeton, to become the foremost authority on statistical theory. Buehler argued that the results indicated that psychoanalysis is powerful and specific therapy for a fairly wide range of psychic ailments, and that there was need to do research as to what that range encompassed. "Not so," said Morgenstern; "if you go by the figures, then there are either no emotional illnesses at all or the trust of the patient in any method makes the patient feel better, regardless of method." "In either case," said another dinner guest, an eye surgeon, "there is as yet no valid Freudian psychotherapy which a physician can recommend or use in good conscience."

But most bothersome of all for the Viennese physician was that you could never know whether Freud and his disciples talked healing the sick or "art criticism." One minute they were trying to cure a specific ailment, whether fear of crossing the street or impotence. The next moment they were applying the same method, the same vocabulary, the same analysis to Grimm's *Fairy Tales* or *King Lear*. The physicians were perfectly willing to concede that, as Thomas Mann put it in his speech at Freud's eightieth birthday, "Psychoanalysis is the greatest contribution to the art of the novel." Freud as the powerful, imaginative, stimulating critic of culture and literature, of religion and art, was one thing; it was readily conceded by a good many that he had opened a window on the soul that had long been nailed shut. This is what made him "the most important man in Austria." But was psychoanalysis then likely to be therapy, any more than were Newton's physics or Kant's metaphysics or Goethe's aesthetics? Yet this was precisely what Freud and his followers claimed. It was a claim the Viennese physicians, by and large, could not accept.

Freud himself was deeply hurt by any hint that his theory was "poetry" rather than "science." He is known to have bitterly resented Thomas Mann's birthday speech even though he himself had asked Mann to be the speaker. But, of course, whatever the validity of psychoanalysis as science, Freud was a very great artist. He was probably the greatest writer of German prose in this century—it is so clear, so simple, so precise as to be as untranslatable as first-rate poetry. His anonymous case histories portray a whole person in two paragraphs better than many long novels, including, I would say, those of Thomas Mann himself. The terms he coined—whether "anal" and "oral" or "ego" and "superego"—are great poetic imagery. Yet this made "scientific medicine" only more uncomfortable, while praising Freud as a poet and artist infuriated him and his followers.

All these things were being discussed and debated endlessly even in my childhood, and far more so, I believe, in earlier years, in the years between 1890 and 1910 when Freud's great books came out and when he moved from being a first-rate neurologist with remarkable clinical results, especially with women, to becoming the leader of a "movement." Again and again the questions came up: of Freud's ethics and of the ethics of psychoanalysis; of its results and how they should be judged or measured; and of the compatibility of cosmic philosophy and clinical therapy. One thing is crystal clear: Freud was not ignored. He was taken very seriously and then rejected.

The emergence of psychoanalysis is often explained, especially in America, as a reaction to the "Victorian repression of sex." Maybe there was such "repression" in America but it is even doubtful whether there was any such phenomenon in England, except for a few short years. It did not exist in the Austria in which young Sigmund Freud grew up and in which he started to practice. On the contrary, late-nineteenth-century Vienna was sexually permissive and sex flourished openly everywhere. The symbol of Freud's Vienna was Johann Strauss's comic opera *Die Fledermaus (The Bat)*, which had its first performance in 1874 when Freud was eighteen. It is an opera of lover-swapping and open sexual pairing in which the wife jumps into the arms of her old boyfriend the moment she thinks her husband is out of the way; in which the maid, one of the main stars, sneaks off to the masked ball to pick up a rich sugar-daddy who will set her up as his mistress and finance her theatrical career; in which another main character—Prince Orlofsky, who gives the ball where all this takes place—is a homosexual whose main aria, in which he invites his guests to love "each to his own taste," must have been understood by every adult in the audience as "gay liberation." This plot might not be "X-rated" should it come up for approval now; but it certainly would not be classed as healthy family fare. Yet it was set in the resort in which the prudish Austrian Emperor spent his summers rather than in some mythical never-never land. And no one was shocked!

The popular playwright a little later, in the Vienna of the 1880s and 1890s, was Freud's former fellow medical student, Artur Schnitzler, whose best-known and most popular play *La Ronde (Der Reigen)* can be described as a game of musical beds, in which everything but the sex act itself takes place on stage.

To be sure, a woman was not supposed to have affairs before her marriage—though it was the fear of unwanted pregnancy far more than morality that underlay that rule. She married young, of course; but then she was on her own, and only expected to be reasonably discreet. And that no restriction on premarital sex was applied to men was not so much because of the "double standard"—though it did exist—as because men had to postpone marriage until they could support a wife and children, and no one had the slightest illusion that they would remain chaste until then, or that such abstinence would be desirable.

Indeed what created sexual anxieties in so many of the middle-class women, and especially the Jewish middle-class women who were Freud's early patients, was Vienna's openness of sex and its sexually supercharged atmosphere. These women came, for the most part, from the ghettos of small Jewish towns, like the Freuds themselves, whose roots were in one of the small Jewish settlements in Moravia—now a part of Czechoslovakia. In these small ghettos, sex was indeed repressed—for both men and women. Marriages were arranged by a middleman when both bride and groom were children. They married as soon as they reached sexual maturity—and until then they had never seen

each other. From then on, the woman lived a domestic life in which she saw her family but few other people, and no men. Sex was deemphasized—in the synagogue, in the family, in the community. But out of this sexless atmosphere the young Jewish woman was, as the century wore on, increasingly projected without preparation into the erotic whirlpool of Vienna, with its constant balls, its waltzes, its intense sexual competition, its demand that she prove herself sexually all the time, that she be "attractive" and attract, and that she be "sexy." No wonder that these women suffered anxieties and became neurotic over their sex life and sexual roles. Freud himself never referred to the alleged "sexual repression" of Viennese society. That explanation came much later and is, incidentally, of American manufacture. No Viennese would have fallen for it.

Freud was, clearly, not in favor of "sexual freedom." He would have repudiated paternity for the sexual liberation of this century that is so often ascribed to him. He was a puritan and suspected that sex, while inevitable, was not really good for the human race. As for the claim that men have made women into "sex objects," he would have thought it a very poor joke. He was familiar with the old Jewish legend of the evil Lilith, Adam's second wife, and considered it symbolic truth. Lilith seduces Adam away from Eve and makes a sex object out of the male by changing woman into the one female among the higher animals that is at all times sexually available—whereas the females of other higher animals are in heat only a few days each month and are otherwise sexless for all practical purposes. Altogether the Freudian sex drives that create repression and neuroses are independent of culture and mores; they are structured into the relationship between adults and children rather than into the relationships between the sexes in a particular society.

Still, in the Freudian literature a constant theme is sexual anxiety, sexual frustration, sexual malfunction. But the one neurosis that is stressed in every other record of late-nineteenth-century Vienna—or indeed late-nineteenth-century Europe—is totally absent: the money neurosis. It was not sex that was repressed in Freud's Vienna. It was money. Money had come to dominate; but money had also come to be unmentionable. Early in the century, in Jane Austen's novels, money is open—almost the first thing Jane Austen tells the reader is how much annual income everybody has. Seventy-five years later, by the time young Freud begins his adult life, the novelist's characters are consumed with concern for money and wealth—and never discuss it. Dickens still talks about money quite openly, just as he talks about sex quite openly, about illegitimate children and illicit liaisons, about the haunts of vice and the training of young girls to be prostitutes. Trollope, only three years Dickens's junior but already a "mid-Victorian," is still fairly explicit about sex—far more explicit than a "proper Victorian" is supposed to be. Yet most of his novels are about money, and about money which the hero or anti-hero (or, as in *The Eustace Diamonds,* the anti-heroine) has to have but cannot mention. And in the novels of Henry James, Freud's closest contemporary among the novelists of society, money and the secrecy surrounding the lack thereof, is as much the subject as the tension between American and European.

In the Vienna of Freud's time no respectable parent discussed his income with his children; it was a carefully avoided topic. Yet money had become the preoccupation of both. This, as we now know, happens in every society where there is rapid economic development.

In Jane Austen's England—still presumed to be quite static—one's money income was a fact. It could be changed only by marriage or by the right aunt's dying at the right time—the change agents in Jane Austen's books. It could not be changed by individual effort. Seventy years later economic development had made incomes highly mobile. At the same time, however, as in any society in the early stages of rapid economic development, there were now "winners" and "losers." A fairly small group profited mightily and became rich. A much larger group, but still a minority, reached precarious affluence—the Freuds in Sigmund's youth were just a cut above that level, I imagine. A majority had suddenly much greater expectations and were torn out of the static poverty of their small-town lives; but their incomes either did not go up at all or far less than their expectations had risen. It was Adlai Stevenson who first talked of the "rising tide of expectations." But the phenomenon antedates him by 150 years. The classical treatment of it is Thackeray's *Vanity Fair*, written well over a century before Stevenson's phrase and dealing with that "less developed country," the England of 1820 rather than with Asia or South America.

No European country in the last decades of the nineteenth century developed faster—and from a lower base at that—than Austria, and especially the Czech areas (Bohemia and Moravia) from which the Freuds had come and from which the Jewish middle class in Vienna was largely recruited. Thus the secret and suppressed obsession with money—the "poorhouse neurosis," it was commonly called—had become a major affliction, and a common one among the older middle-class people of my young years. (The young people were far less prone to it, for by then Austria was no longer developing and was indeed shrinking economically; the younger people were not obsessed with becoming poor, they were poor.) The poorhouse neurosis showed itself in a constant fear of ending up poor, a constant nagging worry about not earning enough, of not being able to keep up with the social expectations of oneself and one's family—and one's neighbors—and, above all, in constant obsessive talking about money while always claiming not to be interested in it.

Freud clearly suffered from the "poorhouse neurosis"; it is etched even into the letters he wrote his betrothed from Paris while still a young man. Yet for all his ruthless honesty with himself, he never could face up to it. That he misrepresented his professional life as being underpaid, under constant financial pressure, and in financial anxiety—these were misrepresentations that evinced the anxiety neurosis which he could not and did not face and which, in a Freudian slip mechanism, he repressed. This also explains why he did not notice it in his patients and leaves it out of his case histories. It had to be a "non-fact," for the fact itself was much too painful for him.

Freud's complaints about being the victim of anti-Semitic persecution similarly covered up and, at the same time, betrayed another fact Freud could not face: his inability to tolerate non-Jews.

Freud's generation of Central European (and especially Austrian) Jews had wholeheartedly and with a vengeance become German nationalists—in their culture, in their self-identification, and in their political affiliation and leanings. And no one was more consciously a German in his culture than Sigmund Freud. Yet there were no non-Jews in psychoanalysis, or at least no non-Jewish Austrians and Continental Europeans. Freud tried hard to attract them. But those who joined were always driven out.

In the "Heroic Age" of psychoanalysis, between 1890 and 1914, Freud repudiated every one of his non-Jewish followers or associates who was Austrian, German or German-speaking, or even a Continental European male. That he broke with Carl Jung and forced Jung in turn to break with him is one example. He could tolerate non-Jews only if they were foreigners, and even then he preferred women like the French Princess Bonaparte—for women did not, of course, rank as equals in Freud's world. For all their German culture—their constant references to German poets and writers, their humanist culture of the German Gymnasium, their strong Wagnerianism, and their aesthetics of the educated German "humanist" whose taste had been formed by Jakob Burckhart's *Culture of the Renaissance in Italy*—the members of the Freud circle could not rid themselves of their intense Jewishness. Their jokes were Jewish, and it is a Freudian tenet, after all, that jokes speak the truth of the heart. The non-Jew was irksome, difficult, a stranger, an irritation—and soon gotten rid of.

This, however, Freud, grand master of non-Jewish German culture, could not admit, least of all to himself. He needed an explanation that would put the blame on others, hence the Freudian slip of "anti-Semitic discrimination" and near-persecution. It was well known, for instance, that both Wagner-Jauregg, the eminent psychiatrist who headed one neuropsychiatric hospital at the University, and the head of the other neuropsychiatric hospital at the University, and the head of the other neuropsychiatric university hospital—the one that had been offered to Freud but was turned down by him—had wanted to attend the meetings of Freud's Psychoanalytical Society. Both were non-Jews, and both were made decidedly unwelcome. But in Freud's version these two men had rejected him and denied him recognition because he was a Jew. Freud needed a Freudian slip because the reality, that is, the fact of his not being able to break out of his Jewishness, was much too painful for him to face and to accept. And finally, of course, he had to make Moses into an Egyptian who was not a Jew at all—in *Moses and Monotheism*, one of his last major works.

But most important and most revealing is Freud's "Freudian slip" in respect to his being "ignored" by the Viennese physicians. He had to suppress their rejection of him; and he could do it only by pretending, above all to himself, that they were not discussing him, not doubting him, not rejecting him, but ignoring him. I suspect that Freud in his heart shared a good many of their doubts about the methodology of psychoanalysis. But he could not even discuss these doubts. For to do so would have forced him to abandon the one central achievement of his: a theory that was both strictly "scientific" and rationalist, and yet went beyond rationalism into the "subconscious," into the inner space of dream and fantasy and, in Thomas Mann's words, into the unscientific experience of the "novel," that is, into fiction.

Freud was led to psychoanalysis by his realization that the prevailing rationalism of the Enlightenment— of which modern scientific medicine was a distinguished and most successful child—could not explain the dynamics of the emotions. Yet he could not abandon the world and world view of science. To his dying day he maintained that psychoanalysis was strictly "scientific"; he maintained that the workings of the mind would be found to be capable of explanation in rational, scientific terms, in terms of chemical or electrical phenomena and of the laws of physics. Freudian psychoanalysis represents a giant effort to hold together in one synthesis the two worlds of scientific reason and non-rational inner experience. It represents a giant effort to hold together in one person the ultra-rationalist Freud, the child of the Enlightenment, and Freud the dreamer and poet of the "dark night of the soul." This synthesis made psychoanalysis so important, and yet so fragile. It gave psychoanalysis its impact. It made it timely. The systems of the nineteenth century that have had a major impact on the Western world—Marx, Freud, and Keynes—all have had in common the synthesis between the scientific and the magical, and the emphasis on logic and empirical research leading to the *credo quia absurdum*—"I believe because it makes no rational sense."

Freud clearly realized how narrow his footing was. Give one inch and you descend into the Eastern mysticism of Jung, with his invocation of myth as the experience of the race, his reliance on the magical sticks of the *I Ching* and on the fairy tales of shamans, sorcerers, and sybils. And there was the descent into the "orgone box" of another ex-disciple, Otto Reich. Give one inch the other way and you descend into the trivialities of another renegade disciple, Alfred Adler, with his arithmetic of "overcompensation" and his petty envies such as the "inferiority complex" as a substitute for the passion of the Prophets and the *hubris* of the Greek dramatists. Freud had to maintain the synthesis where he had carefully and precariously balanced it, otherwise he would have had either the pure magic of the faith healer or the pure and futile mechanism of

those children of the ultra-rationalist eighteenth century, the phrenologists or the Mesmerians with their electric rods. Freud had to have in one statement both "scientific" method for clinical therapy *and* "cosmic philosophy."

Just how precarious the balance was we know today. For by now it has disintegrated. There is on the one hand the scientific, rationalist clinical exploration of the brain—and indeed, Freud's prediction that the brain and its diseases would be shown to be subject to the same approaches of chemotherapy, diet, surgery, and electrotherapy as the rest of the body is well on its way to being proven. But the phenomena with which Freud dealt—we call them "emotional" today—are increasingly being tackled by methods that do not even pretend to belong to the realm of science, but are clearly in Freud's terms "superstition": transcendental meditation, for instance, or the instant "consciousness-raising" psychodynamic techniques. Whether this is good or bad, I do not know. For unlike Freud's generation, we seem to be able to accept a split of the world into incompatible universes.

However, Freud had to hold the precarious balance. I do not know whether he thought it through. Freud was not given to writing his thought processes down for others to read; no other major thinker so carefully dismantled the scaffolding of his thoughts before presenting the finished building to public view. But he knew that he needed the synthesis. And he must have realized, if only subconsciously, that it would collapse the moment he even discussed the questions the critics raised: the question of methodology; the definition of "results" and the matter of control tests; the problem of getting the same—or similar—therapeutic results from any psychotherapy, including purely magical ones; and the hybrid character of psychoanalysis as both scientific theory and therapy, and myth of personality and philosophy of man. He could only maintain the synthesis by ignoring these questions. And so he had to pretend, above all to himself, that the Viennese physicians ignored psychoanalysis so as to be able to ignore them.

The Freud of the Freudian realities is a much more interesting man, I submit, than the Freud of the conventional myth. He is also, I think a much bigger man— a tragic hero. And while a Freudian theory that can only maintain the synthesis between the world of Cartesian rationality and the world of the dark night of the soul by ignoring all inconvenient questions may be a much weaker theory—and one that cannot ultimately stand— it is also, I submit, a more fascinating and more revealing theory, and a humanly moving one.

The Expansion and Domination of the West

In the fifteenth century the Portuguese began to sail out into the Atlantic Ocean in the first of the great explorations. They were looking for trade opportunities and probed southward along the unknown African coast. Before the end of the century Bartholomew Dias reached the Cape of Good Hope and left a Portuguese imprint, as David Birmingham reveals in "Portugal's Impact on Africa."

The Spanish caught the same fever of exploration, and under their flag Christopher Columbus discovered the New World. Shortly thereafter, they conquered South and Central America. Soon other European nations joined in the great adventure, and the initial leaders lost ground as colonization continued. Between 1600 and 1815 England, France, Austria, Prussia, and Russia became the nations which dominated the West and much of the rest of the world until World War I. Gordon A. Craig and Alexander L. George describe this transition, and stress diplomacy, warfare, bureaucracy, and dedication as the key elements in the supremacy of these nations.

The conquest of the world by the West, however, was not a sudden nor a quickly successful venture. The rapid collapse of the Aztec and Inca empires, after the flash of the Spanish sword and an introduction to European diseases, was exceptional. Elsewhere it was not so easy. In Africa there were obstacles such as waterfalls in the rivers and deadly malarial mosquitos. Penetration beyond the coastline had to await the invention of steamboats and the discovery of quinine as a prophylactic for malaria in the nineteenth century. Superior firearms also aided the Europeans when the conquest of Africa finally was launched.

Meanwhile, a flourishing trade was developing on the west coast of Africa: native chiefs were selling their enemies and captives to white slavers, who in turn carried their human cargo to Europe and the New World. Some 10 million slaves were taken to the Americas alone; in 450 years of slave trafficking, the population of Africa was dramatically reduced. Some native groups possessed the ability for massive resistance. One of the most famous campaigns of imperialism was the Anglo-Zulu War of 1079 in South Africa. The Zulus fought with shields and spears, the British with rifles and cannons. There is no doubt about the Zulu courage, but modern firepower prevailed and the British subdued the Zulu nation. Considering the current troubles in South Africa, the eventual loss of the empire, and the survival of the Zulus, Frank Emery raises a question about the pointlessness of imperialism.

The article by Deborah Birkett on Mary Kingsley, an English trader and anthropologist who traveled through West Africa in the 1890s, reveals not only how Western culture was taken to Africa, but also how the native culture affected Westerners. Kingsley developed a great sympathy and respect for African life and fought for a change in imperial policy. She also was an example of an intrepid woman who ventured forth where others feared to go.

On the subcontinent of India, initial attempts at conquest by British traders in the 1680s ended in defeat. The Mogul Empire was too strong, so the British had to await its weakening in the eighteenth century. The takeover was led by the East India Company, but, as Pico Iyer describes, the British government gradually assumed the direction of affairs. Thus, a commercial venture turned into imperialism. The subcontinent had been home to one of the early riverine civilizations, and since the days of Alexander the Great had been partially ruled by a series of empires and invaders. When the British took over, their influence penetrated to the village level, something other invaders had not accomplished.

The Chinese developed a unique and self-contained society over four millennia. Although there had been contact with Westerners earlier, such as with Marco Polo in the thirteenth century, the initial meeting with Westerners in the modern period took place when Portuguese merchants appeared on the southeast coast of China in 1514. Following the Portuguese came the British and the Dutch by sea, and the Russians by land. The Chinese resisted the penetration and finally lost their autonomy in the nineteenth century through three disastrous wars.

Japan likewise resisted foreign influence and remained a closed society for 200 years. This isolation is the subject of the article by C. R. Boxer. In 1853, however, under the threat of United States warships, the Japanese opened their ports. Interestingly, unlike the Chinese, the Japanese utilized Western technology to resist Western civilization. Japan was able to maintain its own culture and independence, and it became the strongest country in Asia by the end of the century. The unusual blend of a Samurai warrior tradition with Western weapons made the Japanese a devastating enemy of the West during World War II.

The high tide of Western expansion and influence came at the beginning of the twentieth century. Western steel warships ruled the seas, Western railroads crisscrossed the continents, the sun never set on the British Empire, and European languages were spoken worldwide. But this did not last; the West lost its hegemony in the twentieth century. As historian William H. McNeill has written, the West, with its rise and its subsequent decline, can be interpreted as another in a series of empires which have come and gone in world history.

Looking Ahead: Challenge Questions

What makes a great power "great"?

What are the essential elements characteristic of the great powers after 1815?

How did the British defeat the Zulus?

Compare Mary Kingsley and Mary Wollstonecraft as feminists.

How did the British government come to control India?

How did Japan resist foreign influence?

Did the Europeans give anything beneficial to other peoples during their time of imperialism?

PORTUGAL'S IMPACT ON AFRICA

Poverty the spur – Bartholomew Dias' voyage to the Cape of Good Hope five hundred years ago marked the apex of an extraordinary Portuguese expansion overseas and the start of a fateful European impact on South Africa.

15th-century tin-glazed bowl showing a Portuguese sailing ship.

David Birmingham

FIVE HUNDRED YEARS AGO, IN 1488, Bartholomew Dias, a Portuguese seaman, reached the Cape of Good Hope on the furthest tip of South Africa. This was the last stage of the Portuguese exploration of the Atlantic coast and its islands. It was also the beginning of five centuries of often strained relations between Europe and South Africa. Two questions arise out of this turning point in the world's fortunes. The first is how did Portugal, a relatively remote and impoverished land at the far ends of medieval Europe, become the pioneer of Atlantic colonisation? And secondly, what were the long-term consequences of the opening of South Africa to alien influences?

The Portuguese domination of the eastern Atlantic took place in six stages, each of which pioneered a new set of colonial experiments. Bartholomew Dias was the heir to two centuries of trial and error as Portugal sought escape from its chronic poverty. The fact that Portugal was able to succeed in becoming an international power was due primarily to the superb shelter which the harbour of Lisbon provided to mariners on the otherwise inhospitable coast of south-eastern Europe.

Lisbon had been a harbour in Phoenician times when Levantine traders needed a haven on the long haul to Britain. It was also used by the Roman and Arab empires, although their primary interest lay in land-based domination. In the thirteenth century sea-power revived and Genoa succeeded in breaking out of the Mediterranean into the Atlantic. The great economic centres of northern Italy and of lower Germany, (hitherto linked by land-routes through the great markets of Lyons and Nuremburg) were now joined by Genoese on the safer maritime route. Lisbon again became a thriving port. The Portuguese learnt about ship-building from the Low Countries and about sea-faring from Italy and Catalonia. At one time the Portuguese monarchy hired no less than six Genoese admirals, although the most famous of them, Christopher Columbus, sought fame by transferring his allegiance to the rival port of Seville in Castile.

The rise of Lisbon as the maritime gateway between northern and southern Europe led to the growth of an urban middle class with merchant and banking skills learnt from Italy. It was this middle class which became

the driving force behind the Portuguese search for new wealth overseas. It found its patron in the royal prince, Pedro, brother of the vaunted Henry the Navigator. Portugal was unusual in that the nobility, lacking any other source of wealth in a country of agrarian poverty, showed a willingness to engage in merchant adventures. They were greatly helped by the thriving Jewish community of Lisbon, a community spasmodically enhanced by refugees fleeing persecution in other parts of Christendom. Jewish scholars were not hampered by Christian concepts of the world as portrayed in the scriptures and were able to take a much more scientific look at the evidence needed to draw maps and collate intelligence on economic prospects overseas.

The crises which drove Portugal to expansion were always crises over the price of bread. Throughout the Middle Ages Lisbon had been a hungry city. Access to the farm lands of the interior was inhibited by poor river navigation and expensive long-distance cartage. Grain was therefore not sought from domestic sources but from overseas shippers. Both Spain and Britain became key sup-

First published in *History Today*, June 1988, pp. 44-50. Reproduced by kind permission of History Today, Ltd., 83-84 Berwick Street, London W1V 3PJ, England.

pliers of wheat to Lisbon, and England built a six-hundred-year alliance on Portugal's need for northern trade. But in the fourteenth century one new solution to the grain deficit was a colonial venture in the Atlantic.

One thousand miles off the coast of Portugal lay the uninhabited islands of the Azores and Madeira. With the development of better shipping they became more accessible to Lisbon than the much closer interior of mainland Portugal. Colonisation and the setting up of wheat gardens were therefore attempted. Concepts of colonisation were learnt from the Venetians who had established settled colonies around their trading factories in the Near East. The labour supply consisted both of cheap European migrants driven by hunger, and captured slaves raided from the Barbary coast. The necessary capital was raised in the banking houses of Genoa. Patronage was provided by the land-owning nobility under the protection of Prince Henry. The beginnings of temperate cereal colonisation in the Atlantic basin were laid. The system was later to spread to the far side of the ocean, and eventually the Canadian and American prairies became a source of wheat not only for Portugal but also for half of Europe. Stage one of the Portuguese expansion, the wheat-based stage, was successful in the initial objective of supplying bread to overcome the Lisbon deficiency. It was also successful in terms of pioneering a colonial system which carried Europe out into the world.

The second stage of Portuguese expansion involved a more subtle development of overseas investment. Wheat was a comparatively low-yielding agricultural enterprise. A much higher return on capital, on labour and on land could be obtained by turning agrarian produce into alcohol. Alcohol could also be better preserved and could be sold when the price was advantageous rather than when the crop was ripe, as in the case of grain. The second stage of Portuguese expansion therefore attempted to establish a wine industry overseas. The necessary skills were available in the wine industry of Portugal. But Portuguese domestic wine, like Portuguese grain, suffered from severe problems of cartage

A detail from Le Testu's 'Cosmographie Universelle' of 1555, showing Portuguese settlements and trading posts in Southern Africa.

to the coast. Even in the eighteenth century, when port wine became a lucrative export, the shooting of the rapids on the Douro river made transport almost suicidal. The prospect of using colonial islands for the growing of vines was therefore attractive. The territory chosen was the Canary Islands, off the Moroccan coast of Africa.

Morocco was known to the Portuguese after a series of raiding wars associated with the militant crusading Order of Christ, of which Prince Henry was the commander. Despite an initial victory in Ceuta in 1415,

these wars had failed to capture the 'bread-basket' of North Africa which had once fed the city of Rome. Instead, the conquerors therefore set their sight on the off-shore islands. Unlike the Azores, the Canaries were already inhabited and conquest was necessary before plantations could be established. Once conquered, however, the surviving islanders could be compelled to slave servitude. Migrants from Portugal's impoverished backlands sailed in to create vineyards using both local and mainland slaves. Even when the colony was transferred in 1479 from

Portuguese suzerainty to control by the Crown of Castile, Portuguese immigrants continued to provide many colonists for Tenerife.

The Canary Islands were a second, wine-based, stage of Portugal's colonial pioneering. The development of colonial wine industries, for instance in California, South Africa and Australia was slower to take off than the development of wheat colonies. Portugal itself imposed restrictions where the interests of metropolitan producers were put at risk, though Canary wine was extensively smuggled into the Portuguese empire. The Canary Islands were important, however, for another reason. They became the base for the conquest and colonisation of Hispanic America. It was from there that Columbus set sail in 1492, and later a significant proportion of the emigrants who went to the Spanish American colonies were Canary islanders, often of Portuguese ancestry. As a stage in the growth of the economic, political and social ideology of imperialism the Canary islands were of critical significance. The slave vineyards of Tenerife, and the spasmodic raiding of southern Morocco, are a more accurate testimony to the place of Henry the Navigator in history than all the myths about his scientific virtuosity which were put out by the hired praise-singer, the chronicler Azurara.

The third stage of Portuguese experimentation in colonial practices was focused on another set of Atlantic islands, the Cape Verde islands. The Cape Verdes became famous over time for their textile industry. Portugal was almost as severely short of textiles as it was short of wheat. One reason for the development of wine exports was to pay for wooleen materials from England. Cotton was also bought in significant quantities from Muslim suppliers in north Africa and, after the rounding of the Cape of Good Hope, from the great texile industries of India. But the Cape Verde islands offered an opportunity to create a colonial textile industry.

Cotton and indigo plantations were established on the islands for spinning and dying. Labour was purchased on the West Africa mainland. Craftsmen were also brought over from the mainland to introduce the necessary weaving skills. The styles of textile adopted were ones which would sell best in Africa. The industry soon became self-perpetuating. Cloth woven in the islands was sold on the mainland in return for more slaves who would further expand the plantations. The only European input was sea transport. The Portuguese shipped cloth up and down the coast in the cabotage trade. The final profits were taken in slaves, the best of which were carried to Portugal to work on the underdeveloped landed estates of the south. By the sixteenth century some 10 per cent of the population of southern Portugal comprised black immigrants. Many were still slaves but others had married into land-owning families, thus increasing the domestic labour force without having to make reciprocal marriage payments. Blacks also became a significant part of the working population of Lisbon.

Slave-grown cotton became, over the colonial centuries, one of the fundamental bases of European relations with the wider world. From its pioneering beginnings the economic system spread to Brazil, which supplied Portugal, to the 'Sea Island' cotton colonies of the Caribbean, and eventually to the great cotton belt of Georgia and Alabama. This particular branch of Portuguese colonial ideology played a more direct part than any other in the development of the industrial revolution in eighteenth-century Britain.

The fourth stage of Portuguese progress towards the discovery of the Cape of Good Hope involved a fourth set of islands and a fourth type of colonial plantation economy. The tropical island of São Tomé, off the Niger delta, proved to have excellent soil and plentiful rainfall. The merchant community of Lisbon, and especially its Jewish economic pioneers, experimented with the introduction of sugar cane. Sugar required a much higher degree of organisation than the temperate or tropical crops hitherto introduced into the new Atlantic colonies. Cane had to be grown on a sufficiently large scale to justify investing in a crushing mill and boiling vats. It also required a labour force which could be compelled to work intensely hard during the harvest season to ensure that mature cane be crushed with a minimum of delay. Sugar seemed to be ideally suited to a slave economy and labour was therefore bought from the nearby kingdoms of Benin and Kongo. The industry so flourished that the island soon became too small, and sugar planting began to spread to other Portugese colonies, notably in north-eastern Brazil.

The success of São Tomé as a pioneering sugar colony was watched with admiration by the European powers which aspired to emulate Portugal's path to colonial prosperity. The Dutch went so far as to conquer the island, and also part of Brazil. The English set up their own black slave sugar colonies in Barbados and the Caribbean in the seventeenth century, and then turned to Indian-worked sugar colonies in the nineteenth century. But the greatest imitator of them all was France whose sugar island, later called Haiti, became the richest colony of all time. It was also the first one to successfully rebel against the racial pattern of servitude that Portugal had evolved and create an independent black state out of a white-ruled colony.

The fifth stage of Portuguese colonial evolution was concerned not with planting but with mining. The mines which the explorers aspired to reach were the gold mines of West Africa. From about 1400 the Akan mines of the coastal forest had begun to supplement gold production in the medieval fields controlled by the inland kingdoms of Ghana and Mali. Information about the trans-Saharan supply of African gold was widely known in the Christo-Islamic financial circles of the Mediterranean and certainly reached the merchants of Lisbon. In 1471 these merchants discovered a back route to the mines by way of the Gold Coast in West Africa. In order to buy gold, however, the Portuguese had to offer prices, and assortments of commodities, which were competitive with those of the experienced Saharan camel caravans. They found, to their surprise, that labour was in scarce supply in the mines and that slaves from their island plantations could fetch a good price. Thus the islands became entrepôts for the selling of slave miners. The business flourished and within a generation Portugal was buying ten thousand and more ounces of gold each year.

The lure of gold became a permanent feature of colonial ambition. The success of Portugal in West Africa became a driving force for all the European powers overseas. All the great gold-bearing regions of the world were explored and often plundered. Africa initially protected its mineral wealth with well-ordered states and effective armies. America was not so strong, and the peoples of the Caribbean died in the Spanish mines while the empires of Mexico and Peru were overthrown and ransacked. Only in the nineteenth century did Africa succumb to the conquering quest for gold by Europeans. Gold lust led to the great Anglo-Boer war of 1899 in which Britain, by now the strongest of the colonising nations, conquered South Africa.

The sixth and last stage of Portuguese expansion before the discovery of the Cape occurred on the western mainland of Central Africa. In Angola the Portuguese made their one and only attempt to create a colony on *terra firma* and among native inhabitants. The trump card which they played to gain access was religion. By offering to introduce more powerful gods and saints to control the supernatural, the Portuguese were able to build up political allies who protected their commercial interests and allowed a limited development of foreign settlement. Africa's first mainland colony was primarily concerned with the buying of slaves, however, and in less than a century it had been stalled by resistance and overrun by rebellion. The Portuguese therefore adopted Spanish military

tactics and sent squads of *conquistadores* to fortify their trading posts. Justification was supplied by accompanying Jesuits who commended armed conversion and established slave-worked plantations to finance their churches and monastries.

Portugal was initially less successful than its latter-day imitators in achieving territorial conquest. But the Jesuits and the soldiers did cross over to Brazil and began the harsh opening up of the eastern half of the South American continent. The colonists included some three million slaves brought over from Africa against their will. All the previous colonial experiments that Portugal had attempted in the fourteenth and fifteenth centuries – cereal farming, wine growing, cotton picking, sugar planting, gold mining – were introduced into Brazil. Sugar in the seventeenth century and gold in the eighteenth proved the most lucrative. Tobacco was added to the cornucopia. By the end of the colonial period in the Americas, the formerly Portuguese United States of Brazil exceeded the size of the formerly British United States of America.

The six stages of Portuguese expansion into the Atlantic were followed in 1488 by the great expedition to the Cape of Good Hope. This was commanded by a common captain called Bartholomew Dias, for whose services the King of Portugal paid an annuity of six thousand reals. Nothing is known of the captain's experience in tropical waters, but in August 1487 he set out with two small exploring caravels, light enough to be beached, and a bulkier store ship of provisions and trade goods. He carried three stone crosses

with which to claim territory on the African mainland. His objective, via Mina and Kongo, was the desert coast of Namibia, beyond the Angolan waters explored by Diego Cão in the three previous seasons. Dias prepared reports on the available anchorages, and conducted a little trade with local Khoi cattle herders. The Portuguese were not welcome intruders, however, and after selling them some sheep and cows the Khoi prudently turned them away. In the skirmish which followed one Khoi was killed by Bartholomew Dias' cross-bow. Relations between Europe and South Africa thus began as badly as they were to continue. At another bay Dias left his store ship with nine men instructed to investigate the commercial opportunities of the region. So unsuccessful were these trade emissaries that six of them had been killed before the main expedition returned to base. The store ship itself had to be fired for want of an adequate crew to sail it back to Lisbon.

After these unhappy encounters, very reminiscent of the hit-and-run exploits of Henry the Navigator's men on the desert coast of North Africa fifty years earlier, Dias sailed on towards the greener coast of the south. After many false promises in the deeply indented bays he gradually realised that the coast he was following had turned eastward. The enthusiasm generated by this discovery

Noble savages? A 1510 woodcut of some of the native peoples the Portuguese encountered: (left to right) West African negroes; Hottentots from Algoa Bay, South Africa; Arab traders from the East African coast.

IN·GENNEA   IN ALLAGO   IN ARABIA

was slow to capture the imagination of his homesick crews as bay followed bay along the southernmost shore of Africa. No opening towards the north was encountered. Eventually, at Bushman's River, some five hundred miles east of the Cape of Good Hope, Dias was persuaded to turn for home. He planted his first stone totem on March 12th, 1488, and dedicated it to Saint Gregory. He had discovered no new wealth, no fertile land, and no hospitable islands, not even a source of slaves with which to recompense the entrepreneurial King of Portugal for his outlay of risk capital. Worse still he had not conclusively found the sea lane to Arabia and India, although the direction of the coast had become more promising.

On the homeward journey Bartholomew Dias stopped on Saint Philip's day, June 6th, 1488, and apparently planted his second stone cross on the Cape of Good Hope. This was the most famous landmark of his voyage, though not actually the southernmost point of Africa. It was the rounding of this cape which eventually secured Dias his place in history. Dias did not enter Table Bay, site of the later city of Cape Town, but he did enter the Namibian bay later named Luderitz and mounted his third pillar of territorial assertion of Portuguese rights. He finally arrived back in Lisbon in December 1488 having covered 6,000 leagues in sixteen months.

The international repercussions of the Dias voyage were numerous. In 1491 a major colonising expedition was sent to the kingdom of Kongo, in Angola, which seemed a more promising African political and commercial partner than the sparse communities of coastal South Africa. In 1492 Columbus, no longer in Portuguese service, and armed with absurdly false data on the earth's circumference, sailed on behalf of Castile to find a western route to China, since Dias had failed to find an eastern one round the African coast. Not till 1497, nine years after the Dias voyage and five years after Columbus began to explore the Caribbean, did a new Portuguese king, Manuel I, manage to raise the resources, then men and the ships to attempt another merchant adventure in the far south without guarantee of profit. The expedition of Vasco da

Gama, however, did complete the task begun by Bartholomew Dias and opened up the sea route to Asia. Dias himself was called back to royal service and appointed to open a gold trading factory at Sofala in southeastern Africa.

Dias had experience of the gold trade. In 1497 he had accompanied Vasco da Gama on the first leg of his journey down the African coast before turning into the Gulf of Guinea to deliver a cargo of trade cloth and merchant goods to the gold factory of Mina. In 1500 Dias was appointed to accompany the great fleet of Alvares Cabral to the Indian Ocean and set up a similar factory at Sofala. The highland gold of the Zimbabwe mines had recently switched from the old ports of southern Mozambique to reach the international market via the Zambezi route in central Mozambique. Manuel of Portugal hoped that Dias, with his little flotilla of four shallow-draft caravels, would be able to close off the traditional gold route via East Africa to the Muslim precious metal marts of the eastern Mediteranean and divert the Sofala gold round the Cape of Good Hope to Christian bankers and the western Mediteranean. Dias, however, failed to crown his career in such a fashion. After an unscheduled stop on the then unknown coast of Brazil, his boat was lost on the south Atlantic crossing. The trading fortress was indeed built five years later, but Bartholomew Dias was remembered not as a great gold trader but as the first navigator along the coast of South Africa.

The discovery of the Cape of Good Hope was initially of little intrinsic interest. South Africa had few attractions to men seeking trade, minerals, slaves, vacant land and any other kind of entrepreneurial opportunity which would allow an escape from the barrenness of Portuguese provincial society. Few Portuguese visited the Cape, and then only in order to by-pass it and seek the wealthy sea lanes of Asia. Dias' son Antonio and grandson Paulo Dias de Novais invested their capital and energy not in South Africa but in Angola in Central Africa. In 1571 they claimed the rights of Lord-Proprietor in Angola and four years later founded the city of Luanda on a shore that their ancestor had patrolled on his epic voyage.

The Dias family failed, however, to secure their colony and in the 1590s the Hapsburgs repossessed Angola for the united Iberian crown of Spain and Portugal. But despite this check, grandfather Dias had, when reaching the Cape, set eyes on the South Africa that was gradually to become the most powerful of all the foreign colonies of Africa. It was also, five centuries later, to be the one which attracted the largest number of Portuguese migrants

In 1588, a century after Dias visited South Africa, the country had changed little. Black farming and cattle-herding were as prosperous as ever in the east while sheep-rearing and shell-fishing were important in the dryer areas of the west. Portuguese mariners were regularly shipwrecked on the coast and often hospitably received and given food, shelter, clothing and a safe-conduct along the trade paths to a Portuguese harbour in Mozambique. The first signs of the agricultural revolution which was to bring American maize to South Africa as a staple crop may have been noted, but it was not until the eighteenth century that the new farming, and favourable climatic conditions, led to a large demographic increase in the South African population.

By 1688 the seeds of colonial challenge to South Africa's independence had been sown. The Dutch haven at the Cape had begun to be swelled by Calvinist refugees from European persecution. Wheat and vine colonies, reminiscent of the Azores and Canaries, were set up in the fertile plains of Swellendam and Stellenbosch. Settlers already felt restive at the imperial control imposed on them by the metropolitan government of the Dutch West India company. Slavery was accepted as the normal means to acquire labour both in the artisan shops of the city and on the farms. White women were rare among the settlers and concubines of every race were readily accepted and acknowledged as they had been on the old colonial estates of the Portuguese islands. Indeed, the Cape was seen by the settlers as an 'island' and they tried to hedge themselves off from the mainstream of South Africa.

In 1788, three hundred years after Dias, the Cape had become a frontier society very strongly linked to the rest of South Africa. The indigenous population of the western Cape had been either integrated into colonial society in as subservient caste, or driven out to the northern frontiers and labelled 'the people of the bush'. In the east settlers had adopted the cattle ranching, and cattle rustling, way of life of their black neighbours. Co-operation and conflict between them alternated according to the grazing and watering needs of the herds. Traders cast their eyes on the further horizon and dreamed of fortunes made hunting elephants for ivory. A large creole population of varied racial composition resembled the creole societies which has evolved in all the Portuguese island colonies and in Luanda. Instead of speaking a 'pidgin' Portuguese creole, the people of the Cape spoke a Dutch creole, later known as Afrikaans.

By 1888 South Africa had changed again and was on the brink of a social and economic revolution. Diamonds, gold and coal had been found and the agrarian societies, both black and white, were beginning to be mobilised for the industrial exploitation of their mineral wealth on behalf of investors in Europe. The upheaval was immense and led to the entrenchment of both a racial divide between black and white and a cultural divide between English-speakers and Dutch-speakers. The old Cape population with its mixed heritage, black and white, English and Dutch, was unable to provide a bridge when the demands of industrial profit outweighed the political benefits of reconciliation. The great Boer War and the ideology of racial segregation were the consequences.

Finally by 1988, at the time of the fifth centenary of the first European visit to the Cape, an embattled South Africa had been transformed into Africa's foremost industrial nation. The old black population had become totally overwhelmed by white power. Surplus people not needed for industrial production or capitalist agriculture were carried off to encampments on the remote and dry fringes of the country. The remainder were segregated into urbanised black ghettos with limited economic rights and no political voice. Meanwhile the white population grew in size and prosperity in the fertile heartlands. Its latest recruits were six hundred thousand Portuguese immigrants. Like their predecessors, the Atlantic migrants of the fourteenth and fifteenth centuries, they were seeking an alternative to penury in Europe's poorest yet most innovative colonising nation.

FOR FURTHER READING:
Charles Boxer, *The Portuguese Seaborne Empire, 1415-1825* (Hutchinson, 1969); G. V. Scammell, *The World Encompassed* (Methuen, 1981); V. Malgalhaes Godinho, several works in Portuguese and *L'economie de l'Empire Portugaise* (Paris, 1969); Walter Rodney, *A History of Upper Guinea* (Oxford University Press, 1970); David Birmingham, *Trade & Conflict in Angola* (Oxford University Press, 1966).

A frontier society; the Town Hall of a Dutch-administered Cape of Good Hope, 1764, with Table Mountain in the background and a slave-based economy already in evidence.

The Emergence of the Great Powers

I

Although the term *great power* was used in a treaty for the first time only in 1815, it had been part of the general political vocabulary since the middle of the eighteenth century and was generally understood to mean Great Britain, France, Austria, Prussia, and Russia. This would not have been true in the year 1600, when the term itself would have meant nothing and a ranking of the European states in terms of political weight and influence would not have included three of the countries just mentioned. In 1600, Russia, for instance, was a remote and ineffectual land, separated from Europe by the large territory that was called Poland-Lithuania with whose rulers it waged periodic territorial conflicts, as it did with the Ottoman Turks to the south; Prussia did not exist in its later sense but, as the Electorate of Brandenburg, lived a purely German existence, like Bavaria or Württemberg, with no European significance; and Great Britain, a country of some commercial importance, was not accorded primary political significance, although it had, in 1588, demonstrated its will and its capacity for self-defense in repelling the Spanish Armada. In 1600, it is fair to say that, politically, the strongest center in Europe was the old Holy Roman Empire, with its capital in Vienna and its alliances with Spain (one of the most formidable military powers in Europe) and the Catholic states of southern Germany—an empire inspired by a militant Catholicism that dreamed of restoring Charles V's claims of universal dominion. In comparison with Austria and Spain, France seemed destined to play a minor role in European politics, because of the state of internal anarchy and religious strife that followed the murder of Henri IV in 1610.

Why did this situation not persist? Or, to put it another way, why was the European system transformed so radically that the empire became an insignificant political force and the continent came in the eighteenth century to be dominated by Great Britain, France, Austria, Prussia, and Russia? The answer, of course, is war, or, rather more precisely, wars—a long series of religious and dynastic conflicts which raged intermittently from 1618 until 1721 and changed the rank order of European states by exhausting some and exalting others. As if bent upon supplying materials for the nineteenth-century Darwinians, the states mentioned above proved themselves in the grinding struggle of the seventeenth century to be the fittest, the ones best organized to meet the demands of protracted international competition.

The process of transformation began with the Thirty Years War, which stretched from 1618 to 1648. It is sometimes called the last of the religious wars, a description that is justified by the fact that it was motivated originally by the desire of the House of Habsburg and its Jesuit advisers to restore the Protestant parts of the empire to the true faith and because, in thirty years of fighting, the religious motive gave way to political considerations and, in the spreading of the conflict from its German center to embrace all of Europe, some governments, notably France, waged war against their own coreligionists for material reasons. For the states that initiated this wasting conflict, which before it was over had reduced the population of central Europe by at least a third, the war was an unmitigated disaster. The House of Habsburg was so debilitated by it that it lost the control it had formerly possessed over the German states, which meant that they became sovereign in their own right and that the empire now became a mere adjunct of the Austrian crown lands. Austria was, moreover, so weakened by the exertions and losses of that war that in the period after 1648 it had the greatest difficulty in protecting its

From *Force and Statecraft: Diplomatic Problems of Our Times* by Gordon A. Craig and Alexander L. George, pp. 3-16. Copyright
©1983 by Oxford University Press, Inc. Reprinted by permission.

eastern possessions from the depredations of the Turks and in 1683 was threatened with capture of Vienna by a Turkish army. Until this threat was contained, Austria ceased to be a potent factor in European affairs. At the same time, its strongest ally, Spain, had thrown away an infantry once judged to be the best in Europe in battles like that at Nördlingen in 1634, one of those victories that bleed a nation white. Spain's decline began not with the failure of the Armada, but with the terrible losses suffered in Germany and the Netherlands during the Thirty Years War.

In contrast, the states that profited from the war were the Netherlands, which completed the winning of its independence from Spain in the course of the war and became a commercial and financial center of major importance; the kingdom of Sweden, which under the leadership of Gustavus Adolphus, the Lion of the North, plunged into the conflict in 1630 and emerged as the strongest power in the Baltic region; and France, which entered the war formally in 1635 and came out of it as the most powerful state in western Europe.

It is perhaps no accident that these particular states were so successful, for they were excellent examples of the process that historians have described as the emergence of the modern state, the three principal characteristics of which were effective armed forces, an able bureaucracy, and a theory of state that restrained dynastic exuberance and defined political interest in practical terms. The seventeenth century saw the emergence of what came to be called *raison d'état* or *ragione di stato*—the idea that the state was more than its ruler and more than the expression of his wishes; that it transcended crown and land, prince and people; that it had its particular set of interests and a particular set of necessities based upon them; and that the art of government lay in recognizing those interests and necessities and acting in accordance with them, even if this might violate ordinary religious or ethical standards. The effective state must have the kind of servants who would interpret *raison d'état* wisely and the kind of material and physical resources necessary to implement it. In the first part of the seventeenth century, the Dutch, under leaders like Maurice of Nassau and Jan de Witt, the Swedes, under Gustavus Adolphus and Oxenstierna, and the French, under the inspired ministry of Richelieu, developed the administration and the forces and theoretical skills that exemplify this ideal of modern statehood. That they survived the rigors of the Thirty Years War was not an accident, but rather the result of the fact that they never lost sight of their objectives and never sought objectives that were in excess of their capabilities. Gustavus Adolphus doubtless brought his country into the Thirty Years War to save the cause of Protestantism when it was at a low ebb, but he never for a moment forgot the imperatives of national interest that impelled him to see the war also as a means of winning Swedish supremacy along the shore of the Baltic Sea. Cardinal Richelieu has been called the greatest public servant France ever had, but that title, as Sir George Clark has drily remarked, "was not achieved without many acts little fitting the character of a churchman." It was his clear recognition of France's needs and his absolute unconditionality in pursuing them that made him the most respected statesman of his age.

The Thirty Years War, then, brought a sensible change in the balance of forces in Europe, gravely weakening Austria, starting the irreversible decline of Spain, and bringing to the fore the most modern, best organized, and, if you will, most rationally motivated states: the Netherlands, Sweden, and France. This, however, was a somewhat misleading result, and the Netherlands was soon to yield its commercial and naval primacy to Great Britain (which had been paralyzed by civil conflict during the Thirty Years War), while Sweden, under a less rational ruler, was to throw its great gains away.

The gains made by France were more substantial, so much so that in the second half of the century, in the heyday of Louis XIV, they became oppressive. For that ruler was intoxicated by the power that Richelieu and his successor Mazarin had brought to France, and he wished to enhance it. As he wrote in his memoirs:

> The love of glory assuredly takes precedence over all other [passions] in my soul. . . . The hot blood of my youth and the violent desire I had to heighten my reputation instilled in me a strong passion for action. . . . *La Gloire*, when all is said and done, is not a mistress that one can ever neglect; nor can one be ever worthy of her slightest favors if one does not constantly long for fresh ones.

No one can say that Louis XIV was a man of small ambition. He dreamed in universal terms and sought to realize those dreams by a combination of diplomatic and military means. He maintained alliances with the Swedes in the north and the Turks in the south and thus prevented Russian interference while he placed his own candidate, Jan Sobieski, on the throne of Poland. His Turkish connection he used also to harry the eastern frontiers of Austria, and if he did not incite Kara Mustafa's expedition against Vienna in 1683, he knew of it. Austria's distractions enabled him to dabble freely in German politics. Bavaria and the Palatinate were bound to the French court by marriage, and almost all of the other German princes accepted subsidies at one time or another from France. It did not seem unlikely on one occasion that Louis would put himself or his son forward as candidate for Holy Roman emperor. The same method of infiltration was practiced in Italy, Portugal, and Spain, where the young king married a French princess and French ambassadors exerted so much influence in internal affairs that they succeeded in discrediting the strongest antagonist to French influence, Don Juan of Austria, the victor over the Turks at the battle of Lepanto. In addition to all of this, Louis sought

3. EXPANSION AND DOMINATION OF THE WEST

to undermine the independence of the Netherlands and gave the English king Charles II a pension in order to reduce the possibility of British interference as he did so.

French influence was so great in Europe in the second half of the seventeenth century that it threatened the independent development of other nations. This was particularly true, the German historian Leopold von Ranke was to write in the nineteenth century, because it

> was supported by a preeminence in literature. Italian literature had already run its course, English literature had not yet risen to general significance, and German literature did not exist at that time. French literature, light, brilliant and animated, in strictly regulated but charming form, intelligible to everyone and yet of individual, national character was beginning to dominate Europe.... [It] completely corresponded to the state and helped the latter to attain its supremacy, Paris was the capital of Europe. She wielded a dominion as did no other city, over language, over custom, and particularly over the world of fashion and the ruling classes. Here was the center of the community of Europe.

The effect upon the cultural independence of other parts of Europe—and one cannot separate cultural independence from political will—was devastating. In Germany, the dependence upon French example was almost abject, and the writer Moscherosch commented bitterly about "our little Germans who trot to the French and have no heart of their own, no speech of their own; but French opinion is their opinion, French speech, food, drink, morals and deportment their speech, food drink, morals and deportment whether they are good or bad."

But this kind of dominance was bound to invite resistance on the part of others, and out of that resistance combinations and alliances were bound to take place. And this indeed happened. In Ranke's words, "The concept of the European balance of power was developed in order that the union of many other states might resist the pretensions of the 'exorbitant' court, as it was called." This is a statement worth noting. The principle of the balance of power had been practiced in Machiavelli's time in the intermittent warfare between the city states of the Italian peninsula. Now it was being deliberately invoked as a principle of European statecraft, as a safeguard against universal domination. We shall have occasion to note the evolution and elaboration of this term in the eighteenth century and in the nineteenth, when it became one of the basic principles of the European system.

Opposition to France's universal pretensions centered first upon the Dutch, who were threatened most directly in a territorial sense by the French, and their gifted ruler, William III. But for their opposition to be successful, the Dutch needed strong allies, and they did not get them until the English had severed the connection that had existed between England and France

under the later Stuarts and until Austria had modernized its administration and armed forces, contained the threat from the east, and regained the ability to play a role in the politics of central and western Europe. The Glorious Revolution of 1688 and the assumption of the English throne by the Dutch king moved England solidly into the anti-French camp. The repulse of the Turks at the gates of Vienna in 1683 marked the turning point in Austrian fortunes, and the brilliant campaigns of Eugene of Savoy in the subsequent period, which culminated in the smashing victory over the Turks at Zenta and the suppression of the Rakoczi revolt in Hungary, freed Austrian energies for collaboration in the containment of France. The last years of Louis XIV, therefore, were the years of the brilliant partnership of Henry Churchill, Duke of Marlborough, and Eugene of Savoy, a team that defeated a supposedly invulnerable French army at Blenheim in 1704, Ramillies in 1706, Oudenarde in 1708, and the bloody confrontation at Malplaquet in 1709.

These battles laid the basis for the Peace of Utrecht of 1713–1715, by which France was forced to recognize the results of the revolution in England, renounce the idea of a union of the French and Spanish thrones, surrender the Spanish Netherlands to Austria, raze the fortifications at Dunkirk, and hand important territories in America over to Great Britain. The broader significance of the settlement was that it restored an equilibrium of forces to western Europe and marked the return of Austria and the emergence of Britain as its supports. Indeed, the Peace of Utrecht was the first European treaty that specifically mentioned the balance of power. In the letters patent that accompanied Article VI of the treaty between Queen Anne and King Louis XIV, the French ruler noted that the Spanish renunciation of all rights to the throne of France was actuated by the hope of "obtaining a general Peace and securing the Tranquillity of *Europe* by a Ballance of Power," and the king of Spain acknowledged the importance of "the Maxim of securing for ever the universal Good and Quiet of Europe, by an equal Weight of Power, so that many being united in one, the Ballance of the Equality desired, might not turn to the Advantage of one, and the Danger and Hazard of the rest."

Meanwhile, in northern Europe, France's ally Sweden was forced to yield its primacy to the rising powers of Russia and Prussia. This was due in part to the drain on Swedish resources caused by its participation in France's wars against the Dutch; but essentially the decline was caused, in the first instance, by the fact that Sweden had too many rivals for the position of supremacy in the Baltic area and, in the second, by the lack of perspective and restraint that characterized the policy of Gustavus Adolphus's most gifted successor, Charles XII. Sweden's most formidable rivals were Denmark, Poland, which in 1699 acquired an ambitious and unscrupulous new king in the person of Augustus the Strong of Saxony, and Russia, ruled since 1683 by a young and vigorous leader who was to gain the name Peter the Great. In 1700, Peter and Augustus made a pact to attack and despoil Sweden and persuaded Frederick of Denmark to join them in this enterprise. The Danes and the Saxons immediately invaded Sweden and to their considerable dismay were routed and driven from the country by armies led by the eighteen-year-old ruler, Charles XII. The Danes capitulated at once, and Charles without pause threw his army across the Baltic, fell upon Russian forces that were advancing on Narva, and, although his own forces were outnumbered five to one, dispersed, captured, or killed an army of forty thousand Russians. But brilliant victories are often the foundation of greater defeats. Charles now resolved to punish Augustus and plunged into the morass of Polish politics. It was his undoing. While he strove to control an intractable situation, an undertaking that occupied him for seven years, Peter was carrying through the reforms that were to bring Russia from its oriental past into the modern world. When his army was reorganized, he began a systematic conquest of the Swedish Baltic possessions. Charles responded, not with an attempt to retake those areas, but with an invasion of Russia—and this, like other later invasions, was defeated by winter and famine and ultimately by a lost battle, that of Pultawa in 1709, which broke the power of Sweden and marked the emergence of Russia as its successor.

Sweden had another rival which was also gathering its forces in these years. This was Prussia. At the beginning of the seventeenth century, it had, as the Electorate of Brandenburg, been a mere collection of territories, mostly centered upon Berlin, but with bits and pieces on the Rhine and in East Prussia, and was rich neither in population nor resources. Its rulers, the Hohenzollerns, found it difficult to administer these lands or, in time of trouble, defend them; and during the Thirty Years War, Brandenburg was overrun with foreign armies and its population and substance depleted by famine and pestilence. Things did not begin to change until 1640, when Frederick William, the so-called Great Elector, assumed the throne. An uncompromising realist, he saw that if he was to have security in a dangerous world, he would have to create what he considered to be the sinews of independence: a centralized state with an efficient bureaucracy and a strong army. The last was the key to the whole. As he wrote in his political testament, "A ruler is treated with no consideration if he does not have troops of his own. It is these, thank God! that have made me *considerable* since the time I began to have them"—and in the course of his reign, after purging his force of unruly and incompetent elements, Frederick William rapidly built an efficient force of thirty thousand men, so efficient indeed that in 1675, during the Franco-Swedish war against the Dutch, it came to the aid of the Dutch by defeating the Swedes at Fehrbellin and subsequently driving them out of Pomerania. It was to administer this army that Frederick William laid the foundations of the

soon famous Prussian bureaucracy; it was to support it that he encouraged the growth of a native textile industry; it was with its aid that he smashed the recalcitrant provincial diets and centralized the state. And finally it was this army that, by its participation after the Great Elector's death in the wars against Louis XIV and its steadiness under fire at Ramillies and Malplaquet, induced the European powers to recognize his successor Frederick I as king of Prussia.

Under Frederick, an extravagant and thoughtless man, the new kingdom threatened to outrun its resources. But the ruler who assumed the throne in 1715, Frederick William I, resumed the work begun by the Great Elector, restored Prussia's financial stability, and completed the centralization and modernization of the state apparatus by elaborating a body of law and statute that clarified rights and responsibilities for all subjects. He nationalized the officer corps of the army, improved its dress and weapons, wrote its first handbook of field regulations, prescribing manual exercises and tactical evolutions, and rapidly increased its size. When Frederick William took the throne after the lax rule of his predecessor, there were rumors of an impending coup by his neighbors, like that attempted against Sweden in 1700. That kind of talk soon died away as the king's work proceeded, and it is easy to see why. In the course of his reign, he increased the size of his military establishment to eighty-three thousand men, a figure that made Prussia's army the fourth largest in Europe, although the state ranked only tenth from the standpoint of territory and thirteenth in population.

Before the eighteenth century was far advanced, then, the threat of French universal dominance had been defeated, a balance of power existed in western Europe, and two new powers had emerged as partners of the older established ones. It was generally recognized that in terms of power and influence, the leading states in Europe were Britain, France, Austria, Russia, and probably Prussia. The doubts on the last score were soon to be removed; and these five powers were to be the ones that dominated European and world politics until 1914.

II

Something should be said at this point about diplomacy, for it was in the seventeenth and eighteenth centuries that it assumed its modern form. The use of envoys and emissaries to convey messages from one ruler to another probably goes back to the beginning of history; there are heralds in the *Iliad* and, in the second letter to the Church of Corinth, the Apostle Paul describes himself as an ambassador. But modern diplomacy as we know it had its origins in the Italian city states of the Renaissance period, and particularly in the republic of Venice and the states of Milan and Tuscany. In the fourteenth and fifteenth centuries, Venice was a great commercial power whose prosperity depended upon shrewd calculation of risks, accurate reports upon conditions in foreign markets, and effective negotiation. Because it did so, Venice developed the first systemized diplomatic service known to history, a network of agents who pursued the interests of the republic with fidelity, with a realistic appraisal of risks, with freedom from sentimentality and illusion.

From Venice the new practice of systematic diplomacy was passed on to the states of central Italy which, because they were situated in a political arena that was characterized by incessant rivalry and coalition warfare, were always vulnerable to external threats and consequently put an even greater premium than the Venetians upon accurate information and skillful negotiation. The mainland cities soon considered diplomacy so useful that they began to establish permanent embassies abroad, a practice instituted by Milan and Mantua in the fifteenth century, while their political thinkers (like the Florentine Machiavelli) reflected upon the principles best calculated to make diplomacy effective and tried to codify rules of procedure and diplomatic immunity. This last development facilitated the transmission of the shared experience of the Italian cities to the rising nation states of the west that soon dwarfed Florence and Venice in magnitude and strength. Thus, when the great powers emerged in the seventeenth century, they already possessed a highly developed system of diplomacy based upon long experience. The employment of occasional missions to foreign courts had given way to the practice of maintaining permanent missions. While the ambassadors abroad represented their princes and communicated with them directly, their reports were studied in, and they received their instructions from, permanent, organized bureaus which were the first foreign offices. France led the way in this and was followed by most other states, and the establishment of a Foreign Ministry on the French model was one of Peter the Great's important reforms. The emergence of a single individual who was charged with the coordination of all foreign business and who represented his sovereign in the conduct of foreign affairs came a bit later, but by the beginning of the eighteenth century, the major powers all had such officials, who came to be known as foreign ministers or secretaries of state for foreign affairs.

From earliest times, an aura of intrigue, conspiracy, and disingenuousness surrounded the person of the diplomat, and we have all heard the famous quip of Sir Henry Wotton, ambassador of James I to the court of Venice, who said that an ambassador was "an honest man sent to lie abroad for the good of his country." Moralists were always worried by this unsavory reputation, which they feared was deserved, and they sought to reform it by exhortation. In the fifteenth century, Bernard du Rosier, provost and later archbishop of Toulouse, wrote a treatise in which he argued that the business of an ambassador is peace, that ambassadors must labor for the common good, and that they should

never be sent to stir up wars or internal dissensions; and in the nineteenth century, Sir Robert Peel the younger was to define diplomacy in general as "the great engine used by civilized society for the purpose of maintaining peace."

The realists always opposed this ethical emphasis. In the fifteenth century, in one of the first treatises on ambassadorial functions, Ermalao Barbaro wrote: "The first duty of an ambassador is exactly the same as that of any other servant of government: that is, to do, say, advise and think whatever may best serve the preservation and aggrandizement of his own state."

Seventeenth-century theorists were inclined to Barbaro's view. This was certainly the position of Abram de Wicquefort, who coined the definition of the diplomat as "an honorable spy," and who, in his own career, demonstrated that he did not take the adjectival qualification very seriously. A subject of Holland by birth, Wicquefort at various times in his checkered career performed diplomatic services for the courts of Brandenburg, Lüneburg, and France as well as for his own country, and he had no scruples about serving as a double agent, a practice that eventually led to his imprisonment in a Dutch jail. It was here that he wrote his treatise *L'Ambassadeur et ses fonctions,* a work that was both an amusing commentary on the political morals of the baroque age and an incisive analysis of the art and practice of diplomacy.

Wicquefort was not abashed by the peccadilloes of his colleagues, which varied from financial peculation and sins of the flesh to crimes of violence. He took the line that in a corrupt age, one could not expect that embassies would be oases of virtue. Morality was, in any case, an irrelevant consideration in diplomacy; a country could afford to be served by bad men, but not by incompetent ones. Competence began with a clear understanding on the diplomat's part of the nature of his job and a willingness to accept the fact that it had nothing to do with personal gratification or self-aggrandizement. The ambassador's principal function, Wicquefort wrote, "consisted in maintaining effective communication between the two Princes, in delivering letters that his master writes to the Prince at whose court he resides, in soliciting answers to them, . . . in protecting his Master's subjects and conserving his interests." He must have the charm and cultivation that would enable him to ingratiate himself at the court to which he was accredited and the adroitness needed to ferret out information that would reveal threats to his master's interests or opportunities for advancing them. He must possess the ability to gauge the temperament and intelligence of those with whom he had to deal and to use this knowledge profitably in negotiation. "Ministers are but men and as such have their weaknesses, that is to say, their passions and interests, which the ambassador ought to know if he wishes to do honor to himself and his Master."

In pursuing this intelligence, the qualities he should

cultivate most assiduously were *prudence* and *modération.* The former Wicquefort equated with caution and reflection, and also with the gifts of silence and indirection, the art of "making it appear that one is not interested in the things one desires the most." The diplomat who possessed prudence did not have to resort to mendacity or deceit or to *tromperies* or *artifices,* which were usually, in any case, counterproductive. *Modération* was the ability to curb one's temper and remain cool and phlegmatic in moments of tension. "Those spirits who are compounded of sulphur and saltpeter, whom the slightest spark can set afire, are easily capable of compromising affairs by their excitability, because it is so easy to put them in a rage or drive them to a fury, so that they don't know what they are doing." Diplomacy is a cold and rational business, in short, not to be practiced by the moralist, or the enthusiast, or the man with a low boiling point.

The same point was made in the most famous of the eighteenth-century essays on diplomacy, François de Callières's *On the Manner of Negotiating with Princes* (1716), in which persons interested in the career of diplomacy were advised to consider whether they were born with "the qualities necessary for success." These, the author wrote, included

> an observant mind, a spirit of application which refuses to be distracted by pleasures or frivolous amusements, a sound judgment which takes the measure of things, as they are, and which goes straight to its goal by the shortest and most neutral paths without wandering into useless refinements and subtleties which as a rule only succeed in repelling those with whom one is dealing.

Important also were the kind of penetration that is useful in discovering the thoughts of men, a fertility in expedients when difficulties arise, an equable humor and a patient temperament, and easy and agreeable manners. Above all, Callières observed, in a probably not unconscious echo of Wicquefort's insistence upon moderation, the diplomat must have

> sufficient control over himself to resist the longing to speak before he has really thought what he shall say. He should not endeavour to gain the reputation of being able to reply immediately and without premeditation to every proposition which is made, and he should take a special care not to fall into the error of one famous foreign ambassador of our time who so loved an argument that each time he warmed up in controversy he revealed important secrets in order to support his opinion.

In his treatment of the art of negotiation, Callières drew from a wealth of experience to which Wicquefort could not pretend, for he was one of Louis XIV's most gifted diplomats and ended his career as head of the French delegation during the negotiations at Ryswick in 1697. It is interesting, in light of the heavy reliance upon lawyers in contemporary United States diplomacy (one thinks of President Eisenhower's secretary of state and

President Reagan's national security adviser) and of the modern practice of negotiating in large gatherings, that Callières had no confidence in either of these preferences. The legal mind, he felt, was at once too narrow, too intent upon hair-splitting, and too contentious to be useful in a field where success, in the last analysis, was best assured by agreements that provided mutuality of advantage. As for large conferences—"vast concourses of ambassadors and envoys"—his view was that they were generally too clumsy to achieve anything very useful. Most successful conferences were the result of careful preliminary work by small groups of negotiators who hammered out the essential bases of agreement and secured approval for them from their governments before handing them over, for formal purposes, to the *omnium-gatherums* that were later celebrated in the history books.

Perhaps the most distinctive feature of Callières's treatise was the passion with which he argued that a nation's foreign relations should be conducted by persons trained for the task.

> Diplomacy is a profession by itself which deserves the same preparation and assiduity of attention that men give to other recognized professions. . . . The diplomatic genius is born, not made. But there are many qualities which may be developed with practice, and the greatest part of the necessary knowledge can only be acquired, by constant application to the subject. In this sense, diplomacy is certainly a profession itself capable of occupying a man's whole career, and those who think to embark upon a diplomatic mission as a pleasant diversion from their common task only prepare disappointment for themselves and disaster for the cause which they serve.

These words represented not only a personal view but an acknowledgment of the requirements of the age. The states that emerged as recognizedly great powers in the course of the seventeenth and eighteenth centuries were the states that had modernized their governmental structure, mobilized their economic and other resources in a rational manner, built up effective and disciplined military establishments, and elaborated a professional civil service that administered state business in accordance with the principles of *raison d'état.* An indispensable part of that civil service was the Foreign Office and the diplomatic corps, which had the important task of formulating the foreign policy that protected and advanced the state's vital interests and of seeing that it was carried out.

BIBLIOGRAPHICAL ESSAY

For the general state of international relations before the eighteenth century, the following are useful: Marvin R. O'Connell, *The Counter-Reformation, 1559–1610* (New York, 1974); Carl J. Friedrich, *The Age of the Baroque, 1610–1660* (New York, 1952), a brilliant volume; C. V. Wedgwood, *The Thirty Years War* (London, 1938, and later editions); Frederick L. Nussbaum, *The Triumph of Science and Reason, 1660–1685* (New York, 1953); and John B. Wolf, *The Emergence of the Great Powers, 1685–1715* (New York, 1951). On Austrian policy in the seventeenth century, see especially Max Braubach, *Prinz Eugen von Savoyen,* 5 vols. (Vienna, 1963–1965); on Prussian, Otto Hintze, *Die Hohenzollern und ihr Werk* (Berlin, 1915) and, brief but useful, Sidney B. Fay, *The Rise of Brandenburg-Prussia* (New York, 1937). A classical essay on great-power politics in the early modern period is Leopold von Ranke, *Die grossen Mächte,* which can be found in English translation in the appendix of Theodore von Laue, *Leopold Ranke: The Formative Years* (Princeton, 1950). The standard work on *raison d'état* is Friedrich Meinecke, *Die Idee der Staatsräson,* 3rd ed. (Munich, 1963), translated by Douglas Scott as *Machiavellianism* (New Haven, 1957).

On the origins and development of diplomacy, see D. P. Heatley, *Diplomacy and the Study of International Relations* (Oxford, 1919); Leon van der Essen, *La Diplomatie: Ses origines et son organisation* (Brussels, 1953); Ragnar Numelin, *Les origines de la diplomatie,* trans. from the Swedish by Jean-Louis Perret (Paris, 1943); and especially Heinrich Wildner, *Die Technik der Diplomatie: L'Art de négocier* (Vienna, 1959). Highly readable is Harold Nicolson, *Diplomacy,* 2nd ed. (London, 1950). An interesting comparative study is Adda B. Bozeman, *Politics and Culture in International History* (Princeton, 1960).

There is no modern edition of *L'ambassadeur et ses fonctions par Monsieur de Wicquefort* (Cologne, 1690); but Callières's classic of 1776 can be found: François de Callières, *On the Manner of Negotiating with Princes,* trans. A. F. Whyte (London, 1919, and later editions).

THE STRUGGLE FOR LAND

Frank Emery looks at the causes and consequences of the Anglo-Zulu War

Dr Frank Emery

Dr Frank Emery is lecturer in historical geography at University of Oxford

THE Anglo-Zulu War of 1879 is the best known of all the many wars of dispossesion fought in colonial Africa. It retains a clear-cut image because it was marked by dramatic military events that sank deep into public awareness at the time, and they have been remembered to a surprising degree. Three of them were, and still are, outstanding. Not long after the British forces invaded Zululand, one entire column was decimated by the Zulu warriors at Isandlwana. Upwards of 1000 imperial troops, mostly seasoned campaigners, were cut to pieces by what was then usually described as a savage, barbarous foe armed mainly with spear and shield. It had never happened before, and the mother country was shocked to the core. As one survivor said, with masterly understatement, 'there will be an awful row at home about this'.

Then on the same day, as if by right of natural justice, a handful of soldiers defending the base hospital and stores at Rorke's Drift mission station did heroic deeds by beating off 3000 Zulu who attacked it before dusk and through the night of January 22-23, 1879. 'Here they come', shouted the look-out as the *impi* came in sight, 'black as hell and thick as grass'. It is rightly remembered as an epic defensive action against all the odds, packed with tension as the Zulu repeatedly stormed the makeshift barricades. When eventually they drew off after suffering heavy casualties, there was precious little ammunition left with the exhausted troops, 11 of whom were awarded the Victoria Cross. Without this victory the shambles at Isandlwana would have been all the heavier to bear.

As the campaign dragged on under the feeble generalship of Lord Chelmsford, ultra-cautious of Zulu military strength after seeing his men lying dead and ritually disembowelled at Isandlwana, another dire episode filled the headlines. Attached to the British staff was the Prince Imperial of

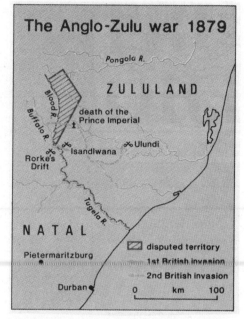

France, Louis Napoleon, a young officer who led a mounted patrol through hostile territory on June 1, 1879. Bold and impetuous, heir to the Bonapartist faction in French politics and carrying the sword of his great-uncle Napoleon, he was ambushed by the Zulu and speared to death. The dismay at this was felt internationally, and it did little good for morale before the Zulu army was eventually defeated in pitched battle at Ulundi on July 4. Superior rifle power, Gatling guns, artillery and cavalry proved too strong for them.

So much for the pattern of military events. The causes of the war are far more difficult to analyze, and historians' interpretations have shifted in emphasis over time. What is undisputed is that a key figure in the path to conflict was Sir Bartle Frere (1815-84), a Proconsul of Empire with a high reputation for his work in India before he went to South Africa in 1877 as Governor of the Cape Colony and High Commissioner. Frere was also a prominent geographer, serving as the President of the Royal

Geographical Society in 1873, and publishing some excellent research on both Indian and African themes. In February 1874 he lectured publicly on Africa, with the confidence of a man who had recently negotiated the anti-slavery treaty at Zanzibar, and as a friend of David Livingstone. Frere argued the case for a more active exploitation of African resources. The external trade of the entire continent, he claimed, was less than that of a third rate European power, a paradox he explained as 'a defect of political cohesion'.

IN his view the best prospects for commercial initiative lay in the equatorial coastlands and again so far as Britain was concerned especially in the southern 'temperate' belt reaching to the Cape. Here powerful inducements to economic growth and European settlement lay in its mineral riches: diamonds, gold, and particularly to his way of thinking, the coalfields of Natal and Zambezia. These fields could supply fuel for steamships in the Indian Ocean and for future railways within the sub-continent. But in order to exploit these resources it was first necessary to create what Frere called 'a welding together of the loose elements of a great South African empire'. He advocated a policy of confederating the British colonies of the Cape and Natal with the Boer republics of the Transvaal and Orange Free State, incidentally expanding their territories as need be at the expense of African indigenous societies. Confederation was to be the mainspring of official British policy in South Africa after 1877, and it became a material reason for the destruction of the Zulu kingdom.

Traditionally the war was seen by historians as due to nothing more than the incompatibility of having such a 'primitive' and warlike people as the Zulu co-existing alongside civilized, peaceful states like Natal and the Transvaal. It is true that earlier in the 19th century under Shaka's leadership the Zulu were the most expan-

From *The Geographical Magazine*, London, England, June 1986, pp. 276-281. Reprinted by permission.

sionist and aggressive Black force in southern Africa. They ruthlessly established their own dominance over neighbouring groups, and created a system of relatively centralized control within the Zulu kingdom. Memories of all this influenced the attitudes of the White south, even though they were scarcely justified by the actions of Cetshwayo kaMpande, the king who was attacked by an imperial British army in 1879. Occupying the throne since 1872, he did little to threaten the status quo or to arouse fears along his borders. Psychologically, however, the recollection of savage conflict involving the Zulu strengthened the general view that war with them was inevitable at some stage, particularly when they began equipping themselves with firearms in the 1870s.

A liberal school of historians since the 1960s has developed a revisionist interpretation based on the specific circumstances that gave rise to the war. The only possible source of friction was an unresolved border dispute with the Transvaal over claims to a strip of land along the Blood River, coveted by both sides. The pastoralist Boers as much as the Zulu were dependent on their great herds of cattle as a mainstay of life, and this contested land was valued for its grazing potential during the dry winter season. Similar frontiers of settlement, in which Black territory was sought by intrusive Whites, were common enough in South Africa at this period. Early in 1878 the dispute was investigated by a boundary commission, and the Transvaal's case was found to rest on dubious evidence. Confirmation of Zulu rights over most of the debatable territory was therefore recommended, thus defusing their apparently hostile stance.

Here the spotlight has to be focused on Frere's decision not to use British power to restore these Zulu rights, but instead to embark on a course of action that brought them to war. It has long been known that Frere deliberately precipitated the Anglo-Zulu War in defiance of the British government's expressed desire to avoid military entanglement in South Africa at that moment. But why exactly did he decide to go it alone? Evidence shows that he exaggerated, for other motives, a sense of concern about the imminence of the Zulu 'menace'. His real aim was to press on with creating a great new British dominion in the form of confederation of the South African states and colonies. He saw it as a personal challenge that could bring him fame and fortune, and he was determined to do all in his power to bring it about.

It was a delicate and difficult task due to local and external complications. In 1877 Britain annexed the Transvaal, a major blunder because it suggested that a confederation strategy was to be forced through by high-handed acts of power politics. It also brought the border dispute with the Zulu fully within British responsibility, at a time when Disraeli's government was distracted from the ideal of confederation by a fresh crisis in Afghanistan. Before moving to Natal, in 1877-78 Frere willingly directed a war in the Transkei that effectively closed the frontier in the Eastern Cape by defeating the Xhosa. With that done, he even drew inspiration from British forward policies in Afghanistan to fuel his own designs on Zululand. It is no exaggeration to say that he tried to emulate the British invasion of Afghanistan in his own machinations against Cetshwayo and in preparation for war.

Frere refused to implement the report on the Transvaal-Zulu border dispute because, having found for the Zulu, it would place Britain in the role of patron of Black rights, not as benefactor of settler interests. White opinion would be alienated, and hopes for confederation dealt a serious blow. From July 1878, therefore, Frere suddenly began to paint a picture of Zulu aggressiveness, with Cetshwayo conspiring to unleash his army of 40,000 warriors, reviving the Zulu military machine as a potential danger to the whole region. Frere needed a war to break Zulu independence, because once the Zulu kingdom was defeated and demolished its territorial rights would cease to be an issue, and prospects for confederation enhanced.

WITHIN this new order, as the radical historians now argue, the way would also be opened for the advance of capitalist production in Southern Africa, an objective of which Frere and his associates were naturally well aware. Given such political and economic imperatives, it explains why Frere manipulated the long delays in telegraphic communication between Natal and London (the cable reached from London only to the Cape Verde Islands at this date, and the gap was bridged by steamship) to forge ahead, despite the known opposition of his masters at Whitehall. He presented Cetshwayo with an ultimatum in December 1878 that he knew the Zulu king could not accept, knowing too that before Disraeli could cable an order to stop the invasion, it would have already begun. A month later the troops went in to start what should really be known as Frere's war. There followed a bitter conflict costing thousands of Zulu and British lives, as well as a bill to the Treasury for over £5 million.

The aftermath of this unjustified and mismanaged war was equally disgraceful, because the post-war settlement imposed by Britain held the seeds of inevitable disruption. Cetshwayo was sent in exile to Cape Town. Zululand was split into 13 chiefdoms, some of them old pre-Shakan units, others newly demarcated. The chiefs were all opponents of the royal house; Cetshwayo's son and brother found themselves under the hostile authority of Zibhebhu, leader of the Ndwandwe clan, who treated them harshly. It was a woeful prescription for divide and misrule.

CETSHWAYO still had a powerful following among his Usuthu clan, and external supporters. He was brought to London in 1882 to put his case to the government (incidentally having lunch with Queen Victoria at Osborne), and he was allowed to return to Zululand in 1883. His status as paramount chief was far from secure, and Zibhebhu's party sparked off a vicious civil war. Cetshwayo was defeated in battle and he died, possibly poisoned, in 1884. White interventionism of the worst kind then followed. Boer and other mercenaries had taken a helping hand in Cetshwayo's overthrow; other Boers now came to help Dinuzulu, the royal heir, in recapturing the lost Usuthu territory. Having succeeded in this, under Lukas Meyer they grabbed for themselves as reward virtually all the old Disputed Territory along the Blood River, and much more, to create their New Republic, which was absorbed into the South African Republic (Transvaal) in 1887.

In that same year Britain annexed Zululand, allowing Zibhebhu back from exile and so undermining Dinuzulu's authority. Entrenched inter-tribal tensions broke out afresh. Civil war followed once again, with Dinuzulu eventually being sent to St Helena for 10 years for high treason. Before his return in 1897, Zululand was incorporated with the self-governing colony of Natal. For a while it was safe from encroachment, due largely to the distractions of the rinderpest pandemic of 1897-8 that wiped out millions of cattle, and of the second Anglo-Boer War of 1899-1902.

The inevitable step was taken of setting up a commission of delimitation, in other words dispossession, which reported in 1905. As a result of its findings more than one-third of Zululand, more than one million hectares, was released for purchase, leaving 1.6 million hectares in Zulu hands. The land was bought by Whites who converted it into sugar and timber plantations along the coastal plain, and cattle farms in the interior. Resentment over this restructuring of their hereditary lands, and other matters flared up in refusal to pay taxes, and the Zulu broke out into open revolt in 1906. The Bambata Rebellion was brief but bloody, being crushed by the colonial authorities.

Who, then, won the Anglo-Zulu War? On the surface it was a military victory for Britain, however clumsily achieved, but victory was negated because confederation policies, the chief pretext for waging the war, were abandoned after 1879. For the Zulu nation the war was a harsh experience of defeat but, as their own historical perception of it makes clear, they suffered even more from the traumatic civil wars within the Zulu polity that continued for 10 years after 1879. The Transvaal Boers did well out of it after they regained their independence in 1881, resting secure from any kind of Zulu threat, real or imagined, as well as acquiring Zulu territory for themselves. In the long term the colony of Natal also benefited by getting their hands on Zulu labour, land, and trade. Those who contributed least to the conflict, in terms of lives and money, gained most, at the expense of dispossessing the Zulu of their kingdom.

Such calculations do not tell the whole story, for the reality is that despite all the pressures placed on them since Frere's ultimatum, the Zulu people survive undaunted. They are now the largest self-identifying 'nation' within the Republic of South Africa, at six million strong outnumbering any other ethnic group, White or non-White. More than this, they are vigorous, well organized politically, and confident. They have come to draw strength from their past.

The Chief Minister of KwaZulu is among the best known spokesmen for the Black majority in their struggle against apartheid. Chief Mangosutho Gatsha Buthelezi is a direct descendant of Chief Mnyamana Buthelezi, commander-in-chief of the Zulu army in 1879; he also has royal blood on his mother's side. He leads Inkatha, a powerful politico-cultural organisation largely, but not wholly, of Zulu membership. Although criticized by the African National Congress and others for his gradualist and non-violent views of negotiating for political change (ironic in such a warrior race as the Zulu), it is inconceivable that Inkatha could be omitted from any serious dialogue on the future of South Africa.

IN 1979 Chief Buthelezi opened a centenary conference at Durban on the history of the Anglo-Zulu War, appearing in all the finery of traditional Zulu dress. Relating the days of his people's des-

pair to the present, he explained the deep difference between Black and White views of South Afrian history. 'A White perspective looks at yesterday as it leads to today. In the Black perspective, we see yesterday and today leading to tomorrow'. Nor are these empty words, because he could fairly claim, in a policy speech to his Legislative Assembly in April 1985, to have brought the region of KwaZulu-Natal to the very threshold of achieving real progress in the politics of power-sharing between Whites and Blacks. In March 1986 a multi-racial *indaba* or debate began in Durban to reach consensus on the creation of a single legislative body to govern the combined area of Natal and KwaZulu. Plans for a joint executive authority with statutory powers are already being considered by Pretoria. It makes Frere's war-mongering in 1879 look all the more sordid and pointless.

WEST AFRICA'S MARY KINGSLEY

Deborah Birkett

'England . . . requires markets more than colonies.' Mary Kingsley's espousal of the African cause was founded on the empathy between second-class citizens in a white, male-dominated society.

IN 1893, FOR A THIRTY-YEAR-OLD British spinster to take a cargo vessel to West Africa was an extraordinary step. The unorthodoxy of Mary Kingsley's response to her stifling domestic life has cast her in the mould of an isolated heroine, removed from the cultural milieu of late nineteenth-century Cambridge in which she was raised. But the long voyage from the confines of her mother's sickroom to the Ogooué rapids was a psychological as well as physical journey. Its roots lay in the dreams and aspirations shared by many middle-class Victorian women who responded in less dramatic and memorable ways. Mary Kinglsey's contribution to the nineteenth-century image of Africa, her work as advisor and campaigner on colonial affairs, and the connections she made between theories of sexual and racial determinism, all reveal a woman firmly rooted in her time, not an individual divorced from it. Her very ordinary ambitions and desires are sometimes swamped amid the foreignness of the landscape in which they were realised.

Mary Kingsley in 1897, ' . . . a maiden aunt dressed as a woman far beyond her mid-thirties.

First published in *History Today*, May 1987, pp. 10-16. Reproduced by kind permission of History Today, Ltd., 83-84 Berwick Street, London W1V 3PJ England.

Her gender was also responsible for the hidden, and now largely forgotten, methods through which she expressed and exercised her power. Although by the time of her death in 1900, while nursing Boer prisoners of war in South Africa, she was considered the leading Africanist of her time, as a Victorian woman she was excluded from many of the forums concerned with African affairs. Her informal and behind-the-scenes politicking has lain buried under the greater weight of government reports and public records.

Although bearing the name of Kingsley, Mary had neither the education, money, nor established class status her literary uncles and cousins enjoyed. Born only four days after Dr George Kingsley married his housekeeper, Mary Bailey, in October 1862, Mary's first thirty years were consumed in tending to her sickly mother and acting as secretary to her father's amateur anthropological work.

When both parents died within weeks of each other in 1892, she felt like 'a boy with a new half crown'. Enticed by the tales of travel and adventure in her father's library, and with the intention of collecting 'fish and fetish', she sailed for West Africa – 'the white man's grave'. But alongside the spirits and jars for preserving her specimens packed in her large black waterproof bag, she took her cultural baggage. The isolation of Mary's early life had forced her onto the companionship of books, and from these she culled an image of the 'Dark Continent' and its exotic 'savage' inhabitants prevalent in both the academic and popular press. So strong were these images, that when the SS *Lagos* drew towards the West African Coast in August 1893, it all seemed so familiar.

Canoeing down the Ogooué rapids and climbing 13,000 foot Mount Cameroon by a route unconquered by any other European brought not only physical but psychological challenges. Her passionate desire to 'penetrate the African mind-forest' made her travel as a trader, living as her African companions and depending entirely upon them for her safety and well-being. In a land where she was first of all white, and only secondly a woman, she found a new kind of freedom which 'took all the colour out of other kinds of living'.

By 1896, after two journeys to West Africa, Mary Kingsley was a celebrity, a regular presence in the daily press and an enormously popular lecturer. Her quest in search of 'fish and fetish' had led her into more far-reaching discoveries, and what she saw and recorded questioned the images she had taken with her. 'One by one I took my old ideas derived from books and thoughts based on imperfect knowledge and weighed them against the real life surrounding me, and found them either worthless or wanting ... the greatest recantation I had to make was my idea of the traders.' Popularly derided as the palm oil ruffians, the European traders in West Africa were mostly single men, some with African wives, caricatured in the British press as debauched and drunken rogues who had reluctantly given up dealing in slaves when 'legitimate trade' offered greater financial inducements. For Mary Kinglsey, however, they were men she was 'proud to be allowed to call friends and know were fellow-countrymen'.

It was not only her trader friends she believed were maligned. Africans, at the hands of the missionary party – eager 'not to tell you how the country they resided in was but how it was getting towards being what it ought to be' – were portrayed unfairly. Kingsley challenged:

> ...the stay at home statesmen, who think that Africans are awful savages or silly children – people who can only be dealt with on a reformatory penitentiary line. This view is not mine ... but it is the view of the statesman and the general public and the mission public in African affairs.

Looking for consistency, practicality and humanity to be understood and explained, rather than vices and immorality to be manipulated and eradicated, she argued for a new approach to anthropological study by looking at African societies from the inside out, to 'think in black'. Long before anthropologists had developed the idea of fieldwork, she argued:

> ...unless you live among the natives you can never get to know them. At first you see nothing but a confused stupidity and crime; but when you get to see – well! ...you see things worth seeing.

Although questioning many of the popular images of Africa, Mary Kingsley was steeped in the racial theories used to justify and support the expansion of British interests in West Africa. She espoused a by now out of fashion polygenesist outlook, believing that Africans and Europeans, as men and women, were essentially rather than evolutionary different. 'I feel certain that a black man is no more an undeveloped white man than a rabbit is an undeveloped hare, and the mental difference between the races is very similar to that between men and women among ourselves'. The fault of the missionary endeavour, she believed, was in trying to Europeanise Africans. Missionary-educated Africans were the curse of the Coast, embracing a secondhand rubbishy white culture rather than traditional African social customs. When writing about her travels, she focused on her contacts with the Fang people of Gabon, 'unadulterated Africans', as she called them, 'in the raw state'.

Her attitude towards women's rights shared this conservative and separatist philosophy. When approached by petitioners for women's admission to the learned societies she brushed aside their entreaties. 'These androgynes I have no time for', she complained. Women and men were different in kind rather than degree, as Africans to Europeans, and these differences should be recognised and encouraged rather than glossed over. While not denying a hierarchy within these differences constructed on racial and sexual lines, she nevertheless argued for areas of specialist knowledge, in line with the popular doctrine of 'separate spheres'. Opposed to the admission of women to societies of travellers, she argued for a separate women's meeting where things could be discussed without the presence of men. 'Women like myself know many things no man can know about the heathen' she told the Secretary of the Royal Geographical Society, 'and no doubt men do ditto'. On her return from West Africa in December 1895, her first venture into print was not, as commonly believed, in defence of European traders or 'real Africans' but in response to an article in the *Daily Telegraph* describing her as a New Woman. Infuriated by this label, she wrote to the Editor denying any such allegiance. 'I did not do anything', she wrote, 'without the assistance of the superior sex' denying the independence she had so desperately sought.

3. EXPANSION AND DOMINATION OF THE WEST

Calabar 1899; Mary Kingsley (centre front) with front-line representatives of the 'pen-pushers and ostrich feathers' of colonialism.

Claude Macdonald, Consul General of the Niger Territories, with his wife, Ethel, and staff — which included Roger Casement (right).

Mary Kingsley's philosophy of separate development of the races and sexes led her into direct opposition to the missionary party and their stress on a common humanity. Her defence of polygamy, domestic slavery, and even cannibalism as appropriate social forms in West Africa, shocked the conservative press and quickly brought her notoriety. But with this came a popular platform from which to air her views. Her first book, *Travels in West Africa*, published in January 1897, was an immediate bestseller. Based on an account of her second journey, its vast amount of new anthropological material established her as the leading West Africanist of the time. But Mary Kingsley was no longer content with confining herself to the issue of enthnology. Soon she was arguing for the recognition of anthropology as a tool of imperialist expansion; to govern the African, she argued, you must first know him. She wrote to the eminent Oxford anthropologist E.B. Teylor:

> ...I will force upon the politicians the recognition of anthropology if I have to do it with the stake and thumbscrew. Meanwhile the heathen unconsciously keeps on supporting anthropology gallantly, and officialdom says it won't have anything but its old toys – missionaries, stockbrokers, good intentions, ignorance and maxim guns. Well we shall see.

The imperial expansion Mary Kingsley envisioned was of a very different kind to that the new Colonial Secretary, Joseph Chamberlain, had in mind. In opposition to his plans for administrative intervention in West Africa and the establishment of the Crown Colony system, supported by the missionary parties, Mary Kingsley advocated informal economic imperialism, looking back to a mythical golden era when British interests in West Africa were protected by European traders and fair commerce between African and European flourished. Economic ties under British merchants rather than administrative control under 'pen-pushers and ostrich feathers' was her aim. She argued:

> England is the great manufacturing country of the world, and as such requires markets, and requires markets far more than colonies. A colony drains from the mother country, yearly, thousands of the most able and energetic of her children, leaving behind them their aged incapable relations. Whereas the holding of the West African markets drains a few hundred men, only too often for ever; but the trade they carry on and develop enables thousands of men, women and children to remain safe in England in comfort and pleasure, owing to the wages and profits arising from the manufacture and export of articles used in that trade.

Only this system – eventually outlined in her 'Alternative Plan' – would, she claimed, also benefit Africans, by leaving their cultural and social organisations intact.

Mary Kingsley's means of raising support and realising her plans were limited, for her gender excluded her from the burgeoning number of forums concerned with African affairs. The admission of women to the Royal Geographical Society in 1892 had drawn such fierce opposition that the decision was hastily rescinded. Other societies of travellers were equally hostile to women's participation. Outspoken women's activities were confined to the field of missionary and philanthropic work, but even here public speaking could be frowned upon. For a woman to actively campaign against the missionary endeavour and on behalf of the palm oil ruffians and heathen Africans threatened her feminity in a way less controversial standpoints would not have done. Mary Kingsley's response was to emphasise her ladyhood, almost to the point of caricature, reminding her audience at public lectures that she appeared as their maiden aunt, dressed as a woman far beyond her mid-thirties. She appealed to a close friend to help her in the maintenance of this public persona, 'I implore if you hear it said in Society that I appear on platforms in African native costume, a billy cock hat, and a trade shirt, to contradict it', she wrote, 'honour bright I'd got my best frock on'.

As the corridors of official power were closed to her, she began to exploit unofficial methods and behind-the-scenes networks. Soon earning the name of 'Liverpool's hired assassin' for her pro-trader politics and clandestine ways of operating, in private she asserted pressure on individual politicians, exploited old networks and created new ones, and encouraged new venturers into the political arena. Her political development was inextricably knitted to the ways and means through which she could work. It is this informal, behind-the-scenes, nature of her politics that has often led to an underestimation of her influence in West African affairs.

Mary Kingsley felt bound to defend the European traders, Africans, and her own reputation against the allegations being paraded in the press. The first public debate in which she became involved was over the 'liquor traffic'. In 1895 a combination of factors – humanitarian and commercial – launched the 'liquor traffic' debate into a new phase, to which Kingsley's own efforts would soon be added. The British fear of the domination of the West African spirit trade by Hamburg firms reached a new height. The return to power of Salisbury in June, with the temperance supporter Joseph Chamberlain as his Colonial Secretary, was cited by Colonel Frederick Lugard, commissioner for the hinterland of Nigeria, as giving 'hope to those interested in the question that the time had at last come when effective steps would be taken to deal with this evil'. The language of the 'liquor traffic' debate became the 'demoralisation of the native' and 'the evil trade' versus 'legitimate commerce' – all reminiscent of earlier anti-slavery arguments – rather than profit and administrative control.

Sir John Kirk's enquiry following the 1895 Brass uprising had reopened the debate around the future control of the Niger Delta, and different interests were vying for influence in the area – the Royal Niger Company under the persuasive leadership of Sir George Goldie, the Niger Coast Protectorate government, Liverpool and Manchester trading houses, the Colonial Office, and the missionary bodies. The liquor traffic was, to a large extent, a pawn in this contest, a highly emotional issue which could be used to draw public support in the propaganda war.

For Mary Kingsley, the temperance party's argument had two main fallacies. Firstly, it painted a picture of an African population easily manipulated and less able to resist the enticements of alcohol than Europeans. Secondly, the curtailment on the importation of trade alcohol to West Africa would inhibit the 'free-trading' practices of the Liverpool merchants, who used it as a form of currency to obtain the palm oil and other raw materials of their trade. The pro-liquor lobby, however, had little ability to raise the sympathies of the general public against the appeal of the temperance party's tales of the degradation wrought by 'trade gin'. In Kingsley, the pro-liquor party found an advocate who could couch their economic arguments in terms more acceptable to the popular palate. While the leading Liverpool merchant

John Holt had earlier complained that the anti-liquor leaders were 'professional agitators and old women', within a few years he would be extremely grateful that someone conforming to this image had come over to the traders' side.

The debate took place as much in extra-governmental forums as behind the walls of the Colonial Office. Lugard spoke to the Colonial Institute, the letters pages of *The Times* were dominated by the altercation between West African bishops and Governors, and missionary societies hosted public discussions. The thrashing out of the issue in these unofficial forums allowed Kingsley, excluded from the official arena, to be fully immersed in the centre of the debate.

Mary Kingsley's first attacks on the temperance party were made from her position as an ethnologist, to counter the image of the African as a 'drunken child'. She was drawn into the fray by an article appearing in the *Spectator* accusing Africans of being 'a people abnormally low, evil, cruel... It is in Africa that the lowest depth of evil barbarism is reached, and that we find the races with the least of humanity about them except the form... they are all degraded'. Kingsley's reply argued for an understanding of African culture:

> I do not believe the African to be brutal, degraded, or cruel. I know from wide experience with him that he is often grateful and faithful, and by no means the drunken idiot his so-called friends, the Protestant missionaries, are anxious, as an excuse for their failure in dealing with him, to make out.

Although a reluctant speaker, Kingsley embarked upon a vigorous and exhausting programme which took her throughout the country, from local geographical societies to 'magic lantern at YMCA'. The popular image of an intrepid lady explorer in the jungle which had initially so angered her could draw large crowds who would then receive political statements sugared in tales of African adventure.

While the propaganda war was being fought out in the pages of the press and on the public platform, in private the correspondence between Kingsley and her temperance adversaries was more wordy and considered. 'I am going for this mission

'Mavungu', the three-foot nail fetish brought back from West Africa on Mary Kingsley's first, 1893, journey, and which stood in her South Kensington flat.

party with feminine artfulness, not 'like a bull at a gate', she told Holt. As Lugard's damning account of the 'witty and amusing Miss Kingsley' appeared in *The Nineteenth Century*, in private his correspondence with her was a more mutual exchange of information and opinion. And while *The Times* paid her the ultimate insult and ignored the publication of her book, widely reviewed elsewhere, she met the editors for dinner. In this manner she hoped to exert private influence where public access was denied.

Kingsley was building up a network of contacts throughout the political spectrum, exploiting the social sphere controlled by women. Her first approach to her Liverpool ally Holt was made by writing to his wife, who had invited her to attend a meeting of the local Literary and Scientific Society. The wife of the Assistant Under Secretary at the Colonial Office, Reginald Antrobus, provided her with invaluable information and insight into Colonial Office wranglings by spying on her husband's papers. The leading Anglo-Irish social hostess Alice Stopford Green's ability to speak French enabled Kingsley to keep in contact with members of the French embassy in London.

Communications with West Africa were also developed, as Kingsley kept in regular contact with Africans on the Coast and hosted them on their visits to London. 'I have quantities of blacks here', she wrote to Holt – including the leading lawyer Samuel Lewis and Edward Blyden, editor of the *Sierra Leone Weekly News*.

The value of this diverse network of contacts would prove itself in the 'hut tax' controversy in the Protectorate of Sierra Leone. The British merchants had always opposed a tax on African property, accurately predicting that the resulting opposition would disrupt trade. When the first outbreak of resistance to payment occurred in early 1898 their fears were proved founded, but a wavering Colonial Secretary was reluctant to remove a tax in the face of persistent support for its implementation by the Governor of Sierra Leone and allegations by humanitarian pressure groups that clamping down on slavery had caused the rebellion. Realising she had once again to fight opponents who appeared to have humanitarian concerns entirely on their side, Kingsley pleaded for an understanding of Africans – sympathy for the black man as she put it, 'not emotional but common sense sympathy and honour and appreciation'.

But the sympathy she invoked also recalled earlier arguments with the temperance lobby over their misunderstanding of the African situation. The pro-hut taxers, she believed, suffered from a similar ignorance of African society, though a different aspect – not the misrepresenation of the African as a 'drunken child', but of the nature and value of indigenous African legal systems. The hut tax, Kingsley argued, offended African law. 'One of the root principles of African law is that the thing that you pay any one a regular fee for is a thing that is not your own – it is a thing belonging to the person to who you pay the fee'. But behind these initial objections lay her deeper objections to an interventionist policy in West Africa. The real cause of the rebellion was the 'reasonable dislike to being dispossessed alike of power and property in what they regard as their own country'. While publicly sticking to her claim that the tax was the root cause of the disturbances, in private she admitted that it was 'merely the match to a train of gunpowder'. By 'sticking severely to native law' however, other arguments would 'come by and by'.

How can the influence of someone who operated in such a behind-the-scenes and informal way be measured? Her prominent position on African affairs led the Colonial Secretary to write to her at this critical time. But he was reluctant to be seen to countenance the opinion of such a controversial figure. He sought her advice, therefore, as covertly as possible. 'He is horribly frightened of being known to communicate with the witch of Endor', Kingsley told Holt. She responded in kind, marking all her letters to him 'Private' and 'Strictly Confidential' – doubly underlined. When Sir David Chalmers was sent out to Freetown as Special Commissioner to investigate the cause of the disturbances, Chamberlain first briefed him on Kingsley's views. Governor Cardew of Sierra Leone paid her frequent visitors on his return to London, and the Acting-Governor Matthew Nathan,

sent out in his place, zealously courted her friendship before his departure. His reading on board ship from Liverpool to Sierra Leone was Mary Kingsley's second book, *West African Studies*. In this manner she was in touch with all those involved in policy-making around the hut tax.

As her political experience grew, her methods of politicking became more sophisticated, subtle and therefore hidden from subsequent history. Not wanting to appear as an one-woman opponent to the hut tax, she encouraged others to commit themselves to print. Using her contacts with leading pressmen such as St Loe Strachey, editor of the *Spectator* and,

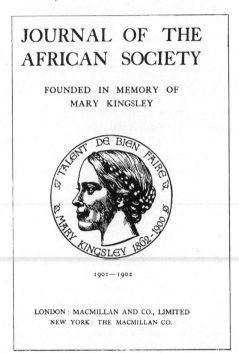

JOURNAL OF THE
AFRICAN SOCIETY

FOUNDED IN MEMORY OF
MARY KINGSLEY

1901—1902

LONDON: MACMILLAN AND CO., LIMITED
NEW YORK: THE MACMILLAN CO.

Kingsley thought, a 'backstairs to Chamberlain, she introduced young journalists into print, most notably E.D. Morel, correspondent for the *Pall Mall Gazette*. She encouraged Holt to write to the papers, but warned him 'don't for goodness gracious sake let the mention of me occur'. As her contacts grew, she increasingly relied on these methods. 'The truth is Mr Holt', she wrote in 1899, 'every bit of solid good work I have done has been done through a man. I get more and more fond of doing things this way. It leaves me a free hand to fight with'. To St Loe Strachey she wrote, 'In the seclusion of private life, in the gentle course of private friendship, I shall do my best in language worse than you have ever heard from me, to weld my

men together and I'll fight to the last shot in my locker against the existing system'. Soon the Colonial Office christened her 'the most dangerous person on the other side'.

Her book, *West African Studies*, published in early 1899, contained a strong attack on the Crown Colony system. 'The sooner the Crown Colony system is removed from the sphere of practical politics and put under a glass case in the South Kensington Museum, labelled Extinct, the better for everyone', she wrote. She described its system of government as a waste of life and money, and a destroyer of African social organisations on which peace and prosperity depended. In its place she drew up an 'Alternative Plan'. This was innovative firstly, in giving governmental and administrative control to European trading interests in West Africa embodied in a Grand Council who appointed a Governor General of West Africa, and secondly, by officially incorporating African opinion – filtered through a council of chiefs – into the administrative network. But although the 'Alternative Plan' was presented as a new option for British control of West Africa, in fact it looked back to a former era rather than forward to a new one. The informal economic ties which Kingsley hoped would form the basis of British imperialism were central to this plan, as was their implementation by a European trading class. The failure of this scheme would depend not only on the impracticality of re-establishing an informal empire in a time of increasing European intervention in West Africa, but also the reluctance of British trading interests to take on the added responsibilities of government. British traders also wanted a non-trading European administrative class to run West African affairs and protect their markets from European and African rivals.

While on the public platform Kingsley appeared as the professional politician, in private she felt more and more drawn to the Africa she had left behind. While maintaining a professional façade of feminine conformity, in the privacy of her Kensington home she decorated her rooms with souvenirs from her journeys – enormous wooden drums and a yard-high nail fetish – and jangled about in her African bangles. To a childhood friend she wrote of the stresses of her two personalities, the public politician and the private African:

> The majority of people I shrink from, I don't like them, I don't understand them and they most distinctly don't understand me... I cannot be a bushman *and* a drawing-roomer. Would to Allah I was in West Africa now, with a climate that suited me and a people who understood me, and who I could understand.

She longed to return to 'skylark' in West Africa and experience a freedom 'this smug, self-satisfied, sanctimonious, lazy, *Times*-believing England' could never give.

Her identity with the African had been strong and heartfelt since her return from West Africa. Emotional revelations of this personal sympathy to close friends found more public expression in the use of terms usually reserved for non-European peoples to describe her own experience. Calling herself a savage and a 'member of the tribe of women', she would even describe herself as 'an African'. 'We Africans are not fit for decent society', she told Alice Stopford Green, and to the Indianist Sir Alfred Lyall, she wrote 'I am a firm African'. She compared her beliefs to those of Africans. 'I desire to get on with the utter Bushman', she declared, 'and never sneer or laugh at his native form of religion, a pantheism which I confess is a form of my own religion'.

This identity was also an expression of her own philosophy of polygenesism and separate development. Arguing for the promotion of women's traditional sphere and African tradi-tional life (although not always consistent in the definition of either), she said the 'African is a feminine race' – misunderstood by a dominant culture. The most candid revelation of these feelings was to Nathan, with whom she was unhappily in love:

> I will import to you, in strict confidence, for if it were known it would damage me badly, my opinion on the African. He is *not* 'half devil and half child', anymore than he is 'our benighted brother' and all that sort of thing. He is a woman... I know those nigs because I am a woman, a woman of a masculine race but a woman still.

Kingsley became increasingly dissatisfied with the isolation of her outspoken position, and the lack of support from disunited traders, and complained to Holt of loneliness. She secretly applied to nurse in South Africa, hoping to cover the Boer War for the *Morning Post* and travel northwards across the Orange River and far away from European settlements to her 'beloved South West Coast'. Letting only a few friends know of her imminent departure, she ended her final lecture at the Imperial Institute with the words 'Fare ye well, for I am homeward bound'. On arriving at the Cape at the end of March 1900, the medical conditions horrified her, and soon she was absorbed in the immediate needs of hospital work. 'All this work here, the stench, the washing, the enemas, the bed pans, the blood, is my world', she wrote to Alice Stopford Green, 'not London Society, politics, that gallery into which I so strangely wandered – into which I don't care a hairpin if I never wander again'. Within two months the typhoid fever that was daily killing four to five of her patients struck Mary, and on June 3rd she died. She was buried, at her own request, at sea. Full military and naval honours accompanied the funeral.

Commentators on Mary Kingsley's life and work have often accredited her with laying the political foundations for the introduction of indirect rule in Northern Nigeria. But it is in the informal sector, and not Colonial Office policy making, that we must look for her political legacy. Morel drew upon her inspiration, and continually agitated against Colonial Office politics, later leading the Congo Reform Movement, an informal pressure group relying on press coverage and public speaking in the Kingsley style. Alice Stopford Green, inheritor of Kingsley's behind-the-scenes politicking, formed the African Society in her memory, as a forum for the exchange of information between traders, academics, and officials involved in West African affairs. John Holt said, 'Miss Kingsley discovered me and made me think'.

FOR FURTHER READING:
Mary Kingsley *Travels in West Africa* (London, 1897; reprinted Virago, 1982); Catherine Barnes Stevenson, 'Female Anger and African Politics' the Case of Two Victorian "Lady Travellers" *Turn-of-the-Century Woman* (1985); K. D. Nworah, 'The Liverpool Sect and British West African Politics 1895-1915' in *African Affairs* (1971); A. Olorunfemi 'The Liquor Traffic Dilemma in British West Africa: The Southern Nigerian Example 1895-1918' in *International Journal of African Historical Studies* (1984). The most recent biography of Kingsley is Katherine Frank *A Voyager Out* (Houghton and Mifflin, 1986).

A whole subcontinent was picked up without half trying

The East India Company went to India not to conquer, but to trade, yet it ended by acquiring a jewel for Victoria's crown

Pico Iyer

The author, born of Indian parents, went to Eton and Oxford. He wrote last on the Assassins (October 1985). His book Video Night in Kathmandu *was published this year by Knopf. Larry Burrows was killed while covering the Vietnam War for* Life.

Images of the British raj in India are everywhere of late. On television reruns, the divided rulers of Paul Scott's *Jewel in the Crown* sip their tea in scented hill stations and swap idle gossip in the palaces of local princes. At movie houses, we can savor all the hot intensities that blast a decorous English visitor the moment she steps ashore after *A Passage to India*, to be engulfed in a whirlwind of mendicants, elephants, snake charmers and crowds. In New York, British director Peter Brook's nine-hour production of an ancient Hindu epic poem, *The Mahabharata*, has lately been playing to packed houses and considerable critical praise. Best-selling books like *Freedom at Midnight* re-create the struggle of two great cultures, mighty opposites with a twinned destiny, as they set about trying to disentangle themselves and their feelings before the Partition of 1947. Across the country, strolling visitors marveled a few years ago at all the silken saris and bright turbans of the Festival of India (SMITHSONIAN, June 1985) and, even more, at the exotic world they evoke: the bejeweled splendor of the Mogul courts; dusty, teeming streets; and all the dilemmas confronting the imperial British as they sought to bring Western ideas of order to one of the wildest and most complex lands on Earth.

Behind all the glamour and the glory, however, lies one of history's mischievous ironies. For the raj, which did not begin until 1858 when the British government officially took over India from a private trading company, was in fact only the final act in a long, crooked and partly accidental drama. Much of the British empire, in fact, was acquired, according to a celebrated phrase, "in a fit of absence of mind."

When the London merchants of what became the East India Company first sent ships to the East in 1601, they were not bound for India at all but for the Spice Islands of the Dutch East Indies, and the English traders who set foot on the subcontinent a little later actually sought to avoid conquest. Directors back in London kept telling them that conquest would only cut into profits. "All war is so contrary to our interest," they reminded field employees in 1681, "that we cannot too often inculcate to you our strictest aversion thereunto."

But India was still part of the fading Mogul empire, which a century earlier had brought Muslim adminis-

3. EXPANSION AND DOMINATION OF THE WEST

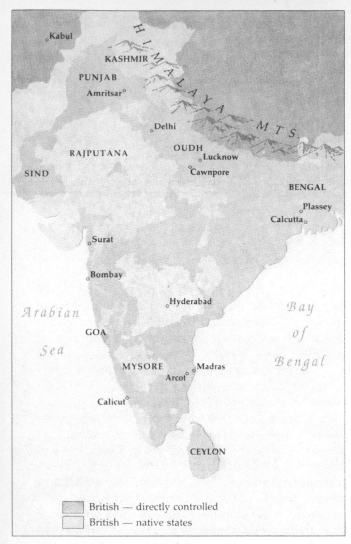

By mid-19th century, British controlled almost all of India either directly or through alliances with partially self-ruling "native states" run by rajas.

trators and conquerors. Just to protect its ability to do business in a land already riddled with fierce animosities, the company found itself forced to defend trading posts with hired soldiers. Before long, the posts became cities (Calcutta, Bombay, Madras) and their soldier garrisons, small private armies. As assets and responsibilities mounted, the merchants, who had come out as supplicants bearing gifts to local princes for an inside track on trade, gradually became soldiers, and then became local rulers themselves.

By the time the company was disbanded in 1858, hardly more than a thousand British officers controlled India, an area the size of Europe in which 200 million people—about a quarter of them Muslim, but a majority Hindu—spoke more than 200 different languages. By then, the company had carried home such Indian terms as "bungalow," "verandah," "punch," "dungarees" and "pyjamas." They had also imported

back to Britain many pukka (first class) habits such as smoking cigars, playing polo and taking showers. Most of all, they had laid the foundations for, and forced the British government to get involved in, what was about to become the most ambitious, and the most anguished, empire in modern history.

The East India Company was originally conceived in September 1599, when a group of London merchants resolved to raise £30,000 for sending ships to the East to collect silks, spices and jewels "upon a purely mercantile bottom." On the last day of the 16th century, Queen Elizabeth I gave her blessing and five British vessels set sail for what is now known as Indonesia. Upon arrival, they found the Dutch far from eager to share their profits. The British therefore turned back to India's west coast, dropping anchor near Surat in 1608, and Sir William Hawkins proceeded to the imperial Mogul court in Agra to seek permission to set up a trading post. But the Portuguese, who had staked some claims on the subcontinent when Vasco da Gama landed in 1498, proved quite as reluctant as the Dutch were to part with their monopoly.

Trading requests, backed up by force

As the Mogul emperor dithered about giving permissions and the Portuguese connived, the British took to backing up their local requests with threats of force. By 1639, English traders were established on the east coast, too, leasing for £600 a year a harborless beach just five miles long and one mile wide, which they christened Fort St. George (later Madras). In 1661 they picked up another site when, for a paltry annual rent of £10, King Charles II handed over a barren island called Bombay, which had been part of his dowry from Catherine of Braganza. A generation later, after some skirmishes, the company gained permission to set up shop in a stinking mudflat in Bengal; it quickly developed into Fort William (Calcutta, now a city of ten million, grew up around it).

The India that these British traders came to do business in was a thoroughly bewildering place, a vast expanse of land filled with millions of peasants ruled by a small number of princes—mostly Muslim—with power derived from a court whose opulence could put any in Europe to shame. The Moguls, a band of intruders of Mongolian, Turkish and Persian origin, had formally established their empire in India in 1526; by the time the British arrived, they ruled most of northern India save for a few fiefdoms still controlled by tribute-paying Hindu rajas. Though ruthless, the Moguls had cultivated tastes, especially for Persian-style gardens, poems and miniatures. The young emperor Jahangir, for example, boasted of slaughtering 17,000 animals and nearly 14,000 birds, yet he was a great patron of the arts. His successor, Shah Jahan,

Carrying on the customs of the Mogul rulers, British hunted tigers from the backs of elephants, although letting the great beasts trample and gore the hunting trophies was a rare and grisly experience.

secured his throne by murdering rivals, yet he was also the romantic who built an exquisite shrine, the Taj Mahal, to the memory of a beloved wife.

Jahangir's father, Akbar, the greatest Mogul emperor, prudently married Hindu princesses, observed Hindu festivals and even placed Hindus in high office. Thus, even those he displaced were inclined to see him not as the head of a Muslim state, but simply as the Muslim head of a nonpartisan India. When Akbar died in 1605, however, the court degenerated into a series of vicious successional struggles animated by an operating principle known as *takht ya takhta* (throne or coffin). Aurangzeb, whose 49-year rule began in 1658, applied special taxes to Hindus and reputedly demolished Hindu temples, sowing the seeds of the furious Hindu-Muslim animosities that would shadow British India till the end and that poison relations between India and Pakistan to this day.

Against this turbulent background, the British were free to ply their trade as they wished, selling silver and devices like clocks and firearms in return for cotton, spices, silk, indigo, jewels and opium. Before long the East India Company was one of the largest employers in London. In India, its major settlements developed into self-sufficient communities, with forts, warehouses, residents and even their own law courts. To defend these "civil servants," each of the trading posts also kept a company of "military servants."

The highest authority in each company settlement was a Governor-in-Council (the Governor of Madras from 1687-92 was one Elihu Yale, who a bit later bequeathed his fortune to help found a small college in New Haven) and these officials developed a taste for the regal extravagance of local potentates. By 1700, the Governor of Bombay would emerge from his private quarters only in palanquined splendor, attended by 40 servants and preceded by underlings waving silver wands. Each course at dinner was announced by a fanfare of trumpets, and some state dinners ran to 600 different dishes.

Most junior employees, later known as griffins, arrived in India expecting to earn just £10 a year as "writers," or clerks. In anticipation of becoming factors or merchants, however, they took out loans and basked in affluence inconceivable at home (p. 48). The day's work was generally confined to the hours between 9 A.M. and noon; the rest of the day was given over to eating, napping, gambling, drinking—and more drinking. During long, sweltering evenings, they smoked hookahs, sometimes loaded with opium, and were pleasantly distracted at titillating nautch dances.

If the rewards of a posting to India were high, the risks were higher. "Two monsoons are the age of a man" ran a gloomy company saying, and many a company man did not survive his first six months of punishing heat and dust. If he were not laid low by malaria, cholera or smallpox, he was likely to be undone by such exotic threats as snakebite, heatstroke, jungle fever or local dancing girls. None of this was helped, of course, by amateur doctors who thought the best cure for cholera was a red-hot iron on the heel. Small wonder that Bombay became known as the "burying ground of the English."

As the Mogul empire began to collapse, a host of contenders swarmed into the vacuum. In 1739, Nadir Shah of Persia marched on Delhi, slaughtered many of its people and carried its treasures, including the Peacock Throne, back to Tehran. The Afghans, too, made intermittent raids from the northwest, and the Marathas, a predatory band of horsemen, were carving sizable chunks out of the middle of the empire. And for all the company's attempts to discourage interloping, more and more free-lance adventurers kept flocking in from Europe, equipped with forged trading passes and a hunger for a quick killing.

The threat that most unsettled the English, however, came from the French, who in the 1750s were engaged in a global war with Britain. In 1746, the French boldly seized Madras and in 1750 their Governor, Joseph François Dupleix, ingeniously set about hiring and training native troops, known as sepoys. Dressed in smart uniforms and transformed into soldiers, these men became the envy of local princes, who were soon turning over tracts of land in exchange for French-trained sepoys. In this way France came to control a large part of southern India. The British cause seemed doomed—until a suggestion arose from a moody young man who had come over as a clerk just seven years before: Why not create a counterforce of sepoys and seize the provincial capital of Arcot, which was under French control? Then, with a vastly outnumbered force of 500 and three small field guns, Robert Clive (p. 129) made good on his plan, and the French challenge in India was effectively stifled.

Hardly had the British begun to catch their breath than another threat emerged up the coast, where the new nawab of Bengal, Siraj-ud-Daula, attacked Calcutta. Leading 30,000 foot soldiers, 20,000 horsemen and 400 trained elephants against a crumbling and ill-fortified garrison defended by scarcely 200 men, he took Fort William without much difficulty. That night, the European captives were locked up in a brig known as the Black Hole, an 18-by-14-foot room with a door on one side and, on the other, a small iron-barred window leading onto a verandah. The stifling air and crush of bodies in the room were compounded by the sweltering summer heat. When morning broke on June 21, 1756, the cell was packed with corpses.

Many scholars today believe that early claims made for the Black Hole of Calcutta—describing 123 dead out of 146—may have been inflated by a factor of three. Even so, the British could hardly fail to be psychologically chilled and outraged by an episode that dramatized all their worst fears of dark suffocation. Two British captives were said to have survived only by sucking the sweat off their shirts. Sixteen-year-old Mary Carey was rumored to have stayed alive—while her husband, her mother and her 10-year-old sister all died—by drinking her own tears.

One year after the Black Hole, Clive sailed up the coast from Madras and led 800 troops and roughly 2,000 sepoys against a force of more than 50,000 at Plassey. There, defying the odds again, he routed Siraj-ud-Daula. He also defied company rules by playing politician and installing as the new nawab an elderly Mogul general named Mir Jafar. By now, the crumbling Mogul empire was in no position to resist; indeed, in 1765, the emperor actually made Clive his dewan (revenue collector) for the whole state of Bengal. Thus the company found itself controlling one of the richest provinces in the land, source of almost two-thirds of all Britain's imports from Asia.

After the takeover of Bengal, relations between the British and the natives changed radically. Company merchants were now free to roam the province, helping themselves to the fruits of the land through joint ventures with Indian partners. Suddenly they were in a position to expect presents themselves. They could not only live with the local rulers, they could live like them, too.

With their "Honorable Masters" nine months' passage and 7,000 miles away, the company men, unsupervised and uncircumscribed, began "shaking the pagoda tree" to their heart's content. Clive was given £211,500 by the nawab he had installed and, 18 months later, another grant assuring him of £27,000 a year for life—at a time when a gentleman in England could live well on £800 a year. Even that much was perhaps Clive's due. But one Mr. Watts was rewarded for his bravery at Plassey with £117,000. Another British merchant was given a very profitable saltworks complete with a staff of 13,000 workers. Still another set up his own mint. Even so, for every British fortune made, ten native fortunes were accumulated.

As news of such profligate doings reached London, the city was scandalized. But every young man wanted a position in India, and company panjandrums in England, no strangers to corruption themselves, were soon accepting £2,000 or more in bribes to secure them such positions. "Animated with all the avarice of age and all the impetuosity of youth," Edmund Burke would tell assembled members of Parliament, traders "roll in one after another; wave after wave; and there is nothing before the eyes of the native but an endless hopeless prospect of new birds of prey and passage."

Most outrageous of all to many in the British squire-archy was that once they got back home, the self-appointed nawabs—nabobs, as the corrupted term had it—were beginning to overturn Britain's age-old social structure. Clive, for example, had gone to India the unpromising son of a penurious country gentleman. By the time he returned in 1760, he was the equivalent of a millionaire and a local hero rich enough to repair his family home, buy another nearby, purchase an estate in Ireland and snap up a house in London's fashionable Berkeley Square. Just for good measure, he also helped himself to a "rotten borough" seat in Parliament. Yet the company was sinking toward bankruptcy. In 1773, the directors had to appeal to the Bank of England for a £1.4 million loan.

Though the government granted the loan, it made an attempt to curb the company's authority. Under the Regulating Act of 1773, all business in India was to be overseen by a Governor General in Calcutta, who would put an end to both "private trade" and those infamous "presents." Eleven years later, Parliament established a six-man Board of Control, including two members of Parliament, to sit above the company directors. This was the first step that would eventually lead to the raj, the period of official British government control.

Warren Hastings (p. 129), the first Governor General, could not have been further removed from the idle and indulgent nabobs: even as de facto ruler of British India from 1772-85, he rode eight miles each day before breakfast, drank nothing stronger than tea, took cold baths and turned in at 10 every night. Under the Governor General's highly principled eye, extra-curricular profits were quickly cut down, earned salaries somewhat increased.

More than just instilling a new sense of discipline, Hastings brought a sense of civility. He was an educated man, schooled in Persian and Bengali and firmly convinced that the company should treat local customs with respect. He skillfully persuaded Indian princes to form alliances with the company, and under his influence scholars introduced the rest of the world to India's fascinating cultures. To support this approach, he began importing a new kind of British official, young men willing to study local languages and traditions, more devoted to king and country than to self. In time, such types became the backbone of the body that would be the brightest creation of the British raj: the Indian Civil Service.

More and more men streamed into the subcontinent: not just *boxwallah* traders now, but soldiers, scholars and sophisticated young administrators. And as they tried to make themselves at home in alien land, the newcomers laid the foundations of that closed society of splendor and heartache that would later so

Naughty nautch parties featured food, drink, sweet music and sometimes debauchery, since many dancing girls were also prostitutes. When more Englishwomen began arriving, such pleasures, as well as easy racial mixing, sharply declined.

fascinate E. M. Forster and Paul Scott. For where the rough-and-ready merchants of old had lived like local princelings, the new arrivals preferred to live like well-heeled Britons. Tom-toms were gradually replaced by fife-and-drum corps, curries by English dishes and local clothes by the latest (or almost latest) London fashions. Country houses complete with tidy gardens began to spring up along the Hooghly River in Calcutta. Places like the Bread and Cheese Bungalow, the Jockey Club and Eden Gardens began to crop up around the City of Palaces. The city of Calcutta came to resemble a sweet-and-sour Bath.

Each morning before the heat of midday, in this imported version of England intensified and exaggerated by its distance from home, the entire beau monde would travel en masse to the local racecourse, and every day at dusk would take the air in carriages along the Embankment. Days would pass in one long round of social calls and afternoon naps, evenings in card games, recitals, balls and dinner parties (complete with sherbet: ice from Maine was delivered by sailing vessel). Musical entertainments like *The Poor Soldier* began to be staged at local theaters, with farces bravely attempted in which women's roles were taken by "awkward giants with splay feet, gruff voices and black beards." Before long, even that last deficiency was being taken care of: each October, shiploads of eligible young women began arriving with the cooler weather in what later came to be known as the Fishing Fleet; each spring, a few Returned Empties sadly took the long, unmarried journey home.

British-Indian society still shone with an air of gilded gentility. Silken canopies graced the private boxes at Calcutta theaters, while palanquins with golden bells and embroidered curtains were carried down St. Thomas Road. One typical bachelor in Calcutta in the 1780s kept 63 servants. Even a man at war did not consider relinquishing his sense of privilege: a captain going to battle in 1780 was generally accompanied by a steward, a cook, a "boy," a horsekeeper, a grass cutter, a washerman and, of course, a mistress. He also had to bring along at least 15 coolies to transport his tent and large bed, camp stools, folding table, maybe six trunkfuls of tableware, cases of wine, a hamper of live poultry, a goat and, not surprisingly, an extra tent for supplies.

Hyder Ali and Tipu Sultan

Such extravagance and eccentricity were hardly confined to the British side, of course. Against them were arrayed colorful adversaries like Hyder Ali and his son Tipu Sultan, who in the 1760s seized control of the predominantly Hindu state of Mysore and proceeded to run it as their own private fiefdom. For decades, father and son were a constant menace to the British presence in the south, now and then setting fire to the country houses on the outskirts of Madras and leading their mercenary *lootywallahs* on one pillaging expedition after another.

Not far away, the British faced another kind of resistance from courtly Muhammad Ali, whom they had installed as nawab of Arcot. Though constantly entwined in shady deals and entangled in ceaseless financial wrangles, the tall and dignified gentleman somehow contrived to live like a king for 50 years. Each day, palanquins filled with Europeans determined to collect money owed would line up outside his Chepauk Palace in Madras; each night, the same men could be seen retreating, still unpaid but thoroughly won over by his apologies and charming ways. At his death, the Ali left behind outstanding debts of more than £30 million.

As the 18th century drew to a close, British India became more and more divided by its own distinctive caste system and plagued by scurrilous gossip and social rivalry. The first great victim of snobbery was, ironically enough, Hastings. In spite of—or maybe because of—his success in bringing some order to India, the Governor General was challenged by jealous rivals and in 1787, after returning to London, he faced impeachment charges in effect blaming him for everything that had gone wrong in India. After a spectacular, protracted trial he was acquitted. Lord Cornwallis, the patrician soldier who had surrendered to George Washington at Yorktown just five years earlier, was sent to India as a replacement. To some degree, Cornwallis extended his predecessor's program of moral reform, establishing auditors to oversee expenses, enforcing an absolute distinction between those who governed and those who traded. Yet he had few of Hastings' wide sympathies: summarily removing from high office in Calcutta every native but one, he sought to stamp out the threat of corruption by attacking the spirit of cooperation.

Lord Wellesley, who took over as Governor General in 1798, was quite another sort of imperial aristocrat. Realizing that his overseers at home were preoccupied with the threat from Napoleon, and rationalizing his assertiveness by pointing to the French march into Egypt in 1798, he briskly set about extending British authority. His troops defeated Tipu Sultan, trounced the long-troublesome Marathas and annexed Indian territory left and right by pressing permanent alliances on local princes. By the time he was recalled in 1805, the grip of the British could be felt across the entire subcontinent.

That year, Wellesley, without the knowledge of the directors back home, set up in Calcutta a kind of Oxbridge-on-the-Hooghly named Fort William College. Here young Englishmen were to learn such languages as Arabic, Persian, Urdu and Sanskrit while cultivating a deeper understanding of local traditions. Thus Wellesley came to embody both the main strains, im-

Fiercest Englishman in India, Robert Clive won crucial battles, went home filthy rich but unhappy.

National Portrait Gallery, London

First Governor General, Warren Hastings tried to reform British rule and was slandered for his trouble.

perialism and Orientalism, that would compete for preeminence throughout the raj. The company was in control of much of India; now it had to decide whether to treat the place as treasure chest, military base, branch office or incipient independent nation. As the British set about "improving" India, for better and for worse, they were driven partly by their arrogant sense of rectitude, partly by an earnest sense of duty, the mixed feelings that would give the raj its tragic, bittersweet tang.

Through it all, the company was more and more supervised by Parliament. In 1813, despite a renewed charter, it was stripped of its Indian trading monopoly. Twenty years later, the company was again allowed to survive, but its assets were liquidated, its ships dispersed and its directors left with little power. At the same time, Indians were allowed to hold increasingly higher administrative posts.

Yet for all its diminishing power, the last 50 years of the East India Company's presence in India in some respects marked a kind of golden age. This was due in large part to a group of thoughtful Englishmen who saw themselves as guardians of a fledgling state and who were committed to preparing the Indians for eventual self-government. The Britons' duty, according to one of them, Mountstuart Elphinstone, was "to prevent people making laws for [India] until they see whether it wants them."

Typical of the best of these men was Charles Metcalfe, of Eton and Fort William College, a solitary and introspective soul who first proved his mettle at 23 when he was sent to deal with Maharaja Ranjit Singh. Famous for his harem, his opium addiction and his possession of the Koh-i-noor diamond, the one-eyed Singh had established a powerful kingdom among the warlike Sikhs, which was guarded by a well-trained army led by European mercenaries. Yet somehow, in an unexpected development that was to become one of the most moving and oft-repeated features of the raj, the British scholar and the flamboyant Indian chieftain struck up a friendship and they sealed it with a treaty of mutual respect.

In recognition of this diplomatic coup, Metcalfe was made Resident at Delhi at the tender age of 27, which meant he presided over an area half the size of Britain. By encouraging agriculture, Metcalfe virtually quadrupled revenues in only six years; more important, perhaps, he abolished the slave trade and outlawed capital punishment, at a time when the former was still going strong in the United States and the latter was often still the lot of a 40-shilling thief in Britain. "Our dominion in India is by conquest," Metcalfe wrote. "It is naturally disgusting to the inhabitants and can only be maintained by military force. It is our positive duty to render them justice, to respect and protect their rights."

While such men sought to nurture Indian culture,

another group steadfastly believed that Britain had a very different kind of moral mission in India—to rescue the locals from the darkness of heathen superstition. No longer were Hinduism and Islam merely regarded as strange and distasteful; now they were seen as positively immoral. Even William Wilberforce, Britain's leading crusader against slavery, told Parliament in 1813 that he hoped to see the subcontinent "exchange its dark and bloody superstition for the genial influence of Christian light and truth."

Ritual murder and self-immolation

Both conflicting impulses came together in one of the last of the company's great Governors General, William Bentinck, who was determined to promote British interests, but only by increasing Indian happiness. After canvassing the opinions of Hindus, he outlawed the custom of suttee, whereby Hindu widows were required to fling themselves upon their husband's funeral pyre. Perhaps the most urgent challenge Bentinck faced was the rising threat of thuggee, the practice of ritual murder that by the 1820s was claiming some 20,000 victims a year. Working in small groups, the Thugs (our word originated here) would fall in with travelers and journey by their side for days or even weeks at a time, often under the pretext of protecting them. Then one night, when the moment was right, the Thugs would suddenly fall upon their companions and strangle them with consecrated bandanas before flinging them into graves as offerings to Kali, goddess of destruction. More than 40 Thug groups existed in India—one man alone boasted 719 murders —until Bentinck, through a system of informers, brought them to justice.

As the British came to govern more and more of India, they developed an even stronger feeling of racial superiority, the spirit of paternalism carrying not only concern but all the condescension that the word can imply. The increased separation of the races had been intensified by the growing presence of upper-class British women on the subcontinent. Women led more insulated lives than their husbands and, rarely seeing the locals, were apt to fear or disdain them. By now, therefore, Indians were no longer sharing nautch parties with their British neighbors and company men were no longer paying courtesy calls on local maharajas. The view of many memsahibs was sadly reflected in the dismissive judgment of one Mrs. Graham, circa 1809, in her *Journal of a Residence in India*: "These [Indian] people, if they have the virtues of slaves, have their vices also. They are cunning and incapable of truth; they disregard the imputation of lying and perjury and would consider it folly not to practise them for their own interest."

For their part, many Indians were increasingly alarmed by all this. Their outrage was hardly soothed when the British responded to a humiliating defeat in the First Afghan War and the disastrous retreat from Kabul with a flurry of saber-rattling and territorial acquisition. In 1848 they annexed the Punjab. In 1856 they took over the large, corrupt and troubled province of Oudh. And they continued to show less and less respect for local customs.

In 1857, native grievances flared up in one dramatic blaze. The final explosion was sparked by a relatively small charge: the introduction of a new kind of Enfield rifle, whose cartridges, it was rumored, had to be greased not with wax and vegetable oil, as before, but with animal fat. The British were sensitive to the fact that no Hindu would touch cow's fat and no Muslim would touch pig's fat; somehow, though, their orders granting permission to use vegetable oil either got confused or distorted. When 85 sepoys were thrown into jail for refusing to accept the new cartridges, their enraged comrades stormed the prison and the whole blood-crazed mob set to murdering every foreign man, woman or child they could lay hands on.

While a few pockets of the country got caught up in the bedlam of the mutiny, most parts remained fairly calm. Nobody, however, could ignore the tales of atrocities on both sides. Perhaps the most famous event was the sepoy siege of Lucknow (opposite). At Cawnpore (now Kanpur), hundreds of European women and children surrendered on guarantee of safe passage—and all were promptly and brutally slaughtered. In response, the British staged mass hangings and bayoneted mutinous sepoys on sight. Near Amritsar, the incident of the Black Hole was horribly repeated, and reversed, as one Major Cooper executed 237 captives, only to find that another 45 had died of suffocation in the tiny police station to which he had committed them. After five months of bloodshed, when the mutiny was put down by the British and loyal Indian troops, the government of Great Britain took over all responsibility from the British East India Company.

Commerce now formally gave way to empire. And despite the protestation of one of its chief executives, John Stuart Mill, the company that had been signed into being by Queen Elizabeth I was now signed into extinction by Queen Victoria. Its army was reorganized into the Indian Army; its Governor General, Lord Canning, became the first Viceroy of India. Thus began the last act of a drama that would culminate 90 years later in Gandhi's campaign of nonviolent resistance and in Paul Scott's heart-torn figures stranded in an imperial twilight. By the time India gained independence in 1947, it was hard for anyone to recall that the whole adventure had begun almost 350 years before with a group of merchants in search of nothing more than a "quiet trade."

SOUTHERN BARBARIANS AND RED-HAIRS IN FEUDAL JAPAN

C.R. Boxer

'This government of Japan may well be accounted the greatest and power-fullest Tyranny, that ever was heard of in the world; for all the rest [of the people] are as slaves to the Emperor (or great commander as they call him), who upon the least suspicion (or jealousy) or being angry with any man (be he never so great a man) will cause him upon the receipt of his letter to cut his belly, which if he refuse to do, not only he, but all the rest of their race shall feel the smart thereof.' (Richard Cocks, chief of the English 'Factory' or trading-agency at Hirado, to the Earl of Salisbury, December 10th, 1614).

The rightful Emperor of Japan was an ostensibly highly venerated but powerless ruler at Kyoto, who claimed unbroken descent from the Sun-Goddess. He was called by foreigners the *Dairi*, or *Mikado*, and was sometimes described as a 'Pope' or spiritual monarch. The real power rested with the Shogun, or Generalissimo (originally, *sei-i-tai-shogun*, or 'barbarian-subduing generalissimo'). This title of 'great commander' as Cocks termed it, was hereditary in the House of Tokugawa, since the unification of the island-empire, after centuries of internecine warfare, by Tokugawa Ieyasu in 1600. Europeans who had resided for any length of time in Japan knew the true state of affairs; but they invariably referred to the incumbent Shogun as the Emperor, since he was the supreme executive ruler, and

styled himself as such in correspondence with foreigners. The 'belly-cutting' mentioned by Cocks was the long-established Japanese custom of ritual suicide by *seppuku*, or *hara-kiri*, as it is more commonly termed in Europe.

All the Europeans who visited feudal Japan were impressed by the readiness with which capital punishment was inflicted on all and sundry for the most trifling offences. The celebrated English pilot, Will Adams, who lived in Japan from 1600 until his death in 1620, wrote that the Japanese were 'in justice very severe, having no respect of persons. . . . No thief for the most part put in prison, but presently executed'. Another contemporary, the Spaniard, Bernardino de Avila Girón, observed: 'Name a Japanese and you name an executioner; and yet they say it is cruel to punish children'—a contrast which significantly illustrates the difference between Japanese and European attitudes. Richard Cocks, after passing the mutilated corpses of criminals on a roadside journey in 1616, commented, 'If it were not for this strict justice, it were no living among them, they are so villainous desperate.'

Westerners who came to Japan from the time of its 'discovery' by three Portuguese castaways in 1543 until the expulsion of all foreigners save the Dutch and the Chinese in 1639, can be divided into two main categories. Those who visited the country briefly or for long periods, but who did not

marry and settle down there; and those who became 'naturalised Japaners'. This latter category included the English pilot, Will Adams, with his homes at Hirado and Yokosuka, the Portuguese pilot, Balthazar de Sousa, 'who had a fine house with spacious and pleasant grounds' at Nagasaki in 1626, and the Dutch shipmates of Will Adams, Melchior van Sandvoort and Jan Joosten.

Before their official expulsion from the country in 1613-14, some of the missionaries, both Jesuits and friars, had lived in Japan for many years and acquired an excellent knowledge of the people, the language, and the country. The most remarkable among them was Padre João Rodriques *circa* 1562-1633, nicknamed *Tçuzzu*, or 'the Interpreter'. He lived in Japan from 1577 to 1610, acting as a confidential interpreter to the *Taiko*, Toyotomi Hideyoshi, 1536-1598, who first unified Japan, and later to the Shogun, Tokugawa Ieyasu, 1542-1616, until he fell out of favour, was banished to Macao, and was replaced by Will Adams. His membership of the Church Militant prevented Rodriques from giving objective accounts of Buddhism and Shinto. But his appreciation of Japanese art and literature in all their forms, his expert knowledge of the tea-ceremony and of many other distinctive aspects of Japanese culture, were not to be attained by any other Westerner in Japan until Von Siebold,

First published in *History Today*, October 1981, pp. 20-25. Reproduced by kind permission of History Today, Ltd., 83-84 Berwick Street, London W1V 3PJ England.

B.H. Chamberlain and E.M. Satow in the nineteenth century.

Another long-time resident of Japan with an excellent knowledge of the language, the culture, and the people, was the Italian Jesuit priest, Organtino Gnecchi-Soldi, 1533-1609. Within thirty years of his death, he entered into Japanese folklore in an anonymous chapbook entitled *Kirishitan Monogatari* (*Tale of Christianity*). He was described as being 'somewhat similar in shape to a human being, but more like a long-nosed goblin, seven feet high, with a black skin, large protruding red nose shaped like a conch-shell and with teeth longer than those of a horse'. Under the name of *Urugan Bateren* (Padre Organtino), he figures in modern Japanese literature, including Akutagawa Ryunosuke's short story 'When the Gods Smile'. After being proscribed on pain of death for centuries, the Jesuits and their religion are now in high favour in contemporary Japan. Many streets in Nagasaki have been given names evocative of 'the Christian Century'; and *Kirishitan* souvenirs are mass-produced for the tourist market.

The Japanese authorities at first showed themselves strangely reluctant to proceed to extremes against the European missionaries who had clearly and deliberately flouted the laws, manners, and customs of the 'Land of the Gods'. After the Shogun's proscription of Christianity and banishment of the missionaries in 1614, many of the Jesuits and friars thought that the *Bakufu* ('curtain government') would not enforce the death-sentence against such European missionaries as they found in hiding, but would merely deport them to Manila or to Macao. Even unconverted Japanese had often told them that Hideyoshi had been criticised by many of the *daimyo* (feudal lords) for crucifying some Spanish Franciscan missionary-friars in 1597. These critics had included Tokugawa Ieyasu; so it was widely assumed that the death-penalty would not be enforced against those who were caught in hiding. No missionary was in fact executed in Ieyasu's lifetime; but after his death, his son and successor, Hidetada, ordered the execution of four European missionary-priests in 1617. This marked an intensification of the persecution, which became yearly more wide-ranging, thorough, and severe. The problem of Christianity in

Japan was no longer one of acceptance by the 'blind heathen', but the necessity for clandestine and underground adaption and survival.

During the years when the Portuguese were established at Nagasaki and the trade with Macao was maintained by an annual 'Great Ship' (*Náo* in Portuguese; carrack in English), Japanese painters of the Kano School produced richly decorated *byobu*, or folding-screens. These screens made a 'most delightful show', as an English traveller noted in 1637; and many of them were exported to Macao and to Goa, whence a few reached Europe. They depicted the *Nambanjin* (literally 'Southern Barbarians'), arriving in their huge *Kurofune* ('Black Ship'), and disembarking at Nagasaki. The Portuguese traders from Macao were depicted in their exotic costumes of richly embroidered Chinese silks, tailored after the Indo-Portuguese fashions prevailing at Goa. The black African slaves, servants and sailors were also richly dressed, but went barefoot as a mark of their servile status. They are shown performing acrobatic feats in the shrouds and rigging, holding sunshades over their masters ashore, or leading exotic animals for presentation to Japanese dignitaries. Portuguese Jesuits and Spanish friars also figure in these screens, accompanied by their Japanese acolytes, but it is the black slaves who steal the show. The Japanese were clearly fascinated by these tall, jet-black Negroes, mostly from Mozambique.

Black slaves were even able to buy—or otherwise acquire—Japanese girls to take back with them to Macao; much to the disgust of the Jesuit missionaries, who strongly denounced but failed to stop the practice. These girls were mostly sold into servitude for a trifling sum by their own parents. Many of them came from the Shimabara Peninsula near Nagasaki, where the peasantry lived on the barest subsistence-line or below it. The Italian merchant-adventurer, Francesco Carletti, who visited Japan in 1597/98, was (or professed to be) horrified by this 'most shameless immorality" of the Portuguese. They hired the girls by the day, or the week, or the month, or for years on end, as they felt inclined, 'and in some cases married them themselves'. The Dutch and English who traded at Hirado from

1609 onwards, behaved in the same way. The *Diary* of Richard Cocks, 1614-1623, is replete with references to these women.

The English voluntarily left Hirado in 1623, since they could not cover their expenses. The Portuguese were expelled from Japan in 1639, on pain of death if they tried to return. They did return next year, and they were all executed save for thirteen of the lowest members of the crew, who were spared to take back to Macao the news of the execution of sixty-one members of the Embassy in August 1640. In 1641 the Dutch were removed from Hirado to Deshima, a small artificial fan-shaped islet joined by a bridge to the town of Nagasaki, which had been built for the confinement of the Portuguese in 1635. Here they remained until after the opening of the country to foreigners in 1853-68.

The Dutch on Deshima have often been criticised for their real or alleged indifference to the rich cultural panorama of Tokugawa Japan, and for concentrating on balance-sheets rather than on artistic and intellectual interests. But what else could have been expected from the representatives of a monopolistic commercial company which confessedly had 'trade as its compass and profit as its lodestar'? Moreover, not all of the Dutch on Deshima were merely dollar-grubbing and dollar-grinding merchants, whose only diversions were the pipe and the bottle. Many of them were just that. But there was also a fair number of intelligent men, who took some interest in Japanese culture. They made the best of their very restricted opportunities, which were compounded by the fact that they were strictly forbidden to learn the language.

Engelbert Kaempfer, a German physician who was in the country in 1690-92, produced a remarkably accurate description of Japan, which was published posthumously in English in 1728, under the rather misleading title of *A History of Japan*. A Japanese author, writing in 1804, commented: 'The existence of this Holland Factory at Deshima has called into being books like Kaempfer's, which depicts our country's situation so well, that I, never having been in the Kwanto, still know what that district is like, because I have read this Dutch book. And so the Europeans know. Is this not terrible?' Nowadays, Japanese historians avidly study the records of the Dutch East India Company from Hirado and Deshima, still preserved in the archives at the Hague, in order to glean information about social and other conditions in Tokugawa Japan, which the more percipient Dutch observers noted, but which are not available in Japanese sources since they were taken for granted by indigenous contemporaries.

The Japanese showed themselves to be as complaisant about providing the Dutch on Deshima with women, as they had originally been with the Portuguese. Kaempfer took a rather jaundiced view of the system as operated by the Nagasaki officials, although he did not object to much to the immorality involved as to the prices charged. 'They also take care to furnish our people on demand with whores; and truly our young sailors unacquainted as they commonly are with the virtues of temperance, are not ashamed to spend five or six dollars for one night's pleasure, and with such wenches too, whom a native of Nagasaki could have for two or three *mas* [small silver coin], they being none of the best and handsomest'. As the average Dutch sailor's basic pay was then the equivalent of five or six dollars a month, this was certainly not a cheap night's 'rest and recreation' for Jan Maat (Jack Tar).

Needless to say, it was not only

young sailors who patronized these prostitutes; their clients included respectable middle-aged Dutch merchants, as no foreign women were allowed on Deshima. The Swedish botanist and traveller, C.P. Thunberg noted that in his time (1775-76), 'One of these female companions cannot be kept for less than three days, but she may be kept as long as one pleases, a year, or even several years together.' Most of the daily fee was paid to the brothel-keeper; but the girls sometimes got rich presents from their Dutch lovers, whom they in turn obliged by smuggling expensive goods, such as watches, into the town for sale at high prices. Children were seldom born of these unions. When they did produce offspring, the fathers were allowed to provide for the education of their children, but could not take them out of Japan. Thunberg adds in this connection: 'During my stay in this country, I saw a girl of about six years of age, who very much resembled her father, a European, and remained with him on our small island, the whole year through.' These romances were sometimes continued by correspondence, long after the lovers had parted with no hope of seeing each other again. Some of these letters from Japanese prostitutes to their former Dutch lovers are still preserved in the Netherlands.

The Dutch did not employ Negro

slaves, but they did have Indonesian slaves and servants on Deshima. These likewise intrigued the Japanese, and are often depicted in colour-prints of the so-called *Nagasaki-e*, a form of Pop-Art produced for sale to Japanese tourists. These Indonesians were also allowed to have the services of prostitutes if they could afford to pay them. On one occasion, these ladies smuggled out some of their patrons, disguised in women's clothes, and took them to the brothel-quarter of Maruyama, where a good time was had by all until they were discovered and severely disciplined. One of the questions most commonly asked of Western men in Japan is "What do you think of Japanese women?" There has never been any doubt about the answer since the first Southern Barbarian to land at Tanegashima in 1543 asked for and received the local swordsmith's daughter in exchange for his own arquebus.

NOTES ON FURTHER READING

C.R. Boxer, *The Christian Century in Japan, 1549-1650.* (University of California Press, 1951, 1981); *Jan Compagnie in War and Peace, 1602-1799* (Heinemann (Asia), Hong Kong, 1979). Michael Cooper, S.J., *They Came to Japan. An Anthology of European Reports on Japan, 1543-1640* (Thames and Hudson, and University of California Press, 1965). George Elison, *Deus Destroyed. The Image of Christianity in Early Modern Japan* (Harvard University Press, 1973).

Twentieth-Century Warfare

L. S. Stavrianos, in his *Global History*, blames the two world wars and the Great Depression for the decline of Western influence in the world. The great loss of life, the cost, and the internecine fighting among the nations of the West took their toll. After 1945 the empires broke up.

Given the history of warfare on earth, people sometimes wonder if the urge to fight is an inborn aspect of human nature. We excuse ourselves at times by saying that war represents a loss of good sense, but Michael Howard, author of "The Causes of Wars," argues that

wars start when both sides think that there is an advantage in fighting; going to war, therefore, is a rational act. Yet, as Edmund Stillman says in regard to World War I, the goals of the warring nations were very questionable compared to the cost of 10 million dead soldiers and a legacy of barbarism. Of course, no one could predict such losses at the outset.

World War I, nonetheless, left not only millions of young men dead, but also left the younger generation disillusioned. In response, this cynical "lost generation" embraced the excesses of the Jazz Age. The collapse of the Western economy in the 1930s, starting in the United States and spreading to other countries, was an additional blow. The economic depression was cured only by the enormous spending that was generated to fight World War II.

It is also difficult to believe in the rationality of war when you consider the career of Adolf Hitler. His megalomania drove Europe once again into the abyss in 1939. According to John Lukacs, Hitler almost won the war in 1940 after his blitzkrieg armies defeated the Western European nations in a few months of fighting. There was talk of a negotiated peace, but the conflict continued. The British, under Churchill's guidance, hung on, and the United States entered the war on the Allied side following Japan's attack on the American naval base at Pearl Harbor late in 1941.

World War II was interpreted by the Allies as a just war, a fight between good and evil. This was confirmed toward the end of the fighting in Europe when Allied soldiers overran the Nazi death camps and discovered that 6 million Jews had been exterminated. The destruction of the Jews is justly condemned and remembered, but others suffered too. Jeremy Noakes points out that some 25,000 Gypsies were also executed and subjected to the infamous medical tortures of the Nazis. The Gypsies are such a vagabond people that no one has paid much attention to their suffering. Only 5,000 of them survived the conflict.

The Germans and Italians were defeated by conventional fighting, and the Japanese surrendered quickly following the dropping of the atomic bombs on Hiroshima and Nagasaki by the United States. The atomic bomb added a new and awesome dimension to warfare. The bomb was the result of the work of nuclear physicists, many of whom had been driven out of Europe to the United States by the excesses of the Italians and Germans. Alan Lightman recounts this segment of their history.

Some scientists argued that the Japanese should have been given a warning about the atomic bomb, or a demonstration of what might happen if it were dropped. In earlier wars, even World War I to an extent, it was a part of military ethics to safeguard women, children, and non-combatants. With the advent of submarine warfare in World War I and the high altitude bombing raids in World War II, such ethics could no longer be sustained. Thus began total war—one nationality against another. The American air force ostensibly chose military targets for the atom bombs, but in effect entire cities were obliterated. In the 40 years since the dropping of the atom bomb, Hiroshima has recovered and looks like many other modern cities. Michael Dillon notes, however, that long-term scars and sadness remain.

For all of its horror, it may be that the threat of atomic warfare has prevented World War III. Warfare on a lesser scale, of course, has continued. The United States, the most powerful nation emerging from World War II, was involved in Korea and Vietnam where it fought wars of limited goals. In Korea the United States fought the Chinese and North Koreans to a standstill, without allowing the fight to escalate into a global conflict. In Vietnam a decade later, the United States again fought a limited war, but this time lost to a determined enemy using guerrilla tactics. The selection from *Time*, written 20 years after the fall of Saigon, claims that Americans have yet to face the critical questions of the war.

In similar fashion, the Soviet Union fought unsuccessfully in Afghanistan for 9 years. It was unable to defeat a guerrilla force armed with American missiles. But it is not just the great powers that have been involved in such fights. Iran and Iraq recently agreed to an armistice after 8 years of fruitless warfare that witnessed the revival of poison gas as a weapon. The use of poison gas had been banned by civilized nations since World War I. With all of these examples, it is difficult to believe that warfare could ever be justified. The technology of weaponry has increased to such a point that any fighting that goes beyond a small scale could be disastrous. In an atomic world, as President Dwight D. Eisenhower once commented, there is no alternative to peace.

Looking Ahead: Challenge Questions

What causes war?

Can war be prevented? How?

Is fighting in the nature of human beings?

Has anything worthwhile been obtained by fighting wars?

Is it true that those with the best weapons always win?

How has the atom bomb acted as a deterrent?

Were there rational purposes behind the wars of the twentieth century?

The Causes of Wars

Michael Howard

Michael Howard, a Wilson Center Fellow, holds the Regius Chair of Modern History at Oxford University. He was born in London, England. Before receiving his B.A. from Oxford (1946), Howard served in the Cold-stream Guards in Italy during World War II, was twice wounded, and was awarded the Military Cross. He received his Litt. D. from Oxford in 1976. Among his many works, he has written War in European History *(1976) and* War and the Liberal Conscience *(1978), and he has translated, with Peter Paret of Stanford, Karl von Clausewitz's classic study* On War *(1976).*

Since the mid-18th century, many European and American theorists have attempted to explain war as an aberration in human affairs or as an occurrence beyond rational control. Violent conflicts between nations have been depicted, variously, as collective outbursts of male aggression, as the inevitable outcome of ruling-class greed, or as necessary, even healthy, events in the evolutionary scheme. One exception to the general trend was the 19th-century Prussian strategist Karl von Clausewitz, who declared, in an oft-quoted dictum, that war was the extension of politics "by other means." Here, historian Michael Howard argues further that war is one of Reason's progeny—indeed, that war stems from nothing less than a "superabundance of analytic rationality."

No one can describe the topic that I have chosen to discuss as a neglected and understudied one. How much ink has been spilled about it, how many library shelves have been filled with works on the subject, since the days of Thucydides! How many scholars from how many specialties have applied their expertise to this intractable problem! Mathematicians, meteorologists, sociologists, anthropologists, geographers, physicists, political scientists, philosophers, theologians, and lawyers are only the most obvious of the categories that come to mind when one surveys the ranks of those who have sought some formula for perpetual peace, or who have at least hoped to reduce the complexities of international conflict to some orderly structure, to develop a theory that will enable us to explain, to understand, and to control a phenomenon which, if we fail to abolish it, might well abolish us.

Yet it is not a problem that has aroused a great deal of interest in the historical profession. The causes of specific wars, yes: These provide unending material for analysis and interpretation, usually fueled by plenty of documents and starkly conflicting prejudices on the part of the scholars themselves.

But the phenomenon of war as a continuing activity within human society is one that as a profession we take very much for granted. The alternation of war and peace has been the very stuff of the past. War has been throughout history a normal way of conducting disputes between political groups. Few of us, probably, would go along with those sociobiologists who claim that this has been so because man is "innately aggressive." The calculations of advantage and risk, sometimes careful, sometimes crude, that statesmen make before committing their countries to war are linked very remotely, if at all, to the displays of tribal "machismo" that we witness today in football crowds. Since the use or threat of physical force is the most elementary way of asserting power and controlling one's environment, the fact that men have frequently had recourse to it does not cause the historian a great deal of surprise. Force, or the threat of it, may not settle arguments, but it does play a considerable part in determining the structure of the world in which we live.

I mentioned the multiplicity of books that have been written about the causes of war since the time of Thucydides. In fact, I think we would find that the vast majority of them have been written since 1914, and that the degree of intellectual concern about the causes of war to which we have become accustomed has existed only since the First World War. In view of the damage which that war did to the social and political structure of Europe, this is understandable enough. But there has been a tendency to argue that because that war caused such great and lasting damage, because it destroyed three great empires and nearly beggared a fourth, it must have arisen from causes of peculiar complexity and profundity, from the neuroses of nations, from the widening class struggle, from a crisis in industrial society. I have argued this myself, taking issue with Mr. A. J. P. Taylor, who maintained that because the war had such profound consequences, it did not necessarily have equally profound causes. But now I wonder whether on this, as on so many other matters, I was not wrong and he was not right.

■

It is true, and it is important to bear in mind in examining the problems of that period, that before

From *The Wilson Quarterly*, Summer 1984, pp. 90-103. Reprinted by permission of the publishers from THE CAUSES OF WARS, by Michael Howard, Cambridge, Massachusetts: Harvard University Press. Copyright © 1983 by Michael Howard.

1914 war was almost universally considered an acceptable, perhaps an inevitable and for many people a desirable, way of settling international differences, and that the war generally foreseen was expected to be, if not exactly brisk and cheerful, then certainly brief; no longer, certainly, than the war of 1870 between France and Prussia that was consciously or unconsciously taken by that generation as a model. Had it not been so generally felt that war was an acceptable and tolerable way of solving international disputes, statesmen and soldiers would no doubt have approached the crisis of 1914 in a very different fashion.

But there was nothing new about this attitude to war. Statesmen had always been able to assume that war would be acceptable at least to those sections of their populations whose opinion mattered to them, and in this respect the decision to go to war in 1914—for continental statesmen at least—in no way differed from those taken by their predecessors of earlier generations. The causes of the Great War are thus in essence no more complex or profound than those of any previous European war, or indeed than those described by Thucydides as underlying the Peloponnesian War: "What made war inevitable was the growth of Athenian power and the fear this caused in Sparta." In Central Europe, there was the German fear that the disintegration of the Habsburg Empire would result in an enormous enhancement of Russian power—power already becoming formidable as French-financed industries and railways put Russian manpower at the service of her military machine. In Western Europe, there was the traditional British fear that Germany might establish a hegemony over Europe which, even more than that of Napoleon, would place at risk the security of Britain and her own possessions, a fear fueled by the knowledge that there was within Germany a widespread determination to achieve a world status comparable with her latent power. Considerations of this kind had caused wars in Europe often enough before. Was there really anything different about 1914?

∎

Ever since the 18th century, war had been blamed by intellectuals upon the stupidity or the self-interest of governing elites (as it is now blamed upon "military-industrial complexes"), with the implicit or explicit assumption that if the control of state affairs were in the hands of sensible men—businessmen, as Richard Cobden thought, the workers, as Jean Jaurès thought—then wars would be no more.

By the 20th century, the growth of the social and biological sciences was producing alternative explanations. As Quincy Wright expressed it in his massive *A Study of War* (1942), "Scientific investigators . . . tended to attribute war to immaturities in social knowledge and control, as one might attribute epidemics to insufficient medical knowledge or to inadequate public health services." The Social Darwinian acceptance of the

inevitability of struggle, indeed of its desirability if mankind was to progress, the view, expressed by the elder Moltke but very widely shared at the turn of the century, that perpetual peace was a dream and not even a beautiful dream, did not survive the Great War in those countries where the bourgeois-liberal culture was dominant, Britain and the United States. The failure of these nations to appreciate that such bellicist views, or variants of them, were still widespread in other areas of the world, those dominated by Fascism and by Marxism-Leninism, was to cause embarrassing misunderstandings, and possibly still does.

For liberal intellectuals, war was self-evidently a pathological aberration from the norm, at best a ghastly mistake, at worst a crime. Those who initiated wars must in their view have been criminal, or sick, or the victims of forces beyond their power to control. Those who were so accused disclaimed responsibility for the events of 1914, throwing it on others or saying the whole thing was a terrible mistake for which no one was to blame. None of them, with their societies in ruins around them and tens of millions dead, were prepared to say courageously: "We only acted as statesmen always have in the past. In the circumstances then prevailing, war seemed to us to be the best way of protecting or forwarding the national interests for which we were responsible. There was an element of risk, certainly, but the risk might have been greater had we postponed the issue. Our real guilt does not lie in the fact that we started the war. It lies in our mistaken belief that we could win it."

∎

The trouble is that if we are to regard war as pathological and abnormal, then all conflict must be similarly regarded; for war is only a particular kind of conflict between a particular category of social groups: sovereign states. It is, as Clausewitz put it, "a clash between major interests that is resolved by bloodshed—that is the only way in which it differs from other conflicts." If one had no sovereign states, one would have no wars, as Rousseau rightly pointed out—but, as Hobbes equally rightly pointed out, we would probably have no peace either. As states acquire a monopoly of violence, war becomes the only remaining form of conflict that may legitimately be settled by physical force. The mechanism of legitimization of authority and of social control that makes it possible for a state to moderate or eliminate conflicts within its borders or at very least to ensure that these are not conducted by competitive violence—the mechanism to the study of which historians have quite properly devoted so much attention—makes possible the conduct of armed conflict with other states, and on occasion—if the state is to survive—makes it necessary.

These conflicts arise from conflicting claims, or interests, or ideologies, or perceptions; and these perceptions may indeed be fueled by social or psychological drives that we do not fully understand and that one day we may learn rather better how to control. But the problem is the control of social conflict *as such,* not simply of war. However inchoate or disreputable the motives for war may be, its initiation is almost by definition a deliberate and carefully considered act and its conduct, at least at the more advanced levels of social development, a matter of very precise central control. If history shows any record of "accidental" wars, I have yet to find them. Certainly statesmen have sometimes been surprised by the nature of the war they have unleashed, and it is reasonable to assume that in at least 50 percent of the cases they got a result they did not expect. But that is not the same as a war begun by mistake and continued with no political purpose.

■

Statesmen in fact go to war to achieve very specific ends, and the reasons for which states have fought one another have been categorized and recategorized innumerable times. Vattel, the Swiss lawyer, divided them into the necessary, the customary, the rational, and the capricious. Jomini, the Swiss strategist, identified ideological, economic, and popular wars, wars to defend the balance of power, wars to assist allies, wars to assert or to defend rights. Quincy Wright, the American political scientist, divided them into the idealistic, the psychological, the political, and the juridical. Bernard Brodie in our own times has refused to discriminate: "Any theory of the causes of war in general or any war in particular that is not inherently eclectic and comprehensive," he stated, ". . . is bound for that very reason to be wrong." Another contemporary analyst, Geoffrey Blainey, is on the contrary unashamedly reductionist. All war aims, he wrote, "are simply varieties of power. The vanity of nationalism, the will to spread an ideology, the protection of kinsmen in an adjacent land, the desire for more territory . . . all these represent power in different wrappings. The conflicting aims of rival nations are always conflicts of power."

In principle, I am sure that Bernard Brodie was right: No single explanation for conflict between states, any more than for conflict between any other social groups, is likely to stand up to critical examination. But Blainey is right as well. Quincy Wright provided us with a useful indicator when he suggested that "while animal war is a function of instinct and primitive war of the mores, civilized war is primarily a function of state politics."

Medievalists will perhaps bridle at the application of the term "primitive" to the sophisticated and subtle societies of the Middle Ages, for whom war was also a "function of the mores," a way of life that often demanded only the most banal of justifications. As a way of life, it persisted in Europe well into the 17th century, if no later. For Louis XIV and his court war was, in the early years at least, little more than a seasonal variation on hunting. But by the 18th century, the mood had changed. For Frederick the Great, war was to be

pre-eminently a function of *Staatspolitik,* and so it has remained ever since. And although statesmen can be as emotional or as prejudiced in their judgments as any other group of human beings, it is very seldom that their attitudes, their perceptions, and their decisions are not related, however remotely, to the fundamental issues of *power,* that capacity to control their environment on which the independent existence of their states and often the cultural values of their societies depend.

■

And here perhaps we do find a factor that sets interstate conflict somewhat apart from other forms of social rivalry. States may fight—indeed as often as not they do fight—not over any specific issue such as might otherwise have been resolved by peaceful means, but in order to acquire, to enhance, or to preserve their capacity to function as independent actors in the international system at all. "The stakes of war," as Raymond Aron has reminded us, "are the existence, the creation, or the elimination of States." It is a somber analysis, but one which the historical record very amply bears out.

It is here that those analysts who come to the study of war from the disciplines of the natural sciences, particularly the biological sciences, tend, it seems to me, to go astray. The conflicts between states which have usually led to war have normally arisen, not from any irrational and emotive drives, but from almost a superabundance of analytic rationality. Sophisticated communities (one hesitates to apply to them Quincy Wright's word, "civilized") do not react simply to immediate threats. Their intelligence (and I use the term in its double sense) enables them to assess the implications that any event taking place anywhere in the world, however remote, may have for their own capacity, immediately to exert influence, ultimately perhaps to survive. In the later Middle Ages and the early Modern period, every child born to every prince anywhere in Europe was registered on the delicate seismographs that monitored the shifts in dynastic power. Every marriage was a diplomatic triumph or disaster. Every stillbirth, as Henry VIII knew, could presage political catastrophe.

Today, the key events may be different. The pattern remains the same. A malfunction in the political mechanism of some remote African community, a coup d'état in a minuscule Caribbean republic, an insurrection deep in the hinterland of Southeast Asia, an assassination in some emirate in the Middle East—all these will be subjected to the kind of anxious examination and calculation that was devoted a hundred years ago to the news of comparable events in the Balkans: an insurrection in Philippopoli, a coup d'état in Constantinople, an assassination in Belgrade. To whose advantage will this ultimately redound, asked the worried diplomats, ours or *theirs?* Little enough in itself, perhaps, but will it not precipitate or strengthen a trend, set in motion a tide whose melancholy withdrawing roar will strip us of our friends and influence and leave us isolated in a world dominated by adversaries deeply hostile to us and all that we stand for?

There have certainly been occasions when states have gone to war in a mood of ideological fervor like the French republican armies in 1792; or of swaggering aggression like the Americans against Spain in 1898 or the British against the Boers a year later; or to make more money, as did the British in the War of Jenkins' Ear in 1739; or in a generous desire to help peoples of similar creed or race, as perhaps the Russians did in helping the Bulgarians fight the Turks in 1877 and the British dominions certainly did in 1914 and 1939. But, in general, men have fought during the past two hundred years neither because they are aggressive nor because they are acquisitive animals, but because they are reasoning ones: because they discern, or believe that they can discern, dangers before they become immediate, the possibility of threats before they are made.

◼

But be this as it may, in 1914 many of the German people, and in 1939 nearly all of the British, felt justified in going to war, not over any specific issue that could have been settled by negotiation, but *to maintain their power;* and to do so while it was still possible, before they found themselves so isolated, so impotent, that they had no power left to maintain and had to accept a subordinate position within an international system dominated by their adversaries. "What made war inevitable was the growth of Athenian power and the fear this caused in Sparta." Or, to quote another grimly apt passage from Thucydides:

> The Athenians made their Empire more and more strong... [until] finally the point was reached when Athenian strength attained a peak plain for all to see and the Athenians began to encroach upon Sparta's allies. It was at this point that Sparta felt the position to be no longer tolerable and decided by starting the present war to employ all her energies in attacking and if possible destroying the power of Athens.

You can vary the names of the actors, but the model remains a valid one for the purposes of our analysis. I am rather afraid that it still does.

Something that has changed since the time of Thucydides, however, is the nature of the power that appears so threatening. From the time of Thucydides until that of Louis XIV, there was basically only one source of political and military power—control of territory, with all the resources in wealth and manpower that this provided. This control might come through conquest, or through alliance, or through marriage, or through purchase, but the power of princes could be very exactly computed in terms of the extent of their territories and the number of men they could put under arms.

In 17th-century Europe, this began to change. Extent of territory remained important, but no less important was the effectiveness with which the resources of that territory could be exploited. Initially there were the bureaucratic and fiscal mechanisms that transformed loose bonds of territorial authority into highly structured centralized states whose armed forces, though not necessarily large, were permanent, disciplined, and paid.

◼

Then came the political transformations of the revolutionary era that made available to these state systems the entire manpower of their country, or at least as much of it as the administrators were able to handle. And finally came the revolution in transport, the railways of the 19th century that turned the revolutionary ideal of the "Nation in Arms" into a reality. By the early 20th century, military power—on the continent of Europe, at least—was seen as a simple combination of military manpower and railways. The quality of armaments was of secondary importance, and political intentions were virtually excluded from account. The growth of power was measured in terms of the growth of populations and of communications; of the number of men who could be put under arms and transported to the battlefield to make their weight felt in the initial and presumably decisive battles. It was the mutual perception of threat in those terms that turned Europe before 1914 into an armed camp, and it was their calculations within this framework that reduced German staff officers increasingly to despair and launched their leaders on their catastrophic gamble in 1914, which started the First World War.

But already the development of weapons technology had introduced yet another element into the international power calculus, one that has in our own age become dominant. It was only in the course of the 19th century that technology began to produce weapons systems—initially in the form of naval vessels—that could be seen as likely in themselves to prove decisive, through their qualitative and quantitative superiority, in the event of conflict. But as war became increasingly a matter of competing technologies rather than competing armies, so there developed that escalatory process known as the "arms race." As a title, the phrase, like so many coined by journalists to catch the eye, is misleading.

◼

"Arms races" are in fact continuing and open-ended attempts to match power for power. They are as much means of achieving stable or, if possible, favorable power balances as were the dynastic marriage policies of Valois and Habsburg. To suggest that they in themselves are causes of war implies a naive if not totally mistaken view of the relationship between the two phenomena. The causes of war remain rooted, as much as they were in the preindustrial age, in perceptions by statesmen of the growth of hostile power and the fears for the restriction, if not the extinction, of their own. The threat, or rather the fear, has not changed, whether it comes from aggregations of territory or from dreadnoughts, from the numbers of men under arms or from missile systems. The means that states employ to sustain or to extend their power may have been transformed, but their objectives and preoccupations remain the same.

"Arms races" can no more be isolated than wars themselves from the political circumstances that give rise to them, and like wars they will take as many different forms as political circumstances dictate. They may be no more than a process of competitive modernization, of maintaining a status quo that commands general support but in which no participant wishes, whether from reasons of pride or of prudence, to fall behind in keeping his armory up to date. If there are no political causes for fear or rivalry, this process need not in itself be a destabilizing factor in international relations. But arms races may, on the other hand, be the result of a quite deliberate assertion of an intention to *change* the status quo, as was, for example, the German naval challenge to Britain at the beginning of this century.

This challenge was an explicit attempt by Admiral Alfred von Tirpitz and his associates to destroy the hegemonic position at sea which Britain saw as essential to her security, and, not inconceivably, to replace it with one of their own. As British and indeed German diplomats repeatedly explained to the German government, it was not the German naval program in itself that gave rise to so much alarm in Britain. It was the intention that lay behind it. If the status quo was to be maintained, the German challenge had to be met.

■

The naval race could quite easily have been ended on one of two conditions. Either the Germans could have abandoned their challenge, as had the French in the previous century, and acquiesced in British naval supremacy; or the British could have yielded as gracefully as they did, a decade or so later, to the United States and abandoned a status they no longer had the capacity, or the will, to maintain. As it was, they saw the German challenge as one to which they could and should respond, and their power position as one which they were prepared, if necessary, to use force to preserve. The British naval program was thus, like that of the Germans, a signal of political intent; and that intent, that refusal to acquiesce in a fundamental transformation of the power balance, was indeed a major element among the causes of the war. The naval competition provided a very accurate indication and measurement of political rivalries and tensions, but it

did not cause them; nor could it have been abated unless the rivalries themselves had been abandoned.

It was the general perception of the growth of German power that was awakened by the naval challenge, and the fear that a German hegemony on the Continent would be the first step to a challenge to her own hegemony on the oceans, that led Britain to involve herself in the continental conflict in 1914 on the side of France and Russia. "What made war inevitable was the growth of *Spartan* power," to reword Thucydides, "and the fear which this caused in *Athens*." In the Great War that followed, Germany was defeated, but survived with none of her latent power destroyed. A "false hegemony" of Britain and France was established in Europe that could last only so long as Germany did not again mobilize her resources to challenge it. German rearmament in the 1930s did not of itself mean that Hitler wanted war (though one has to ignore his entire philosophy if one is to believe that he did not); but it did mean that he was determined, with a great deal of popular support, to obtain a free hand on the international scene.

With that free hand, he intended to establish German power on an irreversible basis; this was the message conveyed by his armament program. The armament program that the British reluctantly adopted in reply was intended to show that, rather than submit to the hegemonic aspirations they feared from such a revival of German power, they would fight to preserve their own freedom of action. Once again to recast Thucydides:

> Finally the point was reached when German strength attained a peak plain for all to see, and the Germans began to encroach upon Britain's allies. It was at this point that Britain felt the position to be no longer tolerable and decided by starting this present war to employ all her energies in attacking and if possible destroying the power of Germany.

What the Second World War established was not a new British hegemony, but a Soviet hegemony over the Euro-Asian land mass from the Elbe to Vladivostok; and that was seen, at least from Moscow, as an American hegemony over the rest of the world; one freely accepted in Western Europe as a preferable alternative to being absorbed by the rival hegemony. Rival armaments were developed to define and preserve the new territorial boundaries, and the present arms competition began. But in considering the present situation, historical experience suggests that we must ask the fundamental question: *What kind of competition is it?* Is it one between powers that accept the status quo, are satisfied with the existing power relationship, and are concerned simply to modernize their armaments in order to preserve it? Or does it reflect an underlying instability in the system?

My own perception, I am afraid, is that it is the latter. There was a period for a decade after the war when the Soviet Union was probably a status quo power but the

West was not; that is, the Russians were not seriously concerned to challenge the American global hegemony, but the West did not accept that of the Russians in Eastern Europe. Then there was a decade of relative mutual acceptance between 1955 and 1965; and it was no accident that this was the heyday of disarmament/arms-control negotiations. But thereafter, the Soviet Union has shown itself increasingly unwilling to accept the Western global hegemony, if only because many other people in the world have been unwilling to do so either. Reaction against Western dominance brought the Soviet Union some allies and many opportunities in the Third World, and she has developed naval power to be able to assist the former and exploit the latter. She has aspired in fact to global power status, as did Germany before 1914; and if the West complains, as did Britain about Germany, that the Russians do not *need* a navy for defense purposes, the Soviet Union can retort, as did Germany, that she needs it to make clear to the world the status to which she aspires; that is, so that she can operate on the world scene by virtue of her own power and not by permission of anyone else. Like Germany, she is determined to be treated as an equal, and armed strength has appeared the only way to achieve that status.

■

The trouble is that what is seen by one party as the breaking of an alien hegemony and the establishment of equal status will be seen by the incumbent powers as a striving for the establishment of an alternate hegemony, and they are not necessarily wrong. In international politics, the appetite often comes with eating; and there really may be no way to check an aspiring rival except by the mobilization of stronger military power. An arms race then becomes almost a necessary surrogate for war, a test of national will and strength; and arms control becomes possible only when the underlying power balance has been mutually agreed.

We would be blind, therefore, if we did not recognize that the causes which have produced war in the past are operating in our own day as powerfully as at any time in history. It is by no means impossible that a thousand years hence a historian will write—if any historians survive, and there are any records for them to write history from—"What made war inevitable was the growth of Soviet power and the fear which this caused in the United States."

But times *have* changed since Thucydides. They have changed even since 1914. These were, as we have seen, bellicist societies in which war was a normal, acceptable, even a desirable way of settling differences. The question that arises today is, how widely and evenly spread is that intense revulsion against war that at present characterizes our own society? For if war is indeed now *universally* seen as being unacceptable as an instrument of policy, then all analogies drawn from the past are misleading, and although power struggles may continue, they will be diverted into other channels. But if that revulsion is not evenly spread, societies which continue to see armed force as an acceptable means for attaining their political ends are likely to establish a dominance over those which do not. Indeed, they will not necessarily have to fight for it.

My second and concluding point is this: Whatever may be the underlying causes of international conflict, even if we accept the role of atavistic militarism or of military-industrial complexes or of sociobiological drives or of domestic tensions in fueling it, wars begin with conscious and reasoned decisions based on the calculation, made by *both* parties, that they can achieve more by going to war than by remaining at peace.

Even in the most bellicist of societies this kind of calculation has to be made and it has never even for them been an easy one. When the decision to go to war involves the likelihood, if not the certainty, that the conflict will take the form of an exchange of nuclear weapons from which one's own territory cannot be immune, then even for the most bellicist of leaders, even for those most insulated from the pressures of public opinion, the calculation that they have more to gain from going to war than by remaining at peace and pursuing their policies by other means will, to put it mildly, not be self-evident. The odds against such a course benefiting their state or themselves or their cause will be greater, and more *evidently* greater, than in any situation that history has ever had to record. Society may have accepted killing as a legitimate instrument of state policy, but not, as yet, suicide. For that reason I find it hard to believe that the abolition of nuclear weapons, even if it were possible, would be an unmixed blessing. Nothing that makes it easier for statesmen to regard war as a feasible instrument of state policy, one from which they stand to gain rather than lose, is likely to contribute to a lasting peace.

SARAJEVO

The End of Innocence

After fifty years of explanations, it is still difficult to see why a political murder in a remote corner of the Balkans should have set off a war that changed the world forever

Edmund Stillman

A few minutes before eleven o'clock in the morning, Sunday, June 28, 1914, on the river embankment in Sarajevo, Gavrilo Princip shot the archduke Franz Ferdinand and brought a world crashing down.

After fifty years and so much pain, Sarajevo is worth a pilgrimage, but to go there is a disappointing and somehow unsettling experience: this dusty Balkan city, in its bowl of dark and barren hills, is an unlikely setting for grand tragedy. Blood and suffering are endemic to the Balkans, but Sarajevo is so mean and poor. Why should an age have died *here*? Why did the double murder of an undistinguished archduke and his morganatic wife touch off a world war, when so many graver pretexts had somehow been accommodated—or ignored—in the preceding quarter-century? It was an act that no one clearly remembers today; indeed, its details were forgotten by the time the war it engendered was six months old. Nowadays, even in Sarajevo, few pilgrims search out the place where Princip stood that morning. Nearby, on the river embankment, only a dingy little museum commemorates the lives and passions of the seven tubercular boys (of whom Princip was only one) who plotted one small blow for freedom, but who brought on a universal catastrophe. Within the museum are faded photographs, a few pitiable relics of the conspirators, a fly-specked visitors' book. A single shabby attendant guards the memorials to a political passion that seems, well, naïve to our more cynical age. "Here, in this historic place," the modest inscription runs, "Gavrilo Princip was the initiator of liberty, on the day of Saint Vitus, the 28th of June, 1914." That is all, and few visitors to present-day Yugoslavia stop to read it.

There is so much that goes unanswered, even though the facts of the case are so well known: how the failing Hapsburgs, impelled by an unlucky taste for adventure, had seized Bosnia and Herzegovina from the Turks and aggravated the racial imbalance of the Austro-Hungarian Empire; how the southern Slavs within the Empire felt themselves oppressed and increasingly demanded freedom; how the ambitious little hill kingdom of Serbia saw a chance to establish a South-Slavic hegemony over the Balkans; and how Czarist Russia, itself near ruin, plotted with its client Serbia to turn the Austro-Hungarian southern flank. But there is so much more that needs to be taken into account: how Franz Ferdinand, the aged emperor Franz Josef's nephew, became his heir by default (Crown Prince Rudolf had committed suicide at Mayerling; Uncle Maximilian, Napoleon III's pawn, had been executed in Mexico; Franz Ferdinand's father, a pilgrim to the Holy Land, had died—most improbably—from drinking the waters of the Jordan); how the new heir—stiff, autocratic, and unapproachable, but implausibly wed in irenic middle-class marriage to the not-quite-acceptable Sophie Chotek—sensed the danger to the Empire and proposed a policy that would have given his future Slav subjects most of what they demanded; how the Serbian nationalists were driven to panic, and how the secret society of jingoes known as "The Black Hand" plotted Franz Ferdinand's death; how seven boys were recruited to do the deed, and how one of them, Gavrilo Princip, on the morning of June 28, 1914, shot Franz Ferdinand and his Sophie dead.

But why the mindlessness of the war that followed, the blundering diplomacies and reckless plans that made disaster inevitable once hostilities broke out? It is all so grotesque: great and shattering consequences without proportionate causes. When the inferno of 1914–18 ended at last, the broken survivors asked themselves the same question, seeking to comprehend the terrible thing that had happened. To have endured the inferno without a justifying reason— to be forced to admit that a war of such terror and scope had been only a blind, insouciant madness—was intolerable; it was easier to think of it as an unworthy or a wrongful cause than as a ghastly, titanic joke on history. After the event Winston Churchill wrote: "But there was a strange temper in the air. Unsatisfied by material prosperity the nations turned restlessly towards strife internal or external. . . . Almost one might think the world wished to suffer." Yet if this opinion had been widely accepted, it would have been a judgment on human nature too terrible to endure. And so a new mythology of the war grew up— a postwar mythology of materialist cynicism almost as contrived as the wartime propaganda fictions of the "Beast of Berlin" or the wholesale slaughter of Belgian nuns. It embraced the myths of the munitions manufacturers who had plotted a war they were, in fact, helpless to control; of Machiavellian, imperialist diplomacies; of an ever-spiraling arms race, when in fact the naval race between England and Germany had, if anything, somewhat abated by 1914. But no single cause, or combination of such causes, will explain the First World War. Neither the Germans, the Austrians, the Russians, the French, the Italians, nor the British went to war to fulfill a grand ambition—to conquer Europe, or the world, or to promote an ideology. They did not even seek economic dominion through war. The somber truth is that Western civilization, for a hundred years without a major war and absorbed in a social and technological revolution—progress, in short—turned on itself in a paroxysm of slaughter.

On both sides the actual war aims, so far as they were articulated at all, were distressingly small. Merely to humiliate Serbia and to "avenge" a man whose death few particularly regretted, the Austro-Hungarian Empire began a war which cost it seven million casualties and destroyed its fabric; to prevent a senile Austria-Hungary from gaining a precarious (and inevitably short-lived) advantage in the poverty-stricken western Balkans, imperial Russia lost more than nine million men—killed, wounded, or taken prisoner. To support an ally, and to avoid the public humiliation and anxiety of canceling a mobilization order once issued, Germany lost almost two million dead, Alsace-Lorraine, a third of Poland, and its growing sphere of influence in Central Europe and the Middle East. England, to keep its word to Belgium, committed eight million men to the struggle, and lost nearly one million dead. France, to counter its German enemy and to avenge the peace treaty it had accepted in 1870, endured losses of 15 per cent of its population and initiated a process of political decline from which it may not yet have emerged.

This was the price of World War I. Two shots were fired in Sarajevo, and for more than four years thereafter half the world bled. At least ten million soldiers were killed, and twenty million were wounded or made prisoners. But the real legacy of the war was something less tangible—a quality of despair, a chaos, and a drift toward political barbarism that is with us to this day. We have not recovered yet.

In the summer of 1914 the armies marched out to Armageddon in their frogged tunics, red Zouave trousers, and gilded helmets. Five months later they were crouching in the mud, louse-ridden, half-starved, frozen, and bewildered by the enormity of it all. "Lost in the midst of two million madmen," the Frenchman Céline was to write of the war, "all of them heroes, at large and armed to the teeth! . . . sniping, plotting, flying, kneeling, digging, taking cover, wheeling, detonating, shut in on earth as in an asylum cell; intending to wreck everything in it, Germany, France, the whole world, every breathing thing; destroying, more ferocious than a pack of mad dogs and adoring their own madness (which no dog does), a hundred, a thousand times fiercer than a thousand dogs and so infinitely more vicious! . . . Clearly it seemed to me that I had embarked on a crusade that was nothing short of an apocalypse."

The savagery of the war and the incompetence of the military commanders quickly became a commonplace. The generals proved wholly unprepared for quick-firing artillery, machine guns, field entrenchments, railroad and motor transport, and the existence of a continuous front in place of the isolated battlefield of earlier centuries. They were helpless in the face of a combat too vast, too impersonal, too technical, and too deadly to comprehend. Quite aside from their intellectual shortcomings, one is struck by the poverty of their emotional response. Kill and kill was their motto. No one in command was daunted by the bloodletting, it seems. No more imaginative battle tactic could be devised than to push strength against strength—attacking at the enemy's strongest point on the theory that one side's superior *élan* would ultimately yield up victory. Verdun in 1916 cost the French some 350,000 men and the Germans nearly as many; the German penetration was five miles, gained in a little more than three months. The Somme cost the Allies more than 600,000 casualties, the Germans almost half a million; the offensive gained a sector thirty miles wide and a maximum of seven deep in four and a half months.

That it was an insane waste of lives the combatants realized early, but no one knew what to do. The waste of honor, love, courage, and selfless devotion was the cruelest of all: at the first Battle of Ypres, in the opening days of the war, the young German schoolboy volunteers "came on like men possessed," a British historian records. They were sent in against picked battalions of British regulars who shot them to pieces on the slopes of Ypres with the trained rifle fire for which they were famous. The incident has gone down in German history as the *Kindermord von Ypern*—"the Slaughter of the Innocents at Ypres." No other phrase will do.

It was a strange world that died that summer of 1914. For ninety-nine years there had been peace in Europe: apart from the Crimean War, only eighteen months of all that time—according to Karl Polanyi—had been spent in desultory and petty European wars. Men apparently believed that peace was man's normal condition—and on those occasions when peace was momentarily broken, war was expected to be comprehensible and salutary, an ultimately useful Darwinian selection of the fittest to lead. To us, after the profuse horrors of mustard gas, trench warfare, Buchenwald, the Blitz, Coventry, and Hiroshima, to name only a few, this is incomprehensible naïveté. But that we have been disillusioned and have awaked to our condition is due to the events of 1914–18.

In the nineteenth century the belief in progress—automatic progress—went deep. The American anthropologist Lewis Morgan had sounded a note of self-confident hope for the entire age when he said, in 1877, "Democracy in government, brotherhood in society, equality in rights and privileges, and universal education, foreshadow the next higher plane of society to which experience, intelligence and knowledge are steadily tending." The emphasis here was on *steadily*: nothing could stop the onward march of mankind.

And the progress was very real. The age that died in 1914 was a brilliant one—so extravagant in its intellectual and aesthetic endowments that we who have come after can hardly believe in its reality. It was a comfortable age—for a considerable minority, at least—but it was more than a matter of Sunday walks in the Wienerwald, or country-house living, or a good five-cent cigar. It was an imposing age in the sciences, in the arts, even in forms of government. Men had done much and had risen high in the hundred years that came to an end that summer. From Napoleon's downfall in 1815 to the outbreak of war in 1914, the trend had been up.

"As happy as God in France," even the Germans used to say. For France these were the years of the *belle époque*, when all the world's artists came there to learn: Picasso and Juan Gris from Spain, Chagall and Archipenko from Russia, Piet Mondrian from the Netherlands, Brancusi from Romania, Man Ray and Max Weber from America, Modigliani from Italy. All made up the "School of Paris," a name which meant nothing but that in this Paris of the *avant-guerre* the world of the arts was at home.

"Paris drank the talents of the world," wrote the poet-impresario of those years, Guillaume Apollinaire. Debussy, Ravel, and Stravinsky composed music there. Nijinsky and Diaghilev were raising the modern ballet to new heights of brilliance and creativity. The year 1913 was, as Roger Shattuck puts it in *The Banquet Years*, the *annus mirabilis* of French literature: Proust's *Du Côté de chez Swann*, Alain-Fournier's *Le Grand Meaulnes*, Apollinaire's *Alcools*, Roger Martin du Gard's *Jean Barois*, Valéry Larbaud's *A. O. Barnabooth*, Péguy's *L'Argent*, Barrès's *La Colline inspirée*, and Colette's *L'Entrave* and *L'Envers du music-hall* appeared that year. "It is almost as if the war *had* to come in order to put an end to an extravaganza that could not have been sustained at this level." That was Paris.

Vienna was another great mongrel city that, like Paris, drank up talent—in this case the talents of a congeries of Austrians, Magyars, Czechs, Slovaks, Poles, Slovenes, Croats, Serbs, Jews, Turks, Transylvanians, and Gypsies. On Sunday mornings gentlemen strolled in the Prater ogling the cocottes; they rode the giant red Ferris wheel and looked out over the palaces and parks of the city; or they spent the morning at the coffeehouse, arguing pointlessly and interminably. It was a pleasure-loving city, but an intellectual one, too. The names of the men who walked Vienna's streets up to the eve of the war are stunning in their brilliance: Gustav Mahler, Sigmund Freud, Sandor Ferenczi, Ernst Mach, Béla Bartók, Rainer Maria Rilke, Franz Kafka, Robert Musil, Arthur Schnitzler, Hugo von Hofmannsthal, Richard Strauss, Stefan Zweig—these hardly begin to exhaust the list. (There were more sinister names, too. Adolf Hitler lived in Vienna between 1909 and 1913, an out-of-work, shabby *Bettgeher*—a daytime renter of other people's beds—absorbing the virulent anti-Semitism that charged the Viennese social atmosphere; so did Leon Trotsky, who spent his evenings listening contemptuously to the wranglings of the Social Democratic politicians at the Café Central.)

England was still gilded by the afterglow of the Edwardian Age: the British Empire straddled the earth, controlling more than a quarter of the surface of the globe. If the realities of trade had begun to shift, and if British industry and British naval supremacy were faced with a growing challenge from the United States and Hohenzollern Germany, the vast British overseas investments tended to hide the fact. England had its intellectual brilliance, too: these were the years of Hardy, Kipling, Shaw, Wells, the young D. H. Lawrence and the young Wyndham Lewis, Arnold Bennett, Gilbert Murray, A. E. Housman, H. H. Munro (Saki)—who would die in the war—and many others, like Rupert Brooke, Robert Graves, Siegfried Sassoon, and Wilfred Owen, who were as yet hardly known.

As for the Kaiser's Germany, it is melancholy to reflect that if Wilhelm II himself, that summer in 1914, had only waited —five years, ten years, or twenty—Germany might have had it all. But Wilhelm was shrewd, treacherous, and hysterical, a chronic bully whose mother had never loved him. His habitual style of discourse was the neurotic bluster of a small man who has had the bad luck to be called upon to stomp about in a giant's boots. Wilhelm II lived all his life in the shadow of "the Great Emperor," his grandfather Wilhelm I, who had created a united Greater Germany with the help of his brilliant chancellor, Prince Otto von Bismarck; he wanted to make the world stand in awe of him, but he did not know, precisely, how to go about it.

If only he could have been patient: Austria-Hungary was really a German satellite; the Balkans and the Middle East looked to Berlin; Germany's industrial hegemony on the continent was secure, and might soon have knocked Britain from her commanding place in the world's trade. By 1914, fourteen Germans had won Nobel Prizes in the sciences (by contrast, their nearest competitors, the French, had won only nine).

But the lesson is something more than a chapbook homily on patience. Wilhelm's personal anxiety merely expressed in microcosm the larger German anxiety about the nation's place in the world. Something strange lay beneath the stolid prosperity of the Hohenzollern Age—a surfeit with peace, a lust for violence, a belief in death, an ominous mystique of war. "Without war the world would quickly sink into materialism," the elder Von Moltke, chief of the German General Staff, had proclaimed in 1880; and he, his nephew the younger Von Moltke, and the caste of Prussian militarists they represented could presumably save the world from that tawdry fate. But this belief in war was not a monopoly of the Right: even Thomas Mann, spokesman of German humanism, could ask, in 1914, "Is not war a purification, a liberation, an enormous hope?" adding complacently, "Is not peace an element in civil corruption?"

There had been peace in the world for too long. From Berlin, in the spring of 1914, Colonel House wrote to Woodrow Wilson: "The whole of Germany is charged with electricity. Everybody's nerves are tense. It only requires a spark to set the whole thing off." People were saying: "Better a horrible ending than a horror without end." In expressing this spirit of violence and disorientation, Germany was merely precocious. It expressed a universal European malaise.

The malaise was evident everywhere—in the new cults of political violence; in the new philosophies of men like Freud, Nietzsche, and Pareto, who stressed the unconscious and the irrational, and who exposed the lying pretensions of middle-class values and conventions; and in the sense of doom that permeated the avant-garde arts of the prewar years. Typical of this spirit of rebellion was the manifesto set forth in 1910 by the Italian Futurist painters: it declared that "all forms of imitation should be held in contempt and that all forms of originality glorified; that we should rebel against the tyranny of the words 'harmony' and 'good taste' . . . ; that

a clean sweep be made of all stale and threadbare subject matter in order to express the vortex of modern life—a life of steel, pride, fever, and speed . . ."

In England and France, as in Germany and Italy, the darker strain was there. When the war came, a glad Rupert Brooke intoned:

Now God be thanked Who has matched us with His hour.

A fever was over Paris as the spring of 1914 slipped into summer. Charles Péguy—Dreyfusard, Socialist, man of good will and reason, to his intellectual generation "the pure man"—had caught this other darker spirit as well. That spring he had written:

Heureux ceux qui sont morts dans les grandes batailles . . .
Happy are those who have died in great battles,
Lying on the ground before the face of God . . .

By September of that year he himself was dead.

No doubt we shall never understand it completely. What is absolutely clear about the outbreak of the First World War is that it was catastrophic: the hecatombs of dead, the appalling material waste, the destruction, and the pain of those four years tell us that. In our hearts we know that since that bootless, reckless, bloody adventure nothing has really come right again in the world. Democracy in government, brotherhood in society, equality in rights and privileges, universal education—all those evidences of "the next higher plane of society" to which experience, intelligence, and knowledge seemed to be steadily tending—gave way to mass conscription and the central direction of war, the anonymity of the trenches, the calculated propaganda lie: in short, between 1914 and 1918 Europe evolved many of the brutal features of the modern totalitarian state. And twenty-one years after the last shot was fired in the First World War, a second war came: a war of even greater brutality, moral degradation, and purposeful evil, but one where the issues at last matched the scale on which men had, a quarter-century earlier, blindly chosen to fight. Here was a deadly justice. That such a war should be fought at all was the direct outcome of the spiritual wasteland that the first war engendered.

Woodrow Wilson, greeting the Armistice, was able to proclaim to his fellow Americans that "everything" for which his countrymen had fought had been accomplished. He could assert that it was America's "fortunate duty to assist by example, by sober, friendly counsel, and by material aid in the establishment of a just democracy throughout the world."

But today we know that the poet Robert Graves more truly expressed the spirit of the nightmare from which the world awakened in 1918 when he wrote, "The news [of the Armistice] sent me out walking alone along the dyke above the marshes of Rhuddlan . . . cursing and sobbing and thinking of the dead."

The DANGEROUS SUMMER of 1940

For a few weeks Hitler came close to winning World War II. Then came a train of events that doomed him. An eloquent historian reminds us that however unsatisfactory our world may be today, it almost was unimaginably worse.

John Lukacs

John Lukacs is Professor of History at Chestnut Hill College, Philadelphia, and the author of many books, including the recent *Outgrowing Democracy: A History of the United States in the 20th Century.*

I n the summer of 1940 Adolf Hitler could have won the Second World War. He came close to that. Had he won, we would be living in a world so different as to be hardly imaginable. So let us contemplate that dangerous summer. It was then that the shape of the world in which we now live began to take form.

There was a curious, abstract quality to the Second World War when it started. On the first day of September in 1939, Hitler's armies invaded Poland. In 1914

the Germans had gone to war not knowing what the British would do. In 1939 the British had given Poland a guarantee to deter Hitler, to make it clear that a German attack on Poland would mean a British (and a French) declaration of war against Germany. Until the last minute Hitler hoped that the British did not mean what they said. In a way he was right. The British and the French governments kept their word and declared war nearly three days after the German armies had driven into Poland. Yet the British and French armies did virtually nothing.

Before long the phrase "Phony War," invented by American journalists, came into the language. Poland was overrun: but in this war, it really was All Quiet on the Western Front. The French and the

British troops spent the freezing winter that followed standing still, the French occasionally peering across the wooded German frontier from the concrete casemates of the Maginot Line. If not a phony war, it was a reluctant one.

There was a curious, abstract quality in the mood of the American people too. When the First World War broke out in Europe, not one in ten thousand Americans thought that their country would ever become involved in it. In 1914 the American people and their President Woodrow Wilson, took a naive kind of pride in their neutrality. When, on September 3, 1939, Franklin Roosevelt addressed the American people, he said the United States would stay neutral: but Roosevelt then added that he could not "ask that every American remain neu tral in thought as well." Most Americans were not. They abhorred Hitler, yet they had no desire to commit themselves on the side of Britain or France or Poland. They followed the conflict on their radios: it was exciting to hear the voices of famous correspondents crackling through the transatlantic ether from the blacked-out capitals of a Europe at war. Many Americans uneasily felt—felt, rather than said—that sooner or later their country would become involved in the war. They did not look forward to it.

Besides, the Phony War got curiouser and curiouser. It had started between Germany and Poland and Britain and France; but three months later the only fighting that was going on occurred in the snowy forests of Finland, a winter war between Finland and Russia. American sympathies for Finland arose. The British government noticed this. It was toying with the idea of coming to the aid of Finland, for many reasons, including the purpose of impressing American opinion. But the winter war came to an end. Churchill now wished to open a far-flung front against Germany, in Norway. Hitler forestalled him. On a freezing, raw morning in early April, his troops invaded Denmark and Norway. They conquered Denmark in a few hours and Norway in a few weeks.

Hitler's triumph in Norway—which he conquered nearly undisturbed by the British navy and largely unvexed by the hapless Allied troops put ashore and then withdrawn again—had an unexpected effect. The great portly figure of his nemesis had arisen—an old-fashioned figure of a man, whose very appearance rose like a spectral monument out of the historical mist. As a member of the Chamberlain government, Winston Churchill had been responsible for much of the Norwegian fiasco. Yet the representatives of the British people had had enough of Chamberlain's reluctant warfare. They helped Winston Churchill into the saddle of the prime ministership—by coincidence, on the very day when the German onslaught in Western Europe had begun.

It was the first of several great coincidences that summer: the kind of coincidences that people weaned on scientific logic dislike and others, with a touch of

poetry in their souls, love. Or as the great Portuguese proverb says: God writes straight with crooked lines. But, as often happens in this world, we see the meaning only in retrospect. At the time, there was no guarantee that Churchill would last. He could have disappeared after a few weeks: a brave, old-fashioned orator, overtaken by the surging tide of the twentieth century, swept under by the wave of the future. When his horse is shot out under him, the best rider must fall.

On the tenth of May, at dawn—it was a radiant, beautiful morning, cloudless across Europe from the Irish Sea to the Baltic—Hitler flung his armies forward. They were the winged carriers of an astonishing drama. Holland fell in five days; Belgium in eighteen. Two days after the German drive had begun, the French front was broken. Another eight days, and the Germans reached the Channel. Calais and Boulogne fell. Dunkirk held for just ten days. Most of the British Expeditionary Force barely escaped; all their equipment was lost. Five weeks from the day they had started westward, German regiments were marching down the Champs Elysées. Three more days, and a new French government asked for surrender.

Here was a drama of forty days unequaled in the history of war for centuries, even by the brilliant victories of Napoleon. Hitler himself had a hand in designing that most astonishing of successful campaigns. He also had a hand in designing an armistice that the French would be inclined to accept.

He hoped that the United States would stay out of the war. His propaganda minister Joseph Goebbels ordered the toning down of anti-American items in the German press and radio. When the German army marched into an empty Paris, its commanders made a courtesy call on the American ambassador, who, alone among the envoys of the Great Powers, chose to stay in the capital instead of following the torn French government during its sorry flight to the south. The Hotel Crillon, headquarters of the German military command, was across the street from the American Embassy. The German general in charge received the

American military and naval attachés at ten in the morning. He offered them glasses of what he described as "the very best brandy in the Crillon." His staff approached the American ambassador with calculated and self-conscious courtesies, to which William C. Bullitt responded with all the tact and reserve of a great envoy of classical stamp. Two months later Bullitt was back from France in his native city of Philadelphia, where, in front of Independence Hall, he made a stirring speech, calling the American people to rally to the British side against Hitler. His speech did not have much of a popular echo.

Hitler hoped that the British would think twice before going on with the war. Their chances, he said, were hopeless; and he repeated that he had no quarrel with the existence of the British Empire. He hoped that the British would make some kind of peace with him.

They didn't. Their savior Churchill had arisen; and behind Churchill—slowly, cautiously, but deliberately—rose the massive shadow of Franklin Roosevelt. In the summer of 1940—still a year and a half before Pearl Harbor and his declaration of war against the United States —Hitler already knew that his principal enemy was Roosevelt, whom he came to hate with a fury even greater than his hatred for Churchill (and, of course, for Stalin, whom he admired in many ways till the end).

Roosevelt and Churchill knew each other. More than that, they had, for some time, put their hopes in each other. For some time Franklin Roosevelt—secretly, privately, through some of his envoys, personal friends whom he trusted—had encouraged those men in London and Paris who were convinced that Hitler had to be fought. Foremost among these was Winston Churchill. In turn, Churchill knew what Roosevelt thought of Hitler; and he knew that what Britain needed was the support of the giant United States. The two men had begun to correspond, in secret. On the day German armor appeared on the cliffs across from Dover, an American citizen, an employee of the American Embassy in London, was arrested by detectives of Scotland Yard. This young man, Tyler Kent, was a convinced and committed isolationist. He knew of that secret correspondence and had tried to inform pro-Germany sympathizers in London.

At that time—and for some dangerous weeks thereafter—Winston Churchill's position was not yet fixed in strength. He had, after all, a mixed reputation: yes, a great patriot, but an enthusiast for losing causes. He had been flung out of power during the First World War because of his advocacy of the failed Dardanelles campaign. There were many people within his own Conservative party who distrusted him. When, during the first eight weeks of his prime ministership, he entered the House of Commons, they sat on their hands. King George VI himself had not been quite happy to hand over the reins to him on that tenth of May. John Colville, Churchill's later faithful and admiring private secretary, reported in his diary that day that "this sudden coup of Winston and his rabble was a serious disaster and an unnecessary one. . . . They had weakly surrendered to a half-breed American whose main support was that of inefficient but talkative people of a similar type. . . ."

On the dark first day of the Dunkirk evacuation, there was a near break between Churchill and the Foreign Secretary, Lord Halifax. Halifax wanted to consider at least the possibility of some kind of a negotiation with Hitler and Mussolini. Churchill said no. "At the moment our prestige in Europe was very low. The only way we could get it back was by showing the world that Germany had not beaten us. If, after two or three months, we could show that we were still unbeaten, our prestige would return. Even if we were beaten, we should be no worse off than we should be if we were now to abandon the struggle. Let us therefore avoid being dragged down the slippery slope. . . ." But he himself was not so far from the edge of a slippery slope. All this looks strange and unreal now. But it is the task of the historian to see not only what happened but also what could have happened. At the end of May and throughout June 1940, the continuation of Churchill's brave position and leadership were still problematic. His great phrases in his great public speeches had not fallen into the void: but their meaning had yet to mature.

During that beautiful and deadly early summer of 1940, Franklin Roosevelt, too, had to contend with a difficult problem. This was the divided mind of the American people. We have heard much lately —because of nostalgic inclinations due to the trauma of a divided nation during the Vietnam War—about the Second World War having been a Good War, when this giant nation was united in purpose and in concept. Even after Pearl Harbor this was not exactly true. During the summer of 1940 it was not true at all. There was a small minority of Americans that was convinced the United States should abet and aid the nations warring against Hitler at almost any price. There was another, larger, minority of isolationists that wanted the United States to keep out of this war, at all costs. And there was a large and inchoate majority that did not like Hitler, and that was contemptuous of the Japanese, but their minds were divided: yes, the United States should oppose the enemies of democracy; no, the democracy of the United States should not engage in a foreign war. There were people who understood that these sentiments were contradictory. Others did not. Yet other Americans began to change their minds —slowly, gradually, at times imperceptibly. But not until after the dangerous summer of 1940.

There was a strange unreality in the American scene during the early summer. The few people from Europe and Britain who landed in New York during those dazzling May and June days found themselves in quite another world—in the gleaming lobbies of the great New York hotels, among the glistening stream of automobiles and taxis, before the glowing glass windows of the incredibly rich department stores, around which flowed the masses of a confident, prosperous, largely undisturbed American people. It was as if the astonishing speed of the devolving events in Western Europe was too fast to grasp. It was not until the fall of France that the startling new specter of a German Europe cohered. The press, for example, including the internationalist newspapers of the East Coast, had not really prepared people for that. Until the fall of Paris its reporters gave undue credit to the resistance of the French and British armies:

for the wish is the father of the thought in newspaperdom as well as elsewhere.

There was another problem. A difficulty between Churchill and Roosevelt had arisen. In their confidential correspondence Churchill was wont to sign himself "Former Naval Person." Yet oddly, of the two, Roosevelt was more of a naval person. Even after the fall of France, he believed, and said, that "naval power was the key to history," that Hitler, because of his naval inferiority, was bound to lose this war. For the European theater, this was wrong in the long run. The internal-combustion engine had changed the nature of warfare; for the first time in five hundred years, armies could move faster on land than on the seas. Eventually Hitler's armies had to be destroyed on land, and mostly by the Russians. Had the German armies not been chewed up by the Russians, the Western allies, with all of their sea and air superiority, could not have invaded France in 1944.

What is more important, Roosevelt was wrong in the short run too. If worst came to worst, he thought, and told Churchill, the British navy could come across the Atlantic to fight on. But Churchill could not guarantee that. As early as May 15 he wrote Roosevelt that if American help came too late, "the weight may be more than we can bear." Five days later, when the Germans had reached the Channel, he repeated this. "If members of this administration were finished and others came in to parley amid the ruins, you must not be blind to the fact that the sole remaining bargaining counter with Germany would be the fleet, and if this country was left by the United States to its fate no one would have the right to blame those then responsible if they made the best terms they could for the surviving inhabitants." The day after Paris fell, Churchill let Roosevelt know that "a point may be reached in the struggle where the present ministers no longer have control of affairs and when very easy terms could be obtained for the British Islands by their becoming a vassal state of the Hitler empire." This was exactly what Hitler had in mind. As in the case of France, his plan called for a partial occupation of the British island, with the fleet in British ports but demobilized, and with a Germanophile British government somewhere within the reach of the German occupation forces.

Nevertheless, Roosevelt's inclinations were strong and clear. He tried to cajole and to warn Mussolini against entering the war on Hitler's side. Roosevelt knew that this kind of diplomacy represented another move away from neutrality and that Mussolini was still popular among the large Italian-American populations in the important cities of the East: but Roosevelt discounted that. When, on June 10, Mussolini chose to declare war on France and Britain, Roosevelt changed the draft of a speech he was to give at the University of Virginia in Charlottesville. He added a sentence: "The hand that held the dagger," he intoned, "has struck it into the back of its neighbor." Few phrases could be more unneutral than that. When he heard this, Churchill growled with satisfaction. But Roosevelt's hands were, as yet, not free.

He had to prepare himself for an unprecedented nomination for an unprecedented third-term election as President. And against him a new American coalition had begun to gather: it came to be called America First, composed by all kinds of men and women who thought, and said, that American support to Britain was illegal, futile, and wrong. A leader of this movement was Charles A. Lindbergh, a great American hero. Its actual members were recognizable, while its potential popularity was not measurable. It is wrong to consider America First as if it had been a fluke, a conventicle of reactionaries and extremists. There were all kinds of respectable Americans who opposed Roosevelt and who were loath to engage themselves on the British side. They included not only Herbert Hoover but John Foster Dulles, with whom the Lindberghs were dining on the evening the French asked for an armistice—in other words, surrender. Anne Morrow Lindbergh was about to publish her book about the spirit of the times, entitled *The Wave of the Future*, arguing, by no means crudely or unintelligently, that the old world of liberal individualism, of parliamentary democracy, was being replaced by something new, before our very eyes. Another

book, from the hands of a young Kennedy, a Harvard undergraduate, was also in the making. Its conclusions were more cautious than Anne Lindbergh's, but some of its underlying suggestions were not entirely different. His father was Roosevelt's ambassador to Britain. Joseph P. Kennedy, Sr., was no admirer of Hitler, but he was a convinced isolationist who loathed Churchill and believed the British resistance to Hitler was futile. His son, John F. Kennedy, was a secret contributor to America First.

Then came the second great coincidence. On the twenty-second of June the French delegates signed their capitulation to Hitler. It was his greatest triumph —and the lowest point in Britain's fortunes in a thousand years. Yet, that very week, the British cause was lifted by an unexpected stroke of fortune, in Philadelphia of all places. There the Republican party had met in convention and nominated Wendell Willkie for their presidential candidate: and Willkie was not an isolationist. There had been many reasons to believe that the Republicans would nominate an isolationist: perhaps Robert A. Taft from Ohio or Arthur H. Vandenberg from Michigan. The Midwest, with its large German-American and Scandinavian-American populations, mostly Republicans, was strongly isolationist. Willkie came from Indiana; and after Hitler's invasion of Scandinavia, some of that Scandinavian-American Anglophobe isolationism began to melt away. Yet the isolationist conviction was still a strong, unchanneled current among the milling Republican delegates on the floor, in that boiling arena of Philadelphia's Convention Hall. But a carefully orchestrated and arranged effort, with the galleries chanting, "We want Willkie," carried the day.

None of this would be possible in our day of the mechanized primary system. It was still possible forty-six years ago. It was the achievement of the internationally minded, anti-populist, financial and social leadership of East Coast Republicans, of readers of the New York *Herald Tribune* over those of the Chicago *Tribune*, of Anglophiles over Anglophobes. The difference between the world view of Willkie and Roosevelt was one of degree, not of kind. Had the Republicans nominated an isolationist,

Roosevelt would probably still have won, but the nation would have been sorely and dangerously divided; and Roosevelt would have been constrained to go slow, very slow; constrained to deny his very convictions and inclinations, to the mortal peril of the British, the sole remaining champions of freedom during that dangerous summer of 1940.

This Willkie business was a great help to Britain. Churchill knew that, and he had been smart enough to do nothing about it. He remembered the aggressive British propaganda in the United States during the First World War. "We shall not dance attendance at American party conventions." He let Hitler do the job of turning the sentiments of Americans around, so that their captain could begin to change the course of the mighty American ship of state from armed neutrality to defiance and war.

Hitler now dawdled—for one of the very few times during the war. Europe lay at his feet. He went off on a vacation, touring places in northern France where he had soldiered during the First World War. He made a short, furtive visit to an empty Paris at dawn. He suggested a European version of the Monroe Doctrine: Europe for the "Europeans," America for the Americans. He did not draft the directive for the invasion of Britain until the middle of July—and even then with some reluctance. On July 19 he made a long and crude speech, offering a last chance of peace to Britain. In London the German "peace offer" was let drop with an icy silence, somewhat like a blackmailing note left at the door of a proud old mansion.

A proud old mansion: but would it stand? Could it stand? Above the gray seas patrolled the pilots, across the soughing waves drove the British flotillas, watching. Were the Germans about to come? And the Americans? There was a trickle of war goods moving eastward across the Atlantic, propelled by a current of American sympathy: but sympathy was not yet resolution, and that current not yet a flood. The bombing of England that turned the hearts and minds of many Americans around had not yet begun. For six weeks after the fall of France, the Americans, as Churchill said later to a confidant, "treated us in that rather distant and sympathetic manner one adopts toward a friend we know is suffering from cancer." There were many people in America—not only isolationists but men high in the Army general staff—who doubted whether Britain would or could hold out against Hitler. In some of the country clubs around Boston and Philadelphia and New York, the members went around to collect secondhand shotguns for the British, whose Home Guard was still bereft of weapons. Some of the Home Guard were given old golf clubs and sticks, presumably to hit prowling Germans on the head. If and when the invasion came, "you can always take one with you," Churchill had planned to say.

Then came the third coincidence, so enormous and shattering in its consequences that, even now, many people, including a number of historians, are unaware of its ultimate portent.

Six weeks had now passed since France had fallen; and Britain still stood, inviolate, increasingly aglow with the spirit breathed by Churchill's words. Franklin Roosevelt made up his mind. He took an important step. He brought in a few confidants who assured him that he, in his constitutional capacity as Commander-in-Chief, could go ahead. This was at the very end of July. Two days later Roosevelt announced to his cabinet that the United States would "sell directly or indirectly fifty or sixty old World War destroyers to Great Britain." Churchill had asked for such a deal in May. The destroyers were not, in themselves, as important as the gesture, the meaning of the act itself for the world. It meant *the* decisive departure from American neutrality. What Roosevelt did not know, and what Churchill did not know, was that, at the same moment, Hitler had taken his first decisive move in ordering the German army staff to plan for an invasion of Russia.

There was method in Hitler's madness. What did he say to the close circle of his commanders on that day? "England's hope is Russia and America." Against

America he could do nothing. But "if hope in Russia is eliminated, America is also eliminated," he said. He was not altogether wrong. Eliminating Russia would destroy British hopes for an eventual conquest of Germany in Europe, and it would strengthen Japan's position in the Far East. In the United States it would also strengthen popular opposition to Roosevelt. There were many Americans who hated and feared communism: the elimination of communist Russia would make Roosevelt's continued intervention on the side of Britain increasingly futile and unpopular. Russia, Hitler said on July 31, 1940, was not yet "a threat." But he was not sure about his prospects of conquering England. Air warfare against England was about to begin; but "if results of the air war are not satisfactory, [invasion] preparations will be halted." So at the end of July 1940, Hitler, after some hesitation, began to consider invading Russia at the very moment when Roosevelt, after some hesitation, made his decision to commit the United States on the British side.

This last day of July in 1940 was not merely an important milestone. It was the turning point of the Second World War. There followed the climax of the Battle of Britain in the air, which, for Hitler, was indecisive. So far as the American people went, the bombing of Britain solidified their gradually crystallizing inclination to stand by the British. Britain held out; and in November 1940 Roosevelt easily won the majority of his people for a third term. That was the first American presidential election watched by the entire world. When Mussolini attacked Greece at the end of October, Hitler berated him: he ought to have waited until after the American election. When Hitler agreed to invite Stalin's minion Molotov, the Soviet commissar for foreign affairs, to Berlin, Stalin set the date of the visit after the American election.

What followed—Lend-Lease, the Selective Service Bill, the Marines sent to Greenland and Iceland, Roosevelt's order to the Navy to shoot at any appearance

of Axis naval craft—was a foregone conclusion. Hitler was shrewd enough to order German commanders to avoid incidents with the United States at all costs. He did not want to furnish Roosevelt with the pretext of a serious naval incident. Eventually his Japanese allies were to accomplish what he was reluctant to do. Five hundred days after that thirty-first of July came another great coincidence. In the snow-covered wasteland before Moscow, the Russians halted the German army just when, in the sunny wastes of the Pacific, the Japanese attack on Pearl Harbor propelled the United States into the war. The Germans and the Japanese would achieve astounding victories even after that: but the war they could not win.

One year before Pearl Harbor Roosevelt had announced that the United States would be the "arsenal of democracy." Churchill had told the American people: "Give us the tools, and we will finish the job." Did he mean this? We cannot tell. It was far from certain that Hitler could be defeated by the supply of American armaments alone. What was needed was the employment of immense American armies and navies in the field. And even that would not be enough. Hitler's defeat could not be accomplished without the armed might of Russia, whereby victory in Europe had to be shared with Russia.

Forty-six years later we have a government that neither remembers nor understands this. Churchill understood the alternative: either all of Europe ruled by Germany, or the eastern portion of it controlled by Russia. It was not a pleasant alternative. In world politics few alternatives are altogether pleasant. Yet half of Europe was better than none. Had it not been for Franklin Roosevelt during that dangerous summer of 1940, even this alternative would have been moot. Had the United States been led by an isolationist president in 1940, Hitler would have won the war.

SOCIAL OUTCASTS IN NAZI GERMANY

An obsession with Aryanism and eugenic theory was the catalyst for Nazi policies of repression and extermination against gypsies and other 'asocials' — the forgotten victims of the Third Reich.

Jeremy Noakes

A German gypsy family on the road in the 1920s.

OF ALL NAZI ATROCITIES, THE extermination of the Jews has, rightly, commanded the most attention from historians and the general public. But this understandable preoccupation with the horrors of Nazi anti-Semitism has led people to overlook the fact that the Jews formed only one, albeit the major, target in a broad campaign directed against a variety of groups who were considered to be 'alien to the community' (*Gemeinschaftsfremd*), and who often were defined in biological terms. Only recently have historians begun to focus their attention on this hitherto neglected sphere of Nazi policy and action.

Nazism arose in the aftermath of defeat and revolution. In the view of its leaders, and notably of Hitler, the main cause of Germany's collapse had not been military defeat but the disintegration of the home front weakened by years of incompetent leadership, corroded by pernicious ideas of liberal democracy, Marxism and sentimental humanitarianism, and sapped by biological decline which was the result of ignoring the principles of race and eugenics. Their main domestic goal was to create out of the German people, riven by divisions of class, religion and ideology, a new and unified 'national community' (*Volksgemeinschaft*) based on ties of blood and race and infused with a common 'world view'. They believed this united national community would then possess the requisite morale to enable Germany to make a bid for the position as a world power to which she had long aspired. The members of this national community, the 'national comrades' (*Volksgenossen*), were expected to conform to a norm based on certain criteria. A national comrade was expected to be of Aryan race, genetically healthy (*erbgesund*), socially efficient (*leistungsfähig*), and politically and ideologically reliable, which involved not simply passive obedience but active participation in the various organisations of the regime and repeated ges-

First published in *History Today*, December 1985, pp. 15-19. Reproduced by kind permission from History Today, Ltd., 83-84 Berwick Street, London W1V 3PJ England.

tures of loyalty (the Hitler salute, etc.).

On coming to power the Nazis were determined to discriminate against, or persecute, all those who failed to fulfill these criteria and were therefore regarded as being outside the national community. There were three main types of these outsiders which, although they overlap, can be conveniently considered as separate categories. Firstly, ideological enemies – those who propagated or even simply held beliefs and values regarded as a threat to national morale. Secondly so-called 'asocials' – the socially inefficient and those whose behaviour offended against the social norms of the 'national community'. And thirdly, the biological outsiders – those who were regarded as a threat because of their race or because they were suffering from a hereditary defect. It is with the last two of these categories that this article is concerned.

The third category, that of biological outsiders, consisted of two main groups: those considered undesirable because of their race (the non-Aryans), and those who were unacceptable on eugenic grounds because of hereditary defects which posed a threat to the future of the German race and/or rendered them socially ineffective. Although the racial and eugenic theories which defined these groups were in some respects distinct – not all eugenists were anti-Semitic for example – they shared common origins in biological theories of the late nineteenth century and a common perspective in viewing mankind primarily in biological terms. Individuals were not seen as possessing validity in themselves as human beings and were not judged in terms of their human qualities, but their significance was assessed first and foremost in terms of their physical and mental efficiency as members of a 'race' and they were seen primarily as collections of good or bad genes.

The theory of eugenics – the idea of improving the 'race' through the encouragement of selective breeding – had become increasingly influential in many countries during the 1920s and 1930s and Germany was no exception. It flourished against a background of concern about declining birthrates and particularly about the destruction of a generation of the healthiest members of the nation in the First World War. There was also growing concern about the impact of modern improvements in welfare, hygiene, and medical care in ensuring the survival of increasing numbers of those with hereditary defects who were thereby allegedly producing a deterioration of the race. Moreover, during this period it was fashionable to attribute many social ills to heredity – habitual criminality, alcoholism, prostitution, and pauperism. Even some on the Left were attracted by eugenics. They tended to make a sharp distinction between the 'genuine' working class and the *Lumpenproletariat*, the 'dregs' of society. Eugenics appeared to offer the prospect of eliminating the *Lumpenproletariat*, traditionally seen since Marx as the tool of reaction.

During the 1920s a number of doctors and psychiatrists in Germany began to propose a policy of sterilisation to prevent those with hereditary defects from procreating. Such a policy of 'negative selection' had already been carried out on a limited scale in the United States where the technique of vasectomy had been developed and was first applied by a prison doctor in 1899. With the economic crisis which began in 1929 such proposals gained increasing support among those involved in the welfare services, since they appeared to offer the prospect not only of substantial savings in the future but also of facilitating the release of some of those in institutional care without fear of their producing defective offspring. Towards the end of 1932 the Prussian authorities prepared a draft law permitting the voluntary sterilisation of those with hereditary defects. Those who drafted the law had felt obliged to make sterilisation voluntary since they believed that public opinion was not yet ready for compulsion. The logic of the eugenist case, however, required compulsion and, significantly, the Nazi medical experts who took part in the preceding discussions had demanded compulsion. The sterilisation issue was given priority by Hitler himself who overruled objections from his Catholic Vice-Chancellor, von Papen. On July 14th, 1933, within six months of its coming to power, the new regime had issued a Sterilisation Law ordering the sterilisation – by compulsion if necessary – of all those suffering from a number of specified illnesses which were alleged to be hereditary.

Apart from the moral issues raised by the question of compulsory sterilisation as such, the criteria used to define hereditary illness were in many respects exceedingly dubious. Thus, while there could be no doubt about the hereditary nature of some of the diseases specified, such as Huntingdon's Chorea, others such as 'hereditary simple-mindedness', schizophrenia, manic depressive illness, and 'chronic alcoholism' were not only more difficult to diagnose but their hereditary basis was much more questionable. Moreover, even if it were granted, the elimination of these diseases through the sterilisation of those affected was an impossible task in view of the role played by recessive genes in their transmission. Finally, although an impressive apparatus of hereditary courts was established to pass judgment on the individual cases, the evidence used to justify proposals for sterilisation sometimes reflected more the social and political prejudices of the medical and welfare authorities involved than objective scientific criteria. Thus a reputation for being 'work-shy' or even former membership of the Communist Party could be used as crucial supporting evidence in favour of sterilisation. From 1934 to 1945 between 320,000 and 350,000 men and women were sterilised under this law and almost one hundred people died following the operation. After the war few of those sterilised received any compensation for what they had suffered since they could not claim to have been persecuted on political or racial grounds. The new measure appears to have had at least tacit support from public opinion. It was only when people found members of their own families, friends and colleagues affected by it that they became concerned.

The Nazis claimed that sterilistion was an unfortunate necessity for those with hereditary defects and that once it was carried out the sterilised were thereby in effect restored to full status as 'national comrades'. In practice, however, in a society in which health, and in particular fertility, were key virtues the sterilised were bound to feel discriminated against, and the fact that they were forbidden to marry fertile partners underlined this point. However, for those who were not merely suffering from hereditary defects but were socially ineffective as well the future was far bleaker. Already in 1920 a distinguished jurist, Karl Binding, and a psychiatrist, Alfred Hoche, had together published a book with the title: *The Granting of Permission for the Destruction of Worthless Life. Its Extent and Form.* In this book, written under the impression of the casualties of the First World War, the two authors proposed that in certain cases it should be legally possible to kill those suffering from incurable and severely crippling handicaps and injuries – so-called 'burdens on the community' *(Ballastexistenzen)*. This proposal assumed, first, that it was acceptable for an outside agency to define what individual life was 'worthless' and, secondly, that in effect an individual had to justify his existence according to criteria imposed from outside (i.e. he had to prove that his life was worthwhile). These assumptions were indeed implicit in the biological and collectivist approach to human life which had become increasingly influential after 1900.

With the take-over of power by the Nazis it was not long before this biological and collectivist approach began to be transferred from theory into reality. In addition to the sterilisation programme, this took the form, firstly, of a propaganda campaign designed to devalue the handicapped as burdens on the community in the eyes of the population and, secondly, of a programme of systematic extermination of the mentally sick and handicapped – the so-called Euthanasia Programme, a misleading title since the term 'euthanasia' was in fact a Nazi euphemism for mass murder.

The euthanasia programme began in the spring or early summer of 1939 when the parents of a severely handicapped baby petitioned Hitler for the baby to be killed. He agreed to the request and ordered the head of his personal Chancellery, Phillip Bouhler, to proceed likewise in all similar cases. Bouhler set up a secret organisation to carry out the programme which initially covered children up to three years old, later

extended to twelve-sixteen years. By the end of the war approximately 5,000 children had been murdered either by injection or through deliberate malnutrition. In August 1939 Hitler ordered that the extermination programme be extended to adults, for which the *Führer*'s Chancellery set up another secret organisation. So large were the numbers involved – there were approximately 200,000 mentally sick and handicapped in 1939 – that a new method of killing had to be devised. Experts in the Criminal Police Department came up with the idea of using carbon monoxide gas. After a successful trial on a few patients, gas chambers were constructed in six mental hospitals in various parts of Germany to which patients were transferred from mental institutions all over the *Reich*. By the time the programme was officially stopped by Hitler in August 1941 under pressure from public protests some 72,000 people had been murdered.

During the next two years under a separate programme also run by the *Führer*'s Chancellery under the code number 14F13, the reference number of the Inspector of Concentration Camps, another 30-50,000 people were selected from concentration camps and gassed on the grounds of mental illness, physical incapacity, or simply racial origin, in which case the 'diagnosis' on the official form read 'Jew' or 'gypsy'. In the meantime, however, the majority of the personnel who had developed expertise in operating the gas chambers had been transferred to Poland and placed at the disposal of the SS for the death camps which opened in the winter of 1941-42. These notorious death camps – Belsen, Treblinka, Sobibor, Majdanek, and Auschwitz-Birkenau – were intended to destroy the other biological outcasts of Nazi Germany, the non-Aryans, of whom the Jews formed by far the largest group. However, the understandable preoccupation with the Holocaust has tended to divert attention from another group which came into this category – the gypsies. For they also suffered genocide at the hands of the Nazis.

Long before the Nazis came to power the gypsies had been treated as social outcasts. Their foreign appearance, their strange customs and language, their nomadic way of life and

lack of regular employment had increasingly come to be regarded as an affront to the norms of a modern state and society. They were seen as asocial, a source of crime, culturally inferior, a foreign body within the nation. During the 1920s, the police, first in Bavaria and then in Prussia established special offices to keep the gypsies under constant surveillance. They were photographed and fingerprinted as if they were criminals. With the Nazi take-over, however, a new motive was added to the grounds for persecution – their distinct and allegedly inferior racial character.

Nazi policy towards the gypsies, like the policy towards the Jews, was uncertain and confused. Initially they were not a major target. With their small numbers – 30,000 – and generally low social status they were not seen as such a serious racial threat as the Jews. They were, however, included in the regulations implementing the Nuremberg Law for the Protection of German Blood and Honour of September 15th, 1935, which banned marriage and sexual relations between Aryans and non-Aryans. From then onwards they were the subject of intensive research by racial 'experts' of the 'Research Centre for Racial Hygiene and Biological Population Studies'. The aim was to identify and distinguish between pure gypsies and the part-gypsies *(Mischlinge)* who had been lumped together in the records of the Weimar police. Whereas in the case of the Jews the *Mischlinge* were treated as less of a threat than the 'full' Jews, among the gypsies the *Mischlinge*, some of whom had integrated themselves into German society, were treated as the greater threat. The leading expert on the gypsies, Dr Robert Ritter, insisted that:

> The gypsy question can only be regarded as solved when the majority of a-social and useless gypsy *Mischlinge* have been brought together in large camps and made to work and when the continual procreation of this half-breed population has been finally prevented. Only then will future generations be freed from this burden.

In December 1938 Himmler issued a 'Decree for the Struggle against the Gypsy Plague', which introduced a more systematic registration of gypsies based on the research of the racial experts. Pure gypsies received brown papers, gypsy *Mischlinge* light blue ones and nomadic non-gypsies grey ones. The aim was 'once and for all to ensure the racial separation of gypsies from our own people to prevent the mixing of the two races, and finally to regulate the living conditions of the gypsies and gypsy *Mischlinge*'. After the victory over Poland the deportation of gypsies from Germany to Poland was ordered and in the meantime they were forbidden to leave the camps to which they were assigned and which were now in effect turned into labour camps. In May 1940 2,800 gypsies joined the Jewish transports to Poland. However, this deportation programme was then stopped because of logistical problems in the reception areas.

During 1941-42 gypsies and gypsy-*Mischlinge* were included in the discriminatory measures introduced against Jews within the Reich and they were also removed from the Armed Forces. However, while there was unanimous contempt for the gypsy *Mischlinge*, Nazi racial experts had a certain admiration for the way in which the pure gypsies had sustained their separate identity and way of life over the centuries, an achievement attributed to their strong sense of race. Dr Robert Ritter suggested that the 'pure bred' gypsies in Germany (*Sinti*) and in the German-speaking areas of Bohemia and Moravia (*Lalleri*) should be assigned to an area where they would be permitted to live according to their traditional ways more or less as museum specimens, while the remainder should be sterilised, interned, and subjected to forced labour. Himmler sympathised with this view and in October 1942 issued orders for appropriate arrangements to be made. However, he ran into opposition from Bormann and probably Hitler and so, on December 16th, 1942, he issued an order for the German gypsies to be transferred to Auschwitz. Between February 26th and March 25th, 1943, 11,400 gypsies from Germany and elsewhere were transported to a special gypsy camp within Auschwitz. Here, unlike other prisoners, they were able to live together with their families, probably to facilitate the medical experiments which were carried out in a medical centre established in their camp by the notorious Dr Mengele. Of the 20,000

gypsies in all transported to Auschwitz, 11,000 were murdered there, while the others were transferred elsewhere. At the same time, thousands of gypsies were being murdered throughout occupied Europe, notably by the *Einsatzgruppen* in Russia. It has been estimated that half a million European gypsies died at the hands of the Nazis. Of the 30,000 gypsies living in Germany in 1939 only 5,000 survived the war.

The gypsies offended against the norms of the 'national community' not only on the grounds of their non-Aryan character (although ironically since they had originated in India they could legitimately claim to be more 'Aryan' than the Germans!), but also on the grounds of their 'a-social' behaviour. The 'a-socials' formed another major category of social outcasts. The term 'a-social' was a very flexible one which could be used to include all those who failed to abide by the social norms of the national community: habitual criminals, the so-called 'work-shy', tramps and beggars, alcoholics, prostitutes, homosexuals, and juvenile delinquents. The Nazis introduced much tougher policies towards such groups, in some cases – as with the Sterilisation Law – implementing measures which had been demanded or planned before their take-over of power. Above all, there was a growing tendency for the police to acquire more and more control over these groups at the expense of the welfare agencies and the courts. It was the ultimate ambition of the police to take over responsibility for all those whom it defined as 'community aliens' (*Gemeinschaftsfremde*). To achieve this goal, in 1940 it introduced a draft 'Community Alien Law' which, after being held up by opposition from other government departments, was finally intended to go into effect in 1945. According to Paragraph 1.i of the final draft:

> A person is alien to the community if he/she proves to be incapable of satisfying the minimum requirements of the national community through his/her own efforts, in particular through an unusual degree of deficiency of mind or character.

The official explanation of the law maintained that:

> The National Socialist view of welfare is

that it can only be granted to national comrades who both need it and are worthy of it. In the case of community aliens who are only a burden on the national community welfare is not necessary, rather police compulsion with the aim of either making them once more useful members of the national community through appropriate measures or of preventing them from being a further burden. In all these matters protection of the community is the primary object.

In September 1933, the Reich Ministries of the Interior and Propaganda initiated a major roundup of 'tramps and beggars' of whom there were between 300,000 and 500,000, many of them homeless young unemployed. Such a large number of people without fixed abode was regarded as a threat to public order. However, the regime lacked the means to provide shelter and work for such vast numbers. Moreover, there were advantages in having a mobile labour force which could if necessary be directed to particular projects. The Nazis, therefore, initially made a distinction between 'orderly' and 'disorderly' people of no fixed abode. Those who were healthy, willing to work, and with no previous convictions were given a permit (*Wanderkarte*) and were obliged to follow particular routes and perform compulsory work in return for their board and lodging. 'Disorderly' persons of no fixed abode on the other hand could be dealt with under the Law against Dangerous Habitual Criminals and concerning Measures for Security and Correction of November 24th, 1933, and the Preventive Detention Decree of the Ministry of the Interior of December 14th, 1937, which introduced the practice of preventive detention. Many tramps were also sterilised.

After 1936, as a result of the economic recovery, Germany faced a growing labour shortage and the regime was no longer willing to tolerate either numbers of people of no fixed abode or the 'work-shy'. Apart from their significance for the labour force, such people contradicted basic principles of the national community – the principle of performance and the principle of being 'integrated' (*erfasst-eingeordnet*). As one Nazi expert put it:

> In the case of a long period without work on the open road where he is

entirely free to follow his own desires and instincts, he (the tramp) is in danger of becoming a freedom fanatic who rejects all integration as hated compulsion.

As a result, persons of no fixed abode increasingly came to be regarded as a police rather than a welfare matter. Even before 1936 some people designated as 'work-shy' had been sent to concentration camps forming the category of 'a-socials' who wore a black triangle. A big round-up had taken place before the Olympic games and in 1936 two of the ten companies in Dachau were composed of this category. In the summer of 1938 an even bigger round-up took place under the code word 'Work-shy Reich' in the course of which approximately 11,000 'beggars, tramps, pimps and gypsies' were arrested and transferred largely to Buchenwald where they formed the largest category of prisoner until the influx of Jews following the 'Night of Broken Glass' on November 8th. It has been estimated that some 10,000 tramps were incarcerated in concentration camps during the Third Reich of whom few survived the ordeal. This harsh policy towards the 'a-socials' appears to have been popular with many Germans and was welcomed by local authorities who were thereby able to get rid of their 'awkward customers'.

Having set up a utopian model of an ideologically and racially homogeneous 'national community', the Nazis increasingly sought an explanation for deviance from its norms not in terms of flaws within the system itself and its incompatibility with human variety but rather in terms of flaws which were innate within the individual. As an anti-type to the racially pure, genetically healthy, loyal and efficient 'national comrade', they evolved the concept of the 'degenerate a-social' whose deviance was *biologically* determined. As the Reich Law Leader, Hans Frank, put it in a speech in October 1938:

National Socialism regards degeneracy as an immensely important source of criminal activity. It is our belief that every superior nation is furnished with such an abundance of endowments for its journey through life that the word 'degeneracy' most clearly defines the state of affairs that concerns us here. In a decent nation the 'genus' must be regarded as valuable *per se*: consequently, in an individual degeneracy signifies exclusion from the normal *genus* of the decent nation. This state of being degenerate, this different or alien quality tends to be rooted in miscegnation between a decent representative of his race and an individual of inferior stock. To us National Socialists criminal biology, or the theory of congenital criminality, connotes a link between racial decadence and criminal manifestations. The complete degenerate lacks all racial sensitivity and sees it as his positive duty to harm the community or member thereof. He is the absolute opposite of the man who recognises that the fulfillment of his duty as a national comrade is his mission in life.

These ideas represent a variation on concepts which had emerged from research into so-called 'criminal biology' which had been going on in the Weimar Republic. Nor was this simply a matter of theory. For the Nazis had actually begun to apply the principles of criminal biology in the sphere of juvenile delinquency. This was another area in which the police usurped the responsibility of the welfare agencies and the courts. In 1939 they exploited the Preventive Detention Decree of 1937 to set up their own Reich Central Agency for the Struggle against Juvenile Delinquency and the following year established a Youth Concentration Camp in Moringen near Hanover. Perhaps the most significant feature of the camp was the fact that the youths were subjected to 'biological and racial examination' under the supervision of Dr Ritter, now the Director of the Criminal-Biological Institute of the Reich Security Main Office. Then, on the basis of highly dubious pseudo-scientific criteria, they were divided into groups

according to their alleged socio-biological character and reformability. This process of socio-biological selection pioneered in Moringen was an integral part of the concept of the Community Aliens Law. Thus, according to the official justification of the Law:

The governments of the period of the System (Weimar) failed in their measures to deal with community aliens. They did not utilise the findings of genetics and criminal biology as a basis for a sound welfare and penal policy. As a result of their liberal attitude they constantly perceived only the "rights of the individual" and were more concerned with his protection from state intervention than with the general good. In National Socialism the individual counts for nothing when the community is at stake.

Defeat preserved Germans from being subjected to the Community Aliens Law and a future in which any deviation from the norms of the 'national community' would be not merely criminalised but also liable to be defined as evidence of 'degeneracy', i.e. biological inadequacy, for which the penalties were sterilisation and probably eventual 'eradication' (*Ausmerzen*) through hard labour in concentration camp conditions. The Third Reich's policy towards social outcasts stands as a frightful warning both against the application of pseudo-science to social problems and against the rationalisation of social prejudices in terms of pseudo-science.

FOR FURTHER READING:
Gitta Sereny, *Into that Darkness* (Picador Books, 1977); D. Kenrick and G. Puxon, *The Destiny of Europe's Gypsies* (Chatto, 1972); J. Noakes, 'Nazism and Eugenics: The Background to the Nazi Sterilization Law of 14 July 1933' in R.J. Bullen et.al., eds., *Ideas into Politics. Aspects of European History 1880-1950* (Croom Helm, 1984); E. Klee, *'Euthanasie' im NS-Staat. Die 'Vernichtung lebensunwerten Lebens'* (Frankfurt, 1983); D. Peukert, 'Arbeitslager und Jugend-KZ: die Behandlung Gemeinschaftsfremder im Dritten Reich', in D. Peukert & J. Reulecke, *Die Reihen fast geschlossen. Beiträge zur Geschichte des Alltags unterm national sozialismus* (Wuppertal, 1981).

TO CLEAVE AN ATOM

Fission has given us a new kind of power and a new kind of war.

Alan P. Lightman

In the spring of 1962 our family built a fallout shelter in the backyard. The President of the United States had been coming on the television set, pointing his finger at us and telling us to go out and build a shelter. Some months earlier the government had distributed 25 million copies of a booklet called "Fallout Protection: What To Know and Do about Nuclear Attack." I was 13 and terrified that I would not live to be 14, and it was my pleading each night at the dinner table, as my three younger brothers sat quietly, that convinced my parents to dig up the backyard and put in a bomb shelter. It cost $3,000, exactly the price of the "H-Bomb Hideaway" featured in *Life* in 1955. The thing was finished just in time for the Cuban missile crisis.

A short-legged man who loved hiking created the first man-made nuclear chain reaction, on December 2, 1942, in a disused squash court at the University of Chicago. His name was Enrico Fermi. In Fermi's chain reaction, a subatomic particle called a neutron hits the nucleus of a uranium atom, cleaving it in two and releasing energy in the process. A uranium nucleus has quite a few

neutrons of its own, and, after the split, a few of these go flying off individually along with the two main fission fragments. Each of the spawned neutrons eventually strikes a fresh uranium nucleus, splitting it in half, releasing more energy and more neutrons, and the activity rapidly multiplies, going faster and faster. The uranium nuclei are like a lot of cocked mousetraps on the floor, each loaded with several Ping-Pong balls waiting to jump into the air when the spring is triggered. Toss a single ball into the middle to get the thing started, and soon Ping-Pong balls will be zinging everywhere. Fermi kept his chain reaction from getting out of hand by constantly removing some of the neutrons, just as the frantic release of the mousetraps can be slowed by catching some of the balls in midair before they land on cocked traps. Fermi was almost unique in 20th-century physics for being superb in both theory and experiment. He had, with others, conceived of nuclear chain reactions in early 1939. The whole idea of fission was only a few months old at the time.

Before 1938, everyone believed that atomic nuclei remained more or less whole, with the nuclei of some elements

gradually disintegrating, a few small bits at a time. The emission of these bits is called radioactivity. Henri Becquerel, a French physicist, first discovered radioactivity from uranium in 1896, and, soon after, the husband and wife team of Pierre and Marie Curie observed it from another element, radium, which lost weight little by little as it hurled out tiny particles.

In the early 1900s, scientists didn't know where in the atom radioactivity originated. Atoms were pictured as solid spheres of evenly distributed positive electrical charge, embedded with negatively charged particles called electrons. The electron, discovered in 1897, was clearly a subatomic particle. Its existence already contradicted the old Greek notion that the atom was indivisible. But the details of an atom's innards were largely unknown. Then, in a brilliantly straightforward experiment in 1911, Ernest Rutherford discovered the atomic nucleus. Rutherford fired subatomic particles at a sheet of gold. The projectiles he used were alpha particles, found by the Curies in their studies of radioactivity and known to be about $1/50$ the weight of gold atoms. If the positive charge in an atom were thinly scattered throughout its volume, as believed, then the alpha particles should have met little resistance in passing through the target gold atoms. But some bounced straight back, apparently having struck something highly concentrated. What Rutherford had discovered was that the atom is mostly empty space, with a very tiny center of positive charge, about which the electrons orbit at great distance. The dense center, the nucleus of the atom, contains all of the atom's positive charge and more than 99.9 percent of its weight. It is roughly a hundred thousand times smaller than the atom as a whole. The booming-voiced Lord Rutherford strongly preferred simple, rough-and-ready experiments, and this was surely one. He also had an excellent nose for making predictions. His experiments had shown that the atom's positively charged particles, called protons, reside in the central nucleus. Rutherford went on to correctly predict that protons share their nuclear living quarters with other, uncharged particles, later called neutrons.

One of Rutherford's collaborators from 1901 to 1903 was a man named Frederick Soddy, who later won the Nobel Prize in chemistry. They worked together on radioactivity. Soddy was impressed by the energy carried away in excited particles emerging somewhere from the depths of the atom. As early as 1903, he commented in the *Times Literary Supplement* on the latent internal energy of the atom and, in 1906, wrote elsewhere that there must be peaceful benefits for society, given the key to "unlock this great store of energy." Soddy had unusual foresight. So did H.G. Wells, who stayed well abreast of scientific developments and paid close attention to the remarks of such men as Soddy. Wells, however, made darker forecasts. In 1914 he published a lesser known novel by the title of *The World Set Free*, describing a world war in the 1950s in which each of the world's great cities are destroyed by a few "atomic bombs" the size of beach balls.

In many ways, the discovery of nuclear fission got underway in 1934. That was the year that Irène Curie, daughter of Marie and Pierre, and her husband, Frédéric Joliot, discovered "artificial" radioactivity. Before then, all radioactive substances had been gathered from minerals and ores. Joliot and Curie found they could *create* radioactive elements by bombarding

nonradioactive ones with alpha particles. Apparently, certain stable atomic nuclei, content to sit quietly forever, could be rendered unstable if they were obliged to swallow additional subatomic particles. The forcibly engorged atomic nuclei, in an agitated state, began spewing out little pieces of themselves, just as in "natural" radioactivity. Enrico Fermi, then working in Rome, immediately took his lead from the Joliot-Curie work but decided to see if neutrons rather than alpha particles could be used to produce radioactive nuclei. Alpha particles are positively charged and therefore partly repelled by the positively charged nucleus, but the uncharged neutrons, Fermi reasoned, would have an easier time making their way into the nucleus. When these experiments proved successful, Fermi bombarded the massive uranium nucleus, containing over 200 neutrons and protons, to see what would happen. He automatically assumed, as did others, that neutron bombardment of uranium would create nuclei close in weight to uranium. Then, in late 1938, the meticulous radiochemists Otto Hahn and Fritz Strassmann found in the remnants of bombarded uranium some barium—an element that weighs about half as much as uranium. There had been no barium in their sample to begin with. Apparently some uranium nuclei had been cut in two.

In December 1938, Hahn sent a letter describing his curious results to Lise Meitner, his coworker of 30 years. Meitner had been a respected and much loved physicist at the Kaiser Wilhelm Institute in Germany, but she was Jewish and had fled to Sweden five months earlier. At Christmas her nephew, physicist Otto Frisch, happened to pay her a visit and described the encounter: "There, in a small hotel in Kungälv near Göteborg, I found her at breakfast brooding over a letter from Hahn. I was skeptical about the contents—that barium was formed from uranium by neutrons—but she kept on with it. We walked up and down in the snow."

During their walk, Frisch and his aunt puzzled over how a single, slowly moving neutron could split in half an enormous uranium nucleus. It was well known that the protons and neutrons in an atomic nucleus are held together by strongly attractive forces—otherwise the electrical repulsion of the protons for each other would send them

flying away. How could so many attractive bonds be broken by a single neutron? Frisch and Meitner realized that the answer lay in an idea put forth by the master Danish physicist Niels Bohr. In 1936, Bohr had suggested that the particles in an atomic nucleus behave in a collective way, analogously to a drop of liquid. Frisch and Meitner reasoned that if such a drop could be slightly deformed from a spherical shape, the repulsive forces of the protons would begin to win out over the other, attractive forces. The attractive nuclear force between two nuclear particles weakens very rapidly as their separation increases, while the repulsive electrical force weakens far more slowly. Flatten a sphere of particles and each particle, on average, gets further away from its neighbors. Flatten it enough and the repulsive forces dominate, splitting it in two and sending the two halves flying apart at great speed. Frisch and Meitner calculated that the uranium nucleus was very fragile in terms of these deformations and that a small kick from a diminutive neutron might send it over the brink. According to their figures, the energy release should be enormous. Frisch went back to Copenhagen a few days later and barely managed to get the news to Bohr as the latter was boarding the Swedish-American liner MS Drottningholm for New York. The soft-spoken Bohr instantly slapped his head and said, "Oh, what fools we have been!" In describing the process, Frisch coined the word *fission*, by analogy with cell division in biology.

It remained for three groups of physicists, including Leo Szilard at Columbia and Walter Zinn, to demonstrate in March of 1939 that neutron fission of a uranium nucleus shakes loose several new neutrons. This proved that chain reactions were possible, as Fermi had conjectured. It remained for Bohr at Princeton to calculate that only a rare form of uranium called U-235, making up about one percent of the element in nature, could sustain a chain reaction. That was why the world hadn't already blown up on its own. To build a chain reactor, U-235 had to be culled and concentrated. It could be done. It could be done by the Germans. On August 2, 1939, Albert Einstein sent a letter to President Roosevelt: "Sir: Some recent work by E. Fermi and L. Szilard . . . leads me to expect that the element uranium may be turned into a new and important source of energy in the immediate future . . . and it is conceivable . . . that extremely powerful bombs of a new type may thus be constructed . . . ."

Powerful, yes. Fissioning a gram of uranium will produce about 10 million times the energy as burning a gram of coal and air or detonating a gram of TNT. Why is nuclear energy so much more potent than any form of energy known before? TNT explosions and coal-burning release chemical energy, which has been harnessed by people in one form or another for thousands of years. Chemical energy derives from rearranging the electrons in the outer parts of atoms. Nuclear energy, of the kind we've been discussing, derives from rearranging the protons in the nucleus of the atom. Because protons are confined to a much smaller volume than electrons, their electrical "springs" are much more compressed and thus much more violent upon release. Roughly speaking, nuclear energy is more powerful than chemical energy by the same factor as the atom is larger than its nucleus. (An even more powerful form of nuclear energy works by fusing small nuclei rather than fissioning large ones.)

As Soddy predicted, nuclear energy has indeed been used for peaceful purposes. The first atomic power generating plant began operation in Lemont, Illinois, in 1956. Unfortunately, nuclear power, which initially promised to be "too cheap to meter," has not yet proven its mettle economically. The 82 nuclear plants now licensed in the United States supply only about 13 percent of our total electric power needs

and continue to suffer from problems with management and design. Some countries in Europe have done better, but coal and oil are still the principal workhorses of the 20th century.

What nuclear energy has dramatically changed is the meaning of war. Each new weapon in its time seemed a giant advance over its predecessors: the Roman catapult, the medieval English longbow, gunpowder artillery in the 14th century, TNT in 1890—but these strides were Lilliputian by comparison to the leap from chemical to nuclear weapons. Ninety-seven out of 101 of the V-1 buzz bombs aimed at London on August 28, 1944, were intercepted—a remarkable success in defense. Had these been nuclear bombs, the four that landed, in fact just one of the four, could have annihilated the whole of the city. The United States and the Soviet Union today each possess 10,000 such bombs, which can be launched on short notice. In our nuclear age, those ancient words of war, *defense* and *victory*, have suddenly lost their meaning. Nuclear weapons demand that we find new concepts for war and peace and weapons themselves.

Even in peacetime, nuclear weapons have violated our sense of security. In a recent survey of high school students across the country, done by Educators for Social Responsibility, 80 percent thought there would be a nuclear war in the next 20 years, and 90 percent of these felt the world would not survive it. How does one measure the psychological effects of these visions?

There is of late a widespread perception that technology, and nuclear technology in particular, has gained a momentum of its own and is hurling the

world toward destruction. According to this belief, we humans are mere bystanders, helplessly awaiting our fate. I believe that our apparent helplessness regarding the nuclear weapons buildup originates from the *abstractness* of the danger more than our inability to stop it. After the destruction of Pompeii in A.D. 79, Mount Vesuvius exploded nine more times before another major eruption in 1631 destroyed many villages on its slopes and killed 3,000 people. For six months prior, earthquakes shook the villages. Why did people continue to go about their business next to a working volcano? About 700 people were killed in the great San Francisco earthquake of 1906, and experts expect the area is due for another big one. Why do people continue to build their houses on the San Andreas fault? In these examples, as in nuclear war, the disaster has an all-or-nothing character, and its likelihood seems either small or incalculable. Of course, we cannot simply remove ourselves from nuclear weapons as we can from volcanoes and geological faults, but the psychology may be the same. Evidently, even with a choice to do otherwise, people will live in a dangerous situation, as long as the danger can be abstracted away.

The discovery of nuclear fission has gotten the world profoundly stuck, to use Freeman Dyson's word. Stuck in a buildup of nuclear weapons, stuck in outdated concepts for war and peace, stuck in human nature. If we can get ourselves unstuck, a thousand years from now people may well remember this era not so much for opening up the atom as for opening up ourselves.

REBORN FROM HOLOCAUST

Michael Dillon

Michael Dillon teaches Chinese and Japanese in Tameside, Greater Manchester

ON the morning of August 6, 1945, *Enola Gay,* a Boeing B-29 Superfortress of the US Air Force, flew over the centre of Hiroshima and released the first atomic bomb ever to be used in action. It exploded in mid-air, 580 metres above the Industrial Promotion Hall. A clock, now in the city's museum, shows its hands fused to its face at 8.15, the precise time of the blast.

Up to a radius of 2500 metres almost everything was reduced to ashes; buildings 1000 metres further out were destroyed completely and there was substantial destruction much further away. People within 3.5 kilometres of the hypocentre suffered burns even if they survived the blast. Strangely, the Industrial Promotion Hall, though damaged, was left erect. It remains to this day, renamed the Atom Bomb Dome. It is still impossible to be certain about the total number of casualties but, according to the plaque at the foot of the Dome, more than 200,000 deaths can be attributed to the bomb.

Hiroshima's response to such catastrophic devastation was robust. In January 1946, just five months after Japan's surrender, a Reconstruction Committee was formed under a town planner, Toshio Nakashima with the aim of rebuilding Hiroshima so that it should become the most modern city in Japan with 'wide streets, skyscrapers and open parks'. During that grim early period of reconstruction, a symbol gave the people cause for hope: two cherry trees that stood a little to the south of the Town Hall had been blackened by the explosion. One morning in April 1946,

white blossoms suddenly appeared on the charred branches and thousands flocked to see them.

A brief walk around the city confirms the success of the 1946 plan. Like all Japanese cities razed during the war, Hiroshima today is a prosperous town built of steel, glass and concrete, and ablaze with neon signs at night. Anyone who did not know its history would not be able to guess what happened there.

Unlike most of Japan's largest cities, however, which seem to have developed without any overall sense of planning since the war, the central part of Hiroshima at least still retains much of the character of the pre-war city. The area that is now called Peace Park and encompasses that part of the city most completely devastated by the bomb, looks very similar to photographs taken of the same scene during the 1930s. Although the buildings and bridges

have been rebuilt with modern materials, the essential shape of the old city has been preserved, as has the uninterrupted view of the mountains to the north.

The dominant feature of the Peace Park is the Atom Bomb Dome, a powerful reminder of that day 40 years ago. The Park also houses the Peace Memorial Museum and the A-Bomb Cenotaph, a marble tomb with the list of names of all known victims. Despite these reminders, the Park is a place of enjoyment and leisure: families and couples walk by the river and sit in the sun, while groups of school children queue up to be photographed in front of the Cenotaph. Beneath the central pillars of the museum, a group of *takenokozoku,* or 'bamboo-shoot kids', dressed as early 1960s rockers, jive around a cassette recorder.

Inside the museum, the atmos-

phere changes. Exhibits show in detail, through relics, diagrams, photographs and a scale model of the ruined city, the effect of heat, blast and radiation on people, buildings and everyday objects. Tape-recordings of survivors' voices and paintings of their impressions of the explosion personalize the tragedy, and exhibits from Nagasaki are a reminder that Hiroshima was not alone. However many photographs the visitors may have already seen, to stand in Hiroshima and see the remains of twisted metal, fused brick and stone and the imprint of a human shadow on a stone step produces an indescribable emotion. Commentary and captions in the museum are presented with commendable understatement, yet visitors walk around in stunned silence.

There are several ironies associated with the bombing. Although Hiroshima had been a military base

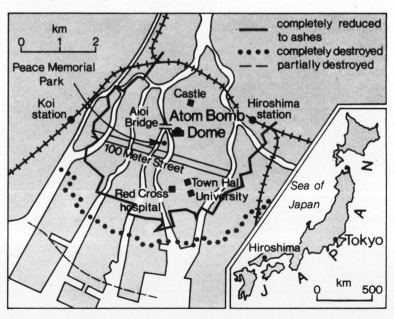

From *The Geographical Magazine*, London, England, August 1985, pp. 402-403. Reprinted by permission.

159

since the war with China in 1894–5, it also had one of the highest concentration of devout Buddhists. They would have nothing to do with ritually impure aspects of daily life such as butchery, the leather trade, and the disposal of refuse or bodies. The small army of *eta* (outcasts) who performed these services was considered as unclean as the tasks themselves and were forced into ghetto areas, or *buraku,* outside the city centre. Thus they suffered less than the rest of the population.

The atom bomb itself produced a new class of outcasts, the *hibakusha,* 'the bombed', who have since undergone serious social and economic deprivation along with the physical or mental suffering. Thousands of horror stories could be told about the effect of the blast, fire and radiation on the victims, but a simple tale illustrates the depth of the psychological damage. Mrs Onoyo Yamamoto lost four of her children in the bombing, but her one-year-old son survived. Interviewed 26 years later, she said that her son had suffered no apparent physical ill effects from the explosion and had grown up and become engaged to be married. But his future parents-in-law, finding that his mother was a hibakusha, forced their daughter to break off the engagement.

Although the scars and the sadness remain, Hiroshima thrives economically. The population today is 900,000, many of them employed in Hiroshima's main industries: shipbuilding, machinery and automobile manufacture. One of Hiroshima's main contributions to the post-war economic miracle of Japan is the Mazda car plant, the single largest employer in Hiroshima. Occupying two million square metres, it claims to be the largest automotive plant in the world.

Mazda accounts for perhaps 25 per cent of the total industrial production of the city, employs 27,700 people directly, and a further 18,000 who work for the company via subcontractors. Four assembly lines run under centralized computer control which allows different models to be produced on each line. Almost 1.5 million vehicles are produced each year at a rate of one every 15 seconds. Seventy per cent of Mazda's production is exported.

HIROSHIMA has made an outstanding success of modernizing its city and its industries. It has the soaring buildings, wide avenues and open spaces planned in 1946. But the city authorities and the people are acutely conscious of their responsibility to warn others of the horrors that must not be repeated. Before I left Hiroshima, Mr Sakata Hiroo, of the International Relations Department of the Mayor's Office, told me that his department wanted every foreign visitior to take home something of the spirit of Hiroshima so that the world would never forget.

In October 1976, the commander of the original mission to bomb Hiroshima flew a restored B-29 bomber at an air display in Texas. The culmination of the entertainment was a mock atom-bomb drop from the aircraft, complete with a simulated mushroom cloud. Clearly, reminders are still necessary.

Lessons from a Lost War

What has Viet Nam taught about when to use power—and when not to?

The customary reward of defeat, if one can survive it, is in the lessons thereby learned, which may yield victory in the next war. But the circumstances of our defeat in Vietnam were sufficiently ambiguous to deny the nation [that] benefit.
—Edward N. Luttwak
The Pentagon and the Art of War

Ten years after the fall of Saigon, the debacle in Southeast Asia remains a subject many Americans would rather not discuss. So the nation has been spared a searing, divisive inquest—"Who lost Viet Nam?"—but at a heavy price. The old divisions have been buried rather than resolved. They seem ready to break open again whenever anyone asks what lessons the U.S. should draw from its longest war, and the only one to end in an undisguisable defeat.

Was that loss inevitable, or could the war have been won with different strategy and tactics? Was the war fought for the right reasons? Did its aftermath prove or explode the domino theory? The questions are not in the least academic. They bear on the all-important problem of whether, when and how the U.S. should again send its troops to fight abroad.

Pondering these questions, Secretary of Defense Caspar Weinberger argues, citing Viet Nam, that "before the U.S. commits combat forces abroad, there must be some reasonable assurance that we will have the support of the American people and . . . Congress." Secretary of State George Shultz replies that "there is no such thing as guaranteed public support in advance." The lesson Shultz draws from Viet Nam is that "public support can be frittered away if we do not act wisely and effectively." And this open dispute between two senior members of the Reagan Cabinet is mild compared with the arguments among policy analysts, Viet Nam veterans and the public about what kinds of wars can be won or even deserve public support in the first place.

A number of experts doubt that the U.S. can evolve any common view of Viet Nam and its lessons for many years to come. Says Graham Martin, the last U.S. Ambassador to South Viet Nam: "I estimated at the end of the war that it probably would be at least two decades before any rational,

> "I want to rail against wind and tide, kill the whales in the ocean, sweep the whole country to save people from slavery."
> —TRIEU AU, VIET NAM'S "JOAN OF ARC" A.D. 248

> "France has had the country for nearly 100 years, and the people are worse off than at the beginning."
> —FRANKLIN D. ROOSEVELT 1944

> "Kill ten of our men and we will kill one of yours. In the end, it is you who will tire."
> —HO CHI MINH 1946

objective discussion of the war and its causes and effects could be undertaken by scholars who were not so deeply, emotionally engaged at the time that their later perceptions were colored by biases and prejudices." William Hyland, editor of *Foreign Affairs* magazine, thinks an even longer perspective may be required: "We always want to make historical judgments two days after the fact. Historians need 100 years."

But the U.S. is unlikely to have anywhere near that much time to decide what lessons to draw from Viet Nam and how to apply them. The initial impulse after the American withdrawal was to avoid any foreign involvement that might conceivably lead to a commitment of U.S. troops. Scholars differ on how seriously this so-called Viet Nam syndrome inhibited an activist U.S. foreign policy, but in any case it is fading—witness the enthusiastic approval of the Grenada invasion in late 1983 (to be sure, that was a rare case in which the U.S. was able to apply such overwhelming force that it could not have failed to win quickly). Says Maine's Republican Senator William Cohen: "The legacy of Viet Nam does not mean that we will not send our sons anywhere. It does mean that we will not send them everywhere." Even some fervent doves agree that memories of Viet Nam should not keep the U.S. from ever fighting anywhere. Sam Brown, onetime antiwar leader who now develops low-cost housing in Colorado, remains convinced that if it were not for the protests against U.S. involvement in Viet Nam that he helped organize, "we would have three or four other wars now." Even so, concedes Brown, some "wrong lessons" might be drawn, among them "the risk that we won't be prepared if our national interest is genuinely threatened."

But if the specter of Viet Nam no longer inhibits all thought of projecting U.S. military power overseas, it still haunts every specific decision. In the Middle East, Weinberger's fears of entrapment in a drawn-out conflict fought without public support caused him at first to oppose sending Marines to Lebanon and then to insist on their withdrawal after terrorist attacks left 266 U.S. servicemen dead. Shultz objected that the pullout would undercut U.S. diplomacy in the area, and still regards it as

POWER

B-52 dropping bombs on guerrillas, 1966: Was it a matter of too much force, or not enough?

a mistake. But Ronald Reagan ordered the withdrawal anyway and won the approval of voters, even though critics portrayed the pullout as a national humiliation. The reason, suggests Democratic Political Analyst William Schneider, is that the President sensed the persistence of a popular attitude toward foreign military commitments that is summarized by the Viet Nam-era slogan "Win or Get Out." Says Schneider: "In Grenada we won. In Lebanon we got out. So much for the Viet Nam syndrome."

The Viet Nam experience colors almost every discussion of Central American policy. Nebraska Governor Bob Kerrey, who won a Congressional Medal of Honor and lost part of a leg fighting with the Navy SEAL commandos in Viet Nam, maintains that if memories of the ordeal in Southeast Asia were not still so strong, "we'd be in Nicaragua now." In Congress, Kerrey's fellow Democrats fret that the Administration's commitment to resist the spread of Marxist revolution throughout the isthmus could eventually bog down American troops in another endless jungle guerrilla war.

Reaganites retort, correctly, that while Viet Nam is halfway around the world and of debatable strategic importance to Washington, Central America is virtually next door, an area where U.S. interests are obvious. Moreover, the amounts Washington is spending to help the government of El Salvador defeat leftist guerrillas and to assist the *contra* rebels fighting the Marxist Sandinista government of Nicaragua are pittances compared with the sums lavished on South Viet Nam even before the direct U.S. military intervention there. Still, the Administration every now and then feels obliged to deny that it has any plan or desire to send U.S. troops to fight in Central America. Weinberger last November coupled his remarks about the necessity of popular support for any foreign military commitment with a pledge that "the President will not allow our military forces to creep—or be drawn gradually—into a combat role in Central America."

"Master fear and pain, overcome obstacles, unite your efforts, fight to the very end, annihilate the enemy."
—GENERAL GIAP
1954

"I could conceive of no greater tragedy than for the U.S. to [fight] an all-out war in Indochina."
—DWIGHT D. EISENHOWER
1954

"You have a row of dominoes set up, you knock over the first one and [the last one] will go over very quickly."
—EISENHOWER
1954

"We do commit the U.S. to preventing the fall of South Viet Nam to Communism."
—ROBERT MC NAMARA
1961

One of the few propositions about Viet Nam that commands near unanimous assent from Americans is the obvious one that the U.S. lost— and a growing number would qualify even that. Richard Nixon, in his new book, *No More Vietnams,* argues that "we won the war" but then abandoned South Viet Nam after the Communist North began violating the 1973 Paris accords that supposedly ended the fighting. Though the former President's self-interest is obvious, parts of his analysis are supported even by the enemy. U.S. Army Colonel Harry Summers Jr., who considers Viet Nam "a tactical success and a strategic failure," was in Hanoi on a negotiating mission a few days before Saigon fell. Summers recalls telling a North Vietnamese colonel, "You know, you never defeated us on the battlefield." The foe's reply: "That may be so, but it is also irrelevant." In essence, the U.S. was outlasted by an enemy that proved able and willing to fight longer than America and its South Vietnamese allies.

Given the weakness of South Viet Nam, the determination of the North and the extent of the aid it could count on from the Soviet Union and neighboring China, even some hawks concede that Hanoi's victory might have been inevitable. Says Military Analyst Luttwak: "Some wars simply cannot be won, and Viet Nam may have been one of them." Nonetheless, the main lesson they would draw from the war is that the U.S. threw away whatever chance for victory it may have had through blunders that must not be repeated.

The most detailed exposition of this view comes from Colonel Summers, whose book, *On Strategy: A Critical Analysis of the Vietnam War,* has become must reading for young officers. Summers argues that the U.S. should have sealed off South Viet Nam with a barrier of American troops to prevent North Viet Nam from sending troops and matériel through Laos and Cambodia to wage war in the South. Instead, he says, the U.S. "wasted its strength" fighting the guerrillas in the South, a hopeless task so long as they were continually reinforced from the North and one that American troops had no business trying to carry out in the first place. The U.S., he contends, should have confined itself to protecting South Viet Nam against "external aggression" from the North and left "pacification," the job of rooting out the guerrillas, to the South Vietnamese. By in effect taking over the war, the U.S. sapped the initiative and ultimately the will of its Southern allies to carry out a job only they could do in the end.

Luttwak carries this analysis a step further by pouring scorn on the tactics used in the South: "The jet fighter bombing raids against flimsy huts that might contain a handful of guerrillas or perhaps none; the fair-sized artillery barrages that silenced lone snipers; the ceaseless firing of helicopter door gunners whereby a million dollars' worth of ammunition might be expended to sweep a patch of high grass." This "grossly disproportionate use of firepower," says Luttwak, was not just ineffective; it alienated South Vietnamese villagers whose cooperation against the guerrillas was vital. At least equally important, "Its imagery on television was by far the most powerful stimulus of antiwar sentiment" back in the U.S. Former CIA Director William Colby agrees that the U.S. got nowhere as long as it tried to defeat guerrillas with massed firepower and only began to make progress when it shifted to a "people's war" in which the

South Vietnamese carried the main burden of the fighting. By then it was too late; American public sentiment had turned irreversibly in favor of a fast pullout.

According to Hyland, "The biggest lesson of Viet Nam is that we need to have a much better notion of what is at stake, what our interests are, before we go into a major military undertaking." Weinberger voiced essentially the same thought last fall in laying down several conditions, beyond a reasonable assurance of public support, that must be met if U.S. troops are again to be sent into battle overseas: "We should have clearly defined political and military objectives, and we should know precisely how our forces can accomplish those." Other criteria: "The commitment of U.S. forces to combat should be a last resort," undertaken only if it "is deemed vital to our national interest or that of our allies," and then "with the clear intention of winning" by using as much force as necessary.

Weinberger's speech, delivered after he had talked it over with President Reagan, is the closest thing to an official Administration reading of the lessons of Viet Nam. But some rude jeers greeted the Weinberger doctrine. Luttwak, for example, called Weinberger's views "the equivalent of a doctor saying he will treat patients only if he is assured they will recover." Columnist William Safire headlined a scathing critique ONLY THE 'FUN' WARS, and New York Democrat Stephen Solarz, who heads the House Subcommittee on Asian and Pacific Affairs, pointed out, "It is a formula for national paralysis if, before we ever use force, we need a Gallup poll showing that two-thirds of the American people are in favor of it."

More important, what is a "vital interest"? To some Americans, the only one that would justify another war is the defense of the U.S. against a threat of direct attack. Decrying "this whole practice of contracting our military out just for the survival of some other government and country," Georgia Secretary of State Max Cleland, who lost an arm and both legs in Viet Nam, insists, "There is only one thing worth dying for, and that is this country, not somebody else's."

Diplomats argue persuasively that a policy based on this view would leave the U.S. to confront Soviet expansionism all alone. No country would enter or maintain an alliance with a U.S. that specifically refused to fight in its defense. But in the real world, an outright Soviet attack against a country that the U.S. is committed by treaty to defend is quite unlikely. The decision whether or not to fight most probably would be posed by a Communist threat to a friendly nation that is not formally an ally. And then the threat might well be raised not by open aggression but by a combination of military, political and economic tactics that Moscow is often adept at orchestrating and Washington usually inept at countering: the front groups, the street demonstrations, the infiltrated unions, the guerrilla units. One reason the U.S. sent troops to Viet Nam is that it lacked other alternatives to help its allies prevail against this sort of subversion. In fact, developing a capacity to engage in such political action and shadowy paramilitary activities might help the U.S. to avert future Viet Nams.

Merely defining U.S. interests, in any event, can prove endlessly complicated. Geography alone is no guide in an age of ocean-spanning missiles. Economics may be vital in some areas like the Persian Gulf, where the flow of oil must be maintained,

Y.R. OKAMOTO—LBJ LIBRARY

POLITICS
Defense Secretary McNamara brooding after troop call-up, 1965: Would Americans have backed a bigger war?

"But it will be just like Berlin. The troops will march in; the bands will play; the crowds will cheer; and in four days everyone will have forgotten. Then we will be told we have to send in more troops."
—JOHN F. KENNEDY
1961

"There just isn't any simple answer. We're fighting a kind of war here that I never read about at Command and Staff College. Conventional weapons just don't work here. Neither do conventional tactics."
—FROM GRAHAM GREENE'S *THE UGLY AMERICAN*

"You let a bully come into your front yard, the next day he'll be on your porch."
—LYNDON B. JOHNSON
ON SEVERAL OCCASIONS

unimportant in others like Israel, where political and moral considerations are paramount. There may be times too when U.S. intervention, even if it seems justified, would be ineffective. Not much is heard these days of the once fashionable argument that in Viet Nam the U.S. was on the wrong side of history because it was fighting a nationalistic social revolution being waged by a regime that was, deep down, benign; Hanoi's brutality within Viet Nam and its swift move to establish hegemony over all of Indochina removed all doubt that the foe was and is not only totalitarian but imperialistic besides. Today, with the focus on Central America, the argument is often heard that economic and social misery have made leftist revolution inevitable. To those who maintain that revolution is the only way to progress, the counterargument is that whatever social and economic gains may be achieved by Communist takeovers usually carry an extremely high price tag: the establishment of tyranny.

About the only general rule that foreign-policy experts can suggest is not to have any general rule, at least in the sense of drawing up an advance list of where the U.S. might or might not fight. They still shudder at the memory of a 1950 definition of the U.S. "defense perimeter" in Asia that omitted South Korea—which promptly suffered an outright Communist invasion that took three years and 54,000 American lives to repel. Walt Rostow, who was Lyndon Johnson's National Security Adviser, recalls how the late Soviet Foreign Minister Andrei Vishinsky "told a group of Americans that we deceived them on Korea." Says Rostow: "I believe that's correct."

The decision on where American military intervention might be both necessary and effective can only be made case by case, based on a variety of factors that may be no easier to judge in the future than they were in Viet Nam: the nature and circumstances of war, the will and ability of the nation under attack to defend itself, the consequences of its loss. Any such debate is sure to revive another long buried but still unresolved controversy of the Viet Nam era: whether a Communist takeover of one country would cause others to topple like a row of dominoes. Hawks insist that this theory was vindicated by Communist triumphs in Laos and Cambodia after the fall of Saigon. Opponents point out that the Asian "dominoes" that most concerned the U.S.—Thailand, Burma, Malaysia, Singapore, Indonesia, the Philippines—have all survived as non-Communist (in several cases, strongly anti-Communist) societies. Rostow, now a professor of political economy at the University of Texas, offers a counterrebuttal. Those countries might have gone under if Saigon had fallen in 1965, he contends. The U.S. intervention in Viet Nam bought them ten years to strengthen their economies and governments and, says Rostow, "bought time that was used extremely well by Asians, especially Southeast Asians."

Be that as it may, the evidence would seem to argue against any mechanical application of the domino theory. It originated in the 1950s, when world Communism was seen as a monolithic force headquartered in Moscow, with Peking a kind of branch office. Today China, never really comfortable with its Hanoi "allies," has resumed its ancient enmity toward Viet Nam; both Washington and Peking are aiding guerrillas battling against the Soviet-backed Vietnamese in Kampuchea. That does not mean that the domino theory has lost all validity everywhere, but its applicability is also subject to case-by-case application.

The most bedeviling of all the dilemmas raised by Viet Nam concerns the issue of public support. On the surface it might seem to be no issue at all: just about everybody agrees that Viet Nam proved the futility of trying to fight a war without a strong base of popular support. But just how strong exactly? Rostow argues that the only U.S. war fought with tremendous public backing was World War II. He points out that World War I "brought riots and splits," the War of 1812 was "vastly divisive" and even during the War of Independence one-third of the population was pro-revolution, one-third pro-British and one-third "out to lunch." Rostow proposes a 60-25-15 split as about the best that can be expected now in support of a controversial policy: a bipartisan 60% in favor, 25% against and 15% out to lunch.

A strong current of opinion holds that Lyndon Johnson guaranteed a disastrously low level of support by getting into a long, bloody war without ever admitting (perhaps even to himself) the extent of the commitment he was making. Colonel Summers, who considers Viet Nam a just war that the U.S. could and should have won, insists that any similar conflict in the future ought to be "legitimized" by a formal, congressional declaration of war. Says Summers: "All of America's previous wars were fought in the heat of passion. Viet Nam was fought in cold blood, and that was intolerable to the American people. In an immediate crisis the tendency of the American people is to rally around the flag. But God help you if it goes beyond that and you haven't built a base of support."

At the other extreme, former Secretary of State Dean Rusk defends to this day the Johnson Ad-

"In the final analysis it is their war . . . We can help them . . . but they have to win it, the people of Viet Nam."
—KENNEDY 1963

"We are not about to send American boys 10,000 miles away to do what Asian boys ought to be doing for themselves."
—JOHNSON 1964

"Hell no, we won't go!"
—ANTIWAR CHANT 1965

"I'm not going to be the first President who loses a war."
—RICHARD NIXON 1969

"Peace is at hand."
—HENRY KISSINGER 1972

ministration's effort "to do in cold blood at home what we were asking men to do in hot blood out in the field." Rusk points out that the war began with impressive public and congressional support. It was only in early 1968, says Rusk, that "many at the grass-roots level came to the opinion that if we didn't give them some idea when this war would come to an end, we might as well chuck it." The decisive factor probably was the defection of middle-class youths and their parents, a highly articulate segment that saw an endless war as a personal threat—though in fact the burden of the draft fell most heavily on low-income youths.

Paradoxically, though, Johnson might well have been able to win public support for a bigger war than he was willing to fight. As late as February 1968, at the height of the Tet offensive, one poll found 53% favoring stronger U.S. military action, even at the risk of a clash with the Soviet Union or China, vs. only 24% opting to wind down the war. Rusk insists that the Administration was right not to capitalize on this sentiment. Says he: "We made a deliberate decision not to whip up war fever in this country. We did not have parades and movie stars selling war bonds, as we did in World War II. We thought that in a nuclear world it is dangerous for a country to become too angry too quickly. That is something people will have to think about in the future."

It certainly is. Viet Nam veterans argue passionately that Americans must never again be sent out to die in a war that "the politicians will not let them win." And by win they clearly mean something like a World War II–style triumph ending with unconditional surrender. One lesson of Viet Nam, observes George Christian, who was L.B.J.'s press secretary, is that "it is very tough for Americans to stick in long situations. We are always looking for a quick fix." But nuclear missiles make the unconditional-surrender kind of war an anachronism. Viet Nam raised, and left unsolved for the next conflict, the question posed by Lincoln Bloomfield, an M.I.T. professor of political science who once served on Jimmy Carter's National Security Council: "How is it that you can 'win' so that when you leave two years later you do not lose the country to those forces who have committed themselves to victory at any cost?"

It is a question that cannot be suppressed much longer. Americans have a deep ambiguity toward military power: they like to feel strong, but often shy away from actually using that strength. There is a growing recognition, however, that shunning all battles less easily winnable than Grenada would mean abandoning America's role as a world power, and that, in turn, is no way to assure the nation's survival as a free society. Americans, observes Secretary of State Shultz, "will always be reluctant to use force. It is the mark of our decency." But, he adds, "a great power cannot free itself so easily from the burden of choice. It must bear responsibility for the consequences of its inaction as well as for the consequences of its action."

—By George J. Church.
Reported by David S. Jackson/Austin and Ross H. Munro/Washington, with other bureaus.

The Dismal Chronology of Foolish War

Strategists will argue for years about the military lessons of the Gulf war. Both sides made mistakes. Both were constrained by shortages of money and limits on the weapons they were allowed to buy. Iran was more lavish with its young men's lives; Iraq more ruthless in its use of military technology.

The Iraqis invaded Iran on September 22, 1980. The attack reached its targets in a couple of weeks, at which point the Iraqis stopped and offered to negotiate. The Iranians were in no mood to talk. They settled down to hold the line, mustering hordes of "Revolutionary Guards" to strengthen an army weakened by revolutionary purges.

At the end of 1981 the Iranians drove the Iraqis from most of the captured territory. But their repeated offensives could never break through to the Iraqi cities of Basra and Baghdad. In February 1984 they sent more than a quarter of a million men into the first of many "final offensives." It took some pockets of land but the Iraqis stopped it, almost certainly with poison gas.

The main action switched in 1984 to the waters of the Gulf, with 37 Iraqi air attacks on ships plying to and from Iranian ports. The Iraqis probably hoped to provoke an Iranian blockade on all oil movements which would bring down the West's wrath. The Iranians mostly attacked ships serving Kuwait and Saudi Arabia, hoping to deter those countries from subsidising Iraq. Iran got the worse of it: the tanker war slashed its oil revenues.

In February 1985 the Iraqis attacked on land but soon ran out of steam. An Iranian counter-offensive was halted,

again with the help of chemical weapons. The war of the cities got worse. Iraq had the better air force, and more missiles. It hit out at military and civilian targets; the military ones included, first, Iran's Kharg Island oil terminal, which went on working, then the trans-shipment terminals at the mouth of the Gulf.

In February 1986 Iran's soldiers crossed the Shatt al-Arab waterway and captured the Faw peninsula. Yet another "final offensive" began in December 1986, presumably helped by weapons supplied by American officials hoping vainly to ransom hostages out of Lebanon. Iran's eager martyrs died like flies through February, and this was probably Iraq's blackest hour. Basra was threatened. Western analysts invented the dictum that "Iraq cannot win and Iran cannot lose." Yet the onslaught, in the end, failed, and Iran faltered. The failure of this offensive was probably the turning-point of the war. Two small attacks in March and April were easily broken up.

At that point the superpowers became more deeply involved. In April 1987 the Kuwaitis were allowed to charter three Russian tankers to lift their oil. In May the Americans matched that by deciding to put the

Stars and Stripes on Kuwaiti tankers and escort them through the Gulf. For a time it looked as if the big countries might be drawn into the fighting. One Russian ship was fired on by Iranian gunboats, another hit a mine on May 16th. Next day an Iraqi aircraft mistakenly fired a missile into an American destroyer, the *Stark,* killing 37 men. In July the *Bridgeton,* the first reflagged Kuwaiti tanker to sail under American escort, hit a mine. Britain, France, Italy, Holland and Belgium all sent a small number of warships to the Gulf in the Americans' wake, as escorts or minesweepers.

In September and October the Americans dealt lethally with Iranian gunboats and oil rigs that had been used against shipping. Yet, despite the mayhem in the Gulf, oil kept flowing in almost normal quantities from Kuwait and Saudi Arabia. They and the other Arab states kept cash and war supplies flowing to Iraq.

Curiously, it was an Iranian victory that signalled the end. In March this year Iran took the insignificant northern Iraqi town of Halabja. Its casualties—many caused by chemical weapons—were heavy, and it was driven out again this month. By then it had been pushed back east of Basra, and the pre-war borders were pretty much restored.

Lessons for learning
- Armies matter more than terri-

From *The Economist,* July 23, 1988, pp. 36-37. © 1988, The Economist, reprinted by permission of The New York Times Syndicated Sales Service.

tory. The Iraqis' greatest mistake was to stop and try to negotiate once they had made their first advance. Their army was doing well, the enemy was disorganised. The cost of giving the Iranians time to mobilise more young men was eight years' more fighting.

• Don't trust air power. The tanker war did cut Iran's oil revenue. Iraq's stronger air force might in theory have been better used against power plants and refineries; but such attacks, notably in 1986, had no great military effect. Iran never had air superiority anywhere, but almost won.

• Poison gas works well. Almost all countries say they want to ban chemical weapons. That will be harder now that this war has proved it effective. Gas is easy to make, and deadly: it

helped stop at least two big Iranian offensives. Countries fighting for their lives, as Iraq was, will try anything that works.

• Sea mines can cause havoc. The Iranians may not have planted many mines, but their effect was great. Only when Iranians were actually caught planting them did the western navies in the Gulf retaliate. A serious mining campaign before the western navies arrived might have blockaded oil traffic from Kuwait and Saudi Arabia. The Americans discovered that helicopters were no substitute for the mine-sweepers they replaced.

• Merchant ships are easy targets. Tiny Iranian gunboats beat up huge vessels, sometimes superficially, sometimes causing great damage. Convoys

are one answer, but hard to organise. Arming merchant ships is difficult and expensive.

• The best attack may be good defence. After their first successful offensive, the Iraqis succeeded mainly by good defensive tactics, yielding a little ground but inflicting so many casualties that even the Iranians could take no more martyrdom.

• War is hell, not just for soldiers. This one ended with the final horror, and mystery, of the shooting down by an American cruiser of an Iranian airliner carrying 290 civilians. Civilians do die in wars, which are about killing people: warriors must act quickly, mistakes are inevitable. This entire dreadful conflict was in many ways a mistake from start to finish.

Weapons, deadly weapons

Swords, stirrups and longbows: the hardware sometimes counts

"MAN", according to an old saying, "is the most important weapon on the battlefield." Usually that's true, but not always. Sometimes a new bit of technology comes along that makes the difference between defeat and victory.

Around 1500 BC the Hittites did rather well east of the Mediterranean because they had iron swords that could cut their opponents' bronze ones to pieces. A couple of millennia later the Byzantine cavalry clobbered all their enemies until the losers learned that stirrups make it far easier for a mounted man to ram a spear into his adversary. In 1415 English longbows swept the field at Agincourt. British ingenuity scored again in 1940, when radar broke Hitler's air weapon and won the Battle of Britain.

Some weapons just missed being decisive. The repeating rifle might have turned the tide in the American civil war had the Confederate cavalry got their hands on it a year earlier. The newly developed machinegun might have won the war of 1870 for the French had they used it as an infantry weapon rather than a small artillery piece. The tank might have broken the hideous stalemate of trench warfare in the first world war had the British held back their invention until they could field greater numbers and then followed up the first surprise attack with a powerful infantry advance.

In Afghanistan the decisive struggle turned out to be for control of the air. The mujaheddin often hid in mountainous retreats that were impossible for the Soviet army to reach with armoured units. The Russians' best hope of hitting the guerrillas was to strike at them from helicopters and bombers. Small shoulder-fired rockets designed to home in on the heat of aircraft exhausts took some toll of this Russian air power; the guerrillas got Russian-made SAM-7s early on in the war. But the Russians knew their own missiles—and the best ways of avoiding them. Russian air power continued to prevail.

The war that Stingers won

Then came the American Stingers, and a sharp tilt in the war in favour of the guerrillas. The Stinger is the best missile of its type in the world today. It has a longer range than the SAM-7, and is manoeuvrable enough for fighters to have trouble outflying it. It can do much better at telling the difference between the aircraft it is aimed at and flares fired as decoys to lure it away. It can pick out aircraft hugging the ground, despite the radar-confusing background. Most deadly of all, its heat-seeking nose is sensitive enough to home in on any part of an enemy aircraft; the SAM-7 and other early models would work only if pointed at something as hot as a jet's exhaust.

At first the Americans held back the Stingers for fear the Russians would capture one; eventually they realised that the Russians would get the technology sooner or later anyway. By the spring of 1986 the first Stingers had reached Afghanistan. The Russians soon began to suffer heavy losses. Air bases were made virtually unusable for weeks at a time. Increasingly dependent on artillery and tanks, Soviet soldiers became virtual prisoners in the corners of Afghanistan where those weapons could be brought to bear. This week the Russians went home—vanquished by a rugged resistance and a clever piece of modern machinery.

The Retreat of the West

Following World War II the colonial empires ended, and new nations inspired by Western ideas about nationalism, liberalism, socialism, and capitalism stepped onto the world stage. The West, exhausted and weakened by warfare, stepped aside. There was little choice. Between 1944 and 1980 90 countries became independent. The United Nations started with 51 members after World War II, and in 1980 it listed 152.

In looking at what happened in Africa, where the new nations often lacked economic balance, Westerners generally thought that nationalism had failed. In June 1987, for example, the Central African Republic sentenced its former dictator, Jean-Bedel Bokassa, to be shot to death. He was responsible for over 20 murders and for spending $100 million on his coronation as emperor in 1977. His poor, landlocked republic had a population of only 3 million people. Michael Crowder points out, however, that the condemnation by Westerners is often made within the framework of Eurocentric hopes. He claims that there have been accomplishments worth noting in the African nations as well.

The most remarkable revolt against Western control came in India under the leadership of Mohandas Gandhi. He wanted independence for India, but chose nonviolent demonstrations to achieve his goal. India became independent, but it was split into two nations—one for the Hindus (India) and the other for the Muslims (Pakistan). In part, this triumph over British imperialism was due to the exhaustion of the British after World War II, and the fact that the British were willing to dismantle their empire. Gandhi, moreover, worked within a British frame of ethics; they too abhorred the bloodshed of the contest. The difficulty is that the British left behind a nation with an enormous population which spoke 16 different languages. India has been torn by civil strife ever since it gained independence, as Mustafa Malik demonstrates in his article.

After World War II the British also retreated from the Middle East and worked to erect the independent state of Israel. There was world sympathy for the Jews who had suffered during the Holocaust, and the United Nations agreed to the establishment of a Jewish homeland. Unfortunately, there were Arabs already there who felt that they had an equal claim to the land. Christians, in addition, had an interest in the area because of their heritage, and thus a three-way religious controversy developed.

As it has turned out, the Middle East has suffered a series of wars between the Jews and Arabs, between Iran and Iraq, and between Afghanistan and the Soviet Union. One reason for the continuing conflict is the Islamic religious fervor, which rejects both the capitalism of the West and the communism of the Soviet Union. Tom Hundley emphasizes that outsiders too often misread the motives of Islamic politicians and forget the power of religion as a motivating force.

In Asia Western influence was eliminated from the southeast with the Vietnam War, and from China with the triumph of Mao Tse-tung. A closed China underwent a Marxist revolution that included a remarkable attack on Chinese culture and history. As Sarah Ballard reveals in her article, even sports in China came under this attack. Ultimately, the attack failed and Mao died. Since then China has opened its doors to visitors, capitalized on its

cultural assets, promoted athletic competition with the rest of the world, and sought Western technology. Recent events, however—namely, the massacre of students in Tiananmen Square in June 1989—cast considerable doubt on China's intention to undergo significant political change.

There is also change in the Soviet Union as the current leader Mikhail Gorbachev seeks to open up the nation to the world and to loosen the economic bonds in order to improve its economy. *The Economist*, the British version of *Newsweek*, classifies the Soviet Union as a third-class power in all areas except military proficiency. By contrast, Japan, a country reformed by the United States after World War II, has developed one of the largest economies in the world. It has become the foremost creditor nation and the leader in nonmilitary grants to underdeveloped countries.

The difficulties in the Soviet Union, the economic rise of Japan, and the changes in China all illustrate the shift in power after World War II. The West no longer dominates the world, but the Western nations remain important. The United States still acts as a policeman to the world and leads in the number of Nobel laureates. The Soviet Union, East Germany, and the United States dominate the Olympic Games. The English language, as *The Economist* states, has become a world language that is used by one-fifth of the people around the globe.

Yet, compared to the way it was in 1900, the world at the end of the twentieth century is much more pluralistic; there are many voices, not just a few. On the world stage there are black, yellow, and brown actors, not just white ones. The problems are more complex because of this, and interdependence is stronger than ever before.

Looking Ahead: Challenge Questions

Why did the colonial empires come to an end?

What were the legacies of colonialism in Africa? In India?

Why is the Middle East in turmoil?

What went wrong with communism in China and the Soviet Union?

Why did the cultural revolution fail in China?

How did Japan take over from the United States the title of leading creditor nation?

How is Gorbachev different from earlier Soviet leaders?

What is significant about English as a world language?

Whose Dream Was It Anyway? Twenty-Five Years of African Independence

Michael Crowder

Michael Crowder is visiting Professor at the Institute of Commonwealth Studies, University of London.

When the Union Jack was lowered at midnight and the green white and green flag of Nigeria raised in its place on October 1st 1960, there was considerable optimism in the British press about the future of that erstwhile British colony. The leaders of its three political parties were all by their own declarations committed to the practice of liberal democracy Westminsterstyle. The constitution that enshrined the ideals of Westminster had been patiently negotiated over a decade between the British and the leaders of the three main political parties. The former colonial masters left with the warm words of the new Prime Minister ringing in their ears: 'We are grateful to the British officers whom we have known, first as masters, and then as leaders, and finally as partners and always as friends'.[1] Many stayed on under the new Nigerian leadership, particularly those in commerce and industry, especially as Nigerians had only taken over the political infrastructure of the state from the British. The economic infrastructure remained largely intact in the hands of big British firms like UAC. The prospects for the country seemed rosy with its apparently sound agricultural base and the promise of additional foreign earnings from its proved oil reserves. An optimism about Nigeria pervaded most of the British press for the next five years. The riots that were taking place in Tivland at the very time the new flag of Nigeria was being raised were conveniently ignored by many pressmen intent on conveying an appropriate euphoria to their British readers. Indeed, the Prime Minister of the Federation, Sir Abubakar Tafawa Balewa, remarked wryly on the adulation of the world's press that 'even some of the big nations of the world are expecting us to perform miracles and solve their problems for them'.[2] That adulation had indeed been fair-

ly universal but *West Africa* did note that one foreign visitor to the Independence Celebrations did not share the 'general satisfaction and optimism' and that was Mr. Sisnev, the correspondent of *Trud*, but it concluded 'even if Nigeria sounds too good to be true, the Nigerian story is one of the most remarkable and creditable in the modern world'.[3] *Time* talked of Nigeria's 'impressive demonstration of democracy's workability in Africa'.[4]

Despite the many internal strains which the country experienced in its first few years of independence, including the suspension of the constitution of one of its three constituent regions and the jailing of the leader of the opposition for treason, the British press appeared to share the belief that as one Nigerian newspaper put it: 'Nigerians seem to have perfected the art of walking to the brink of disaster without falling in.'[5] Indeed the British Prime Minister and his officials were apparently so ignorant of the real breakdown of law and order in the country that in January 1966 they flew to Lagos to attend the Commonwealth Prime Ministers Conference on the Rhodesian question.[6] A day after they flew back to London, the Prime Minister of Nigeria was assassinated and the first military regime was installed. In the twenty years that followed, Nigeria has suffered four more military coups, at least one failed coup, a three year long civil war, a brief return to an elective form of government that made a mockery of liberal democracy, and an oil boom that permitted lavish spending and corruption on a massive scale, followed by the near bankruptcy of the country, which today is economically on its knees. As a result, Nigerians of all classes have developed a deep cynicism about their leaders, both civilian and military, and certainly have little faith in the liberal democracy and mixed economy that were the legacy of their colonial rulers.

I have chosen Nigeria as an example of the disillusion that has attended the first twenty-five years of independence not only among the former colonial rulers who transferred pow-

I am grateful to Lalage Bown and Roland and Irene Brown for helpful comments on a first draft of this paper which was originally presented in the series of lectures on Africa since Independence sponsored by the Yale University African Studies Program in Spring of 1986 under the title 'Things Fall Apart?'.

Reprinted from *African Affairs*, January 1987, pp. 7-24.

er but also among those who inherited that power, because it contains a quarter of the population of the African continent. Its experience has unhappily not been atypical but rather the norm for the majority of African countries.

The same optimism that attended Nigeria's independence attended that of the Francophone countries, and the British territories in East, Central and Southern Africa. In each case, what was transferred was a constitution inspired by the metropolitan model. All these states committed themselves in their national anthems and the mottoes on their coats of arms to variations of freedom, justice and equality.

Of all these states only one has realised the pious hopes of those who transferred power: Botswana, which alone has suffered no *coup* or *coup manqué* and has maintained intact its liberal democratic constitution in both spirit and practice.[7] The story everywhere else has been the same. Majority parties voted to establish one party states which western apologists were quick to justify as reflecting true African democracy encouraging the politics of consensus where two or multiparty democracy was divisive.[8] In reality, such moves usually proved but a cloak for the establishment of personal rule, as Jackson and Rosberg have put it.[9] Even military regimes that intervened were seen by optimists as mere correctives for temporary aberrance in the practice of democracy by young nations. Military coups were invariably staged in the name of cleansing the state, after which the soldiers would return to the barracks. And this they did in Sudan, Ghana, the former Upper Volta and Nigeria, only to fling wide the barrack gates again as it became clear that the politicians had learnt nothing except how to abuse power more successfully. The excesses of the second Obote regime in Uganda were reputedly greater than those of Amin himself.[10]

Coupled with the abuse of the inherited constitutions and the acquisition of personal power through manipulation of the ballot box or the barrel of the gun has been the expropriation of the resources of the state by the few and the apparent progressive immiseration of the masses as a result. The famines that have caught the world's attention in the past few years have increasingly been laid at the doors of the politicians and military leaders rather than nature. And yet, grasping at straws, westerners refuse to see their dreams shattered. Nigeria's return to democracy in 1979 was seen as a vindication by those who believed that Africans could and would adhere to the ideals of Western liberal democracy. Similar optimism attended the return to civilian rule under Obote, with the British government even helping to train the army he used to establish a worse record with Amnesty International than Amin.[11]

But by 1985, a quarter of a century after the *annus mirabilis* of African independence, the dream had been shattered and replaced by a profound disillusion whereby Africa had become the world's basket case, a permanent *mezzogiorno* for which there was little if any hope. Ghana and Uganda, the jewels in Britain's African colonial crown had, despite their extensive educated elites, sunk in the former case into an economic slough of despond and in the latter into anarchy. In the chanceries of the West, officials wished Africa would just go away and this has been reflected most dramatically in Britain, still the country with the largest investments in sub-Saharan Africa, which has reduced its support for the study of Africa to a level lower than it has been for the past twenty years.[12]

The universal wisdom has become that African independence has been an abysmal failure. Thus the conservative London *Daily Telegraph* in a recent editorial wrote that Uganda 'the one-time pearl of Africa can fairly be described as having become a symbol of everything that has gone wrong in that continent over the past 20 years or so. Since independence it has experienced violence (with hundreds of thousands killed), poverty, misgovernment on an enormous scale, and terrible suffering. Steadily the pillars of government, of law and even economic life have been destroyed. . . '.[13]

But is this not to judge the past twenty five years in terms of a dream manufactured in Europe not Africa, and a dream that took no cognisance either of contemporary African realities, nor, more important and less forgivable, of the legacy of colonial rule?

Was not this dream of a model Africa in which Africans would faithfully adhere to the liberal democratic institutions transferred at independence and uphold a mixed economy in which the interests of the ordinary people would be served in reality a pipe dream in the context of a plethora of states that had for the most part only been cobbled together fifty odd years before? Will not historians be kinder in their judgement of these sometimes unlikely states created by the colonial rulers when they come to assess the post independence period than the journalists and political scientists who wring their hands in despair today? Will they not judge the experience of independence in terms of the African experience of colonial rule, which has been undergoing serious revision by historians as the true secrets of the colonial rulers emerge from the archives? Will they not compare favourably the impressive economic transformations that even the most impoverished of African states in question have undergone since independence with the little that was done for them under colonial rule? Given the little attention that any of the European colonial powers gave to building national political and economic structures during the period of their rule will not historians of the future see the very survival of these states as something of an economic and political miracle?

In this essay, therefore, I want to try and project myself forward and see what sort of perspective historians may have on what so many see today as 'the African disaster'.

I suggest they will look at the developments of the past twenty five years as part of a continuum in which independence will not be seen as a historical dividing line. All that has happened in the past quarter of a century will be set much more firmly in the context of the colonial experience than is the custom for present-day political scientists and journalists to do. So I first want to examine how the colonial experience has affected the way Africa has developed over the past twenty-five years and I shall suggest that there are many more parallels to be found between the colonial state and the independent state than are usually conceded.

I believe that historians will consider that contemporary judgements about the so called failure of Africa are really judgements made in terms of a Eurocentric dream for an independent Africa in which liberal democracy would be the norm, a dream that was shared only by a few elitist politicians like the Danquahs,[14] who were pushed aside in the struggle for independence by politicians with mass following like Nkrumah. I shall suggest that most African politicians did not share this dream and at best thought as Nyerere did that liberal democracy would only be a slowly acquired habit,[15] and at worst like Nkrumah only paid lip service to it.[16]

Finally I believe that future historians will set against the obvious failures of independent African states the very real achievements they have made in comparison with the record of their colonial masters.

THE COLONIAL LEGACY

In considering continuities between the colonial period and independence, let us look at the sort of model the colonial state provided in terms of the *Daily Telegraph* editorial. The violence which the editorialist posited as characteristic of contemporary African states was no stranger to the colonial state. The many studies of resistance to colonial occupation have shown that for the most part the colonial state was conceived in violence rather than by negotiation. This violence was often quite out of proportion too the task in hand, with burnings of villages, destruction of crops, killing of women and children, and the execution of leaders.[17] Some military expeditions were so barbaric that they caused outrage in the metropolitan press, as did the Voulet and Chanoine expedition in Niger.[18] The colonial state was not only conceived in violence, but it was maintained by the free use of it. Any form of resistance was visited by punitive expeditions that were often quite unrestrained by any of the norms of warfare in Europe. The bloody suppression of the Maji Maji and Herero uprisings in German East and South West Africa are well enough known. The less known atrocities committed in the suppression of the Satiru revolt in Northern Nigeria by the Sultan of Sokoto's forces acting on commission for the British in 1906 were such that the missionary Walter Miller wrote that 'it would be worth Leopold of Belgium's while to pay ten thousand pounds to get hold of what we know of this'.[19] As Edward Lugard, brother of the British High Commissioner in Northern Nigeria, wrote: 'they killed every living thing before them', Women's breasts had been cut off and the leader spitted on a stake.[20]

Lest these be thought too distant events in the colonial record to have much bearing on the present, one must recall that a man aged eighteen at the time of Satiru, would only have been 72 at the time of Nigeria's independence. Furthermore, the use of violence to suppress protest continued throughout the colonial period and into the period of decolonisation. The bloody massacre of Tirailleurs Sénégalais protesting against delays in paying their benefits and effecting their demobilisation at Thiaroye in Dakar in 1944 sent shock waves throughout the French African empire,[21] as did the revelations about the brutal treatment of Mau Mau prisoners by the British at the Hola Camp in Kenya through the British African colonies.[22] The colonial state, it must be remembered, maintained troops for internal security, not for defence against external aggression. These armies were of course used for this latter purpose when the occasion arose, most notably in the two world wars where African soldiers experienced violence on an unprecedented scale.[23] So too did civilians when their territory became part of the theatre of war. As Terence Ranger wrote of the impact of the First World War on East Africa 'it was the most awe-inspiring, destructive and capricious demonstration of European 'absolute power' that Eastern Africa ever experienced'.[24] It must be remembered too that the colonial rulers set the example of dealing with its opponents by jailing or exciling them, as not a few of those

who eventually inherited power knew from personal experience.[25] Indeed if the colonial state provided a model for its inheritors it was that government rested not on consent but force. Indeed when Nyerere was once pressed on the subject of preventive detention in his country he was quick to point out that Tanzania had inherited the practice from British colonial times.[26]

If we take up the second theme of the *Telegraph* leader, that of poverty, this was certainly no stranger during the colonial period. The colonial state was certainly not run for the benefit of its inhabitants. The roots of rural poverty, as Palmer and Parsons' volume of essays of that name on Southern Africa demonstrate, lie deep in the policies of the colonial powers.[27] In the white settler colonies the best land was appropriated from the African farmer who was crowded into less fertile reserves often with disastrous ecological results.[28] Where the main agent of exploitation was the African farmer, he was forced to produce the crops that the colonial rulers required rather than those he needed. Through taxation, compulsory crop cultivation, forced labour and requisition, and in the case of the Portuguese territories physical coercion, the farmer produced the cash crops that the big companies overseas required even at the risk of impoverishment of the land and famine. For many Africans taxation of any kind was a complete innovation. Many others had only paid indirect taxes. And where direct taxation was imposed, it was rarely, if ever, as high as that of colonial state, which at its most oppressive extracted taxes directly in the form of cash, labour and compulsory crop cultivation, and indirectly through duties on imported goods.[29] Robert Shenton in his recent book on *The Development of Capitalism in Northern Nigeria* has shown how British taxation policies designed to increase cultivation of cotton and groundnuts in some cases took up to 50% of a farmer's income from him and led to shortages of subsistence crops which in turn led to famines. As he shows, the colonial rulers themselves were fully aware of the consequences of their policies.[30] Similarly later colonial government marketing boards were used as a means of taxing further the potential earnings of the farmer. Yet critics of the independent African regimes seem to suggest that this neglect and exploitation of the farmer was new rather than a major legacy of colonial rule.[31]

Urban poverty and the slums associated with it were not a function of independent Africa but were established features of colonial rule. I recall arriving in Nigeria for the first time in 1953 and nearly retching as I crossed from the Mainland to Lagos Island by Carter Bridge, so rank was the stink from the slums beneath its piers. The bidonvilles of Dakar were a colonial creation of which Senghor was so ashamed that after independence he built a high wall around them so that visitors to his country should not see them as they entered Dakar from the airport.

The third theme in the *Telegraph* editorial is the misgovernment that has characterised independent African governments. Here again we must remind ourselves how little opportunity Africans had of participating in the machinery of government of the colonial state until a few years before its demise. In British Africa only a few chiefs under British indirect rule were allowed any initiative in the administration before 1945. Otherwise all Africans in the administration, whatever the colonial regime, fulfilled a purely subaltern role without executive initiative. As to legislative functions, again these were limited to local government under the system of indirect rule, and to a handful of elected Africans in Nigeria, Senegal and the Gold Coast. Generally in British and French Africa preparation for taking over the legislative, executive and administrative organs of the colonial state by Africans began only after the Second World War. Even where some effort was made to prepare African administrative cadres, they were often treated as second class members of the administration. In the 1950s, newly appointed African administrative officers in Uganda were specifically barred from access to the confidential files, a point that led to much bitterness on their part.[32] In many African countries not a few inhabitants exercised the right to vote for the first time at the elections that brought their independent governments to power.

The Congo perhaps provides the most notorious example of the lack of preparation for the transfer of the institutions of state, while Guinea provides a different kind of example, where the French actually tried to destroy the very fabric of that state before they departed. They even removed the books from the law library of the Ministry of Justice.[33] Yet the scuttling Belgians received surprisingly little blame in the press for the disasters of the Congo compared with the Congolese themselves. Surely historians of the future will be less preoccupied by the anarchy and savagery that flowed from independence than by the marvel of the survival of the Congo intact as the huge state of Zaire, however far the former corporal who is its current head of state may deviate from the standards of good government as conceived in Brussels, Paris or London.

If the Belgians only prescribed the medicine of democracy for their Congolese subjects on the eve of the transfer of power, we must recall that neither the Spaniards nor the Portuguese rulers of the day had any faith in this type of medication for their own peoples, let alone their African subjects. They had no qualms about their conviction that their states were based on force not consent.

No aspects of post-independence Africa has drawn more criticism by scholars and journalists of the West than the personal power exercised by its leaders. Again it is instructive to look at the colonial model. Colonial governors enjoyed very wide powers without brakes from below. Even in British Africa where some territories had legislative councils these were dominated by an official majority which could be relied on to vote as solidly for any new policy or programme introduced by the Governor as the legislators in today's one party states. In many territories the Colonial Governor ruled by decree or proclamation and even where he had an executive council his decision on policy was overriding since that council's members were all his officials. The Governor also enjoyed to the full the outward trappings of power, living in an imposing palace, driven in large limousines flying the flag, deferred to by all, and on ceremonial occasions dressed in cocked hat and plumes and a quasi-military uniform. In the British territories, he alone was allowed to use red ink to minute or sign official documents.

This again was a model not lost on the inheritors of the colonial state. The model for the successors was invariably derived from that of the colonial masters. Thus ex-Sargeant Jean Bedel Bokassa modelled his coronation as Emperor of Central Africa on that of a former French corporal. Americans will recall Washington Irving's allegorical version of the European folk-tale about Rip Van Winkle. In Irving's version he becomes a Catskill villager who slumbers through the American Revolution to awake to the many changes that

have taken place in his village. Among these is the new sign on the Inn. Before he slept it was a crude picture of George III. The uniform has now been changed and the name transmogrified from King George to George Washington.[34] For a more sinister comparison we might remember that the OGPU of the Russian revolutionary state had its direct antecedents in the Tsar's okhrana.

Another theme in the *Telegraph* leader is the destruction of the pillars of law in African societies. Again we must look back at the colonial model. In French Africa until 1946, all Africans but a few citizens were under a regime of administrative law whereby they were subject to summary justice with no right of appeal. In 1914 Lugard specifically outlawed the representation of defendants by lawyers in the magistrate's courts of the South where a British model judiciary had been installed, albeit with massive problems and defects. In The Congo and Portuguese territories, too, the Africans had no access to metropolitan style legal institutions. These existed only for the European inhabitants or in the case of the Portuguese territories the handful of *assimilados*. They were made available to Africans only on the eve of independence or immediately afterwards.

Again, what is remarkable is that so much of the trappings of spirit of these hastily implanted systems have survived rather than broken down. I am sure all were moved that out of the misery and anarchy that has bedevilled Uganda for the past decade and a half the apparent end should be marked by a bewigged and scarlet robed Chief Justice swearing in the new Conqueror-President Museveni—and what is more that it should have been a white Ugandan in a post that in Uganda has held few promises of retirement benefits.

The final point made by the *Telegraph* leader was that economic life had been destroyed. Of course in terms of exports and imports this has often been the case as countries like Nigeria have built up massive overseas debts, cannot afford imports and have neglected agricultural exports. But as Pius Okigbo, former economic adviser to the Nigerian Government, so forcefully pointed out in a recent lecture, the real problem is that the health of African economies is judged by the outside world in terms of the size of their imports and exports.[35] This too of course is a legacy of the colonial period when the colonial rulers were little concerned with measuring the African domestic economy but were principally interested in the size of its import-export economy. Thus during the Depression of the 1930s there was crisis for the colonial rulers whose income was reduced, for the import-export firms whose crops fetched abysmal prices on the world market, and for those African farmers who were involved in the sector of the agricultural economy. But for the subsistence crop producer and the craftsmen there was something of a boom.[36] Similarly in many countries that are apparently suffering in terms of their import-export economy, there is today something of an internal boom. If African leaders have tended to judge the health of their economies in terms of imports and exports, they are only following a colonial precedent.[37]

The colonial rulers, furthermore, hardly set a good example of operating the economy in the best interests of their subjects: profits were expatriated not invested in local industries, providing a parallel with, though here not a model for, the present salting of ill-gotten gains by African leaders in the banks of Switzerland and other safe havens of the Western world. We must recall too the price rings, the lack of local industrial development and the lodging of the assets of marketing boards in metropolitan banks before we talk too much about mismanagement of the economy by African successor states. As Ralph Austen has recently emphasised, Patrick Manning has demonstrated that considerable economic damage was done to Dahomey by the French 'who used it to subsidise less profitable French possessions, to fulfil their own ambitions, or to respond to the pressures of local European economic interests.'[38] As Austen further emphasises: 'The economic and political malaise afflicting the African continent today with such breadth and severity . . . must have deep roots in a past about which so little is generally known'.[39]

A final point concerning the colonial legacy to Independent Africa concerns the state structures that were handed over at independence. The borders of these states, it may be tedious to remind ourselves, were erected without reference to African realities in the chanceries of Europe. But having created them, colonial powers did little to foster a sense of national unity within them. The French territory of Upper Volta for instance was not created until 1920, was dismembered in 1932 and divided up among its neighbours, only to be re-established in 1947, thirteen years before it became independent, German Kamerun and Togo were divided between the French and British after the First World War, while, although the separate Protectorates of Northern and Southern Nigeria were amalgamated by Lugard in 1914, it was a token amalgamation which did not truly bring them into a meaningful relationship with each other.[40] The two French federations of Equatorial and West Africa were broken up by the French against the wishes of the majority of the constituent colonies on the eve of independence. Furthermore it has been argued, convincingly, that the system of indirect rule, employed by the British, was a divisive one in that it emphasised the integrity of the pre-colonial political unit as against the new colonial state. And up until the mid-forties there were still powerful advocates in the Colonial Office who saw the native authorities as the building blocks of independence.[41]

This has been a deliberately selective view of the colonial past but, I hope, a corrective one that the Cassandras of contemporary Africa would be adviced to take into account.

WHOSE DREAM WAS IT ANYWAY?

We come now to my second theme: how far did Africans share the dream of the colonial rulers for Africa? In the first place, it has to be remembered that the liberal democratic ideal was espoused only by the British and French for their African colonies. Though at home the Belgians shared these ideals, they only very belatedly suggested that they might be appropriately transferred to their colonial subjects.[42] In both Spain and Portugal liberal democracy had succumbed many years since to Fascist regimes, so for their overseas subjects there was not even a metropolitan model of democracy to aspire to. In the case of the Portuguese their African colonies were considered integral parts of the metropolis and, far from instruments of power being transferred to African subjects, control of the state was seized by them by force of arms. There was thus no obligation placed on the victors to maintain any particular form of government.[43]

In all the French Black African states, with the exception of Guinea, and in all the British African states, including

Zimbabwe, the transfer of power was negotiated and made conditional on the acceptance of a liberal democratic constitution inspired by the metropolitan model. What we have to ask ourselves is how far the African parties to these negotiations were ideologically committed to these constitutions? In Francophone and Anglophone Africa educated Africans soon learnt that the pen was mightier than the sword in dealing with their particular colonial masters and turned the democratic ideals and institutions of their masters against them and asked why they espoused democracy at home and denied it abroad. The Senegalese politician Lamine Gueye in his autobiography recalls the irony of the 'Liberté, Egalité et Fraternité' emblazoned on the offices of a colonial administration which practised none of these three virtues as far as their African subjects were concerned.[44] An educated chief like Tshekedi Khama in the then Bechuanaland Protectorate skilfully manipulated British press, parliament and public opinion to block measures of the local administration to which he was opposed. But if we examine his own life closely we find that while he was keen on his own rights, and went to great lengths to defend them, he was none too careful with respect to those of his own subjects.[45] David Williams has hypothesised that the emirs in Northern Nigeria finally agreed to back self-government and independence under the Sardauna of Sokoto because they believed he would be less insistent on the implementation of democracy than the British showed clear signs of being if they continued administering their country any longer.[46]

African leaders may have skilfully pressured the British and French to transfer their models and when finally they agreed to do so accepted them as a condition of gaining independence, just as Nkrumah had to accept a final election as a precondition of independence for Ghana.[47] But did this mean that they implicitly believed in them as anything other than as a means to an end? The answer is surely 'No'. Only thus can we explain the rapid dismantling of these constitutions in form or spirit by nearly all who were party to the independence agreements. A few days after Ghana's independence, Nkrumah gave a press conference in which he assured the world's press that 'We shall help [other African states] by our example of successfully working a parliamentary democracy'.[48] But within a few days more he had moved into Christiansborg Castle, the seat of the colonial governors, arranged for his own portrait to appear on currency and postage stamps, and started on the road to the acquisition of unchecked personal power. The commitment to liberal democracy thereafter tended to be the exclusive concern of the opposition, but how shallow this was may be illustrated by the example of Siaka Stevens of Sierra Leone. His All People's Congress (APC) had campaigned against the ruling Sierra Leone People's Party (SLPP) in part on the basis that it was abusing democracy. Having won the election despite heavy rigging by the Government, and finally acceding to power several coups later, Stevens set about creating the one party state that the SLPP had not quite dared to. It is clear that for all but a few leaders—Seretse Khama of Botswana and Dauda Jawara of The Gambia being the notable exceptions—the commitment to liberal democracy was a transitory one. Nor of course were the military who succeeded them so committed, coming from a very different tradition of dealing with people.

Was it not a staggering piece of arrogant paternalism that the European powers should prescribe for their African dependencies a model that had had such a chequered career on their own continent and criticise them for failing to work it? African leaders were for the most part aware of the many attacks on democracy experienced by Europe during the years that they had been under its tutelage. They had seen how weak democracies could be in the face of a determined fascist leader like Mussolini. Not all were convinced by their masters' condemnations of Hitler. It is not for nothing that a fair number of African boys were named Adolf in the early forties.[49] But democracy remained, in the eyes of the Western press, the panacea for Africa. Thus there was general rejoicing at Nigeria's return to civilian rule in 1979 and general hostility to the military coup that brought it to an end in December 1983, even though there was rejoicing by the general population at the demise of a corrupt and increasingly oppressive regime. A former Labour Minister in the British Foreign Office concerned with Africa, Ted Rowlands, was reported by *West Africa* as appearing to be calling for economic sanctions against Nigeria for 'abandoning democracy'.[50] While the *Daily Express* referring to the new military ruler, General Buhari, wondered whether the Queen 'will take this despot's hand'.[51]

What African leaders surely appreciated more perceptively than those who wished liberal democratic constitutions on them was that liberal democracy had only worked in those countries of Europe where there was relative lack of inequality, a deep-rooted sense of national identity, and a consensus as to the ideal model for the government of the state. Where, as in Zimbabwe, such conditions did not obtain, and where there were two major ethnic groups vying for power, the operation of the liberal democratic constitution became very close in character to the operation of democracy in Northern Ireland. There was certainly genuine belief on the part of those African leaders who advocated the one-party state, however much later they were to pervert it to their own ends, that it would be less divisive than the two-party model of the British or the multi-party model of the French.[52] Nor were African leaders particularly committed to the equitable distribution of resources that their election manifestos promised and their talk of African socialism may have suggested. Since the means to independence was to be through the ballot box, they had necessarily to persuade the electorate by offering to implement programmes that would benefit them. With independence won, the behaviour of African politicians has differed little from that of the majority of office-seekers in promoting personal advancement and profit, with some pork barrelling for their homeboys. Africans were much more hard-nosed, realistic and even cynical about what independence portended. Rosy dreams were left to the departing colonial masters and the metropolitan press. Indeed as *West Africa* remarked almost petulantly at Ghana's independence celebrations 'the Accra crowds were much less demonstrative than expected'.[53] Its then editor, David Williams, tells the story of Sir Milton Margai who was overseeing the arrangements for the independence service in the Freetown Cathedral. When the Bishop suggested he might like to give a second thought to the choice of one hymn which contained what he felt was the inappropriate second verse: 'Though the darkness deepens, Lord with me abide'. 'Exactly' replied Sir Milton.[54] David Williams also tells of how journalists at Nigeria's independence had to file their stories three hours before the ceremonial lowering of the Union Jack in order to have their stories on the British breakfast table. All wrote of the dancing in the streets that followed the raising of the Nigerian flag. In fact when David Williams and a fellow-journalist

toured the streets after the midnight ceremonial they met only desultory groups wending their way home. His colleague shouted out of the car: 'Dance, Dammit, you're meant to be dancing'.[55] To be fair, however, to the British, it must be remembered that the democratic dream was more enthusiastically supported in the corridors of Whitehall than in the offices of the District Officers who, as Sylvia Leith-Ross has shown in her memoirs of Nigeria, were much more apprehensive of its application to the societies among which they worked.[56]

I would like to conclude with the more positive assessment of the last quarter century of African history that I believe will be accorded by historians of the future. I need not record the failures of Africa—these can be read about daily in the papers.

AFRICAN ACHIEVEMENT

I am convinced that historians of the future will find much more to the credit of Africa than current press punditry and academic despondency at present will admit. And I think that their judgement will be made in the context of the colonial record.

Here it is instructive to listen to Julius Nyerere's recent justification *pro vita sua* made just after he relinquished the Presidency of Tanzania.[57] It is instructive not least because Tanzania is usually cited as one of Africa's worst basket-cases in economic terms. In 1961, he recalled, on the eve of independence and after nearly seventy years of colonial rule only 486,000 children were in primary school. Today there are over three and a half million, in his own words 'a tremendous achievement unmatched anywhere else in Africa'. In 1961 80% of the adult population was illiterate. Today, according to the Tanzanian Government, 85% can read and write. In 1961 only 11% of the population had access to clean water— today, Nyerere claims, nearly 50% have access to clean water within 450 yards of their homes. The availability of health services, particularly in the rural areas has improved out of all recognition. The ratio of doctors to population has been reduced from 1:830,000 to 1:26,000. The mortality rate of infants has nearly halved while life expectancy for adults has risen from 35 to 51.

Of course all this was achieved at a tremendous cost to the economy with the accumulation of massive international debts. We know that in many African countries these debts have been amassed not through genuine attempts at betterment of the lives of the people but by large scale squandering of resources and corruption. Two points have to be made about the debts of African countries. In many cases they were built up in a genuine attempt to make up for the sad development record of the colonial governments. We should also remind ourselves that some of the spectacular failures in African development were part of development plans concocted largely in the metropole to buttress the colonial state, for instance the notorious Tanganyika groundnut scheme and the Gambia poultry project. Moreover, in the post-colonial era, many African development plans and projects were the outcome of advice by foreign experts.[58]

The financial strains experienced by the post-independence governments have also been due to a sometimes over-zealous concern to improve the inadequate communications systems left by the colonial powers and to build the foundations of an industrial infrastructure that would make them less dependent on supplies from the First World. Much more directly responsible for these economic problems are facts such as these: in 1979, as Nyerere put it, Tanzania was paying nine times as much for its oil though using less than before the oil crisis began. To buy a seven ton truck in 1981 his country had to produce four times as much cotton, three times as many cashew nuts, ten times as much tobacco, and three times as much coffee as five years earlier.[59]

As Nyerere complained at the Cancun North-South summit in 1981:

Our balance of payment difficulties are enormous and getting greater. This is not because we are trying to live as though we were rich. It is because our already low income is constantly being reduced because of our participation in international trade. . . . We find ourselves always selling cheap and buying dear . . . we are asking for a chance to earn our living in the international system.[60]

I believe that historians will also see these problems in this perspective, and I believe that, in the context of the colonial legacy and the economic vicissitudes of independence (whether self-inflicted or brought about by the caprices of the world market), they will marvel that by and large the post-colonial state in Africa has remained intact, often despite the machinations of erstwhile colonial powers or the conflicting interests of East and West as in the cases of Biafra, Chad and Angola. They will marvel that the map of Africa has remained largely the same as it was at independence and that there have been so few wars between the post-colonial states though they were left with so many of the problems that in Europe have been the cause of war: ill-defined frontiers, split ethnic groups and so forth. In the thirty years period 1914-1944, as we know, Europe was ravaged by two major wars, as a result of which the boundaries of Europe were twice redrawn. In the thirty year period following the independence of Sudan in 1956, there has been marginal readjustment of the African map, and surprisingly little interstate hostility and when it has broken out it has usually been quickly resolved. Many potentially explosive situations have been defused by the little-known but often highly effective Conciliation Committee of the Organisation of African Unity.

Against the internal violence of Chad and Uganda we must set the large number of African countries where such violence has been minimal, and remember that even the three year lonng Biafran civil war in Nigeria came to an end without recrimination and in a spirit of reconciliation on the part of the victors that was without precedent in Europe or the Americas. We must also recall that when for instance South Africans use the examples of Uganda or Chad to argue against the transfer of power to their own African majority, the surprising thing is that the most secure group in Africa since independence has in fact been the whites themselves. We must further remind ourselves that some of the most extreme forms of violence perpetrated in post-colonial Africa have been by the whites of Rhodesia and South Africa.

If it seems that I have presented this case as though it were that of a defence lawyer, this has been deliberate. Africa has in a very real sense been on trial for the desperate situation in which she has found herself twenty-odd years after independence. The blame for this situation has almost universally been placed upon African leaders. I have tried to show that

that blame properly should be divided between these leaders and their colonial predecessors. I have also tried to show that the criteria by which Africa is being judged are Eurocentric ones. Finally I have suggested that historians of the future will set against the many failures of African leaders since independenced their very real achievements which the Western press so often ignores. I rest my case.

FOOTNOTES

1. Sir Abubakar Tafawa Balewa, Speech made on Independence Day, 1 October 1960 in *"But always as Friends": Northern Nigeria and the Cameroons, 1921-1957*, (London, George Allen and Unwin, 1969), Frontispiece.

2. *West Africa* 19 November 1960.

3. *ibid*.

4. *ibid*.

5. See Michael Crowder *The Story of Nigeria* (London, Faber, 1978), p. 259.

6. To be fair the usually well informed magazine *West Africa* raised no alarm in its columns either on the eve of the Conference nor during it, even though its own representative 'Griot' was touring the country at the time.

7. See Michael Crowder 'Botswana and the Survival of Liberal Democracy in Africa' in Prosser Gifford and Wm. Roger Louis eds. *African Independence: the Origins and Consequences of the Transfer of Power in Africa* (Newhaven: Yale University Press) (forthcoming).

8. See for example James S. Coleman and Carl G. Rosberg Jr. eds. *Political Parties and National Integration in Tropical Africa* (Berkeley and Los Angeles, University of California Press, 1964), especially their 'Introduction'.

9. Robert H. Jackson and Carl G. Rosberg *Personal Rule in Africa. Prince, Autocrat, Prophet, Tyrant.* (Berkeley, Los Angeles and London, University of California Press), 1982.

10. The first indications that this might be the case came to public attention as a result of the Namugongo massacre of May 1984, when both Baganda Muslims and Christians were murdered, thus giving it a genocidal character. I am grateful to Michael Twaddle for this reference.

11. See comments on the Amnesty International Report in *The Times* 28 June 1985.

12. See Michael Twaddle 'The State of African Studies' *African Affairs* 85, 340, July 1986 especially p. 444 and Richard Hodder-Williams, 'African studies: back to the future', *African Affairs* 85, 341. October 1986, pp. 593-604, with their gloomy prognoses for the future.

13. 'Agony in East Africa'. Editorial in *Daily Telegraph* 28 January 1986.

14. See L.H. Ofosu-Appiah *The Life and Times of Dr. J.B. Danquah*, (Accra, Waterville Publishing House, 1974), in particular Danquah's letter of protest against the Removal Order served on him, 12 March 1948, p. 61, in which he wrote that 'the people directly charged with the administration of Government should be directly responsible to the people, with power in the people to change the personnel of Government when they feel that the Government or Cabinet of the day had failed them, or served its time. This constitutional goal I am pledged to pursue without flinching. . .'

15. Julius K. Nyerere interviewed by William E. Smith in 'A Reporter at Large: Transition'. *New Yorker*, 3 March 1986.

16. On the very day of Independence Nkrumah was presenting himself as a committed democrat.

17. See H.L. Wesseling 'Colonial Wars and Armed Peace, 1870-1914' *Itinerario V*, 1981, 2, pp. 53-69.

18. See Finn Fugelstad *A History of Niger 1850-1960* (Cambridge, Cambridge University Press, 1983), p. 61.

19. Walter Miller to Sir Frederick Lugard, 24 September 1907 in Rhodes House Library, Oxford, Mss. Brit. Emp. s. 62. 'Lugard Papers'. Cited in Robert Shenton *The Development of Capitalism in Northern Nigeria* (London, James Currey, 1986), p. 27.

20. *ibid*. Edward Lugard to Sir Frederick Lugard. 21 May 1908.

21. Myron Echenberg ' "Morts pour la France": the African Soldier in France during the Second World War' *Journal of African History*, 26, 4, 1958, p. 376.

22. It also convinced Britain's new Colonial Secretary, Iain Macleod, that 'swift change was needed in Kenya'. Quoted in Jeremy Murray-Brown *Kenyatta* (London, George Allen and Unwin, 1972), p. 299. See also A. Marshall Macphee *Kenya* (London, Ernest Benn, 1968), pp. 151-3.

23. See for example the special issues of the *Journal of African History* on the two world wars: 'World War I and Africa', 19, 1978, No 1; and 'World War II and Africa', 26, 1985, No 4. David Killingray and Richard Rathbone

eds. *Africa and the Second World War* (London, Macmillan, 1986).

24. T.O. Ranger *Dance and Society in Eastern Africa 1890-1970: the Beni Ngoma* (London, Heinemann, 1975), p. 45.

25. For instance Jomo Kenyatta of Kenya, Hastings Banda of Malawi, Kwame Knrumah of Ghana, Sultan Mohammed V of Morocco, Seretse Khama of Bostwana.

26. William P. Smith 'A Reporter at Large'.

27. Robin Palmer and Neil Parsons eds. *The Roots of Rural Poverty in Central and Southern Africa* (London, Heinemann, 1977).

28. For instance Robin Palmer *Land and Racial Domination in Rhodesia*, (London, Heinemann, 1977) but see also Paul Mosley *The Settler Economies: Studies in the Economic History of Kenya and Southern Rhodesia 1900-1963* Cambridge, (Cambridge University Press, 1983) where he expresses reservations about the conventional view of settler economies in Africa.

29. While it is difficult to calculate the relative burden of taxation imposed on their subjects by those pre-colonial policies which raised revenue through direct taxes and that exacted by the colonial state, it is significant that many inhabitants of pre-colonial polities that did impose direct taxation in cash or kind, for example in Niger, French Soudan and Chad, were forced to migrate in order to earn enough to pay their taxes. See Elliott P. Skinner *The Mossi of the Upper Volta* (Stanford, Stanford University Press, 1964), pp. 156-8 for the early impact of taxation by the French on the Mossi, who were later to be one of the chief suppliers of migrant labour in West Africa.

30. See in particular Chapter 6 of Shenton *The Development of capitalism in Northern Nigeria*.

31. See Robert H. Bates, Essays on the Political Economy of Rural Africa (Cambridge, Cambridge University Press, 1983), especially Part III, though he has trenchant criticisms of the effect of the colonial agricultural regime on the peasant.

32. Personal Communication from Professor Lalage Bown based on direct observation in the Eastern Province of Uganda 1955-60.

33. Personal communication from Irene Brown. Most of the examples of what the French did on leaving Guinea are not published but fall into the category of 'on dit que'. See, however, Claude Rivière *Guinea: the Mobilisation of a People* (Ithaca, Cornell University Press, 1977), p. 83, where he says of the departing French that some destroyed equipment before they left, others carried away files, while one group of soldiers set fire to their barracks.

34. Marcus Cunliffe 'The Cultural Patrimony of the United States' in Prosser Gifford ed. *The Treaty of Paris (1793) in a Changing States System* (Lanham, Maryland, University Press of America and Washington D.C., Wilson Center, 1985), p. 177.

35. Pius Okigbo 'The Nigerian Economy in the next decade: possibilities of self-reliance'. St. Antony's College Oxford, African Affairs Seminar, 13 March 1986. Discussion.

36. See S.M. Jacobs 'Report on Taxation and Economics of Nigeria', 1934 in Rhodes House Library Mss. Afr. t. 16 where he writes '. . . Nigeria in *all internal respects* has not suffered from an economic depression. Her production of yams, cassava, fish, corn, and her exchange of all her produce goes on as before'. Quoted in Shenton *The Development of Capitalism in Northern Nigeria* p. 101.

37. The health or otherwise of a colonial economy was measured almost exclusively in terms of imports and of agricultural and mineral exports since there was little attempt by the colonial authorities to assess the volume of production of food crops for local consumption or of locally manufactured goods, for example cloth, pots and iron work.

38. This point from Patrick Manning's *Slavery, Colonialism and economic Growth in Dahomey, 1640-1960* (Cambridge, Cambridge University Press, 1982), (see especially Chapter 10) is made by Ralph Austen in 'African Economies in Historical Perspective', *Business History Review*, Spring 1985, p. 103.

39. Austen in *ibid* p. 101.

40. See Michael Crowder 'Lugard and Colonial Nigeria: Towards an Identity' *History Today* 36, February 1986, pp. 23-29.

41. R.D. Pearce *The Turning Point in Africa: British Colonial Policy 1938-1948* (London, Frank Cass), 1982, especially Chapter 3.

42. Crawford Young *Politics in the Congo: Decolonisation and Independence* (Princeton, New Jersey, Princeton University Press, 1965), Chapters 3 and 4.

43. In Guinea-Bissau, for instance, the PAIGC carried out a General Election in the liberated zones in 1972 two years before the Portuguese recognised the independence of its former colony, an independence which the Guinea-Bissau leaders had anyway effectively proclaimed in September 1973. See Basil Davidson 'Portuguese-speaking Africa' in *Cambridge History of Africa* 8 (Cambridge, Cambridge University Press, 1984), p. 788-9. Another example would be the Algerian Revolution though here there was a deliberate move to revalidate many of the institutions and much of the legislation of the erstwhile colonial regime because the FLN had failed to build political institutions of its own during the long and bitter struggle with the French. See Clement Henry Moore 'The Maghrib' in *ibid*. pp. 580-82.

44. Lamine Gueye *Itinéraire africaine* (Paris, 1966), p. 79.

45. See Michael Crowder 'Tshekedi Khama: Statesman' in R.F. Morton and Jeff Ramsay eds. *Botswana: Making of a Nation* (Gaborone, Longman) (forthcoming).

46. David Williams: Personal Communication.

47. Ofosu-Appiah *Danquah* pp. 130-1.

48. *West Africa* 16 March 1957.

49. I have come across one Nigerian named Hitler, a Motswana named Mussolini, and been told of two sons of a Togolese called respectively Bismarck and Goebbels.

50. *West Africa* 16 January 1984.

51. Cited in *ibid*.

52. Julius Nyerere immediately comes to mind. Another example is Mamadou Dia, the former Prime Minister of Senegal.

53. *West Africa* 16 March 1957. 'Ghana takes it calmly'. Two and half years later *West Africa* used a similar headline 'Lagos takes it calmly' for its report on the independence celebrations of Nigeria.

54. David Williams. Personal Communication.

55. *ibid*.

56. Sylvia Leith-Ross *Stepping Stones: Memoirs of Colonial Nigeria, 1907-1960* (London, Peter Owen), 1983, in particular Section V covering the years 1951-55.

57. Interview with William E. Smith 'A Reporter at Large'.

58. See the admirable critique of the role of foreign experts in African development in Paul Richards *Indigenous Agricultural Revolution* (London, Hutchinson University Library for Africa), 1985.

59. Julius Nyerere in interview with William E. Smith 'A Reporter at Large'.

60. *ibid*.

INDIA'S
Estranged Communities

Continued community strife suggests that the Indians' view of themselves should be redefined

Mustafa Malik

Journalist Mustafa Malik was born in Assam, India. Over the past twenty years, his articles have appeared in U.S. and South Asian newspapers.

At midnight on August 14, 1947, the viceroy's house in New Delhi resounded with ceremonies inaugurating India's independence from British rule. The father of the new nation agonized on a straw pallet in a stench-filled Calcutta slum hundreds of miles away; Mohandas Karamchand Gandhi, beloved as the *Mahatma* (great-soul), could not bear to join the celebrations while Hindus, Sikhs, and Muslims killed one another in Punjab. Riots had started over Hindu and Sikh resistance to a partition of British India to carve out Pakistan. Almost a million people were to die in what remains the worst communal carnage in South Asian history.

Under the Pakistan plan, monotheistic Muslims, who had complained that their religious and cultural identity would be in danger in a country dominated by polytheistic Hindus, would have their own homeland. The Sikhs, whose syncretic faith combined Muslim monotheism and castelessness with the Hindu doctrines of rebirth until attaining salvation through good deeds, decided to remain in India. They had been persecuted by Islamic rulers in the Middle Ages and had since sided with the Hindus in many battles against the Muslims.

What the Mahatma had not been prepared for was his discovery that the people he had served and loved so long could be so ugly. "I have come to the conclusion," he wrote to a longtime associate, "that our way was nonviolent only superficially, our hearts are violent."

If the Mahatma had been alive this past August, he might have boycotted the gala celebrations of India's fortieth independence anniversary; those violent hearts were in action all year round. On average, India had a riot per day last year, either between Sikhs and Hindus or between Hindus and Muslims. The year-round death toll was at least 1,837.

Growing estrangement between Hindu and Muslim

Although the subcontinent's Muslim-majority regions in the west and northeast broke away to form Pakistan—the northeastern part of which later emerged as independent Bangladesh—India still has eighty million Muslims, who make up 11 percent of the country's population. Most Indian Muslims had supported the Pakistan movement, thereby incurring Hindu wrath. After 1947, they became demoralized. Indian society was 83 percent Hindu and nursed a grudge toward the Muslims after losing the long and bitter fight to prevent the creation of Pakistan.

For more than a decade after independence, however, violence between Hindus and Muslims in India remained at a low level. Throughout the 1950s, Indian Muslims kept their heads down. The individual Indian Muslim felt guilty about his or his fellow Muslims' support for Pakistan, and because the memories of the 1947 riots were still fresh, it was deemed prudent to maintain a low profile. Also, Indian National Congress old guards, who believed in religion-neutral politics, were at the helm in politics and administration, and they were a shield against Hindu-Muslim hostilities.

Relations between the two communities began to

deteriorate during the early 1960s, despite several quiet interludes. Today the estrangement is nearly complete in many cities, where an incident between a Hindu and a Muslim can quickly turn into a communal conflagration.

The issues that trigger rioting may have religious or cultural bearings; for example, should a Muslim decide to sacrifice a cow (to commemorate Abraham's plans to sacrifice his son to God) the Hindus would challenge him because the cow is sacred for them; or Hindus might play music near a Muslim prayer congregation, angering the Muslims who view this activity as an obstruction to their prayer. Sometimes a clash between a Hindu and a Muslim over daily, mundane affairs draws the two communities into mayhem.

One such incident occurred last May 16 in the northern Indian city of Meerut. A man was killed in a property dispute. Had the fight occurred between Muslims or between Hindus, it would have resulted in a regular court case involving two families. But here the victim was a Hindu and his assailants Muslims. Two days later when Hindu police came hunting for suspects in a Muslim neighborhood at the breaking of a religious fast, Muslims protested. A series of riots followed in which Hindu civilians and Hindu local and state police engaged the minority Muslims in an orgy of bloodletting. Civilians fought pitched battles with knives, sticks, and axes, while police shot Muslim men, women, and children, and rounded up hundreds of others. On the night of May 22, state police took more than fifty Muslim captives to a canal, shot them, and dumped their bodies into the water. At least five more Muslims were tortured to death in jail, and dozens of other detainees remain unaccounted for to this day.

Incidents such as this are typical. In many ways, today's situation is more disturbing than ever. The predominantly Hindu law enforcement agencies and local administrations often blatantly support the Hindu rioters. The ruling Congress Party, now confined to Hinduism's traditional stronghold of northern India, has shed its role as protector of minorities and begun to woo militant Hindu groups to court the Hindu vote. This has bolstered Hindu militancy, nudging Muslims further into the fold of their own militant groups.

Sikh alienation

Sikhs took a break from communal strife after independence. They, too, have returned to the fray since 1981, this time against their former allies, the Hindus. The current phase of the Sikh-Hindu feud began over a host of Sikh complaints and demands. Some demands were religious. Sikhs sought holy-city status for Amritsar, site of their holiest shrine, the Golden Temple; a radio transmitter to broadcast their scriptures; the right to carry swords on passenger aircraft (their religion requires them to always carry swords); and so on. Some demands were economic: a larger share of river water and more hydroelectricity for Punjab, where Sikhs are a majority; better job opportunities for Punjabi youths, especially in the armed forces; more powers for Punjab's government; and so on.

Many of these demands just could not be fulfilled, not in the short term, anyway. Other demands that could have been met encountered resistance and stalling tactics from the Indian government and many Hindus. The Sikhs stepped up their agitation and escalated it into a demand for a sovereign Sikh homeland, "Khalistan" (the Land of the Pure). Today, about twenty separatist groups operate in Punjab, many of them killing innocent Hindus and Sikhs who oppose secession. In 1987, an average of three people were killed daily in clashes over the Sikh secessionist movement, more than double the rate of the previous year. The average Sikh, like the average Muslim, feels alienated from Indian life. For centuries, Sikhs and Hindus intermarried, attended each other's social events, and operated businesses together. They rarely do so now. "Punjab's tragedy," writes one of India's best-known columnists, "is that there are no Punjabis anymore in Punjab." There are only Sikhs and Hindus (Nayar & Singh, 1987).

The most ominous aspect of today's communal strife, whether between Hindus and Muslims or between Hindus and Sikhs, is not its dimension; it is the apparent resignation among many Indians toward the problem. In earlier decades, Indian intelligentsia considered communal riots a grave problem and vigorously debated a sociopolitical solution. Today the government considers it a law-and-order issue to be addressed by the police, the military, and occasional political rhetoric.

The public too is getting used to it. "It's our tradition, unfortunately," a Hindu professor at a West Bengal college said to me during a 1982 train ride from Calcutta to New Delhi. "Don't Americans have their black-white problem?" He was more interested in talking about capitalism, socialism, and the place of the Bengali epic *Meghnad Badh* (the slaying of Meghnad) in world literature than in discussing the mounting Hindu-Muslim and Hindu-Sikh strife.

Muslim persecution

Tradition, of course, partly explains today's Hindu-Muslim animosity. Interfaith violence was introduced to India by Muslim invaders nearly a millennium ago. The most egregious of them, Sultan Mahmud of Afghanistan (971-1030), raided northern India seventeen times over a span of three decades, plundering cities, massacring Hindus, and destroying temples. Some of the Turkish-Muslim invaders and rulers who followed Mahmud over the next eight centuries also persecuted Hindus and Sikhs.

Muslim atrocities mark some of India's darkest hours because Indians had never known interfaith violence. India had fostered three great religions

—Hinduism, Buddhism, and Jainism—without any bloodshed. Hinduism, the mother faith, had been one of the world's most tolerant and adaptable creeds. Through its policy of adaptation, Hinduism, despite its caste segregation, had overcome powerful Buddhist and Jaina challenges. Also, Hindus boasted a much higher spiritual and intellectual heritage than the culturally impoverished Turkish Muslims. The spiritual and metaphysical discourses of Hindu Brahman priests were among the most advanced in the world. Hindu progress in astronomy, mathematics, medicine, chemistry, textile manufacturing, and handicraft had made Indian civilization one of the world's richest. The outrages committed by the mostly illiterate, fanatical Turkish Islamic hordes created revulsion throughout Hindu society.

That revulsion has left an abiding imprint on the Hindu psyche and has been translated into a vague anger against Indian Muslims, most of whom are offspring of local converts. The Hindus' ire against Muslims was reinforced by the creation of Pakistan. Today, that anger is being fanned again by communal Hindu organizations such as the Rashtriya Swyamsevak Sangh (RSS), Viswa Hindu Parisad (VHP), and Shiv Sena. On the other hand, the new generation of Muslims, who played no role in the creation of Pakistan, feel no guilt about being Muslim in India—and no need to "keep their heads down." Instead, feeling an urge to preserve their communal and cultural identity against the threat of assimilation into Hindu culture, they join their own communal groups such as Jamaat-i-Islami and the Muslim League.

Whatever the cause of Hindu-Muslim riots, the backward Muslim minority, which usually is out of favor with the predominantly Hindu police and local administrations, suffers the most violence. One may wonder what has become of Hindu religious tolerance. Has it been snuffed out by the memory of Muslim persecution a millennium ago and the Pakistan movement of the 1940s?

Feudal and colonial legacy

Apart from the history of communal strife, India's feudal and colonial legacy must accept a large share of the blame for Hindu-Muslim animosity. The gulf between the communities is the result of disparate economic progress over the past centuries. During the Middle Ages, Muslim invaders and their descendants made up India's administrative, military, and feudal establishments. Another segment of the Muslim population, comprising the bulk of Indian Muslims, emerged from native low-caste Hindus who had converted to Islam. Islam's social equality had offered them an escape from Hindu caste discrimination. Islam did not, however, improve their economic fortunes very much; converts clung to their old low-paying callings. Higher-caste Hindus were left to pursue trade, commerce, and most other middle-class occupations.

When the British conquered India, Muslims were thrown out of top administrative and military echelons. They had few other skills and little inclination to compete with Hindus for middle-class jobs and gradually faded away as a social and economic force. By the time British rule was challenged by Indian nationalism, what had remained of the Indian Muslim community was composed of poor peasants, artisans, clerics, and a sprinkling of landed gentry. Hindu upper castes, on the other hand, pulsated with capital, education, and progressive thinking.

The colonial rulers, trying to play the "Muslim card," declared the Muslims a separate political entity and offered the Muslim elite legislative quotas and other perks. The faint Muslim aristocracy and feeble intelligentsia, finding it hard to compete with the large and vibrant Hindu middle classes, readily accepted the bait and pressed for more.

Eventually, Muslim leaders escalated their demands, requiring the establishment of a homeland, Pakistan. But the secession of Muslim-majority regions weakened the Muslim community that remained in India, which now became more defensive and withdrawn. Withdrawal from the mainstream of India's economic and social life accentuated Indian Muslims' economic and social backwardness. Muslims today are largely poor, uneducated, and xenophobic, and are perceived by Hindus as an obstacle to India's social and cultural progress.

Many Indian social thinkers, however, viewed economic disparity as the main—if not the sole—cause of the Hindu-Muslim cleavage, and therefore concluded that a socialist democratic system would take care of the problem. Sociological thinking in modern India developed in the shadow of the independence struggle, which identified itself with other movements against Western colonialism and was anchored in socialism.

Democracy and a centrally planned economy, it was argued, would afford the backward groups better economic opportunities, provide for an equitable distribution of wealth, and narrow the gaps between economic classes. Because Muslim estrangement is the result of the community's economic backwardness, it was reasoned, that problem, too, will be resolved in this process. India's first Prime Minister Jawaharlal Nehru, a Fabian socialist, was among the earliest exponents of this theory. "The real thing to my mind," he asserted, "is the economic factor. If we lay stress on this and divert public attention to it we shall find automatically that religious differences recede into the background and a common bond unites different groups."

India's forty-year history appears to belie the socialist hypothesis. Despite a considerable overall growth rate (about 5 percent during the five-year plan that ended in 1985), the gaps between economic classes remain as wide as ever, and the Muslims languish in the lower ranks of the 40 percent of Indians who are below the poverty line. India, like most other underdeveloped socialist economies, is gradually realizing that distributive justice means little in a society that has little to distribute.

Islamic obscurantism

In their penchant to explain the Hindu-Muslim cleavage in terms of a historic "class struggle," Indian social thinkers generally have ignored what probably is the most potent cause of Muslim backwardness. The Islam that once plunged Muslims into world conquest and social reforms stressed man's responsibilities as God's "viceroy on Earth." With the loss of empires, Muslims began to emphasize more their duties as worshipers of God. The outlook that this later Islam tends to inculcate is world-denying. Muslims are taught to rely more on God than on their own efforts for their well-being. A true Muslim is not supposed to even worry about his material well-being. Man's sustenance is predetermined by God.

My former brother-in-law is a scholar from India's famous Deobond Islamic academy and a devout Muslim. Last fall he divorced my sister because she and I had insisted on bringing their children to the United States to seek a better life than his eighty dollar monthly income could allow them. His argument: Quest for wealth would cause the children to stray from the path of God. So what if they have to live humbly for the few fleeting years they have on this planet? And besides, isn't the American businessman, officeworker, or cabdriver really wasting his life scrambling for the means of living and never trying to find out what—if anything—living is about?

The average Indian Muslim is not a Deobond scholar. He does not even know the meaning of the Arabic scriptures he recites five times a day in his prayers. Yet the idea that life here on earth is not important dulls his interest in modernity, society, statecraft, and environment.

Most Hindus, and many Indian social thinkers, take little note of this phenomenon, and hence complain that "the Indian Muslims behave as stateless citizens and as if they are temporarily living in this country" (Durrany, 1984). The Muslim could tell them that he is on this planet on a brief sojourn. In fact, Muslim backwardness is not just an Indian problem. It is worldwide. In Nigeria, Malaysia, the Philippines, and Indonesia, Muslims are economically and educationally behind other ethnic groups with whom they share territory. Middle Eastern Muslims present a more revealing picture. Petrodollars have swung open the door to the resources generated by the Western work ethic and education, but Western education and industry still elude them.

The Sikh example

The Sikh-Hindu feud is a more telling indictment of the theory linking communal strife to a historic "class struggle." Just as the British conquered much of the rest of India from minority Muslims, they seized Punjab from a minority Sikh government. After Sikhs lost the Punjab kingdom, they confined themselves to agriculture and soldiering.

Punjabis are an industrious people. Industry is also encouraged by the Sikh faith. And so, if Muslims in the rest of India wallowed on the lowest rung of the economic ladder, the Sikhs quickly ascended to the highest. The Punjabis, especially the Jat Sikhs, spearheaded India's "green revolution" of the 1960s, contributing more than 50 percent of the nation's central food reserve. In per hectare rice and wheat yield, Punjab has broken the world record. Its per capita income is double the Indian average, and wage rates are the highest in the country. A Punjabi's average life expectancy of sixty-five years dwarfs the Indian average of forty-seven years.

The greatest benefit of the green revolution has, of course, accrued to the farmers who own the larger farms and can better afford modern technology. Yet, compared to the rest of India, even ordinary Punjabis are better off. Higher wage-rates and steadier employment ensured by double- and triple-cropping have quadrupled Punjabi farm workers' income since the onset of the green revolution.

Sikh secessionists, like secessionists everywhere else, have economic grievances. Yet the Sikh struggle clearly defies the definition of "class struggle." (Or can it be revised to include the reverse class struggle of the bourgeoisie to "expropriate" the less privileged?)

Religion versus community

Then what have the Indians been fighting so long and relentlessly for? Religion? Not really. Few of the people who have been in the vanguard of communal movements are known for religious piety or concern.

Mohammad Ali Jinnah, the father of the Muslim nationalist movement that led to the founding of Pakistan, was a thoroughly Westernized, Oxford-educated barrister who seldom practiced the Islamic faith. The orthodox Deoband group of theologians opposed the creation of Pakistan. Their leader, Maulana Hussein Ahmad Madani, maintained that territorial nationalism is alien to Islam, which calls for an international religious community. The more politicized but fundamentalist Jamaat-i-Islami believes in Islamic statecraft. But it also stayed away from the Pakistan movement because, lamented Syed Abul A'la Maodoodi, Jamaat's founder, in the whole movement "there was not one who could be credited with an Islamic point of view."

The same is true of Hindu communalism. V.D. Savarkar, the theoretician of the anti-Muslim RSS, was a practicing atheist. He asserted that one does not need to follow a creed to become a Hindu; declaring oneself Hindu was enough. The two dominant Hindu communal organizations, the RSS and VHP, are essentially concerned with organizing Hindus to promote Hindu culture, boost morale, and preserve India's territorial integrity. These groups are sidestepping key precepts of traditional Hinduism, such as caste segregation, supremacy of the clergy, and renunciation of mundane pursuits.

Hindu communalists view Hindus—not Indians —as a nation. India, the "sacred abode" of that nation, is the "Mother-Goddess." Promoting the 3,500-year-old Hindu culture and defending India's territorial unity, according to them, are Hindu religious duties; hence, they struggle against the "disruptive" strains in Indian society: Muslim, Christian, and Sikh cultures.

Muslims and Sikhs remain unreconciled to this conception of Indian nationalism and civilization. They seek to assert their communal identities and to preserve what they consider their social and cultural heritage.

The March 1985 Hindu-Muslim riots in Ahmedabad offer an example. Liquor is banned, but an underground business thrives in Ahmedabad. Disputes arise now and then between Hindu manufacturers and Muslim carriers over remuneration. Often, police join the fray over the bribes they have to be paid to overlook the illicit trade. One such dispute turned into a major Hindu-Muslim riot, in which Alam Zeb, a notorious liquor-gang leader, emerged as leader of the Muslims. His courage and intense loyalty to his community is credited with saving many Muslim lives. Later, Zeb was killed by police in a dispute over bribes. When his body was brought to Bombay for the funeral, fifty thousand Muslim mourners came down the street carrying placards extolling his heroism and service to the cause of Islam. A plaque on his grave reads:"Shaheed-i-Millat Alam Zeb"—Martyr of the (Islamic) Nation Alem Zeb. To appreciate the irony one should recall that liquor is among the few strictly forbidden commodities in Islam.

Communalism versus nationalism

The Indian's communal affinity often outweighs his allegiance to his class, caste, region, or tongue. Communal symbols are sometimes the most prized values among the lower-class people, who cannot boast of wealth, aristocracy, or white-collar jobs. Communal affinity outweighs class comradery with members of other communities. The word "communalism" is used in a special sense in the Indian context. It means the belief among members of a religious community that they not only share a common faith but are also bound by common economic, political, social, and cultural ties. Naturally, it also implies consciousness of the discreetness of their ways of life from those of other communities.

In 1986, when the *Deccan Herald* of Mysore, India, ran a short story entitled "Mohammed the Idiot," the anger among Indian Muslims was universal. One of the processions in protest was composed of horribly poor Muslims from Mysore's Gandhi Nagar slums. They were challenged, not by the mill-owners or middlemen, who supposedly are their "class enemies," but by the Harijans, the former untouchables who form the lowest layer of Hindu society. The savage fighting that followed left four persons dead, about two hundred vehicles vandalized and more than four hundred homes looted, burned or damaged.

"What startles the objective observer," lamented an analyst at the mass-circulated *Indian Express,* "is the fact that whether the victims are Hindus or Muslims, they are comrades in poverty and privation. But not even this common bond deterred them from going at each other's throats in the name of religion" (Subha Rao 1987).

Communal fervor also cuts across caste, linguistic, and territorial barriers. When Prime Minister Indira Gandhi, a Hindu Brahman, was killed by two Sikhs in 1984, Hindus irrespective of caste, tongue, region, or occupation cried out in anguish, and many called for revenge. More than two thousand Sikhs were killed in the carnage that followed. On the other side of the fence, Sikhs, from Amritsar, India, to London, to New York, to Vancouver, Canada, extolled the bravery of the Sikhs who assassinated Mrs. Gandhi in retaliation for her order to storm the Golden Temple, which had been used as a sanctuary for Sikh terrorists.

The many linguistic groups in India have fought long and hard for official recognition of their languages. Yet when a choice had to be made between mother tongue and communal values, the tongue often has lost out. That brings us back to the Sikh-Hindu imbroglio. After India became independent, the Jawaharlal Nehru government set about redrawing boundaries of Indian states to afford every major linguistic group a state. Naturally, the Sikhs of Punjab demanded a state for the Punjabi-speaking people. But as soon as it became apparent that Sikhs would outnumber Hindus in the proposed Punjab state, several Hindu organizations began campaigning against a Punjab state. In a desperate attempt to build a case against it, millions of Punjabi-speaking Hindus routinely lied to census takers and declared their mother tongue to be Hindi. Many had to announce in Punjabi (because that was the only language they spoke) that their native tongue actually was Hindi! Hindu resistance to a Punjab state marked the beginning of Sikh-Hindu estrangement.

Hindus and Muslims in Bengal shared common territory for millennia until, again, communalism put their geographical ties to a test. The division, reunification, and redivision of Bengal is a classic example of communal values winning over territorial loyalty. In 1905, the British colonial government divided the old Bengal into two provinces for administrative convenience. Attached to Assam, East Bengal (today's Bangladesh) turned out to be a Muslim-majority province. Hindu communal groups, apprehensive of Muslim dominance in the new province, launched virulent agitation against the partition, forcing the British to reunify Bengal in 1911.

In Punjab, Hindus and Sikhs initiated the first

division of their historic province in 1947 to ensure the exclusion of the Sikh- and Hindu-majority districts from Pakistan. That partition pitted Punjabi-speaking Sikhs against Hindus in the worst carnage in Indian history. The Indian part of Punjab was redivided in 1966 to create the present Sikh-majority state. And now, a new communal bloodbath has begun between Punjabi-speaking Sikhs and Punjabi-speaking Hindus over the secession of the Indian Punjab.

Jump-starting a nation

The Indian leaders who spearheaded the independence struggle were educated in British schools. While they detested Western colonialism, they greatly admired Western concepts of nationalism and democracy and their corollary institutions, such as religion-neutral parties, elections, and legislatures. They were a proud people and could not imagine why their great country could not emulate the achievements of other nations. In their pride and enthusiasm to create a brave new world, they apparently overlooked their countrymen's deep attachment to their indigenous communal and ethnic values. Of course, India needed to be freed from the colonial yoke, and there was no viable alternative to territorial nationalism and a democratic political order. Yet they erred in assuming that Indians' communal or ethnic ties would "automatically recede into the background," as Nehru had predicted.

This assumption led them to adopt a political system that is more suited to a homogenous nation like Britain. It has a strong central government run by a parliamentary majority; if the people do not like the deeds of a government, they theoretically can send a new parliamentary majority with a new mandate at the next election.

In the multicommunal, multiethnic India, the recipe does not work. Communal and ethnic minorities can never expect to gain a parliamentary majority, and so their grievances cannot ordinarily be redressed through the ballot box. This frustration partly explains the minority challenge to the system: the Gurkha rebellion in Darjeeling; the Munda-Oraon-Ho-Santhal uprising in Bihar, Orissa, Madhya Pradesh, and West Bengal; the Naga (mostly Christian) protests in Nagaland; and the caste riots in several states. Communal conflicts, however, appear to be the most formidable of all centrifugal challenges. Sikh communalism, meanwhile, has assumed the garb of a nationalist movement.

An answer appears to lie in the decentralization of political powers. One may wonder whether, had India's founding fathers been educated at Harvard and Yale instead of Oxford and Cambridge, the country might have started off with an American political model, with wide powers given to the states and checks and balances established between government branches—which appears to be more suited to India's needs. It would allow Muslims and ethnic minorities to exert influence on authorities and states where they live in substantial numbers. That would diffuse the consternation that sparks the communal conflicts. It appears now that Sikh separatism in particular cannot be overcome without transfer of substantial powers to Punjab.

While these or other constitutional and political formulas might alleviate the fissiparous trends, they are unlikely to cure the cause of communal and ethnic discord. The answer appears to lie in a redefinition of Indian nationalism. Indians are not a nation like the British, French, Italians, or even Americans. A population of eight hundred million speaking fifteen major languages and sixteen hundred dialects, belonging to several major religions and countless sects, and embracing numerous castes, subcastes, and tribes, they are a nation of nationalities, communities, and cultures. Communal relations can be improved and Indian nationalism truly served, only through the appreciation of the diversity of cultural and religious values that make India unique. Calls for resistance to "disruptive" cultural trends need to be replaced by pleas for respect for ethnic and communal customs, heritage, pride, and susceptibilities. This is a tall order that cannot be filled by a leader, group, or political party. It is the job of a nationwide interparty, interfaith, intercaste campaign.

Additional Reading

N. Gerald Barrier, ed., *Roots of Communalism*, South Asia Books, Columbia, Mo.

Bipan Chandra, *Communalism in Modern India*, Vikas Publishing House, New Delhi, 1986 edition.

Khurramshah Durrany, "The Dilemma of Identity Dogs Indian Muslims," *The Hindustan Times*, New Delhi, Jan. 10, 1984.

S. Gopal, ed., *Jawaharlal Nehru: Selected Works*, vol. 5, New Delhi, 1972.

Kuldip Nayar and Khushwant Singh, *Tragedy of Punjab*, Vision Books, New Delhi, 1987.

Satya M. Rai, "Gandhi and the Communal Politics in India" in *Gandhi and Politics in India*, edited by Verinder Grover, Deep & Deep Publications, New Delhi, 1987.

V.N. Subha Rao, "A Moment of Madness in the City of Palaces," *Ethnic Conflicts in South Asia*.

P.N. Rashtogi, *Ethnic Tensions in India*, Mittal Publications, Delhi.

Khalid B. Saeed, *Pakistan—The Formative Phase —1857–1948*, London, 1968.

Ghanshyan Sgah, *The 1969 Communal Riots in Ahmedabad: A Case Study in Communal Riots in Post-Independence India*, edited by Asghar Ali, Sangam Books, Hyderabad, India, 1984.

Islam: Religion Has Potential to Reshape World

Tom Hundley

Knight-Ridder Newspapers

Wearing blue tennis shoes, fatigues and a red headband that proclaims "Nobody is greater than God," Mustafa Haidari, a 22-year-old Iranian foot soldier in the legions of Ayatollah Khomeini, explained that he is "fighting to uphold the dignity of Islam."

In the last five weeks alone, tens of thousands of Iranian soldiers have been slaughtered on the marshy flatlands along the Shatt al Arab waterway in a holy war between Iraq and Iran that has dragged on for 6½ years. But for Haidari, who is serving his second tour on this battlefield, death is an invitation.

"The people of Iran," he explained, "respect the blood of martyrs."

Martyrs, holy wars, suicide bombings and hijackings—ever since a mob of students seized the U.S. Embassy in Tehran seven years ago, Americans have been buffeted by a bewildering succession of headlines linked to the "Islamic fundamentalism" of Mustafa Haidari and the Iran of Ayatollah Khomeini.

Even today, the headlines are often dominated by the latest kidnappings in Beirut, and yet another American presidency is paying a heavy price for getting too close to Iran, the eye of this whirlwind.

But what is happening in the Moslem world is something far more profound than religious fury or the revival of a 1,400-year-old faith. That is the message that emerges from interviews with specialists as well as with ordinary people across the Islamic heartland.

From Morocco to the Philippines, from the Sudan to Yugoslavia, there is a growing sense among the world's 850 million Moslems that their traditional Islamic values are under attack from alien ideologies—specifically, from the competing secular ideologies of the United States and the Soviet Union.

The response has been a powerful resurgence of religious sentiment fueled by a belief that Islam offers an alternative to the "materialistic capitalism" of the West and to the "godless communism" of the Soviet Union.

Because Islam's appeal transcends ethnic and national boundaries, and because its basic ideological foundations are already deeply imbedded in one-fifth of the world's population, the Islamic movement's potential for reshaping global politics is enormous.

Often characterized in the West as Islamic fundamentalism, it is actually a broad-based but highly fragmented social movement aimed at bringing the political systems of Moslem countries in line with deeply held personal beliefs.

On another battlefield in another holy war a thousand miles from the Persian Gulf war, Malik Mujahid Nazir expresses the depth of his beliefs with certainty: "If we die fighting the Russians, we will be awarded paradise."

But Nazir, a barrel-chested man with a ferocious black beard, is confident that his Khugani tribesmen will defeat the Soviet troops that have been occupying their lands in Afghanistan since 1979.

Fourteen hundred years of history and divine will are on the side of the Afghan rebels known as the mujahideen, he tells a visitor to the dusty refugee camp at the foot of the Hindu Kush mountains on the Pakistan border.

"At the time of our Holy Prophet, the Moslem armies were able to overcome enemies who greatly outnumbered them. It is our faith that those who stand in the way of Allah will be defeated."

Sipping from a bottle of Coca-Cola, ignoring the swarming flies that have invaded the camp's mud- and dung-walled guest house, Nazir explains why he and the Afghan rebels are so driven by their faith.

"We call our resistance jihad (holy war) because the Russians have attacked our beliefs. They are taking away our Islamic traditions and trying to convert Afghanistan to communism," Nazir says through an interpreter.

"The Russians also want to destroy the purdah system and permit the free mixing of males and females. We believe such things generate many vices. They want to make it possible for a father to sleep with his daughter."

These sentiments might sound simplistic or naive to a Western audience, but among the world's Moslems they would strike a responsive cord.

Viewed against this background, it is easy to understand why Marvin Zonis of the University of Chicago's Middle East Institute has called the Islamic movement "the single most impressive polit-

Reprinted from *Fort Collins Coloradoan*, February 15, 1987.

ical ideology which has been proposed in the 20th century since the Bolshevik Revolution."

Palpable signs of the Islamic movement's strength can be seen throughout the Moslem world.

In Iran, the Islamic revolution has been relentless. Each week thousands of young men heed the call for volunteers to fight Iraq in a war that has been portrayed as a struggle against the enemies of Islam.

Portraits of the Supreme Guide, Ayatollah Khomeini, hang in every public place. Revolutionary Guards, identifiable by their drab olive parkas, seem to be in charge of running everything from the Tehran airport to the ever-expanding cemetery reserved for the war's martyrs on the southern outskirts of the city.

Iran has been totally transformed by the reign of the ayatollahs, while elsewhere in the Islamic world, newspapers seem to be devoting much more space to Islamic affairs. Television is crowded with religious programming. And ever greater numbers of pilgrims are inspired to visit the holy shrines in Mecca and Medina.

In smart sections of Cairo, boutiques featuring "Islamic fashions" are doing a brisk business as more women return to the hijab, the modest head-covering. Beards, a Moslem sign of piety, are undergoing a revival among young men.

Alcohol, once freely available in Pakistan, may now be consumed only by foreigners—after they fill out two forms in triplicate swearing that they are not Moslems. Under Islamic law, violators face public flogging. Kuwait, which once turned a blind eye to the private use of alcohol by foreigners, has recently cracked down.

Mosque construction is booming. Turkey had 20,000 mosques at the end of World War II; today it has 72,000, outpacing population growth by 40 percent despite the government's official policy of secularization. Bahrain, a compact nation with only 250,000 citizens, has more than a thousand mosques. Saudi Arabia, a nation of 9 million, which already has 20,000 mosques, recently announced plans to add 2,000 more. Even the Soviet Union, whose southern region is populated by 44 million Moslems, has tolerated a mild surge in new mosques.

Perhaps the most telling sign of the Islamic movement's strength is its popularity among the educated. At universities, administrators say students are flocking to Islamic studies programs. They are pressuring the universities to "Islamicize" the curricula of traditional fields such as economics and law—that is, to teach them in accordance with Moslem religious traditions. And at many campuses, male and female students have demanded to be segregated by sex.

"I don't like it, but we are surrounded," said Ahmed el-Shafti, an economics professor at Cairo University. "This religious sentiment is widespread among the young. It's serious and you cannot ignore it or repress it. We have to come to terms with it."

Iran remains the symbolic heart of the Islamic movement. Although the perceived extremism of Ayatollah Khomeini and the excesses of his theocratic regime have tarnished Iran's reputation in the eyes of much of the Moslem world, the 1978-79 Iranian revolution remains the one shining triumph of Islam over the West in the modern era.

The Iranian experience, though closely identified with the Moslem minority Shiite sect, was a jolt of adrenaline shot through the entire body of Islam. Moslems everywhere began to assert themselves with militant determination against regimes that they view as repressive, corrupt and anti-Islamic. The result has been a continuing string of violent confrontations:

• Before 1978, Lebanon's Shiites were politically irrelevant even though they were the largest of that country's many religious cantons. Today, Shiite militias control west Beirut and most of southern Lebanon. One Shiite faction, the Hizballah, Party of God, has orchestrated a string of deadly attacks against U.S. targets and continues to hold a number of kidnapped Westerners.

• In Egypt, Islamic extremists in the army gunned down President Anwar Sadat; five years later, the government of Hosni Mubarak is still rooting out extremist elements within the military.

• In Saudi Arabia, the monarchy was stunned in 1979 when Mecca's Grand Mosque, Islam's holiest shrine, was seized by extremists whose proclaimed mission was to cleanse Islam of the corruption of the royal family.

• In Syria, President Hafez Assad laid siege to one of his own cities in an effort to crush an Islamic fundamentalist movement. Thousands were killed, but the fundamentalists remain the single biggest threat to the regime's stability.

• In Pakistan, seven years after a mob burned the U.S. Embassy, opposition politicians continue to press the Islamic government of Mohammad Zia ul Haq to distance itself from the United States.

The Islamic world, the locus of so much unrest, is of vital strategic interest to the United States: Egypt is the linchpin of U.S. efforts to resolve the Arab-Israeli conflict, the Persian Gulf states contain 60 percent of the world's proven oil reserves, and Pakistan is considered a "front-line state" in the struggle to contain Soviet expansion.

But successive U.S. administrations have attempted to deal with the Islamic movement as an element of superpower rivalry, rather than come to grips with it as an independent force. U.S. embassies in Moslem countries have become isolated fortresses bristling with anti-terrorism devices—a stark symbol of the failure to heed the depth and intensity of the Islamic movement.

This failure has been costly: 52 Americans held hostage in Iran for more than a year, 68 killed in embassy bombings in Beirut and Kuwait, 241 Marines killed in Beirut by a suicide bomber, and more than a dozen Americans kidnapped in Lebanon over the last three years, eight of whom are still being held.

The continued misreading by U.S. policymakers of the politics of the Islamic movement, its key players and what motivates them is one of the more obvious factors in the controversy over the Reagan administration's secret arms sales to Iran.k

Because only the excesses of the Islamic movement tend to make news in the United States, many Americans equate it with violence and fanaticism. But fanatics and extremists represent only the fringe.

Islam, in fact, emphasizes economic and social justice. From the beginning, the faith of Muhammad strove to improve the lot of society's have-nots: women, slaves, orphans and the poor.

For strict Moslem fundamentalists, distinctions between U.S. capitalism and Soviet communism are irrelevant. As American scholar Daniel Pipes, director of Foreign Policy Research Institute in Philadelphia, has observed, "The two Western cultures are alike—and different from Islam—in many ways. Men wear pants, women wear skirts and everyone sits on chairs. The intelligentsia in both countries listen to the same classical music, attend the same plays, and admire the same oil paintings."

"Mr. Reagan and Mr. Gorbachev are the same face," says Maulana Noorani, a Pakistani cleric. "America and Russia both want to destroy Islam. We must resist. We must make Islam the third superpower."

THE 10 YEARS
OF CHAOS 運 動

***Three noted
Chinese sportsmen
tell how their
careers were
derailed by the
Cultural
Revolution***

SARAH BALLARD

HUANG JIAN HAD BEEN THE coach of China's national track and field team. He had trained two high jumpers who broke records and brought glory to China when it was an unknown in international sport. Now he's standing alone on a platform in front of a jeering mob, bent forward from the waist, his back straight and his arms stretched out and back from his sides in the "airplane position." The mob knows he's an intellectual and has been led to believe he's a spy and a traitor as well. It would like nothing more than to see him drop to his knees from the pain of holding the airplane position. Most intellectuals are skinny and weak and topple after 10 minutes. Huang lasts for an hour. "I was proud because they could see I was a sportsman," he says of that day in the mid-1960s.

China's Great Cultural Revolution has been called "a settling of accounts on a cosmic scale." The powerless avenged themselves against the powerful, the young against the old, students against their teachers, children against their parents, friends against friends. Before it ran its 10-year course, hundreds of thousands died, more were mentally or physically crippled, uncounted treasures of Chinese antiquity were destroyed, the national economy ground to a halt, the old Communist Party structure was dismantled, the universities were closed, and, in the end, a populace that for decades had endured hardship, often terrible, grinding hardship, in the name of Mao Tsetung and his revolutionary vision, had become disillusioned.

The Cultural Revolution officially began in 1966, when Mao set out to rekindle China's revolutionary fire, which he believed was being extinguished by revisionist intellectuals, opportunistic bureaucrats and "capitalist roaders." He declared war on the Four Olds—old ideas, old culture, old customs and old habits—and he unleashed the Red Guards, an army of several million student zealots, ages 9 to 18. They roamed the country, ferreting out and "reeducating" enemies of the people wherever they found them.

Not surprisingly, considering the forces Mao had unleashed, the Cultural Revolution soon outgrew his capacity to control it. In July of 1968 he disbanded the Red Guards, sent perhaps as many as 14 million of them to work in the countryside and replaced them as the arbiters of the people's behavior with the People's Liberation Army. Still, except for a relaxation of tension in 1970, '71 and '72, the storm raged on until Mao's death in '76.

The earliest indication to the outside world that athletes had been drawn into the vortex of the Cultural Revolution was the sudden withdrawal of China's No. 1-ranked table-tennis team from the 1967 World Championships in Stockholm. News from inside China emerged slowly in those days, but the rumors were stunning. In the case of the table-tennis players, they were later found to have been mostly true. Chuang Tse-tung, the world champion from 1961 through '66 and China's first modern sports hero, along with other team members and their coaches, had been jailed for having "followed the capitalist road" of Mao's political rival, Liu Shao-ch'i.

Nothing more was heard of Chuang for three years; he had been given up for dead by the world's table-tennis fans when suddenly he appeared in a Chinese exhibition match. By 1972 he was rehabilitated and the leader of a table tennis delegation that toured the U.S. during the period of Ping-Pong diplomacy that marked the reopening of relations between the U.S. and China.

Once again, however, Chuang had hitched his wagon to the wrong political star. His protector was Chiang Ch'ing, Mao's ultraleftist wife, and when she and the rest of the infamous Gang of Four fell after Mao's death, Chuang fell with them. It's said that, upon being jailed again, he tried to hang himself in his cell, but he was cut down by his captors before he succeeded.

Today Chuang, now known as Zhuang Zedong, is a table-tennis coach at a Beijing recreation center for children. He's lucky to be alive—and luckier still to be out of the sometimes dangerous Chinese limelight. Less fortunate were two of his colleagues: Jung Kuo-tuan, the world table-tennis champion in 1959, and Fu Chi-fang, a coach of that era. Tainted by "foreignism" because they were returned Chinese, Jung and Fu both were persecuted. And both committed suicide.

Some of the survivors of the Cultural Revolution are now powers in the Chinese sports establishment. Two of them, Yuan Weimin, a former volleyball player, and Zhang Jian, who was a gymnast, were athletes in their prime when the Cultural Revolution began. Both made successful comebacks as coaches and now have been rewarded for their success with elevation to the higher ranks of the sports hierarchy. Huang, the track coach who held the airplane position for an hour, is back at his old job of guiding China's track and field team, this time as it prepares for the Seoul Olympics.

Yuan's office is in the Sports Federation headquarters in Beijing. At 49, he's a national hero and, as a vice-minister of the Commission for Physical Culture and Sports, one of the highest-ranked sports officials in China, yet his office could belong to the vice-principal of an aging, inner-city American high school. The only indication there of Yuan's importance is the two telephones sitting on his desk, one of which is red.

"For 10 years everything stopped everywhere in China," says Yuan. "But since 1978, when the National People's Congress set a new policy of openness and reform, 152 Chinese athletes have won 230 world titles. We have had exchanges with 139 countries and 5,000 visits abroad by 60,000

athletes. That's a very large step in a very short time."

Yuan was spared the worst excesses of the Cultural Revolution because he was the son of an average peasant and, therefore, was considered politically reliable according to Mao's caste system. On the other hand, in 1966 Yuan was a setter on the national volleyball team and a student at Nanjing Sports Institute. Being a student made him an intellectual and, therefore, politically suspect. As a result, while he was not persecuted by the Red Guards as other intellectuals were, he did become the victim of a sort of circumstantial ostracism: He was unable to play volleyball because all of the team members had been sent home, unable to be a student because his institute—and all others—had closed down, and unable to work for eight years because the work for which he was trained, coaching, didn't exist.

"The Cultural Revolution arrived when I was at my peak as a player," says Yuan. "Afterward I tried to play. Although the spirit was willing, the flesh was not able. Those were my twilight years. During that time I spent much time studying by myself about volleyball teaching. I didn't involve myself in the fighting."

When the Cultural Revolution passed, China's athletes were in sorry shape. All had been sent home when the universities and training centers in the big cities were closed down, and if home was a poor farming area, which it often was, they were not only without training for at least five years, but they were also malnourished and prey to injury. City dwellers didn't fare much better. For example, a good 400-meter runner whose former coaches refused him protection on account of his bad class background, was sent to the countryside for three years. He tried to stay in shape by bounding and running in place, but when he attempted a comeback, the years of poor diet and heavy farm labor took their toll in torn tendons, and his athletic career was finished.

Beginning in 1976, Yuan's job was to restore women's volleyball to its previous level—fast. He did much more than that. Applying strict discipline and rigorous training methods, he led the Chinese women's national team from obscurity (14th in '76) to world dominance in five years. His teams won the World Cup in '81, the world championship in '82 and the Olympic gold medal in '84.

When he returned from the Los Angeles Games, Yuan was a hero. He was promoted to vice-minister of the Commission for Physical Culture and Sports and, in 1985, to membership on the Party's Central Committee. His book, *My Way of Teaching*, which was published in 1987, sold out the day it hit the bookstore shelves.

"What I failed to fulfill as a player, I tried to fulfill as a coach," Yuan says.

Zhang is a former gymnast who is now deputy

director of the training bureau of the State Commission for Physical Culture and Sports. He's a small man with a flat stomach and broad shoulders who looks younger than his 45 years, not handsome but virile, a man of action. He wore running shoes to my interview with him, and throughout it he perched on the cushion of an overstuffed sofa in the VIP reception room of the Beijing Gymnasium, as if awaiting a signal to vault its antimacassared arm and be gone.

Zhang, who's from Kunming, the capital of Yunnan Province in southwest China, is the son of a forest worker (good class background) and a minor local official (good political background). The Cultural Revolution closed the book on Zhang's career as a gymnast, just as it did on Yuan's in volleyball, but Zhang scarcely felt the loss, even though his team finished fourth at the World Championships in 1962. "If I look back, I think the Cultural Revolution was a pity, because I'd begun to do well. But at the time I was very happy to have a rest," he said.

With no discernible regret, Zhang described the years from 1966 to '70 as a sort of prolonged spring vacation. "I traveled for four years from place to place, seeing all the famous sights in China," he said. "I didn't think much about politics. I only cared about free time to relax and make plans. I had free train tickets and free lodging and an allowance. I traveled with a gymnast from the women's team, and we were married in 1968."

The only Chinese allowed to travel in those years were the Red Guards, who in addition to being given train tickets, got free lodging and an allowance as they "learned revolution by making revolution." Zhang doesn't say he was a Red Guard, but chances are he was at least a fellow traveler. In any case, a year after the Red Guards were disbanded, Zhang was made a coach.

An ancient Chinese saying, "Become an official and get rich," has renewed validity in today's China, although prosperity, especially in the crowded cities, may take the form of a three-room apartment in a postwar building and not much more. Unlike some bureaucrats, however, sports officials have to earn their perks. Zhang got his by scouting gymnastic talent in Jiangxi Province and producing Tong Fei, who won a gold medal at the 1982 World Cup, two silvers at the Los Angeles Olympics and two golds and a silver at the '85 World Championships.

"I was looking for talent in a school and noticed that one boy came to the window every day to watch practice," said Zhang. "So I went outside to catch him, and coached him for 14 years." When Tong made the national team in 1979 and went to Beijing to train, Zhang went with him as the new national coach. Now Zhang finds such talent harder to come by. "Our family planning policy is one family, one child," he said. "Today young athletes cannot endure suffering as well because children are overprotected by their parents. Any athlete who wants to become a star has to endure something."

Yuan, the volleyball player, and Zhang, the gymnast, were comparative bystanders at the time of the Cultural Revolution. Certainly their athletic careers were ruined, and, at least to Yuan, the years they spent waiting for the chaos to subside so they could get on with their work seemed endless. But they were spared the vengeance of the mobs that Huang, the track coach, endured.

Huang's ordeal at the hands of the Red Guards was harsh because, besides being a college graduate himself, he was the son of a professor of foreign languages at Fudan University in Shanghai. Furthermore, though Huang had been born in China, he'd been raised in the Soviet Union. An intellectual background combined with foreign contacts, including a wife who is half Soviet, half Chinese, made him a prime target for the anti-intellectual and xenophobic hysteria that characterized the early years of the Cultural Revolution.

In an open letter written by one of his best friends, Huang was accused of spying. The letter led to his being fired, criticized in wall posters and vilified at mass meetings. "Everything I did was wrong, nothing was right," Huang says. "Now it seems like a joke." For thousands of less hardy Chinese, the betrayal by friends and coworkers and the loss of dignity in front of ignorant mobs was unbearable. Suicide was the only recourse.

After the mass meetings came solitary confinement. For a year and three months Huang, a cheerful and gregarious man, spoke to no one save his Red Guard captors. In winter he was confined to an unheated basement, in summer to a stifling attic. His only exercise was a half hour of walking in a confined space each day. A light was kept burning over his bed all night, and during the day, he was expected to read from Mao's writings.

"Because I know Americans like pranks, I will tell you about a prank," says Huang. "As a coach I was in the habit of taking a rest after lunch and before training. So to have my rest in prison, I surrounded myself with the books of Chairman Mao, and then I put my head on my hand and slept. My ruse was successful for only one day. On the second day, a Red Guard said, 'What are you doing?' I said, 'I'm reading.' The Red Guard said, 'You're lying. I just listened to you snoring for 15 minutes.'" After that Huang had to recite Mao's works out loud.

"When they tried to force me to write a confession, I didn't fight with them," says Huang. "I only debated. After one year and three months they got nothing, so they sent me to the country."

Following three years of hard farm labor on short rations, Huang was allowed to return to Beijing, but his lot scarcely improved. For the next six years no one would give him work. He was paid the universal subsistence allowance, which even today, in a much improved economy, is still very low, but not until 1976, after Mao died and the Gang of Four had fallen, was Huang allowed to return to his old job.

"I endured because from the age of two until 24 I lived in the Soviet Union," he says. "My father worked in the underground with Chou when it was very dangerous. In 1928 my father was sent to the Sixth Party Congress in Moscow, and a year later my mother and I were sent there to join him. Two bodyguards went along to protect us. When Kuomintang [Nationalist Chinese] soldiers searched the train at the border, the bodyguards hid me in a basket and covered me with many old and dirty things. At first they were afraid I would cry. When I didn't cry, they were afraid I had suffocated, but when we were across the border, they found I was merely asleep. My mother always says, 'Even then you liked to sleep.'

"World War II was very hard in the Soviet Union. Everybody was hungry. So I am well-suited to any bad situation." Huang points to a small scar in the crook of his left elbow. "I gave blood every month to get money and a ration card. What most attracted me was that with the ration card I could get canned meat from America, which was delicious. I was very young, and to me the United States was famous only for this meat."

In the early 1930s, Huang's parents returned to their work in the revolutionary underground in China, leaving him to be raised at the International Children's Garden, outside Moscow, with other orphans of revolutionary storms. He was a good-natured but unruly boy who loved sports. In 1938 Chou, who had been wounded, went to Moscow for medical treatment, and he paid a visit to the Children's Garden. When the great man asked the children what they wanted to be when they grew up, Huang, who was 11, had no answer. "I was ashamed because I had never thought about the future," he says. "Then all the children shouted, 'He's an athlete!' When I heard that I thought maybe it was right, but I didn't know what Chou would think. To my surprise, he said, 'I like sports, too. When I was doing underground work, the enemy couldn't catch me because I could run fast and far.' "

That was all the endorsement Huang needed. After graduating from a Soviet sports high school, he taught physical education at a Soviet agricul-

tural institute. By studying nights on his own he gained entrance to the Moscow Physical Education Institute, and in 1951, degree in hand, he was ready to return to China, which was knee deep in Soviet experts in the early 1950s. With his Moscow training, Huang soon became the leading track coach. His greatest successes were his high jumpers—a woman, Cheng Feng-jung, and a man, Ni Chih-chin. Cheng set a world record in '57, as did Ni in '61, but his mark was never officially recognized because by then China had dropped out of the IAAF, the world governing body of track and field.

Today Huang lives with his wife and two cats in a small apartment in a Beijing building reserved for the coaches of national teams. The hallways and stairwells are dark and grimy, but the interior of their apartment is tidy and filled to overflowing with souvenirs of his eventful life. Stuffed toy animals, painted Russian dolls, photographs and trophies line the shelves in the foyer.

Huang counts himself lucky. "Looking back, I think my experience wasn't the worst," he says. His father, for instance, was jailed for eight years. Huang's best performer now is another high jumper, but he's injured, so Huang cannot hope for a medal in Seoul. "We have some good women in the shot put," he says, "but in other events we can get maybe a sixth or an eighth."

And how does he feel about the 10 lost years and the friends who turned against him? "Most of them regret what they did to me," he says. "People were forced to do it out of fear and pressure from other people. I look at it with historical perspective, and I forgive them."

The Cultural Revolution is now referred to in China as the 10 Years of Chaos. Its survivors are like aging veterans of an unpopular war: They tell their stories—sometimes, as Huang does, with humor—to a younger generation already growing weary of the recounting. For the time being, until the political pendulum begins its next swing, the young adults of China have put the pursuit of material comfort ahead of political idealism and revolutionary virtues. Still, the Cultural Revolution was a traumatic national experience, and its psychic scars linger even in the young.

Yu Daihua, a 33-year-old translator for the All-China Sports Federation, expressed a sadness that his elders, Zhang, Yuan and Huang, had avoided putting into words. "If you live in the community, it's difficult to speak; you can only feel. I think earlier it was man against nature, man against animals. Then man got guns, and it was no longer man against animals. I think it is now man against man." Yu paused to think. "We could have been much faster in reform."

Marx had it wrong. Does Gorbachev?

Seweryn Bialer

Seweryn Bailer is director of the Research Institute on International Change at Columbia University. He is a leading figure in Soviet studies.

"The most awful tyranny is that of the proximate Utopia where the last sins are currently being eliminated and where, tomorrow, there will be no more sins because all the sinners will have been wiped out."

—*Thomas Merton*

Mikhail Gorbachev has set a course for the Soviet Union unprecedented in its history. Entranced, the rest of the world speculates about his success or failure—and the consequences. But almost everything about the course of Communism has defied prediction—even the prediction of its founders.

Almost a century and a half ago, Marx and Engels started their famous manifesto with the words: "A specter is haunting Europe, the specter of a Communist revolution." Marx expected revolution in economically and culturally developed countries, where industrial workers, in the majority, would lead the way. Once started, it would sweep simultaneously across most of the industrial nations. Finally would come the global Utopia that—until now—has been the confidently declared vision of Communist leaders. But Marx was wrong from the start. Instead of industrial Europe, the revolution came in Russia, the most improbable of lands.

Along came Lenin

Russia was economically and socially the most primitive European country, with underdeveloped industry, backward agriculture and a population overwhelmingly illiterate. Industrial workers, those Marx thought would lead the revolution, were only 1.5 percent of the population. The peasants, seen by Marx as a reactionary class doomed to extinction, accounted for more than 80 percent. There was no mass uprising for

Communism. The revolution was accomplished by a small minority that ruled dictatorially after it achieved power. But it might not have happened at all had it not been for the pragmatic genius of V. I. Lenin.

It was Lenin who saw the opportunity in Russia's turmoil and who was ready to abandon the Marxian vision of revolution to exploit it. By October, 1917, much of the work had been done for him. The nation was devastated by World War I. Its peasants were land hungry, the intelligentsia rebellious. The many peoples of the Russian Empire were frustrated in their national aspirations. Demonstrations for food and pressure from democratic parties and the nobles had forced the hapless Nicholas II to abdicate nine months before. The result was a power vacuum in which the forces of democracy were unable to consolidate. Russia was ripe for Lenin's slogan of "Peace and bread." When he seized the moment, it was, in his words, "the most democratic country in the world." What he overthrew was not the Czar, but a disunited democracy.

Lenin and his supporters believed in the Marxian Utopia of a perfect society. In its name they fought ruthlessly to victory, at the cost of hundreds of thousands of lives in the internal conflict that continued after settlement of the European war. How did he justify the bloodletting? Under the czars, he said, masses had died of the diseases of injustice, such as tuberculosis. With socialist victory, a decade of recovery would more than justify the revolutionary sacrifice. Today, after the loss of tens of millions of lives in the collectivization of agriculture, the great purge of 1936-38 and Stalin's mass terror, Lenin's words are especially empty. Even before he died in 1924, he had been forced to recognize the flaws in his vision. As his grip weakened with his health, he died a deeply troubled man. With success had come failure.

This is the reality his successors have lived with and tried to correct in many ways. True, Soviet Russia has become a gigantic industrial power. But over all, it is still the most backward of major European countries—and now half a score of Asian countries are moving forward. It is of course a giant territorial power, the world's biggest. Before Lenin's death, some of the far-flung lands of the Czarist Empire were brought into the Soviet fold. They came not by authentic revolution, however, but by the force of the Red Army. That process was finally completed under Stalin through the Nazi-Soviet pact in 1939, leading to the Soviet occupation of Lithuania, Estonia, Latvia, Bessarabia and eastern Poland.

Victory in World War II produced in Europe a buffer zone of Communist states along the Soviet border. From the Central and East European countries a new Soviet empire was forged. But the only European country where an authentic revolution took place, Tito's Yugoslavia, became an implacable enemy of Stalin's. This pattern was repeated in the greatest historical triumph of Communism: The victory of Mao Tse-tung's revolution in China. Instead of producing a Communist alliance of the world's largest country and its most populous one, the Soviet Union and China became bitter adversaries. The Marxian Utopia planted on the alien soil of Russia by Lenin thus discredited forever the idea of revolutionary socialism in civilized countries.

By far its greatest achievement was to transform the Soviet Union into a great military power. The country in search of secular Utopia became the world's largest military-industrial complex. Until the current reforms, the Soviet Union remained economically, politically, psychologically, in a state of war in peacetime, under the harsh policy of war Communism developed by Lenin. The search for Utopia brought enormous power but also uncounted tragedies, sacrifices and horrors.

Today, 70 years after the revolution, Russia is again in crisis. This one is different from the one that made Bolshevik victory possible. It does not endanger the survival of the Soviet regime. Yet is real and serious and is so recognized by the leadership and political elite and by the educated strata of the country. It is a crisis of effectiveness, of the regime's ability to attain the goals of political leadership and to fulfill the modest aspirations of its citizens. It is a crisis that in the final analysis casts into question even the regime's most cherished achievement, its global superpower status.

This crisis became visible and acute during the stagnant period of Brezhnev's rule and the interregnum that followed his death. Brezhnev presided over a leadership that was the oldest in Soviet history and longer in office than that of any major country with the exception of China. It was he who brought his nation to strategic parity with the U.S. and undeniable global power. Yet in his preoccupation with military might and foreign expansion, he let the Soviet system run down dangerously at home. Economically, the weakness appears in a slowing of growth and, for the first time in Soviet history, a widening technological gap between the Soviets and their capitalist adversaries. Politically, the crisis became evident in the staggering scope of official corruption, loss of control over gigantic, self-protecting bureaucracies, and the alienation of society from the regime. Workers shirked on the job, and alcoholism became rampant. The system of rewards took on two characteristics disastrous for a country that wants to modernize. It provided immense benefits for those in power and withheld incentives for good work and initiative. The welfare state suffered from being ridiculously overdeveloped and painfully underdeveloped at the same time. It provided staggering subsidies for staple food, housing and transportation when these were in short supply. Yet such welfare services as health care were so poor as to border on criminality. The country with the world's largest professional class denied its members not only political influence but professional autonomy and freedom of cultural expression. There had to be a reckoning if the decline was to be reversed, or even prevented from becoming worse. It came with the emergence, after the long paralysis in the Kremlin, of a young, imaginative and politically skilled leader in Mikhail Gorbachev.

Finally, a break with the past

It is by now clear that he is a determined reformer who could potentially change the Soviet system as much as only Stalin did in the past. His goal is the modernization of Russia. But it is apparent that he understands the concept of modernity differently from his predecessors. For Stalin, Khrushchev and Brezhnev, modernity meant new factories, construction, a larger labor force, improved technology and, above all, increased output of basic resources and products. They saw the road to modernity primarily in quantitative terms, with emphasis on production of tangible things rather than as an economic, social and political process. They had graduated from the school of Soviet prewar industrialization, the mobilization of World War II and postwar reconstruction.

For Gorbachev and others in the new political elite, modernity means something quite different, as it does to scientists and economists as well. To them, the key importance of high technology is a given. More important, the perception of the *process* of modernization centers not on things but on people, their attitudes and skills, and the conditions necessary for creativity and commitment. In this deepest sense, Gorbachev must be recognized as the first modern leader of the Soviet Union. To achieve modernization as he envisions it, he believes it necessary to destroy or circumvent the economic, social, cultural and partly the political institutions inherited from Stalin. *Glasnost*, democratization, legal reforms, devolution of economic power are for him the necessary means to modernize Russia.

5. RETREAT OF THE WEST

Gorbachev's course is not the first modernization of the Soviet Union. Before him, a generation back and daring for his time, came Nikita Khrushchev. This uneducated peasant's son, a graduate of Stalin's terror machine, repudiated his master and undermined two pillars of the Stalinist system—mass terror and unlimited, arbitrary, personal dictatorship. Today, Gorbachev continues what Khrushchev tentatively began by attempting to dismantle Stalinist institutions in the economy, society, culture and partly even in politics. In his objectives and design, he has already moved beyond what Khrushchev intended. Khrushchev was after all an ideologue. He still had illusions of a perfect society under Communism. He promised the Soviet people that they would live under "full Communism" and overtake and surpass America by the 1980s. Gorbachev still uses frequently the sacred words: Socialism, Communism, Leninism in their positive sense. What is absent, however, is the central ingredient of the doctrine, the ultimate goal in the name of which millions were killed and generations were sacrificed. The new Soviet leader no longer seems to pursue heaven on earth, the goal of the perfect society. The present political and cultural process, if it continues, signifies the end of Utopia in Soviet official thought.

America and the West have a stake in Gorbachev's anti-Stalinism on its own merits. His program promises a better life for the people of the Soviet Union. It may also provide greater autonomy for the nations of East-Central Europe. It could improve Soviet-American relations and wind down the nuclear-arms race. There is a further reason to wish Gorbachev well. For what if he does not succeed, what then? There is a warning in the words of the 19th-century writer Charles Caleb Colton: "Attempts at reform, when they fail, strengthen despotism, as he that struggles tightens those cords he does not succeed in breaking."

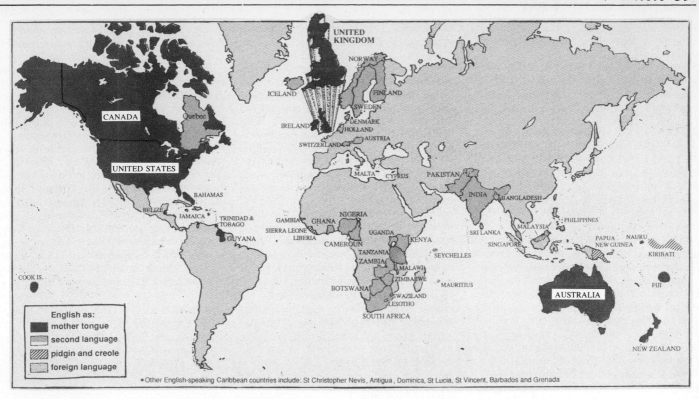

English as:
mother tongue
second language
pidgin and creole
foreign language

*Other English-speaking Caribbean countries include: St Christopher Nevis, Antigua, Dominica, St Lucia, St Vincent, Barbados and Grenada

The new English empire

English is the first truly universal language wider in its scope than Latin was or Arabic and Spanish are. These five pages examine why

The worldwide spread of English is remarkable. There has been nothing like it in history. Spanish and French, Arabic and Turkish, Latin and Greek have served their turn as international languages, in the wake of the mission station, the trading post or the garrison. But none has come near to rivalling English.

Four hundred years ago, English was the mother tongue of 7m speakers tucked away on a foggy island in Western Europe. Today, about 330m people throughout the world speak it as a mother tongue. That leaves it a distant second to Guoyo (Mandarin Chinese), which is estimated to have 750m speakers. But in international diffusion and acceptance, English is in a class of its own. Add to its 330m mother-tongue speakers the same number using English as a second language (ESL) and the same number again with reasonable competence in English as a foreign language (EFL), and you approach 1 billion English speakers.

As an official language, English serves more than 40 countries; French serves 27, Arabic 21 and Spanish 20. English is the language of international shipping and air travel. It is one of the two working languages of the United Nations (French

is the other). And it has become the language of both international youth culture and science (two-thirds of all scientific papers are published in English).

Its appeal is irresistible: advancement in the civil or diplomatic service almost anywhere will be aided by a good grasp of English; preliminary trade negotiations between a Hungarian and a Kuwaiti will probably be conducted in English; half of all foreign-language courses in the Soviet Union are English courses; and a quarter of China's 1 billion people is engaged in studying English, in one way or other.

English, then, is a world language. What befits it for that role? It is chiefly, of course, thanks to the power of Britain in the nineteenth century and America in the twentieth. But English has spread far beyond its spheres of political influence in a way that French and Spanish have not. Luckily, English fits its role well, thanks to the structure of the language.

English is relatively easy to pronounce: it has few of the tongue-knotting consonant-clusters of Russian or the subtle tone-shiftings of Chinese. The basic syntax is fairly straightforward, too. Words can be readily isolated (Turkish words cannot), and they are relatively "stable"

(having few of the inflections of Russian). English dispensed long ago with informal vocatives (*du*, *tu*) and with the gender-system (*der*, *die*, *das*; *le*, *la*) that most other European languages rejoice in and most students of them despair at.

The Roman alphabet is supple and economical (more efficient than the Arabic alphabet; easier to learn than the ideography of Chinese). The problem is spelling, which, for historical reasons, is out of kilter with pronunciation. *Ough* can be pronounced in at least seven different ways (*though*, *rough*, *thought*, *cough*, *hiccough*, *plough*, *through*).

The huge vocabulary, on the other hand, is no drawback to its use as a world language, though many people have sought to disqualify it on that ground. No one needs Shakespeare's command of the language for everyday communication. The more adept speaker can always adjust his register to suit the less adept.

English, in short, is easy to speak badly—and that is all that is required of a world language, if what you mean by a world language is an attenuated code, a means of transmitting and receiving simple information. English is the official language of the European Free Trade

Association, composed of six countries none of which has English as a mother tongue. Its secretary-general says: "using English means we don't talk too much, since none of us knows the nuances."

As a means of more complex social exchange, however, English is, on the face of it, less well suited to being a true world language. Here, its vast vocabulary does begin to prove a formidable obstacle. Idioms—as in all languages—confront the learner with their opacity. English is particularly well endowed with idioms: *a dark horse*, *a horse of a different colour*, *hold your horses* and *from the horse's mouth*. And English has the added irritation of a plethora of phrasal and prepositional verbs. *Put someone down*, *put someone up*, *put up with someone*, *put someone up to something*: such "simple" phrases are much harder for students to grasp than the corresponding "advanced" vocabulary (*humiliate someone*, *accommodate someone*, *tolerate someone* and *incite someone to something*).

More recondite still is idiom itself—the deep, sometimes unanalysable determinants of natural construction and usage. Why is it acceptable to say "You'll succeed provided that you prepare sufficiently" but not "You'll fail provided that you prepare insufficiently"? Why do people say "a *very* affected lady"; "*much* affected by your kindness", and "*greatly* affected by a change in pressure"? Why should "I haven't got a clue" mean "I don't know" but "You haven't got a clue" mean "You're a fool"?

Whose English?
Even in England, "standard English" has always been a will-o'-the-wisp. True, the language of south-eastern England began to acquire its prestige in Chaucer's time and, by the early days of the BBC, was so well established that the job of a radio announcer was closed to anyone whose accent was regional or not upper-middle class. But many linguists now reject the notion of a blanket uncountable noun "English", with its suggestion of a relatively homogeneous language. They use instead the unlovely term "Englishes" which, in effect, challenges the very notion of an ideal English *tout court*.

Englishes are:
● **Pidgins and creoles.** Pidgins are makeshift. They started as elementary systems of communication between traders, explorers or soldiers and suppliers, guides or slaves. The outsider's language—the "base" language—usually contributes 80% or more of the vocabulary, often in distorted form. *Pidgin* itself probably began life as a pidgin English word for *business*, hence the expression "That's not my pigeon". Syntax and pronunciation are often simplified by the constraints of the local vernacular.

A creole is a pidgin that has become a mother-tongue and developed into a sophisticated and well equipped language. The main fully-fledged English creoles are broad Creole in Jamaica, Krio in Sierra Leone and Tok Pisin in Papua New Guinea. English pidgins and creoles fall into two families: the Atlantic (in West Africa, the Caribbean, and parts of Nicaragua, Florida and Georgia); and the Pacific (spoken by Australian Aborigines, in Papua New Guinea and other Pacific islands, and formerly along the coast of China).

Educated creole speakers can shift back and forth along a kind of linguistic spectrum that stretches to standard English; their shift is mimicked by the communities as a whole. If the experience of black American English during the nineteenth century is anything to go by, all creole speakers may be drifting towards standard English (though, as if in rearguard action, a distinctive and energetic creole literature is emerging in both the Atlantic and Pacific families).

● **English as a foreign language.** EFL is big business. American universities offer PhDs in the teaching of it. In Britain, it earns dollops of foreign currency and goodwill. There is a quiet war going on between Britain and America over the international EFL market, with Australia increasing its share of EFL-teaching.

The plum, China, has fallen to Britain: the BBC's "Follow Me" is probably the most widely followed teaching course in history. But the most lucrative market, Western Europe, seems to be changing from British English to American. The countries of Latin America keep faith with the American variety; even the partial-exception is swinging away from its traditional preference for British English; that odd-man-out is, or was, Argentina.

It is impossible to be sure how many foreigners "know" English; 330m is a convenient speculation (though whatever number you choose, it is certainly rising rapidly every year). The reason is that the "linguistic spectrum" is wider in EFL than in any other kind of English. At one end lie the excited unintelligibiiities of a souvenir-seller in Siena or Sao Paulo: at the other, the accented, but serene, fluency of a teacher from Tel Aviv or Tübingen.

● **English as a second language.** This is the English of the Commonwealth, the Philippines, Pakistan, and of American Hispanics, Québecois, black South Africans, Afrikaners and so on. ESL is usually modelled on British English rather than American. The Philippines is the main exception; Liberia and Sierra Leone are partial exceptions.

English acts as an instrument of national unity, a relatively neutral *lingua franca*. Tribal rivalries can be allayed more easily when neighbouring peoples—Hausas, Yorubas and Ibos, for instance—can speak the same language. Understanding

Pay attention on your language

ESL is the most diverse form of English. "Mother-tongue interference" changes standard English—and ESL-speakers have an enormous number of mother tongues. Even within a single community, not all local ESL peculiarities will hold good for all speakers; or, even, for any one speaker. An Indian professor is unlikely to omit the word *is* when lecturing to a university class; but might well do so when rebuking the *dhobi wallah* for inattention to the laundry.

With those qualifications, some common features of ESL are:
● **Pronunciation.** Many consonants are hard for ESL speakers to distinguish or reproduce. Speakers from south Asia, for instance, tend to use the *v* and *w* sounds interchangeably. *It vas a wery vet veekend in Nowember* is how a dull British or American ear might register a statement made by an Indian. An Indian might also confuse the sounds of *k* and *g*, or *p* and *b*—*gruel and baneful* for *cruel and painful*—and so would an African, though often in the opposite direction: *picketed and crumpling* for *bigoted and grumbling*. Consonant clusters are often broken up by an "epenthetic" vowel—*spot* comes out as *si-pot* in Kashmir—or reduced: *bend* and *bent* and *burnt* are often sounded as *ben* in African English. Vowels are no easier. *Cutting* and *curtain* both sound like *cotton* in West Africa (and the Caribbean) and like *kettin* in East and southern Africa. The slurred or neutral vowels of standard English are seldom heard in ESL. In West Africa, *gorilla* sound something like *go'-rill-o'*. Jamaica, to a Jamaican, is *juh-mée-kuh*. And the stress-system of ESL often goes against that of mother-tongue English. ESL imitating indigenous African and Asian languages tends to have a smoother "syllable-timed" rhythm, closer to that of French than to the "stress-timed" undulations of standard English. When ESL speakers do add stress, accordingly, it is often in an unconventional position; *imitáting*, *pósition*, *capítalist*.
● **Vocabulary.** Standard English words may be extended in meaning; in parts of Africa, *carpet* might also be used to refer to a linoleum floor-covering, and *bluffing* can be used to mean "showing off". Standard English forms might be distorted; Indian English has *dissentment* for *dissent*. African and Indian English are much given to pluralising uncountable English nouns: *funs*, *slangs* and so on. In India, you might buy *two breads* or put *two woods* on the fire.

(comprehension) breeds understanding (tolerance).

As the sun set on the British Empire, each newly independent country had to commit itself to an official language. English was usually entrenched as the language of education, the law and the civil service. Sometimes, it could be edged out—as in Tanzania by Swahili (a *lingua franca* anyway) and in Pakistan by Urdu (another *lingua franca*, though one spoken as a mother tongue by only 5m of the country's 90m inhabitants compared with 60m who use Punjabi as theirs). But such edging-out has not proved easy. Malaysia imposed Bahasa Malaysia (a standardised form of Malay) as a national language in the 1960s. Not only was this of doubtful fairness to the Chinese and Tamil minorities, it has also meant that young Malays, educated in Bahasa Malaysia to secondary school and beyond, are finding it hard to get places at English-speaking universities abroad.

India, with a dozen or more main indigenous languages, and more than 150 languages in all, resolved at independence to establish Hindi as its sole official national language by 1965. Hindi is the mother tongue of about a third of the population. But in 1965, the government conceded that English should, for the time being, remain an "associate official language". Professional advancement and social prestige among middle-class urban Indians still depend upon skill in English. In the southern states, where the indigenous languages are unrelated to Hindi, many people are reluctant to learn the northerners' tongue when it is more useful (and no harder) to learn English.

Indian English shows how one variety of the language can take on a life of its own while still remaining comprehensible to speakers of standard English (indeed, British English continues to coexist with the new indigenous form). Just as Australia, with its robust cultural self-confidence, has ceased looking over its linguistic shoulder at London, so India can now fairly lay claim to possessing a separate English (in a way that Nigeria, say, cannot yet do). Indian English occurs in writing, not just in speech, and might be adopted even by an author accustomed to writing standard British English.

The influence of Indian English is felt far beyond the Indian subcontinent. Foreign students studying at Indian colleges take it home with them. Thousands of Indian teachers elsewhere in Asia and in Africa spread it abroad. School and college textbooks are written in Indian English—they are even sometimes "translated" into Indian English from British and American English. This pleads eloquently on behalf of English's claim to be a true international language, not just a national language used internationally.

● **English as a mother tongue.** A Scot might say "Will I write a letter of complaint?" where an Englishman or North American would say "Should I write a letter of complaint?" Scots also, like South Africans, may say "Where do you stay?" when asking where you live. A Miami Beach realtor (estate agent), if she ever had occasion to refer to a hot-water bottle, might call it a *haat wáa-derr báa-dill*. A Cockney shop assistant (sales-clerk) calls hers a *'o' wáw-uh bó-oo*. Cornishmen and Newfoundlanders speak of farmers as *varmers*.

The broadest divide in mother-tongue English lies between British English and American English. There are systematic differences of spelling (*colour/color, manoeuvre/maneuver*) and of pronunciation (*hostile* [Britons and Canadians distinguish it from *hostel*] and *ballet*). There are "morphological" differences: *aluminium/aluminum, zip/zipper, at a loose end/at loose ends*. Above all, there are lexical and idiomatic differences—*drawing pin/thumbtack, unit trust/mutual fund*.

These are straightforward enough. But the same word may have different meanings on different sides of the Atlantic (see table). Or a word or phrase may have a common transAtlantic meaning, but have an additional sense in one variety that it lacks in the other. In British English, *majority* does service for a "relative majority" as well as for an "absolute majority". In American English, it means only an "absolute majority"; a "relative majority" is a *plurality*.

This asymmetry is best demonstrated by words or phrases that have suffered "semantic taint" on one side of the Atlantic but not on the other. A *rubber* refers to an eraser in British English; in American English, to a condom. An American sociological study called "Women on the Job" had to be retitled when published in Britain.

Such differences take only a little application to identify and remember. But other subtleties are harder to master—even to define. Wilde's dictum about "two great countries divided by a common language" applies mostly to this twilight zone. Two examples must suffice, both tentative. First, the "register" of the word *toilet*: it seems to have a coarser ring to it in American English. Second, the size of a *pond*: in British English, any pool of water wider than about 40 yards would probably be called a *lake*; American English, on the other hand, provides for much larger ponds.

Noah Webster and H. L. Mencken both thought that British and American English were diverging. That may have been true once, but is no longer. The changes can be traced by comparing the various vocabularies to do with communication. Before 1776, sailing terms were almost identical in both American and British English. In the nineteenth and early twentieth centuries, in a proud

---

New words might be created from English elements. In West Africa, a *been-to* is a person who has been overseas. In India, to *airdash* is to fly from place to place. And so-called "calquing" (an element-by-element translation of an indigenous idiom or compound word) flourishes: *plenti han* (plenty hands) for *centipede*; *grass-bilong paul* (grass belong fowl) for feathers.

Words that are archaic or regional in British English may be part of the mainstream vocabulary of both ESL and West Indian creole (where *buss* is used to refer to a kiss, and *bubby* to a breast). In India, the police might *nab a miscreant*, or you might greet a friend with the question "How is your good self?", and show him your new *timepiece*.

Most conspicuous of all, to the outsider, are those words taken unselfconsciously into ESL from the speaker's mother tongue, whether to designate western things or purely local ones. In India, the *mali* (gardener) might sleep on a *charpoy* (string bed).

● **Syntax.** The word *him* or *im* might be used (as in Jamaican creole) to cover the forms *he, him, his* and even *she* and *her*. Among proficient speakers, articles and basic verbs may be left out (especially if the mother tongue lacks or habitually omits them). *We are going to see new hotel this morning,* a Nigerian architect might tell his draughtsmen.

Word-order is often unconventional. It may remain uninverted in a direct question—"What you will do if I go away?"—or be irregularly inverted in an indirect question: "He asked why are you wanting to go away?" A frequent ESL feature, in both Asia and Africa, is the use of unvarying tags at the end of a sentence: "He is a very clever boy, isn't it?"

The subtleties of the English tense system seldom correspond to those of an ESL- or EFL-speaker's mother tongue. Hence such common constructions in south Asia, as: "When you will come and help me here, I can get finished." "I am telling you—I am not knowing how to help you." And the randomness of English pronouns gives rise to many defiant local preferences. Standard adverbs may be omitted; in West Africa, you might hear "The taxi will pick me at 10 o'clock". Or one may be inserted where standard English has none, or be substituted for the standard one. In India, a politician might *voice out a protest*, and the press might urge people to *pay attention on this protest of his*.

assertion of linguistic independence, American English chose to go its own way: hence the differences in *railway/railroad* vocabulary (*goods train/freight train, sleepers/cross-ties*) and in *motor car/automobile* terms (*boot/trunk, wing/fender*). But technical vocabularies are coming together again. Aerospace terminology has fewer transAtlantic variations than that of motor cars; computer terminology shows hardly any differences at all. America's *program* and *disk* have ousted Britain's traditional *programme* and *disc*.

The current "convergence" of British and American Englishes is mainly the result of British adoption of American usages. The American pronunciation of *suit, lute* and *absolute* has almost ousted the traditional standard British pronunciation with its *y*-sound after the *s* or *l*. (Curiously, *pursuit* remains resolutely *pur-syóot* in British English and *nuclear* showed no signs of going *nóo-clear*).

In vocabulary and meaning, too, American English calls the shots. The American sense of *billion* has been widely adopted in Britain. Many American imports to Britain have been quietly absorbed: *teenager, babysitter, commuter; striptease, brainwash, streamline; lean over backwards, fly off the handle, call the shots.* Even *stiff upper lip* seems to be American in origin.

Estas neniu alternativo

As a world language, English has two half-serious rivals and one serious alternative. The two half-serious rivals are Esperanto and Basic English.

Esperanto, 100 years old in 1987, has around 100,000 fluent speakers in some 85 countries; as many as 8m people have a smattering. It is one of the oldest of such "constructed languages" and is certainly the best survivor. Four or five others have got beyond the linguistic drawing-board and between five and 35 more have been devised. Esperanto's syntax and sound system are both regular and simple; its vocabulary is largely European. More than 10,000 publications have been produced in Esperanto; these include not just technical studies and works of non-fiction but some creative writing, too, especially poetry.

Most experts agree that Esperanto has nowhere to go. Why should a non-Anglophone student devote language-learning time and resources to Esperanto rather than to English? Esperanto is so Eurocentric in its vocabulary and structure that it cannot claim to be much freer of cultural bias than English is. In any case, the culture inherent in English is part of its appeal: at least a few novice students of EFL look forward to the treasures of Shakespeare, Mark Twain and Yeats. And those language students who have less exalted ambitions—refining their appreciation of Bob Dylan's lyrics, following "Dynasty" without the subtitles, securing the local McDonald's franchise, emigrating to America—have even less reason to be diverted from their English studies.

Basic English, devised in the 1930s, enjoyed only a brief vogue. It is a slimmed-down English, with 850 core words and a moderately simplified syntax. It could, perhaps, rival Esperanto in ease of acquisition. But radical changes to English grammar would be needed, and so would a drastic reform of spelling. But the less like English Basic English becomes, the less likely it is to gain acceptance.

The real alternative to English as a world language is the interpreting machine. One day, perhaps, there will be a portable black box—the size of a largish pocket calculator?—with flawless powers of voice recognition and simultaneous translation. Put it on the desk between you and your Japanese counterpart, and let talks proceed.

A new kind of colonisation

English has a happily eclectic vocabulary. Its foundations are Anglo-Saxon (*was, that, eat, cow*) reinforced by Norse (*sky, get, bath, husband, skill*); its superstructure is Norman-French (*soldier, Parliament, prayer, beef*). The Norman aristocracy used their words for the food, but the Saxon serfs kept theirs for the animals. Its decor comes from Renaissance and Enlightenment Europe: sixteenth-century France yielded up *etiquette, naive, reprimand* and *police*; Italy provided *umbrella, duet, bandit* and *dilettante*; Holland gave *cruise, yacht, trigger, landscape* and *decoy*. Its elaborations come from Latin and Greek: *misanthrope, meditate* and *parenthesis* are all first attested during the 1560s; in this century, English adopted *penicillin* from Latin, *polystyrene* from Greek, and *sociology* and *television* from both. And English's ornaments come from all round the world: *slogan* and *spree* from Gaelic, *hammock* and *hurricane* from Caribbean languages, *caviar* and *kiosk* from Turkish, *dinghy* and *dungarees* from Hindi, *caravan* and *candy* from Persian, *mattress* and *masquerade* from Arabic.

Redressing the balance of trade, English is sharply stepping up its linguistic exports. Not just the necessary *imotokali* (motor car) and *izingilazi* (glasses) to Zulu; or *motokaa* and *shillingi* (shilling) to Swahili; but also *der Bestseller, der Kommunikations Manager, das Teeshirt* and *der Babysitter* to German; and, to Italian, *la pop art, il popcorn* and *la spray*. In some Spanish-speaking countries you might wear *un sueter* to *el beisbol*, or witness *un nocaut* at *el boxeo*.

Indeed, a sort of global English wordlist can be drawn up: *airport, passport, hotel, telephone; bar, soda, cigarette; sport, golf, tennis; stop, OK,* and increasingly, *weekend, jeans, know-how, sexappeal* and *no problem.* The presence of so many words to do with travel, consumables and sport attests to the real source of these exports—America.

Foreign governments rarely welcome this lexical dumping. Is there a secret clause in the constitution of the Fifth Republic which requires a French president to protest at the defilement of his noble language by *les anglicismes?* According to one calculation, *Le Monde* perpetrates an anglicism once every 166 words—not just the established *le dancing, le parking* and *le camping*, but now *le fast food, le hot money* and *le jumbo jet.* The recommended alternatives for these phrases—*prêt-à-manger, capitaux fébriles* and *le gros-porteur*—seem to lack a certain *je ne sais quoi.* More important, they miss the point: that things and ideas American should be American in name, too, if you want to preserve the nation's "linguistic integrity". French cultural traditions are under threat more from fast food the thing than from *fast food* the phrase.

While French presidents protest, there is no record of an American president or a British prime minister complaining at the defilement of English by the infiltration of gallicisms. (Indeed, the word *gallicism* is much rarer in English than *anglicisme* is in French; there is no term at all for the obverse of *franglais*).

Note, however, two caveats in dealing with *anglicismes.* First, they are not always recent: *le biftek* goes back to at least 1807, *le snob* to 1857 and even *le self-made man* to 1878. (English, note, has two useful near-synonyms for that last phrase—namely, *parvenu* and *nouveau riche.*) Second, *anglicismes* do not always mean what they appear to mean. *Un smoking* is not a smoking jacket but a dinner jacket; *un egghead* means an idiot and *un jerk*, a good dancer.

Although most transAtlantic lexical traffic runs eastwards, *central heating* and *weekend* crossed the Atlantic from east to west before 1900. They have been followed by *miniskirt, opposite number, hovercraft, the Establishment, smog, brain drain* (appropriately) and, probably, *gay*, in the sense of homosexual.

The future of English

Mr Robert Burchfield, who recently retired as chief editor of the "Oxford English Dictionary", once suggested that the varieties of English (ESL as well as mother-tongue English) might one day become separate languages, just as Latin, after the fall of the Roman Empire, broke up into French, Italian, Spanish, and so on. Almost 100 years before Mr Burchfield, another language scholar, Henry Sweet, wrote:

> In another century . . . England, America and Australia will be speaking mutually unintelligible languages.

Such a divergence did not occur then because, though communications were slow in those days, language changed slowly, too. Such a divergence is not likely to take place in the next 100 years

The exchange rate

British	American
camp bed	cot
cot	crib
fruit machine	slot machine
slot machine	vending machine
waistcoat	vest
vest	undershirt

because, though language is changing faster today, so, are communications, and hence mutual linguistic influences.

True, a few new dialects might develop, joining the ranks of English creoles that are unintelligible to most mainstream English speakers. British and American English are never likely to become indistinguishable but they are never likely to become mutually unintelligible either. Indian English will remain widely comprehensible elsewhere. It is precisely because of its international intelligibility that English is so earnestly courted by governments and citizens alike.

This does not mean English is in the process of unbuilding the Tower of Babel, as the extreme proponents of a universal language want. Equivocation, lies and babble flourish as much in communities united by one language as they do in those divided by two. Nor is English replacing other languages, as opponents of its spread fear. For the most part, it is supplementing them, allowing strangers to talk to each other. A more temperate and useful role this—and one that English fulfils creditably and deservedly, in all its variety of varieties.

The Price of Success:
Japan's Foreign Policy Dilemma

Robert A. Scalapino

Robert A. Scalapino is Robson Research Professor of Government, Director of the Institute of East Asian Studies, and Editor of Asian Survey *at the University of California, Berkeley.*

The phenomenal economic success of Japan in the past three decades is too well known to require elaboration. From a war-ravaged, bare subsistence economy, Japan has risen to have the second or third largest economy in the world, depending on how one ranks the USSR. No one doubts that this nation has the capacity today to influence global economic conditions second only to the United States. Yet Japan's extraordinary growth now lends itself to problems at home and abroad.

It may seem curious that a people with one of the highest per capita incomes in the world consider themselves underprivileged. But complaints are mounting from the Japanese citizenry, ninety percent of who view themselves as part of the middle class. The unhappiness centers on the quality of life. Housing, congestion, and the general strain of urban existence are increasingly accounted serious problems. Japanese leaders have acknowledged the need for basic reforms either as a part of, or apart from, economic restructuring. Taxes, education, social services and land policies have all been placed on the agenda. Most of the requirements were underlined in the Maekawa Report commissioned by Prime Minister Nakasone some two years ago, but implementation of that report has been disappointingly slow.

Meanwhile, Japanese foreign policies have been under unprecedented assault. The economic complaints voiced by the United States and other trading partners of Japan form a consistent pattern. The chief charges are lack of access to the Japanese domestic market, Japanese saturation of foreign markets and a wide range of tactics including dumping employed in an effort to obtain or hold market share, and Japanese reluctance to advance a generous aid program to developing nations, or to be forthcoming in technology transfer and investment in sectors vital to such nations.

The Japanese have ample criticisms of others in response, especially the West in general and the United States in particular. West Europe is often referred to as decadent, and the United States is described as a young adolescent threatening its health by various excesses, including that of spending beyond its means. "Has not the mismanagement of the American economy, together with the loss of competitiveness in many fields and the historic disinterest of US producers in the foreign market accounted for America's current plight?" query Japanese spokesmen.

There is sufficient blame to be shared by all major parties. The primary criticisms of Japan are valid despite the process of change in Japanese policies that is underway. A central difficulty lies in the fact that in addition to structural alterations in the economy, Japan is being asked to undertake what amounts to a profound cultural transformation, going from an in-group, exclusivist, introverted way of life to one featuring genuinely internationalist attitudes and policies. This transformation, moreover, is being demanded at a time when the old policies are still sufficiently successful to make external pressures for rapid change far greater than those generated at home

At the same time, the transgressions of the United States and West Europe cannot be ignored. Nor are they likely to be quickly or easily remedied. Nothing is more difficult than for a democratic society to accept immediate sacrifices on behalf of long-term benefits. The Western democracies have handled their recent affluence with minimal regard for the global industrial revolution that surrounds them, a revolution demanding adjustments both rapid and profound. Their decision-making processes and more importantly, their intellectual capacity to grasp a meaningful vision of the future seem inadequate to the tasks so essential to continued well-being at home and in the international community. Indeed, the democratic system—both in Japan and in the West—is in some degree at odds with both the tempo and the thrust of the economic changes required in our revolutionary age.

Currently, a single word—internationalization—is in vogue with Japanese policy makers. The principal policies being advanced are those of expanding the domestic market at home and advancing economic assistance programs abroad to the developing nations, especially those in East Asia. Efforts are being made to further reduce the barriers to the Japanese financial as well as commodity marketplace. A new focus upon improving the Japanese quality of life involving increased expenditures for social services, tax reform and revisions in policies relating to agriculture and land—two huge problems—is underway. The results thus far have been very modest, and it remains to be seen whether the government of Takeshita Noboru can overcome deeply entrenched domestic obstacles to effect real change.

Japan has promised to recycle some $20 to $30 billion of its huge reserves, providing assistance to such countries as those of Southeast Asia. Some observers have called this a second Marshall Plan, but as yet, it does not match that plan either in scope or design. Much of the funds are to be allocated from the Japanese private sector or through international agencies to which Japanese monies have already been committed. Moreover, if this assistance results in worse trade imbalances between the borrowing nations and

Japan with the funds used to buy Japanese machinery or components, or in increasing Japanese "round-about" imports to the United States via Japanese ventures operating abroad, it will not have resolved current problems.

The primary method of approaching the US-Japan trade imbalance at present is that of currency reevaluation, as is well known. By the end of 1987, the yen had been appreciated extensively, standing at 122 to $1. While efforts to stem devaluation strengthened the dollar in the opening weeks of 1988, it was by no means clear that the dollar would be stabilized at roughly its present position. Some experts predicted that a further 10 percent drop of the dollar, even at a rate of 100 yen to the dollar, was possible in the not too distant future. Japanese producers, despite earlier cries of alarm, have been able to adjust relatively well to the present situation. But up to now, dollar devaluation has had a smaller impact on the trade imbalance than had been predicted, although if it continues, that impact will take effect at some point. One truth is evident: the massive US trade imbalance cannot continue indefinitely, and only by some combination of export expansion and import reduction can correction be achieved. The only issue—and one of major consequence to the world as well as the United States—is the timing and means of adjustment.

Meanwhile, attention to the central problem, that of the US budget deficit, has resulted in what most foreign observers regard as disappointingly small steps toward correction. Once again, an elemental truth has to be faced: imbalance can only be remedied through some combination of expenditure curtailment and revenue enhancement, a fact that most US politicians are willing to acknowledge intellectually and shun politically.

Given the fact that remedial measures to the central economic problems confronting Japan and the United States are likely to fall short of sufficiency in the period immediately ahead, relations between the two nations will resemble those of a troubled marriage. Japan, along with many other nations, especially those that have targetted the American market, fears a rising tide of US protectionism. Nearly 40 percent of Japan's exports enter the American market today, and a similar or higher percentage applies to such countries as South Korea and Taiwan. Having long served as the single greatest resource for the export-oriented nations, the United States now demands reciprocity, including the rapid dismantling of the protectionist policies—formal and informal—that are widespread throughout Asia and elsewhere.

Yet the troubled Japanese-American marriage is most unlikely to end in divorce. The level of economic interdependence—indeed, integration—is too high to make any such course of action viable. As the recent controversy over semiconductors illustrated, it is difficult for the United States to punish Japan without punishing an important segment of the American economy. Both US and Japanese industries are going out of country at an accelerating rate, and in the case of Japan, more than 600 companies employ 160,000 Americans in the US at present, with those figures destined to expand dramatically. Beyond this, the vast Japanese real estate holdings, and the purchases of US bonds making the funding of the US debt possible testify to the intimacy (and the hazards) of the economic relationship. Quarrels will continue, sometimes at a violent

level, and certain threatening legislative and administrative actions may well take place, but just as the United States and the Soviet Union must resolve security issues, so must the US and Japan resolve economic issues without destroying the economies of each other and the world. To be sure, neither of these supreme challenges rests wholly with the principal parties, but the importance of bilateral agreements cannot be denied.

The economic aspect, however, is only one facet, albeit, a supremely important facet of Japan's foreign policy. Security issues and political relationships also constitute important aspects of Japan's relationship to the world. For more than three decades, Japanese security has rested on treaty relations with the United States, with the US committed to the defense of Japan in case of aggression on it. In recent years, Japan has created a small (272,000) technologically-advanced Self Defense Force that some observers rate as the sixth or seventh strongest military force in the world. In 1988, Japan will spend some $30 billion, or 1.013 percent of its GNP on further military refinements. While a comparatively low percentage of the GNP, this constitutes one of the world's highest actual defense expenditures. Today, the Japanese commitment is to surveillance by air for several hundred miles off its shores and for 1,000 nautical miles by the sea to the east and south.

In contrast to the economic arena, defense cooperation between Japan and the US has never been closer. Joint military exercises and joint defense planning for contingencies are now well established. American requests for greater burden sharing are still forthcoming, and in partial response, Japan has steadily increased its financial commitments to the upkeep of American forces and facilities in Japan. Japan's security commitments, moreover, form a part of the soft regionalism that now prevails in Northeast Asia. While formal ties except those of a bilateral nature with the United States are lacking, exchanges of visits and information between Japan and both Chinese and South Koreans responsible for security have been taking place.

As Japanese defense expenditures have grown, various Asian nations have expressed alarm about the possibility of the restoration of Japanese militarism. They point to some revival of nationalism in Japan including visits to Yasukuni Shrine, the hallowed sanctuary for Japan's war dead, and revisions in Japanese textbooks aimed at softening Japan's actions during the war with China that commenced in 1937 and extended into World War Two. The People's Republic of China has taken the lead in voicing concerns about "bad elements of Japanese society that would revive militarism," but similar alarms have been sounded in various Southeast Asian countries.

A new pride (some would say arrogance) exists in Japan's recent accomplishments together with a growing resentment of external criticisms. The old feelings of inferiority and guilt held so strongly by the World War Two generation are fading. But this neo-nationalism does not carry with it a militaristic overtone, at least at present. According to opinion polls, the Japanese public, including all younger generations, continue to support the present level of military preparation only, desiring neither an escalation nor a decline. The three non-nuclear principles (no use, no manufacture, no presence on Japanese soil) continue to evoke overwhelming public support. And the social status of the military (as well as their political power) continues to be low. Moreover, the Asia of the 1980s is not the Asia of the 1930s. There is no vacuum of power or colonial enclave against which to operate. Instead, the Japanese recognize the continuing Asian antipathy to any sign of Japanese military resurgence and the degree to which this would affect Japanese economic relations with the region.

Thus, there is no likelihood that the Japanese constitutional restrictions on the military will be revised in the foreseeable future, or that efforts will be made to increase in major degree the percentage of GNP spent on defense. The current Japanese response to security issues was well illustrated by Tokyo's actions regarding the Persian Gulf crisis. Despite its heavy dependence upon gulf oil, Japan rejected any military involvement, opting instead for furnishing an advanced navigational detection system to enable better guidance of ships through routes cleared of mines. In addition, it announced the commitment of low interest loans to Oman and Jordan.

The latter action underlines a favorite Japanese phrase, namely, "comprehensive security." This phrase symbolizes the thesis that security also has strong economic and political components, and that Japan can best play an economic role, with assistance used for political as well as developmental purposes. In recent years, Japan has "rewarded" strategically crucial countries like Egypt and various ASEAN (Association of Southeast Nations) states with loans. Conversely, it has "punished" a state like Vietnam after its Cambodian invasion by restricting economic relations—although not to the extent desired by some ASEAN states, since private trade continues. Indeed, a struggle within Japan is unceasing between those who adhere to the historic Japanese principle of separating economics from politics, doing business wherever it is offered and conducting an essentially "market foreign policy," and those who argue that Japan must use its economic power to advance its own political-security interests and those of its allies. While the latter school has made advances in recent years, the former position—deeply entrenched in Japanese attitudes and practices—retains great potency.

Policies toward the two big, neighboring Communist states illustrate some of the dilemmas confronting Japanese foreign policies today. In modern times, Japan has revealed ambivalent attitudes toward China. On the one hand, it has held Chinese culture in esteem, and acknowledged its deep historic debt to that nation. On the other hand, it has had doubts as to whether China can get its act together, at least in the near future. In addition, while Japan does not want a chaotic China, it also does not want a China that is making progress too rapidly, fearing a spillover of Chinese nationalism into the broader Asian arena and the advent of economic competition too swift to be accomodated.

Chinese leaders have their own desires and reservations regarding Japan. They recognize that Japan can and should play a major role in assisting China's rapid modernization. But they are disappointed in Japanese concentration on trade and reluctance to transfer technology or pursue joint ventures. Yet the PRC (People's Republic of China) finds it difficult to create the economic conditions that would induce the Japanese private sector—and that of other nations—to place a higher priority on such activities. Two

additional issues—Taiwan and "Japanese militarism"—currently complicate Japan's relations with China. The ties between these two nations are destined to be delicate: there is ample reason for cooperation and at the same time, continuing problems inhibit genuine trust. The events of the 20th century, together with the very different stages of development characterizing these two societies, would dictate policies differently fashioned, even if a significant ideological-political gulf did not add further complications.

Japan's relations with the Soviet Union pose a different set of issues. The chemistry between Japan and Russia has been bad for more than one hundred years, with direct military conflicts recurrent. Until recently at least, the USSR has followed unremittingly harsh policies toward Japan, the by-words being "one must use tough treatment on the Japanese." In response, the Japanese have shown little inclination to concede to Soviet positions, and public opinion polls verify the fact that of all nations, the Soviet Union is least respected, most feared. Yet the Japanese public today does not regard a direct Soviet attack upon Japan as likely despite the augmented Soviet military presence in Japan's near vicinity. Only in the context of a global war is the threat of invasion perceived to be serious. It should also be noted that Japanese trade with the USSR has been increasing, and is expected to average around $4.5-5 billion during the next few years, with the export of whole Japanese plants playing an important role in the Soviet quest for modernization.

The Gorbachev era, moreover, may offer opportunities for some improvements in relations, although that is by no means certain. Thus far, Soviet overtures have come primarily in the form of higher level visits and more skillful diplomats assigned to Japan. As yet, there is no sign that Soviet leaders are prepared to give major ground on the issue of the four northern islands off Hokkaido, occupied and partially fortified by the Soviets. On balance, there seems little likelihood of dramatic improvements in Japanese-Soviet relations. Another variable of significance, however, will be the course of the American-Soviet dialogue. Should a new era of superpower detente ensue, Japan would feel safer in advancing economic relations with Moscow at a more rapid rate, and possibly searching for compromises on territorial-security issues.

As relations with the major states and regions are explored, the overweaning issue that haunts the Japanese people is what kind of world will exist in the decades ahead and what should be the role of Japan in that world? While Japan as a nation is moving rapidly towards an internationalist policy, with rare exceptions the Japanese as a people do not yet have an internationalist outlook. Insularity and parochialism, together with a strong adherence to class and generational distinctions, have been too long and too deeply embedded in Japanese culture to disappear in a few decades. The Japanese remain a very private people, introverted and most comfortable in familiar surroundings, with long-established reference groups. Yet as noted, a new mood is gradually emerging in Japan, one of greater self-confidence, with the Japanese prepared to stand comparisons with others and to interact with them, bearing an increased responsibility for world order.

It is in this context that Japan's global role is debated. Two broad options have been largely discarded, at least in their pure forms. The neutralist-pacifist route has long been championed by the Japan Socialist Party, but even it has recently moved to modify somewhat its traditional stance. Soviet military power remains formidable in the near vicinity, and Soviet interests—some of them in conflict with Japan—will continue to be advanced. The Korean peninsula, so vital to Japanese interests, remains unpredictable, but most unlikely to be responsive to the appeals of a weak, isolated neighbor. And in the middle and long run, China is also a nation with which to reckon, a nation that even now exhibits a strong nationalism and views pacifism contemptuously. Unless Japan is prepared to hand over the determination of its vital interests to others, the neutralist-pacifist route is most unpromising, and the overwhelming majority of Japanese people recognize that fact.

An opposite course is no more viable, namely, a foreign policy characterized by a high posture, assertive and independent, defining Japan's national interests apart from those of others. This policy, which can be labelled Gaullist, has an appeal to a small band of ultra-nationalists, but under the present or foreseeable circumstances, it has no chance of being adopted as the foundation of Japanese foreign policy. The backlash from Asia, already feeling threatened by the relatively modest Japanese security commitments, would be immense. Japan's economic relations in Asia and elsewhere would be undermined. The repercussions at home would also be severe, with consensus breaking down on many fronts. And Japan could never counterbalance Soviet or American military power, whatever sacrifices it induced from its citizens. Once again, these views are shared by the great majority of the Japanese people and policy makers.

The remaining option is one that builds from the past, enlarging the Japanese role in diverse ways while retaining the basic linkages that currently exist. The foundation of Japanese foreign policy will continue to be an alliance with the United States, as I have indicated. Yet within that alliance, as within all other alliances of this period, the quotients of equality and independence on the part of both partners will increase. Further differentiation of policies will take place, greater reciprocity will be necessary, and continuous consultation will be required.

Within this policy, moreover, two significant variables are possible. One found expression in an earlier Japanese phrase, "omnidirectional foreign policy." Such a course, while retaining close ties with the United States, would seek to place primary emphasis upon international economic relations. Japan would continue to turn outward, crossing ideological boundaries in playing an ever growing role in the economic modernization of the world, while continuing to pursue a relatively low political and military posture, counting upon American leadership, but feeling free to diverge from the United States when national interests appeared to dictate that need.

The other variant is that most recently espoused by Prime Minister Nakasone, namely, a policy of accepting greater political and military responsibilities, acknowledging that Japan must gradually assume the role of a major power with a growing stake in global affairs. Such a course does not relegate economic policies to an inferior position, but it adds to Japanese foreign policy additional political and security elements, thereby raising Japan's voice in the international community. It also presumes a close, continuing consultative relationship with the United States while not precluding a separate stance on some issues.

In both of these variants, a reassertion of Japanese nationalism is to be seen, as well as a reflection of the global trend away from the tight alliances of the past toward the looser alignments of the present. Japanese public opinion remains divided over which variant is preferable, a division reflected within elites. Japan's future course will probably involve some mixture of the two, influenced by the international climate of the time at least as much as by internal considerations. Yet whatever the specific course taken, a policy of minimal involvement is ruled out by the incontrovertible fact that no major nation is more dependent upon global trends than is Japan.

World Problems and Interdependence

One of the unpredicted benefits of space exploration was the ability to view our own blue planet from outside the atmosphere. The idea of "spaceship earth" impresses upon each of us the responsibility that we have for the well-being of the planet. The burning of the Amazonian rain forests, the use of fluorocarbons, dumping trash into the sea, hunting whales and elephants to extinction—these actions and others can change our environment and our quality of life. Many of our problems have global dimensions, and what we do may have worldwide consequences.

One issue of concern is population growth. We now have over 5 billion people, and will reach the 6 billion mark by the end of the century. Unchecked growth might lead to a scarcity of resources and prove the predictions of economist Thomas Malthus correct after all. Like fruit flies, human beings would reproduce to the limit of their container and then die from starvation. Is that our fate? Nick Eberstadt reviews current thinking about the "population explosion," and concludes that the reactions of leaders are more important than the size of the population and its growth rate.

The Chinese, who have over a billion people in their country, embarked on an ambitious one-child-per-family program which has been remarkably successful in slowing the nation's growth. Greater longevity because of better care for the elderly, however, has prevented them from stopping the growth entirely. Within China and elsewhere urbanization has continued, and at the end of the century one-half of the world's population will be living in cities. Eighty percent of the urban growth will be in the Third World; Mexico City and São Paulo will have populations of 25 million or more. We have little knowledge about managing such megacities, with their predictable massive problems of food supply, water, sanitation, transportation, and air pollution.

In Brazil, 30 years ago, the government built a "new town"—a completely planned city—for their capital. Although it was not a total failure, the much-heralded futuristic city of Brasilia failed to meet expectations. One difficulty was that the planners did not consider carefully the characteristics of the society. They did not need the carefully crafted roads for automobiles in a country where few such vehicles existed. Such errors can be predicted, or corrected, but there are more subtle difficulties in dealing with culture.

In Japan, for example, because of tradition and attitudes, women are constricted in the workplace. Not only is this a waste of a resource, as *The Economist* points out, but also this situation will create future stress in the population. Stress caused by the accommodation of the

old and new is everywhere in the world. The Bedouins, the age-old nomads of the desert, have now taken to the cities of the Middle East. Yet, as Longina Jakubowska writes, their older traditions still have some power. For instance, women cannot run off with their lovers; if they do, tribal honor must be upheld and the transgressors punished.

Although this example may seem quaint to the Western mind, foreign attitudes deserve contemplation and respect, if for no other reason than to avoid surprise. Take, for example, the furor over Salman Rushdie's novel *The Satanic Verses*. Rushdie, a British citizen, wrote in what Muslims considered to be a profane fashion about Muhammad and the Koran. To Islamic people this act was worthy of death, but in the West it was a matter of freedom of speech. Who was right, and on what basis? In a world of interdependence and global problems, such conflicts should be avoided. But how?

Another potentially devastating global problem is the greenhouse effect, which climatologists say is already underway and irreversible. It may cause a rise in sea levels and a change in agricultural areas, possibly with surprising swiftness. As the temperate zone moves northward, the environment of the United States could be dramatically altered. Richard A. Houghton and George M. Woodwell look at the possibilities.

The American naturalist John Muir once said that when you tug at a single thing in nature, you will find it attached to the rest of the world. So it is with the human species in this new modern world. To understand our condition, and to act with intelligence and compassion, we need to learn the history of world civilizations. The American Historical Association, as Akira Iriye summarizes, has undergone a transition from being a historical association for American history to being an organization in America for history. This is indicative of a broadening intellectual interest. The earth is filled with wonders and perils, and we need to know its history for our own salvation and inspiration.

Looking Ahead: Challenge Questions

What are the major problems in the world today?

How could these problems be solved?

What are the complications of population control?

Compare the situation of women in Japan with that of women in Bedouin society.

What values clashed in the case of Salman Rushdie?

Do you have a solution to the Rushdie problem?

What caused the greenhouse effect and can it be stopped? How?

Why is history important?

Population and Economic Growth

The world's population, increasing by more than one million human beings a week, reached a total of five billion in 1986. Since the time of Thomas Malthus (1766–1834), scholars and philosophers have worried that population growth, if unchecked, would doom mankind to famine, disease, and dire poverty. Today, that threat seems acute among some of the rapidly growing peoples of the Third World. Here, Harvard's Nick Eberstadt examines the diverse economic effects of the much-publicized "population explosion." His surprising conclusion: The size and growth rate of a poor country's population are seldom crucial to its material prospects. What matters most, he contends, is how well a society and its leaders cope with change.

THE THIRD WORLD

Nick Eberstadt

Nick Eberstadt, is a Visiting Fellow at the Harvard University Center for Population Studies and a Visiting Scholar at the American Enterprise Institute for Public Policy Research. Born in New York City, he received a B.A. from Harvard (1976), an M.Sc. from the London School of Economics (1978), and is a doctoral candidate at Harvard's John F. Kennedy School of Government. His most recent book is Poverty & Policy in Marxist-Leninist Countries *(forthcoming).*

The world's poorer nations are in the midst of an unprecedented "population revolution." The revolution is occurring not in the delivery room, but in the minds of men who run governments. In Africa, Asia, and Latin America, political leaders of the Left and Right have variously agreed that one thing is crucial: shaping the size and growth rate of their populations.

These officials, along with many Westerners, have come to embrace the idea that slowing the birthrate in the Third World is essential to economic progress, and, indeed, will foster rapid modernization. As early as 1967, President Lyndon B. Johnson endorsed this view. "Five dollars in family planning aid," he said, "would do more for many less-developed countries than $100 of development aid."

Family planning programs, directed by governments and implemented on a massive scale, seemed feasible only after the 1957 invention of the birth control pill by Gregory Pincus, an American scientist at the Worcester Foundation for Experimental Biology. Third World governments, however, were long reluctant to make population control a top priority: They rebuffed U.S. efforts to win backing for the idea at the 1974 United Nations (UN) World Population Conference in Bucharest. A delegate from Communist China, the planet's most populous nation, declared that "the large population of the Third World is an important condition for the fight against imperialism." Many Third World delegates argued that Washington and its well-to-do Western allies were simply trying to divert attention from their obligations to the poor nations. To Washington's chagrin, the conference voted, as an Algerian delegate put it, "to restore the paramountcy of development over the matter of negatively influencing fertility rates."

A Plea for Modesty

"After the brouhaha of Bucharest, however," recalls Charles B. Keely, of the Population Council in New York, "the population establishment, led by the United Nations Fund for Population Activities, set about its business; and soon family planning programs and a government role in them became the accepted wisdom in most developing nations."

Today, with UN encouragement, more than 40 Third World regimes, including the governments of six of the world's 10 largest nations, are developing or implementing "population plans." Overall, some 2.7 billion people live under regimes committed to carrying out such policies. They comprise about three-quarters of the population of the less-developed regions of the earth, and nearly three-fifths of the entire world population.

In the past, national governments often performed tasks with demographic consequences—the regulation of immigration, for example, or the eradication of communicable diseases. But the demographic impact of such efforts was always secondary to their intended purpose (e.g., the preservation of national sovereignty, the promotion of public health). The policy of harnessing state power to the goal of altering the demographic rhythms of society per se suggests a new relationship between state and citizen.

In South Asia, for example, General Hossain Mohammad Ershad's regime in Bangladesh is committed to reducing the fertility rate of the nation's 95 million people to 2.5 births per family by the year 2000. In West Africa, the government of Ghana (pop. 13 million) is aiming for 3.3 births per family. Parents in Bangladesh, however, seem to be having an average of six children and Ghana's parents an average of perhaps seven children. Statistics on Third World nations are unreliable, but the families of Bangladesh today appear to be as large as ever, and Ghanaians seem to be having *bigger* families than in the recent past. If Bangladesh and Ghana are to attain their targets, both governments must oversee a 50 percent reduction in their people's fertility during the next 15 years.

How such a radical alteration of personal behavior in so intimate a sphere—the bedroom—is to be achieved is not clear. But if these governments are serious about meeting their goals, they will need to resort to direct, far-reaching, and possibly even forceful intervention into the daily lives of their citizens. Among the nations that already have turned to coercion is India, where hundreds of thousands of men and women were sterilized against their will during the mid-1970s.

Unfortunately for the ordinary people in all of the 40 countries devoted to activist population plans, their governments have acted on the basis of a serious misconception.

The fact is that there is much less to the "science" of population studies than most politicians realize or proponents concede.

Do slower population gains *cause* economic development, or vice versa?

What other factors are involved?

None of the studies done by population specialists answer these questions. In the same year that Lyndon Johnson voiced his faith in family planning, Simon Kuznets, Harvard's late Nobel laureate in economics, called for "intellectual caution and modesty" on population issues. Scholarship, he declared, "is inadequate in dealing with such a fundamental aspect of economic growth as its relation to population increase." Kuznets's plea was, as we know, largely ignored.

I
THE PERILS OF DEMOGRAPHY

Writers and thinkers have debated the "population question" for centuries. Plato argued that the ideal community would limit itself to exactly 5,040 citizens; Aristotle warned that overpopulation would "bring certain poverty to the citizens, and poverty is the cause of sedition and evil." John Locke, on the other hand, suggested in 1699 that large numbers were a source of wealth. In 1798, Thomas Malthus, the spiritual father of today's pessimists, published *An Essay on the Principle of Population*, the famous treatise in which he argued that population would inevitably outstrip "subsistence." During the 1930s, John Maynard Keynes and other economists warned that *falling* birthrates would exacerbate unemployment, erode living standards, and spark a food crisis—precisely the threats that pundits see in today's high birthrates in the Third World.*

Few of the basic issues in this centuries-old debate have been

*Among the less-heralded intellectual forebears of today's "science" of population studies are the 19th-century social Darwinists, who warned that "inferior" nations, ethnic groups, or social classes might outprocreate their betters. Toward the turn of the century, an English anthropologist named Francis Galton founded the pseudoscience of eugenics, claiming that he could identify individuals and entire "races" endowed by heredity with superior qualities. One eugenicist, Madison Grant, president of the New York Zoological Society, urged America to "take all means to encourage the multiplication of desirable types and abate drastically the increase of the unfit and miscegenation by widely diverse races."

resolved. One lesson that can be drawn from the recurring arguments, however, is that the population question has usually engaged man's fervor more than his intellect.

That is not surprising. After all, the debate involves many matters of deep personal conviction. To talk about population issues is to touch upon the nature of free will; the rights of the living and the unborn; the roles of the sexes; the obligation of the individual to his society or to his God; the sanctity of the family; society's duties to the poor; the destiny of one's nation or one's race; and the general prospects of mankind.

These are fundamentally questions of conscience or creed, not of science. Avowed political ideology is not always a reliable indicator of a country's stance on "population policy." Communist China's "one-child" policy, with its harsh penalties for large families, represents the contemporary world's most drastic current effort to curb population growth [see box, p. 213]. But Prime Minister Lee Kuan Yew of Singapore, who governs a nominally open society with a nominally democratic government, has embraced policies with many of the same precepts.

Around the world, today's campaign against "overpopulation" resembles nothing so much as a religious crusade. Faith, far more than facts, inspires the politicians and intellectuals, North or South, who fervently believe that they have found a "magic bullet" solution to the problems of economic development.

This zeal emerges in the messianic pronouncements of some of today's most influential thinkers on population control. They often evoke the specter of a population apocalypse—and justify the enormous sacrifices they favor by holding out the prospect of demographic salvation. Thus, Stanford biologist Paul Ehrlich began his 1968 best seller *The Population Bomb* with the prophetic words: "The battle to feed all of humanity is over. In the 1970s the world will undergo famines—hundreds of millions of people will starve to death in spite of any crash programs embarked upon now."

Changing the Date

That dire prediction was echoed in 1972 by an international group of researchers gathered under the aegis of the Club of Rome. Their much-publicized report, *The Limits to Growth*, predicted a population "collapse" more devastating than that caused by the Black Death in medieval Europe unless global ecological and population trends were reversed. A feat of that magnitude presumably could only be accomplished with far-reaching and praetorian social controls. And in 1973, Robert McNamara, then president of the World Bank, warned that "the threat of unmanageable population pressures is very much like the threat of nuclear war.... Both threats can and will have catastrophic consequences unless they are dealt with rapidly and rationally."

Few of these true believers are nonplused when events prove them wrong. Like disappointed prophets of the millennium, they simply move the day of reckoning forward or refashion their dire predictions in terms too vague to be disproved.

In recent years, faith in such prophets has waned somewhat in Western official and academic circles. In 1986, for example, the U.S. National Research Council, which had published an alarmist assessment of global population trends in 1971, issued a much more sober-minded study, *Population Growth and Economic Development: Policy Questions*. Family planning programs, it concluded, "cannot make a poor country rich or even move it many notches higher on the scale of development."

But Third World governments are still attracted by the prospect of "scientifically" advancing their national welfare through population control. And Charles Keely's "population establishment"—at the UN, in academe, and in numerous private think tanks in America and Western Europe—is still sounding the alarm. Almost always, popular journalism reflects their convictions. "The consequences of a failure to bring the world's population growth under control are frightening," *Time* declared in 1984. "They could include widespread hunger and joblessness.... heightened global instability, violence, and authoritarianism."

Population studies cannot be expected to provide solutions to such problems. Just as no one would demand that historians create a unified "theory of history," it is asking too much of demographers to expect them to provide overarching "laws of population." For all the mathematical rigor of some of its investigations, population studies is a field of social inquiry, not a natural science. Researchers may uncover relationships between population change and prosperity, poverty, or war in particular places at particular times, but none of these findings can be generalized to cover the world at large.

Indeed, it is difficult even to forecast the long-term growth rates of human populations with any accuracy. During the 1920s, Raymond Pearl, one of America's leading population biologists, predicted that U.S. census-takers would not count 200 million Americans until the start of the 22nd century. In fact, the United States passed that mark during the 1960s. During the 1930s, France's foremost demographers agreed that the French population was certain to fall between five and 30 percent by 1980. However, despite the losses it sustained during World War II, France's population *rose* by about 30 percent.

An Embarrassment of Theories

Some long-range estimates of population trends have been quite accurate. But long-term forecasts for particular regions or countries are still frequently wrong. In 1959, for example, the UN's "mid-range" prediction envisioned India's 1981 population at 603 million, too low by nearly 20 percent.

Despite improvements in the software and computers that demographers use, it is actually getting harder to foresee the demographic future. One reason is that new medicines and public health programs have enabled even the poorer nations to make deep cuts in their death rates quickly and inexpensively—if their governments choose to spend the money.

The unpredictable "human factor" also affects fertility. In England and Wales, it took almost 80 years during the 19th and early 20th centuries for the birthrate to fall by 15 points, from about 35 to 20 births per 1,000 people. Following World War II, Japan experienced a 15-point drop between 1948 and 1958 without any aggressive government intervention, and birthrates may have dropped by 20 points in China during the 1970s.

So every nation follows its own path: Personal choice and national culture seem stronger influences than any pat structural parameters of social science.

Low fertility, for example, is often said to go hand in hand with high levels of health. Yet life expectancy in contemporary Kenya, where women now seem to bear more than eight children on average, is almost exactly equal to that of Germany during the mid-1920s, when that country's total fertility rate was only 2.3 children per woman. Nineteenth-century France experienced a drop in fertility even though the nation's death rates were considerably higher than those in Bangladesh today.

Another demographic truism is that people in poor nations have more children than those in wealthier lands. The limits of that generalization are suggested by the World Bank's *World Development Report 1985*. According to those statistics, Zimbabwe's level of output per capita and its birthrate are *both* about twice as high as the corresponding measures in Sri Lanka.

Demographers have, in a sense, an embarrassment of theories. As historian Charles Tilly puts it, they offer "too many explanations in general terms which contradict each other to some degree, and which fail to fit some significant part of the facts."

There is also a "fact" problem, evident, for example, in the treatment of Somalia in the *World Development Report 1985*. The report presents an estimate of 5.1 million for Somalia's 1983 population—implying a margin of error of 100,000, or about two percent. It also puts Somalia's birthrate at 50 per 1,000 for both 1965 and 1983—again implying a two percent margin of error. The unhappy surprise is that Somalia has no registration system for births whatsoever, and has never conducted a census. The World Bank's numbers were essentially invented: guesses dignified with decimal points.*

Somalia, of course, is an extreme example. Almost every modern nation has by now conducted at least one census of its people. Even so, it would be a mistake to take for granted the precision of estimates by the World Bank or by the many other international organizations that publish them. Only about 10 percent of the Third

World's population lives in nations with near-complete systems for registering births and deaths. And the published economic data on most poor nations are even less reliable.

What Is Overpopulation?

Nevertheless, the general outlines of the population trends that some scholars and political leaders call a "crisis" are not hard to sketch. Until the 20th century, births and deaths were roughly balanced in most of the Third World, with both at relatively high levels. During this century, improved sanitation and health care have cut death rates dramatically, especially among children, while birthrates have stayed relatively high. As a result of these changes, the Third World did indeed experience a "population explosion," growing from two billion souls in 1960 to 3.6 billion in 1985, according to the UN's best estimates.

Based on the West's experience, some specialists assume that Third World birthrates will now begin to fall until a new equilibrium between births and deaths, and more stable population growth, is achieved. That interpretation seems consistent with current trends, for example, in many of the nations of Latin America. But it is far from clear that such a "demographic transition" will occur quickly or even of its own accord. That uncertainty has spurred political leaders from Karachi to Mexico City to try to curb "overpopulation" by government action.

But what is overpopulation? There are no workable demographic definitions. Consider these possible indicators:

• *A high birthrate.* The U.S. birthrate during the 1790s was about 55 per 1,000 people, more than 20 points higher than the latest World Bank estimates of the birthrates for India, Vietnam, Indonesia, or the Philippines.

• *A steep rate of natural increase (births minus deaths).* By this measure, the United States was almost certainly overpopulated between 1790 and 1800. Its annual rate of natural increase then was

---

MEXICO

"Poor Mexico, so far from God, so close to the United States," mourned President Porfirio Diaz a century ago. Yet the proximity that he lamented has, in one way, proved a godsend to his successors and to millions of Mexicans.

Every year, an estimated one to six million *mojados* (wets) illegally cross the Rio Grande in search of work on farms or in factories. After saving the lion's share of their earnings for a few months, most return to their villages; later, they head north again. The unemployment rate in Mexico officially averages 8.5 percent, but "underemployment" is said to reach 40 percent. In a land of some 79 million people, the working-age population grows by 3.2 percent annually.

Those statistics, argue many U.S. scholars and politicians, are all one needs to know about the causes of illegal immigration. "With unemployment increasing and hundreds of thousands of field hands moving illegally into the United States, the crisis nature of Mexico's annual population increase became evident" in 1972, writes Marvin Alisky, an Arizona State University political scientist. The "crisis" prompted Mexico's government to mount an expensive family planning campaign, publicized in a TV soap opera, "Maria la Olvidada" (Maria the Forgotten One), a victim of her husband's machismo. Officials were helped by the Mexican Catholic Church, which broke with Rome to implicitly endorse the program. With their priests' consent, millions of Mexicans felt free to begin using modern contraceptives. Within 10 years, overall annual population growth slid from an estimated 3.6 percent—very high for such a relatively prosperous nation—to 2.3 percent, or about the same rate as in Egypt.

•

The fact is that many Mexicans would trek north even if there were no "population pressure." One big reason: Wages in the United States are three times as high as those in Mexico.

Even so, the illegal influx probably would be smaller were it not for Mexico's long series of wrong turns in economic policy. In some ways, Mexico is one of Latin America's success stories, with a record of rapid economic growth since World War II surpassed only by Brazil's. But growth has not created a corresponding number of jobs. During the 1960s, the Mexican economy expanded by more than six percent annually; yet, according to one study, its demand for labor rose by only 2.3 percent per year.

Under President Miguel Alemán Valdes (1946–52), Mexico, like many other Third World nations, adopted a policy of "import substitution," seeking

---

*Over the years, the World Bank also issued seemingly precise data on Ethiopia. In 1985, after Ethiopia conducted its first census, the Bank was obliged to drop its estimate of the nation's birthrate by 15 percent and to boost its figure for Ethiopia's population by more than 20 percent.

three percent—almost exactly the rate that the World Bank ascribes to Bangladesh today, and considerably higher than the rates prevailing in Haiti and India. Today, population is growing faster in the United States than it is in Cuba, Eastern Europe, or the Soviet Union, all of them in economic torpor.

- *Population density.* By this measure, in 1980 France was more overpopulated than Indonesia, and the United Kingdom was in worse shape than India. The world's most densely populated nation in 1980: Prince Rainier's Monaco.
- *The "dependency ratio" (the proportion of children and the elderly to the "working-age" population).* According to 1980 World Bank data, the world's *least* overpopulated lands were crowded Singapore and the United Arab Emirates, where immigration was helping to achieve an ultrarapid population growth rate of 11 percent a year.
- *Poverty.* Inadequate incomes, poor health, malnutrition, overcrowded housing, and unemployment are the unambiguous images of poverty. But it is a profound error to equate these social and economic ills with problems of population. Upon closer examination, it becomes clear that many of these Third World woes are closely related to ill-advised government policies, such as those that discriminate against farmers in favor of city dwellers or stifle private initiative. More generally, what are often mistaken for "population problems" are usually manifestations of state-imposed restrictions that prevent ordinary individuals from pursuing what they see as their own welfare and the welfare of their families.

II

THE POOREST OF THE POOR

The catchall term "Third World" conceals at least as much as it

to nurture steel, chemicals, and other industries to reduce the need to buy manufactured goods from abroad.

Alemán and subsequent presidents imposed stiff tariffs on foreign goods, exempting only the foreign-made tools and machinery that Mexico's infant industries needed to get started. They offered cheap loans to Mexican entrepreneurs. Bowing to labor union pressure, the government also required industrial employers to contribute heavily to new pensions, schooling, and profit-sharing programs for their workers.

All of these measures artificially boosted the cost of labor relative to capital, encouraging Mexico's industrialists to replace workers with machinery.

At the same time, protectionism eased competitive pressures on Mexican factory managers, especially those in state-run enterprises, to control costs and improve quality. Mexico's exports suffered; more jobs were lost. To make matters worse, the government neglected Mexican agriculture, which employed the bulk of the nation's workers. As the wage gap between farmers and factory workers widened, many Mexicans deserted the countryside, subsisting in the city slums without work or in marginal occupations—shining shoes, peddling fruit or flowers—in the hope of landing the elusive "high-paying job." The population of greater Mexico City soared to 17 million.

Paradoxically, the discovery of vast new oil reserves in Mexico in 1976 hurt its basic economic health. As in Nigeria and Venezuela, swelling oil revenues made it easy to import foreign products without relying on exports of domestic goods to pay the bills. Succumbing to the "oil syndrome," President José Lopez Portillo (1976–82) went on a spending spree, borrowing heavily, expanding the government payroll, and boosting industrial subsidies.

Today, five years after world oil prices began to fall, Mexico is $98 billion in debt. Despite its continuing promises of reform to the World Bank and other lenders, the government of President Miguel de la Madrid Hurtado appears to have done little to relieve the productivity-constricting restraints it has imposed upon the national economy.

Encouraging citizens to seek jobs in the United States may simply be seen, in Mexico City, as a substitute for taking painful economic measures at home.

—N. E.

reveals about the 133 nations it encompasses. Any classification that lumps together Hong Kong and Chad, or Iran and Jamaica, or Cuba and South Africa, loses much of its meaning. Even within a single country, social, cultural, and economic differences can be profound. India, for example, has a single central government, but at least six major religions, six alphabets, and a dozen major languages. Life expectancy is thought to be 20 years greater in Kerala, India's healthiest state, than in impoverished Uttar Pradesh. The fertility rates in these two states of India differ by almost three children per woman.

Such variations, to say nothing of the dubious social and economic statistics available for many less-developed countries, suggest that the best way of gaining some insight into the population question may be to examine a few specific cases.

Let us begin by looking at the most troubled populations of the modern world: the nations at the low end of the national income spectrum. By the reckoning of the World Bank's *World Development Report 1984*, eight of the 34 nations that the Bank classifies as "low-income economies" were poorer in terms of gross national product (GNP) per capita during the early 1980s than they were in 1960. The unhappy eight were: Chad, Nepal, Zaire, Uganda, Somalia, Niger, Madagascar, and Ghana.

By the World Bank's estimate, these nations had a total of over 90 million inhabitants in 1982. Between 1960 and 1982, their economies grew, albeit slowly. Population, however, increased faster—indeed, the rate of population increase is said to have *accelerated* in five of the nations. The Bank's estimates of population growth range from just under two percent annually in Chad to more than three percent a year in Niger.

War, Politics, Chaos

Do these numbers mean that rapid population growth dragged these nations deeper into poverty?

Not necessarily. For one thing, many of the statistics that point to a drop in GNP per capita are suspect or contradictory. Take the numbers for Niger: According to the *World Development Report 1984*, the former French West African colony's GNP per capita fell by about 29 percent between 1960 and 1982. According to other tables in the same report, however, private consumption per capita in Niger *increased* by about three percent during the same years, investment per capita jumped by over 35 percent, and government spending maintained a steady share of GNP. The only logical conclusion: GNP per capita must, in fact, have gone up.

Another set of figures from the same report supports that conclusion. Based on what the report's authors say about the growth of Niger's exports (which include uranium, peanuts, and cotton) and the share of its GNP derived from them, one comes to the conclusion that Niger's GNP per capita *grew* by almost six percent annually between 1960 and 1982. That would add up to a cumulative jump of 240 percent during those years.

What, in truth, are the correct numbers for Niger?

It is impossible to tell from the World Bank's figures.

Let us ignore such inexactitudes for the moment, however, and accept the World Bank estimates of growing poverty in these eight nations as accurate. Would they allow us to conclude that population growth was to blame? No. The figures show only that their economies grew more slowly than population, not *why* they did.

Although the World Bank estimates that the rate of natural increase in these eight nations quickened between 1960 and 1982, the speedup, according to Bank numbers, was chiefly the result of a drop in death rates. In other words, their people suffered less sickness and disease. How could that have reduced their productivity?

The cause of the economic woes of these countries must lie elsewhere. In three of the eight nations—Chad, Somalia, and Uganda—the explanation seems clear enough. Chad has been convulsed by unending civil war since the late 1960s, with Libya joining in; Uganda remains in chaos even though Idi Amin's barbarous eight-year rule ended in 1979; Somalia has been fully mobilized for war against Ethiopia for nearly a decade. (The Somali government claims that it spends "only" 14 percent of GNP on defense; U.S. defense outlays are 6.5 percent of GNP.) Politics can fully account for the misfortunes of these three African nations. There seems to be no need in these cases to resort to demographic explanations.

6. WORLD PROBLEMS AND INTERDEPENDENCE

What about the difficulties of Ghana, Madagascar, Nepal, Niger, and Zaire (formerly the Belgian Congo)?

Many development economists argue that rapid population growth retards economic progress by slowing the accumulation of capital needed to build factories, harbors, and roads. However, if the World Bank's figures are accurate, low investment was not a major problem in four out of these five stricken nations.

In Nepal, Zaire, and Niger, the investment ratios for 1983 were all reckoned at 20 percent or more—higher than those in many advanced industrial nations, including the United States (17 percent). Indeed, a number of Third World nations with higher rates of population growth and lower investment ratios outperformed this trio.

Ghana is the only one of the five suffering from capital scarcity today. But that was not always so. By the World Bank's reckoning, Ghana's gross domestic investment ratio in 1960 was 24 percent—more than twice as high as the 1960 estimates for Singapore or South Korea.

If the World Bank's numbers are correct, the economies of these five countries have been afflicted by an extremely low ratio of growth to investment. In other words, heavy capital outlays yielded very meager dividends. (Madagascar's ratio of economic growth to investment appears to be only half the U.S. rate; Zaire's seems to be less than a third as high as Spain's; Ghana's during the 1960s and '70s was about one-tenth that of South Korea.) To find out what has been going wrong in these countries, one must inquire into the economic policies of their political leaders.

A Reign of Error

Take Ghana. During the late 1950s and early '60s, it was one of a select group of nations (including Burma, Chile, and Egypt) that economists were touting as bright prospects in the Third World.

After the West African nation gained its independence from Britain in 1957, Kwame Nkrumah, the charismatic new prime minister, quickly embarked on an ambitious "reform" program. Casting aside such economic considerations as competitiveness and productivity, he decided to seek prosperity by political means. "The social and economic development of Africa," he declared, "will come only within the political kingdom, not the other way round."

Nkrumah aimed to transform Ghana into a prestigious industrial power at all costs. The nation's long-successful small farmers were to foot the bill.

Nkrumah forced the farmers to sell their cocoa, the nation's chief export, at a fixed price to the government, which then sold it abroad at a profit. The proceeds were poured into Nkrumah's industrial development schemes.* By the late 1970s, long after Nkrumah, the self-styled "Redeemer," had been deposed, Ghana's small cocoa farmers were getting less than 40 percent of the world price for their crop—an effective tax of over 60 percent. Not surprisingly, Ghana's cocoa output and cocoa exports plummeted.

As these new policies made their mark on agriculture, Nkrumah took aim at industry. Shortly after independence, he nationalized the nation's foreign-owned gold and diamond mines, cocoa-processing plants, and other enterprises. Ghana's new infant industries were also state-owned. The result was inefficiency on a monumental scale. According to one study, between 65 percent and 71 percent of Ghana's publicly owned factory capacity lay idle 10 years after independence.

To cut the price of imported goods, Nkrumah allowed the Ghanaian cedi to rise in the world currency markets. Unfortunately, that also drove up the price of the products Ghana was trying to sell overseas. The nation's trade balance tilted deeply into the red.

Under these diverse pressures, the nation's visible tax base began to shrink, even as the government budget swelled. Foreign aid did not solve the problem. Deficit spending increased: By 1978, tax revenues paid less than 40 percent of the government's budget. Inflation spiraled, climbing by over 30 percent a year during the 1970s, according to the World Bank. With annual interest rates fixed by law at levels as low as six percent (to reduce the cost of capital), it made no sense for Ghanaians to put their money in the bank.

By 1982, only one percent of Ghana's GNP was devoted to investment. Black Africa's most promising former colony had become an economic disaster.

So Ghana's current economic travails can be explained without recourse to demographic theory. The nation's parlous economic

straits are the result of Accra's 29-year reign of error. Rapid population growth may have compounded the woes caused by mismanagement, or it may have eased these pressures somewhat by creating a better-educated, healthier, and potentially more productive work force. It may have done both. But its overall impact on the course of events does not seem to have been great.

Food for the Hungry

The most haunting evidence of a Malthusian crisis in Africa—a growing number of hungry mouths to feed and ever-diminishing resources—is the images of hunger and starvation that regularly appear on TV news broadcasts. The U.S. Department of Agriculture estimates that farm output per capita in Black Africa dropped by nine percent between 1969–71 and 1979–81. In one African country after another, write Lester R. Brown and Edward C. Wolf of the Worldwatch Institute, "demands of escalating human numbers are exceeding the sustainable yield of local life-support systems—croplands, grasslands, and forests. Each year, Africa's farmers attempt to feed 16 million additional people."

In this bleak view, population pressures are pushing people into marginal lands, which are eventually reduced to desert by overgrazing and deforestation. Indeed, the evidence of food shortages and famine in the nations of the Sahel—from Senegal in the west to the Sudan in the east—is undeniable.

But does all of this mean that population growth per se is causing food shortages in sub-Saharan Africa?

In fact, none of the nations with the poorest records of farm output—Ghana, Mozambique, Uganda (where output per capita dropped by more than 30 percent between 1969–71 and 1979–81), and Angola (where it fell by more than 50 percent)—is in the drought-stricken Sahel. Several African nations have creditable records of improving farm productivity, and they are right next door to the nations with the most severe problems: Prosperous Kenya is contiguous to Uganda, Mozambique adjoins Zimbabwe (formerly Rhodesia), and a common border unites Ghana and the flourishing Ivory Coast. Since the climates and population growth rates of these nations were broadly similar, something else must have been at work.

In the overwhelming majority of cases, the food crisis in Black Africa has obvious political and economic causes. In Uganda, Mozambique, and Angola, coups or revolutions were followed by continuing domestic violence, persecution of minority groups, and, as in Ghana, destructive economic policies. In Ethiopia, where mass starvation has reached its most tragic proportions, the fault lies largely with the

POPULATION GROWTH AND POVERTY

POPULATION
GROWTH RATE,
1973–1983
(per year)

☐

▨ One percent to less than two percent

☐ Two percent to less than three percent

■ Three percent or more

▨ No data

THE WORLD'S TEN POOREST COUNTRIES
Based on 1983 GNP per capita

1 Ethiopia	6 Burkina Faso (formerly Upper Volta)
2 Bangladesh	7 Burma
3 Mali	8 Malawi
4 Nepal	9 Uganda
5 Zaire	10 Burundi

*Nkrumah also received generous aid from abroad during his 10-year rule, including $145.6 million in economic assistance from the United States.

forced collectivization of farming and other cruel and disastrous accomplishments of a 12-year-old Marxist regime, now headed by Mengistu Haile Mariam, turning an ordinary drought into a deadly famine. But Ethiopia is only one of the most extreme cases. During the decades since independence, more and more regimes in Black Africa have adopted misguided policies that have variously restricted trade, discouraged farm production, and depressed local industry.

III

THE 'LITTLE DRAGONS'

On the basis of demographic criteria alone, four of the most likely candidates for severe "population problems" after World War II were Singapore, Hong Kong, Taiwan, and South Korea. As they entered the 1950s, they were among the most densely peopled lands in the world. There were almost four times as many people per square mile in Taiwan as in mainland China; South Korea's population density was nearly twice as high as India's.

These crowded lands were blessed with comparatively little in the way of oil, coal, iron, or other natural resources. Hong Kong and Singapore imported even their drinking water. All four had high fertility levels during the early 1950s: six births per woman was the lowest level. During the period from 1950 to 1980, population grew faster in Taiwan (2.7 percent per year), Hong Kong (2.7 percent), and Singapore (2.9 percent) than in the world's less-developed countries as a whole (an estimated 2.3 percent). South Korea, despite suffering perhaps one million deaths during the Korean War, still grew by an average rate of about two percent annually.

Dependency ratios were high, with the young and the elderly vastly outnumbering workers. Twenty-five years ago, unemployment and underemployment were still pervasive. The signs of poverty and even destitution—sprawling city slums, malnutrition, unemployment—were everywhere.

Many observers expected nothing but grim futures for these impoverished lands. In 1947, General Albert Wedemeyer, dispatched from Washington to assess South Korea's prospects, reported: "Basically an agricultural area, [it] does not have the overall economic resources to sustain its economy without external assistance.... It is not considered feasible to make South Korea self-sustaining."

Such judgments proved almost ludicrously wrong. Today, Singapore, Hong Kong, Taiwan, and South Korea are known as Asia's "little dragons." In all four lands, GNP per capita quadrupled between 1960 and 1980, despite rapid population growth. Unemployment (and, with the exception of South Korea, underemployment) have virtually disappeared. Despite an "adverse" balance of "dependent" age groups to working-age population, each society sharply increased domestic investment per capita. Despite high ratios of population to arable land, measured malnutrition was virtually eliminated. Even without a wealth of natural resources, all four have emerged as major export centers and commercial entrepôts.

What explains these success stories? Edward K. Y. Chen, an economist at the University of Hong Kong, has attempted a breakdown of the "sources of growth" for the four from the late 1950s through 1970. By his accounting, increased "inputs" of capital and labor alone explain less than half the growth of Taiwan, Singapore, and South Korea and barely more than half of Hong Kong's. Improvements in "total factor productivity" (net output per unit of net expenditure) account for the remainder. In short, the economies of the little dragons were simply more efficient than were those of other less-developed nations.

Not that they all found a *single* success formula. Hong Kong's economy is freewheeling and lightly regulated, while Taiwan's Nationalist government owns a number of inefficient large enterprises. South Korea blocks most foreign investment and runs constant balance of payments deficits, while Singapore holds more foreign currency reserves than does oil-rich Kuwait. Hong Kong is a British colony, Singapore a nominal parliamentary democracy, and South Korea a virtual dictatorship. But there are common elements in their success: "outward-looking" export-promotion policies, including reduction of barriers against imports, minimal restraints on interest rates, subsidies to encourage production for foreign markets, and an openness to the adoption of technology from abroad.

The relationship between population change and economic development in the little dragons is more ambiguous. During their decades of astonishing economic growth, all four enjoyed rapid fertility declines. (Rates now range from two children per woman in Hong Kong and Singapore to just under three in South Korea.) Many development specialists credit state-sponsored family planning programs with bringing birthrates down in these countries. But, as we have seen, that explanation may not suffice.

A Nobel Prize winner, Paul Samuelson of the Massachusetts Institute of Technology, once observed that there are always two plausible, and opposite, answers to any "common sense" question in economics. So it is with the effects of population growth.

Such growth may impose costly new burdens on a government, or it may expand the tax revenue base. It may cause food shortages, or it may speed the division of labor by which farm productivity is increased. If it tends to increase unemployment by adding new workers to the labor pool, it also tends to reduce the danger of insufficient consumer demand that so troubled Keynes and many other Western economists during the Great Depression of the 1930s.

The overall impact of population change on a society seems to depend on how the society deals with change *of all kinds*. Indeed, coping with fluctuations in population is in many ways less demanding than dealing with the almost daily uncertainties of the harvest, or the ups and downs of the business cycle, or the vagaries of political life. Societies and governments that meet such challenges successfully, as the little dragons did, are also likely to adapt well to population change. Those that do not are likely to find that a growing population "naturally" causes severe, costly, and prolonged dislocations.

AROUND THE WORLD, 1973–1983

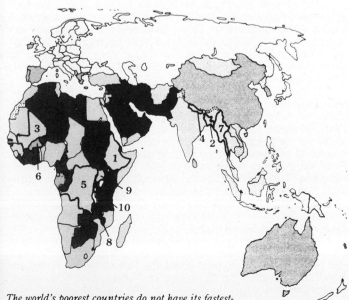

The world's poorest countries do not have its fastest-growing populations. Most destitute is Ethiopia, with a GNP per capita of $120, and a population growth rate equal to Hong Kong's.

IV

HUMAN CAPITAL

Spinning the globe offers a broad perspective on the impact, or lack of impact, of population change. One can also "come down to earth" to examine the behavior of individuals and their families.

Much of today's alarm over population growth springs from simple arithmetic. Every newborn child shrinks the wealth per person of his family and his nation. In a sense, he begins life as a debit in the national ledger.

During his lifetime, the child will require food, clothing, schooling, and medical attention. But there is no guarantee that he will be able to "repay" his debt during his working life. And if his homeland is developing rapidly, his debt actually grows larger, because the cost of raising children soars and the length of their dependency increases as the economy demands more skilled and educated workers.

During the late 1950s and early 1960s, development scholars, notably Ansley J. Coale and Edgar M. Hoover of Princeton, crafted influential economic models that demonstrated that, beyond some ideal point, additional births would indeed impose an intolerable economic burden on society. These "excess" children, they warned, would, in effect, be "living off capital," draining their societies of savings and investment desperately needed to fuel economic growth.

Getting Rich

Economists have since recognized the limitations of these models. Coale, Hoover, and their colleagues made a number of questionable assumptions. Among them: that economic growth results solely from the accumulation of capital; that the rate of return on capital is fixed; and that education, health care, and all other forms of human consumption bear no productive returns.

Today, the old argument has reappeared in a new, albeit more cautious, form. Some development scholars now contend that Third World governments are in effect subsidizing the births of too many children. How? By providing free services, such as public education, that make it cheaper for families to raise children but increase society's costs.

The Soviet Union offers a fascinating example of how such "externalities" work. To prevent any upsurge of unrest in its Muslim republics, Moscow is spending millions of rubles to provide schools, jobs, and health care for its Muslim citizens. Children are indeed a "bargain" for Muslim parents. Not surprisingly, total fertility in Soviet Central Asia remains in the vicinity of six births per woman—higher than the World Bank's current estimates for neighboring Iran, or nearby Pakistan and India. In this case, the development scholars appear to be right about externalities.

Yet such dramatic gaps between public and private costs rarely occur. Only serious failures of the market mechanism, or, as in the Soviet Union, political decisions, make them possible. In either case, such policies are costly. Except under extraordinary circumstances, they cannot be sustained for long—certainly not long enough to have pronounced effects on childbearing patterns.

Another cause of worry among population specialists is the tendency of poor people to have more children than rich people. If the poor and the well-to-do also have nearly the same death rates, as is now the case in most countries, it makes sense to expect that poverty will spread and the gaps between rich and poor widen.

As it happens, however, the record of modern history does not bear out these fears. In Western nations where the poor have borne more children than the well-to-do for a century or more, long-term economic growth has not slowed. And economists' measures of income distribution, though imperfect, give no indication that the gaps in the West between rich and poor have widened over the long term. In fact, most studies suggest that they are narrower today than they were a century ago.

The data on wealth and poverty in the Third World are even less reliable than comparable statistics on the West, but careful long-term studies have been made of two countries, India and Taiwan. The results show no clear evidence of increased inequality in either nation since World War II, despite population growth, and there is a hint of reduced inequality in Taiwan.

The modern world has witnessed two general, though not universal, trends. First, the productivity of individuals has climbed steadily, enough not only to cover rising standards of living, but also to add to national wealth. That is what has happened in North America and Western Europe over the past four or five generations, despite wars and recessions. And these improvements were not financed by "dipping into capital": Assets per capita in these societies are vastly greater today than they were a century ago.

Thus, over the generations, the people in these societies produced more than they consumed. The pattern was repeated during the rapid climb of Japan and Israel into the ranks of economically advanced nations. Following close on the heels of these industrial

A Taiwanese farmer plants his field using a rice transplanter. By allowing crop prices to rise and dispersing industry throughout the countryside, Taiwan has avoided many of the pitfalls of economic development.

powers are Asia's little dragons and an encouraging number of other Third World countries.

Their success highlights the second general trend of the post–World War II era. Despite the rhetoric of Third World partisans in the "North-South" debate, the history of the past 25 years shows that it is possible for the poor, as well as the rich, to become richer. In fact, the productivity of the poor can rise more rapidly than that of the rich. But certain things have to happen.

Adding Value to Time

In his now-classic studies of economic growth, Simon Kuznets discerned two distinctive features of the economic development of the West between the beginning of the 19th century and the middle of the 20th. The first was that increases in GNP could not be explained simply by the growth of population and the accumulation of physical capital. Secondly, he found that while dividends from capital and other property (e.g., farmland) grew as economies developed, the share of GNP from wages, salaries, and earnings grew even more rapidly. Long-term economic development, Kuznets concluded, depended much less on building factories, power plants, and other capital stock than on the improvement of "human capital"—the ability of human beings to put to work a growing body of knowledge, research, and technology.

Theodore W. Schultz, Nobel laureate in economics at the University of Chicago, refined this notion of human capital. In a series of studies beginning during the 1950s, he showed that government outlays on education, health, and nutrition were not unproductive "consumption," as some economists had defined them to be. Usually, these investments in human beings bore productive returns—often very high ones.

Originally trained as an agricultural economist, Schultz had observed that even in impoverished, "backward" societies, poor people tended to make the most of whatever resources were available to them. He argued that even penniless men and women with nothing to invest but their time would often behave like entrepreneurs. The process of economic development, he argued, is in large part the extension of human choice made possible by the rising value of human time. Time, after all, is the single resource that is absolutely fixed in quantity, nonrenewable, and impossible to trade or save.

By helping their people to improve their health and gain better schooling, for example, governments increased the value of human time, and thus of human capital.

Poor people and poor nations can actually enjoy a paradoxical edge in building up human capital. Because of what the late Alexander Gerschenkron of Harvard called the "advantages of backwardness," they can climb the "learning curve" of economic development much more quickly than the pioneers in other societies who preceded them. Whether by importing penicillin invented and manufactured in the West, or by borrowing the technology for manufacturing com-

The nations of the West achieved prosperity despite rapid population growth. Can the Third World follow the same path, without imposing government-sponsored family planning programs? Sharon L. Camp, vice president of the Population Crisis Committee, writing in Population *(Feb. 1985), argued that the West's experience does not apply to the Third World:*

During Europe's [18th–19th century] population explosion, annual rates of population growth rose from about 0.5 percent to about 1.5 percent. In contrast, Third World countries now have higher birthrates and lower death rates than did Europe, and their annual rate of population increase is about 2.4 percent (excluding China). Some African countries are growing by three to four percent a year—a population doubling time of just over 20 years. The analogy with historical Europe is thus suspect. . . .

The post–World War II population explosion in less-developed countries is largely the result of a precipitous drop in death rates spurred primarily by a revolution in public health and improved response to food crises. The speed and magnitude of these changes are unprecedented. In 18th- and 19th-century Europe, by contrast, death rates declined slowly in response to rising standards of living and remained relatively high compared to current rates in many developing countries. . . .

•

The reverse is true of birthrates. During Europe's Industrial Revolution, cultural and other factors kept birthrates well below the biological maximum. Marriage was delayed to the mid-twenties and not uncommonly to the late twenties. Significant numbers of adults did not marry at all or did not survive their reproductive years. In most Third World countries today, marriage is nearly universal and the majority of women are married by their late teens. Although maternal and infant deaths take a large toll, it is not unusual to find women in developing countries who have been pregnant a dozen times and have eight to 10 living children. . . .

Not only are Third World countries growing two to three times faster, many are starting from a much larger population base than did European countries at a comparable stage of economic development. In most developing countries, population density on arable land is at least three times higher than in 19th-century Europe and rural population growth is twice as rapid despite massive urbanization. The combination of a larger population base and a more rapid rate of growth means that the total number of people added to the Third World's population in the last decade alone exceeds the total increase in Europe's population over the whole of the 19th century.

puter chips, they can reap at relatively low cost the advantages that others paid dearly for. This is precisely what Japan and the little dragons did during their post–World War II economic "catch-up."

Demographic events can profoundly influence when and where this catch-up occurs. Migration is an obvious example. When they move from countryside to city, or from one nation to another, most families pursue economic advantages. The Nigerian who leaves his farm for the city of Lagos makes a personal economic calculation. But by putting himself where his time can be used more productively (e.g., in a factory), he enhances national wealth. In the same way, America's immigrants have added vastly to the nation's affluence (and their own) by fleeing lands where, among other things, their labor was less productively employed.

Small-Family Formula

Another important economic event is the recent fall in mortality rates in many less-developed nations. Coming largely as a result of improvements in nutrition, hygiene, and health care, the drop can be seen as an enormous deposit in the human capital "bank." Not only will the productive working lives of many people be lengthened, but the returns from further "social investments" can be higher. Healthy children, after all, can profit more from extra schooling than can malnourished children.

The economic implications of changes in fertility are more ambiguous. Few parents decide whether or not to have children solely on considerations of profitability. If Western parents did so, they would be childless.

On the other hand, personal choices are always constrained by what is economically feasible. And the economics of the family vary enormously from place to place. In the West, where the economic value of human time is high, preparing a child for adult life is a lengthy and expensive proposition. It consumes a great deal of time

that many parents could otherwise devote to work, and few will call upon their young for financial help in their old age. It is not surprising, then, that Western parents tend to have small families.

In a farming society such as Kenya, on the other hand, children may start working in the fields at an early age and help support their parents long after they reach adulthood. In such societies, where the costs of raising a child are low and the benefits high, it may not be financially punitive to have large families. In India, there is a saying: "One son is no sons." In short, parents may have different views of the family than do their political leaders or their governments' technocrats, a fact worth remembering.

V

FAMILY PLANNING

The Third World's population is considered to be "exploding," despite the fact that governments in all but 27 of these 133 nations promote the use of modern contraceptives among their people, and often distribute them at little or no charge.

The political energy and financial resources expended on these family planning programs are considerable. By the World Bank's estimate, Third World governments spend more than $2 billion annually on such efforts. (The actual purchasing power is probably much greater than dollar figures indicate.) International organizations, Western governments, and charitable institutions also make substantial contributions. Between 1969 and 1984, they added another $7 billion (in 1982 dollars). In some less-developed countries, e.g., Bangladesh, governments spend more on family planning programs than on all other health-related services combined.

What do such programs, and national population policies, actually accomplish? How do they affect current living standards and the prospects for economic development?

Today's national family planning bureaucracies are in the business of subsidizing and promoting the use of birth control pills, intrauterine devices (IUDs), condoms, diaphragms, and other modern contraceptives. These methods are not necessarily more effective than some old approaches to family planning: On grounds of effectiveness alone, nothing can improve upon total abstinence or infanticide. Of course, modern contraception is much more acceptable than these extreme alternatives, and it is also more reliable than some widely used traditional techniques of birth control (such as coitus interruptus, the rhythm method, or drinking native contraceptive potions). Moreover, by making it easier to exercise choice, modern contraception reduces unwanted pregnancies that can cause sickness and death among mothers and infants—notably by preventing closely spaced births. So a voluntary family planning effort can be a useful public health service, one of many government activities that can increase choice, reduce mortality, augment human capital, and improve the well-being of individuals and families.

It is not so clear, however, that voluntary family planning always delivers the big reductions in "unwanted" births that Third World governments seek.

Family planning workers from Nepal to Kenya have discovered that making modern contraceptives available to all does not by itself stimulate a revolution in attitudes toward family size. In Kenya, for example, total fertility appears to have *increased* from under six children per couple to more than eight despite nearly 20 years of officially sponsored family planning efforts.

As Lord Peter Bauer of the London School of Economics has observed, people of all nations are quick to buy Western-style cosmetics, soft drinks, and transistor radios. In most Third World countries, birth control pills, IUDs, and diaphragms are just as available, but are in much less demand.

In the Third World, Bauer writes, "the children who are born are generally desired. They are certainly avoidable. To deny this amounts to saying that Third World parents procreate heedless of consequences. This view treats people with . . . contempt."

Indeed, in many parts of the globe, truly effective family planning might actually *increase* the birthrate. In Zaire, Gabon, and other nations of sub-Saharan Africa, for example, families have demonstrated little interest in modern contraception, but considerable concern about *infertility*. In these societies, a wife who cannot bear children faces an unenviable fate. Increasing parents' "freedom to choose" will always serve the purposes of parents, whatever the preference of the government and its advisors.

Of course, the thrust of most family planning efforts in less-developed countries over the past generation has been antinatalist. And the principal international institutions supporting these programs, including the World Bank and the U.S. Agency for International Development, remain firmly in favor of reducing birthrates.

Unquestioning faith in this goal has led some of the world's poorest governments to pour extraordinary amounts of money into family planning. In 1980, for example, the World Bank estimates that Ghana's family planning program spent $68 per contraceptive user, Nepal's $69. The Bank's data also suggest that government outlays for *all other* health programs totaled only $20 per family in Ghana and $8 in Nepal. In these and other poor nations, government officials seem to believe that birth control yields tremendous benefits.

The Bottom Line

That faith extends even into the academic world. Only a handful of researchers have attempted to *measure* the impact of family planning against a "control group" (i.e., a similar population which lacks the service)—standard practice in the health sciences. The few properly conducted studies do not reveal many differences in fertility decline between "control" and "experimental" groups.

In a little-noticed 1984 study, Donald J. Hernandez, a demographer at Georgetown University, attempted to disentangle the effects of family planning efforts from "natural" declines in fertility. Among the nations he examined were four that have been widely hailed as exemplars of successful family planning programs: Two little dragons, Taiwan and South Korea, as well as Costa Rica and Mauritius.

In Mauritius, he found, family planning might have pushed birthrates down by as much as three to six points over 10 years. However, because of shortcomings in his own methodology, Hernandez cautioned against ascribing too much meaning to this calculation.

In Taiwan, South Korea, and Costa Rica—where Hernandez felt that his methodology would produce more reliable results—he estimated that family planning efforts brought birthrates down only by between 0.1 and 1.6 points over periods ranging from four to 11 years. Hernandez rightly concluded that family planning programs may be able to speed the fall of birthrates somewhat where this decline has begun on its own. But such programs experience "little success and considerable failure in initiating fertility reductions independently of socioeconomic and other indigenous factors."*

One sure way to bring birth trends down is to resort to Draconian measures, as several governments have done. But insofar as they have coerced involuntary behavior out of parents, these governments generally have reduced—not raised—standards of living.

A case in point is Romania's radical effort to *increase* fertility during the 1960s. The nation's Communist leaders had long been concerned that declining birthrates (by that time below the net replacement level) would exacerbate the nation's troublesome labor shortages. In 1966, one year after taking the helm of the Romanian Communist Party, Nicolae Ceauşescu announced a series of measures designed to raise the national birthrate. The most important of these was a sudden restriction of access to abortion, at that time Romanians' principal means of birth control.

Taken unawares by the change in rules, Romanian parents had many more children that year than they had been planning. Romania's crude birthrate in 1967 jumped to 27 per 1,000—almost double the 1966 rate of 14 per 1,000. But as parents reverted to traditional methods of contraception (e.g., rhythm, withdrawal, abstinence), fertility dropped back toward the pre-1966 level. Between 1967 and 1972, the crude birthrate fell from 27 to 18.

But Romania is still paying for its artificial birthrate "blip." Infant mortality jumped and maternal death rates more than doubled between 1966 and 1967. Ceauşescu's edict also created a peculiar

bulge in the Romanian age structure. To accommodate the needs of this "cohort" as it passed through the different stages of childhood and youth, Bucharest has been forced to create and then close down kindergartens, elementary schools, and health clinics—a costly proposition. Entirely apart from the damage done to Romanians' physical health, Bucharest's demographic shock may well have done more to retard the pace of economic progress than to hasten it.

Singapore has taken a more constant approach to population policy, and with the opposite end in view. Lee Kuan Yew, Singapore's prime minister since 1959 and the chief architect of its economic success, seems to be deeply impressed by some of the arguments of the prewar eugenicists. "We are getting a gradual lowering of the general quality of the total [world] population," Lee fretted in 1973. "Over the long run this could have very serious consequences for the human race."

For the island republic of Singapore, he sought "zero, possibly even negative [population] growth. Then we can make up for it with selective immigration of the kind of people we require to run a modern higher technology society."

Penalizing Big Families

Lee's vision of the solution was specific. "We must," he said, "encourage those who earn less than $200 a month [then about half of Singapore's households] never to have more than two [children]" so that Singapore might as its economy progressed be spared a "trend which can leave our society with a large number of the physically, intellectually, and culturally anemic."

In August 1972, Lee's government announced a new policy of "social disincentives against higher order births," to take effect the following year. Among the many disincentives were restrictions on maternity leaves for mothers bearing a third or higher-order child and the elimination of family tax deductions for children born fourth or later, as well as official discrimination against these children in public school placement.

The demographic impact of these strictures is unclear. It is true that since 1975—the third year of the "social disincentives" policy—Singapore's fertility rate has fallen. But the rate was already dropping before 1973, and Lee's new edicts do not appear to have hastened the speed of its fall.*

While the demographic consequences of Singapore's population sanctions are murky, some of the social and economic effects are unmistakable. Lee's program has reduced the living standards of Singaporeans who choose to have large families, widening income gaps in the nation. It has also created a new disadvantaged minority: the youngest children born to large families since August 1973.

Under Lee's law, these youngsters stand last in line for spots in the nation's desirable schools and universities, an important consideration in a society that places a premium on schooling. How the new "undesirables" will finally fare, and how their fate will affect Singapore, remains to be seen. The eldest are only 13 years old today.

VI

THE VALUE OF A LIFE

What, finally, can be said with confidence about the impact of population change on social and economic development in the Third World? As we have seen, much less than partisans in the population debate currently claim. So it may be appropriate to conclude with a few observations distinguished more by their tentativeness than by their insight.

First, population growth (or decline) is a relatively slow form of social change. A rate of population increase of four percent a year is extremely high; four percent price inflation a year is, today, generally

---

*Some family planning advocates claim that there is an enormous unmet need for birth control in the Third World, which only a 50 percent boost in outlays can satisfy. That claim is based on the results of surveys showing that many women say they want no more children or wish to delay the birth of their next child, and also say they are not using modern contraceptives. The researchers ignore the fact that many of these women may be using traditional birth control methods. In any case, Western survey methods are rarely reliable—especially among poor, uneducated people in less-developed nations. Moreover, the interrogators never put their questions to men, who, in many societies, have the final say in such matters.

*During the decade before the disincentives were announced, Singapore's birthrate dropped from 22 per 1,000 people to 17 per 1,000. Since 1973, Singaporeans *have* had smaller families. In 1980, fourth and higher-order births accounted for about seven percent of all live births—as against more than 28 percent in 1970. But this pattern was not distinctly different from those in comparable countries. In Hong Kong, which imposes no penalties for having large families, only nine percent of all births in 1980 were children born fourth or later.

CHINA

"Every stomach comes with hands attached," Chairman Mao once said in explaining his laissez-faire attitude toward population growth. In 1982, Beijing's census-takers counted one billion stomachs, nearly double the number in 1949, when Mao took power.

Mao's successors, led by Deng Xiaoping, had already rejected Mao's benign view. In 1979, they launched an ambitious population control program, calling on every couple to have a single child. "Husband and wife," declared the new constitution of 1982, "have a duty to practice family planning."

The intensity of China's "one-child" campaign has varied over time and from locale to locale. Billboards, newspapers, and radio broadcasts trumpet the message. Beijing offers economic rewards (e.g., cash awards and free medical care) to parents who agree to stop having children after their first child, and penalties (e.g., fines equalling 15 percent of family income for seven years) for those having a second child. At the height of the campaign in 1983, Beijing ordered the sterilization of one spouse in every couple with more than one child. Reports of forced abortions in China began reaching the West [see "The Mosher Affair," *WQ*, New Year's '84].

Deng has put population control near the top of the Chinese political agenda because he and his colleagues blame the nation's economic woes—occasional food shortages, unemployment, lackluster economic growth—on its vast human numbers. But studies by Western economists point directly at China's official policies—such as Mao's 1958 Great Leap Forward and the Cultural Revolution of the 1960s. According to K.C. Yeh of the Rand Corporation, for example, the overall efficiency of Chinese industry and agriculture fell by more than 25 percent between 1957 and 1978. If China had merely matched *India's* improvements in productivity during those years, its output per capita in 1978 would have been two-thirds greater than it was.

In the short term, Deng's "one-child" policy will surely work. Fertility, which had already dropped sharply during the 1970s, has continued to decline. By 1984, the Chinese population was growing by only 1.1 percent annually.

What price China will pay for this success is not yet entirely clear. Smaller families by themselves mean a lower quality of life for couples who desire more children. And, in the nation's fields and rice paddies, one-child families find themselves short-handed—especially if the child is a girl. Female infanticide seems to be on the upswing among China's peasants.

Moreover, limiting couples to one child may not be in the best interests of the country's future elderly population. China's parents must be asking themselves today: Will Beijing keep its promise to provide for them in their old age, when *their* child (and spouse) may be supporting four grandparents?

—*N. E.*

For nations that cope poorly in general, any quickening of the pace of change—including the rate of demographic change—is likely to cause difficulties. Yet adapting to novel conditions is in itself an integral part of modern economic development for any society. Development is in a sense a learning process. To the extent that population growth stimulates this learning process, it can accelerate a society's material progress.

Second, demographic change since World War II has typically been both benign and relatively favorable to economic growth. It has come about chiefly because of dramatic improvements in human health, lengthening the life expectancy of people all over the globe. Better health, moreover, can help augment human capital, which is the ultimate basis of economic productivity. Increasing human capital alone does not assure material progress; such progress depends on many other things, including the priorities governments place on developing and utilizing human talents. But it does make it *possible* to quicken the pace of economic advance.

Third, to assume, as many academics and public officials do, that preventing the birth of poor people will help eliminate poverty appears to be a fundamental error. Mass affluence is the result of human productivity and human organization, and it is not at all clear that these factors would be enhanced by falling birthrates, or, for that matter, by rising birthrates.

To make the economic case for aggressive population control, demographers and economists would have to show, in effect, that the cost of raising a child born in a particular society would be greater than his lifetime economic "value." That would be an extraordinarily difficult task. Economists and corporate executives constantly go astray in estimating the economic value of such relatively simple things as machinery, factories, and dams. Imagine how much more difficult it would be to determine the value of an unpredictable, living human being, or to have decided, in 1955, whether a baby born in Ghana was "worth" more than one born in South Korea.

Such population controls, in any realistic sense, would be fruitful *only* if no new technologies were ever created, societies did not change, and individuals were given few options in shaping their futures. That kind of world would be incompatible with the very essence of economic development, which is the successful management of change, and, ultimately, the extension of human choice.

There is little chance that enforced family planning in the Third World or elsewhere will yield benefits without great social costs and a sacrifice of human freedom. This approach reflects, as Peter Bauer notes, a contempt for ordinary people. In most of the countries where they have been tried, population policies, "soft" or "hard," have amounted to little more than attempts to solve through demographic tinkering economic problems that can, in fact, be traced to misguided governmental policies. To make a reduction of the birthrate the focus of so many high hopes is to divert attention and political energy from the real sources of poverty and lagging economic growth in many countries of the Third World.

considered to be blessedly low. And, for all the uncertainties of long-term population forecasting, *annual* shifts in the size and composition of a national population can be predicted with far greater accuracy than can changes in inflation, unemployment, the gross national product, or crop harvests.

BACKGROUND BOOKS

POPULATION AND ECONOMIC GROWTH

"The scourges of pestilence, famine, wars, and earthquakes have come to be regarded as a blessing to overcrowded nations, since they serve to prune away the luxuriant growth of the human race." So wrote the Christian theologian Tertullian during the second century A.D., when the earth's population was only about 300 million—or six percent of what it is today (five billion). Tertullian's observation, and the book in which it appears—Garrett Hardin's **Population, Evolution and Birth**

Control (W. H. Freeman, 1964, cloth; 1969, paper)—remind the reader that the Reverend Thomas R. Malthus (1766–1834) was not the first writer to reflect on the hazards of under- or overpopulation. Hardin pulled together a rich menu on the subject—everything from Han Fei-Tzu's fifth-century B.C. observations on fecundity and prosperity to the government of India's 1962 birth control campaign slogan: "Don't postpone the first, don't hurry up the second, and don't go in for the third."

Malthus's **Essay on the Principle of Population** (1798; Penguin, 1970, paper only) still stands as the single most influential work on population. The English economist's argument is well known: "It may be safely asserted," Malthus wrote, "that population, when unchecked, increases in a geometrical progression [whereas] the means of subsistence, under circumstances most favorable to human industry, could not possibly be made to increase faster than in an arithmetical ratio."

Thus Malthus, as Swedish sociologist Gunnar Myrdal observed 142 years later, "shifted the blame for misery from Society to Nature, from environment to heredity." Myrdal believed that a prudent society could control its own destiny. But in **Population: A Problem for Democracy** (Harvard, 1940), Myrdal foresaw a conflict in democratic countries between private wants (whether to have children) and public needs (to boost or limit population). "The population question," he predicted, "will dominate our whole economic and social policy for the entire future."

Myrdal's prognosis was at least partly correct. The immediate post–World War II years saw the appearance of several population "scare books." William Vogt's **Road to Survival** (William Sloane, 1948), for example, stressed what would become an oft-repeated theme: the interdependence between human beings and their planet. "An eroding hillside in Mexico or Yugoslavia," Vogt said, "affects the living standard and probability of survival of the American people." Vogt also alerted Americans to the increasing multitudes of "Moslems, Sikhs, Hindus (and their sacred cows)," whose populations ballooned due to "untrammeled copulation."

Paul R. Ehrlich's **Population Bomb** (River City, rev. ed., 1975, cloth; Ballantine, rev. ed., 1976, paper) dramatized the threat of overpopulation for the next generation of Americans. Only some five million people, Ehrlich estimated, had inhabited the planet in 6000 B.C. Doubling every 1,000 years, the world's population reached 500 million by A.D. 1650, and then began to accelerate rapidly. It doubled again in just 200 years, hitting one billion by 1850, and reached two billion by 1930. Should the world's population continue to grow by two percent annually (doubling every 35 years), Ehrlich warned, 60 million billion people (or 100 for every *square yard* of the globe's surface) would be swarming the earth by the year 2900.

Ehrlich also publicized many of the environmental hazards commonly associated with overpopulation and industrialization—such as the "greenhouse effect"—all well known today. A slight warming of the globe, resulting from an overabundance of carbon dioxide in the atmosphere, generated by the burning of fossil fuels, could melt the polar ice caps, raising ocean levels by some 250 feet. Asked Ehrlich: "Gondola to the Empire State Building, anyone?"

More recent works on the "population problem" are less apocalyptic, for several reasons. As Rafael M. Salas, executive director of the United Nations Fund for Population Activities, points out in **Reflections on Population** (Pergamon, 2nd ed., 1986), the *rate* of population growth worldwide has dropped dramatically, from 2.03 percent in 1970–75 to 1.67 percent in 1980–85. Demographers now expect the globe's population to hit 6.1 billion by A.D. 2000, and level off at 10.2 billion by the end of the next century. And, "despite rapid population growth," as the National Research Council's scholarly **Population Growth and Economic Development** (National Academy, 1986, paper only) observes, "developing countries have achieved unprecedented levels of income per capita, literacy, and life expectancy over the last 25 years."

Much current research focuses on the environmental (rather than the economic) effects of population growth. The best, most comprehensive surveys include **State of the World 1986** by Lester Brown et al. (Norton, 1986, cloth & paper); the World Resources Institute's **World Resources 1986** (Basic, 1986, cloth & paper); and economist Robert Repetto's **Global Possible** (Yale, 1985, cloth & paper). All of these works emphasize that the "state of the world" varies from country to country. Two of the 23 scientists and environmentalists who contributed to Repetto's book, for example, found that the rate of annual deforestation ranges from a safe 0.6 percent of all woodlands in the Congo and Zaire to a dangerous four to six percent in the Ivory Coast and Nigeria. Limiting population, Repetto says, is just one way to help preserve world resources. Governments, he stresses, must also provide better management of land, forests, and waterways. Underdeveloped countries, meanwhile, need easier access to credit, new technologies, and small-scale investment.

Indeed, these three books sugges that the "spaceship earth" approach t population and development problem may be misguided. As former *New Yo Times*man Pranay Gupte writes in h highly readable **Crowded Earth** (No ton, 1984), "people do not live on th 'globe' but in villages and towns, withi the walls of their houses or shacks c tenements."

Gupte spent 14 months travelin through 38 impoverished countrie around the world to discover how ord nary people cope in overpopulated ar underdeveloped communities.

He spoke, for example, with Ibrahi Mesahi, a grocery store owner in bu tling downtown Lagos. The population Nigeria's capital shot up, largely throu in-migration, from 1.4 million in 1970 3.6 million in 1985. But Gupte fou that Mesahi had no interest in birth co trol, at least not for himself. "I need the help I can get," explained Mesahi. have 10 boys and one girl . . . with n children, at least I can watch them. The are honest."

The author, however, still favo population education programs. "Wher is demonstrated to people that 'small beautiful,'" he says, "their choice will for small families, not large ones."

A 'Satanic' Fury

Iran's Ayatollah Khomeini orders the murder of a novelist in Britain as the 'blasphemy' in a controversial new book convulses the Islamic world

He is old and unwell and hardly ever appears in public. Spokesmen read his pronouncements for him on the radio. His revolution has stalled, its fervor flagging, its reach wider than its grasp. His potential successors are smaller men who constantly bicker among themselves. Last summer, bitterly humiliated, he sipped from what he called the "poisoned chalice" of peace, settling for a cease-fire in a war—a jihad—he had sworn to win. But last week Ayatollah Ruhollah Khomeini proved that, at 88, he still has the power to convulse the Islamic world and to send shivers of fear and loathing through the West.

The object of Khomeini's wrath was an author who appeals mostly to Western intellectuals and whose latest novel may be the least-read book ever to provoke an international furor. Condemning it for blasphemy, devout Muslims are proud to say they have never read Salman Rushdie's "The Satanic Verses." Many of its defenders haven't read the novel, either. Starting last fall, Islamic leaders around the world began to denounce the book's seemingly irreverent treatment of the Prophet Muhammad. Coming to the fray a bit late, Khomeini seized what his fundamentalist followers regard as the moral high ground by ordering Rushdie's murder. "The author of the 'Satanic Verses' book, which is against Islam, the Prophet and the Koran, and all those involved in its publication who were aware of its content, are sentenced to death," Iran's spiritual leader said in a statement read for him on the radio. Anyone who died attempting to kill Rushdie, he promised, would go straight to heaven. As another inducement, Khomeini's disciples put a price on Rushdie's head of more than $5 million.

Later, Iran's relatively moderate president, Ali Khamenei, said the "wretched man" might still be pardoned if he were to "repent and say, 'I made a blunder' and apologize to Muslims and the imam [Khomeini]." By then, Rushdie had gone into hiding somewhere in Britain, shaken by the threat to his life. He answered Khamenei with a statement saying that "I profoundly regret the distress that publication has occasioned to sincere followers of Islam." Iran's official news agency replied that the statement fell "well short" of what was needed for absolution, complaining that it "made no indication of his repentance or that his slanderous book would be withdrawn."

Meantime, "The Satanic Verses" has suddenly become a best seller, exceeding whatever commercial prospects it had before Khomeini hurled his thunderbolt. But Rushdie's American publisher closed its New York office temporarily after receiving several bomb threats, and some of his European publishers reconsidered their plans to bring out the book. As panic spread, three large American bookselling chains, Waldenbooks, B. Dalton and Barnes & Noble, pulled the novel off their shelves, deciding that devotion to free speech was less important than the safety of their employees and customers (next page). Writers and government leaders in the West expressed outrage at Khomeini's action. "Nobody has the right to incite people to violence," said British Foreign Secretary Geoffrey Howe. "We want serious and stable relations with Iran. But [that] will not be possible while Iran fails to respect international standards of behavior."

In Britain, where "The Satanic Verses" was published first, devout Muslims railed against the author. "I think we should kill Salman Rushdie's whole family," a man named Farook Mughal screamed as he emerged from a Friday service at a mosque in west London. "His body should be chopped into little pieces and sent to all Islamic countries as a warning to those who insult our religion." Anti-Rushdie riots led to several deaths in Pakistan and India, where the religious controversy quickly became entangled in politics. In Bombay, where Rushdie was born into a Muslim family 41 years ago, an anonymous phone caller, who said he represented the "Iranian Guards," threatened to murder Indians who criticized Khomeini and to blow up British airliners.

'Thought police': Rushdie, now a British subject who no longer considers himself a Muslim, insisted that his book was not blasphemous. Before he went into hiding, he complained about the influence of Islamic "thought police." Some Muslims deplored Khomeini's call for assassination. Egyptian writer Naguib Mahfouz, who last year became the first Arab to win the Nobel Prize in Literature, said the ayatollah should be condemned for "intellectual terrorism." Sheik Muhammad Hussam al Din, an Egyptian theologian, complained: "This makes Islam seem brutal and bloodthirsty. Blood must not be shed except after a trial, [when the accused has been] given a chance to defend himself and repent."

But even Mahfouz conceded that "sometimes such a book may cause unrest. So I can find an excuse for the state if it prevents publication." As many Muslims saw it, Rushdie's book was a product of the West, and they have a profound distrust of most things Western. Many Islamic countries quickly banned the book. What seemed a deplorable act of censorship to many in the West struck Muslims as an understandable response to a heinous slur on their religion. Mohammad Javad Larijani, Iran's deputy foreign minister, asked: "How can the West advocate respect for human rights on the one hand and on the other be indifferent to the insult against the holiest belief of more than 1 billion people in the world?"

'A dead man': As soon as Khomeini pronounced his sentence of death, zealots in Iran put on death shrouds and offered to form suicide squads to carry it out. This time, Iran had no need to hire professional hit men; rank-and-file believers in many countries said they were ready to shed blood. "If I see him, I will kill him straight away," property developer Abzul Khan said in London. "Take my name and address. One day I will kill him." Most of the furor over Rushdie's book may die down soon; even some of last week's demonstrations seemed quiet, compared with earlier anti-American rampages in countries like Iran and Pakistan. But even if Rushdie issues a more thorough apology, security experts fear that fanatics may stay on his trail indefinitely. "Salman Rushdie is a dead man," said an Iranian exile in Britain. "As long as the *fatwa* [theological ruling] remains, he could be killed at any time. There is no way to protect him. He will be followed for the rest of his life."

After the reverses he has suffered in recent months, Khomeini found in the Rushdie affair a chance to reassert his claim to leadership of the worldwide Islamic movement. Fred Halliday, an expert on Islam at the London School of Economics, describes Khomeini's tactics as "bandwagoning." "The campaign against Rushdie was started by the Saudis," says Dr. Ali Nourizadeh, a former Iranian newspaper editor who now lives in Britain. "It was taken up by the people in Cairo, and then the Pakistanis took the initiative. Suddenly, Khomeini found himself left behind. His reputation has suffered since the cease-fire [in the Iran-Iraq war]. He wanted to prove himself the solid defender of Islam and leader of fundamentalism."

The furor over "The Satanic Verses" also gave Khomeini a chance to revive the faltering revolutionary spirit of his own people. Like China's late Mao Zedong, Khomeini is an aging leader who feels the need for perpetual revolution. Not long ago he expressed the hope that Iran's masses would "maintain their revolutionary and sacred rancor and anger in their hearts and use their oppressor-burning flames against the criminal Soviet Union and the world-devouring United States and

their surrogates." In Rushdie, he found an ideal Western surrogate.

Although Khomeini is obviously frail, even his political enemies believe that his health is relatively good for a man of his age. In recent interviews, his daughter, Zahra Mustafavi, 48, admitted that he takes medicine for heart trouble but denied Western intelligence reports that he has cancer. She said he sleeps on a hard surface, takes walks every day and eats only vegetables and yogurt. He listens constantly to the news on the radio and is so obsessed with cleanliness that he uses a spoon to eat bread and douses himself with cologne six or seven times a day. His daughter told The Washington Post that "his room smells so good, my own memories associate it with heaven."

Hot temper: In meetings with his advisers, Khomeini reportedly listens a lot but has little to say. His son Ahmad is thought to write many of the statements that are issued in the old man's name. "Ahmad is the Mrs. Wilson of modern Iran," says Iranian-affairs expert Gary Sick, referring to the wife of President Woodrow Wilson, who virtually ran his administration during her husband's final illness. Some outside analysts suspect that Khomeini is becoming senile. His daughter concedes that his temper sometimes gets the better of him, especially when he thinks Islam has been insulted. Earlier his month he ordered prison terms and whippings for four Iranian radio executives who had aired a broadcast in which a young woman suggested that Muhammad's daughter may not be the best role model for modern women. Kohmeini even considered executing the radio men before his daughter helped persuade him to authorize a pardon.

There is no challenge to Khomeini's commanding stature inside Iran. When the ayatollah called for Rushdie's death, his followers eagerly offered reward money, including bonuses that would be paid if an Iranian carried out the sentence. People in the hometown of Ali Akbar Hashemi Rafsanjani, the speaker of Iran's Parliament and a potential leader after Khomeini's death, put up $3 million in blood money.

In a sense, the succession to Khomeini has already been settled. His designated spiritual heir is Ayatollah Hussein Ali Montazeri, whose stand on many issues is more moderate than Khomeini's. (Montazeri recently declared: "We are not going to solve anything by torturing, imprisoning and executing our opponents.") It currently appears that the strongest political figure in the immediate post-Khomeini era will be Rafsanjani, a relative pragmatist who argued for an end to the holy war against Iraq. But Montazeri lacks charisma and is politically weak, while Rafsanjani has some determined challengers.

For years, foreign analysts described

At Stake: The Freedom to Imagine

Booksellers let the mullahs call the shots

BY LAURA SHAPIRO

Salman Rushdie spent most of last week hiding out, but before he disappeared he tried to reclaim "The Satanic Verses" as a work of the imagination. "The idea that this is somehow an attack on . . . religion shows an absolute failure to understand what fiction is," he told host Jeff Greenfield on ABC's "Nightline." "Fiction is—" But Greenfield had to turn to another guest. Rushdie never did finish that sentence; by now, a global uproar has shifted the terms of the debate from literature to religious politics.

Yet "The Satanic Verses" is a work of literature, not just an object of political notoriety—and the distinction underscores dramatically what is at stake here. Last week B. Dalton (which owns Barnes & Noble) and Waldenbooks, the largest bookstore chains in the country, effectively bowed to Muslim demands and pulled the book from the shelves. In France, West Germany, Greece and Turkey, local publication of the novel has been postponed or canceled; in Canada, new imports of the book have been halted at least temporarily and one major chain, Coles Book Stores Ltd., has stopped selling it. PEN America, the Authors Guild and numerous writers have spoken out strongly in support of Rushdie, and celebrities including Norman Mailer, Susan Sontag and E. L. Doctorow plan a public reading of "The Satanic Verses" this week in New York. Nonetheless, the sight of so many powerful members of the publishing community caving in to demagoguery has been chilling.

The passages that have inflamed Muslims around the world constitute only a part of this huge, brilliant novel. Rushdie, who was born to a Muslim family in Bombay but has spent much of his life in London, sees "The Satanic Verses" as a book about migrants like himself, hybrids in a sometimes unwelcoming society. With glittering language and effects he has created a fanciful exploration of good and evil starring a couple of Indian actors named Gibreel and Chamcha, who fall from a plane into England. Gibreel dreams himself into the persona of the archangel Gabriel; Chamcha grow horns and hooves and temporarily turns into the Devil. An extravagant cast of characters leads us from the deserts of ancient Arabia to the slums of modern London, and a tortuous plot ends on a pleasingly sentimental note. Rushdie suffers from one of those cumbersome literary reputations that hold his work to be awe-inspiring but impenetrable; don't believe it. This is a master storyteller.

Right now, of course, the most famous sequences in the book are those describing the birth of a religion that looks very much like Islam (next page). These events—dreamed by Gibreel in the course of a drawn-out mental breakdown—are derived from traditional accounts of Muhammad's life, but Rushdie spins them into fantasy and embroiders them with highly irreverent touches of sex, humor and politics. The prophet is called Mahound, a term for the Devil, and at least one of his followers—a "bum from Persia" named Salman—becomes convinced that Mahound is little more than a charismatic charlatan. In a chapter that has particularly infuriated Muslims, a dozen prostitutes take on the names and identities of Mahound's wives; their business booms.

"Muslims aren't prudish, there's a lot of frank discussion of sex and bodily functions in Islamic literature, but the context makes all the difference," says William Graham, professor of the History of Religion and Islamic Studies at Harvard. "Here, episodes from standard early Islamic works are interspersed with what are in this context degrading images. It's as if you took the Bible, and in the middle of the Sermon on the Mount, you showed Jesus fantasizing copulation with whores. It's that kind of juxtaposition that many Muslims find so offensive."

Rushdie's background—he is no longer a practicing Muslim—makes his book all the more volatile, Islamic specialists say.

"Historically, Muslims have been much more tolerant of nonbelievers than have Christians," says Graham. "But apostates traditionally have been viewed and treated harshly. There's a sense among Muslims that to know and then to reject the truth is particularly perverse."

This isn't the first time Rushdie's work has aroused controversy. Indira Gandhi threatened to sue for libel over a passage in his 1981 "Midnight's Children" that implied she was responsible for her husband's death, and his 1983 "Shame," based loosely on Pakistani politics, was banned in that country. He says he was aware that "The Satanic Verses" would provoke the Muslim community, but he doesn't think of his work as blasphemous; he certainly did not anticipate the virulence of the response. "I take Muhammad to be in the first place a genius and in the second place a completely sincere mystic," he says. "Something quite extraordinary happened to him, about which he himself had great doubts. It wasn't all this kind of simply sitting at the feet of the archangel Gabriel and taking dictation. It's fascinating, and also an absolutely proper subject for a writer."

Litmus test: In a sense, the content of the book has ceased to matter; the novel has become a kind of litmus test for Islamic morality. "You don't have to read the book; the point is to take a position," says an Islamic expert. "How can you criticize this whole situation without seeming anti-Muslim?" For lovers of literature in the West, too, "The Satanic Verses" had become a test of faith, albeit of a different sort. "We've fought long and hard against censorship," said Bonnie Predd, executive vice president of Waldenbooks, as bookstores packed away their copies of Rushdie's novel. "But when it comes to the safety of our employees, one sometimes has to compromise." It's politics that we call the art of compromise, however; literature cannot afford that luxury. It would have cost the bookstores far less—in every sense except financially—if they had hired security guards and stationed one by every shelf, rather than pack up a single book. "How fragile civilization is," wrote Rushdie last month, after Muslims in Britain set fire to his novel. "How easily, how merrily a book burns!"

Donna Foote also contributed to this report.

the factions in Iran as "moderates" and "radicals," an oversimplification that has been discredited by the tangled course of Teheran politics. Today's oversimplification pits "pragmatists" against "purists." In general, the pragmatists, including Rafsanjani and President Khamenei, favor an opening to the West in order to rebuild Iran's economy. The purists include Prime Minister Mir Hussein Moussavi and Interior Minister Ali Akbar Mohtashami, who is blamed for masterminding the suicide attack on the U.S. Marine barracks that killed 241 Americans in 1983. Most of the purists want a kind of Islamic socialism that stresses "self-sufficiency," which means independence from the West.

Blurred lines: The lines between the factions often blur. President Khamenei is not considered a pragmatist on foreign policy, while Mohtashami, a radical on most issues, comes close to outright capitalism on trade. And Rafsanjani's alleged moderation does not keep him from ruthlessness. Partly at his instigation, at least 1,000 of the regime's opponents have been executed since the end of the war last August—one of the bloodiest phases of Khomeini's revolution. "Among them were a large number of prisoners of conscience and others serving prison terms, imposed after unfair trials, for their nonviolent political activity," reports Amnesty International.

Rafsanjani, who also is in day-to-day charge of the armed forces, has been riding so high lately that many analysts expect him to become president of Iran when Khamenei leaves office next summer. Rafsanjani may even be able to turn the largely ceremonial job into something more powerful than the prime minister's post. The hard-liners may have kicked up a fuss over Rushdie's book as a way of curbing the speaker's power, by launching a new campaign against the West. "This Rushdie issue is being used as a instrument of Iranian politics," says Marvin Zonis, a University of Chicago expert on the Middle East. If so, Khomeini has given a boost to the hard-liners, perhaps deliberately. "He's clearly been upset that one group headed by Rafsanjani is consolidating power," argues Zonis. "Khomeini likes creative chaos, so now he's abetted the cause of the conservatives."

Children in charge: The Rushdie furor comes at a time when Iran's economy is in serious trouble. Oil revenues have fallen from $20 billion in 1983 to a level of about $8 billion predicted for this year. One analyst, Pauline Jackson of the London-based Iran Monitor newsletter, estimates that the country needs $15 billion a year "just to keep ticking over." Last year Ayatollah Montazeri wrote a letter to Prime Minister Moussavi complaining that the hard-liners' "lack of expertise" and other failings had "totally paralyzed the country's economic situation." He charged: "The actual

Passing Judgment: Poetry or Blasphemy?

Among the most inflammatory passages in "The Satanic Verses" are those in which a character named Salman describes his disenchantment with a new religion called Submission (English for Islam) and its prophet, Mahound. The following excerpts satirize a belief at the very heart of Islam: that the Koran is the word of God, revealed to Muhammad by the archangel Gabriel.

"Amid the palm-trees of the oasis Gibreel appeared to the Prophet and found himself spouting rules, rules, rules, until the faithful could scarcely bear the prospect of any more revelation, Salman said, rules about every damn thing . . . . It was as if no aspect of human existence was to be left unregulated, free. The revelation . . . told the faithful how much to eat, how deeply they should sleep, and which sexual positions had received divine sanction, so that they learned that sodomy and the missionary position were approved of by the archangel, whereas the forbidden postures included all those in which the female was on top. . . . And Gibreel the archangel specified the manner in which a man should be buried, and how his property should be divided, so that Salman the Persian got to wondering what manner of God this was that sounded so much like a businessman. This was when he had the idea that destroyed his faith, because he recalled that of course Mahound himself had been a businessman, and a damned successful one at that, a person to whom organization and rules came naturally, so how excessively convenient it was that he should have come up with such a very businesslike archangel . . . .

"After that Salman began to notice how useful and well timed the angel's revelations tended to be, so that when the faithful were disputing Mahound's views on any subject, from the possibility of space travel to the permanence of Hell, the angel would turn up with an answer, and he always supported Mahound . . . It would have been different, Salman complained . . . if Mahound took up his positions after receiving the revelation from Gibreel; but no, he just laid down the law and the angel would confirm it afterwards . . .

"What finally finished Salman with Mahound: the question of the women . . . . Listen, I'm no gossip, Salman drunkenly confided, but after his wife's death Mahound was no angel, you understand my meaning. But in Yathrib he almost met his match. Those women up there: they turned his beard half-white in a year.

The point about our Prophet . . . is that he didn't like his women to answer back, he went for mothers and daughters . . . . He didn't like to pick on someone his own size. But in Yathrib the women are different, you don't know, here in Jahilia you're used to ordering your females about but up there they won't put up with it . . . . Well, our girls were beginning to go for that type of thing, getting who knows what sort of ideas in their heads, so at once, bang, out comes the rule book, the angel starts pouring out rules about what women mustn't do, he starts forcing them back into the docile attitudes the Prophet prefers . . . .

How the women of Yathrib laughed at the faithful, I swear, but that man is a magician, nobody could resist his charm; the faithful women did as he ordered them. They Submitted: he was offering them Paradise, after all."

---

running of the country is in the hands of immature children who hold grudges."

If the hard-liners hoped to close off Rafsanjani's opening to the West, they succeeded, at least for the moment. Britain, which had been rebuilding its diplomatic relations with Teheran, put everything on hold. Other West European countries and the United States protested; the Dutch foreign minister canceled a trip to Teheran because of Khomeini's "totally unacceptable . . . call for international terrorism." The diplomatic freeze sets up another obstacle to the release of American and European hostages held by pro-Iranian terrorists in Lebanon. And it will force Rafsanjani and his relatively enlightened allies to tread warily in the weeks ahead. Most analysts believe, however, that the setback to pragmatism is only temporary.

Elsewhere in the Islamic world, politics also shaped the response to Rushdie's book. In Indonesia, the most populous Muslim country, the controversy caused barely a ripple, in part because the press hardly mentioned the book and in part because the government insists on religious toleration. In India, where three people died in riots, pro-Pakistani Muslims in the Kashmir Valley turned their protest against the book into an anti-Indian demonstration. In Pakistan, where six protesters were killed by police as they tried to storm a U.S. cultural center, the campaign against Rushdie also was aimed at the relatively secular government of Western-educated Prime Minister Benazir Bhutto, a woman in the man's world of Islam. Although Bhutto dutifully denounced "The Satanic Verses," one opposition leader accused her of going easy on Penguin, Rushdie's British publisher, because it also had published her own book, "Daughter of the East." Bhutto's militantly Islamic rivals could use the Rushdie issue to cause her trouble for months to come.

'On different planets': To Westerners, the furor demonstrated again that, even in the Age of Communications, the cultural gap between East and West has not been closed. "It indicates just how impenetrable the Muslim world is and what a fundamentally different value system operates there," said Zonis. "We are really on different planets." Like a character from his own novel, Rushdie now found himself hiding out on an alien planet—in this case, a familiar Western world with Eastern assassins lurking in every shadow. Would his statement of regret be enough to clear the air eventually? "Nobody knows what effect the statement will have or even how much credence should be attached to what they've been saying," a British government official said of the Iranians. "Have they got to ask Khomeini to retract the verdict and take it all back in order for Rushdie to be safe? Nobody knows." "Maybe in four or five years," predicts Halliday, "he'll be able to walk freely on the streets of Manhattan. Not much else." For the moment, at least, Salman Rushdie is a fugitive from his own past—and from the frenzied legions of the ayatollah.

RUSSELL WATSON *with* DONNA FOOTE *in London,* RAY WILKINSON *in Cairo,* JANE WHITMORE *in Washington and bureau reports*

JAPANESE WOMEN

A world apart

If women are second-class citizens in most industrial countries, they are third-class ones in Japan. Far from scaling the peaks, they have failed to reach even the foothills in politics, the bureaucracy and business. This waste of the talents of 60m Japanese will cost the country increasingly dear

OTHER than for this article, your correspondent has not interviewed a Japanese woman in almost a year of writing about Japan's politics, economics, business and science. Women are entering the country's workforce in increasing numbers: two-fifths of those employed are women, and more married women now go out to work than stay at home. But most have no prospect of an interesting or rewarding career. They have to limit their ambition to dead-end jobs where the pay packet provides the only satisfaction.

For many families, especially in Tokyo, two incomes are a necessity. A tiny house that is 1½ hours from the city centre costs about 20 times the average annual salary of a white-collar worker. Middle-class parents feel obliged to put aside money for the private tutors who will give their children an edge in university entrance examinations. They also need to save for their own retirement in a country where the social-security system is primitive and people live even longer than Swedes, Europe's Methuselahs. (Life expectancy at birth is 75.2 years for men and 80.9 for women in Japan, compared with 71.6 and 77.6 in Britain and 71.6 and 78.8 in the United States.)

These pressures combine to push Japanese women out to work. It helps too that today's women have fewer children, more vacuum cleaners and marginally more accommodating husbands than their mothers did. But if they expect to be given the same opportunities as men, they are quickly disillusioned. The average pay of a working woman in Japan is about half that of the average man. This is true even when fringe-benefits reserved mainly for men, like subsidised housing or sports-club memberships, are disregarded.

The gap between the wages of men and women is actually widening. This is because the great majority of women who are now entering the workforce are doing so in lowly, low-paid and often part-time jobs. The principle of equal pay for equal work is still far from universal, and in newspapers about one job advertisement in 20 still specifies that only men need apply.

A bad business

Big companies treat their women employees more fairly than other businesses in Japan, but this is faint praise. In taking on people straight from university, about 20% of them still pay female graduates less than male graduates. A recent survey of 1,000 large Japanese companies showed that only 150 of them have any women at all at *kacho* (section-chief) level. Fewer than 20 of the 1,000 companies have women in positions above that level.

Nissan, the Japanese motor multinational, has only one woman in a managerial position. Other particularly bad offenders are the large banks and the trading companies. They doll female employees up in cutesy uniforms, have them self-effacingly serve the tea, but appoint no more than a token number to managerial jobs. None of Japan's internationally famous blue-chip companies has ever had a woman as a board member, not even as a token.

Mrs Kiyoko Fujii, who runs the wom-en's affairs division of the prime minister's office, says that only 7.3% of working women have a subordinate. The rest are at the bottom of the pyramid. The proportion has barely changed since 1975. The tiny number of women who have achieved great things have almost all succeeded at the expense of marriage and children. That is a painful choice which Japanese men never have to make.

The custom of lifetime employment at large Japanese companies also puts women at a disadvantage. The emphasis on promotion by seniority rather than by merit discriminates against those who temporarily quit their jobs to raise a family.

Aspiring young women find few exemplars to encourage them. Although women have had the vote since General Douglas MacArthur insisted upon universal suffrage in 1946, the country has since then had only three female cabinet ministers and eight parliamentary vice-ministers. There is none of either now. The governing lower house of parliament (the Diet) is 98.6% male. The only women parliamentarians are to be found in the ranks of the opposition and in the House of Councillors, a body that has little prestige and less influence.

When asked recently if his faction of the ruling Liberal Democratic party would field any female candidates in future Diet elections, Mr Noboru Takeshita said no: campaigning "is too physically tough for women". (The 64-year-old prime minister was later made to eat his words by the indefatigable Ms Takako Doi, leader of Japan's second largest political party, the Socialists).

From *The Economist*, May 14, 1988, pp. 19-20, 22. © 1988, The Economist, reprinted by permission of The New York Times Syndicated Sales Service.

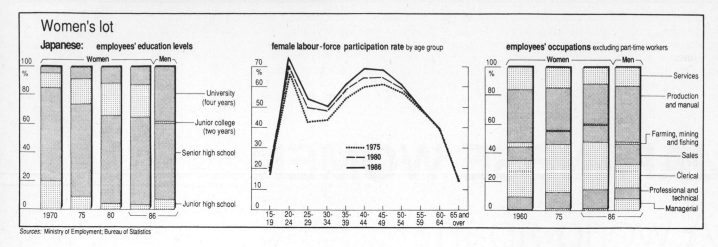

Women's lot

Japanese: employees' education levels

female labour-force participation rate by age group

employees' occupations excluding part-time workers

Sources: Ministry of Employment; Bureau of Statistics

Things become a little better as you go down the power scale, but only a little. Though just 1.4% of representatives at prefectural councils are women (none of Japan's 48 prefectures has a female governor), 3.2% of municipal councillors and 7.7% of ward councillors are women.

The civil service is scarcely any better, although it generally tries to set an example—by, for instance, taking two Saturdays off a month and not requiring its female employees to wear uniforms. Of 1,669 new recruits to the government's administrative ladder last year, 128 were women. Of the service's 6,500 middle-ranking administrators, the people who actually run things, only 36 are women. The number of women in higher levels than that can be counted on the toes of one foot.

Time warp

Why are women doing so badly? The answer is a combination of traditional attitudes at home and traditional attitudes at work. Both are changing as the country becomes more exposed to foreign influences. Japan is nonetheless still 30 years behind America when it comes to women's lib, and it is not showing the same enthusiasm to catch up as it has done in technology and finance.

Japanese women are cramped by a culture that conditions them from an early age to accept the role of obedient wife and doting mother. Feminists in the West who complain about the pernicious influence of such sexually exclusive terms as "mankind" and "chairman" would find certain (admittedly ancient) kanji far more chauvinist.

The ideogram for "man" combines a rice-paddy with a pair of sturdy legs, the symbol for power. That for "woman" represents a kneeling, subservient figure. The "woman" character thrice repeated means "noisy"; combined with the symbol for "force", it means "evil". Women are brought up to speak a form of Japanese far fuller of honorifics and intimations of the speaker's inferior status than that used by men. The character "-ko" which terminates virtually every woman's name (as in

Michiko, Akiko, Taeko, Hiroko, Mariko or Keiko) means "child". Most companies still seek to discover whether a female employee lives at home or not. A single woman who does not live with her parents is regarded as morally suspect.

Other long-standing forms of sexual discrimination in the workplace and in education are more familiar in the West, though they take on an exaggerated form in Japan. Women are not encouraged to go to universities. Though about 35% of women receive tertiary education (as against 40% of men), two-thirds of them get it at junior or "two-year" colleges, which virtually no men attend. The two-year colleges are not usually considered by employers as university education: home economics and the humanities are stressed in their curriculum. Fewer than 20% of the women who do go to university (compared with 70% of the men) are enrolled in law, economics or the applied sciences, employers' favourite courses.

The employment pattern of the female workforce is the industrial world's deepest "M". Up until marriage Japanese women work: just under three-quarters of women aged 20-24 are employed, with most of the rest engaged in some form of higher education. Marriage, for almost all women, comes between the ages of 24 and 27, with 25 still considered to be tekireiki, the optimal age. (One Japanese saying compares women to Christmas cakes, unwanted after the 25th. After a woman has passed that age unwed, parents frequently bring in professional match-makers.) Japan has the highest marriage rate in the world. Fewer than 2% of women remain spinsters.

A Japanese women typically has two children today compared with five in the empire-building days before the second world war, so the period between the birth of the first child and the packing off to school of the last has been cut in half, to under ten years. But women still tend to withdraw from the workforce in those years. Only about half of all women in the 25-35 age group are in paid employment. As many as 70% of women return to work in their

40s, usually in part-time jobs. By then they have stepped off the seniority ladder.

Japan has 20,000 day-care centres, looking after 2m children. They still carry a social stigma, and are generally open only from nine till five—fine for a part-time worker in a local office or shop, impossible for a commuter with a serious job. Even if more husbands wanted to help look after their children (and a recent survey found a mere 10% of male undergraduates thought men ought to help around the house), they would find it hard to do. Japan is a conformist society, and a male office worker courts unpopularity if he declines to spend noisy drinking-evenings with colleagues and clients. Home-life happens only on Sundays—and even then the man of the house often takes himself off to play golf. It is rare to see any but the youngest Japanese couples dining together in restaurants.

Japanese women are getting fed up. Divorces are increasingly common, and 60% of them are initiated by women. But the divorce rate is still much lower than in other industrial countries, in part because a divorced woman is likely to find herself in an unenviable position. According to Ms Yoriko Madoka, who writes books with names like "Divorce with a Smile" and runs a counselling service for women in Tokyo, the woman receives no settlement at all in about half of the divorces. For most of the rest, the settlement takes the form of a lump sum payment of ¥2m-3m ($15,000-22,000).

Almost all divorces are mutually agreed. Few find their way to the courts, where procedures are extraordinarily slow and costly (one recently finalised divorce case had dragged on for 35 years). Under Japanese law, women do not have any claim on household property. Men are expected to treat their ex-wives decently but this is more a moral than a legal requirement.

Semi-equal opportunities

Though the status of women remains distinctly inferior in Japan, sexual discrimination in the workplace is at last receding—not least because Japanese companies face ever more competition and must take their talent where they can find it. To bolster the rights of working women, Japan's Equal Employment Opportunities Law was passed by the Diet in 1985—after seven years of wrangling. The law was approved only just in time for Japan to fall within the United Nations' women's decade—a decade in which all member countries were supposed to come up with equal-rights legislation. Keidanren, Japan's employers' federation (none of whose board members is a women), opposed the law. So did Nikkeiren, the employers' economic think-tank. The law has now been in effect for two years.

Its most obvious short-coming is a lack of teeth. The law does not require employers to guarantee women equal treatment. It commits them to "strive towards" it. Though it prohibits various kinds of discrimination, the law provides no penalties for violators. Defenders of this approach say that it is more effective in Japan than it would be in the West because Japanese companies tend to do what the government asks them to do (but only when it suits them?)

The Labour Ministry has established "mediation offices" in each of Japan's prefectures. They are under-employed. A couple of courts have ruled against pay discrimination, but their rulings have rested on the constitution rather than the law. And the snag with the law is that, in seeking to protect women in Japan, it often has the effect of discriminating against them.

A classic example is the way overtime work by women is limited. The restrictions were originally introduced, laudably enough, to stop the exploitation of women in sweat-shops, but today they make it harder for women to make their way up the corporate ladder. The limits no longer apply to women in managerial and professional positions, but most other female employees (some of whom would like to climb to the top) are still prevented from working more than 24 hours' overtime a month and from working at all between 10pm and 5am.

The strict demarcation between "clerical jobs" (*ippan shoku*) and "general" or managerial jobs (*sogo shoku*) remains unaffected by Japan's equal-rights legislation. The *ippan shoku* grade is almost exclusively female. Duties include simple clerical work, telephone answering and, above all, making and serving tea—a chore never performed by a male employee. Even in the office of the director of the women's affairs bureau of the Ministry of Labour and in the women's section of Recruit, Japan's largest employment agency, your correspondent has been served tea by humble and bowing young women.

Promotion out of the grade, or recruitment into *sogo shoku* work (the only way to climb towards the boardroom), is generally by examination. Until 1986 most companies would not even allow women to take the examinations. Such blatant discrimination is now disappearing: about 30% of companies claim to have introduced new rules to conform with the law. But the number of women admitted to *sogo shoku* work is dismally small. Sumitomo bank claims to have the largest number of women in the *sogo-shoku* grades: 50 out of about 12,000. Nomura Securities has around ten. Marubeni, among the largest of the trading houses, has five. These numbers are higher than before the law went into effect. But Ms Eiko Shinotsuka of Ochanomizu University fears that even they may be tokenism. She notes that the ratio of female to male pay in Britain rose for a bit after the equal-opportunities law was passed but then started to decline again.

The price of chauvinism

In economic terms, the way Japan treats its women is shockingly wasteful. Half the country's human resources—and they are the only resources Japan possesses—are being squandered. More than 90% of women get a full 12 years of education, usually at public expense, and most are then slotted into menial, dead-end jobs.

This profligate waste of talent can no longer be afforded in a country where the population is aging rapidly. Only 10% of Japanese are more than 65 years old now but, on current trends, by 2025 the proportion will be 25%. The country needs to encourage all people of working age, women as much as men, to develop their full potential.

Changes for the better are likely to come fastest in service industries where discrimination is less entrenched than in manufacturing. In financial services in particular Japanese firms are beginning to find that their discriminatory attitudes are a business handicap. At home, talented young Japanese women are snapped up by foreign banks and securities houses establishing operations in Japan. Abroad, Japanese bankers and brokers find themselves at a loss when they have to deal as equals with the increasing number of women who occupy senior jobs in the City of London and Wall Street.

There are signs of improvement in the status of women. Japan has recently gained its first female high-court judge, its first female captain of a coastguard patrol boat, its first female guards at the parliament building. Customs enforcement at Narita Airport is run by a woman, as is the international-operations centre of the Bank of Tokyo. Nikko Securities has just appointed a woman, Miss Haruko Fukuda, to the board of its European subsidiary. About 80,000 women are presidents of (mostly tiny) companies—twice as many as five years ago. The Defence Academy will take women from 1990. All the statistics—labour-force participation rates, women's length of service at companies and the proportion of women who go to university for the full four years—clearly show an advance on what they were 20 or even ten years ago.

The boom in consumption in Japan is among the forces helping to better the lot of women. They are the big spenders in a society where most men are "thousand-yen husbands": the amount of their daily pocket-money. Department stores in particular feel they must have women in executive positions to advise them on how to please their customers and to anticipate changes in taste and fashion. Seibu has 100 women top managers; Takashimaya more than 200. The director of Takashimaya's consumer-products division is a woman. Brother got a team of women to design a new sewing machine.

What remains depressing is the pessimism of young Japanese women who possess skills that would guarantee them success elsewhere. In Japan they accept that it is impossible for a woman to combine a satisfying home and working life, and they often have scant hopes of getting either. The young Japanese male comes in for plenty of abuse. "They are more conservative than their fathers", is a complaint made by almost any young woman who is asked for her opinion.

Ms Kaori Abe, a student at Sophia University in Tokyo, says that when she proposed a few women for membership of a newspaper discussion group, she was rebuffed by the male members. They were not keen on having too many "strong-minded women" around the place, though they were quite happy with a few demure and pretty ones.

A Matter of Honor

Bedouin cultural codes and sense of honor persist despite the passing of the people's nomadic life-style

Longina Jakubowska

Longina Jakubowska teaches anthropology at the University of the Pacific in Stockton, California.

The world modernizes: Technology and consumerism spreads: a nomad hauls his herd in a truck; television antennas stick through tent roofs; a Walkman covers the ears of a shepherd. And today, no one is surprised. The Bedouin —pastoral Arab nomads who have roamed the deserts for centuries—hardly exist as such anymore. Most live in cities today.

The word *Bedouin* is derived from the Arabic *bada'* (desert). The Bedouin derived their livelihood from herding animals—camels, goats, sheep. Their lifestyle was a direct adaptation to the desert ecology; their movements and activities determined by the needs of their animals. Scarce reserves of underground water and sparse, unpredictable rainfall obliged movement over a large territory to ensure that herds had enough pasture and consequently people enough food. Nomads rarely consumed meat, considered a luxury, since doing so would deplete their capital. They mostly lived off animal by-products (predominantly, processed milk), as well as dried fruits, dates, and some grains. There was a time when most of their needs were fulfilled by animal products—tents were woven from camel and goat wool, and gear was made from leather.

Given the limited resources of the desert, the nomads faced the constant challenge of maintaining a precarious balance between water supplies, pasture, and animal populations. Depletion of either meant demise. The land was sparsely populated and the lonely black tents of small Bedouin groups dotted the desert. Space and freedom of movement were essential to the nomadic existence, but the Bedouin nomads did not wander aimlessly; their movements were calculated, conducted seasonally, and limited to a territory they claimed as their ancestral tribal land. Territorial rights were closely guarded; infringements could, and frequently did, result in extended disputes or even an occasional war.

Fiercely independent, the Bedouin avoided involvement in the wars of others, even those conflicts that affected their own region. They remained disinterested in the politics of the entities surrounding them, until the middle of this century when the Bedouin became absorbed or encapsulated by the state structures. The process of settling the nomads in more permanent locations was strongly encouraged by all state governments in the Middle East and is now well under way. Nomadism is perceived as incompatible with modernity, and the nomads are also considered difficult to control. Yet the traditional Bedouin lifestyle still lingers in some areas, usually those which the state considers marginal.

"Settling-down" involves more than simply moving into houses. It necessitates a total restructuring of the society to be settled and a redefining of the sense of identity—which for the Bedouin is closely linked with the notion of honor.

The contrast between the Bedouin past and the present is striking. The change occurred rapidly, in less than one generation. Encased in the trappings of modernity, technological gadgets, and Western clothing, the Bedouin present a very different image today from that of the past. Most have moved to towns and adjusted to the market economy. They hold salaried jobs, work in construction, operate agri-

The honor and authority of the father is central to Bedouin family and society.

cultural machines, and drive trucks. There is, however, continuity in their attitude toward employment. They prefer independence, the ability to set their own time schedule, and they frequently operate family businesses. Occasionally, forgetting the hardships of nomadic life, they reminisce nostalgically about when the Bedouin worried only about the rainfall and pasture, and tell stories to their children about the challenge and glory of *hel* (camel racing).

Contrary to expectations, settling-down has not greatly improved the quality of life for either Bedouin men or women. If anything, their behavior has become even more circumspect, and female honor is guarded even closer. Compared with the sparsely populated desert, Bedouin towns are crowded, which greatly increases social interaction and potential sources of conflict. To maintain the code of modesty, women are forced to remain either inside their houses or to veil heavily, in a manner similar to peasant women. Since men are absent from the village most of the day, and since the behavior of women forms an intricate part of the honor code, there is even greater social control imposed on women. Furthermore, due to present patterns of employment, women are now completely excluded from involvement in the process of production, which diminishes their participation in decision-making and consequently harms their position in society.

So far the Bedouin exhibit considerable resiliency and cultural continuity. They remain the unquestionable ideal of the Arab ethos—honorable, pure, brave, independent, hospitable, and honest. It is widely believed that the Bedouin dialect is the untainted version of Arabic, the language in which the Prophet Muhammad spoke. Although highly praised, the Bedouin are also feared for their unequivocal honor code which does not allow for mistakes.

The consequence of an elopement

Changes in material culture and in the externals of life-style can be misleading: The beliefs and value systems taught to the generation of Bedouin born and brought up in the sedentary modern environment remain those of the nomadic tradition. The trial described below occurred a few years ago in southern Israel, but it could have happened in any other country in the Middle East, for the issues involved are of vital importance to the Bedouin cultural ethos. Despite the numerous changes that many of these societies experienced, the notion of honor has been altered little.

The trial took place early on a spring morning. The rains had stopped and the arid hills were, at least temporarily, green again. The busy morning activities in the small encampment of Sheikh Abu Rashid had subsided. Everything indicated that something unusual was about to happen. A long black tent, many times the size of the domestic tents that some of the Bedouin present remembered living in, had been erected. Firewood had been gathered in piles, animals stood nearby—unknowingly waiting to be slaughtered, and the rhythmic sounds of coffee mills could be heard. Everyone present awaited the arrival of the guests. The preparations that were under way in the camp (which consisted of tin shacks and wooden plank huts) were similar to those for a wedding, yet the joy of wedding preparations, usually marked by the shrilled ululations of women rejoicing because their sons were soon to become men, was missing.

There was another significant difference. Although Sheikh Abu Rashid was giving the last directions to his male and female kinfolk about placement of the mattresses and pillows in the grand tent for the visitors to recline on, none of the implements—the tent, the firewood, the animals, nor the numerous other supplies including tea and coffee and even the mattresses, belonged to him. All were brought by the men who were to be tried, the family of Ataywah. A Bedouin court, or *manshed*, was about to be convened.

In a distant hut, surrounded by the sheikh's female relatives, a young girl called Azizah was anxiously awaiting the events of the day. Some weeks ago she and her boyfriend had run away to the Negev desert hoping their families would agree to their marriage. It occasionally would happen; elopements were rare but legitimate means of eliciting consent to marriage. According to tradition, marriage unions were arranged by the respective families of groom and bride, as marriage is not a matter for the individual but the family to decide. There were concerns about access to wells and pastures, previous marriage arrangements to finalize, and weakened ties that needed strengthening; in short, alliances to be made. In the absence of other forms of social integration, kinship and marriage serve as the primary means of political and social action. Women link families together. This link, however, is highly vulnerable, and women are placed under a constant cloud of suspicion regarding their loyalty (or suspected disloyalty) to either their paternal or husband's families.

Azizah did not rebel against the norms underpinning the Bedouin institutions, but rather against a particular choice of husband her father had made on her behalf. She miscalculated, however, the degree of his involvement in the marriage negotiations and the extent of his commitment. Once the agreement was made it became a matter of honor to keep it.

Whatever credits or discredits a woman earns reflect back on her paternal family. An unruly daughter can damage family reputation. Public disclosure of the inability to exert control over one's women is disgraceful. Fathers are aware of the inherent power in command of women and frequently mediate between daughters' preferences and their own goals. In this case, however, marriage to a man chosen by the daughter, a man from the Ataywah, was incongruent with the father's family politics. Public opinion is a double-edged sword. Mustering public sympathy could have turned events to Azizah's advantage, but it would also have exposed her father's honor. The only means of saving his and the family's face was to bring a legal case against the family of the offender, the young man she eloped with.

The importance of the codes of honor

In the Bedouin social framework, an individual's actions reflect on his paternal kin. Family, which includes generations and can reach hundreds of members, is the strongest unit of identification. The farther the distance between kin, the "weaker the blood" between them, the lesser are the responsibilities toward one another and the accountability for

each other's behavior. This system of organization, called the segmentary lineage system in anthropological literature, is best illustrated by the Bedouin proverb:

Me against my brother,
My brother and I against my cousin,
My cousin and I against a stranger.

Family lineage, called *hamula*, places a person in the social structure, gives identity, and offers protection and security. It circumscribes, however, freedom of individual action and imposes obligations and strict rules of behavior. The price of misconduct on the part of an individual is paid by the group.

The behavior of the young man was irresponsible and implicated his hamula. The verdict of guilt was already pronounced and the result of the trial known beforehand. His family had few excuses to make on his behalf and had to carry the burden of the trial —including its costs—and reparations to the girl's family. The financial as well as social losses were considerable and would take years to repay. There were no possibilities of appeal—to maintain their respectability the family had to act in a socially prescribed responsible fashion. Serious transgressions of norms and recidivist behavior, which threaten the economic well-being and the social standing of the family, could result in the offender's expulsion from the larger group. This grave consequence served as the final safeguard for the family. It had happened only a few times in the living memory of the Bedouin present. Such an outcast, expelled from under the protective umbrella of the hamula, becomes a person without roots or identity; without kin, he loses his social existence. The Bedouin apply a very revealing term to such a person, *enshamma*, meaning literally and metaphorically "the one under the sun."

One may wonder why, knowing the serious potential repercussions, the young man risked public condemnation. The possibility of public exposure and confrontation at the beginning of the affair was rather small, and he had made every effort to avoid it. However, the girl's father was so unrelenting that the couple had sought refuge with the well-respected Sheikh Abu Rashid, leader of a powerful tribe, relying on his reputation in the Negev to mediate a noncontroversial settlement in the dispute.

On the surface, the issue concerned arranging a marriage. Using an important personality as a broker was common in such negotiations. However, this was no longer only a question of marriage; the problem now addressed a principle of honor. The girl's father had refused to grant his permission to the marriage both before and after the elopement and demanded restitution of his honor, insulted by an unlawful act of taking his daughter against his wishes. Since the offensive act, the elopement, was a public statement, so had to be the admission of guilt. The guilty party had to show humility and restore the honor of the offended.

Honor is the basis of the moral code of an individ-

Women's roles are closely defined, and their behavior, which can bestow honor or dishonor upon one's family, is under constant scrutiny.

ual in Bedouin society. It is inherently personal, but as the individual constitutes an integral part of the kinship group, his honor extends to the kin. Honor is obtained not by performing unusual acts but by the ability to live according to the ideal. Honor is maintained through a series of challenges and ripostes; success garnishes respect; failure to react entails disgrace. Even blood can be spilled in defense of honor. "Blood can be washed only by blood," the Bedouin say. A wounding or killing is a stain on the family honor; restitution can be accomplished only through a similar retaliatory act.

Blood feuds are spectacular examples of the honor code binding Bedouin kin groups. Although they occur rarely in the extreme, they command attention, appeal to the imagination, and linger in Bedouin memories. Events that occurred in a distant past are handed down to each generation. The Bedouin culture always emphasized the oral tradition; skillful storytellers once held great respect. Historical time was changed; events of hundreds years ago appeared as yesterday's happenings. Stories of blood feuds, of warriors fighting inadvertent circumstances told at the evening fires become relevant to the present. They form the integral part of the Bedouin ethos, the code of honor.

Sheikh Abu Rashid had little choice when the eloping couple approached him. He was expected to offer hospitality, protection, and to mediate in the dispute. Refusal would endanger his reputation. Heredity does not guarantee leadership among the Bedouin. So although Sheikh Abu Rashid came from a long line of tribal chiefs, he had to earn his title —by demonstrating charisma, powers of persuasion, and by gaining fame for his wisdom.

Hospitality among the Bedouin is proverbial. It also is the rule of the desert. Bound by ecological constraints and the frequent shortage of resources, the nomads customarily extend help to those in need. Visitors are fed, given shelter, and even clothing if necessary. Bedouin glorify hospitality. One is obliged by it even at the risk of starvation. Every Bedouin child can recall a tale that recounts the suffering of an impoverished nomad who, although his very life depended on it, slaughtered the last camel to feed the unsuspecting but hungry guest. For his sacrifice he was held in the highest esteem. Furthermore, guests receive immunity and protection from their hosts. Hospitality is a sacred duty. Even one's enemies are granted this privilege and are entitled to safety of passage. Any attack on the guest would be perceived as an affront to the host.

It was common for eloped couples to seek refuge from their families at the powerful Bedouin houses. When Azizah and her young man arrived in the encampment of Sheikh Abu Rashid they were promptly separated from each other and housed in different places. Sheikh Abu Rashid could not afford,

The "advantages" of modern life are affecting the core values of Bedouin society and could introduce an unprecedented separation between the generations.

for his own sake, the reputation of his kin, and the proceedings of the case, to be placed under the slightest suspicion of fostering improper sexual behavior. He breathed easier upon learning that the girl's virginity was intact. Had the couple been involved sexually, the matter would have been even more grave.

The honor of Bedouin men is dependent upon the sexual conduct of women in their family. Male kin are required to protect female virtue. While male honor is flexible—depending on the man's behavior, it can be acquired, diminished, lost, or regained —female honor is rigid. A sexual offense on the part of a woman causes her honor to be lost, and it cannot be restored. Thus the core of male honor is the protection of one's female relatives' honor. According to the Bedouin ethical code, a transgression of sexual norms is a crime that may result in capital punishment.

Azizah's father pressed for court proceedings. *Manshed*, the highest Bedouin court, is convened extremely rarely, once in a few years or even a decade. Usually every effort is made not to escalate the conflict so that it can be resolved on a much smaller scale at lower levels of Bedouin social structure. Manshed deals with the most serious matters and achieves the greatest exposure, which was why the girl's father insisted on its taking place. As one Bedouin said when addressing the sources of conflict in Bedouin society, Bedouin fight either over land or over women, and both concern honor.

The trial

Attendance at the manshed was enormous —over a hundred people arrived. As each visitor entered the tent, ceremonial greetings were exchanged and tea served. There were no women in sight, and adolescent boys quietly and busily attended to all the guests. The court was open to all men. Only the assailants' party, the family of Ataywah, was conspicuously missing. It was represented by Sheikh Abu Rashid. There was no set hour for the beginning of the proceedings, which began when all the important participants were present, notably the famous sheikhs of the area and authorities on Bedouin law. There was no set procedure either. All could voice their opinions. Knowledge and oratory skills prevailed in reaching the decision, which took until the late afternoon. The discussion of the case was intertwined with chatting about recent political events, questions about each other's families. It was interrupted by people taking leave for noon prayers and greeting those who were still arriving.

When a sense of consensus was reached, a tentative verdict was announced, the hearing of which could make an inexperienced observer shudder. The man's tongue was to be cut, for he talked to the girl; his hands were to be cut, for he touched her; his legs were to be cut, for he walked with her. Then a prolonged and heated bargaining started. It soon became clear that nobody had any intention of mutilating the culprit's body; the verdict was an expression of the severe nature of the crime committed. Instead the punishment was translated into monetary measures. The bargaining had all the makings of a ritual. There was more to follow. For every mile the man traveled with the girl, he was also to pay. All came to an enormous sum of 100 million lira, approximately $500,000. It was lowered considerably during further bargaining: in honor of the prophet Muhammad, on behalf of the people present and the costs of tea and coffee consumed by them, which they would have refused to drink otherwise.

A stream of new guests arrived in the afternoon. They came late intentionally, announced their names aloud, and refused to drink the customary cup of tea unless an additional sum of money was forgone. Only one representative of a hamula was allowed to make an appeal. The amount withdrawn from the one penalty depended on the respect commanded by his family. The family of the offender, although not present at the proceedings, kept a close watch over its developments. Through sending messengers and calling upon their allies, people were lobbied to make a plea on behalf of the Ataywah.

By the evening, the sum was lowered to $100,000, but the bargaining did not cease yet. Dinner followed and this called for further negotiations. Meanwhile an elaborate meal was served, for which fifteen sheep were slaughtered, but the guests refused to eat until the punishment was revised again.

It was late at night when the sheikhs pronounced their final verdict. Azizah was to come back to her family. The young man was found guilty of kidnap-ping, for such was the preferred interpretation of the affair, and had to pay 15 million lira ($75,000) to the girl's family. Also the family's car in which they eloped had to be returned to them. Sheikh Abu Rashid and two other prominent figures agreed to oversee the fulfillment of the sentence.

The punishment was severe. The young man, employed as a construction worker at the time, did not have the means to pay the penalty himself. The elopement proved to be a costly affair. The cost of materials and food supplied for the trial, together with the monetary amount of compensation, exceeded his probable lifetime earnings. These expenses were divided equally among his hamula, the members of which from now on were obliged to commit their meager resources to paying the family debt, the debt of honor. The social costs were even greater. His family had to call upon old alliances and political favors, reserved for a time of crisis.

The girl returned to her father's household. Her future looked bleak. After causing so much discord, it was unlikely that she would still be welcomed as a match for the marriage her father arranged for her. Most probably Azizah would be married as a second wife, or else wedded to an elderly widower (which is certainly not regarded as the best option).□

--------------- **Additional Reading** ---------------

Lila Abu-Lughod, *Veiled Sentiments: Honor & Poetry in a Bedouin Society*, University of California Press, 1986.

P.C. Dodd, "Family Honor & the Forces of Change in Arab Society," *International Journal of Middle East Studies*, 4 (1973): 40-54.

Emanuel Marx and Avshalom Shmueli, eds, *The Changing Bedouin*, Transaction Books, 1986.

Global Climatic Change

Evidence suggests that production of carbon dioxide and methane from human activities has already begun to change the climate and that radical steps must be taken to halt any further change

Richard A. Houghton and George M. Woodwell

RICHARD A. HOUGHTON and GEORGE M. WOODWELL have collaborated for more than 20 years on topics of environmental concern. Houghton is an ecologist and a senior scientist at the Woods Hole Research Center in Woods Hole, Mass. For the past 10 years he has been concerned with the global carbon cycle and has specialized in the response of ecosystems, particularly forests, to climatic change. Woodwell is also an ecologist and is the director of the Woods Hole Research Center. He and Houghton hope to be able, along with their Woods Hole colleagues, to advance improved models for the management of renewable resources.

The world is warming. Climatic zones are shifting. Glaciers are melting. Sea level is rising. These are not hypothetical events from a science-fiction movie; these changes and others are already taking place, and we expect them to accelerate over the next years as the amounts of carbon dioxide, methane and other trace gases accumulating in the atmosphere through human activities increase.

The warming, rapid now, may become even more rapid as a result of the warming itself, and it will continue into the indefinite future unless we take deliberate steps to slow or stop it. Those steps are large and apparently difficult: a 50 percent reduction in the global consumption of fossil fuels, a halting of deforestation, a massive program of reforestation.

There is little choice. A rapid and continuous warming will not only be destructive to agriculture but also lead to the widespread death of forest trees, uncertainty in water supplies and the flooding of coastal areas. When the ice now covering the Arctic Ocean melts, further unpredictable changes in the global climate will ensue. There may be controversy over whether the data are adequate and whether the warming is caused by changes in the atmosphere. Yet there is an unusually powerful consensus among climatologists that the dominant influence on global climate over the next centuries will be a warming driven by the accumulation of heat-trapping gases. The consequences are threatening enough so that many scientists, citizens and even political leaders are urging immediate action to halt the warming.

The fact that heat-trapping gases have been accumulating in the atmosphere is well established. Since the middle of the 19th century the amount of atmospheric carbon dioxide has increased by about 25 percent. The increase has come about because human activities, especially the burning of coal and oil and the destruction of forests, have released greater quantities of carbon dioxide into the atmosphere than have been removed by diffusion into the oceans or by photosynthesis on land.

The increase in carbon dioxide appears trifling when one considers that the total amount in the atmosphere is a little more than .03 percent by volume. But in spite of its low concentration, carbon dioxide and several other gases present in even smaller amounts have an important role in determining the temperature of the earth. In contrast to both nitrogen and oxygen, which together make up more than 99 percent of the atmosphere, these trace gases absorb infrared radiation, or radiant heat. Since in this regard they act much like the glass over a greenhouse, they are commonly referred to as greenhouse gases.

Because the total amount of greenhouse gases is small, their concentrations are easily changed. An increase in the concentration of any one of them increases the atmosphere's capacity to retain heat and raises the temperature at which the atmosphere comes into equilibrium with the energy it receives from the sun. In recent years investigators have recognized that the atmospheric burden of greenhouse gases other than carbon dioxide, such as methane (CH_4), nitrous oxide (N_2O) and the chlorofluorocarbons (CFC's), is also growing at an increasing rate. By the mid-1980's, in fact, these gases had reached levels at which their combined effect approached that of carbon dioxide.

In this article we emphasize the role of carbon dioxide and methane because they are the principal contributors to the current warming, because their concentrations are strongly influenced by biological processes and because slowing or stopping the global warming will require control of carbon dioxide emissions in particular.

Global warming due to the accumulation of heat-trapping gases, particularly carbon dioxide, was predicted at the turn of the century by Svante Arrhenius in Sweden and Thomas C. Chamberlin in the U.S. Systematic research on the atmospheric accumulation of carbon dioxide began only in 1958. Since then Charles D. Keeling of the Scripps Institution of Oceanography has provided a continuous record of the carbon dioxide level at various stations, the best-known of which is at Mauna Loa in the Hawaiian Islands.

Information on the earth's temperature has been more difficult to accumulate. Strong evidence for global warming became available by late 1988. The most direct evidence lies in temperature records from around the world. James E. Hansen of the National Aeronautics and Space Administration's Goddard Institute of Space Studies and his colleagues have analyzed temperature records going back to 1860. Their analyses suggest that the average global temperature has increased by from .5 to .7 degree Celsius since that year. The greatest increase has taken place in the past decade; this recent warming is both statistically significant and consistent with their experience based on theory and on models of the global climatic system.

Thomas M. L. Wigley and his colleagues, working independently at the University of East Anglia in England, have also shown the increase in average global temperature. The rise has

not been observed in all regions: a recent analysis of climate records by Kirby Hanson and his colleagues at the National Oceanic and Atmospheric Administration shows no trend in temperature for the contiguous U.S. Such regional variation is not unexpected; the contiguous U.S. covers only 1.5 percent of the globe's surface.

The observed rise in global temperature has not been steady and is clearly not simply a response to the accumulation of greenhouse gases. There was, for example, a decline in the mean global temperature between 1940 and 1965 in spite of the continued increase of heat-trapping gases in the atmosphere. Nevertheless, Phil D. Jones, one of Wigley's collaborators, has just recently reported that the global temperature has risen about .5 degree C since the beginning of the century and that the six warmest years on record were 1988, 1987, 1983, 1981, 1980 and 1986 in that order.

If a .5-degree temperature change seems insubstantial, one should remember that in 1816, the "year without a summer," the mean global temperature drop was also less than one degree. It was nonetheless sufficient to cause frosts in June in New England and widespread crop failures [see "The Year without a Summer," by Henry Stommel and Elizabeth Stommel; SCIENTIFIC AMERICAN, June, 1979]. The heat and drought that have afflicted North America and other regions of the earth in recent years are consistent with the predictions of a global warming trend.

There are other indications of an accelerated warming. According to Arthur H. Lachenbruch and B. Vaughn Marshall of the U.S. Geological Survey, the depth to permafrost in the Alaskan and Canadian Arctic has increased in recent decades. The average temperature of Canadian lakes has increased; the annual maximum extent of sea ice surrounding the Antarctic continent and in the Arctic seas appears to be declining; inland glaciers throughout Europe and elsewhere have receded.

These observations are consistent with predictions made by climatologists on the basis of theory aided

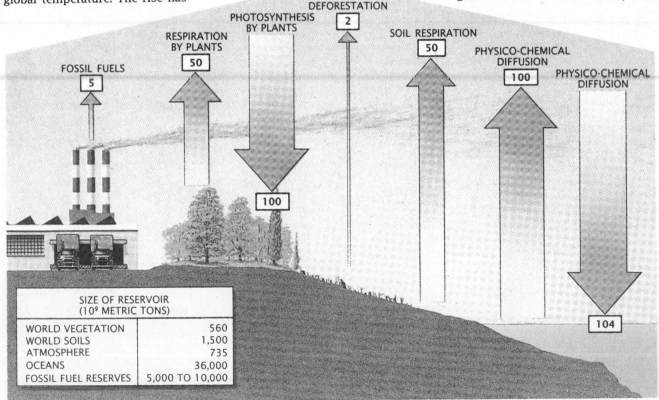

SIZE OF RESERVOIR (10⁹ METRIC TONS)	
WORLD VEGETATION	560
WORLD SOILS	1,500
ATMOSPHERE	735
OCEANS	36,000
FOSSIL FUEL RESERVES	5,000 TO 10,000

ANNUAL CARBON FLUXES are shown in units of one billion (10^9) metric tons. Photosynthesis on land removes about 100 billion tons of carbon from the atmosphere annually in the form of carbon dioxide. Plant and soil respiration each return about 50 billion tons. Fossil-fuel burning and deforestation release into the atmosphere respectively about five and two billion tons. Physicochemical processes at the sea surface release about 100 billion tons into the atmosphere and absorb about 104. The net atmospheric gain is about three billion tons annually. The table lists the world's major carbon reservoirs.

by general circulation models. Several such global models exist and, although analyses based on them do not agree in detail, the general predictions are consistent with theory and experience. Climatologists expect that the greatest warming will occur at higher latitudes in winter. In these latitudes the warming, according to the models, will probably be at least twice the global average. In addition it is expected that the upper atmosphere will cool as the lower atmosphere warms and that there will be less precipitation and less moisture in the soil at lower latitudes. All these trends have been reported in recent years.

Data such as those are always open to further analyses, interpretation and augmentation. They invariably appear to suffer from inadequacies of measurement and uncertainties about whether the period over which the measurements were taken was long enough to be significant. Investigators are currently improving the data and the analyses, but the fact remains that the observations described above, taken together with the rising concentration of greenhouse gases, constitute strong evidence that the process anticipated nearly a century ago by Arrhenius is under way.

One can learn much about potential future changes in climate by examining past climatic change. A mere 15,000 years ago glaciers covered much of North America and northern Europe. Were changes in the composition of the atmosphere involved in the great climate swings that brought glacial and interglacial periods? The answer is not completely clear, but one of the most important advances in recent years has been the ability to determine atmospheric composition in previous eras from tiny samples of air trapped in glacial ice. In particular, determination of the atmospheric composition during periods of glacial expansion and retreat has been made possible by data obtained from an ice core drilled by a joint French-Soviet team at the Antarctic Vostok station.

The Vostok core, as it is called, was 2,000 meters in length, long enough to sample ice dating through the past 160,000 years [*see illustration on next page*]. The data show fluctuations in temperature of up to 10 degrees; such fluctuations are derived from changes in the isotopic ratios in the core. It is well established, for example, that the ratio of the two common isotopes of oxygen, ^{18}O and ^{16}O, in cores of marine sediments reflects past temper-

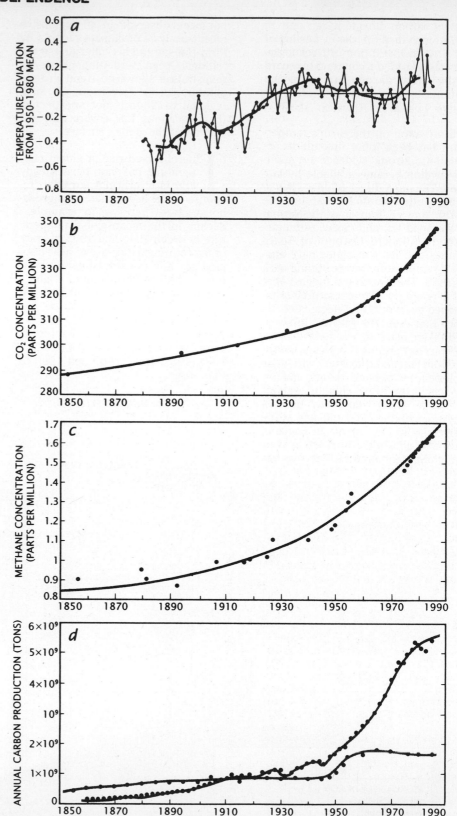

CORRELATION among the global temperature change, level of heat-trapping gases and carbon dioxide emissions is shown in the first three graphs for the past 140 years. In graph *a* both the annual mean temperature (*spiky curve*) and the five-year running mean (*smooth curve*) are plotted. Graphs *b* and *c* show the atmospheric carbon dioxide and methane content respectively. Pre-1958 data come from analyses of air trapped in bubbles of glacial ice from various sites around the world. The annual production of carbon from fossil-fuel burning (*black*) and from change in land use (*color*) is shown in *d*; the last data were obtained from historical sources.

ature changes.

The Vostok data also show how the abundances of atmospheric gases have fluctuated with temperature over the past 160,000 years: the higher the temperature, the greater the concentration of carbon dioxide and vice versa. To be sure, the correlation of carbon dioxide with temperature does not establish whether changes in atmospheric composition caused the warming and cooling trends or were caused by them. Although the carbon dioxide content follows temperature very closely during periods of deglaciation, it apparently lags behind temperature during periods of cooling.

Although there is tight statistical coupling between carbon dioxide and temperature throughout the record, the temperature changes are from five to 14 times greater than would be expected on the basis of the radiative properties of carbon dioxide alone. This relation suggests that quite aside from changes in greenhouse gases, certain positive feedbacks are amplifying the response. Such feedbacks might involve ice on land and sea, clouds or water vapor, which also absorb radiant heat.

Other data from the same Vostok core sample show that methane also closely follows temperature and carbon dioxide. The methane concentration nearly doubled, for example, between the peak of the penultimate glacial period and the following interglacial period. Within the present interglacial period it has more than doubled in just the past 300 years and is rising rapidly. Although the concen-

VOSTOK ICE-CORE DATA reveal a correlation between certain gas concentrations and temperature over the past 160,000 years. The ice core, 2,200 meters long, contains bubbles of air with carbon dioxide and methane that were trapped at different depths (*top scale*) and hence at different times (*bottom scale*). Several independent methods have established that the deuterium concentration in ice is a good measure of past temperature; both temperature and deuterium level are plotted in *a*. More traditional is the use of the oxygen isotope ^{18}O to track temperature; curve *b* is almost identical with *a*. The remarkable agreement with the shape of the Vostok-station carbon dioxide curve *c* argues that carbon dioxide can also serve as a global thermometer. Data on Antarctic methane compiled in 1985 and 1986 from several stations (*d*) strengthens the conclusion that levels of greenhouse gases are positively correlated with temperature and may actually influence it.

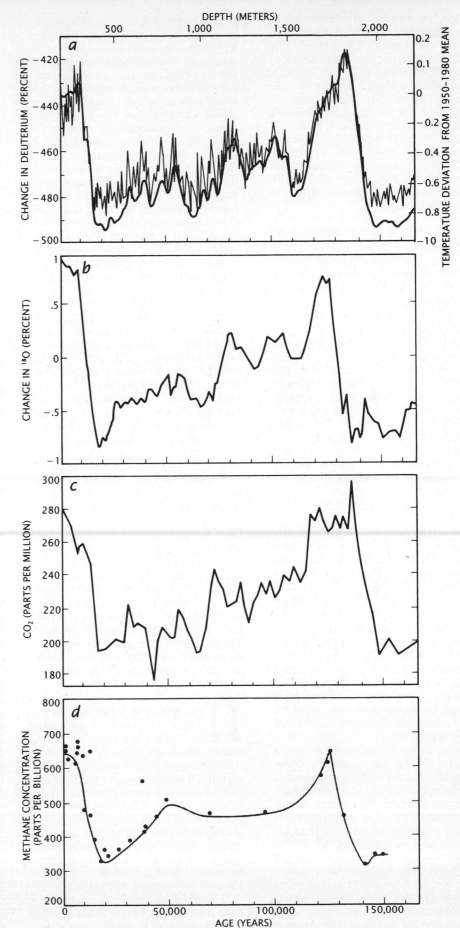

tration of atmospheric methane is more than two orders of magnitude lower than that of carbon dioxide, it cannot be ignored: the radiative properties of methane make it 20 times more effective molecule for molecule than carbon dioxide in absorbing radiant heat. On the basis of Hansen's radiative-convective model, which includes chemical feedbacks, methane appears to have been about 25 percent as important as carbon dioxide in the warming that took place during the most recent glacial retreat 8,000 to 10,000 years ago.

How can a global rise in temperature be expected to cause greater releases of carbon dioxide and methane into the atmosphere? In the process of photosynthesis terrestrial plants remove about 100 billion tons of carbon from the atmosphere per year, or about 14 percent of the total atmospheric carbon content. An approximately equal amount of carbon is returned to the atmosphere through the processes of plant respiration and decay of organic matter. Because the fluxes are a substantial fraction of the carbon dioxide already in the atmosphere at any time, a change of a few percent in either the photosynthetic or the respiratory flux would soon significantly alter the atmospheric carbon dioxide content. Will global warming produce such an imbalance?

The answer is unclear and probably will remain so until after the climate has changed considerably more than it has already. Nevertheless, the general picture is probably as follows. The rate of photosynthesis is affected by many factors, particularly the availability of light, water and nutrients. It is not, however, very sensitive to temperature change. The rates of plant respiration and decay, on the other hand, do strongly depend on the temperature. A one-degree temperature change in either direction often alters rates of plant respiration by from 10 to 30 percent.

These observations suggest that a global warming will speed the decay of organic matter without appreciably changing the rate of photosynthesis. That will increase the release of carbon dioxide into the atmosphere. A warming will also result in more methane, because methane is produced by respiration in regions where oxygen is not freely available, such as swamps, bogs and moist soils. In recent years there has been a rise in the concentration of atmospheric methane of more than 1 percent per year. The increase

is both rapid and significant because, as noted above, methane is 20 times as effective as carbon dioxide in trapping heat. The wet soils where methane is produced as a result of anaerobic decay probably represent the world's major source of methane. The global warming that has already occurred has undoubtedly stimulated anaerobic decay and the production of methane as well as carbon dioxide.

It is possible to estimate the size of the resulting increase in carbon production at least crudely. A significant fraction (from 20 to 30 percent) of global respiration on land takes place in the forest and tundra of the middle and high latitudes, where the warming is expected to be greatest. If we assume that the mean global warming to date has been .5 degree C, and that in the middle and high latitudes the rise has been one degree, then plant respiration in these latitudes and the decay of organic matter in soils has increased significantly. If the increase in respiration is between 5 and 20 percent over 20 to 30 percent of the total area respiring, then total global respiration will increase between 1 and 6 percent above normal. Once again assuming that the annual flux of carbon into the atmosphere is 100 billion tons and that the rate of photosynthesis remains unchanged, the warming that has already taken place has meant an injection of between one and six billion tons of carbon per year. Over the past century from 20 to 30 billion tons of carbon may have been released in this manner.

That estimate is probably high, because the average warming may have been less than assumed and because photosynthetic response will tend to reduce the release of carbon dioxide. Yet the estimate is probably not high by as much as a factor of two, and it serves to emphasize the importance of biotic feedback mechanisms.

How does the value just computed compare with amounts of carbon released by other known processes? The release from the burning of fossil fuels is approximately 5.6 billion tons per year; deforestation adds an amount estimated at between .4 and 2.5 billion tons per year. The total carbon injected into the atmosphere from these two sources added to a temperature-enhanced respiration is not known, but it appears to be more than six billion tons annually and may approach 10 billion.

The release of carbon due to changes in the respiratory rate could fluctuate appreciably; a gradual warming,

such as that experienced over most of this century, would change the respiratory rate slowly enough so that year-to-year changes would be inconspicuous. On the other hand, a sudden warming or cooling over a period of several years might result in an observable change in the carbon dioxide content of the atmosphere. In the past 15 years the annual rate of accumulation of atmospheric carbon dioxide has been about 1.5 parts per million, equivalent to a global accumulation of about three billion tons of carbon.

According to data recorded on Mauna Loa and at the South Pole by Keeling, however, over the past 18 months the accumulation rate has risen to about 2.4 parts per million, equivalent to about five billion tons of carbon. Keeling expects that the surge will prove transitory, as a lesser surge in 1973 and 1974 did. Nevertheless, the implication we assign to the observations at the moment is that the surge is a result of the high temperatures that have marked the 1980's, delayed by the time necessary to warm the soil. Whether this interpretation is correct remains to be seen.

Any climatic change can also be expected to affect the ability of the terrestrial biota, in particular forests and soils, to retain carbon. At warming rates that are lower than the rates at which forests develop, forests may actually expand, and with them the capacity to store carbon. But if the warming rate exceeds the rates at which forests migrate into more climatically favorable regions, widespread mortality of trees and other plants is likely to follow. The net result of such destruction of forests is difficult to predict, but it will probably mean a further release of carbon dioxide through the decay of plants, animals and organic matter in soils.

The amount of carbon dioxide that could be injected into the atmosphere would depend heavily on the rate of climatic change in the forested zones of the middle and high latitudes. Although it is impossible to make any accurate calculation, an upper limit is given by the amount of carbon in these forested latitudes: approximately 750 billion metric tons, or about the same amount of carbon as there is in the atmosphere currently.

Is it possible that a global warming could stimulate the growth of forests? In this case the spread of forests to high latitudes and tundra regions would result in a greater uptake of carbon dioxide from the atmosphere and a greater accumula-

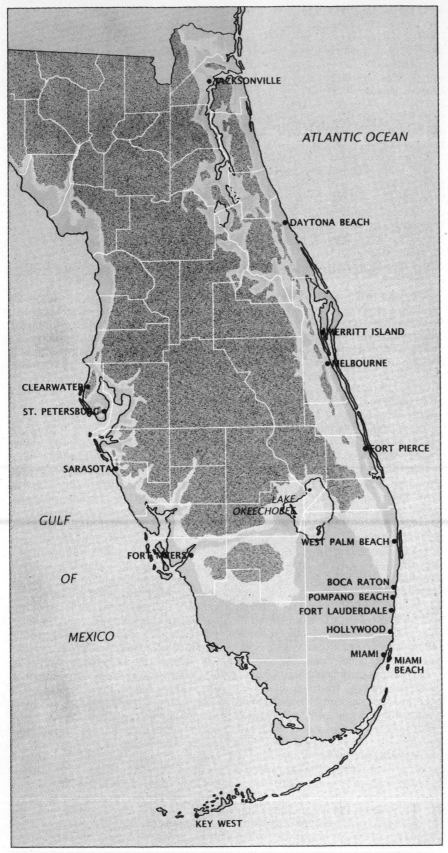

ATLANTIC OCEAN

JACKSONVILLE

DAYTONA BEACH

MERRITT ISLAND

MELBOURNE

CLEARWATER

ST. PETERSBURG

FORT PIERCE

SARASOTA

LAKE OKEECHOBEE

GULF

WEST PALM BEACH

FORT MYERS

OF

BOCA RATON

POMPANO BEACH

FORT LAUDERDALE

HOLLYWOOD

MEXICO

MIAMI

MIAMI BEACH

KEY WEST

"GLOBAL WARMING FLOODS FLORIDA" could be a tabloid headline if the polar ice caps began to melt. Florida is shown here as it might look if sea level rose 4.6 meters above or 7.6 meters above the present level. In either case Miami and Lake Okeechobee are submerged. A rise of four to five meters might be expected if the West Antarctic Ice Sheet broke up under global warming.

tion of carbon dioxide in the soil. Such a transition is unlikely. Forests require centuries to develop, especially where soils are thin and nutrients are in short supply. They also require climatic stability and sources of seeds. The climatic transitions currently under way, unless they are checked, are rapid by any measure and can be expected to continue into the indefinite future. They do not offer the conditions under which forests are able to develop on new land and remain for long periods.

Might the warming at least stimulate existing forests to store additional carbon in plants and soil? Perhaps. The boreal forest and other coniferous forests may indeed be sufficiently resilient to respond to warming with increased photosynthesis and growth. Whether the carbon taken up by photosynthesis will be stored or simply released through increased respiration remains an open question.

There is also the possibility that the tundra, the treeless plain found in arctic and subarctic regions, will respond to a warming in surprising ways, including an increase in the production of carbon and its storage in peat. The nature of the response will largely hinge on the availability of water. A wetter tundra might store additional carbon in soils; a drier tundra might release it through the decay of organic matter in long-frozen soil or soil that is normally frozen for most of the year. W. Dwight Billings of Duke University believes global warming will speed the decay of peat in tundra soils and precipitate that ultimate breakdown of the tundra known as thermal karst erosion, which allows flowing water to erode the tundra in great acre-size chunks. Not only is the tundra devastated but also substantial amounts of carbon dioxide and methane that were stored in the peat as carbon are released into the atmosphere.

The evidence indicates that under rapid planetary warming respiration rates will increase more than photosynthesis rates. The changes will lead to the release of additional carbon dioxide and methane into the atmosphere. The magnitude of the release will hinge strongly on the rate of warming: the faster the warming, the larger the release. Such behavior is consistent with (but not proved by) the data from the Vostok core.

What will be the consequences of a continued global warming? In 1985 a group of meteorologists meeting under the auspices of the World Meteorological Organization (WMO) and the United Nations Environment Programme (UNEP) demonstrated that without the respiratory feedback mechanisms addressed above, the combined effect of the greenhouse gases would warm the earth by an average of from 1.5 to 4.5 degrees C before the middle of the next century. The conclusion was recently confirmed in a review written by more than 50 scientists who met in Villach, Austria, in 1987 and was published by the WMO and the UNEP.

Seldom has there been such a strong consensus among scientists on a major environmental issue. The warming, unless consciously checked by human effort, will be rapid and will be felt differentially over the earth. Winter temperatures in the middle and high latitudes can be expected to rise by more than twice the world average. If the mean global temperature were to rise by from two to three degrees C by the year 2030, the winter temperature increase in Minneapolis might approach from four to six degrees C, or about one degree per decade. Summer temperatures would also rise, but less severely. A one-degree change in temperature is equivalent to a change in latitude of from 100 to 150 kilometers. The prairie-forest border, which is now south and west of Minneapolis, might be expected to migrate north at a rate of between 100 and 150 kilometers per decade, or between 400 and 600 kilometers by the year 2030.

Such changes are likely to be difficult for most of the world's peoples. First, the changes will be continuous. Unless the warming stops, efforts to adapt to climatic changes are likely to be responses to conditions that no longer exist. Second, the changes in climate will be irreversible for any time of interest to us or our children. There is no way to cool the earth or to lower sea level; we cannot return quickly to an atmosphere with lower concentrations of greenhouse gases. The best we can do is to reduce current emissions. If that step is taken immediately, a further warming of more than one degree can be expected as the full effects of the heat-trapping gases already present are felt.

Finally, the effects are open-ended. Although most modeling to date simulates a doubling of the atmospheric carbon dioxide content, there is simply no reason to assume that the concentrations will stop at twice the current levels. Estimated reserves of recoverable fossil fuels in themselves are enough to increase the atmospheric concentration of carbon dioxide by

a factor of from five to 10.

Can anything be done to slow the climatic change that is now under way? The immediate need is to stabilize the greenhouse-gas content of the atmosphere. Regardless of its source, over the past decade carbon has been accumulating in the atmosphere at a rate of about three billion tons annually. (The remainder is being absorbed by the oceans or stored in forests and soils.) If current fluxes were reduced by three billion tons annually, the atmospheric carbon dioxide level would be stabilized for a few years. The stabilization would not be permanent, however. The rate of accumulation in the oceans is determined by how fast they can absorb carbon dioxide from the atmosphere; this in turn depends on the difference in carbon dioxide concentration between the atmosphere and the ocean. As the flux of excess carbon is reduced, the difference is also reduced and the ocean becomes less capable

of absorbing excess carbon; carbon dioxide emissions would have to be reduced still further to prevent additional atmospheric accumulation.

The largest source of carbon dioxide emissions is the combustion of fossil fuels, which releases about 5.6 billion tons of carbon into the atmosphere annually. Industrial nations contribute about 75 percent of these emissions; steps toward stabilizing the composition must begin in the industrialized world. A recent study carried out under the auspices of the World Resources Institute and led by José Goldemberg, president of the University of São Paulo in Brazil, suggests that the consumption of energy from fossil fuels in the developed nations could be halved by a program of conservation and improved efficiency alone.

Although developing nations produce less carbon dioxide, their contributions are growing; if economic development follows conventional patterns, their potential contributions are very large. The second step toward the

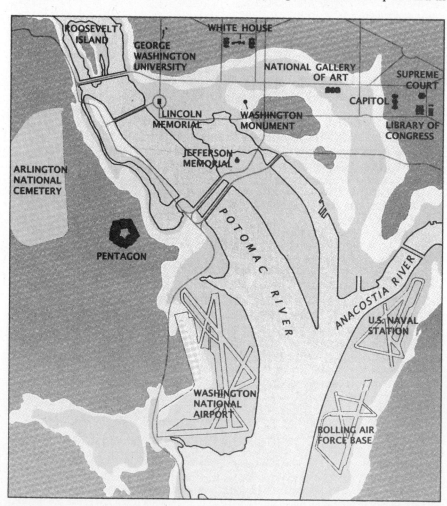

WASHINGTON, D.C., is depicted here under the same conditions as in the preceding illustration. Washington National Airport and the Lincoln Memorial are inundated. The 7.6-meter contour reaches almost to the Capitol steps and to the White House.

stabilization of greenhouse gases will require innovations in economic development that lessen dependence on fossil fuels.

The other known major source of carbon dioxide is deforestation, predominantly in the Tropics. By 1980 about 11,000 square kilometers of forest were being cleared annually, with the result that in 1980 between .4 and 2.5 billion tons of carbon (as carbon dioxide) were released into the atmosphere. The rate of deforestation has increased over the past decade. If the present release of carbon is near the upper end of the above range, halting deforestation would reduce carbon emissions by the three billion tons per year needed immediately to stabilize atmospheric composition.

Reforestation will also help to stabilize the composition of the atmosphere. The reforestation of from one to two million square kilometers (about the area of Alaska) will result in the annual storage of one billion tons of carbon. Although this area is large and productive land in the Tropics is at a premium, there may be as much as 8.5 million square kilometers of once forested land available for reforestation. Of this land, about 3.5 million square kilometers could be returned to forest if permanent agriculture were to replace shifting cultivation. Another five million square kilometers of deforested land are currently unused, and there reforestation could in principle be implemented immediately. Forests established to store carbon would, of course, have to be maintained: neither harvested nor destroyed by toxic effects or change in climate.

Each of the measures to stabilize the atmospheric carbon dioxide level would have salutary effects locally, regionally and nationally, quite apart from its effects on climatic change. An improvement in energy-use efficiency, a step that might have been taken long ago with benefits to all, would bring economic and material advantages to both individuals and nations. An improvement in efficiency would lessen reliance on fossil fuels; this in turn would reduce sulfur and nitrogen oxide emissions, acid deposition and the release of other toxins. Halting deforestation would help to maintain the genetic diversity of the planet, reduce erosion, stabilize local and regional climates, cleanse water and air and preserve opportunities for future generations.

No one remedy by itself is likely to stabilize the levels of carbon dioxide and methane in the atmosphere. If the accumulation of carbon dioxide in the atmosphere persists, the carbon burden will have shifted from three billion tons annually to five billion tons and will be that much more difficult to address. The measures that are required can begin at home, although it is clear the world must join in the effort if it is to be effective. There are precedents for international action on similar issues. The Limited Test Ban Treaty of 1962 was an agreement among certain nations to avoid atmospheric tests of nuclear weapons. It has been effective. Nations that did not sign it (France and the People's Republic of China) have yielded to international pressure and now conduct weapons tests underground. The Vienna Convention for the Protection of the Ozone Layer and the Montreal Protocol, the latter negotiated in 1987, have moved the world far toward the elimination of chlorofluorocarbons.

There is no reason to assume that similar progress cannot be made with carbon-based fuels and deforestation. With that end in view a series of steps has already been undertaken: 50 specialists in international diplomacy and law met recently under the auspices of the Woods Hole Research Center to outline approaches that might work. The greatest problem is gaining the active and effective support of the developing nations, which are poised for a massive increase in fossil-fuel consumption. Development need not, however, follow historical paths. To cite one example, the low-latitude countries stand to gain immeasurably as techniques for exploiting solar energy are perfected. Solar-powered electrolysis of water can produce hydrogen, which in turn can run automobiles and other machinery. There are few places in North America where domestic hot water cannot now be produced by solar energy at little or no cost throughout most of the year. Nor is it to the advantage of nations to allow their forests to be destroyed.

Conferences are under way in the developing nations to explore alternatives to the present course. The first was held in New Delhi in February; the second is planned for São Paulo in September under the leadership of Goldemberg. The conferences will explore the possible responses of developing nations to a world in which conventional energy sources are limited. There are extraordinary opportunities for industrial innovations, particularly in energy efficiency and solar power. But developing countries cannot be expected to shoulder the entire burden; the developed nations, which are responsible for most of the problem, must do their share.

These issues will persist throughout the next century and dominate major technical, scientific and political considerations into the indefinite future.

FURTHER READING
GLOBAL DEFORESTATION: CONTRIBUTION TO ATMOSPHERIC CARBON DIOXIDE. G. M. Woodwell, J. E. Hobbie, R. A. Houghton, J. M. Melillo, B. Moore, B. J. Peterson and G. R. Shaver in *Science*, Vol. 222, No. 4628, pages 1081–1086; December 9, 1983.
THE FLUX OF CARBON FROM TERRESTRIAL ECOSYSTEMS TO THE ATMOSPHERE IN 1980 DUE TO CHANGES IN LAND USE: GEOGRAPHIC DISTRIBUTION OF THE GLOBAL FLUX. R. A. Houghton, R. D. Boone, J. R. Fruci, J. E. Hobbie, J. M. Melillo, C. A. Palm, B. J. Peterson, G. R. Shaver, G. M. Woodwell, B. Moore, D. L. Skole and N. Myers in *Tellus*, Vol. 39B, Nos. 1–2, pages 122–139; February–April, 1987.
GLOBAL TRENDS OF MEASURED SURFACE AIR TEMPERATURE. James Hansen and Sergej Lebedeff in *Journal of Geophysical Research*, Vol. 92, No. D11, pages 13345–13372; November 20, 1987.

THE INTERNATIONALIZATION OF HISTORY

Akira Iriye

Akira Iriye, professor of history at the University of Chicago, was president of the American Historical Association in 1988. He earned his Ph.D. at Harvard University, where he studied with Ernest R. May, John K. Fairbank, and Oscar Handlin. His major field of interest is modern international history. He is the author of Power and Culture: The Japanese-American War, 1941–1945 *(1981) and* The Origins of the Second World War in Asia and the Pacific *(1987). Professor Iriye is currently at work on two topics: changing conceptions of war and peace in the twentieth century and U.S.–Asian relations since 1945.*

That history is a cosmopolitan discipline seems to be accepted today at least as a vision by a large number of historians. Recent presidents of the American Historical Association have alluded to and confirmed this vision. Bernard Bailyn has called historical scholarship "an international enterprise" and noted the increasing "transnational communication of parallel information"; John Hope Franklin has written that "scholarship knows no national boundaries"; and William H. McNeill has spoken of "the moral duty of the historical profession" to cultivate "a sense of individual identification with the triumphs and tribulations of humanity as a whole."[1] History, it seems, has come a long way in the last one hundred years. When this organization was established, "history" mostly referred to European and especially American history, and the mission of the association was said to consist in the preservation of historical manuscripts and in the promotion of "American history, and of history in America." George Bancroft, president of the association in 1885, declared that the AHA devoted itself "to the affairs of the United States of America."[2]

In the intervening years, as Arthur S. Link noted in his centennial presidential address given four years ago, there has been "growing diversity in the membership and leadership of the AHA," and there has developed a "catholicity of interest" in all aspects of the past and in all parts of the world.[3] Today, the association's 13,000 members represent diverse methodologies and specializations, many ethnic groups, nearly all ages, and scores of countries.[4] This last seems to me to be of special significance, for, although our organization is called the American Historical Association, it has been an international community of historians. From its inception, it has been open to historians of all countries, and today scholars from over forty countries belong to it. More than five hundred members have overseas mailing addresses; while some are undoubtedly American historians residing abroad, their number must be more than matched by foreign scholars living in the United States. Some of the distinguished foreign historians have been elected honorary members of the AHA. Starting with Leopold von Ranke in 1885, the honorary membership has been offered to scholars in all parts of the globe. Visiting historians regularly participate in our annual conventions. Moreover, the AHA has sponsored, and sent delegations to, many international conferences.

These are impressive beginnings and attest to the openness and vitality of the American historical profession, which seems unsurpassed anywhere in the world. I am sure I speak for all scholars of foreign origin in the United States when I express my deep gratitude for this openness. But I strongly believe that the AHA should dedicate itself not only to reaffirming but also to expanding the tradition of openness and cosmopolitanism. Today, further efforts are required to internationalize the discipline. At one level, this will necessitate the establishment of closer ties between the American and overseas historical communities. At another level, the effort will entail the search for historical themes and conceptions that are meaningful across national boundaries. At still another level, each historian will have to become more conscious of how his or her scholarship may translate in other parts of the world. I would like to comment briefly on these three aspects of internationalization.

The establishment of closer ties with foreign historical communities requires dedicated and enterprising initiatives, such as those demonstrated by one of our past presidents, Lewis Hanke, who a few years ago undertook a survey of American history as taught and practiced in other countries. In the process, he communicated with over five hundred foreign scholars specializing in the history of North America, and his initiatives have left a valuable legacy to build on for further internationalizing the profession.[5] As one step in this direction, the American Historical Association, the Organization of American Historians, and the American Studies Association have created a joint committee on international scholarly exchange. It will seek to strengthen ties to overseas historians, especially in American history, by suggesting specific ways in which they may better communicate with Americanists in the United States. It makes sense to pay particular attention to American history because the United States is the center of this subfield, and yet specialists in the United States do not always possess information on what Americanists do in other countries. And Americanists overseas do not enjoy as much opportunity as they would like to interact with historians here. There are even indications that the number of Americanists in Britain and some other European countries, as well as Japan, may be declining.[6] If so, the question of what the American historical profession can do to reverse this trend should be on its agenda for the immediate future. On the other hand, in socialist countries such as the Soviet Union, Yugoslavia, East Germany, and the People's Republic of China, American studies may have entered a period of growth. Clearly, it is imperative to encourage such a development. To take perhaps the most notable example, the ties between the American and Chinese historical communities have become very close in the last several years. Senior Americanists from the United States,

many of them members of our association, have visited China under the auspices of the Council on International Exchange of Scholars, the American Council of Learned Societies, the Committee on Scholarly Communication with the People's Republic of China, or other organizations. They have lectured to large Chinese audiences, organized workshops in American studies to which Chinese scholars from all over the country were invited, and donated books to university libraries throughout China. Historians in China, for their part, have established American studies associations, and Chinese scholars now here have organized themselves into an association of Chinese historians in the United States. It is to be hoped that similar attempts will be made in other countries as well and that the AHA will become more directly involved in furthering such scholarly ties.

It is not enough, however, merely to promote the study of the United States in other countries by duplicating what American historians do at home. Such an exchange is a one-way transaction. More fruitful exchanges would be, and have been, those in which American historians from the United States come into contact not only with Americanists overseas but with other historians as well, thereby broadening their perspectives and accustoming themselves to thinking of American history not just as national history, or even as part of transatlantic history, but also as an aspect of human history.

This notion of the interconnectedness of human history is the second topic I would like to consider. International exchanges will mean little if historians from various countries meet, exchange specialized information, and part without having jointly explored wider issues of history. It seems to me that, even when they exchange localized knowledge, they should keep in mind the questions of what such information may mean to the rest of humanity. This is another way of suggesting that historians from different parts of the world should make an effort to discuss problems whose significance transcends local boundaries. The best examples of international scholarly collaboration have come when scholars have translated their respective specialized and fragmented knowledge into more universal language and explored the meaning of, for instance, feudalism, slavery, or modernization in different countries. The list of "internationalizable" topics is endless. Such fundamental questions as human beings' relationship to nature, the definitions of beauty and truth, social justice, freedom against power, and the struggle to preserve memory should provide thematic points of contact between scholars of various countries. Historians can collaborate in comparing these themes in different parts of the world, thereby affirming that history belongs to the whole of humanity, not just to its segments.

As these remarks indicate, the internationalization

of history may be the same as the promotion of comparative history, in the sense that we are comparing ideas and institutions in different parts of the world. There is a tendency, however, at least in some works of comparative history, to emphasize differences between nations and cultures or the particularity of indigenous social developments. Often, a comparison of social, political, or intellectual trends in countries ends up reiterating their unique natures.[7] The more one compares ideas and institutions in one part of the world with those in another, the stronger their differences tend to appear. This is perhaps unavoidable, but it seems to me that to confirm local, national, or cultural distinctions is counter to the ideal of internationalization. To the extent that we seek to internationalize history, it would be unfortunate if our work merely nationalized it in the sense of stressing the uniqueness of each country's historical development. Sometimes, it may be necessary to try to denationalize history in order to internationalize it, that is, to find themes and responses common to a plurality of nations rather than those limited to specific subcategories of humanity.

It may be said that the study of history, at least modern history, has experienced a tension between nationalization and internationalization. I believe both are important perspectives, and to illustrate I would like to cite my own field of specialization, international history. At one level, international history is but a sum total of national histories: it deals with the behavior of nations toward one another. Most major works in the field are studies of this kind, written in terms of national security, national interest, national power, national prestige, national styles of foreign policy, and the like.[8] Because the interests and relative power of nations provide key conceptual frameworks, it is not surprising that most monographs in international history are studies of crises, tensions, struggles, and wars among nations. This may also explain why there are far more studies of war than of peace. A focus on conflict seems inevitable so long as the nation remains the basic unit of inquiry. This is what I mean by nationalization.

At the same time, international history has sought to go beyond the national level of analysis and to treat the entire world as a framework of study. In addition to examining the behavior of each nation, historians have proposed various conceptions of the world system, or the international system, a structure that establishes conditions for the existence of individual nations and to which their policies are responses. Thus scholars have written of "the concert of Europe," "Bismarck's European order," and the like. These were all definitions of international order accepted by the major powers with varying degrees of enthusiasm, and whose stability or instability spelled the difference between world peace and war. Whereas these systems

are conceptual constructs defined basically in terms of power, some scholars have stressed international economic systems, or regimes, referring to such examples as the British-sustained and gold-based system of international economic exchange in the nineteenth century and the Bretton Woods system after World War II. International order, therefore, may be characterized both as a power system and as an economic regime. The study of how such a system or regime affected various countries, how it was supported or destroyed by them, has provided a key set of issues for international historians, and these issues have been subjects of joint research for scholars from different nations.

Perhaps one of the most important areas that awaits extensive investigation is the relationship between a given international power system and a global economic regime. The two are often, but not always, interchangeable. In the nineteenth century, it could be argued that *Pax Britannica* was both a power and an economic definition, upheld by Britain's navy and commerce. It may also be that imperialism was a system both of power and economic relations in which hegemonic nations controlled the affairs of dependent populations. but sometimes there can be a gap between an international system defined in power terms and a global economic order. During the 1920s, for instance, power balances in Europe and Asia were sustained by Britain, France, and Japan, whereas the United States was the undisputed leader in the world economy. Thus there was a gap between international power relations and the global economic system. Today, the power aspect of the international order may be characterized by the nuclear balance between the two superpowers, but that does not correspond to the structure of global economic transactions. What such gaps may imply for the stability or instability of the world as a whole is a problem that can be profitably and cooperatively explored by historians in all countries.

Ultimately, I think international historians must also concern themselves with cultural issues. One might well ask whether it is even possible to speak of a cultural dimension to the international system. In addition to discussing the rise and fall of the great powers, or the creation and collapse of an economic regime, can we also talk about the emergence and erosion of global cultural trends? On the surface, it might seem impossible to do so, if for no other reason than that culture denotes something private, local, parochial—in Bailyn's phrase, "interior world views—shared attitudes and responses and 'mind-sets.' "[9] Thus defined, culture is specific as to time and place, so that to talk of culture in the context of something as broad and vague as international order may be an absurdity. Still, it is worth exploring whether or not connections exist between inner worlds and the external world, for, after all, the relationship between private and public affairs has long defined a key historical issue.

International historians have in fact been examining cultural issues even when they do not explicitly write about them. To take a recent, well-known example, Paul Kennedy's *Rise and Fall of the Great Powers*, despite its conventional-sounding title, is filled with pertinent insights in this regard.[10] While the book does compare the relative military and economic positions of various nations, it suggests that the search for power is a pervasive human condition. While the great powers rise and fall, one thing seems to remain constant: the power orientation of men and women everywhere, at least when they organize themselves into national entities. In this sense, the book is about a fundamental transnational drive, defining the culture of people living in international society. At the same time, Kennedy implied that power is not all that they have chosen to invoke in defining their relations with one another. Toward the end of the book, he cited Friedrich List and Adam Smith as exponents of two contrasting conceptions of international affairs, List postulating a power definition in which a state's raison d'être is to amass power to prepare for possible war, and Smith stressing economic transactions that do not necessarily imply hostile relations. The contrast between a List and Smith, between an image of sovereignty and one of interdependence, between an assumed state of conflict and one of harmony in the world, is not limited to Western thinkers. The same dichotomy informed the classical Chinese conception of *wu* (power) versus *wen* (civilization), and undoubtedly other societies have developed similar polarities. The reality, of course, may not fit so neatly into a simple opposition, but the point is that both List's and Smith's formulations are ideological productions, assuming certain images of international order, and suggest that neither power relations nor economic transactions are mindless, automatic responses but that the choice to pursue power or stress economic interests is conditioned by suppositions about culture and its relation to the world community.

Of these suppositions, none has been more prevalent than the ideas of nationalism and internationalism. Gustave Hervé, an influential French author, noted in 1910 that, as capital moved across national boundaries and as people crossed frontiers, the distinction between domestic and foreign goods and populations was diminishing. In time, international regulations would come to be promulgated to govern their behavior. Capitalists and workers, thus internationalized, would try to avoid disastrous competitions that led to war. The nineteenth century, Hervé asserted, "was a century of nationalism. The twentieth century will be a century of internationalism. . . . There will eventually be a United States of Europe and of America, perhaps a United States of the world."[11] This kind of internationalism, an echo of Adam Smith,

gained currency particularly in the United States in the first decades of the century. And American historians, perhaps because they are uncomfortable with purely power-oriented formulations of foreign affairs and believe in economic interdependence, have produced many valuable studies of internationalism. The late Warren Kuehl, one of the pioneers in this endeavor, asserted on many occasions that no study of international history would be complete without due attention to forces that make for internationalism.[12] And it is gratifying that recently U.S. and Soviet historians have been holding a number of symposia to explore the meaning of internationalism.[13]

Internationalism is clearly a conceptualization, what we may call an ideology, but so is nationalism. Max Weber, writing at about the same time as Hervé, vehemently denied that, because economic development had created an international community. nationalism had become an anachronism; on the contrary, "the economic community is . . . only another form of the conflict of nations with each other."[14] Weber postulated the primacy of nationalism and interstate conflict even when the world was becoming more and more internationalized economically. But he defined nationalism as "the assertion of one's own 'Kultur,' " thus indicating that he did not subscribe to a crude power determinism, any more than he accepted what he viewed as a naive economic internationalism. We may grant that Weber's conception of international affairs was more realistic than Hervé's, but it was still a conceptualization, an idea that assumed localized orientations and priorities of human behavior. Nationalism, in a sense, was accepted as the prevalent ideology of the time in whose terms states were pictured to be organizing themselves.

The ideology of nationalism has spread to other parts of the world, but again it has been moderated by currents of internationalist thinking. To cite just one example, Fukuzawa Yukichi, the Meiji intellectual leader, while stressing, in a widely read book published in 1875, national sovereignty as the cardinal goal of Japan, argued that, ultimately, national power hinged on the level of acceptance of modern civilization. Drawing a distinction between the Japanese people's behavior toward one another and toward foreigners, he wrote that individual Japanese were quite honest and courteous at home but that this tendency was not sufficient to establish just and equal relations with other countries. Dealing with foreigners (*gaikoku kosai*) was a serious weakness with the Japanese, one that they must somehow overcome if they chose to live in the international community. The answer lay in civilizing themselves, by which Fukuzawa meant industrialization, modern learning, and the spirit of independence. How individual personalities and energies could be channeled into promoting these objectives was his main concern and, one suspects, the concern of many others in Japan and elsewhere at an early stage of nation-building.[15] It is illuminating that the Japanese word for diplomacy, *gaiko*, is an abbreviation of what Fukuzawa termed *gaikoku kosai*, indicating that diplomatic affairs must be comprehended in terms of their grounding in people's dealings with foreigners. In such a conception, the international system is inseparable from the individual attitudes and orientations that constitute a culture. One may also note that, over a hundred years after Fukuzawa penned these thoughts, one still hears a great deal about Japan's cultural isolation in the international community, in sharp contrast to its superior economic position in the world. But to speak of cultural isolation assumes that there is an international cultural order in terms of which one is judged to be isolated.

Is there in fact such an order? I would suggest that here is another important area of inquiry in which historians of various countries can cooperate to develop wider perspectives. It is obvious that they must draw on the insights and methodologies of anthropologists, sociologists, and practitioners of other disciplines who have long been interested in the phenomenon of cultural diffusion and transformation. Those perspectives will be invaluable as historians attempt to trace the forces that make for, or militate against, the creation of an international cultural order. International historians in particular may have much to learn from art historians who, after all, have explored the transfer of artistic styles and tastes from one part of the world to another. Perhaps they could help us understand how these phenomena might be linked to political and economic trends. Recent writings in art history have, moreover, emphasized the need to go beyond national frameworks and to look for transnational artistic themes. Some art historians have, in the meantime, developed the theme of hegemonic order, the production of predominant modes of artistic expression acceptable to the elites in society.[16] Perhaps we could borrow from such a vocabulary and examine if, over the centuries and through the decades, there have developed hegemonic cultural orders in the world. It is an exciting prospect to explore the relationship between an international power system, a global economic regime, and a world cultural outlook.

Speaking of hegemonic order brings me to the third and last item that I wish to discuss very briefly, namely, the problem of cultural consciousness on the part of the historian. John King Fairbank, another former president of our association, has emphasized how "culture bound" we all are.[17] Although, as a recent study on Fairbank shows, he started out believing in the universal applicability of certain principles and values, he became increasingly more skeptical, for instance, of judging developments in China with an American yardstick.[18] He thus cautioned against asserting American ideological hegemony. Such self-criticism provides an obligatory methodological underpinning for what we do; we should of course be aware of the cultural presuppositions that may affect the ways in which we represent past phenomena. But such caution need not mean that all we can do with confidence is to examine ourselves. As Philip Curtin has noted, "self-knowledge by itself is . . . a form of selfishness that can be dangerous to social health."[19] While it may be true, as Paul Ricoeur wrote more than twenty years ago, that cultures, defined in terms of their respective values and symbols, are fundamentally "incommunicable," we must not assume that we cannot encounter other cultures and in the process transform our "privileged" knowledge into something less privileged and therefore more universal.[20]

It seems to me that our methodological self-consciousness should not prevent us from translating historical works into many languages. I believe that whatever we do as historians will be of little value unless it has some meaning to readers in other parts of the world, unless it is read in different cultural languages, as it were. And, in this regard, Fairbank himself has contributed enormously not only to the Western understanding of Asia but also to Asia's understanding of itself, and not just in conceptual frameworks indigenous to the West. His pessimism seems to be more in the realm of trying to influence official relations among countries than in searching for intellectual common ground where Americans and Asians, and others as well, may seek to promote better mutual understanding. In similar fashion, a generation of Japan specialists in the United States has engaged in intellectual dialogue with their counterparts in Japan with the result that it is no longer clear which contributions are made by U.S. historians and which come from Japanese.

The distinction between Japanese and American history lost meaning for me in August 1945 when, upon Japan's defeat, school children of my generation were told by the American Occupation authorities that whatever we had learned of history up to that point was all wrong and that we must now restudy the past without taking anything for granted. This was a most liberating experience and persuaded us that national history could best be understood when it was examined from without as well as from within, that, in this quest for a less distorted view of the past, it made no difference who you were so long as you were willing to learn from various perspectives. In very much the same way, when I came to the United States shortly after the end of the Occupation, I was treated like any other student of history. I was grateful that my professors in college and graduate school never considered my being an outsider a handicap for the study of history. By the same token, the blackening out of passages in school textbooks that were objectionable to the Occupation authorities had impressed on us how easily the past could be manipulated by temporal power. The recent rewriting of history textbooks in Japan is but the latest manifestation of this. Those in China, Korea, and other countries who remember the wartime atrocities have justifiably protested against such revisions, and this outside intervention may be one of the healthiest developments of the internationalization of history, for it indicates that forming a less parochial view of the past may depend on international cooperation.

Herbert Norman, the Canadian historian of Japan whose tragic death in 1957—when he chose suicide to put an end to interminable investigations of his past political beliefs and behavior—in many ways symbolized the limits imposed by temporal authority on the freedom of historical inquiry, once wrote, "History is the discipline that makes the whole world kin and is for humanity what memory is for the individual."[21] To which I would like to add a quote from Milan Kundera: "The struggle of man against power is the struggle of memory against forgetting."[22] It seems to me that memory is a precious gift in all countries and cultures, and that the historical profession here and throughout the world has the task of ensuring that this gift will be constantly reaffirmed so that the past can be transmitted to and confronted by the present. Of course, there will not be one past but as many pasts to remember as there are individuals, but the totality of remembered pasts forms the legacy of civilization to which we are all heirs. No profession would seem to be as well equipped as the historical community to recognize and reconfirm this faith in common humanity.

NOTES

1. Bernard Bailyn, "The Challenge of Modern Historiography," AHR, 87 (February 1982): 13; John Hope Franklin, "A Life of Learning: Charles Homer Haskin Lecture" (ACLS Occasional Papers, No. 4; April 1988), 16; William H. McNeill, "Mythistory," AHR, 91 (February 1986): 7.

2. George Bancroft, quoted in AHA Perspectives, April 1984.

3. Arthur S. Link, "The American Historical Association, 1884–1984," AHR, 90 (February 1985): 7.

4. I am indebted to the AHA executive director, Samuel Gammon, for membership and other information.

5. Lewis Hanke, Guide to the Study of United States History Outside the U.S., 1945–1980, 5 vols. (White Plains, N.Y., 1985).

6. Chronicle of Higher Education, 35 (April 10, 1988): 1; Peter Parish, "American History Abroad: Britain," OAH Newsletter, 16 (May 1988): 6–7.

7. See a perceptive comment on this point in Carl Degler, "In Pursuit of an American History," AHR, 92 (February 1987): 1–12.

8. For recent assessments of international history, see Gordon A. Craig, "The Historian and the Study of International Relations," AHR, 88 (February 1983): 1–11; Warren I. Cohen, "The History of American-East Asian Relations," Diplomatic History, 9 (Spring 1985): 102–12.

9. Bailyn, "Challenge of Modern Historiography," 22.

10. Paul Kennedy, The Rise and Fall of the Great Powers (New York, 1988).

11. Gustave Hervé, L'Internationalisme (Paris, 1910), 172, 176.

12. Warren Kuehl, "Webs of Common Interests Revisited," Diplomatic History, 10 (Spring 1986): 107–20.

13. Charles Chatfield, "Report on Consultation on Peace Research in History," Dialog, 8 (January 1987): 275–83; personal communication, Chatfield to author, July 5, 1988.

14. Max Weber, Gesammelte Politische Schriften (Munich, 1921), 14.

15. Fukuzawa Yukichi, Bunmei von no gairyaku (An outline of theories of civilization), Iwanami edn. (Tokyo, 1986), 237–60.

16. For example, T.J. Clark, The Painting of Modern Life (Princeton, N.J., 1984).

17. John K. Fairbank, China Watch (Cambridge, Mass., 1987).

18. Paul M. Evans, John Fairbank and the American Understanding of Modern China (New York, 1988).

19. Philip D. Curtin, "Death, Span, and Relevance," AHR, 89 (February 1984): 3.

20. Paul Ricoeur, History and Truth, Charles A. Kelbley, trans. (Evanston, Ill., 1965), 282. I am grateful to Frank Ninkovich for calling my attention to this book and otherwise providing me with valuable comments on this essay.

21. Quoted in Roger Bowen, Death Is Not Enough (Vancouver, 1986), 109.

22. Milan Kundera, Book of Laughter and Forgetting, Michael Henry Heim, trans (New York, 1980), 3.

Index

Credits/ Acknowledgments

Cover design by Charles Vitelli

1. Industrial and Scientific Revolutions
Facing overview—Dover *Pictorial Archives* Series. 7-11—Illustrations by John U. Nef and Dover *Pictorial Archives* Series. 13—from *The Textile Manufactures of Great Britain,* by George Dodd, London, 1844. 15—(top) from *Book of English Trades,* London, 1804; (bottom) from *Cotton Manufacture in Great Britain,* by Edward Baines, London, 1835. 16—(left top and bottom) from *The Book of English Trades;* (right top) from *Days at the Factories,* by G. Dobb, London, 1843; (right bottom) from *Penny Magazine,* November 1944. 17-19—Mansell Collection. 21—Peabody Museum, Harvard University. 22—The Bettmann Archive. 23—National Aeronautics & Space Administration. 26—Smithsonian Institution Libraries. 27—Pitti Collection, Italy. 28—(top)Ann Ronan Picture Library; (bottom) Rare Book Collection, Perkins Library.

2. Cultural Ferment of the West
Facing overview—Library of Congress. 69—(left) by courtesy of Bristol City Art Library; (center and right) HT Archives. 70—(left) Metropolitan Museum of Art, New York; (center) Mansell Collection; (right) Historical Society of Pennsylvania. 71—New York Historical Association. 72—from *The Arts of the Young Republic* by H. E. Dickson (University of North Carolina Press, 1968).

3. Expansion and Domination of the West
Facing overview—Virginia State Library. 100, 101—Weidenfeld Archives. 103—HT Archives. 105—Mansell Collection. 116, 118—by courtesy of the Royal Commonwealth Society. 120—by courtesy of P. H. River Museum, University of Oxford. 124—Bowring Cartographic. 125, 127—Larry Burrows Collection. 129—Larry Burrows Collection, National Portrait Gallery.

4. Twentieth-Century Warfare
Facing overview—U.S. Navy Photo. 151—from *Die Zigeuner,* by Hermann Arnold, Freiburg, 1965.

5. Retreat of the West
Facing overview—United Nations photo by J. Isaac.

6. World Problems and Interdependence
Facing overview—World Bank Photo Library. 210—Government Information Office. 223, 225, 226—Photographs by Longina Jakubowska. 229-231, 233-234—*Scientific American,* April 1989.

ANNUAL EDITIONS: WORLD HISTORY, VOLUME II
Article Rating Form

Here is an opportunity for you to have direct input into the next revision of this volume. We would like you to rate each of the 46 articles listed below, using the following scale:

1. **Excellent: should definitely be retained**
2. **Above average: should probably be retained**
3. **Below average: should probably be deleted**
4. **Poor: should definitely be deleted**

Your ratings will play a vital part in the next revision. So please mail this prepaid form to us just as soon as you complete it.
Thanks for your help!

Annual Editions revisions depend on two major opinion sources: one is our Advisory Board, listed in the front of this volume, which works with us in scanning the thousands of articles published in the public press each year; the other is you—the person actually using the book. Please help us and the users of the next edition by completing the prepaid article rating form on this page and returning it to us. Thank you.

Rating	Article	Rating	Article
	1. An Early Energy Crisis and Its Consequences		24. Southern Barbarian and Red-Hairs in Feudal Japan
	2. Cottage Industry and the Factory System		25. The Causes of Wars
	3. From Astronomy to Astrophysics		26. Sarajevo: The End of Innocence
	4. Galileo's Science and the Trial of 1633		27. The Dangerous Summer of 1940
	5. The Alchemical Roots of Chemistry		28. Social Outcasts in Nazi Germany
	6. Life's Recipe		29. To Cleave an Atom
	7. New Light on Edison's Light		30. Reborn From Holocaust
	8. The Green Revolution		31. Lessons From a Lost War
	9. Driving Toward a World Car?		32. The Dismal Chronolgy of Foolish War
	10. The Conquering Machine		33. Weapons, Deadly Weapons
	11. Scientists Go North		34. Whose Dream Was It Anyway?
	12. Luther: Giant of His Time and Ours		35. India's Estranged Communities
	13. The Body of Bach		36. Islam: Religion Has Potential to Reshape World
	14. The Great Compromise: Drafting the American Constitution, 1787		37. The 10 Years of Chaos
	15. What Was Revolutionary About the French Revolution?		38. Marx Had It Wrong. Does Gorbachev?
	16. Scotland's Greatest Son		39. The New English Empire
	17. The First Feminist		40. The Price of Success: Japan's Foreign Policy Dilemma
	18. Freudian Myths and Freudian Realities		41. Population and Economic Growth: The Third World
	19. Portugal's Impact on Africa		42. A "Satanic" Fury
	20. The Emergence of the Great Powers		43. Japanese Women: A World Apart
	21. The Struggle for Land		44. A Matter of Honor
	22. West Africa's Mary Kingsley		45. Global Climatic Change
	23. A Whole Subcontinent Was Picked Up Without Half Trying		46. The Internationalization of History

(Continued on next page)

ABOUT YOU

Name_____ Date_____

Are you a teacher? ☐ Or student? ☐

Your School Name _____

Department _____

Address _____

City _____ State _____ Zip _____

School Telephone # _____

YOUR COMMENTS ARE IMPORTANT TO US!

Please fill in the following information:

For which course did you use this book? _____

Did you use a text with this Annual Edition? ☐ yes ☐ no

The title of the text? _____

What are your general reactions to the Annual Editions concept?

Have you read any particular articles recently that you think should be included in the next edition?

Are there any articles you feel should be replaced in the next edition? Why?

Are there other areas that you feel would utilize an Annual Edition?

May we contact you for editorial input?

May we quote you from above?

ANNUAL EDITIONS: WORLD HISTORY, VOLUME II

BUSINESS REPLY MAIL

First Class   Permit No. 84   Guilford, CT

Postage will be paid by addressee

The Dushkin Publishing Group, Inc.
Sluice Dock
DPG **Guilford, Connecticut 06437**

No Postage
Necessary
if Mailed
in the
United States

5244